The Poetical Works of Alain Chartier

London, Brit. Mus. Additional MS 21247 (*Df*), fol. 1r
(Reproduced by permission of the Trustees)

The Poetical Works of
Alain Chartier

EDITED BY

J. C. LAIDLAW

Fellow and Tutor of Trinity Hall and
Lecturer in French in the University of Cambridge

CAMBRIDGE UNIVERSITY PRESS

Published by the Syndics of the Cambridge University Press
Bentley House, 200 Euston Road, London NWI 2DB
American Branch: 32 East 57th Street, New York, N.Y.10022

© Cambridge University Press 1974

Library of Congress Catalogue Card Number: 73–77177 ✓

ISBN: 0 521 07940 3

First published 1974

Printed in Great Britain
at the University Printing House, Cambridge
(Brooke Crutchley, University Printer)

Contents

Preface

This edition would not have been completed without constant help and encouragement from different sources, above all from my wife and family. I wish to express my sincere thanks to Dr S. C. Aston who supervised the research which was a preliminary to this work and whose continuing help has been invaluable; to Dr L. T. Topsfield and Dr P. Rickard who read parts of the edition in draft; to Professor Ll. J. Austin and my other colleagues in the Faculty of Modern and Medieval Languages in Cambridge; to Professor M. M. Pelan and Dr N. C. W. Spence for their encouragement when I worked with them in Belfast; to Professor Jean Frappier and Professor T. B. W. Reid, to the late Professor A. Ewert and the late Professor John Orr for their wise and helpful advice; to the Literary and Linguistic Computing Centre in Cambridge. I am also grateful to the University of Cambridge, to the Queen's University of Belfast, to the Rijksuniversiteit te Utrecht, to the Centre National de la Recherche Scientifique, to the Institut de Recherche et d'Histoire des Textes, and particularly to the Master and Fellows of Trinity Hall for their material help.

My wife and Dr R. E. V. Stuip have given invaluable help with the proofs. Mrs R. Hebblethwaite and Mrs J. P. McCall typed parts of the edition with great care. They have all saved me from making more than one error; for those which remain I am responsible.

My debt to earlier critics is considerable. For any student of Alain Chartier the works of André du Chesne, G. du Fresne de Beaucourt, Arthur Piaget and Pierre Champion are indispensable reading. It is perhaps invidious to single out these men, since the work of other scholars is also important. The extent of my indebtedness to them all is revealed in the footnotes and bibliography.

'Difficile est longum subito deponere amorem', said Catullus. Although the context is different, the sentiment is not dissimilar. I hope that this edition, which has demanded time and devotion, will be worthy of an author whose poetical works have not been edited adequately for more than three and a half centuries and who deserves to be better known and understood.

J. C. L.

1

The life of Alain Chartier

Stat magni nominis umbra.

Lucan

Alain Chartier[1] came from Bayeux, as is attested by an inscription in his own hand on the fly-leaf of his copy of Sallust, *De Coniuratione Catilinae et de Bello Iugurthino*: 'De libris alani aurige de baiocis'.[2] His name is most frequently found in that form in Latin documents and in the manuscripts of his Latin works. An alternative form, 'Alanus quadrigarii', found in two manuscripts,[3] does not seem to have had the blessing of the author himself. In French, several forms exist of his surname; 'Chartier', 'Charretier' or 'le Charretier' are all found.[4] Very often a manuscript or an account-book will be inconsistent in the form which it uses. Chartier, being the most usual and shortest form, has been adopted here.

Alain Chartier was born into a family which owned property in Bayeux and which seems to have been prominent in the town's affairs for two generations at least before his birth. An act of 1455 indicates that his father was Jean Chartier who in 1387 settled money on a church in Bayeux and was alive in 1404. It is far from certain that the house described in that act is the one in which Alain Chartier was born.[5] Jean Chartier had at least

---

[1] See G. du Fresne de Beaucourt, 'Les Chartier: recherches sur Guillaume, Alain et Jean Chartier', *Mémoires de la Société des Antiquaires de Normandie*, 3e Série, VIII (XXVIII), 1870, 1–59, an important biographical study which cleared up many misconceptions and included much information unknown until then; P. Champion, *Histoire poétique du XVe siècle*, I, Paris, 1923, 1–165 (*Bibliothèque du XVe siècle*, XXVII), a full and readable account of Chartier's life and works; E. J. Hoffman, *Alain Chartier, his Works and Reputation*, New York, Wittes Press, 1942, a critical appraisal of earlier work; Pascale Hemeryck, *Alain Chartier, poète et penseur, d'après 'Le Debat des deux fortunes* (sic) *d'amour' et les œuvres latines*, Paris, 1970 (Thèse de l'Ecole Nationale des Chartes); C.J.H. Walravens, *Alain Chartier, études biographiques, suivies de pièces justificatives...*, Amsterdam, Meulenhoff-Didier, 1971, a detailed account and criticism of earlier work, which includes the texts of many documents. Details of the other works consulted are given in notes or in the bibliography.

[2] Paris, Bibl. Nat., f.lat. 5748, fol. 1r. The page is reproduced as the frontispiece of Champion, *Histoire poétique*. See p. 24.

[3] 'Alanus quadrigarii regis orator et secretarius' in both *Ke* and *Lf*. For an explanation of the sigla used, see J. C. Laidlaw, 'The Manuscripts of Alain Chartier', *Modern Language Review*, LXI, 1966, 188–98. A complete list of the manuscripts is given on pp. 45–8.

[4] 'Le Charretier' is the least common form but is given in *Ea*, an early manuscript (fol. 1r).

[5] The text of the act of 1455 is given in Vicomte de Toustain, 'Notice historique et généalogique sur la famille d'Alain Chartier', *Revue nobiliaire historique et biographique*, n.s., II, 1866, 5–13. C. J. H.

three sons: Alain, Guillaume and Thomas. All three were destined to fill high offices. Alain and Thomas both became *notaires et secrétaires du roi*; it is probable that brother succeeded brother.[1] Guillaume Chartier was Bishop of Paris from 1447 until his death in 1472 and also served as a royal councillor. Alain was probably the eldest of the three brothers;[2] it is not known whether Jean Chartier had any more children. Despite the coincidence of period and surname, the chronicler Jean Chartier, *moine et chantre de Saint-Denis*, was probably not of the same family.

The date of Alain Chartier's birth is unknown.[3] The only evidence available, the chronology of his career in royal service, allows no more than an approximate estimate. If it is assumed that he entered royal service when he was between twenty and thirty years of age, it follows that he was born between 1380 and 1390.

Nothing is known about Chartier's early education. It is clear that he studied at the University of Paris: the *Epistola ad Universitatem Parisiensem* begins with the words 'Alma mater...'.[4] In a document dated 4 July 1425 he is described as a Master of Arts[5] but it is not certain that he was a Master of the University of Paris. It is true that Chartier is described as 'Maistre' in a number of documents earlier than 1425 which relate to his employment as a royal notary and secretary. Yet no positive conclusion can be drawn from them about the date when he took his degree for all royal secretaries seem to have been called 'Maistre' by courtesy whether they were Masters of Arts or not.[6] In one collected manuscript of his works, Chartier is described as a 'docteur en decret'.[7] The statement must be treated with caution, occurring as it does only once.

The earliest known reference to Alain Chartier occurs in the household

---

Walravens (*Alain Chartier, études biographiques*, 95–113) has published documents concerning the Chartier family and has republished the act of 1455. In these documents the usual form of the surname is 'Le C(h)ar(r)etier'. The controversy concerning the house is discussed in detail (*ibid.*, 15–18).

[1] See pp. 14–15.

[2] In the act of 1455 Guillaume Chartier is described as 'filz et heritier aisné de Jehan le Caretier'. The phrase was taken by Du Fresne de Beaucourt to mean 'eldest son and heir'. Piaget's interpretation 'son and eldest heir' (*Romania*, xxx, 1901, 43) fits better the facts known about the careers of Alain and Guillaume Chartier. See Champion, *Histoire poétique*, 1, 3, n. 3.

[3] The date of his birth has been long debated. For a full account see Walravens, *Alain Chartier, études biographiques*, 10–14.

[4] A. du Chesne (ed.), *Les Œuvres de Maistre Alain Chartier*, Paris, P. le-Mur, 1617, 490–2; H. Denifle and Æ. Chatelain, *Chartularium universitatis parisiensis*, IV, Paris, Delalain, 1897, 381–2. See also Champion, *Histoire poétique*, 1, 25.

[5] Denifle and Chatelain, 'De legatione Alani Chartier in Germaniam', *ibid.*, XIII–XIV.

[6] A. Coville, *Gontier et Pierre Col et l'humanisme en France au temps de Charles VI*, Paris, Droz, 1934, 12.

[7] *Pk*, fol. 231r.

accounts of Yolande of Anjou, Queen of Jerusalem and Sicily, who played an important role in the politics of France during the early fifteenth century. Her influence on her son-in-law, Charles of France, Count of Ponthieu and later Charles VII, was particularly strong. The young prince was betrothed on 18 December 1413 to Marie of Anjou, daughter of King Louis II and Queen Yolande. In accordance with the custom of the time Charles, then aged ten, went to live in the household of his future bride and spent the next five years under the almost continuous tutelage of Queen Yolande.

The account of the Queen's household for the period 19 February 1408/9 to 19 September 1414 includes on fol. 39r a list of: 'Autres debtes deues pour ladicte despence aux gens et officiers de l'ostel de ladicte dame et ses enfans de tout le temps dont ces presens comptes font mencion'; Chartier, here called 'Alain le charetier', is listed twice both among those who have a note acknowledging the debt owed to them and among those who do not; the sums involved amount to 96 *sous*.[1]

The information is tantalising for it is not clear at what time or for what reason Queen Yolande incurred these debts. We do not know when Alain Chartier entered her household, whether it was before or after the betrothal. Nor do we know whether he served the Queen or one of her children; it is clear from other passages in the account-book that Charles of France was included among the 'children' of the Queen.

The young prince became Dauphin in April 1417 and set up his own household soon afterwards. Two pieces of information show that Alain Chartier became a member of it. The second account of Queen Yolande's household, which runs from 19 September 1414 to 31 December 1418, contains no mention of Alain Chartier.[2] On the other hand, the earliest known letters which Chartier signed in his capacity as a royal notary and secretary fall within the period, being dated 16 and 27 September 1417.[3] Chartier's name is absent from the later household accounts of Queen Yolande and of her son King René, which run from the beginning of 1418/19 until January 1438/9. The references which they contain to a 'Maistre alain' are not, as might be supposed, to Master Alain Chartier but to Master Alain Lequeu.[4]

[1] Paris, Archives Nationales, KK 243, ff. 2r–40r, especially ff. 39r and 39v.
[2] KK 243, ff. 42r–59v.
[3] G. du Fresne de Beaucourt, *Histoire de Charles VII*, I, Paris, Libr. de la Soc. Bibl., 1881, 437–8. See also the chronological table on pp. 18–21.
[4] KK 243, ff. 60r–90r; Paris, Bibl. Nat., f.fr. 8588, ff. 43r–83v; Paris, Archives Nationales, KK 244. See J. C. Laidlaw, 'Master Alain Chartier and Master Alain Lequeu', *French Studies*, XXII, 1968, 191–200; the article includes chronological tables which give details of the careers of the two men.

Chartier's earliest poems are associated with his period of service at the court of Queen Yolande. The *Debat des Deux Fortunés d'Amours* dates from 1412 and the *Lay de Plaisance* from a slightly earlier period.[1] There is no mention of the house of Anjou in either poem. Indeed, the *Debat des Deux Fortunés d'Amours* was sent to Jean, Count of Foix, for reasons which will be discussed later. The importance of the house of Anjou in encouraging the arts is well known and it is possible that Alain Chartier benefited from its patronage and encouragement. Among the councillors of Louis II at this time was Guillaume Saignet, whose judicial and political career left him time to pursue his literary interests;[2] Saignet and Chartier were to serve together as ambassadors of Charles VII in 1425.[3]

The exact date of Alain Chartier's appointment as a royal notary and secretary is unknown. The two letters which he signed in September 1417 were written in Paris: the first was from the Dauphin to the people of Tournai; in the second the Dauphin confirmed the grant of a privilege to the inhabitants of Villeneuve-Saint-Georges. One, perhaps two letters, signed by Chartier early in the following year were also written in Paris and were from the Dauphin to the people of Lyons. In the prologue to the *Quadrilogue Invectif*, which was written in 1422 before the death of Charles VI, Alain Chartier described himself as 'Alain Charretier humble secretaire du roy et de mon tresredoubté seigneur monseigneur le regent'.[4] Yet it is to be noted that no letter of Charles VI has been found which bears Chartier's signature. Chartier's name is not included in a list of the royal secretaries, given in letters patent of Charles VI signed at Paris on 2 August 1418,[5] nor among those secretaries who figured in an ordinance which listed the members of the King's household and was compiled a month later, again in Paris.[6] Both lists, however, were drawn up after the Burgundians had occupied the capital and after Alain Chartier had left the city. The letters patent inveigh against those secretaries who were not supporting the King and the Duke of Burgundy; the ordinance was enacted in the presence of the Duke himself. In the absence of evidence to the contrary, Chartier's own statement that he was a secretary of Charles VI must be accepted.

[1] See pp. 28–32.
[2] A. Coville, *La Vie intellectuelle dans les domaines d'Anjou-Provence de 1380 à 1435*, Paris, Droz, 1941, esp. pp. 319–57.
[3] See p. 9.
[4] E. Droz (ed.), *Alain Chartier: le Quadrilogue invectif*, Paris, 1950[2], 1 (*CFMA*).
[5] Paris, Archives Nationales, v² 2, pièce 3.
[6] London, Public Record Office, Diplomatic Document 1652, especially fol. 3r. There is a copy of the list in Paris, Bibl. Nat., f.fr. 7853, fol. 48v.

The next known royal letter signed by Alain Chartier was written at Bourges on 13 June 1418.[1] The previous four months had seen the advance of the English into Normandy and the Burgundian attack on Paris; the Dauphin had fled the city on 29 May. It is possible that Chartier was in the party which escorted the Dauphin from Paris. Whether he went then or immediately afterwards, it seems clear that he *chose* to follow the Dauphin into 'exile', as Chartier himself called it in the first line of his *Livre de l'Esperance*.

Chartier continued to serve as secretary to the Dauphin, later Charles VII, for the next eleven or so years until his death in 1430. The surviving letters[2] of Charles VII, as Dauphin and King, are the principal source of information about the career of Alain Chartier during the period. The information which they give is deceptive and incomplete: deceptive because many of the documents reveal no more than that Chartier was at a given place on a given day; incomplete because no list has yet been made of the letters issued from the royal chancellery at the period.

Those letters which bear Alain Chartier's signature show that he shared the itinerant life of the court, as it progressed round the castles and towns of Berry and Touraine which were loyal to the 'roi de Bourges'. Examination of the contents of these letters does not suggest that Chartier had any special responsibility within the Chancellery. The earliest are directed to different towns and institutions and often solicit their support for the Dauphin's cause. Some deal with finance, others with grants or appointments, others with the day-to-day business of government. Of particular importance is a series of letters written in September and October 1419 after the murder at Montereau of John (the Fearless), Duke of Burgundy. They include a letter sent to Philip, Duke of Burgundy, on 15 October; the letter was accompanied by an account of the events preceding the murder and by detailed instructions for the Dauphin's envoy to the new Duke. In signing, perhaps drawing up, these documents, Alain Chartier allied himself irrevocably to the cause of the Dauphin whom he had chosen to serve.[3]

During the years 1425 to 1428, Alain Chartier served on a number of occasions as a royal ambassador. In the letters of credence which name him he is generally the last of the envoys mentioned and he played the sub-

---

[1] Du Fresne de Beaucourt, *Histoire de Charles VII*, I, 95, n. 1; A. Thomas, *Romania*, XXXIII, 1904, 394.
[2] The term is used in its broadest sense and includes a wide range of documents – charters, grants, proclamations, orders, exemptions, instructions etc.
[3] They have been edited by C. J. H. Walravens (*Alain Chartier, études biographiques*, 164–84).

ordinate, though by no means unimportant, role of secretary and orator. In the fifteenth century it was traditional for an oration in Latin to be given in the course of an embassy. The texts have survived of three such orations by Alain Chartier, two delivered before the Emperor Sigismund in 1425, the third before James I of Scotland three years later.[1]

Alain Chartier appears to have been absent from court on diplomatic business for the greater part of 1425. The evidence available about his activities in that year is at times contradictory; it can be and has been interpreted in different ways.

The chief source of information is Le Mans, Bibl. Mun., MS 163, a formulary dating from the middle of the fifteenth century. Since it is a formulary, it must be used with caution; many of the letters which it contains are cut short to end simply 'Datum etc.', and tell nothing about the place and time at which the letter was written. Again, the presence of a letter in a formulary is not of itself a guarantee that the letter was sent or was not redrafted. Nevertheless, the formulary must be used as the only source so far available and must be relied on unless good reason is shown to the contrary.

The Le Mans MS contains copies of four letters which interest us here.[2] Three are from the King of France; the fourth is addressed to the Pope by a prince whose identity has been the subject of some debate. The first letter was given at Espaly on 31 December in a year which is not specified. The others contain no details of where or when they were written.

In two letters of credence Artaud de Granval, Abbot of Saint-Antoine de Vienne, and Alain Chartier are named as envoys from Charles VII to Sigismund, King of Hungary and Holy Roman Emperor, and to Nicholas Garai, Count Palatine of Hungary. The Count Palatine or *nádor* was the chief dignitary after the King; it is known that the *nádor* Nicholas Garai frequently accompanied Sigismund on his journeys.[3] The letters mention Thomasinus de Narduchio, an envoy sent by Sigismund to the French court. In a third letter, from Charles to Sigismund, Narduchio is recommended as the bearer of a detailed reply to Sigismund's message.

---

[1] They are edited in D. Delaunay, *Etude sur Alain Chartier*, Rennes, Oberthur, 1876, 218–42, 252–64; and in Hemeryck, *Alain Chartier, poète et penseur*.

[2] Ff. 21v–22r; 23r; 23v–24r. The letters have been published by C. J. H. Walravens (*Alain Chartier, études biographiques*, 115–18), from the Le Mans MS and a later copy of it, Paris, Bibl. Nat., n.a.fr. 1001. The letters had earlier been cited by Du Fresne de Beaucourt (*Histoire de Charles VII*, II, 1882, 344–7) from the Paris MS.

In his account of the embassies in 1425, Dr Walravens concludes that Chartier did not take part in the mission to the Pope, but probably did pay a second visit to the Emperor (*ibid.*, 27–33).

[3] D. Sinor, *History of Hungary*, London, Allen and Unwin, 1959, 104.

Narduchio may well have accompanied Granval and Chartier on their journey to the imperial court.

At the beginning of 1425 Sigismund was in Vienna or close by.[1] Artaud de Granval and Alain Chartier must have seen the Emperor and Nicholas Garai in late January or early February. Discussion of the objects of their mission can be deferred since the two ambassadors were to visit Sigismund's court a second time later that year.

Information about the embassy's progress and the time it was expected to last is given in a letter to Alain Chartier written at Issoudun on 31 January (1425) by three ladies of the court.[2] The letter shows that Chartier was then absent from the court and in a position of some danger, for it mentions the possibility of his being killed or captured. The reasons for the letter were literary, not diplomatic: certain persons at court had taken advantage of Chartier's absence to criticise the *Belle Dame sans Mercy* which he had recently completed and to demand that he be made to answer for it. Chartier was summoned to face his accusers at a hearing on 1 April. The three ladies expressed their belief that he would not fail to appear in person.

Alain Chartier took his critics seriously enough to write the *Excusacion aux Dames* in which he defended his earlier poem. A request to the ladies forms part of the first stanza:

> Escoutés les durez nouvelles
> 4   Que j'ouÿ le jour de l'estraine.

In 1425 New Year's Day fell on 8 April: the French court reckoned the year from Easter.[3] The dates when the letter was written and received, and the date fixed for the hearing, suggest that Chartier had been expected back at court in March but had been delayed, and that the letter had taken longer to reach him than had been foreseen. The *Excusacion* must have been written in April or soon afterwards and the hearing arranged for 1 April must at the very least have been postponed. Chartier's poem provoked from the ladies a *Responce* in verse.[4] Examination of the *Excusacion* and the *Responce* together suggests that both poems were written at a time when Alain Chartier was absent from court.

---

[1] See Walravens, *Alain Chartier, études biographiques*, 29–30, who reprints the tables of W. Altmann (and J. Aschbach).

[2] A critical edition of the letter is on pp. 360–1.

[3] P. Champion (*Histoire poétique*, I, 71, n. 3) considered that the *Excusacion* dated from 1 January 1425.

[4] A. Piaget, 'La Belle Dame sans merci et ses imitations', *Romania*, XXX, 1901, 22–48, esp. 31–5. See also p. 23.

The ladies' reply wasted no sympathy on the poet; it is not certain whether the Court of Love likewise condemned him. Pierre de Nesson in his *Lay de Guerre* described Chartier as:

> Lui qui jadis fut, anmy d'Issouldun,
> Present son roy et trestout le commun,
> Publicquement banni a son de trompe.

If Nesson is referring to a sentence of the Court of Love, then it could have been carried out in May or June 1425: in both those months the court spent some time at Issoudun.[1] It is clear that the banishment mentioned cannot have been a legal sentence for Alain Chartier continued in royal service. Indeed, the whole episode recounted by Nesson may have been a joke. In *Ff*, in a marginal note to the lines just cited, it is stated that Nesson had bribed a drunken crier to go round Issoudun, announcing the sentence of banishment.[2] The two poets clearly knew one another well; the final stanzas of the *Debat du Herault, du Vassault et du Villain* show that Chartier might on occasion poke fun at Nesson.[3]

The diplomatic evidence indicates that Chartier was also absent from the court for most of the summer of 1425. On 3 May Artaud de Granval and Alain Chartier were in Venice and appeared before the Senate on that day.[4] Their intention was to offer the mediation of Charles VII in a dispute over Zara which had gone on since 1409 between Venice and the Emperor Sigismund. French mediation had brought about the only previous suspension of hostilities, a truce between 1413 and 1418. The mission to Sigismund undertaken by Granval and Chartier had sought to win imperial support for the cause of Charles VII and perhaps also the help of Sigismund in making peace with England;[5] it seems clear that among the conditions for such support laid down by Sigismund was mediation in the dispute over Zara. We cannot be certain, however, that this was the sole purpose of the mission to Venice, for no copy has survived of the ambassadors' instructions.

The French offer of mediation was accepted on 3 May. Venetian sources show that Artaud de Granval then returned to the imperial court and

[1] *Ibid.*, 36–7; see also Du Fresne de Beaucourt, *Histoire de Charles VII*, II, 93–4.
[2] *Ff*, fol. 211: 'Est assavoir que Nesson, estant le roy a Issodun, trova une crie de la ville faisant ung cry de par le roy et estoit ladicte crie yvre; si fist Nesson bannir maistre Alain par mocquerie par tous les carrefours et de ce parle Guerre en ce lieu.'   [3] See pp. 37–8.
[4] P.-M. Perret, 'L'ambassade de l'abbé de Saint-Antoine de Vienne et d'Alain Chartier à Venise d'après des documents vénitiens (1425)', *Revue historique*, XLV, 1891, 298–307. See also Walravens, *Alain Chartier, études biographiques*, 119–20.
[5] See pp. 9–10.

that he was in Venice again on 23 October when he reported how the negotiations had progressed. Alain Chartier is not mentioned in Venetian documents after 3 May 1425.[1]

Evidence from other sources shows that Alain Chartier must have gone back to the court of Sigismund with Artaud de Granval. On 4 July the Pope approved a request made by Charles VII that Chartier, described for the first time as rector of the parish of Saint-Lambert-des-Levées in the diocese of Angers, should be allowed to defer his admission to full orders as the incumbency required. In the king's letter Chartier is described as: 'pro certis ejusdem regis peragendis negociis ad serenissimum principem Sigismundum Romanorum regem augustum ambaxiator seu nuncius destinatus.'[2]

Several manuscripts of Chartier's Latin works contain a second oration to Sigismund, together with a *Persuasio ad Pragenses de Reductione ad Fidem*.[3] In *Kc* the title ends enigmatically: 'Persuasio... unde rorata presente cesare'. If the correction plausibly suggested by Thomas is accepted, the title should end 'Bude perorata...'.[4] The Emperor Sigismund spent much of the summer of 1425 in Buda (Ofen).[5] The second oration may have been delivered at the same time.

In *Kc Lo* and *Lr*, the *Persuasio* ends with a list of Charles VII's ambassadors to Sigismund. There are four names: Artaud de Granval, Guillaume Saignet, Alain Chartier and Thomas de Narduchio. The four are named again in a letter addressed to the Pope by an unspecified prince, which is copied in the Le Mans formulary; they have been sent to the writer by Charles VII, described as 'quondam Francorum regis fillius (*sic*)', and have been discussing with him the question of negotiating a peace between France and England. The name of Thomas, or rather Thomasinus, de Narduchio had already been mentioned in the letters of credence given to Granval and Chartier. He had also been entrusted with a message from Charles VII to Sigismund and was to that extent Charles' envoy. Guillaume Saignet's name, on the other hand, has not occurred before. If, as it would

[1] Perret and other biographers of Chartier have assumed that he returned to France thereafter. Hoffman suggested that a second embassy might have taken place without coming to a definite conclusion. See also p. 6, n. 2.

[2] Denifle and Chatelain, 'De legatione Alani Chartier in Germaniam'; see also A. Thomas, 'Un document peu connu sur Alain Chartier (5 juillet 1425)', *Romania*, XXXV, 1906, 603–4. C. J. H. Walravens (*Alain Chartier, études biographiques*, 120) has republished the document, correcting the date from 5 to 4 July. [3] The title is quoted from *Lk*.

[4] A. Thomas, 'Alain Chartier en Hongrie', *Romania*, XXXVIII, 1909, 596–8.

[5] W. Altmann, *Die Urkunden Kaiser Sigmunds (1410–1437)*, II, Innsbruck, Wagner, 1897–1900, 1–32, esp. 18–27; see also Walravens, *Alain Chartier, études biographiques*, 30.

appear, the original embassy had been prolonged, then a further envoy could have been sent out to bring fresh instructions to Granval and Chartier.

The letter to the Pope is headed in the formulary 'Lettres du roy au pape'. Misled by the rubric, Du Fresne de Beaucourt thought that the letter was from Charles VII. Pointing out the mistake, Valois made the tentative suggestion that the letter was from the Duke of Savoy.[1] It is more likely that Sigismund was its author; his prestige fitted him well for the role of mediator between France and England.

The writer asks the Pope to give credence to whatever Artaud de Granval may tell him concerning the peace negotiations and other business, and seeks the Pope's help and support. Granval is the writer's personal envoy – he will see the Pope alone.[2] The fact that the four ambassadors are named in the letter suggests that they may have gone with Granval to Rome; otherwise there would have been little need to list them. It is unlikely that Granval would have travelled without the company of the embassy's secretary at the very least.

To decide when the embassy to the Pope took place is less easy. The journey to Rome could have been combined with that to Venice in May. It could have taken place in the late summer or early autumn, perhaps before Granval's second visit to Venice in October. Whenever it was that Pope Martin V received Artaud de Granval in private audience, their conversations had small effect on the war between France and England.

The mediation of the French ambassadors over Zara had no more success. On his return in October, Artaud de Granval persuaded the Venetians to receive the imperial Chancellor and the two sides reached agreement on some of the points at issue. Their decisions were not ratified by Sigismund, however, and war was resumed. It is possible that Alain Chartier accompanied Artaud de Granval to Venice and that the two returned to France together. Chartier may, on the other hand, have returned direct to France; he was certainly back at court on 3 December, when he signed a letter of appointment.

An embassy to Philip, Duke of Burgundy, followed almost at once. Plans for it seem to have been made as early as 27 December, when the inhabitants of Tournai were informed that such a mission was being

---

[1] N. Valois, *Histoire de la pragmatique sanction de Bourges sous Charles VII*, Paris, Picard, 1906, xxxvi, n. 7 (*Archives de l'histoire religieuse de la France*). For this reference I am indebted to Mr Satoshi Hosokawa.

[2] The phrase 'idem abbas unicus personaliter E.V.S. accederet' suggests a private audience but need not imply that Granval went to Rome alone. C. J. H. Walravens (*Alain Chartier, études biographiques*, 32–3, 118) takes the contrary view.

undertaken 'pour le bien de paix et union de ce royaume'. The mission was delayed, however, for Georges de la Tremoïlle, who had been designated as the King's envoy, was captured and held to ransom at the end of December; it was more than two months before he was released. On 26 March 1426 he presented letters to the *consaux* of Tournai asking them to give him the money necessary to complete his mission.[1] Their reluctance to meet all his demands was finally overcome by Alain Chartier on 2 April. After a full and persuasive account from him of La Tremoïlle's capture and the difficulties caused thereby, the town agreed to make up the necessary sum. La Tremoïlle and Chartier arrived in Bruges soon after to see the Duke of Burgundy; it was not until 2 May that Alain Chartier returned alone to Tournai to give to the *consaux* an account of what the embassy had accomplished on behalf of the town and of the kingdom in general.

Despite the length of their stay in Bruges, the two ambassadors had had little success. No Latin oration, such as had been delivered during the embassies to Sigismund, seems to have been delivered on this occasion; the oration may have been replaced by a poem in the vernacular. Rubrics in four manuscripts associate the *Lay de Paix* with the Duke of Burgundy; the testimony of the manuscripts is to some extent reinforced by the fact that their texts of the poem belong to divergent traditions. The assertion in *Nq* that the poem dates from the time of the Congress of Arras can be discounted. That the *Lay de Paix* was written at the Duke's request, as *Fe* would have it, is much less likely than that it was given or sent to him, as *Pe* and *Qo* suggest.[2] It is unlikely that the poem was written with this particular embassy in mind: in the first stanza of the *Lay de Paix* Peace addresses herself

A vous, Princes nez du lis precïeux,

and not to the Duke of Burgundy in particular. The *Lay de Guerre*, written by Pierre de Nesson after the *Lay de Paix* and probably in 1429,[3] is of no real help in dating Chartier's poem.

---

[1] H. Vandenbroeck, *Extraits analytiques des anciens registres des consaux de...Tournai, 1422–1430*, Tournai, Malo et Levasseur, II, 1863, 195–7, 203–4. The relevant extracts have been republished by C. J. H. Walravens (*Alain Chartier, études biographiques*, 120–2).

[2] The rubrics are given in full in the descriptions of the manuscripts.
   C. J. H. Walravens (*ibid.*, 72–3) also finds it impossible to date the poem, but thinks it unlikely that it was offered to the Duke.

[3] A. Piaget and E. Droz, *Pierre de Nesson et ses œuvres*, Paris, 1925, 12–20 (*Documents artistiques du XVe siècle*, II). In the poem Nesson mentions the death of the (ninth) Earl of Salisbury, which took place in August or September 1428. The *Lay de Guerre* was probably completed before Chartier's death in March 1430.
   P. Champion (*Histoire poétique*, I, 184–5) considered that the *Lay de Guerre* had been written

In 1428 Alain Chartier undertook his last embassy on behalf of Charles VII, to the court of James I of Scotland. In the early years of his administration Charles had sent several embassies to Scotland both to negotiate alliances and to seek military aid. Scottish soldiers had served Charles well and their commanders had been rewarded with estates and high offices. In 1428, when his political and economic position was near desperate, Charles turned again for help to James I. The three ambassadors whom he sent were chosen in accordance with the importance of the mission. Regnault de Chartres, Archbishop of Rheims, had been in Scotland three years before and was the most experienced diplomat in the royal service. Sir John Stewart of Darnley was the Constable of the Scottish troops in France; his services had been rewarded in the previous year by the grant to him of the County of Evreux, at that time in enemy hands. The secretary and orator assigned to the embassy was Alain Chartier. It may be that his literary fame had preceded him; an envoy of his talents would be welcomed by the author of the *Kingis Quair*.[1]

An embassy seems to have been contemplated as early as October 1427. In that month, Stewart of Darnley was paid 500 *livres* 'pour lui aidier a faire son veaige en Escoce'. Alain Chartier is reported to have resigned his canonry of Notre-Dame de Paris two months later in favour of his brother Guillaume.[2] Nevertheless, the two powers issued to the ambassadors were not sealed until 7 April 1428. The first gave to the ambassadors authority to negotiate a renewal of the ancient alliance between the two countries. In the second, the envoys were authorised to arrange a marriage between the Dauphin Louis and the eldest daughter of James I,[3] whose name was apparently unknown at the French court. 'Margareta' has been added, in a space left blank, by a hand which may be that of Chartier himself; the form adopted by the Scottish court was in fact 'Mergareta'.

The embassy may have travelled in two parts. The Latin oration which Chartier delivered before James I indicates that Alain Chartier arrived at the Scottish court before his companions: he apologises for their absence.[4]

just after the *Lay de Paix* which was composed when the princes met at Angers in October 1424. The latter date is possible but by no means certain; peace initiatives were not infrequent at the time. 1425, suggested by E. Droz (*Alain Chartier: le Quadrilogue invectif*, viii), is open to the same objection.

[1] W. W. Skeat (ed.), *The Kingis Quair*, Edinburgh, Blackwood, 1911[2] (*STS, new series, 1*).
[2] See pp. 15 and 26.
[3] Edinburgh, Register House, Treaties with France, nos. 8 and 7. The two powers, together with Paris, Archives Nationales, J 678, pièces 24–6, mentioned below, have been published by C. J. H. Walravens (*Alain Chartier, études biographiques*, 125–38).
[4] Delaunay, *Etude*, 259–60.

An undated entry in the accounts of the Burgh of Linlithgow for 1428 refers to expenses incurred on behalf of the Archbishop of Rheims and the Lord of Darnley on their first arrival; Chartier is not mentioned.[1]

At Perth, on 17 July 1428, James I nominated three representatives to negotiate the marriage, to arrange matters affecting the future Dauphiness and to seek the renewal of the alliances with France.[2] Agreement was reached without delay for a new treaty of alliance was signed that same day;[3] by letters patent issued at Perth on 19 July, James I gave his consent to the marriage and promised to send to France 6,000 men-at-arms.[4] The only question which remained to be settled, that of the Lady Margaret's dowry, seems to have been beyond the competence of the French ambassadors; arrangements were made for a Scottish embassy to be sent to France later in the year to discuss the matter further.

It is not known when the French ambassadors left Scotland. The embassy sent by James I was present at the French court in October. In a letter signed at Chinon on 30 October, Charles VII ratified the marriage agreement reached in Scotland; some further conditions were agreed and provisions were made for the dowry of the future Dauphiness.[5] Alain Chartier, whose name is mentioned in the rehearsal of the negotiations, may have been present.

The embassy to Scotland was not without its effect on Chartier's literary reputation. The part which he played in negotiating her marriage must be the ultimate source of the celebrated but apocryphal anecdote according to which the Dauphiness Margaret kissed the sleeping Chartier on the mouth. She excused herself saying: 'Je n'ay pas baisé l'homme, mais la precieuse bouche de laquelle sont yssuz et sortis tant de bons motz et vertueuses parolles.'[6] The Dauphiness did not arrive at the French court until 1436, six years after Chartier's death.

During November 1428 Alain Chartier signed two royal letters, the

---

[1] G. Burnett (ed.), *The Exchequer Rolls of Scotland*, IV, Edinburgh, H.M. General Register House, 1880, 485.
[2] Paris, Archives Nationales, J 678, pièces 21–3.
[3] J 678, pièce 24.   [4] J 678, pièce 25.
[5] J 678, pièce 26; it incorporates a copy of pièce 25.
[6] Jehan Bouchet, *Les Annalles d'Acquitaine...*, Paris, Jehan Mace, 1537, fol. S.i.v. According to Bouchet, one reason why the incident aroused comment was because Chartier's face was ugly. Chartier's ugliness, like the anecdote, became proverbial.
   C. J. H. Walravens (*Alain Chartier, études biographiques*, 57–8), though rejecting the anecdote, is more favourable to the suggestion that Chartier was, or had grown, ugly. The passages from Chartier's works and from another source cited by Dr Walravens point to Chartier's having grown thin and prematurely old, not ugly; even these quotations need not all be taken literally, but could in some cases be exaggerated for effect.

first at Chinon on the 6th, the second at Selles on the last day of the month. No later official document has been found bearing his signature. Nevertheless, it is clear that he was still at court at the end of July 1429. His *Epistola de Puella*,[1] in which he set down for a foreign prince his impressions of Joan of Arc, was written after the prince's envoy had spoken to him in Bourges. The letter gives an enthusiastic account of the Maid's exploits and achievements and mentions both the relief of Orleans in the previous April and the coronation of Charles VII at Rheims on 17 July. Suggestions that Chartier may have fallen from favour about this time[2] appear to have no foundation. Indeed, if an epitaph and a rubric in *Nm* are to be believed, Chartier may have become a member of the royal council. Promotion from the rank of secretary to that of councillor was not unusual and Chartier had served his master faithfully; such advancement might explain the fact that no document later than November 1428 has been found signed by him.

While there is some evidence that Alain Chartier did resign his post as *notaire et secrétaire du roi*, the source in question is less informative than it appears at first sight. Some fragments, taken from bindings, are bound together in Paris, Bibl. Nat., n.a.lat. 2615. At the very top of fol. 7v, from which a vertical strip has been cut, there is written:

> harretier eut les bourses
> Et apres les resigna
> rretier son frere et apres le (*sic*).

The brother mentioned must be Thomas Chartier described as a *notaire et secrétaire du roi* in the act of 1455 which has already been discussed.[3] No further conclusions can be drawn from the fragment, however.

---

[1] Io. Lamius, *Deliciae eruditorum...*, IV, Florentiae, Vivianii, 1737, 38–42; J. Quicherat, *Procès de condamnation et de réhabilitation de Jeanne d'Arc*, V, Paris, 1849, 131–6 (SHF); Delaunay, *Etude*, 206–10; Hemeryck, *Alain Chartier, poète et penseur*.

The title above has been adopted instead of *Epistola ad Imperatorem*, given in *Lf*, and the only title found in any manuscript of the work. Although C. J. H. Walravens (*Alain Chartier, études biographiques*, 83–4) and others have taken the contrary view, Quicherat is surely correct in thinking that the opening words of the letter 'Illustrissime princeps' are not those which would be addressed to the Emperor. Miss P. Hemeryck (*op. cit.*, 211–22) argues thoughtfully and convincingly that the letter was sent to the Duke of Milan.

[2] See Margaret S. Blayney, 'Alain Chartier and Joachism?', *Modern Language Notes*, LXX, 1955, 506–9. It is argued that Chartier may have been disgraced because he presented Joachist ideas in the *Livre de l'Esperance*. Since the work is unfinished, there is no guarantee that it was published before Chartier's death.

C. J. H. Walravens (*Alain Chartier, études biographiques*, 49–53) concludes that the suggestions have no foundation, but advances different reasons in a full discussion of the problem.

[3] See pp. 1–2.

As will be shown later, Alain Chartier was probably entitled to both the *gages* and the *bourses* which attached to the office.[1] His resignation may have been a partial one, to ensure his brother's succession, in which case Alain Chartier would have retained the *gages* attached to the office; it may have been a complete resignation, that of the *gages* being listed elsewhere in the original manuscript. Whether it was partial or complete, it may have been only a precautionary measure taken, for example, before the embassy to Scotland – Chartier's supposed resignation of his Canonry of Notre-Dame de Paris in favour of his brother Guillaume in December 1427 was alleged to have been made in case he failed to return from that embassy.[2]

Alain Chartier died at Avignon on 20 March 1429/30, and was buried there in the Church of Saint-Antoine.[3] Two fifteenth-century epitaphs are known: the first was apparently written soon after his death and is a literary exercise rather than a tomb inscription; the second dates from April 1458 and was intended to be engraved on a memorial.

The later epitaph was commissioned by Guillaume Chartier, then Bishop of Paris. A copy has survived of the contract drawn up between Johannes de Fonte, a stonemason, and Guillaume Chartier for the setting up in the church of a stone, bearing both an 'ymago seu forma' and an inscription to be provided by the Bishop; in the contract Alain Chartier is described as 'reverendissimus quondam magister Alanus, archidiaconus Parisiensis'.[4] The stone itself has not survived.

In the early eighteenth century an antiquarian, Joseph-François de Remerville, noted in the church an inscription which has subsequently disappeared; it seems to have been destroyed when the church was renovated between 1730 and 1745. The inscription read:[5]

HIC JACET

Virtutibus insignis, scientiâ et eloquentiâ Clarus
Alanus Chartier, ex Bojocis (*sic*) in Normaniâ natus,
Parisiensis Archidiaconus et Consiliarius, Regio
jussu ad Imperatorem, multosque Reges Ambasciator

---

[1] See p. 25.   [2] See p. 26.

[3] A very full account of the different dates which have been suggested is published by C. J. H. Walravens (*Alain Chartier, études biographiques*, 40–8).

[4] Abbé Requin, 'Jean de Fontay et le tombeau d'Alain Chartier', *Bulletin archéologique du Comité des Travaux Historiques et Scientifiques*, 1892, 434–43.

[5] Abbé Expilly, *Dictionnaire géographique, historique et politique des Gaules et de la France*, 1, Paris, 1762, 341. The epitaph was reprinted in 1870 by Du Fresne de Beaucourt and by Piaget in 1894 (see p. 16, n. 1); in both cases the epitaph is laid out in a mixture of short and long lines and the date is given in Roman numerals.

saepiùs transmissus, qui libros varios stilo
elegantissimo composuit, et tandem obdormivit in
Domino in hac Avenionensi Civitate, anno
Domini 1449.

The form and the style of the epitaph suggest that it is not the epitaph commissioned by Guillaume Chartier.[1] At the same time, it is largely accurate in the information which it gives. It seems likely that Remerville copied an epitaph which had itself been refashioned from an earlier, probably the original, version; such refections are not unknown. The date in the epitaph is clearly wrong, for reasons that will be discussed presently. The statement that Alain Chartier was a royal councillor is corroborated by the rubric in *Nm*.

A much earlier epitaph, in Latin hexameters, was published in 1929 by R. Busquet from a register of Yves Roussel, a notary in Arles.[2] Busquet considered the hand of the epitaph to be almost identical with the hand in which documents dated between 1430 and 1433 are copied in the same register: the quire which includes the hexameters also contains a copy of a judgement made on 14 February 1432. The text itself is faulty and Busquet suggested a number of emendations, which are given here in brackets:

Ortibus excelsis egressus (expulsus) Fulgure Phebes (Phebus)
Palladis auxilio qui (que) vicit (vincit) menia, picti
Munere Mercurii refulgens tempore toto,
Sublimibus volitans (Sublimis voliturus), ab alis fatus (factus) Alanus
5 Haurige licuit ductoris carpere nomen,
Infima qui novit nitente (nitenti) luminis haustu,
Junxit qui lilii facundia federa regis,
Imperium Franco qui valuit (valuit qui) nectere regno
Quid fatear tanto (tantis) decorum laudibus? Ipsi (Ipse)
10 Sileo, non validus decores pendere miros,
Aut morum cumulos, aut gestus dicere celsos,
Aut mentis arduos (ardua) censendi singula fagos (sagax)
Hoc jacet in lacu (in tumulo), poscens a judice grates,
In superum requie, pulsa caligine, nitens,
15 Corporis ac tenues animi reverberat visus.
Millibus ex annis centum quater atque vigintim (et triginta)
Exulat a seclo, motrisque gracia (mortique graciis), datis,

---

[1] A. Piaget, 'L'épitaphe d'Alain Chartier', *Romania*, XXIII, 1894, 152–6.
[2] R. Busquet, 'Une épitaphe d'Alain Chartier', *Mémoires de l'Institut Historique de Provence*, VI, 1929, 179–87. The text of C. J. H. Walravens (*Alain Chartier, études biographiques*, 213–14), based on a re-examination of the register, is slightly different: 4 *aliis*; 7 *lilie*; 9 *tanta*.

Marcii vicesima saliens in eternum summum;
Pro cujus anima sacras effundere preces
20 Postulat ut velint carmen hoc legere grati.

The style of the epitaph, learned but contrived, shows that its author was a man of some literary pretensions. The copyist was clearly not the author of the piece; the text which has been preserved may be an imperfectly memorised version of the original.

The epitaph's most tantalising feature is the date, which in the register reads 20 March 1420. The date is wrong just as clearly as 1449, the date in the Remerville epitaph, is wrong. Can these contradictions be resolved?

At this period Arles and Avignon both used the style of the Nativity in dating documents. The practice of the French court, on the other hand, was to begin the New Year at Easter; Guillaume Chartier would almost certainly have followed the so-called *mos gallicus*. If it is assumed that Chartier died on 20 March 1430, that is before Easter, then the date would be so described in Arles or Avignon but would be expressed by a French prelate as 20 March 1429, that is 1429/30. The contradictions can be resolved if it is accepted that *triginta* was miscopied as *vigintim* and that M CCCC XXIX was wrongly carved or wrongly copied, whether by mason or antiquary, as M CCCC XLIX.[1] Mistakes in the transcription of Roman numerals were not infrequent even in the fifteenth century.[2]

That Alain Chartier died in 1429/30 is confirmed by circumstantial evidence. The canonry of Notre-Dame de Paris once held by Alain Chartier was the subject of a law-suit between 1440 and 1444;[3] from the depositions of both plaintiff and defendant it is clear that Chartier had been dead for some years. Jean Regnier, who was in captivity from January 1432 until May 1433, apparently sang just after his release a song composed by

Maistre Alain, duquel Dieu ait l'ame
Lequel cy gist soubz une lame;[4]

Regnier's *Livre de la Prison* may have been revised at a later date, however. Guillaume Chartier is described about 1432 as rector of the parish of Saint-Lambert-des-Levées, a charge previously held by his brother.[5]

---

[1] P. Hemeryck (*Alain Chartier, poète et penseur*) has independently reached the same conclusion. The date 20 March 1430 is that accepted by C. J. H. Walravens (*Alain Chartier, études biographiques*, 45) but for slightly different reasons.

[2] See M. Roy (ed.), *Œuvres poétiques de Christine de Pisan*, I, Paris, 1886, xxii, col. 2 (*SATF*).

[3] See p. 26.

[4] E. Droz (ed.), *Les Fortunes et adversitez de Jean Regnier*, Paris, 1923, 154 (*SATF*).

[5] *Gallia christiana*, VII, 1744, col. 150. See p. 9.

What Chartier's business was in Avignon and how long he had been there are not known. He was buried in the church of the regular canons of Saint-Antoine, a church dependent on the Abbey of Saint-Antoine de Vienne. Is it coincidental that Alain Chartier had spent the greater part of 1425 on diplomatic business in the company of its Abbot, Artaud de Granval?

As the preceding account shows, detailed information about the career of Alain Chartier is available only for the last twenty years of his life. Perusal of the chronological table[1] which follows will show that there are periods within those twenty years about which nothing at all is known. That is the case, for example, with the years 1423 and 1424. It may well be that during those years Chartier was engaged on normal secretarial business at the court in France. Nevertheless, in the absence of a catalogue of the letters of Charles VII, one cannot be certain that this was so. Further information about the career of Alain Chartier is most likely to come from such a catalogue.

Chronological table

19 February 1408/9– 19 September 1414	At some time between these dates, service in the household of Queen Yolande (A.N., KK 243, ff. 39r–v).
16 September 1417	*Paris*: signed a letter from the Dauphin Charles to the people of Tournai (Du Fresne de Beaucourt, *Histoire de Charles VII*, I, 437–8).
27 September 1417*	*Paris*: signed a letter confirming an exemption granted to Villeneuve-Saint-Georges (A.N., Y 10, ff. 14v–15r – copy).
31 January 1417/18	*Paris*: signed a letter from the Dauphin to the inhabitants of Lyons (L. Caillet, *Etude sur les relations de la commune de Lyon avec Charles VII et Louis XI (1417–1483)*, 1909, 304–5 (*Ann. de l'Univ. de Lyon*, n.s., *Droit, Lettres*, XXI)).
1 February 1417/18	*Paris*: signed a letter from the Dauphin to the town of Lyons (Du Fresne de Beaucourt, *Histoire de Charles VII*, I, 74, n. 4).[2]
13 June 1418	*Bourges*: signed two letters from the Dauphin to the town of Lyons (Thomas, *Romania*, XXXIII, 394).[3]
29 June 1418	*Aubigny*: signed a letter from the Dauphin to the town of Lyons (*ibid.*).

[1] The table is based on that in A. Thomas, 'Alain Chartier chanoine de Paris, d'après des documents inédits', *Romania*, XXXIII, 1904, 387–402, esp. 394–5; it was first published in J. C. Laidlaw, 'Master Alain Chartier and Master Alain Lequeu', *French Studies*, XXII, 1968, 191–200, esp. 195–8, and is reprinted here with some corrections and additions. The additions are marked with an asterisk; all except the first were kindly sent to me by Mr Satoshi Hosokawa. The abbreviations A.N. and B.N. refer to the Archives Nationales and the Bibliothèque Nationale in Paris.

C. J. H. Walravens (*Alain Chartier, études biographiques*, 149–211) has edited all but one of the letters and documents which I listed in 1968, and has published two further letters.

[2] C. J. H. Walravens (*ibid.*, 152, n. 1) is doubtful whether such a letter existed.

[3] The second letter was discovered by Dr Walravens (*ibid.*).

29 September 1418	*Maillezais*: signed a letter from the Dauphin to the Governor and Council of Dauphiné (B.N., Anjou et Touraine 9, no. 3827 – copy).
31 October 1418	*Chinon*: signed a letter from the Dauphin (Thomas, *Romania*, XXXIII, 394).
24 November 1418*	*Loches*: signed an order of payment (B.N., Clairambault 55, p. 4209, no. 136).
13 December 1418*	*Poitiers*: signed a letter (A.N., X^{Ic} 118, no. 135).
4 February 1418/19*	*Bourges*: signed a letter (A.N., X^{Ic} 117, no. 71).
6 May 1419	*Mehun sur Yevre*: signed a letter dealing with finances (London, B.M., Additional Charter 3519).
20 May 1419	*La Ferté Hubert*: signed a letter from the Dauphin proclaimed in various towns ([L. F. J. de la Barre], *Mémoires pour servir à l'histoire de France et de Bourgogne*, Paris, J.-M. Gandouin et P.-F. Giffart, 1729, 253–4).
11 September 1419	*Montereau fault Yonne*: signed letters to the town and to the University of Paris (Thomas, *Romania*, XXXIII, 394; A.N., X^{Ia} 8603, ff. 55v–56r – copy).
15 September 1419	*Nemours*: signed letters from the Dauphin to the Duke and to the Duchess of Burgundy (Thomas, *Romania*, XXXIII, 394; originals in B.N., Moreau 1425, nos. 84–5).
September 1419 (?)	Signed instructions for the Comte d'Aumale, the Dauphin's envoy to the Duke of Burgundy (*ibid.*, no. 93).
27 September 1419	*Gyen*: signed a letter from the Dauphin to the town of Carcassonne (Le Sieur Besse, *Recueil de diverses pièces servant à l'histoire du roy Charles VI*, Paris, A. de Sommaville, 1660, 317–26).
15 October 1419	*Loches*: signed a letter from the Dauphin to the Duke of Burgundy (Thomas, *Romania*, XXXIII, 394).
October 1419 (?)	Signed an account of the events which had led to the murder of John the Fearless. The account seems to have been intended to accompany the letter of 15 October (B.N., Moreau 1425, no. 94).
21 October 1419*	*Bourges*: signed a letter (A.N., X^{Ic} 119, no. 118 – vidimus).
13 November 1419	*Bourges*: signed a letter from the Dauphin to the Abbot of Mont-Saint-Michel (S. Luce, *Chronique du Mont-Saint-Michel*, 1, Paris, 1879, 93–5 [*SATF*]).
27 December 1419	*Bourges*: signed a letter from the Dauphin to the Parlement of Poitiers (Thomas, *Romania*, XXXIII, 394).
2 January 1419/20	*Bourges*: signed a letter by which the Dauphin authorised a payment to the Bâtard d'Alençon (B.N., f.fr. 20372, no. 80).[1]
27 February 1419/20*	*Bourges*: signed a letter (A.N., X^{Ic} 122, no. 3).
February or March 1419/20	Nominated Canon of Paris by the Bishop, Gérard de Montaigu (Thomas, *Romania*, XXXIII, 394).

[1] Dated 1419 by Dr Walravens (*ibid.*, 159).

17 June 1420*	*Poitiers*: signed a letter giving powers to the Cardinal Duke of Bar (S. Luce, *Jeanne d'Arc à Domrémy*, Paris, Champion, 1886, 307–10; original in B.N., Lorraine 200, no. 4[2])[1].
23 June 1420	*Poitiers*: signed a letter by which the Dauphin appointed the Duc d'Alençon and the Comte d'Aumale as his lieutenants in Normandy (Luce, *Chronique du Mont-Saint-Michel*, I, 102–5).
31 January 1420/1	*Celles en Berry*: signed a letter whereby the Dauphin bestowed confiscated lands on the Duke of Orleans (A.N., K 59, no. 32).[2]
1 July 1421	Listed as one of the Dauphin's creditors in an account covering the previous six months (A.N., KK 50, fol. 19r).
6 September 1421	Confirmed as a Canon of Paris by the Dauphin (Thomas, *Romania*, XXXIII, 395).
1 January 1421/2	Listed as a creditor of the Dauphin in an account for the second half of 1421 (A.N., KK 50, fol. 48v).
19–23 January 1421/2	*Limoges*: signed a letter in Latin addressed to the consuls of the town (Thomas, *Romania*, XXXIII, 395).[3]
1 July 1422	Listed as one of the Dauphin's creditors in an account for the first six months of the year (A.N., KK 50, fol. 76v).
30 November 1422	Listed again as a creditor in an account for the previous five months (*ibid.*, fol. 80[bis]v).
11 December 1422	*Mehun sur Yevre*: signed a letter in Latin from Charles VII to the town of Toulouse (Thomas, *Romania*, XXXIII, 395).
3 January 1422/3	*Bourges*: signed a royal letter in favour of La Rochelle (*ibid.*).
8 February 1422/3	*Bourges*: signed a letter in Latin dealing with the confiscation of lands near Toulouse (Cl. Devic et J. Vaissete, *Histoire générale du Languedoc*, Toulouse, Privat, x, 1885, cols. 2024–6).
2 March 1422/3	*Bourges*: signed two letters in Latin in favour of Jehan de Vaily (A.N., X[Ia] 8604, ff. 112v–113r – copy).
23 October 1424	*Pont du Sec*: signed a letter in favour of Mont-Saint-Michel (B.N., f.fr. 25710, no. 29).
27 October 1424	*Lodun*: signed a letter dealing with finances (B.N., f.fr. 26047, no. 339).[4]
31 December 1424	*Espaly pres du Puy*: named in letters of credence as one of the King's ambassadors to the Emperor Sigismund and to Nicholas Garai, Count Palatine of Hungary (Thomas, *Romania*, XXXIII, 395).
1425	Named as one of the King's ambassadors in letters of credence to Pope Martin V (*ibid.*).
3 May 1425	*Venice*: named as one of the French envoys in a report made by the Doge to the Venetian Senate (*ibid.*).

[1] Dated 27 June by Dr Walravens (*ibid.*, 190–2).
[2] Dated 1420 by Dr Walravens (*ibid.*, 186–7).
[3] The time has been narrowed down by Dr Walravens (*ibid.*, 194, n. 35).
[4] The letter is not among those published by Dr Walravens.

4 July 1425	Object of a request to Pope Martin V (Thomas, *Romania*, xxxv, 603).
3 December 1425	*Mehun sur Yevre*: signed a letter appointing Jean, Sr. de Graville, Captain of Mont-Saint-Michel (Luce, *Chronique du Mont-Saint-Michel*, I, 233–5).
2 April and 2 May 1426	*Tournai*: passed through the town on those dates in the course of an embassy to the Duke of Burgundy (Thomas, *Romania*, xxxiii, 395).
24 November 1426	Mentioned in a list of beneficiaries submitted for approval to Pope Martin V (Thomas, *Romania*, xxxvi, 306–7).
December 1427	Resigned his Canonry of Paris in favour of his brother (Thomas, *Romania*, xxxiii, 395).
7 April 1428	*Chinon*: named as one of the King's envoys to James I of Scotland in two sets of instructions (Edinburgh, Register House, Treaties with France, nos. 7–8).
17 July 1428	*Perth*: mentioned as an envoy in a treaty of alliance negotiated between Scotland and France (Thomas, *Romania*, xxxiii, 395).
30 October 1428	*Chinon*: mentioned in similar terms when the treaty was ratified by Charles VII (*ibid.*).
6 November 1428	*Chinon*: signed a letter giving confiscated lands to the Count of Vendôme (A.N., K 63, no. 3).
30 November 1428	*Selles*: signed an order of payment (B.N., f.fr. 25710, no. 60).
20 March 1430	*Avignon*: death of Alain Chartier (Busquet, 'Une épitaphe', 179–87).

So far as is known, Alain Chartier spent the years from about 1410 to 1430 in royal service. Although nothing has been discovered about the position which he filled in the household of Queen Yolande, a great deal of information is available about the duties and privileges attached to the office of *notaire et secrétaire du roi*. Some discussion of that office must precede an examination of Chartier's poetical works, of the order in which they were written and of the circumstances which gave rise to them.

The *notaires du roi* made up a select body which had an important part to play in government.[1] The number of notaries was in theory restricted to fifty-nine, 'dont le roi était le soixantième'; that the King should have consented to be described in that fashion shows the esteem in which they were held. The notaries dealt with the general correspondence of the Chancellery. Among their number they included a smaller body of secretaries who were alone empowered, as their name suggests, to sign

---

[1] On the *notaires et secrétaires du roi*, see O. Morel, *La Grande Chancellerie royale...*(*1328–1400*), Paris, Picard, 1900 (*Mémoires et documents publiés par la Société de l'Ecole des Chartes*, III). Most of the observations made about the notaries are also valid for the first part of the fifteenth century. See also Paris, Bibl. de l'Arsenal, MS 4544.

secret letters. The two posts were cumulative; it was not possible to be a secretary without also being a notary.

A royal secretary would be acquainted with the day-to-day business of government and with the detail of royal policy. He would, by virtue of his office, be in close contact with the monarch, with the chief officers of state and with the royal council. Secretaries often served as ambassadors and might on occasion become members of the council; it is likely therefore that they played their part in formulating policy.

During the embassies in which he took part, Alain Chartier must have become well acquainted with some of the most important churchmen, courtiers and soldiers in the service of Charles VII. As ambassadors travelled, they would have ample time to discuss the contemporary political situation and to seek for solutions to the problems facing France. Chartier's later political works, for example the *Livre de l'Esperance*, must have benefited greatly from the opportunities presented by an embassy for discussion, for meditation or for reading. The *Excusacion* was composed in 1425 during an embassy;[1] it may not be the only work to have been written when Chartier was away from the court on diplomatic business.

The atmosphere at the court of France and particularly in the Chancellery must have been conducive to scholarship. The position of *notaire et secrétaire du roi* was an attractive one which a writer would be well qualified to fill. During the fourteenth and fifteenth centuries the royal notaries and secretaries included a number of men of letters, some distinguished for their Latin scholarship, some for their skill in writing in the vernacular. Guillaume de Machaut was for a time secretary to John of Luxemburg, King of Bohemia; it is probable that he went on to serve Jean II or Charles V of France in the same capacity.[2] Earlier the *Roman de Fauvel* had been written by Gervais du Bus, a notary in the royal household;[3] the *Roman du comte d'Anjou* was composed about the same time by a Jehan Maillart who may well have been the secretary of that name who served Philippe IV le Bel and his sons.[4] The secretaries of Charles VI included Jean de Montreuil and Gontier Col.[5] Both men were greatly interested in humanistic scholarship, as is shown by their concern to widen their knowledge of the Latin classics, to establish better texts of classical

[1] See pp. 7–8.
[2] E. Hoepffner (ed.), *Œuvres de Guillaume de Machaut*, I, Paris, 1908, xxxiv–xxxvii (*SATF*).
[3] A. Lângfors (ed.), *Le Roman de Fauvel par Gervais du Bus*, Paris, 1914–19, lxxi–lxxii (*SATF*).
[4] M. Roques (ed.), *Jehan Maillart: le Roman du comte d'Anjou*, Paris, 1931, v–vi (*CFMA*).
[5] Coville, *Gontier et Pierre Col*, 11.

authors, famed and less well known, and to cultivate through their correspondence an elegant and refined Latin style. They were associated further-
more with other prominent men of letters: with Nicolas de Clamanges
whose interests matched their own and with whom they exchanged letters;
with the keeper of the papal library at Avignon and with the humanists
connected with that court; with Jean Gerson and Christine de Pisan, the
plaintiffs in the quarrel over the *Roman de la Rose*. Christine de Pisan was
herself the widow of a royal secretary and her son, Jean Chastel, followed
his father's profession; indeed, it was he who was named by the ladies as
one of their two advocates in the *Responce* which, as has already been
mentioned, was sent by the ladies to Alain Chartier in the spring or early
summer of 1425.[1]

Alain Chartier's works, whether in Latin or in French, betray the
influence of these writers, of their techniques, their ideas and preoccupa-
tions. Although he nowhere acknowledges directly that he had known
them, it is probable that he met at least some of them during his career
in royal service. It would have been difficult for him to avoid meeting
Gontier Col for example; many royal letters written at Paris about the
year 1417 bear the latter's signature.[2]

Interest in literature at the court was not confined to the officials of the
Chancellery. The King and the different royal Dukes were patrons of the
arts and the many manuscripts extant which were presented to them are
an indication of the support which they gave to literature in particular.
The *Cent Ballades* were composed by a group of nobles towards the end of
the fourteenth century;[3] the work was widely known and it may not be
a coincidence that the first line of the *Belle Dame sans Mercy* is strangely
similar to the opening lines of the collection. The works of Jean de
Garencières, soldier and poet, were apparently less well known.[4] Nevertheless they were read and appreciated by the young Charles d'Orléans,
who knew Garencières well. The only known manuscript of the poems of
Garencières, *Ph*, contains the works of two other poets, Alain Chartier
and Charles d'Orléans. Chartier may have met them both in Paris before
the battle of Agincourt, where the one was to meet his death and the other
to be captured. The part played by the Duchess of Orleans in the *Livre*

---

[1] See pp. 7–8.

[2] Coville, *Gontier et Pierre Col*, 22–3; Paris, Archives Nationales, JJ 169–71.

[3] G. Raynaud (ed.), *Les Cent Ballades, poème du XIVe siècle, composé par Jean le Seneschal avec la col-
laboration de Philippe d'Artois, comte d'Eu, de Boucicaut le Jeune et de Jean de Crésecque*, Paris, 1905
(*SATF*).

[4] Y. A. Neal, *Le Chevalier poète Jehan de Garencières (1372–1415)*, I–II, Paris, Nizet, 1953.

des Quatre Dames suggests some link between Chartier and the house of Orleans; his sympathies lie with the Orleanists.[1]

While Chartier can hardly have met Oton de Granson who was killed in a judicial duel in 1397, it is clear that he knew his works: Granson is one of the few poets whom he mentioned by name.[2] Poems by Granson were copied frequently with poems by Chartier so that for long their works were confused.[3] On the other hand, Chartier seems to have been personally acquainted with Pierre de Nesson who wrote the *Lay de Guerre* in imitation of the *Lay de Paix* and is mentioned in the *Debat du Herault, du Vassault et du Villain*. The relationship between the two poets will be discussed when the debate is examined.[4]

The magnificent royal library, largely founded by Charles V and enlarged by Charles VI, was close at hand while Chartier was at the court in Paris. The records of the library mention one manuscript which was given to a royal secretary.[5] It is likely that Alain Chartier was allowed access to the library. Only one manuscript, the copy of Sallust already mentioned, is known to have belonged to Alain Chartier. The inscription on the fly-leaf in his own hand indicates that the volume had formed part of the library of Guillaume de Boisratier, Archbishop of Bourges, and had been given to Chartier by the Bishop of Valence, Jean de Poitiers, after the Archbishop's death, that is after 1421.[6] Although Chartier's library doubtless contained more books than the Sallust, that volume alone is revealing enough: it is a manuscript of the eleventh century of the kind prized by the humanists. It is in fact listed and discussed in modern editions of the two works by Sallust which it contains.[7]

In drawing this picture of life at court, too much emphasis has perhaps been laid on the opportunities which the court, its society and its facilities, afforded to Chartier the author. That there was another side to the picture is shown by the bitterness and disillusion which characterise his *De Vita Curiali*.[8] Court life is presented as irregular, disorganised and unjust; the

---

[1] See pp. 35–6 and lines 3276–343.   [2] *Le Debat de Reveille Matin*, line 231.

[3] A. Piaget, *Oton de Grandson, sa vie et ses poésies*, Lausanne etc., Payot, 1941, 107–26, esp. 108–9 (*Mémoires et documents publiés par la Société d'Histoire de la Suisse romande*, IIIe série, 1).

[4] See pp. 37–8.

[5] L. Delisle, *Le Cabinet des manuscrits*, I, Paris, Imprim. Nat., 1868, 51.

[6] 'Salustius. In Catilinario & Jugurta. De libris Guillielmi Boisratier de bituris *famosi Olim, nunc autem de libris alani aurige de baiocis.*
   Habui hunc librum a domino episcopo valencinen. dono.'
   That part of the inscription which is in Chartier's hand is printed in italics.

[7] E.g. B. Ornstein (ed.) et J. Roman, *Salluste: Conjuration de Catilina, Guerre de Jugurtha*, Paris, 1924 (*Collection Guillaume Budé*).

[8] F. Heuckenkamp (ed.), *Le Curial par Alain Chartier*, Halle s. S., Niemeyer, 1899.

typical courtier as envious, self-seeking and unscrupulous. While certain of Chartier's observations were doubtless exaggerated for effect, it must be remembered that in his letters *Ad Ingratum Amicum* and *Ad Invidum et Detractorem* he expressed a similar disillusion with members of the society in which he moved.[1] The letters make it clear that he had experienced injustice and disfavour.

Material considerations may have had their part in Chartier's discontent. The position of *notaire et secrétaire du roi* was an attractive one, in untroubled times. It entitled the holder to the privileges and exemptions attaching to membership of the royal household. Chief among these were exemption from the *tailles* and from ordinary jurisdiction. The stipend was made up of *gages*, a fixed daily payment, and *bourses*, a share in the dues levied on the documents issued by the Chancellery; there were also certain payments in kind. A judgement dated 14 March 1410/11 speaks of 'officium predictum secretariatus et notariatus cum bursis vadijs (*alias* gagiis) et mantellis ac alijs proficuis et emolumentis'.[2]

Taken together, these payments made up a more than adequate salary. Alain Chartier was probably paid both *gages* and *bourses*:[3] he had the latter for he was to resign them in favour of his brother;[4] an entry dated July 1422 in the account-book of the *Chambre aux Deniers* implies that he was also entitled to *gages*.[5] The entry is found under the heading: 'Item debtes pour gaiges comptez aux offices oudit chappitre d'escuierie'. It reads:

> A maistre alain charretier pour ce (i.e. ses
> gaiges) audit mois (de juillet) vi^{xx}l.

The three other entries in the book which relate to Chartier all occur under the heading *Fourriere* and refer to monies owed by the Dauphin for 'hostellages chevaulx et busche' or some combination of these; the debts are listed in three six-monthly accounts which begin on 1 January 1420/1 and end on 1 July 1422. The sums involved are not inconsiderable: on 1 July 1421, 67l. 2s. 8d. is owing; six months later there is a debt of 12l. 6s. 0d.; the debt listed on 1 July 1422 amounts to 82l. 16s. 0d.[6]

---

[1] The first letter is printed in Du Chesne, *Les Œuvres de Maistre Alain Chartier*, 488–9, the second in Walravens, *Alain Chartier, études biographiques*, 268–73; both letters have been edited by P. Hemeryck (*Alain Chartier, poète et penseur*).

[2] Paris, Bibl. de l'Arsenal, MS 4544, ff. 39v–41v, esp. 39v.

[3] The point must be made for it was not uncommon to separate the payments and thus divide one office between two holders. In that way a notary could nominate his successor. Successive kings forbade the practice but in vain. See Morel, *La Grande Chancellerie royale*, 83–4.

[4] See pp. 14–15.

[5] Paris, Archives Nationales, KK 50, ff. 80^{bis}r–v; the account runs to 30 November.

[6] KK 50: ff. 19r, 48v and 76v.

Most of the other account-books for the period of Chartier's service have disappeared. It is likely that his name figured in them likewise for the finances of Charles VII remained in a precarious state throughout the period under consideration. While the entries in the accounts of the Dauphin and of Queen Yolande have their value for us today, they must have been seen by Alain Chartier in a different light.

Those holders of royal offices who were in holy orders were frequently presented to ecclesiastical benefices as a reward for their services. The careers of earlier royal secretaries such as Guillaume de Machaut or Jean de Montreuil illustrate this well.[1] Alain Chartier likewise received preferment to a number of benefices during his career. He can have received no material benefit from some of them since they were situated in areas under enemy control.

In February or March 1419/20 Chartier was nominated a Canon of Notre-Dame de Paris by the Bishop, Gérard de Montaigu.[2] After the death of the Bishop on 20 September 1420, the Dauphin exercised his right of regale and confirmed Chartier in that office on 6 September 1421. The canonry is said to have been resigned by him in December 1427 in favour of his brother Guillaume. It is not clear whether the resignation was genuine or was simply a precaution taken lest Chartier might not return from his embassy to Scotland; divergent views were taken by the two parties to a dispute involving the canonry which began in 1440 and was not settled until 1444. In the contract for the epitaph commissioned by Guillaume, Alain Chartier is described not as *canonicus* but as *archidiaconus parisiensis*. When he became Archdeacon of Paris has not been discovered.

In the account of the embassies undertaken by Chartier in 1425, reference was made to a request concerning him which was submitted to the Pope on 4 July of that year. Chartier, who had been rector of the parish of Saint-Lambert-des-Levées in the diocese of Angers since the previous year, was allowed to defer his admission to full orders, as the incumbency demanded, until his return from the imperial court. It is to be presumed that Chartier was duly admitted to holy orders and inducted to the charge on his return. A later incumbent of the same parish was Guillaume Chartier who was described as such about 1432. It is not known whether the parish was resigned by Alain Chartier in the same way that he resigned his

[1] Hoepffner, *Œuvres de Guillaume de Machaut*, I, xix–xxvi; Coville, *Gontier et Pierre Col*, 73–4.
[2] The canonry and its part in the later law-suit are discussed in detail by A. Thomas in *Romania*, XXXIII, 1904, 387–402. The documents have been republished by C. J. H. Walravens (*Alain Chartier, études biographiques*, 139–46).

canonry of Paris, or whether Guillaume was presented to the parish only after his brother's death.

A French embassy to the papal court at Easter 1425 had been instructed to concede to Martin V his demands concerning preferment to benefices. In November of the following year, the Pope agreed at Charles VII's request to maintain in their office twenty-five persons who had been appointed to them by ordinary patrons. Alain Chartier is included 'pro canonicatu et prebenda ecclesie Turonensis, quos tenet'.[1] He is one of twelve royal councillors and secretaries to whom this favour was granted. As the document indicates, he already held those offices.

A further benefice to which Chartier was nominated at about this time was the Chancellorship of Bayeux. In all the documents relating to the embassy to Scotland, he is so described. While Chartier must have taken pride in the honour since Bayeux was his native town, he can have derived no more revenue from the office than he did from being a Canon or Archdeacon of Paris; neither city was then in territory under the King's control.

[1] Paris, Archives Nationales, X$^{\text{1a}}$ 8604, 86r–87r and 89v–90r. The documents are analysed in Valois, *La Pragmatique Sanction de Bourges*, 38–42 and 52–5. See also A. Thomas, 'Encore Alain Chartier', *Romania*, XXXVI, 1907, 306–7.

2

The Poems

Storys to rede ar delitabill,
Suppos that thai be nocht bot fabill.

John Barbour

The preceding account of Chartier's life includes references to most of the
poems which can be dated accurately; they will provide a convenient
framework into which the other poems can be fitted. In discussing the
order in which the poetical works were written,[1] the statements made by
the poet about himself will be of importance. Chartier states in some
poems that he has no lady and has never known love; in others he is in
love; in others he mourns the death of his beloved and in his grief abandons
poetry. Such statements cannot be assumed to be reliable and straightforward. In evaluating them, some assessment will be made of the poems,
their form, their intention and their quality. The chapter is not intended,
however, to present a detailed analysis and appreciation of Chartier's
poetical works. It would be premature to do so in the absence of satisfactory
critical editions of Chartier's works in French prose.

'LE LAY DE PLAISANCE'

The *Lay de Plaisance* is one of Alain Chartier's earliest works.[2] It is a
poem for the New Year written

> 1   Pour commencer joyeusement l'annee...

The joy with which lovers greet one another is described and contrasted
with the attitude of the poet. He has no lady and has never been granted
true love:

---

[1] The reasons for accepting that a particular poem is authentic are given in the introduction to the
edition of the poem.

[2] Pierre Champion (*Histoire poétique*, I, 8–10) was of the same opinion. In dating the poem 1 January
1413 or 1414, he relied on statements in the *Livre des Quatre Dames*, composed in 1416; according
to them Chartier had been in love for two years. It is shown below that the *Debat des Deux Fortunés
d'Amours* was written in 1412 or 1413. The *Lay de Plaisance* is almost certainly an earlier work
than the *Debat*. New Year's Day is Easter Day (see pp. 7 and 17).

> Dame qui soit ne sera huy penee
> Pour m'estrener, ne moy pour dame nee,
> 16 Dont je doy bien piteusement plourer.

Although his mood is sad, he advises the friend whom he addresses in the second stanza to cultivate *Plaisance*, which is to be interpreted as 'pleasure' or a 'pleasing, cheerful disposition'. The next nine stanzas are in definition and praise of *Plaisance*, which is necessary in love and is to be contrasted with *Mirencolie*. In the final stanzas the friend is enjoined to serve both *Plaisance* and *Amours*; if he does so, he will be the more acceptable and honoured as a lover.

Both the tone and the construction of the *Lay de Plaisance* confirm that it is an early work. The sections defining *Plaisance* and praising its worth are not well developed, being repetitive and at times obscure. The obscurity almost certainly results from the poet's need to force his thoughts into the difficult mould of the *lay*. The *Lay de Plaisance* is copied in a relatively small number of manuscripts and appears not to have been widely known or esteemed.

'LE DEBAT DES DEUX FORTUNÉS D'AMOURS'

The *Debat des Deux Fortunés d'Amours*, also known as the *Debat du Gras et du Maigre*, is almost certainly an early work.[1] It is a substantial poem, 1246 lines long, in which Alain Chartier displays more control over his material and much greater technical skill than in the *Lay de Plaisance*. In plan and also in metre, the *Debat des Deux Fortunés d'Amours* resembles a number of narrative poems by earlier writers; it is particularly close to the *Debat de Deux Amans* written by Christine de Pisan between 1400 and 1402.[2] The *Acteur* or Author plays a similar part in both works.

The two *Fortunés d'Amours* speak in turn; the fat knight, who maintains that more benefits than ills are to be derived from the service of love, is followed by his thin companion whose view is the reverse. These long speeches are followed by short replies from each knight before the problem is sent for arbitration. The author's role is that of observer and reporter: he sets the scene as the poem begins and ends, and he is the narrator of those passages which link the speeches delivered by the fat and thin knights; he is asked by the audience to make the debate ready

[1] The contrary view has generally been taken. See p. 31, n. 1.
[2] Roy, *Christine de Pisan*, II, 1891, xiii.

for presentation to the arbiter. Although the author's role is restricted and passive, his character is not undeveloped.

The poet hesitates to join in the conversation of the company in which he finds himself. It is partly because the joyous mood of the knights and ladies gathered in the castle contrasts with his own, but chiefly because he is timid and lacks experience:

> Ne ou parler d'elles ne me boutoye,
> Mais mon penser et ma langue arrestoye
> Et de faillir a parler me doubtoye,
> 16 Ardant d'apprendre
> Et d'aucun bien recevoir et comprendre
> En si hault lieu ou Honneur se doit prendre,
> Ou j'estoye le plus nice et le mendre.

When, towards the end of the poem, a search is made for a person suitable to record the debate, it is emphasised that he was

> 1232 Seul clerc present, escoutant par derriere
> Tout le debat, les poins et la maniere.

A final quatrain, which mentions the name Alain and with which the poem is signed, as it were, also emphasises the inexperience of a poet

> 1246 Qui parle ainsi d'amours par ouïr dire.

The arbiter to whom the poem was to be sent was Jean de Grailli, Count of Foix, who was at that time absent 'en ost armé'. The poem shows that Alain Chartier had some knowledge of Jean de Grailli and his affairs. The Count's amorous device 'J'ay belle dame' and the fact that his arms were quartered are worked into the closing lines. At three points he is described as the heir of (Gaston) Phoebus.[1]

Possible dates for the composition of the *Debat des Deux Fortunés d'Amours* are between 1412 and 1420, or between 1425 and 1430. Jean de Grailli was the eldest son of Archambaud, Captal of Buch and of Isabelle, Countess of Foix in her own right.[2] On 22 February 1411/12, after the death of her husband, Isabelle confirmed her son as Count of Foix. Jean de Grailli was appointed Captain-General of the royal forces in Languedoc soon afterwards and was presently engaged in conflict with the Arma-

---

[1] Gaston III, Count of Foix (1331–91).

[2] See L. Flourac, *Jean 1er comte de Foix, vicomte souverain de Béarn, lieutenant du roi en Languedoc,* Paris, Picard, 1884.

gnacs. In 1420, after various complaints about his administration, he was deprived of his office by the Dauphin. Relations between the Dauphin, later Charles VII, and the Count of Foix were strained, not to say hostile, until the two became reconciled early in 1425.

In fact the date can be narrowed still further. The device 'J'ay belle dame' makes up one of the short lines and is therefore in an emphatic position. The short line next following is also emphatic:

1207   Or l'a il (*sc.* Jean) belle.

It was taken by Gaston Paris to refer to Jean de Grailli's second marriage, to Jeanne d'Albret early in 1423; if this were the case, the poem would date from 1425 or 1426, in which years Jean de Grailli was engaged on several military expeditions.[1]

The case of the Count's first wife, Jeanne de Navarre, must also be considered, however. Perhaps the beauty of her person was such as to merit Chartier's description; as heiress apparent to the throne of Navarre, she was also an excellent match. If it is to her that Chartier is referring, then the poem must have been written between February 1411/12 and July 1413, when the Countess died. During 1412 the Count of Foix was at war with the Armagnacs: one expedition seems to have lasted from April until August or later; another foray took place in October.[2] It is probable that the poem was composed in 1412 at a time when the French court was anxious to win and keep the support of the house of Foix. The house of Anjou which had extensive interests in Provence would also favour this policy;[3] indeed, Louis of Anjou, King of Sicily, was present at the meeting of the Council at which the appointment of Jean de Grailli as Captain-General was approved.[4]

It would not be surprising in these circumstances that Alain Chartier, then in the service of Queen Yolande, should in 1412 have invited Jean, Count of Foix to serve as arbiter of the *Debat des Deux Fortunés d'Amours*. The literary evidence already discussed supports that date, which will be confirmed by the account of the *Livre des Quatre Dames* which follows.

Doubtless the *Debat des Deux Fortunés d'Amours* was intended to be presented to Jean de Grailli; no trace of a presentation copy has been found. One manuscript, *Ga*, contains only the poem, but its text is imperfect.

---

[1] G. Paris, 'Note additionnelle sur Jean de Grailli, comte de Foix', *Romania*, xv, 1886, 611–13. Later critics have been of the same opinion, though some doubt was cast on the traditional date by D. Poirion (*Le Poète et le prince...*, Paris, Presses Univ. de France, 1965, 267, n. 81).

[2] Flourac, *Jean 1er comte de Foix*, 51 and 54.

[3] Coville, *La Vie intellectuelle dans les domaines d'Anjou-Provence*, 5–10.

[4] Flourac, *Jean 1er comte de Foix*, 233–7.

Although the *Debat des Deux Fortunés d'Amours* was apparently better known than the *Lay de Plaisance*, neither poem seems to have enjoyed as wide a circulation as those written later. Whether there is some connection between the early date of these two poems and the relatively small number of copies in which they have survived, is uncertain.

'LE LIVRE DES QUATRE DAMES'

The *Livre des Quatre Dames* is the longest and most ambitious of Chartier's poetical works, being almost three times as long as the *Debat des Deux Fortunés d'Amours*. The prologue to the poem is in octosyllabic lines arranged in twelve stanzas of twelve or sixteen lines; the metre of the body of the poem recalls that of the *Debat des Deux Fortunés d'Amours*. There are other similarities in plan and treatment.

The four ladies are met by the poet as he walks in the countryside on the first morning of May. They are all in distress, having been affected each in a different way by a recent battle against the English. The battle, which had been disastrous for France and from which a number of French knights had fled, can only be Agincourt. The criticism meted out to fugitives and laggards in the speeches of the First and Fourth Ladies echoes that in contemporary accounts.[1] Nevertheless, the name of the battle is not given within the poem itself; in only one manuscript, *Pc*, is it named in the rubric of the poem. After the four ladies in turn had described their plight to the author, he returned to Paris:

> 3450 Envers Paris m'en retournay,
> Car sans y estre, bon jour n'ay.

The poem must therefore have been begun after 25 October 1415, the date of the battle, and finished before May 1418 when Chartier fled Paris to join the Dauphin. A poem of 3531 lines must have taken a considerable time to compose; it cannot have been completed before 1416.

The theme with which the *Livre des Quatre Dames* opens is a commonplace one. A prey to Melancholy, the poet seeks solace in the spring landscape. He walks alone as is his custom; the joy which he takes in contemplating the scene around him is dispelled as he recalls the reasons for his grief. The skill with which this very detailed description is handled suggests from the beginning that the *Livre des Quatre Dames* will mark an advance

---

[1] Mlle Dupont (ed.), *Mémoires de Pierre de Fenin*, Paris, 1837, 62–7 (SHF); L. Douët-D'Arcq (ed.), *La Chronique d'Enguerran de Monstrelet*, III, Paris, 1859, 103–21 (SHF).

on the earlier poems. The greater assurance of the poet is shown by his concern to amplify the introduction and by his confidence that, in doing so, he can retain the interest of his audience or reader: it is also apparent in the poet's willingness to analyse his own mood and to take an active rather than passive role in the action.

He is now in love and the victim of injustice at the hands of *Amours*. His lady is unaware of his love and he himself is too timid to declare his love to her or to recount the grief which besets him. His diffidence is further emphasised when he ventures the opinion that he is one of many who love her and that he is the least of them. His only consolation is that he has chosen well. In a passage which is probably more extravagant than true, he adds that since childhood he has suffered nothing but pain and trouble.

An account of his love-affair now follows. Of his heart he writes:

> 320 Je l'y ay mis
> Puis deux mois et m'en suy desmis,
> Et si ay a Amours promis
> Lui quicter, et m'en suy soubmis
> 324 A son bon vueil,
> Lui prïant qu'il change le dueil
> Que passé a deux ans recueil,
> Qui appert au doy et a l'oeil,
> 328 Par le refuz
> De celle a qui servant je fuz,
> Qui mist en mon cuer fers et fustz
> D'un dart amoureux dont confuz
> 332 Je me rendi.
> Par deux ans sa grace actendi...

Thus his present lady is not the only one to whom Chartier has lost his heart. He had loved another, and had waited for two years to have some token of her love, but to no avail. If these statements are accepted as true, then two or three years at least must separate the *Livre des Quatre Dames* from the *Debat des Deux Fortunés d'Amours* in which the poet 'parle d'amours par ouïr dire'. The dates suggested for the two poems are consistent with such an interval.

Chartier's lady, to whom he has now abandoned his heart, is mentioned again at the end of the *Livre des Quatre Dames*. It had originally been suggested that the poet himself should act as arbiter in the debate between the four ladies. After each has expounded in turn her claim to be considered the most worthy of pity, that proposal is set aside in favour of Chartier's own suggestion that his lady should be asked to arbitrate; a lady would in any case be a more fitting judge of a dispute involving members of her own sex. The poet now recalls his own diffidence in matters concerning love; we learn that, in a conversation with the lady which had taken place almost a year before, he had asserted:

> Qu'amant doit estre un an en crainte
> Sans oser descouvrir la plainte
> De quoy sa pensee est actainte.
> 3424 Bien lui souvient
> De ces paroles, se devient;
> Maiz s'en memoire lui revient,
> El scet que le bout de l'an vient.

A little earlier (lines 3396–7), he had said that it would soon be a year since he had fallen in love with his lady. That statement contradicts lines 320–33 quoted above; from them it seemed that Chartier had surrendered his heart to his lady some two months previously. The discrepancy can be explained by taking into account the time spent in writing the poem.

The *Livre des Quatre Dames* concludes with a request that the lady, who is not named, should judge the dispute. The poet hopes that she will not be displeased with the gift of his book and apologises in advance for any defects which it may contain. In its diffidence the apology recalls that with which the *Debat des Deux Fortunés d'Amours* had ended:

> 3475 Il m'est commis que je demande
> Vostre avis, Belle,
> D'une questïon bien nouvelle
> Dont en ce livre la querele
> J'ay mise en rime tele quele,
> 3480 Au long escripte.

The 'book' referred to here and at other points in the concluding lines may be the poem itself; it may also be a presentation copy intended to be given to the lady. The length of the *Livre des Quatre Dames* is such that it could conveniently be copied to make up a volume of small format. Six manuscripts are known which contain only the poem. *Dd* and *Df*, although they are too late in date for either of them to be the presentation copy, do contain, among a series of delicate miniatures, one depicting the presentation to the lady of the *Livre des Quatre Dames*.

Who Chartier's lady was, whether she was real or not, is impossible to determine. The information given about her is presented in such a way that, if she existed, she alone could have recognised herself. It is almost as difficult to identify the Four Ladies. No personal details are given of the Third Lady whose lover is still missing after the battle, nor of the Fourth Lady whose lover fled the field. Although the First Lady's lover, who was killed in the battle, is described as being:

> 706   De hault sang et royal lignage,

such a description fits more than one of the nobles who lost their lives at Agincourt.

More details are given of the Second Lady's lover, who now lies captive in England. In describing her love for him, the Second Lady mentions the great humility which he showed in loving her; she further stresses that, before he was twenty, he had often been the object of attacks by Fortune who had harried him since the age of ten:

>   Car sans mesprison,
> 1196   Mort d'amis, guerres et prison,
>   Couroux et pertes,
>   Blasmes par mensonges appertes,
>   Traÿsons, mauvaistiez couvertes
> 1200   A essaiees et expertes...

Before the battle her lover had been ill – she paints a pleasing picture of him composing ballades on his sick-bed – but had insisted on going to battle in order to forestall criticism. Since his capture she has had no letters from him nor indeed any news of him. The ladies of England are asked to intercede on his behalf.

The information given about the prisoner points to Charles d'Orléans. Charles was born on 24 November 1394 and was thus not quite twenty-one at the time of Agincourt.[1] The quarrel between the Burgundian and the Orleanist factions had turned into open hostility for the first time in the summer of 1405 when he was ten years old. The Second Lady refers to the ten years of civil war which ensued in lines 3293ff., especially in line 3298. During that time Fortune smiled but rarely on Charles d'Orléans: the murder of his father, Louis d'Orléans, in November 1407 is referred to by the Second Lady in lines 3260–3; December 1408 saw the death of his mother, Valentina Visconti; his wife, Isabelle de France, died in September 1409. And so Charles, at the age of fourteen, was left both an orphan and a widower. He subsequently married Bonne, daughter of the Count of Armagnac; their happiness was to be short-lived for Charles was captured

---

[1] See P. Champion, *La Vie de Charles d'Orléans (1394–1465)*, Paris, Champion, 1911 (*Bibliothèque du XVe siècle*, XIII).

at the battle of Agincourt. The Second Lady mentions her husband's great humility in loving her; if she were Bonne d'Armagnac, she might be referring both to the difference in rank between her husband and herself and also to the fact that Charles' first wife had been a daughter of Charles VI. While it is not known whether Charles d'Orléans was ill just before the battle, it is well established that he was already a poet of some repute.[1]

All four Ladies are fierce in their criticism of those who did not join the army or who fled the field, the First and Fourth Ladies being most outspoken. The way in which their two speeches combine expressions of private grief with bitter attacks on the behaviour of the noble and knightly classes is a striking and novel feature of the poem. As early as 1416, Alain Chartier was developing those ideas which he was to expound more forcibly and at greater length in prose, for example in the *Quadrilogue Invectif* of 1422 or in Latin works of the same period.

'LE BREVIAIRE DES NOBLES'

The duties incumbent on the nobility form the subject of the *Breviaire des Nobles*. Chartier's concern in the poem is to define and describe *noblesse*: he does so in a time-honoured and convenient way, by dividing the quality into twelve constituent virtues which are treated each in a separate ballade.[2] Since the definition and description of these virtues are theoretical and general, the poem cannot be dated.[3] In content, it recalls some of the lyrics of Christine de Pisan, particularly her *Autres Ballades*.[4] The idea of writing a sequence of ballades was not an original one and may have occurred to Chartier through his acquaintance with the lyric poetry of Christine de Pisan or with the *Cent Ballades*.[5]

[1] It is interesting to note that about 1442 the *librairie* of Charles d'Orléans contained 'Ung viel livre des Quatre Dames, en papier, couvert de viel parchemin' (P. Champion, *La Librairie de Charles d'Orléans*, Paris, 1910, 30); the way the manuscript is described suggests that he had owned it for some time.

[2] A similar plan was used by Christine de Pisan in the *Livre de la Paix*, when she defined *vertu* in terms of *prudence* and six other virtues. See Charity C. Willard (ed.), *The 'Livre de la Paix' of Christine de Pisan*, 's-Gravenhage, Mouton, 1958, 64.

[3] E. Droz (*Alain Chartier: le Quadrilogue invectif*, viii) suggested 1424 as a possible date.

[4] For example *Autre Ballade* L, a description of the duties of a *gentilhomme*. See Roy, *Christine de Pisan*, I, 264–6.

[5] See p. 23.

The poems

'LE LAY DE PAIX'

Possible dates for the composition of the *Lay de Paix* have already been discussed and rejected.[1] The poem resembles the *Breviaire des Nobles* in that Peace, like Nobility, is discussed on a general level. Although the *Lay de Paix* is addressed to the 'Princes nez du lis precïeux', it is not certain that it was inspired by any particular event. The poem was probably composed before Chartier's embassy to the Duke of Burgundy but could have been written considerably earlier than April 1426.

'LE DEBAT DU HERAULT, DU VASSAULT ET DU VILLAIN'[2]

The plight of France is discussed in more specific terms in the *Debat du Herault, du Vassault et du Villain*. The greater part of the poem is taken up by a debate between a *Herault* and a *Vassault*. They both agree that the present situation is desperate, but, whereas the *Vassault* is discouraged and disillusioned, the *Herault* advocates positive action and a return to the values of earlier generations. Their debate is overheard by a *Villain* who interrupts it rudely to present the views of the peasantry. The grievances and prejudices of the three are set down in appropriately forthright language and in simple rhymes.

While in subject the poem bears some resemblance to the *Quadrilogue Invectif*, it is a much less developed and polished production than the prose work. The suggestions that the *Debat du Herault*... dates from 1422 like the *Quadrilogue Invectif*[3] or that it was written between 1421 and 1425[4] can be discounted: the allusions in the poem are far from specific. The references to the English, however, do suggest that it dates from after the invasion of 1415.

The *Debat du Herault*... has some puzzling features. The last two stanzas, which indicate that the poem is by Chartier, are attached to the poem rather inconsequentially. They mention Pierre de Nesson, the 'vaillant bailly d'Aigueperse', but the words attributed to him show him to be anything but valorous.[5] Chartier adds, tongue in cheek, that he has told his copyist not to show Nesson the poem:

---

[1] See p. 11.

[2] The debate has until now been known as the *Debat Patriotique*. See p. 421.

[3] Champion, *Histoire poétique*, I, 42; Droz, *Alain Chartier: le Quadrilogue invectif*, viii.

[4] Walravens, *Alain Chartier, études biographiques*, 68–71.

[5] Lines 429–32. It is not known when Nesson was appointed to that office; no other reference to it has been found. One would like to be sure that it was not just a nickname.

436 ...quant je l'ay fait escripre,
J'ay a l'escripvain deffendu
Du moustrer. Au fort, s'on lui baille,
Bien assailly, bien deffendu;
440 Face, s'il scet, de pire taille!

Chartier's 'bon compaignon Neczon' is being challenged to go one better, or rather, one worse. The little else that is known about relations between Chartier and Nesson has already been discussed. The story of the drunken crier and the sentence of banishment also pointed to a relationship good-humoured enough to allow both gibes and practical jokes.

Curiously, the *Debat du Herault*... survives in only one manuscript, *Of*, where it is copied just before two poems by Nesson. It cannot have circulated widely, and it may not have been its author's intention that it should.

'LE DEBAT DE REVEILLE MATIN'

Like the *Debat du Herault*..., the *Debat de Reveille Matin* contains little information about the date when it was written. The subject of the poem, a Sleeper being compelled to listen to, and to comment on, the grievances and aspirations of a sleepless Lover, recalls a passage in the *Debat des Deux Fortunés d'Amours*:

388 S'il va couchier joieux, n'en faictes doubte.
Si arraisonne
Son compaignon a qui sa foy s'adonne,
Et toute nuit la teste lui estonne...

Chartier, in presenting the debate between the *Amoureux* and the *Compaignon*, assumes his customary role of reporter and observer. The terseness of the introduction and the conclusion to the poem suggest on the part of the author a diffidence similar to that which characterises the opening and closing lines of the *Debat des Deux Fortunés d'Amours*.

On the other hand, the *Debat de Reveille Matin* is markedly different in form and conception from that poem. The stanzas are of eight octosyllabic lines rhyming *ababbcbc*. Chartier almost certainly knew poems by Oton de Granson in which the same stanza form is used.[1] This type of octave was also chosen by Chartier for the *Belle Dame sans Mercy* and the *Excusacion aux Dames*. In the *Debat du Herault*... a second variety is found, with the rhyme-scheme *ababcdcd*.

[1] For example in the two *Complaintes de Saint Valentin*. See Piaget, *Oton de Grandson*, 183–93 and 221–5.

If the *Excusacion* is excepted, the octave was used by Chartier for the purpose of debate. In the *Debat de Reveille Matin* and the *Belle Dame sans Mercy* two protagonists speak alternate stanzas, once the debate proper has begun. Much of the *Debat du Herault*... follows that pattern, although there longer and shorter speeches also occur to give variety. The method of presentation of the debate is thus very different from the technique of the *Debat des Deux Fortunés d'Amours* or the *Livre des Quatre Dames*, in which the characters deliver long set speeches and in which the author, as he prepares the transition from one speech to another, assumes the role of commentator in addition to that of observer. These two poems are also much longer than the three debates now under consideration. These last are reminiscent of the earlier *debat*. It is in the development of this older form of the *debat*, in which he allies shrewdness of observation with dialogue of high quality, that Chartier is at his most original. One would like to know whether Chartier wrote the two types of debate at the same period or whether the more concise and original form succeeded the two long debates which recall similar poems by Christine de Pisan or Guillaume de Machaut;[1] although the latter order may seem the more likely, one cannot be certain.

'LA BELLE DAME SANS MERCY' AND 'L'EXCUSACION AUX DAMES'

The *Debat de Reveille Matin* was almost certainly written before the *Belle Dame sans Mercy*[2] which dates from 1424.[3] The two poems differ above all in tone and in outlook. The mood of the *Debat de Reveille Matin* is good-humoured; when the poet contrasts the extreme protestations and yearning of the sleepless courtly Lover with the prosaic statements and wise saws of his somnolent Companion, he does so sympathetically and indulgently. While the *Debat de Reveille Matin* may contain hints of irony and perhaps also of self-mockery, these are less developed than in the *Belle Dame sans Mercy*. The author plays an important role in the latter poem, a significant proportion of the work being devoted to a description of his mood and to an account of the events which preceded the debate. The poet is in mourning following the death of his lady and is far from

[1] For example the *Debat de Deux Amans* (Roy, *Christine de Pisan*, II, 49–109) or the *Jugement dou Roy de Behaingne* (Hoepffner, *Œuvres de Guillaume de Machaut*, I, 57–135).
[2] Champion (*Histoire poétique*, I, 63–4) takes that view. The poem is dated 1425, a year later than the *Belle Dame sans Mercy*, by Droz (*Alain Chartier: le Quadrilogue invectif*, viii).
[3] See p. 7.

anxious to join the gathering which he comes on 'par droicte destinee' (line 55). As he watches the particular Lover and Lady whose conversation is to form the centre-piece of the poem, the poet recalls his own love. The line and a half of direct speech uttered then:

> (Si dis a par moy:) 'Se m'aist Dieux,
> 120 Autel¹ fumes comme vous estes',

are clearly emphatic for they occur at the end of a stanza and are the only lines of direct speech within a long piece of narration. Line 120 is just as clearly ambiguous; the comparison between Chartier himself and the Lover may entail a comparison between the Lady and Chartier's dead mistress but need not do so. It is just as difficult to be certain about the tone and mood in which the two characters conduct their debate. A debate has affinities with a play; its different sections can be interpreted in different ways or given differing degrees of emphasis.

The character of the Lover is better developed and more finely drawn than that of his counterpart in the *Debat de Reveille Matin*. His protestations are even more extravagant and are couched in language of fitting eloquence. The Lady shuns rhetoric; while her speeches recall those of the Companion in their use of proverbial expressions, her attitude to the Lover is far less sympathetic than had been that of the Companion to his bedfellow. The Lady's wit and intelligence are more than proof against all the Lover's fervour and all the rhetoric which he can marshal. The good-natured banter of the *Debat de Reveille Matin* has become disillusion and self-mockery.

The poem can also be seen as a criticism of courtly attitudes and conventions. It was so interpreted by some contemporary readers who condemned it as an attack on courtly society and particularly the ladies. In his *Excusacion aux Dames*, written in the spring of 1425, Chartier excused himself and his poem.

'LA COMPLAINTE'

The allusion in the *Belle Dame sans Mercy* to the death of Chartier's lady makes it possible to assign his *Complainte* to the same period. The poem is written in stanzas of twelve or sixteen lines which rhyme: *aa(a)baa(a)bbb(b) abb(b)a*. The scheme is similar to that employed in the prologue to the *Livre des Quatre Dames* save that two rhymes, rather than three, are used

¹ Certain manuscripts have the alternative reading *Autelz*; see p. 335.

in each stanza and that decasyllabic, not octosyllabic, lines are used; the longer line is in keeping with the gravity of the subject. Chartier addresses his complaint to untimely Death who has taken his mistress from him and who has thereby deprived the world and the poet of one who was the sum of all beauties and all virtues. This moving poem, in which Chartier's rhetorical and poetic skills are combined most effectively, was well known; its influence can be traced in many a later poem.[1]

'RONDEAULX ET BALADES'

The lady's death was also the inspiration of a number of lyric poems, a rondeau (XVII) and two ballades (XXIV and XXVII). The other twenty-five lyrics treat different aspects of the poet's experience: in one (XXVI), he is newly fallen in love and he describes how it came about on Saint Valentine's Day; elsewhere (XXI), he protests his love for his lady and his intention to serve her; he is too timid to declare his love to his lady (I, II); more often he asks for her mercy and dwells on the effects which he may suffer if it is refused (VII, IX, XV); elsewhere, he tells of the pains of separation (X, XIII) and, in one poem (XI), he tells how his lady has accepted another in his stead. The small collection of lyrics which has survived was written over a number of years. Some recall the aspirations of his earliest poems and are almost certainly contemporaneous with them, while others are of a much later period. The order in which the lyrics are presented in the manuscripts appears to be haphazard.

The opening stanzas of the *Belle Dame sans Mercy* include the following lines:

> Je laysse aux amoreux malades
> Qui ont espoir d'alegement
> Faire chançons, diz et balades,
> 28 Chascun a son entendement.
>
> Desormais est temps de moy tayre,
> Car de dire suis je lassé.
> Je vueil laissier aux autres faire:
> 36 Leur temps est; le mien est passé.

A similar sentiment is expressed in a ballade (XXIV) written after his lady's death:

> 6 ...plus ne fais dit ne chançon nouvelle,
> ...j'ay mis soubz le banc ma vïelle.

[1] See p. 53.

41

Such statements might be assumed to be either temporary or conventional reactions to grief; in fact none of the poems of Alain Chartier, narrative or lyric, appears to be later than the *Belle Dame sans Mercy* or the *Excusacion*.

The following list sets the poems in the order suggested by the discussion.

?	*Le Lay de Plaisance*
1412–13	*Le Debat des Deux Fortunés d'Amours*
1416	*Le Livre des Quatre Dames*
?	*Le Debat du Herault, du Vassault et du Villain*
?	*Le Breviaire des Nobles*
? (before 1426)	*Le Lay de Paix*
?	*Le Debat de Reveille Matin*
1424	*La Complainte*
1424	*La Belle Dame sans Mercy*
1425	*L'Excusacion aux Dames*
c. 1410–1425	*Rondeaulx et Balades*

3

The Manuscripts

Attempt the end, and never stand to doubt;
Nothing's so hard, but search will find it out.

Robert Herrick

The works of Alain Chartier have survived in almost two hundred manuscripts; one hundred and thirteen contain the poetical works in French which are edited here. There is no evidence that any of these manuscripts was copied under Chartier's supervision or that he himself had his works collected together; he may have had copies made of the *Debat des Deux Fortunés d'Amours* for submission to the Count of Foix or of the *Livre des Quatre Dames* for presentation to an unknown lady.[1] Almost all the surviving manuscripts were copied after his death.

When a list of the manuscripts was published in 1966,[2] it was shown that they can be divided into groups which reflect the contents of the manuscripts. It is not surprising to find that works on similar subjects are often copied together. However, the size of a work, as much as its subject, determines the sort of manuscript in which it is copied. The longest poems, such as the *Debat des Deux Fortunés d'Amours* or the *Livre des Quatre Dames*, are rarely found in large collections, but tend to be copied separately or as part of a collection of two or three poems. For the most part, Chartier's works in French prose and his works in Latin are copied in manuscripts which do not contain any of his poetical works in French. The *Dialogus Familiaris Amici et Sodalis* is the only Latin work to be included in any of the manuscripts which are discussed here; it is found in two manuscripts of the poetical works.[3] The *Quadrilogue Invectif* is the

---

[1] See pp. 31 and 34.

[2] J. C. Laidlaw, 'The Manuscripts of Alain Chartier', *Modern Language Review* LXI, 1966, 188–98. *Fg* and *Lt* are to be added to that list. The article gives details of the number of manuscripts known to earlier critics. Just after the article appeared, the following edition became available: J. E. White, Jr., *The Major Poems of Alain Chartier: A Critical Edition*, Chapel Hill, 1961 (University of North Carolina Ph.D. Thesis); see 'Rassegna bibliografica: Quattrocento', *Studi Francesi* IX, 1965, 526. White's edition contains all Chartier's poetical works except the ballades and rondeaux.

White listed and classified 144 manuscripts of Chartier's works; the number is reduced to 128 when manuscripts wrongly included or listed under more than one press-mark are subtracted. The classification of the manuscripts is often wrong.

The edition is discussed below (p. 58, n. 2).   [3] *Ob* and *Of*.

only work in French prose which is copied at all frequently beside the poetical works; the *Curial* and the longer *Livre de l'Esperance* are found more rarely.

The sigla allocated to the manuscripts consist of a capital and a small letter: the capital letter gives information about the contents of the manuscript and is allotted according to the scheme given below; the small letter distinguishes the manuscript from others of like content.[1] The scheme has been extended to include the early printed edition of Chartier's works.

A–G MSS containing a single work in French by Alain Chartier:

   A *Le Quadrilogue Invectif* 11 MSS, *Aa–Al*

   B *Le Breviaire des Nobles* 10 MSS, *Ba–Bk*

   C *Le Curial* 8 MSS, *Ca–Ch*

   D *Le Livre des Quatre Dames* 6 MSS, *Da–Df*

   E *Le Livre de l'Esperance* 12 MSS, *Ea–Em*

   F *Le Lay de Paix* 7 MSS, *Fa–Fg*

   G Other single poems 9 MSS, *Ga–Gj*

H MSS containing the *Quadrilogue Invectif* and the *Livre de l'Esperance* 9 MSS, *Ha–Hj*

J MSS containing the *Quadrilogue Invectif*, the *Dialogus Familiaris* and the *Livre de l'Esperance* 7 MSS, *Ja–Jg*

K–L MSS containing Latin works:

   K MSS in Paris libraries 13 MSS, *Ka–Kn*

   L MSS elsewhere 19 MSS, *La–Lt*

M–O MSS containing one or more French works:

   M All in prose 2 MSS, *Ma–Mb*

   N All in verse 17 MSS, *Na–Nr*

   O In prose and verse 16 MSS, *Oa–Oq*

P–Q MSS containing French works in verse or in prose and verse, together with 'imitations'[2] of the *Belle Dame sans Mercy*:

   P MSS in Paris libraries 15 MSS, *Pa–Pp*

   Q MSS elsewhere 17 MSS, *Qa–Qr*

T MSS containing one or more lyrics 16 MSS, *Ta–Tq*

X Early printed editions, whether of a single work or a collection.[3]

---

[1] The letter *i* has not been used.

[2] The term was first applied by A. Piaget to the works written during the controversy provoked by Chartier's poem. See A. Piaget, '*La Belle Dame sans merci* et ses imitations', *Romania*, XXX, 1901, 22–48, 317–51, and later articles in that journal.

[3] For a list of the editions see Walravens, *Alain Chartier, études biographiques*, 222–62; see also J. C. Laidlaw, 'André du Chesne's Edition of Alain Chartier', *Modern Language Review*, LXIII, 1968, 569–74, and section 2 of the bibliography *infra* (p. 504).

   A description of *Xa*, the first collected edition, published in 1489, is given on pp. 142–4. Other sigla, used on p. 57, are as follows: *Xd*, the Du Chesne edition of 1617; *Xf*, the separate edition of the *Lay de Paix*; *Xg*, the separate edition of the *Complainte*; *Xp* the only separate edition of the *Debat de Reveille Matin* which has been traced.

List of manuscripts by sigla

The sigla and location of a few manuscripts are given in square brackets, showing that the manuscript has not been traced or is damaged. An approximate date for each manuscript is also given, based where possible on the following time-scale: early fifteenth century (before 1440); mid fifteenth century (1440–70); late fifteenth century (1470–1500); late fifteenth century, early sixteenth century (1485–1515); early sixteenth century (1500–30).

Aa	Paris, B.N., f.fr. 1126	15th c.	*Ab*	Paris, B.N., f.fr. 1129	15th c.
Ac	Paris, B.N., f.fr. 19127	15th c.	*Ad*	Paris, B.N., f.fr. 20021	15th c.
Ae	Paris, B.N., f.lat. 16692	15th c.	*Af*	Chantilly, Musée Condé, 882	15th c.
Ag	Brussels, B.R., IV 29	late 15th c.	*Ah*	London, B.M., Additional 15300	mid 15th c.
Aj	Vatican, Regina lat. 918	15th c.	*Ak*	Paris, B.N., n.a.lat. 2055	17th c.
Al	Escorial, X. III. 2.	15th c.			
Ba	Paris, B.N., f.fr. 2206	16th c.	*Bb*	Paris, B.N., f.fr. 4939	15th c.
Bc	Paris, B.N., f.fr. 25434	15th c.	*Bd*	Coutances, B. Mun., 8	15th c.
Be	Berne, Burgerbibliothek, 205	15th c.	*Bf*	Kortrijk, Stadsbibliotheek, III	early 16th c.
Bg	London, B.M., Royal 14 E ii	15th c.	*Bh*	London, B.M., Royal 15 E vi	1445–7
Bj	London, B.M., Royal 17 E iv	late 15th c.	*Bk*	Poitiers, B. Mun., 215	late 15th c.
Ca	Paris, B.N., f.fr. 2861	15th c.	*Cb*	Paris, B.N., f.fr. 5339	1476
Cc	Paris, B.N., f.fr. 20055	late 15th c.	*Cd*	Douai, B. Mun., 767	16th c.
Ce	Rouen, B. Mun., 930	mid 15th c.	*Cf*	Valenciennes, B. Mun., 304	16th c.
Cg	Oxford, Bodl. L., Bodley 864	15th c.	*Ch*	Göttingen, U.B., Philos. 98	16th c.
Da	Paris, B.N., f.fr. 1507	late 15th c., early 16th c.	*Db*	Paris, B.N., f.fr. 2234	15th c.
Dc	Paris, B.N., f.fr. 2235	15th c.	*Dd*	Paris, B. de l'Arsenal, 2940	early 15th c.
De	Heidelberg, U.B., Pal. Germ. 354	15th c.	*Df*	London, B.M., Additional 21247	early 15th c.
Ea	Paris, B.N., f.fr. 832	15th c.	*Eb*	Paris, B.N., f.fr. 1132	late 15th c., early 16th c.
Ec	Paris, B.N., f.fr. 12435	early 16th c.	*Ed*	Paris, B.N., n.a.fr. 6535	15th c.
Ee	Paris, B.N., f.lat. 18583	mid 15th c.	*Ef*	Besançon, B. Mun., 1791	15th c.
Eg	Copenhagen, Royal L., Thott 57, 2°	mid 15th c.	*Eh*	The Hague, Royal L., 78 E 68	15th c.
Ej	Heidelberg, U.B., Pal. Germ. 484	15th c.	*Ek*	London, B.M., Royal 19 A xii	late 15th c.

El New York, Pierpont   late 15th c.,
      Morgan L., 438   early 16th c.

Fa Paris, B.N., f.fr. 1563   early 15th c.
Fc Paris, B.N., f.fr. 25548   15th c.
Fe Barbentane (Bouches-du-
      Rhône), Library of M. de
      Puget de Barbantane (*sic*) 15th c.

Ga Paris, B.N., f.fr. 2262   15th c.
Gc Paris, B.N., f.fr. 2229   mid 15th c.
Ge Jena, U.B., El. f. 98   late 15th c.

Gg Vatican, Regina lat. 1362
                                late 15th c.
Gj Paris, B.N., f.fr. 2253   16th c.

Ha Paris, B.N., f.fr. 1125   15th c.
Hc Paris, B.N., f.fr. 1549   15th c.
He Paris, B.N., f.fr. 12437 early 16th c.
Hg Valenciennes, B. Mun., 652 15th c.
Hj Brussels, B.R., II 1172   15th c.

Ja Paris, B.N., f.fr. 126   mid 15th c.
Jc Paris, B.N., f.fr. 1124   mid 15th c.
Je Harvard College, Houghton L.,
      Typ 92   1464/5
Jg Vatican, Regina lat. 1338   15th c.

Ka Paris, B.N., f.lat. 3127   1456
Kc Paris, B.N., f.lat. 5961   mid 15th c.
Ke Paris, B.N., f.lat. 8757   mid 15th c.
Kg Paris, B.N., f.lat. 14117   1470/1
Kj Paris, B.N., f.lat. 18532   15th c.
Kl Paris, B. Mazarine, 3893   1472
[*Kn* Paris, B. de l'Université, 229] 15th c.

La Chantilly, Musée Condé, 438 15th c.
Lc Tours, B. Mun., 978   1435/6
Le Einsiedeln, Monastery L., 307 1442

Lg Liège, B. de l'Université,
      Wittert 109   15th c.
Lj Oxford, Bodl. L., e Museo 213
                                    15th c.

Em Vatican, cod. lat. 1005   mid 15th c.

Fb Paris, B.N., f.fr. 11464   late 15th c.
Fd Vatican, Regina lat. 1900   15th c.
Ff Vatican, Regina lat. 1683
                                late 15th c.
Fg Paris, B.N., f.lat. 17447 mid 15th c.

Gb Paris, B.N., f.fr. 15219   15th c.
Gd Paris, B.N., f.fr. 24435   1476/7
Gf New York, Pierpont Morgan
      L., 396   early 15th c.
Gh Berlin, Staatsbibliothek,
      Phillipps 1928   15th c.

Hb Paris, B.N., f.fr. 1133   15th c.
Hd Paris, B.N., f.fr. 12436   late 15th c.
Hf Paris, B.N., f.fr. 24441 mid 15th c.
Hh Berlin, Kupferstichkabinett,
      78 C 8   15th c.

Jb Paris, B.N., f.fr., 1123   15th c.
Jd Moulins, B. Mun., 26   mid 15th c.
Jf London, B.M., Cotton
      Julius E V   mid 15th c.

Kb Paris, B.N., f.lat. 4329   15th c.
Kd Paris, B.N., f.lat. 6254   15th c.
Kf Paris, B.N., f.lat. 10922   15th c.
Kh Paris, B.N., f.lat. 15083   15th c.
Kk Paris, B. Mazarine, 940   15th c.
Km Paris, B. Ste. Geneviève, 1992
                                      15th c.

Lb Rouen, B. Mun., 480   15th c.
Ld Brussels, B.R., 14370-1   15th c.
Lf Florence, B. Riccardiana, 443
                                 late 15th c.
Lh London, B.M., Harley 1883 15th c.

Lk Tübingen, U.B. (Depot der
      ehemaligen Preussischen
      Staatsbibliothek), lat. fol.
      366   15th c.

Ll Uppsala, U.L., C 917   mid 15th c.
Ln Vatican, Regina lat. 1366   15th c.

Lp Vienna, N.B., 3281   15th c.
Lr Toledo, Cabildo Toletano VI 21   ?
Lt Haarlem, Stadsbibliotheek,
   187 C 14   15th c.

Ma Paris, B.N., f.fr. 2265   1457

Na Paris, B.N., f.fr. 2249   late 15th c.
Nc Paris, B.N., f.fr. 25435   15th c.
Ne Paris, B.N., n.a.fr. 6220-4   15th c.

Ng Chantilly, Musée Condé, 685 15th c.

Nj Grenoble, B. Mun., 874 mid 15th c.
Nl Berne, Burgerbibliothek, 473 15th c.

Nn Karlsruhe, Badische Landes-
   bibliothek, 410   15th c.
Np Lausanne, B. cantonale et
   universitaire, 350   *c.* 1430
Nr Clermont-Ferrand, Archives du
   Puy-de-Dôme, 28   15th c.

Oa Paris, B.N., f.fr. 1127   mid 15th c.
Oc Paris, B.N., f.fr. 1130   15th c.
Oe Poitiers, B. Mun., 214   15th c.

Og Escorial, O.I.14   mid 15th c.

Oj Manchester, Chetham's Library,
   Muniment A.6.91 mid 15th c.
Ol Oxford, Bodl. L., Clarke 34   15th c.

On Vienna, N.B., 3391   15th c.

Op Brussels, B.R., 21521-31 late 15th c.

Pa Paris, B.N., f.fr. 833   late 15th c.,
   early 16th c.
Pc Paris, B.N., f.fr. 1131   mid 15th c.

Lm Vatican, Ottoboni lat. 858   15th c.
Lo Wolfenbüttel, Herzog-
   August Bibliothek,
   Helmstedt 376   *c.* 1441
Lq Vatican, cod. lat. 11548   15th c.
Ls Giessen, U.B., 1256   1463/4

Mb Oxford, Bodl. L., Bodley 421 15th c.

Nb Paris, B.N., f.fr. 25293   15th c.
Nd Paris, B.N., n.a.fr. 4511-13   15th c.
Nf Aix-en-Provence,
   B. Méjanes, 168   mid 15th c.
Nh Clermont-Ferrand, B. Mun.,
   249   early 15th c.
Nk Rodez, B. Mun., 57   15th c.
Nm Florence, B. Laurenziana,
   Ashburnham 51   15th c.
No Madrid, B.N., 10307   15th c.

Nq Vatican, Regina lat. 1323
   late 15th c.

Ob Paris, B.N., f.fr. 1128   late 15th c.
Od Paris, B.N., f.fr. 2263   mid 15th c.
Of Berlin, Kupferstichkabinett,
   78 C 7   15th c.
Oh London, B.M., Harley late 15th c.,
   4402   early 16th c.
Ok Munich, Bayerische Staats-
   bibliothek, cod. gall. 10   16th c.
Om Stockholm, Royal L.,
   V. u. 22   late 15th c.
Oo Geneva, Library of Mlle E.
   Droz   15th c.
Oq Paris, B.N., Rothschild
   2796   mid 15th c.

Pb Paris, B.N., f.fr. 924   late 15th c.

Pd Paris, B.N., f.fr. 1642   late 15th c.,
   early 16th c.

Pe	Paris, B.N., f.fr. 1727	mid 15th c.	*Pf*	Paris, B.N., f.fr. 2230	mid 15th c.
Pg	Paris, B.N., f.fr. 2264	15th c.	*Ph*	Paris, B.N., f.fr. 19139	15th c.
Pj	Paris, B.N., f.fr. 20026		*Pk*	Paris, B.N., f.fr. 24440	15th c.
		mid 15th c.			
Pl	Paris, B.N., Rothschild 440		*Pm*	Paris, B.N., f.fr. 1661	late 15th c.
		mid 15th c.			
Pn	Paris, B. de l'Arsenal, 3521	15th c.	*Po*	Paris, B. de l'Arsenal, 3523	15th c.
Pp	Paris, Musée Jacquemart-André, 11	15th c.			

Qa	Besançon, B. Mun., 554	15th c.	*Qb*	Carpentras, B. Mun., 390	15th c.
Qc	Chantilly, Musée Condé, 686	15th c.	*Qd*	Toulouse, B. Mun., 826	
					early 15th c.
Qe	Valenciennes, B. Mun., 417	15th c.	*Qf*	Arnhem, Bibliotheek, 79	
					c. 1480
Qg	Brussels, B.R., 10961–9	late 15th c.	*Qh*	Copenhagen, Royal L., Ny kgl. Saml. 1768. 2º	late 15th c.
[*Qj*	Fribourg, Diesbach Library]	mid 15th c.	*Qk*	The Hague, Royal L., 71 E 49	late 15th c.
Ql	Leningrad, Saltikov-Shchedrin L., Fr. F. V. XIV. 7	15th c.	*Qm*	London, B.M., Royal 19 A iii	late 15th c.
[*Qn*	London, Clumber Sale (Sotheby, 6/12/1937) 941]	*c.* 1490	*Qo*	Milan, B. Trivulziana, 971	15th c.
[*Qp*	Turin, B. Nazionale Universitaria, L II 12]	16th c.	*Qq*	Vatican, Vat. lat. 4794	mid 15th c.
Qr	Vienna, N.B., 2619	mid 15th c.			

Ta	Paris, B.N., f.fr. 1722	16th c.	*Tb*	Paris, B.N., f.fr. 9346	16th c.
Tc	Lyon, B. Mun., 1235	15th c.	*Td*	Berlin, Kupferstichkabinett, 78 B 17	late 15th c.
Te	London, B.M., Royal 20 C viii	early 15th c.	*Tf*	London, B.M., Additional 34360	15th c.
Tg	Oxford, Bodl. L., Canonici Misc. 213	15th c.	*Th*	Washington, Library of Congress, M.2.1. L 25	15th c.
Tj	Paris, B.N., f.fr. 1881	15th & 16th c.	*Tk*	Paris, B. de l'Arsenal, 3059	16th c.
Tl	Brussels, B.R., 11020–35	15th c.	*Tm*	London, B.M., Harley 4397	15th c.
Tn	London, B.M., Harley 4473	15th c.	*To*	London, B.M., Lansdowne 380	early 16th c.
Tp	Wolfenbüttel, Herzog-August Bibliothek, 84.7.Aug.fol.	15th c.	*Tq*	Cambridge, Trinity College, R.3.20	15th c.

In an edition of Chartier's poetical works in French, manuscripts of types *A*, *C*, *E*, *H*, *J*, *K*, *L* and *M* are not of immediate importance and are used only rarely. If the manuscripts of type *T*, which contain only lyrics, are excluded, there remain ninety-seven manuscripts which contain

Chartier's longer poems in French. To these must be added a considerable number of early printed editions.

The number of manuscripts in which a poem is copied varies widely. One manuscript is known of the *Debat du Herault...*, fifty-three of the *Breviaire des Nobles*. These are the extreme figures; for most works between twenty-five and fifty manuscripts are available. The list of poems which follows illustrates the point; the reasons why the works have been accepted as authentic will be given in the discussion which precedes each edition.

Le Lay de Plaisance,	17 MSS	*Le Lay de Paix,*	48 MSS
Le Debat des Deux Fortunés d'Amours,	27 MSS	*Le Debat de Reveille Matin,*	37 MSS
Le Livre des Quatre Dames,	32 MSS	*La Complainte,*	36 MSS
Le Debat du Herault, du Vassault et du Villain,	1 MS	*La Belle Dame sans Mercy,*	44 MSS
Le Breviaire des Nobles,	53 MSS	*L'Excusacion aux Dames,*	31 MSS

Such large numbers of manuscripts cause difficulties: it is not that an editor cannot deal with so many manuscripts; rather is it that the edition which results is burdened with variants and notes, difficult to use because of the mass of information which it presents and extremely costly to print.

It is clear that the number of manuscripts from which a poem is to be edited must somehow be reduced. For this to be done satisfactorily, a way must be found of determining the quality of each manuscript. The thirty-two manuscripts of types *B*, *D*, *F* and *G*, which each contain only a single poem by Chartier, pose no problems in this respect which could not have been solved by conventional means. The remaining manuscripts, those of types *N*, *O*, *P* and *Q*, present greater difficulties. These sixty-five manuscripts contain selections of Chartier's poetical works, selections which are not always comparable in size or type: one manuscript may contain eight poems, another six, a third two; two manuscripts each containing five poems may have no more than two in common. Reference to the table on pages 50–1 will show how widely the selections vary from manuscript to manuscript. The collection in a particular manuscript cannot be assumed to be of consistent quality; it could for example contain an acceptable text of the *Lay de Plaisance* and an unsatisfactory version of the *Breviaire des Nobles*.

Before an outline can be given of the method devised to deal with the

The contents of the collected manuscripts and the first collected edition. A key to the abbreviated titles of the poems is given on p. 437. In the entries under *RB* (*Rondeaulx et Balades*), the numbers indicate how many lyrics are copied in the manuscript in question.

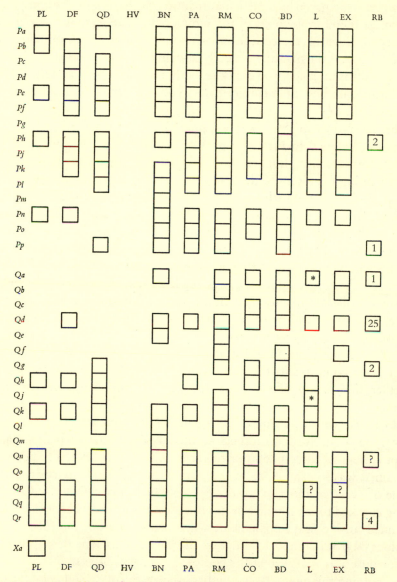

† *Oh* contains an abbreviated version of the *Breviaire des Nobles*.

* *Qa* includes versions of the letters in both prose and verse; *Qj*, which is defective, the metrical version of one letter.

problem, three terms must be defined. The works of Chartier being discussed will be described as *works* or as poems. A *text* will be the copy of a work as it is given by a particular manuscript; for texts to be compared, they must therefore be texts of the same poem. The term *manuscript* will be used to describe the collection of texts in a given volume taken together; because the manuscripts each contain a different selection of texts, they cannot immediately or easily be compared. It is this fact, allied with the large number of manuscripts involved, which complicates the editor's task.

The following method was adopted. It was a method which was primarily designed to meet the problem of assessing the quality of the collected manuscripts, but which could readily be used to deal both with the remaining manuscripts, those of types *B, D, F* and *G* containing single poems, and with the early printed editions, single or collected. Critical editions, from all the available manuscripts, were made of four poems: the *Lay de Plaisance*, the *Lay de Paix*, the *Complainte* and the *Debat de Reveille Matin*. These poems were chosen because they are relatively short and because between them they are copied in a large number of manuscripts. In the four editions use was made of texts from fifty-five of the sixty-five collected manuscripts. Since many of these manuscripts contain copies of more than one of the works edited, it was possible to use the editions as a probe: to see whether the relationships found to exist between the texts of one work in different manuscripts also existed between the other texts common to the manuscripts in question; to see as a result whether the quality of a manuscript was constant from one work to another.

No assessment of a manuscript's quality was made until the texts of at least three poems from it had been studied in some detail; where a manuscript contained three poems or fewer by Chartier, each of the poems it contained was so examined. At the same time, a detailed description was made of every manuscript, all the poems which it contained by Chartier being checked to see whether or not they were complete. The information obtained in that way supplemented that acquired from the four critical editions or from samples of the texts of other poems. The descriptions of the manuscripts are given at the end of the present discussion.

In applying this method, account had to be taken of several complicating factors, some obvious and predictable, others more subtle and not immediately apparent. When the four poems were being edited, it became clear not only that the textual tradition was complex in each case but also that there was evidence of contamination. Examination of the manuscripts confirmed this, in some cases incontrovertibly: *Pd*, for example, gives both the versions available for stanza XVI of the *Excusacion aux Dames*[1] and therefore has one stanza more than the other manuscripts containing the poem; in their texts of the *Lay de Paix*, *Nl* and *Ob* both include extra lines, while the text of the *Complainte* in *Nb* contains a similar addition; the copy of the *Belle Dame sans Mercy* in *Nl* has variants added by the scribe in the margin. In most cases the evidence was less striking; a given text of a particular poem might be found to agree substantially with another text but to contain at the same time an irreducible number of readings which linked it with a third text of an apparently different tradition.

That some contamination should be present is not surprising. There is ample evidence of the popularity of Alain Chartier's poetical works; the large number of manuscripts which survives must represent only a small portion of those which were copied in the fifteenth century. When a scribe wished to copy a new manuscript of Chartier's poetry, he would have had little difficulty in finding an exemplar. If he desired to make a large collection, he would probably have been compelled to draw on more than one manuscript: in the surviving manuscripts the collections of poetical works do not correspond one to another and small collections predominate. Contamination could take place if the two (or more) collected manuscripts used by the scribe each contained a copy of the same poem. This type of contamination might affect only one or two texts in the resulting manuscript. It would be detected only if the texts conflated by the scribe were of markedly different traditions.

Contamination might assume a subtler guise. Where a scribe knew by heart snatches of the poem which he was copying, he might incorporate into his text a word or phrase from the version which he held in his memory. Echoes of Chartier's verse are found in the works of many a later poet and testify to the extent to which his poetry was memorised or adapted. In discussing the works of later poets such as Villon or Blosseville, critics have noted passages which suggest such an influence;[2] examples could also be cited from the work of other poets.[3] It may not

---

[1] The existence of alternative stanzas raises the possibility that Chartier revised his poems. There is insufficient evidence for one to be certain.

[2] A. Piaget, *Romania*, XXI, 1892, 429; K. Chesney, 'Some Notes on the Lyrics of Alain Chartier', *Mélanges Roques*, I, Bade, Paris, Didier, 1950, 27–35, esp. 30–1, 34.

[3] Obvious borrowings from Chartier's *Complainte* are found in an early printed edition of the *Epitaphes des feuz roys Loys .xi...et de Charles...viii...*([E. Picot], *Catalogue des livres de feu M. le baron James de Rothschild*, IV, Paris, Morgand, 1912, 177–9 [no. 2842]). Echoes of the same poem can also

be irrelevant to mention here the case of Triboulet who, as he lay dying, recited farces and the *Belle Dame sans Mercy*.[1]

The fact that contamination exists meant that small use could be made of the classic methods of argument developed by editors as a means of narrowing or justifying a choice between manuscripts or texts. The methods adopted in editing the four poems were determined in part by the proven existence of contamination, in part by certain features characteristic of fifteenth-century French verse. Stemmata were excluded: those which might have been drawn would not have represented the *only* or *necessary* view of the relationships which exist between the texts. Instead, the texts were grouped together so far as this was possible. It proved difficult to fit every text neatly into a group; very often it was found that a text allotted to one group had affinities with texts of another group. Such findings do not necessarily suggest that the text is contaminated. It may well be; on some occasions, it is equally possible that one (or both) of the groups is itself contaminated. The different groups which were drawn up are listed in a table at the end of this discussion.

The examination of the textual tradition of the poems had three main purposes: to describe the relationships between the texts of a particular poem found in different manuscripts; to select those manuscripts which must be used in the edition of Chartier's poetry; and to choose suitable base texts for the edition of each poem. Since no manuscript contains all Chartier's poetical works, the base texts must be drawn from more than one manuscript. An ideal base would be complete, would be metrically regular, would rhyme correctly, would make good sense and would contain few individual readings. Such criteria, of value in discussing the textual tradition of any medieval French poem, are likely to be especially useful where fifteenth-century poetry is concerned.

In Chartier's time, metrical complexity and skill in rhyming were especially valued in lyrical and narrative verse. The formal complexity of poetry at this period can hardly be better illustrated than by the structure of the *lay*; in its twelve stanzas there were deployed no less than eleven stanza-forms, each distinct and elaborate. If the *lay* demanded expertise and virtuosity on the part of its composer, it also required care and diligence from the scribe who copied it. Thus, examination of a *lay* as it is

---

be detected in Villon's *Lay* or rather rondeau (*Testament*, lines 978–89), though the case is less certain.

1 G. Frank, *The Medieval French Drama*, Oxford, Clarendon Press, 1954, 252–3; see also E. Droz, *Le Recueil Trepperel: les sotties*, Paris, Droz, 1935, 217–38, esp. 233 (*Bibl. de la Société des Historiens du Théâtre*, VIII).

copied in a given manuscript can be an unusually good test of that manuscript's quality. The discussions of the textual tradition of the *Lay de Plaisance* and the *Lay de Paix* were likely to be of especial value for that reason.

Rhyme, important in the *lay* where it is used in a metrically complex stanza, takes on a relatively greater importance in poems like the *Complainte* and the *Debat de Reveille Matin* in which the same stanza-form is repeated. From the time of Machaut and particularly Deschamps onwards, poets made increasing use in lyrical and narrative verse of the more complicated rhymes available. Chartier follows that tradition and in his poems there abound all manner of *rimes riches, léonines* and *équivoques*. A good manuscript of Chartier's poetical works, of the *lays* as much as of the narrative poems, should give these rhymes correctly.

Inaccuracy of rhyme is an absolute criterion by which a text may be judged. If for one line of a poem, the texts offer rhymes of different types, simple or complicated, the choice is less easy. The effect of *rimes léonines* and more complicated rhymes may be heightened if ornate and simple rhymes are juxtaposed. In the *Belle Dame sans Mercy*, for example, Chartier will use this device to contrast the speeches and hence the attitude of the Lover and the Lady; stanzas XXVII and XXVIII illustrate this well.

Regularity of metre provides another criterion by which texts may be judged, but one which must be applied with caution. There is clear evidence that Chartier used hiatus, albeit sparingly, for poetic effect. Particularly good examples occur in the *Lay de Plaisance* (line 182) and in the *Complainte* (line 107); at these lines few texts correct the apparent irregularity. Once the use of hiatus as a poetic device has been proved, there is a possibility that hiatus exists in other lines of similar formation and construction. A like problem stems from the fact that Chartier, again for reasons of emphasis, will alter in different lines the syllable count of the same or similar words. An instance is his treatment of words like *veoir* or *veu*, which may count as one or two syllables (*Debat de Reveille Matin*, lines 212, 305; 348, 349).

It is appropriate to mention here that Chartier makes use of morphological doublets, such as *Elle/El* or *telle/tel*, for purely metrical reasons. The fact that he does so may on occasion further complicate the problem of deciding whether a particular line is regular or not: while Chartier may use both the forms available but on different occasions, a scribe may use only one and consistently. Thus, a list of the irregular lines in a given text can only be of value if it has been drawn up after due consideration both of the place which the lines in question occupy in the poem and of the characteristics of the manuscript as a whole.[1]

In discussing a particular text, no account is taken of the date at which it was copied. The manuscripts of Alain Chartier's poetical works were copied between about 1420 and about 1510 for the most part, and it is difficult to place them in a firm chronological order. Even if it could be done, the information would not necessarily be of value for there exists the possibility, not always theoretical, that a late manuscript was copied directly from an early one. To add that a text, good or bad, is found in a late or early manuscript in no way affects the quality of that text. It has been found similarly that the provenance of a manuscript gives no guarantee of its quality. Thus, *Pf* and *Pj*, copied by the same scribe for the wives of the brothers Jean d'Angoulême and Charles d'Orléans, who were not only patrons of the arts but men of letters themselves, include a collection of Chartier's poetical works which is extensive but of poor quality from a textual point of view.

The description of each manuscript in this edition concludes with an assessment of the manuscript's quality and a discussion of its relationship to other manuscripts; the assessment has been made in accordance with the criteria just outlined. In giving particulars of the relationship which a particular manuscript bears to others, frequent reference is made to the groups which were drawn up in the course of editing the four poems previously mentioned. While the following table is intended to be a convenient reference list, it also serves to emphasise that the manuscript tradition of these four poems is extremely complex. The varying number of groups into which the texts of each poem have been fitted has no significance of itself: it is determined by the tradition of the particular poem. Although it is not possible to discuss here the reasons why a text has been allocated to a particular group, the reasons are set out elsewhere in a full account of the textual tradition of the four poems.[2] Where sigla are juxtaposed (e.g. *PkPoXa*), the texts are closely akin; if a comma intervenes (e.g. *Pl, Pp, Ql*), the degree of relationship is less close; where the sigla are separated by a semicolon (e.g. *Pd*; *Po* ; *Nm*), the kinship is distant.

---

[1] The discussion of *Oa* on p. 89 illustrates the point.

[2] J. C. Laidlaw, *The French and Latin manuscripts of Alain Chartier: A Bibliographical Study, together with Editions of Four Poems*, 1963 (Cambridge University Ph.D. Thesis).

Lay de Plaisance[1]	Group I	*OaPeQr*
	Group II	*NfNjNrQo; Pn; Qq*
	Group III	*Ph, Oc, PbQhQk, PaXa, Xd*
Debat de Reveille Matin	Group I	*NfNj, Nr, Pg; Nl; PnQ f*
	Group II	*NcNgPh; QeQr, Pe; No; NnQg; PfPj*
	Group III	*PkPoXa, PaXp; Pd; Xd*
	Group IV	*OaQoQq; Qa*
	Group V	*Pc; Pl, Pp, Ql; Qd, Qb; PbQk*
Lay de Paix	Group I	*FeFfNbNfNjOmPbQoQqXf; Nh, Oc, Nl*
	Group IIa	*OqPc; FbFcNaNeOb; PaPkXa, Xd; Pd; Pp; NqPo; Fg*
	Group II	The texts of Group IIa together with *PlQr, Ol; Pe, Oj, Qd; OfPfPj, Pn; Fd*
	Group III	*FaNp; Oa, OdOe; Ph, QhQk; Nk*
Complainte	Group I	*NfNjNlNrQoXg; NbQq; Tc*
	Group II	*GcGgOl; PcQl; PaPkXa, Xd; Pd; Po; Nm*
	Group III	*PfPj; Ph; Oc*
	Group IV	*PbQhQk; PnQg, Nq, Qc; GhQr; Oa, Pe; Qa, Qd*

An attempt to use the groups of texts as a means of grouping manuscripts together had only limited results; possible reasons for this were outlined earlier when the problem of contamination was discussed. Among the groups of manuscripts drawn up in this way were: *NfNjNlNr, NbQoQq; PcQl; PfPj; PbQhQk*. Where they were found to exist, these closely knit groups of manuscripts were extremely useful: *Nf* and *Nj*, for example, were so obviously superior in quality to the other manuscripts in their group that only these two needed to be considered further.

Generally, however, the decision to accept or to reject a manuscript had to be made on absolute rather than comparative grounds, that is to say that reliance had to be placed above all on the criteria discussed earlier. Such decisions were made easier by the discovery that those manuscripts which contained more than one of the four poems edited were consistent in quality from one poem to another. For example, if the manuscript contained a good text of the *Debat de Reveille Matin*, it also contained good texts of the *Lays* and so on. These findings were corroborated by the samples taken from other texts.

[1] The number of manuscripts listed here does not correspond to the figures quoted above on p. 49: certain manuscripts are damaged or have not been traced. Precise details of the manuscripts and early printed editions are given below in the introduction to the critical editions of these poems (pp. 147–8, 305–6, 320–1, 410–11; see also p. 44, n. 3).

A short list of twenty manuscripts was drawn up before a final selection was made. In making that selection, care was taken to ensure that each poem would be edited from a reasonable number of texts and that those manuscripts which were chosen would represent adequately the various traditions found to exist when the four poems were edited and when other works were examined. In that way fourteen manuscripts were chosen and used in the edition of the poems. Five manuscripts, *Db, Dc, Dd, Df* and *Gf,* include only one work, the *Livre des Quatre Dames* in the case of the first four, part of the *Belle Dame sans Mercy* in the case of *Gf.* A sixth, *Of,* contains the only known copy of the *Debat du Herault . . .* and was used only in the edition of that poem. The eight others, *Nf, Nj, Oa, Oj, Pc, Ph, Qd* and *Ql,* are all collected manuscripts. Fourteen was an arbitrary figure. Several manuscripts, *Dd, Df, Nj, Oj* and *Qd,* and to a lesser extent *Nf, Oa* and *Pc,* are of such fundamental importance that they would have commended themselves to any editor. The others, *Db, Dc, Gf, Ph* or *Ql,* while they are quite good manuscripts, are not so clearly superior to a number of manuscripts which were in the end rejected[1] that another editor might not have chosen differently.[2]

The descriptions of the fourteen manuscripts are more detailed than the other descriptions. They include, for example, an account of scribal practice.

RONDEAUX AND BALLADES

Alain Chartier's lyric poems were excluded from the preceding discussion. Reference to the table on pp. 50–1 shows that, where the lyrics are included in the collected manuscripts, it is generally in small numbers. The largest collections are found in *Nf, Nj* and *Qd,* manuscripts which have already been chosen for use in this edition. *Oa* and *Ph,* of the other manuscripts chosen, also contain lyrics. These five manuscripts will be used in the edition of the lyrics together with *Tc* and *Td,* which contain large collections, and also *To.* None of the remaining manuscripts of type *T* includes more than two lyrics.

[1] Among the manuscripts finally rejected were *Om, Oq, Pe, Pl, Pn* and *Pp.*

[2] J. E. White (*The Major Poems of Alain Chartier*) edited the *Debat du Herault . . .* from *Of.* In the editions of the other poems *Oa* was used as base and variants were given from *Ob, Oc, Pc* and *Pe;* the other manuscripts which he consulted were *Pd, Ph* and *Pk.* All these manuscripts, with the exception of *Of,* are in the Bibliothèque Nationale in Paris.

The manuscripts

THE DESCRIPTIONS OF THE MANUSCRIPTS

The descriptions of the manuscripts have been set out in the following
pattern. Not every description contains material under each heading.

Siglum, location and press-mark

Sigla have been allotted to the manuscripts according to the scheme outlined earlier.
Where a manuscript has been examined only in microfilm, the press-mark is preceded by
a plus sign. The descriptions of all the other manuscripts are based on examination of the
volumes themselves.

Physical description

(1) Date. The following divisions have been adopted:
    Early fifteenth century – before 1440   Late fifteenth century,
    Mid fifteenth century – 1440–70   early sixteenth century – 1485–1515
    Late fifteenth century – 1470–1500   Early sixteenth century – 1500–1530
(2) Material, and format in the case of paper manuscripts.
(3) Overall measurements in millimetres of the folios and, in brackets, of the written area.
(4) Number of folios or pages, and of fly-leaves where they appear to be contemporary with the texts in the volume.
(5) Number of columns. Unless it is stated otherwise, the manuscript is written in single columns and the two sides of a folio are described as recto and verso. When a manuscript is laid out in double columns, the fact is indicated by the abbreviation 'd.c.', and the four columns contained in each folio are given letters *a* to *d*.
(6) Number of lines per column.
(7) Collation. Where a folio has been cancelled, the abbreviation 'canc.' is used. A colon between quires indicates that the end of a work (or of a manuscript where several are bound together) coincides with the end of a quire.
(8) Signatures, catchwords. Unless there is any indication to the contrary, they have been checked to see whether or not the manuscript is complete.
(9) Table of contents, if it appears to be contemporary with the manuscript.
(10) Decoration; binding, if it is contemporary with the texts in the volume; coats of arms.
(11) Water-marks in paper manuscripts. An attempt has been made to identify each mark, using the standard manual.[1] The descriptions are necessarily less detailed where the paper is folded in quarto or smaller.

Notes on hands and on the composition of the manuscript

Notes on the provenance of the manuscript

[1] C. M. Briquet, *Les Filigranes...*, Leipzig, 1923[2], I–IV.

List of the contents of the manuscript

The item number where appropriate, *incipit* and *explicit* are given of works by Alain Chartier. When the title given to a work is not immediately recognisable, the more usual title follows within round brackets. If the work has no title in the manuscript, the title is supplied within square brackets. When a title has been added in a hand later than the text, the fact is noted and the title is given within square brackets.

In the case of the poetical works, any gaps or additions have been listed.[1] Lack of space has made it necessary to omit details of all works other than those by Alain Chartier.

Where a work is wrongly attributed to Alain Chartier, the item is entirely enclosed within round brackets and the reasons for rejecting the attribution are given in a footnote.

Notes on the use made of the manuscript by earlier critics before 1970

For convenience, there follows a list of the works mentioned most often. The abbreviations adopted are given in brackets.

P. Champion, *Histoire poétique du XVe siècle*, I, Paris, 1923, 1–165 (*Bibliothèque du XVe siècle*, XXVII) (Champion)

E. Droz et A. Piaget (eds.), *Le Jardin de plaisance*, II, Paris, 1925 (*SATF*): 218–19 (Bibliography of the ballade 'Il n'est dangier que de villain'); 263–4 (Bibliography of the *Debat des Deux Fortunés d'Amours*); 271–5 (Bibliography of the lyrics)

A. du Chesne (ed.), *Les Œuvres de Maistre Alain Chartier*, Paris, P. le-Mur, 1617 (Du Chesne edition)

L. Kussmann, *Beiträge zur Überlieferung des 'Livre des Quatre Dames' von Alain Chartier*, Greifswald, Abel, 1904 (Kussmann: Bibliography and study of the textual tradition of the *Livre des Quatre Dames*)

A. Piaget, 'La Belle Dame sans merci et ses imitations', *Romania*, XXX, 1901, 22–48, 317–51; XXXI, 1902, 315–49; XXXIII, 1904, 179–208; XXXIV, 1905, 375–428, 559–97 (Bibliography of, discussion of, the imitations of the *Belle Dame sans Mercy*)

A. Piaget (ed.), *Alain Chartier: La Belle Dame sans mercy et les poésies lyriques*, Lille, Genève, 1945 (*TLF*) (Bibliography of, edition of, the *Belle Dame sans Mercy*)

W. H. Rice, 'Pour la bibliographie d'Alain Chartier', *Romania*, LXXII, 1951, 380–6 (Bibliography of the *Breviaire des Nobles*)

J. E. White, Jr., *The Major Poems of Alain Chartier: A Critical Edition*, Chapel Hill, 1961 (University of North Carolina Ph.D. Thesis) (White's edition)

F. Rouy (ed.), *Alain Chartier: Le Livre de l'esperance*, 1967 (Paris Thesis) (Edition of the *Livre de l'Esperance*)

Correction of earlier published descriptions of the manuscript

1 Details are not usually given of the cases where a scribe has repeated a line or lines in error. Full details of lines inserted or rearranged are given only in the descriptions of the *Lay de Plaisance*, the *Debat de Reveille Matin*, the *Complainte* and the *Lay de Paix*. The descriptions of the rondeaux take no account of the refrains. Full details are not always given of the lines missing from texts of the *Livre des Quatre Dames*, especially when their number is large.

Assessment of the quality of the manuscript and of its usefulness in editing the poetical works

The assessment is most detailed in the case of manuscripts chosen for use in this edition. Particulars are given on page 437 of the abbreviations used to refer to individual poems.

Ba   PARIS, BIBL. NAT., F. FR. 2206

16th c.; paper;[1] 2°; 240 × 160 (*c.* 200 × 110); 258 ff.; *c.* 25 lines.

109. Ff. 106v–107r, *Balade.*
     Incipit: Il n'est danger que de villain...
     27 lines. Lacks a line from the third stanza.
162. Fol. 143r, *Extraict du breviere des nobles composé par m^e alain. En ce ne sont recitez que les poinctz principaulz dudit Breviere.*
     Fol. 149r, *Fin du Breviere des nobles.*

     The extract comprises: ballades II, III, and IV (with an envoy of four lines); the envoy of ballade V (here of five lines); ballade VI (line 179 is lacking); the envoys of ballades VII and VIII; the last four lines of the first stanza, the third stanza and the envoy of ballade IX; the third stanza and envoy of ballade X; ballade XI; the second stanza and envoy of ballade XII; the envoy of ballade XIII. The ballades are headed and numbered.

Ba was included in the earlier bibliographies of the ballade and the *Breviaire des Nobles*, but has not been examined before. The latter contains a number of irregular lines and is too abbreviated to be used in an edition of the poem. The text bears some resemblance to that in *Pa*: see the notes to lines 112–13 and 144–7 of the *Breviaire des Nobles*.

Bb   PARIS, BIBL. NAT., F. FR. 4939

15th c.; paper; 2°; 275 × 185 (*c.* 195 × 130); xxvii (=xxviii) plus 170 ff.; 30–5 lines; collation A^{14} (first 3 canc.), B^{18} (first (?) canc.): 1^{14}, 2–3^{16}, 4^{22}, 5^{24}, 6^8: 7^{12}, 8^{10}: 9^{18}, 10^{14}: 11^{16}; catchwords; decoration in red.

Water-marks

(a) A hand, perhaps raised in benediction, the cuff with three tails. 65 mm long, chain-lines 42 mm apart.
(b) An anchor, 63 mm long between sewn chain-lines 44 mm apart.
(c) An anchor, 65 mm long, fixed to chain-line. Briquet 417 (1461).
(d) A five-toothed wheel 18 mm in diameter, with a 'starting-handle' attached; sewn chain-lines 42 mm apart.
(e) A similar mark, but without the starting-handle; sewn chain-lines 48 mm apart.
(f) A five-toothed wheel 22 mm in diameter, surmounted by a 'P'; chain-lines, perhaps sewn, 41 mm apart.
(g) A variety of (f), but with six teeth.

[1] The water-marks are poorly defined, and the manuscript is too tightly bound for the collation to be worked out.

The signatures 'Deciternes' and 'Florimont de robertet'[1] appear frequently.

3. Ff. 107r–113v, *Cy commance le breviaire des nobles fait par maistre Alain Chartier.*
431 plus 8 lines. Lacks lines 112–13, 144–7, 218–21, 347, 394–7.

Bb was included by Rice in his bibliography of the poem but has not been examined before. The text is incomplete and includes a number of irregular lines and poor rhymes.

Bc PARIS, BIBL. NAT., F. FR. 25434

15th c.; paper; 8°; 135×95 (75×55); 143 ff., numbered to 137; 16–17 lines; collation 1[16], 2–3[12]: 4–8[12]: 9–11[12]: 12[8] (last stuck down); decoration in red and yellow. On fol. 55r there is the unidentified device 'Sans mal penser'.

5. Ff. 41r–55r (begins quire 4), *Cy commence le breviaire des nobles composé par maistre alain chartier contenant douze balades morales.*
Complete. The ballades are copied in the order: I–X, XII, XI, XIII. The fifth ballade, *Droiture*, is written in stanzas of seven lines with an envoy of three lines.

Bc was mentioned by Champion and included by Rice in his bibliography. The text has not been examined in detail before. Although it is complete and generally of quite good quality, *Bc* includes some irregular lines.

Bd +COUTANCES, BIBL. MUN., 8

15th c.; paper; 278×205; 149 ff.

1. Fol. 9r, *Cy commence le breviaire des nobles composé par maistre allain charetier.*
Fol. 18r, *Explicit nobilium breviarium Ab alano aurige compositum.*
411 = 421 plus 8 lines. Lacks lines 43, 108, 179, 255–9, 311, 342–53, 443–6. The fifth ballade is written in stanzas of seven lines with an envoy of three lines.

Bd was included by Rice in his bibliography. The text has not been examined before. *Bd* is incomplete and includes a number of irregular lines.

Be +BERNE, BURGERBIBLIOTHEK 205

15th c.; paper; 2°; 570 ff.; *c.* 30 lines.

81–2. Fol. 216r, [*Le Breviaire des Nobles*].
Fol. 222v, *Expliciunt duodecim virtutes nobilitatis.*
433 plus 7 lines. Lacks lines 103–11, 394–7.

---

[1] The name Florimond Robertet and the year 1546 are written in Paris, Bibl. Nat., f.lat. 15071, fol. 97r, but in a careful italic hand (L. Delisle, *Le Cabinet des manuscrits*, II, Paris, Imprim. Nat., 1874, 398).

Be has not been listed or examined before. The poem was not recognised by the cataloguer who treated it as two works.[1] Although it is of quite good quality, the text is incomplete and at times irregular.

Bf KORTRIJK (COURTRAI), STADSBIBLIOTHEEK III

Early 16th c.;[2] paper; 2°; 285 × 210 (235 × 160); 212 ff.; *c.* 55 lines; d.c. of 75 mm; decoration in red and yellow; contemporary binding of stamped leather on boards.

4. Fol. 190d (P. 370), *S'ensieut le beviaire* (sic) *des nobles faict par maistre allain charretier secretaire du roy charle* (sic) *vij* de ce nom.
   Fol. 193a (P. 375), *Explicit le breviaire des nobles.*
   443 plus 8 lines. Lacks lines 315–17. The envoys are headed 'Prince'.

Bf was included by Rice in his bibliography of the poem, being described wrongly as MS 3. The text, which is incomplete, contains a number of irregular lines and some poor rhymes.

Bg LONDON, BRIT. MUS., ROYAL 14 E ii[3]

15th c.; parchment; 460 × 330 (280 × 225); d.c. of 100 mm; 357 ff.; 35–6 lines; miniatures, decorated borders and initials, headings in red.

3. Ff. 332a–335c, *Cy commence le breviaire des nobles Et parle premierement dame Noblesse.*
   445 plus 8 lines. Lacks line 179.

Bg was included by Rice in his bibliography. The text has not been examined before. It is of quite good quality but includes some irregular lines.

Bh LONDON, BRIT. MUS., ROYAL 15 E vi

1445–7; parchment; 470 × 330 (355 × 220); d.c. of 95 mm; 440 ff.; 73–5 lines; miniatures, decorated borders and initials, headings in red; contemporary table of contents.

13. Fol. 402v, *Cy commence la* (sic) *breviaire des nobles.*
    Fol. 404d, *Explicit le livre nommé le Breviaire des nobles.*
    434 plus 8 lines. Lacks lines 53–6, 120, 179, 225, 365, 443–6.

Bh was listed by Rice, but the text has not been examined before. It is incomplete and includes a number of irregular lines and some poor rhymes.

Bj LONDON, BRIT. MUS., ROYAL 17 E iv

Late 15th c.; parchment; 410 × 300 (260 × 185); d.c. of 75–80 mm; 326 ff.; 38 lines; catchwords (at right angles); miniatures, decorated initials.

---

[1] H. Hagen, *Catalogus codicum bernensium (Bibliotheca Bongarsiana)*, Bernae, Haller, 1875, 248–54.

[2] Item 7 (fol. 206a) is concerned with an archery contest at Tournai in 1510.

[3] See Sir G. F. Warner and J. P. Gilson, *British Museum: Catalogue of Western Manuscripts in the Old Royal and King's Collections*, II, 1921. The collations are given of all the Royal manuscripts listed here and the provenance of the manuscripts is discussed in detail.

4. Ff. 319b–322d, *S'ensuit le breviaire des nobles.*

366 plus 8 lines. Lacks lines 73–80, 179, 282–3 (1 line), 290–357, 443–6. Ballade IV has an envoy of four lines. The ballades are copied in the order: I–IV, VI, V, VIII, VII, IX, XII–XIII.

Bj was listed by Rice, but has not been examined before. It is incomplete and includes irregular lines and poor rhymes.

Bk +POITIERS, BIBL. MUN., 215

Late 15th c.; parchment; 149 ff.

Fol. 48r, *Maistre allain charstier* (sic) *dit ou livre de juvencel.*
Incipit: Prouesse faict aux nobles assavoir.

This item comprises the first stanza of the sixth ballade of the *Breviaire des Nobles*, twelve lines in all.[1]

Bk has not been listed or examined before.

Cd +DOUAI, BIBL. MUN., 767

Cd includes an item beginning on fol. 31r which is headed, '...aulcuns coupletz...de pluiseurs escripz et dictiers de feu mesire george chastelain et maistre alain chartier...' None of the poems included in this collection of rondeaux is by Alain Chartier.[2]

Da PARIS, BIBL. NAT., F. FR. 1507

Late 15th, early 16th c.; parchment; 280 × 190 (185 × 105); 74 ff.; 26 lines (quire 1), 24 lines (quires 2–10); collation 1–4⁸, 5⁴, 6–9⁸, 10⁶; catchwords, signatures; miniatures, decorated initial, coat of arms.

On fol. 1r there is a coat of arms which has not been identified: 1 et 4, d'argent, entre 8 croisettes pattées de sable 4 à 4, 5 fusées de gueules posées en fasce; 2 et 3, d'azur semé de fleurs de lys d'or un lion rampant d'or, couronné lampassé et armé de gueules; sur le tout, de gueules un lion rampant d'or. On the same folio is the signature 'Nicolas Moreau Sr D'auteuil...', with the device 'A L'ami son Coeur'.[3]

Fol. 1r, *Cy commancent les quatre dames nommez* (sic) *le joyeulx de espoir.*
Fol. 73v, *Vecy la fin des quatre dames autrement nommez le joyeulx de espoir.*

3489 lines. 42 lines are missing, single lines rather than groups.

Da was examined by Kussmann who listed 35 missing lines. The text contains many irregular lines and individual readings.

[1] The stanza is quoted in *Le Jouvencel*. See C. Favre et L. Lecestre (eds.), *Le Jouvencel par Jean de Bueil*, II, Paris, 1889, 30 (*SHF*).
[2] All the rondeaux save the last are published in Baron Kervyn de Lettenhove, *Œuvres de Georges Chastellain*, VIII, Bruxelles, V. Devaux, 1866, 309–21.
[3] See A. Vidier, 'Un bibliophile du XVIe siècle, Nicolas Moreau Sr d'Auteuil', *Mélanges E. Picot*, II, Paris, Morgand, 1913, 371–3. Neither *Da* nor *Ah*, also owned by Moreau, is among the manuscripts listed by Vidier.

Db PARIS, BIBL. NAT., F. FR. 2234

15th c.; parchment; 210 × 140 (145 × 85); 62 ff., plus 2 parchment end-leaves; 30 lines; collation 1–7^8, 8^6: A^2; signatures, catchwords; coloured initials, spaces for miniatures.

Fol. 1r, [*Le Livre des Quatre Dames*].
Fol. 61v, *Explicit le debat des quatre dames.*

3526 lines. Lacks lines 59, 910, 939, 2459, 2947.

Db was discussed by Kussmann who listed 5 missing lines. The text has been used in the edition of the *Livre des Quatre Dames*. The manuscript is in a clear cursive hand and has been carefully copied.

Dc PARIS, BIBL. NAT., F. FR. 2235

15th c.; parchment; 215 × 150 (145 × 95); 80 ff.; 25 lines; catchwords, signatures a–i; collation A^4: 1–9^8: B^4; miniature, decorated initials, headings in red, coat of arms.

Fol. 5r, [*Le Livre des Quatre Dames*].
Fol. 76r, *Explicit.*

[*Le livre des quatre dames.*] Added in a later hand.

3529 lines. Lacks lines 1953, 2306, 2643. Includes line 3531a, added in a later hand.

Dc was described in the inventory of the Royal Library at Blois in 1518 as 'Les quatre Dames, en rime. *Item* Le livre qui s'apelle les Quatre Dames, en rime et en parchemin'.[1] An inscription on fol. 1v indicates that its was kept 'aux armoyres dessoubz le pulpistre de la cronicque d'angleterre'. This description of the position of the MS in the library agrees with that of the catalogue.[2] On fol. 2r are the device 'A mon atante' and the signature 'Charles', which have been identified by Leopold Delisle as those of Charles VIII.[3] There is a further inscription on fol. 1v, which speaks of 'Les quatre dames appartenant au roy loys xii me'.

The arms of France appear twice on fol. 5r, the second time within the collar of the order of St Michel. The very thick azure field has begun to flake at the edges, revealing traces of red at the point of the shield. The presence of the order of St Michel had led Van Praet[4] to argue that this MS might have formed part of the library of Louis de Bruges, despite the fact that the arms of Louis de Bruges (aux 1 et 4, d'or à la croix de sable; aux 2 et 3, de gueules au sautoir d'argent) were generally depicted with the collar of the order of the Golden Fleece. Since there are traces of an earlier red field at the edges of both the third and fourth quarters, the earlier coat of arms on which the royal arms have been superimposed cannot be that of Louis de Bruges.

Kussmann listed *Dc* in his bibliography. The manuscript has not been examined before.

Dc has been used in the edition of the *Livre des Quatre Dames*, although it contains a considerable number of individual readings. It is copied in a clear and legible cursive hand. The manuscript contains a few corrections in a second hand (*Dc^2*).

[1] H. Omont, *Anciens inventaires et catalogues de la Bibliothèque Nationale*, I, Paris, E. Leroux, 1908, 47.
[2] H. Omont, *op. cit.*, I, 41, 'S'ensuit l'Inventaire des petitz livres et traittiez en francoys…aux armaires soubz le pulpitre de la Cronicque de Angleterre et de la Toison'.
[3] Delisle, *Le Cabinet des manuscrits*, I, 96.
[4] [J. B. B. Van Praet], *Recherches sur Louis de Bruges, seigneur de la Gruthuyse*, Paris, De Bure Frères, 1831, 163–4.

Dd   PARIS, BIBL. DE L'ARSENAL, 2940

Early 15th c.; parchment; 240 × 170 (160 × 85); 2 plus 66 ff.; 29–30 lines; collation A⁷(2): 1–8⁸:B²; catchwords, signatures a–h; miniatures, decorated initials and borders, coat of arms.

The coat of arms in the initial on fol. 1r is unidentified.[1] Two other coats of arms, in the initial on fol. 36v, and on fol. 63v, have been erased. The manuscript formed part of the library of Guyon de Sardière and perhaps also of that of the Duc de la Vallière.[2]

In style and subject, the five miniatures are very like those in *Df*, and they were probably painted by the same artist. The device, 'Au povre prisonnier', figures in the first miniature of both manuscripts.

Ff. 1r–63v, [*Le Livre des Quatre Dames*].

3529 lines. Lacks lines 747, 2402, 3386. Includes line 3531a, added in a later hand.

Dd was discussed by Kussmann, who considered it to be of good quality. It has been used here as base text in the edition of the *Livre des Quatre Dames*. *Dd* is copied in a clear cursive hand. *N* and *u* are generally, but not always, distinguished; *i* is usually dotted. The text has been carefully corrected and punctuated by the scribe. The divisions between words are indicated, in cases where confusion could arise. The scribe has marked the beginning and end of passages in direct speech by a sign in the margin or by writing the line in capitals.

De   +HEIDELBERG, U.B., PAL. GERM. 354

15th c.; paper; 4°; 200 × 135; 50 ff.; 35 lines; quires of 8 leaves; catchwords; red initials; binding dated 1558.

Ff. 1r–44r, *Cy commaince le livre des quatre dames*.

The introduction to the poem is largely complete, but the narrative has been abridged from 841 stanzas to 717 stanzas. In addition, some single lines are omitted.

De was discussed by Kussmann who listed 405 missing lines. The text is too abbreviated to be of use in a critical edition. It resembles those found in *Pf* and *Pj*, but is shorter still.

Df   LONDON, BRIT. MUS., ADDITIONAL 21247

Early 15th c.; parchment; 240 × 165 (140 × 87); 72 ff.; 26 lines; collation 1–9⁸; miniatures, decorated borders and initials; coat of arms; contemporary binding of stamped leather.

The arms on fol. 1r (d'or, à la croix de gueules, chargée de 5 coquilles d'argent, et cantonnée de 16 alérions d'azur) have been identified as those of the family of Montmorency-Laval.[3] In style and subject, the miniatures in *Df* closely resemble those in *Dd* (q.v.).

---

[1] Ecartelé: au 1, de gueules à la fasce d'hermine; au 2, d'azur à la croix anillée d'argent ombrée d'or; au 3, d'or à 9 macles d'azur; au 4, de vair plein. See M. Pecqueur, 'Manuscrits armoriés de l'Arsenal', *Bulletin d'information de l'Institut de Recherche et d'Histoire des Textes*, IV, 1955, 107–76, esp. 124.

[2] Despite the statement to that effect on fol. Av, no trace of *Dd* has been found in the sale catalogues of the La Vallière library. See the descriptions of *Nm* and *Oj*.

[3] A. Piaget, 'La Complainte du prisonnier d'amours', *Mélanges E. Picot*, II, Paris, Morgand, 1913, 155–62. Two of the miniatures are reproduced.

The manuscripts

Ff. 1r–70v, [*Le Livre des Quatre Dames*].

3524 lines. Lacks lines 495, 891, 1723, 2356, 3250–1, 3464.
A second hand has added this quatrain on fol. 71r:

> Car piecza l'ain
> Pour ce belle que prins(?) a l'ain
> Avez le cueur du pouvre Allain
> Ou il n'entre pencer villain.

Kussmann included *Df* in his bibliography, but the manuscript has not been examined before.

Df has been used in the edition of the *Livre des Quatre Dames*. In layout and decoration, it closely resembles *Dd*. The hand, part cursive, part bastard, is different; the scribe has a very characteristic way of writing *ri*. Although careful, he has paid less attention than the scribe of *Dd* to details such as punctuation and rhyme. The text has been corrected but sometimes untidily. Some lines omitted by the scribe have subsequently been added by him at the foot of the page concerned; the absence of other lines is noted in the margin.

Fa PARIS, BIBL. NAT., F. FR. 1563

Early 15th c.; paper; 2°; 265 × 180 (190 × 143); d.c. of 70 mm; 224 numbered ff.; 36–40 lines; collation 1^{20} (last folded back on to board), 2^{16}, 3^{14}, 4^{18}, 5–9^{16}: 10^{12}, 11^8, 12^{10}: 13^{14}, 14^{12} (last canc.): 15^{12}, 16^{12} (last two stuck to board); catchwords; miniatures, coloured initials in first part; contemporary table of contents on fol. 1; contemporary binding of leather on boards, with traces of two clasps.

Water-marks

(a) An anchor 55 mm long, between chain-lines 37 mm apart. Briquet 349 or 350 (1398–1410).
(b) An anchor surmounted by a cross, 69 mm long, chain-lines 38 mm apart. Very like Briquet 365 (1392).
(c) A basilisk, 75 mm long, partly across sewn chain-lines 37 mm apart. Of the type Briquet 2701–9 (1400–35).

The poem by Chartier has been copied on leaves left blank, in a second hand which is a little later than that which has copied the rest of the manuscript.

Fol. 222a, [*Le Lay de Paix*].
Fol. 223d, *C'est ung lay fait par maistre alain secretaire du roy nostre sire.*
276 = 277 lines. Lacks lines 11, 126, 232–6. Lines 109–10 are inverted, and lines 87–8 written as one line.

Fa also contains the *Roman de la Rose* and was described in detail by Langlois.[1] The *explicit* of the *Lay de Paix* was mentioned by Champion. The text in *Fa*, which is related to that in *Np*, is incomplete and contains a number of individual readings.

[1] E. Langlois, *Les Manuscrits du 'Roman de la Rose'*, Lille, Paris, 1910, 20–2 (*Travaux et mémoires de l'Univ. de Lille*, n.s., I: VII).

Fb PARIS, BIBL. NAT., F. FR. 11464

Late 15th c.; paper; 2°; 270 × 190 (170 × 100); 93 = 92 ff. (includes fol. 91bis; there are no ff. 40 or 81); c. 26 lines; collation A²: 1–3¹², 4⁷(5): 5–6¹², 7¹² (tenth lacking), 8–9⁸; catchwords; initials highlighted in red.

Water-marks

(a) A unicorn 90 mm long, between chain-lines 30 mm apart. Akin to Briquet 10426–31, especially 10430–1 (1499–1504).
(b) As (a) but 95 mm long, between chain-lines 33 mm apart.
(c) A bunch of grapes with letters, the mark being in the middle of the open leaf. In design very like Briquet 13113–38 (1486–1552).

On a fly-leaf is written 'Ce livre est a noble Jan Guillemot Sr. de L'argentaye'.

Ff. 76r–82v, [*Le Lay de Paix*].[1]
   270 lines. Lacks lines 1–14, 75, 101, 226. Includes lines 77a, 102a, 224a. Lines 15–16 and 109–10 are inverted.

Fb has not been listed or examined before. Its text is incomplete and includes a large number of irregular lines. The three additional lines are all peculiar to *Fb* which forms part of the group *FbFcNaNeOb*.

Fc PARIS, BIBL. NAT., F. FR. 25548

15th c.; paper and parchment; 4°; 210 × 150 (142 × 85); fly-leaf and (originally) 321 ff.; 20–1 lines (*Lay de Paix*); quires of 16 or 18 leaves (generally with outermost and innermost sheets of parchment); catchwords; contemporary binding of skin on boards, with traces of two clasps.

Water-marks

(a) A fleur-de-lys, chain-lines 42 mm apart.
(b) A unicorn, across chain-lines 40 mm apart.
(c) An anchor surmounted by a cross, chain-lines 39 mm apart.
(d) A 'Y' surmounted by a cross, between chain-lines 42 mm apart. Similar to Briquet 9174 (1449–56) or 9179 (1455–6).

Ff. 244r–250r, [*Le Lay de Paix*].[2]
   264 lines. Lacks lines 1–16, 75, 87, 95, 108, 155, 168, 180, 226, 273. Includes lines 77a, 88a, 96a, 109a, 275a. Lines 64–5 are inverted.

[1] In a note at the top of fol. 76r the poem is identified as the *Libelle de Paix*, '...mais il manque icy quatorze vers...peut estre qu'ils estoient dans la feuille qui paroit avoir esté dechiree'. The collation shows that a leaf is missing at this point. Any traces of it must have disappeared when the manuscript was rebound in 1851.

[2] The poem was copied in a quire of sixteen leaves, the outermost and innermost sheets being of parchment. The first six leaves, together with the last leaf of the preceding quire, have disappeared and have left a gap in the foliation from 237 to 243 inclusive.

Fc has not been listed or examined before. The text is incomplete and includes several additional lines. *Fc*, which forms part of the group *FbFcNaNeOb*, is closely connected with *Ob*.

Fd +VATICAN, REGINA LAT. 1900[1]

15th c.; parchment; 328 × 244; 158 ff.; d.c.; 40 lines.

2. Ff. 151c–153b, [*Le Lay de Paix*].
      280 lines. Lacks lines 30–2, 267. Lines 260–3 and 264–8 are transposed.

Fd has not been listed or examined before. The text, incomplete and disarranged, includes a number of readings peculiar to itself.

Fe +BARBENTANE (BOUCHES-DU-RHÔNE), LIBRARY OF M. DE PUGET DE BARBANTANE[2]

15th c.; paper; 203 × 145; 207 ff.; 24 lines.
    The manuscript has belonged to the Barbantane family since the sixteenth century.

Fol. 62v, [*Le Lay de Paix*].
Fol. 68r, *Sy fine le lay de paix que fist Maistre alain charetier a la requeste de mon seigneur de bourgongne.*
      267 lines. Lacks lines 11, 15, 44, 103–9, 121, 155, 240, 247, 254, 271, 274, 282. Includes line 156a. Line 65 is copied between lines 62 and 63.

Details of this manuscript, which has not been listed or examined before, were provided by the Institut de Recherche et d'Histoire des Textes. Many lines are omitted in *Fe* and the text has been rearranged at one point. *Fe* includes several faulty rhymes and a number of individual readings. It stands in the same tradition as *Nf* and *Nj*.

Ff +VATICAN, REGINA LAT. 1683

Late 15th c.; parchment; 306 × 214; 113 ff.; 30 lines.

3. Fol. 33r, *Le lay de paix (d'Alain Chartier).*[3]
    Fol. 38r, *Explicit le lay de paix (de Me Alain Chartier).*[3]
      272 = 273 lines. Lacks lines 15, 44, 70, 111, 120, 128–9, 142, 150, 155, 225, 267. Includes line 156a. Lines 58–9 are written as one line.

Ff has not been examined or used before. It is closely related to *Pb* and forms part of the larger group *FfNbPbQq*. Many lines are omitted in both *Ff* and *Pb* which further contain a number of readings peculiar to themselves. Individual readings, some irregular, are

---

[1] In the description of this and other Vatican MSS use has been made of E. Langlois, 'Notices des manuscrits français et provençaux de Rome antérieurs au XVIe siècle', *Notices et extraits*, XXXIII: ii, 1889, 1–347.
[2] For a fuller description of *Fe* see F. Lecoy, 'Farce et *Jeu* inédits tirés d'un manuscrit de Barbantane', *Romania*, XCII, 1971, 145–99, esp. 145–6.
[3] Chartier's name has been added in a second hand.

frequent in *Ff*. Although they are closely linked with texts in the tradition of *Nf* and *Nj*, both *Ff* and *Pb* contain readings which link them with texts of other traditions, particularly *Fb* or *Qr*.

Fg PARIS, BIBL. NAT., F. LAT. 17447[1]

Mid 15th c.; parchment; 340×260 (230×165); 86 ff.; single and double columns; *c.* 50 lines; catchwords; signatures a–g, –, h–l; collation 1^8 (first lost), 2–5^8: 6^4, 7^8, 8^4 (third canc.): 9–12^8; initials and headings in red; binding of parchment on boards with traces of two clasps.

An inscription on fol. 86r indicates that *Fg* once belonged to René Vallin of Nantes; it passed to Claude Joly, perhaps in December 1666, and was one of the manuscripts given by him to Notre-Dame de Paris in 1680.[2]

4. Ff. 52c–53d, [*Le Lay de Paix*].[3]
   277 = 278 lines. Lacks lines 15, 121, 157, 190, 194, 264. Lines 35–6 are copied as one line.

Fg has not been listed or described before. The text is incomplete and contains a number of irregular lines. It is generally in agreement with texts of Group II, especially Group IIa, and is most closely linked with *Fc* or *Nq*.

Ga PARIS, BIBL. NAT., F. FR. 2262

15th c.; parchment; 185×115 (125×75); 23 ff.; 27 lines (quire 1), 28 lines (quires 2 and 3); collation 1–2^8, 3^8 (last canc.); catchwords, signatures; miniature, decorated initial, coat of arms.

On fol. 13r is the inscription 'A Monseigneur le Conte de Soisons(?)'. The arms on fol. 23v (de sable, à deux léopards d'or, au filet écoté d'argent posé en barre) are those of the house of Dinteville, differenced perhaps for an illegitimate son.

Ff. 1r–23v, [*Le Debat des Deux Fortunés d'Amours*].
   1235 plus 4 lines. Lacks lines 46, 96, 151, 635, 653, 897, 1149, 1219. Includes line 1130a (Non ferés vous d'elle sa grand bonté).

The manuscript was discussed by Gaston Paris in 1886.[4] Droz and Piaget did not include it in their bibliography of manuscripts containing the poem. *Ga* has not been examined before in detail. Its text of the *Debat des Deux Fortunés d'Amours* is not only incomplete but also contains a large number of irregular lines.

[1] *Fg* is to be added to the list of manuscripts published in *Modern Language Review*, LXI, 1966, 188–98.
[2] Delisle, *Le Cabinet des manuscrits*, I, 431.
[3] The eighth quire, which contains the *Lay de Paix*, is of three leaves and has no signature. Since the recto of the first leaf contains the last few lines of item 3 (*De Sacramentis*) and the last leaf the table of the contents of item 5 (*Gregorii Pastoralis*), it is clear that quire 8 is a constituent part of the manuscript.
[4] G. Paris, 'Note additionnelle sur Jean de Grailli, comte de Foix', *Romania*, XV, 1886, 611–13.

Gb PARIS, BIBL. NAT., F. FR. 15219

15th c.; parchment (quires 1–3), paper and parchment (quires 4–15); 2° and 4°; 240 × 180 (185 × 95); 212 ff.; 24–8 lines; collation 1¹⁰, 2⁸, 3⁶: 4¹⁴, 5¹⁵, 6–7¹⁶, 8¹⁵: 9–14¹⁶, 15⁷(16); catchwords; decorated initials and borders, headings in red in first items.

Water-marks

(a) A fleur-de-lys, 60 mm long, between finely sewn chain-lines 38 mm apart.
(b) An anchor, surmounted by a cross, 63 mm long, between chain-lines 40 mm apart.
(c) An orb, between chain-lines 43 mm apart. The position of the mark across the fold and the direction of the chain-lines suggest that this paper is folded in-quarto. Similar to Briquet 2988 (1427–42).
(d) A unicorn 95 mm long, across chain-lines 40 mm apart. Very like Briquet 10009 (1441–7).

The following names in contemporary hands can be read: 'Jehan guyard' (fol. 1r); 'Jehan francoys' (35r); 'Martin francoys' (211r); 'Metre robert drieu' (210v).

Fol. 188v, [*La Belle Dame sans Mercy*].
Fol. 203v, *Explicit la belle dame sans mercy.*
    796 lines. Lacks lines 262–3, 380, 398. The text contains a few corrections. Some headings have been added in a later hand.

Gb was included by Piaget in his bibliography of the poem; it has not been examined before. The text, which is incomplete, contains some poor rhymes and a large number of irregular lines.

Gc PARIS, BIBL. NAT., F. FR. 2229

Mid 15th c. (before June 1467); paper and parchment (fly-leaves); 4°; 215 × 150 (150 × 80); 2 plus 116 plus 2 ff.; 26 lines; collation A²: 1–14⁸, 15⁴: B²; signatures a–l, k, m–n, (o); catchwords; headings in red, coloured initials.

Water-mark: A coat of arms (3 fleurs-de-lys), surmounted by a crown; approximately 33 mm long, between chain-lines 40 mm apart. Briquet 1701 (1454–65).

In 1467 the manuscript belonged to Jean d'Angoulême.[1] The signature 'Yzabeau d'alebret' occurs on a fly-leaf.[2]

2. Fol. 108r, [*La Complainte*].
    Fol. 111v, *Explicit la complainte.*
        181 lines. Lacks lines 83, 117, 147, 163, 173. Includes lines 119a, 174a. The stanzas are in the order I–IV, VII, V–VI, VIII, X, IX, XI–XII.

Gc has not been listed or examined before. Its text of the *Complainte* is very like those in *Gg* and *Ol*, and is particularly close to that in *Gg*; these three texts are all incomplete and contain many readings peculiar to themselves.

---

[1] It is described in the inventory of his books made on 1 June 1467. See Champion, *La Librairie de Charles d'Orléans*, 121; only the first work, *Le Chevalier des Dames*, is listed.
[2] The same signature appears on a fly-leaf of *Pf*.

Gd PARIS, BIBL. NAT., F. FR. 24435

1476/7; paper;[1] 2°; 280×205 (*c.* 230×100 [item 4]); 195 ff., numbered to 190; 35–40 lines; collation 1⁴: 2–8¹⁰, 9¹²: 10²⁰: 11¹⁴ (first canc.): 12–15¹², 16⁶: 17¹⁸: 18⁴ (last stuck down); catchwords in first item; coat of arms.

On fol. 5r there is an unidentified coat of arms (de sable à 2 léopards d'argent l'un sur l'autre, armés et lampassés de gueules) which was probably added some time after the manuscript was copied. The signature 'Helene de tournon' occurs on fol. 1r. In a note on fol. 190v the scribe signs himself 'Nicholaus plenus amoris'. An inscription on the same folio reads: 'Ce livre est a tristan de sazilly escuier seigneur de la court de auon et l'a faict extraire et coppier d'aultres livres et fut parachevé le viij^e jour de janvier mil quatre cens soyxante et seize.' Underneath is a note that the manuscript was 'donné par M. l'abbé de Castres le 21 octobre 1709'.[2]

4. Ff. 174r–190v (quire 17), [*Le Debat des Deux Fortunés d'Amours*].
   1225 plus 4 lines. Lacks lines 40–3, 95, 407, 440, 723–30, 950, 989.

Gd was included by Droz and Piaget in their bibliography of the poem, but has not been examined in detail before. The text contains a good number of irregular lines and individual readings; it is also incomplete.

Ge +JENA, UNIVERSITÄTSBIBLIOTHEK, El. f. 98

Late 15th c.; paper; 2°; 14–20 lines.

This manuscript, along with two others, was commissioned by the Elector Frederick the Wise to encourage the study of French at his court.[3] An interlinear translation of the poem into Latin is included.

1. Fol. 1r, [*La Belle Dame sans Mercy*].
   Fol. 32r, *Explicit la belle dame sans mercy. Finis.*
       791 = 788 lines. Lacks lines 177–84, 318–20, 757. Lines 589–92 are copied instead of lines 318–20 and are copied again in their correct position. Stanzas XLVII and XLVIII are transposed. Text with headings.

Ge has not been listed or used before. The text contains a number of individual readings and poor rhymes; certain lines, for example lines 557–60 and 645–8, are different from those found in the manuscripts used in this edition of the poem.

---

[1] There are ten water-marks; no details of them are given because the manuscript is dated.
[2] *Gd* formed part of a collection given by Castres to R. de Gaignières in 1709 (Delisle, *Le Cabinet des manuscrits*, I, 350).
[3] This information was provided by the librarian.

Gf   +NEW YORK, PIERPONT MORGAN LIBRARY, 396

Early 15th c.; parchment; 320 × 240; 246 ff.; d.c.; 44 lines; miniatures, decorated and coloured initials.

The manuscript is imperfect.[1]

2. Ff. 227a–229d, *La belle dame sans mercy.*
   Only the first 480 lines have been preserved. Text with headings.

Gf was mentioned by E. J. Hoffman in 1942.[2] It was not included in Piaget's list of manuscripts containing the *Belle Dame sans Mercy.*

The text in *Gf* is of good quality, being generally regular and containing few individual readings. Although it is incomplete, it has been chosen for use in the edition of the *Belle Dame sans Mercy*. The manuscript is written in quite a clear cursive hand. Since the scribe's down-strokes are thick and the parchment absorbent, the text can be difficult to read. There is no clear distinction between *n* and *u*, and the divisions between words are not made in a consistent manner. The 'headings' in *Gf* are in fact instructions to a rubricator.

The text contains some north-eastern forms: e.g. *ricesse* (line 38), *s'efforchoit* (line 89), *s'enlachoit* (line 94). Similar forms are found in *Pc* and *Ql*, to which *Gf* is related.

Gg   +VATICAN, REGINA LAT. 1362

Late 15th c.; paper; 198 × 135; 143 ff.; 21 lines.

2. Fol. 132v, *La Complainte que fist Maistre Alain Charretier pour sa Dame.*
   Fol. 137v, *Explicit la complainte de maistre alain charretier.*
      181 lines. Lacks lines 83, 117, 147, 163, 173. Includes lines 119a, 174a. The order of stanzas is: I–IV, VII, V–VI, VIII, X, IX, XI–XII.

Gg was mentioned by Champion, but has not been examined or used before. The connection between *Gg*, *Gc* and *Ol* was mentioned when *Gc* was discussed. *Gg* is particularly close to *Gc* but does include a number of individual readings, some of which are irregular.

Gh   +BERLIN, STAATSBIBLIOTHEK, PHILLIPPS 1928

15th c.; parchment; 67 ff.; 110–20 × 70–80; 17 lines.

On ff. 1v and 64v is the device 'Je ly tiendray'.

This manuscript is probably that described by Montfaucon in his list of manuscripts belonging to Baron de Crassier in 1733.[3] It later formed part of the Meerman library

---

[1] S. de Ricci and W. J. Wilson, *Census of Medieval and Renaissance Manuscripts in the United States and Canada*, II, New York, H. W. Wilson, 1937, 1440. Their description contains details of the manuscript's provenance.
  See also W. H. Bond and C. U. Faye, *Supplement to the* [same] *Census...*, New York, Bibliogr. Socy. of America, 1962, 344.

[2] Hoffman, *Alain Chartier, his Works and Reputation*, 281, n. 10.

[3] B. de Montfaucon, *Bibliotheca bibliothecarum manuscriptorum nova*, I, Parisiis, Briasson, 1739, 606.
  On *Gh* see also E. Winkler, 'Französische Dichter des Mittelalters: I, Vaillant', *Sitzungsberichte der Kais. Akademie der Wissenschaften in Wien: Phil.-hist. Klasse*, CLXXXVI: i, 1918, 45.

(No. 880), and was acquired by Sir Thomas Phillipps in 1824. The Meerman–Phillipps manuscripts were bought by the German government in 1887.[1]

3. Ff. 47r–52r, [*La Complainte*].
    182 lines. Lacks lines 110, 130. Lines 146–7 are inverted.

Gh has not been listed or examined before. It is closely related to *Qr* and the two texts can be grouped together with *Pn* and *Qg*. *Gh*, *Qr* and *Nr*, a text of a different tradition, have some readings in common. The number of individual readings and irregular lines found in *Gh* is extraordinarily high.

Gj PARIS, BIBL. NAT., F. FR. 2253

16th c.; parchment; 205 × 140 (140 × 90); 38 ff.; 16 lines; collation[2] 1^2, 2^8, 3^{12}, 4^4, 5^{12}; headings in red, coloured initials.

On fol. 2v there is the device 'J'en garde un leal', an anagram of Anne de Graville. The manuscript is perhaps written in two hands (ff. 2v–12v, 37r–38r; ff. 13r–36v).

Fol. 2v, *A ma dame.*
Incipit: En maistre Allain, de ses oeuvres j'ay quis
      A mon juger, le plus fin et exquis. . . .

Gj contains a collection of seventy-one rondeaux, inspired by the *Belle Dame sans Mercy*. Stanzas XXV–XCVII of Chartier's poem are copied in the margins of the manuscript, near to the rondeaux adapted from them.

Gj was not included by Piaget in his bibliography of the *Belle Dame sans Mercy*. The adaptation, which is by Anne de Graville, has been discussed by C. Wahlund.[3] The text of the *Belle Dame sans Mercy* is incomplete and contains a number of irregular lines and some poor rhymes.

Na PARIS, BIBL. NAT., F. FR. 2249

Late 15th c.; paper; 4°; 205 × 135 (140 × 80); 112 ff.; *c*. 30 lines; quires generally of 16 leaves;[4] trace of catchwords.

Water-marks

(a) A coat of arms (a fleur-de-lys, a three-pointed label), surmounted by a passion cross with 3 nails; chain-lines 41 mm apart. Perhaps Briquet 1552 (1468–88).
(b) The arms of France crowned, with a 't' at the point of the shield; chain-lines 35 mm apart.
(c) As (b) but overlapping chain-lines 37 mm apart.
(d) A pot surmounted by a cross; chain-lines 37 mm apart. Perhaps Briquet 12481 (1468).

[1] A. N. L. Munby, *The Formation of the Phillipps Library up to 1840*, Cambridge, U.P., 1954, 25–8: *The Dispersal of the Phillipps Library*, Cambridge, U.P., 1960, 22–6.
[2] The binding is so tight that it is difficult to be sure of the collation.
[3] C. Wahlund, 'La Belle Dame sans mercy', *Skrifter Kongl. Humanistiska Vetenskapssamfundet i Upsala*, v: viii, Upsala, 1897.
[4] The binding is so tight that it is difficult to be sure of the collation.

The signature of 'Nicolas de Livre, Sr. de Humerolles'[1] appears on ff. 1r and 40r. *Na* was given by him to Fauchet[2] (fol. 1r), who in turn gave it to L. de Sainte-marthe[3] (fol. 1r).

3. Ff. 23r–32r, *Cy commance le breviere des nobles.* (*Par Alain Chartier*, added)

442 plus 8 lines. Lacks lines 53–6. The text has been corrected and the author's name added, probably by Livre.

5. Ff. 34r–39r, [*Le Lay de Paix*].

278 lines. Lacks lines 75, 120, 136, 151, 155, 273.

The text of the *Breviaire des Nobles* was listed by Rice in 1951 but the manuscript has not been examined before. The texts of both poems are incomplete; they contain individual readings and a number of irregular lines. So far as the *Lay de Paix* is concerned, *Na* forms part of the group *FbFcNaNeOb*.

Nb PARIS, BIBL. NAT., F. FR. 25293

15th c.; cloth (quires A and B) and parchment; 235 × 175 (145 × 105); 137 = 138 ff. (includes fol. 29bis); 29 lines; collation A²: 1–6⁸, 7⁶: 8–17⁸: B²; catchwords at right angles; miniatures, decorated borders and initials; binding (repaired) of leather on boards.

The manuscript contains on ff. 136v and 137r the following signatures in contemporary hands: 'Charles d'Espinay', 'Anthoine d'Espinay' and 'Rene d'Espinay'. Some of the decorated capitals incorporate the letters 'E' and 'I' joined by a love-knot. On fol. 2r 'forget' is written in a fifteenth- or sixteenth-century hand.

2. Fol. 51r, [*La Complainte*].

Fol. 54r, *Explicit le lay contre la mort.*

184 lines. Lacks line 162. Includes line 119a.

4. Fol. 131r, [*Le Lay de Paix*].

Fol. 135v, *Explicit le lay de paix.*

272 lines. Lacks lines 15, 44, 52–3, 80, 89, 121, 155, 161, 169–70, 196, 232. Includes line 156a. Lines 63–4 are inverted.

Nb has not been listed or examined before. The second item is not recognised in the catalogue.[4] Neither text is complete; both contain a number of irregular lines and many individual readings. The *Complainte* has an extra line which shows that the text is contaminated. *Nb* is closely related to *Qq*.

Nc PARIS, BIBL. NAT., F. FR. 25435

15th c.; paper; 4°; 220 × 145 (c. 170 × 110); single and double columns; 49 ff.; c. 36 lines; collation 1¹², 2¹⁶ (fourteenth canc.): 3¹⁴, 4⁸; catchwords.

---

[1] He published a translation from the Italian in 1575 (*Catalogue général des livres imprimés de la Bibliothèque Nationale*, XCVIII, 1930, 1116).

[2] Probably Claude Fauchet; see Delisle, *Le Cabinet des manuscrits*, II, 363–4.

[3] Probably Louis de Sainte-Marthe, *historiographe du roi* (*cat. cit.*, CLX, 1940, 570–1).

[4] H. Omont, *Bibliothèque Nationale: catalogue général des manuscrits français, anciens petits fonds français*, II, Paris, Leroux, 1902, 556–7.

Water-mark: A cross-bow, between chain-lines 37 mm apart. Similar to Briquet 726 (1447–58).

'Jehan dany (dauy)' is written on fol. 6v in a hand slightly later than the manuscript.

1. Ff. 1r–6v, *Cy comence Resveille.*
   360 lines. Lacks lines 17–24. Text with headings. The outside edge of fol. 1 is damaged and part of the text has disappeared.
2. Ff. 6v–17v, [*La Belle Dame sans Mercy*].
   800 lines. Complete. The order of stanzas is: I–XXXIX, XLVI–LI, XL–XLV, LII–C. From the beginning of quire 2 (line 429), the hand has a more finished appearance and thereafter the stanzas are headed.
5. Ff. 28r–49b[1] (quires 3–4), *Cy comencent les iiii dames.*
   2903 lines. Lacks lines 415, 1700, 1731–2, 1834, 1953, 2228, 2306. Ends at line 2911.

Nc was listed by Piaget in his bibliography of the *Belle Dame sans Mercy*; it has not been examined in detail before. The version of the *Debat de Reveille Matin* in *Nc* lacks stanza III and contains a number of irregular lines; it forms part of the group *NcNgPh*. The text of the *Livre des Quatre Dames* is incomplete. Examination of parts of that poem and of the *Belle Dame sans Mercy* reveals that they are often irregular and contain many poor rhymes.

Nd PARIS, BIBL. NAT., N. A. FR. 4511–13

15th c.; paper; 4°; written area *c.* 155 × 85; 173 ff.; 24–30 lines; catchwords.

Water-marks

(a) The arms of France, within a border, a 't' at the point of the shield; chain-lines 40 mm apart. Very like Briquet 1825 (1466–7).
(b) A unicorn across chain-lines 39 mm apart.
(c) A cock across chain-lines 38 mm apart.

Originally MS 8047 in the Royal Library of France, *Nd* was stolen and cut into three parts, to become Barrois MSS 402, 585 and 396 in the library of the fourth Earl of Ashburnham.[2]

4. Ff. 35r–55v, *Et commence de l'autre cousté de ce fueillet le debat des deux fortunez autrement dit le gras et le meigre.*
   1237 lines. Lacks lines 40, 96, 256, 635, 653.
9. Ff. 116r–173v, *Les quatre dames.*
   3498 lines. 33 lines are missing, single lines rather than groups.

Kussmann discussed *Nd* in his study of the textual tradition of the *Livre des Quatre Dames* and listed 31 missing lines. *Nd* was included by Droz and Piaget in their bibliography of the *Debat des Deux Fortunés d'Amours.* Although the text of the latter poem is generally regular and of quite good quality, that of the *Livre des Quatre Dames* contains many irregular lines and individual readings.

---

[1] The text is in double columns on ff. 29r and 32r–49r.
[2] L. Delisle, *Catalogue des manuscrits des fonds Libri et Barrois*, Paris, Champion, 1888, 237–40.

Ne PARIS, BIBL. NAT., N. A. FR. 6220–4

MS 6221: 15th c.; paper; 2°; 290 × 210 (245 × 160); d.c. of 75 mm; 35 detached ff.; *c.* 60 lines.

Water-marks

(a–c) An anchor surmounted by a cross, three varieties:

(a) 50 mm long, between chain-lines 45 mm apart; (b) 65 mm long, chain-lines 45 mm apart; (c) 55 mm long, chain-lines 43 mm apart. All three are similar to Briquet 396–400 (1420–64).

(d) A 'P' surmounted by a cross, 80 mm long, between chain-lines 38 mm apart. Akin to Briquet 8462–85 (1379–1455).

(e) An angel, 65 mm long, between sewn chain-lines 40 mm apart. Very like Briquet 601 (1410–41).

At first St Victor MS 275 in the Royal Library of France, *Ne* was stolen and divided into five parts which formed Barrois MSS 373, 523, 498, 494 and 492 in the library of the fourth Earl of Ashburnham. The physical description above is based largely on the present MS 6221.[1]

Ff. 24c–26c, *Cy commence le breviaire des nobles.*

442 lines plus rondeau. Lacks lines 239, 315–17.

Ff. 26c–27d, *Lay notable* (= *Le Lay de Paix*).

281 lines. Lacks lines 75, 199, 273. Lines 15–16 are inverted.

Ne has not been listed or examined before. The published catalogue makes no mention of the items by Chartier.[2] The texts of both poems are incomplete and include quite a large number of individual readings. Where the *Lay de Paix* is concerned, *Ne* forms part of the group *FbFcNaNeOb*.

Nf AIX-EN-PROVENCE, BIBL. MÉJANES, 168

Mid 15th c.; parchment; 210 × 160 (155 × 95); 128 pp.; 32 lines; collation 1–8⁸; catchwords; headings in red, coloured initials; contemporary binding of limp skin, bearing the letters 'P' and 'Y', joined by a love-knot.

An inscription on page 1 reads: 'Dono dedit D. Lud. Daniel de Montcalm de Gozon de Candiac etc., An. .MDCCVIII. die xxiv. januarii'. According to a note on page 128, 'Ce manuscrit vient de la bibliotheque de M. le Marquis d'aubais et m'a ete vendu par ses heritiers 4 ll. en 1780'.[3]

---

[1] Delisle, *Catalogue des manuscrits des fonds Libri et Barrois*, 254–61. See also Le Marquis de Queux de Saint-Hilaire, *Œuvres complètes de Eustache Deschamps*, II, Paris, 1880, xvii–xliv (*SATF*). The first work in MS 6221, the lay 'Un mortel lay vueil commencier', is wrongly attributed to Alain Chartier in both these descriptions.

[2] H. Omont, *Bibliothèque Nationale: catalogue général des manuscrits français, nouvelles acquisitions françaises*, II, Paris, Leroux, 1900, 419–20.

[3] For other manuscripts owned by the Marquis d'Aubais see Delisle, *Le Cabinet des manuscrits*, II, 337.

1. Pp. 1–12, *Cy commence le debat de resveille matin.*
    360 lines. Lacks lines 17–24.
2. P. 12, *Cy commence la belle dame Sans mercy.*
    P. 35, *Explicit la belle dame sans mercy.*
    752 lines. Lacks lines 673–720.
3. P. 36, *Copie des lectres envoyees par les dames A alain.*
4. Pp. 36–8, *Copie des lectres envoyees aux dames contre alain.*
5. Pp. 38–46, *Excusacion faicte envers les dames par alain.*
    240 plus 4 lines. Complete.
6. P. 46, *Cy se commence le lay de paix.*
    P. 55, *Cy est la fin du lay de paix.*
    283 lines. Lacks lines 15, 155. Includes line 156a. Lines 225–6 are inverted.
7. P. 55, *Et commence le lay de plaisance.*
    P. 61, *Cy est la fin du lay de paix* (sic).
    196 lines. Complete. Lines 1–2 are inverted.
8. P. 61, *Et commence une complainte contre la mort.*
    P. 67, *Cy est fin de la complainte de la mort.*
    184 lines. Lacks line 117. Includes line 119a. The order of stanzas is: I–III, V–VII, IV, VIII–XII.
9. P. 67, *Cy commence le breviaire des nobles.*
    P. 82, *Cy est la fin du breviaire des nobles.*
    446 lines. Complete, save for the final rondeau.
10. Pp. 82–121, *Et aprez se commence le debat sur la quantité de fortune des biens et des maulz d'amours que aucuns nomment le gras et le mesgre.*
    P. 120, *Cy est la fin du gras et du maigre. Finis.*
    1239 plus 4 lines (on p. 121). Lacks lines 96, 635, 653. Line 583 has been added by a second hand in a space left blank.
11. Pp. 121–7, *Cy apres s'ensuivent aucuns rondeaulz et balades faiz et composez par maistre Alain.*
    A. Pp. 121–2, *Balade.*
       Incipit: Je ne fu né fors pour tout mal avoir...   36 lines
    B. Pp. 122–3, *Autre balade.*
       Incipit: Aucunes gens m'ont huy arraisonné...   35 lines
    C. Pp. 123–5, *Autre balade.*
       Incipit: J'ay ung arbre de la plante d'amours...   35 lines
    D. Pp. 125–6, *Autre balade.*
       Incipit: J'ay voulentiers oy parler d'amours...   41 lines
    E. P. 126, *Rondel.*
       Incipit: Je vy le temps que je souloye...   10 lines
    F. Pp. 126–7, *Rondelet.*
       Incipit: Helas ma courtoise ennemie...   10 lines
    G. P. 127, *Rondinet.*
       Incipit: Du tout ainsi qu'il vous plaira...   10 lines

The collection of lyrics in *Nf* was published by the Marquis Philippe de Chennevières in 1846.[1] *Nf* was included in the bibliographies of the lyrics, the *Debat des Deux Fortunés d'Amours*, the *Belle Dame sans Mercy*, and the *Breviaire des Nobles*. The manuscript has not been examined in detail before.

Nf, which was used in the edition of the four poems, is closely related to *Nj* to which it bears some formal resemblance. They are the best of a larger group of collected manuscripts which includes *Nb Nl Nr Om Qo* and *Qq*. Although *Nf* is slightly inferior in quality to *Nj* – some lines are omitted in *Nf* and the manuscript is a little more individual – its readings complement those of *Nj*. For that reason both manuscripts have been used in this edition.

Nf is written in a well-formed cursive hand; *u* and *n* are generally distinguished and the division between words is clearly made. The scribe used so few abbreviations that they can be difficult to interpret: his intention to write *serement* rather than *serment* (CO 88; PA 183) is only confirmed when the full form is found in BD 350. *Nf* was corrected by the scribe: errors are scored out or cancelled by the placing of dots underneath; where lines are inverted, the correct order is indicated in the margin. Exceptionally, a cancellation increases the evidence that the manuscript may be contaminated:[2] in EX, line 90 ends 'si d̲ noble figure'; in several manuscripts *digne* is an alternative reading for *noble*. The rubrics and coloured capitals, which were added later, can obscure the second letter of a word (BN 359). Certain leaves at the beginning and the end of the manuscript have become wrinkled with damp and are difficult to read.

Ng CHANTILLY, MUSÉE CONDÉ, 685

15th c. (after 1457);[3] paper and parchment (fly-leaves); 2°; 290 × 205 (*c.* 210 × 105); 2 plus 166 ff.; 24 lines (verse); collation 1^{12}, 2^{10}, 3^{12}, 4^6: 5^{10}: 6^{12}: 7^{12}, 8^{12}, 9^{10} (last canc.): 10^{10}: 11^{16}: 12^{18}: 13^{18}: $14^7(9)$; contemporary table of contents on fly-leaf; contemporary binding of stamped leather on boards.

Water-marks

(a) A 'Y', surmounted by a cross, the tail ending in a trefoil; 60 or 70 mm long (two varieties), between chain-lines 40 mm apart.

(b) A fleur-de-lys, 55 mm long, fixed to lightly sewn chain-lines 40 mm apart.

(c) A coat of arms (a fleur-de-lys, a fesse in chief), with a passion cross above; in all 55 mm long, chain-lines 40 or 45 mm apart (two varieties).

(d) The arms of France, surmounted by a crown, with a 'c' below; 75 mm long, chain-lines 40 or 43 mm apart (three varieties). Similar to Briquet 1725 (1463–4).

(e) A man's head, surmounted by a cross; 70 mm long, chain-lines 44 mm apart. Similar to Briquet 15670–84 (1433–1527).

(f) A six-toothed wheel, 24 mm in diameter, with a cross (?) attached, between chain-lines 43 mm apart.

[1] [Marquis Philippe de Chennevières], *Rondeaux et ballades inédits d'Alain Chartier*, Caen, Poisson et fils, 1846.   [2] See pp. 330 and 393.

[3] This date is copied on fol. 120v at the end of item 8, *Les Merveilles de la terre prestre Jehan.*

(g) An ox-head, 60 mm long, between chain-lines 40 mm apart. Similar to Briquet 14329–35 (1441–87).

The manuscript is in at least two hands. In the margin of fol. 2 is scratched the signature of Francoys de Bourbon, younger brother of the Connétable de Bourbon, who was killed at the battle of Marignano in 1515.[1]

2. Ff. 41r–49r (quire 5), *Le Resveille Matin*.
      360 lines. Lacks lines 17–24. The order of stanzas is I–XXVIII, XXXVIII–XL, XXIX–XXXI, XLI–XLII, XXXII–XXXIV, XLIII–XLIV, XXXV–XXXVII, XLV–XLVI.
10. Ff. 140r–157v (quire 13), *La Belle Dame sans mercy*.
      800 lines. Complete. Text with headings.

Ng has not been listed or examined before. The text of the *Debat de Reveille Matin*, which lacks stanza III and is disarranged, contains a number of irregular readings and poor rhymes; it is related to the texts in *Nc* and *Ph*. Part of the text of the *Belle Dame sans Mercy* was examined and found to be of fair quality.

Nh CLERMONT-FERRAND, BIBL. MUN., 249[2]

Early 15th c.; paper; 2°; 290 × 210; 89 ff.; contemporary parchment binding.

Water-marks

(a) A vine-leaf and stalk, 55 mm long, between sewn chain-lines 40 mm apart. Very like Briquet 6194 (1415–19).
(b) A cat's head, 42 mm long, between sewn chain-lines 45 mm apart.
(c) A glove, the cuff having six tails, 70 mm long, between chain-lines (perhaps sewn) 43 mm apart. Very like Briquet 11124 (1426).
(d) A crown, 31 mm broad at base, 60 mm broad at top; fixed to chain-lines 35 mm apart. Most like Briquet 4621 (1392–1433).
(e) An ox-head, surmounted by a cross, between chain-lines 38 mm apart; 85 mm or 90 mm in length (2 varieties). Akin to Briquet 14168–9 (1410–21).
(f) A cat, rather indistinctly formed, across chain-lines 38 mm apart. Like Briquet 3553 (1404–15).

So many leaves have been lost that it is impossible to determine the collation. The size of the written area and the number of lines per page vary widely. The scribe has used now single, now double columns.

17. Ff. 10r–14v, [*Le Breviaire des Nobles*].
      442 plus 8 lines. Lacks lines 167, 325, 352, 378.
19. Fol. 15r, *Le lay de pays*.
      Fol. 16v, *Cy faut le lay de paix*.

---

[1] *Chantilly: Le Cabinet des livres: Manuscrits*, Paris, Plon-Nourrit, II, 1900, 406–9.
[2] See C. Couderc, 'Notice du manuscrit 249 de la bibliothèque de Clermont-Ferrand', *Bulletin de la SATF*, XV, 1889, 98–114.

161 lines. Lacks lines 44, 59, 81–201. The poem is copied in single columns, except for the last 5 lines which form a second column on fol. 16v.[1]

33. Fol. 18b, [*Rondeau*].
   Incipit: Pres de ma damme e loing de mon volo…(*sic*)   10 lines
34. Fol. 18b, [*Rondeau*].
   Incipit: Ou mon desir s'assouvira…   13 lines

Nh was listed in the earlier bibliographies of the lyrics and the *Breviaire des Nobles*. The manuscript is in a poor state of preservation and is illegible in places. The texts of the two long poems are incomplete and include individual readings; a number of lines are irregular or, in the case of the *Breviaire des Nobles*, rhyme badly.

Nj   +GRENOBLE, BIBL. MUN., 874

Mid 15th c.; 205 × 185; parchment; 98 ff.; 24 lines.

1. Ff. 1r–8r, *Cy commence le debat de resveille matin.*
   360 lines. Lacks lines 17–24.
2. Ff. 8v–24r, *Cy commence ma belle dame sans mercy.*
   752 lines. Lacks lines 673–720.
3. Ff. 24r–v, *Copie des lectres envoyees par les dames a Alain.*
4. Ff. 24v–26r, *Copie des lectres de la requeste envoyee par les amans aux dames contre Alain et puis la response par alain.*
5. Ff. 26r–31r, *Excusacion envers les dames faicte par Alain.*
   240 plus 4 lines. Complete.
6. Ff. 31r–37r, *Cy commence le lay de paix.*
   284 lines. Lacks line 155. Includes line 156a. Lines 225–6 are inverted.
7. Fol. 37r, *Cy commence le breviaire des nobles.*
   Fol. 47r, *Fin du breviaire des nobles.*
   446 plus 7 lines. Complete.
8. Ff. 47v–51v, *Cy commence le lay de plaisance.*
   196 lines. Complete. Lines 1–2 are inverted.
9. Ff. 51v–55v, *Cy est une complainte contre la mort.*
   184 lines. Lacks line 117. Includes line 119a. The order of stanzas is: I–III, V–VII, IV, VIII–XII.
10. Ff. 55v–58v, [*Ballades*].
   A. Ff. 55v–56r, *Balade.*
      Incipit: Je ne fu nez fors pour tout mal avoir…   36 lines
   B. Ff. 56r–57r, *Balade.*
      Incipit: Aucunes gens m'ont huy arraisonné…   35 lines
   C. Ff. 57r–v, *Balade.*
      Incipit: J'ay ung arbre de la plante d'amours…   35 lines

---

[1] The poem being copied with some 39 lines per page, the gap of 121 lines is consistent with the loss of three pages or columns. The second quire (ff. 9–17), which contains items 17 and 19, was originally of 10 leaves, but the eighth has been lost. If the text of the *Lay de Paix* in *Nh* was originally complete, then one side of the missing leaf must have been written in double columns.

[1] Another heading, *Rondelet,* is at the foot of fol. 62v.

    u. Fol. 64r, *Rondeau.*

       Incipit: Ainsi que bon vous semblera...   13 lines

    v. Fol. 64v, *Rondelet.*

       Incipit: Quant j. jour suy sans que je voie...   10 lines

12. Ff. 64v–90v, *Cy commence le traictié des biens et des maulz de fortune sur amours que aucuns nomment le gras et le mesgre.*

    1239 plus 4 lines. Lacks lines 96, 635, 653.

Nj was included in the bibliographies of the lyrics, the *Debat des Deux Fortunés d'Amours,* and the *Breviaire des Nobles.* Piaget used *Nj* as base text in his edition of the *Belle Dame sans Mercy* and the lyrics.

    When the four poems were edited, *Nj* was found to give the best text of its group on each occasion; it is generally complete and contains few irregularities of rhyme or metre. *Nj* is similar in layout to *Nf*, to which it is related textually, and both manuscripts have been used in this edition of the poetical works. *Nj* is written in quite a careful and well-formed cursive hand. Although a distinction exists between *n* and *u*, it is not always a clear one; it can be difficult to tell *r* from a minim. The scribe is not consistent in making divisions between words. Errors in the text are either scored out or cancelled with dots set underneath; where lines have been inverted, the correct order is indicated in the margin. In BN 95, the scribe has written ' son los perit'; since the line begins 'Bon los' in some manuscripts, the correction raises the possibility that that text at least may be contaminated.[1] Some of the leaves at the beginning of *Nj* have faded a little.

Nk   +RODEZ, BIBL. MUN., 57[2]

15th c.; paper; 188 × 147; 133 ff.; *c.* 30 lines.

7. Fol. 100r, *Le lay de paix.*

   Fol. 105r, *Explicit le lay de paix.*

    282 lines. Lacks lines 87, 155.

9. Fol. 110r, *Le breviaire des Nobles.*

   Fol. 118v, *Explicit le breviare* (sic) *des nobles.*

    445 = 446 plus 8 lines. Complete.

Nk was included by Rice in his bibliography of the *Breviaire des Nobles,* but has not been examined before. The text of the *Lay de Paix,* which is incomplete, includes individual readings, several of which are irregular. The *Breviaire des Nobles* has similar characteristics and also contains a number of poor rhymes. *Nk* is a manuscript of reasonable, but by no means outstanding, quality.

[1] See the discussion of the textual tradition of the *Breviaire des Nobles,* pp. 393–4.

[2] See G. Raynaud, 'Notice du manuscrit 57 de la bibliothèque municipale de Rodez', *Bulletin de la SATF,* XIII, 1887, 77–82.

Nl +BERNE, BURGERBIBLIOTHEK, 473[1]

15th c.; paper; 138 ff.; 24–30 lines; catchwords.

4. Ff. 17r–33r, *La belle dame sans merci.*
   800 lines. Complete. Text with headings.
5. Ff. 33v–34v, *Copie de la requeste baillee aux dames contre maistre alain.*
6. Ff. 34v–35r, *Copie de lectres envoyees par les dames A maistre alain.*
7. Ff. 35r–40r, [*L'Excusacion aux Dames*].
   240 lines. Complete. Between stanzas XIV and XV is the heading 'Response'.
8. Ff. 40v–47v, *Reveille matin.*
   360 lines. Lacks lines 17–24. Lines 308–9 are inverted.
9. Ff. 48r–51r, *Complainte.*
   183 lines. Lacks lines 117, 126. Includes line 119a. The order of stanzas is: I–III, V–VII, IV, VIII–XII.
10. Ff. 51v–56v, *Le lay de paix.*
    285 lines. Includes line 156a.
11. Ff. 56v–66r, *Le breviaire des nobles.*
    444 lines. Lacks lines 425, 438.
12. Fol. 66v, *Le debat des deulx fortunés d'amours.*
    Fol. 86v, *Finit le debat des deulx fortunés d'amours.*
    1232 lines. Lacks lines 27, 96, 180, 213–16, 635, 653, 1221.
13. Ff. 87r–96v, [*Ballades et Rondeaux*].
    A. Ff. 87r–v, *Balade.*
       Incipit: J'ay ung arbre de la plante d'amours... 35 lines
    B. Ff. 87v–88r, *Aultre balade.*
       Incipit: J'ay volentiers ouy parler d'amours... 41 lines
    C. Ff. 88r–89r, *Aultre balade.*
       Incipit: Je ne fu né fors pour tout mal avoir... 36 lines

Nl was listed in the bibliographies of the *Debat des Deux Fortunés d'Amours* and the *Belle Dame sans Mercy*; it has not been examined before. When the *Debat de Reveille Matin*, the *Lay de Paix* and the *Complainte* were edited, *Nl* was found to contain few irregular lines or individual readings. It is quite closely related to *Nf* and *Nj*, which are of superior quality. The text of the *Lay de Paix* in *Nl* is contaminated for it contains an extra line. The scribe has copied variant readings in the margins of items 4, 11 and 12.

---

[1] For a detailed description of *Nl* and its provenance, see A. de Mandach, 'A la découverte d'un manuscrit d'Amédée VIII à la bibliothèque de Berne avec des textes inédits attribués à Alain Chartier', *Bibliothèque d'humanisme et renaissance*, XXX, 1968, 115–32. That part of the manuscript which includes the poems by Chartier (ff. 17r–114v) is thought to have been copied about 1435–7 and perhaps in Chambéry.

Thirteen ballades and one rondeau follow the three ballades listed in this description (item 13) and these further poems are also attributed to Chartier by Mandach because of their position in the manuscript and on stylistic grounds. While the arguments cannot be rejected absolutely, account must also be taken of the quality of *Nl* and of the collections of lyrics found in other Chartier manuscripts. See pp. 372–3, where the question of attribution is discussed at length.

Nm   +FLORENCE, BIBL. LAURENZIANA, ASHBURNHAM 51 (124–56)

15th c.; parchment; 350 × 215; 19 ff.; 32 lines.

Nm previously formed part of the library of the fourth Earl of Ashburnham. An earlier owner had been the Duc de la Vallière.[1]

2. Ff. 14r–16v, *Cy commence la complainte maistre alain Chartier conseiller et secretaire de Charles vij^e*.

   184 lines. Lacks line 117. Includes line 119a. Lines 173–4 are inverted. The order of stanzas is: I–VI, IX–X, VII–VIII, XI–XII.

3. Ff. 17r–18v, [*Ballade et Rondeaux*].

   A. Ff. 17r–v, *Ensuit Balade dudit Maistre Alain Chartier.*
      Incipit: Aucunes gens m'ont huy arraysonné...   35 lines
   B. Fol. 17v, [*Rondeau*].
      Incipit: Joye me fuit et desplaisir me chace...   13 lines
   C. Fol. 18r, *Rondeau dudit maistre Alain.*
      Incipit: Triste plaisir et douleureuse joye...   10 lines
   D. Fol. 18r, *Autre Rondeau dudit maistre Alain.*
      Incipit: Riche d'espoir et pouvre d'autre bien...   10 lines
   E. Fol. 18v, [*Rondeau*].
      Incipit: Je n'ay pouair de vivre en joye...   10 lines
   F. Fol. 18v, [*Rondeau*].
      Incipit: Mort sur les piez faignant avoir plaisir...   10 lines

Nm was included in the bibliography of the lyrics published by Droz and Piaget, but has not been examined in detail before. The text of the *Complainte* is individual both in its stanza-order and in its readings. Examination of the lyrics confirms that impression. *Nm* contains some valuable attributions.

Nn   +KARLSRUHE, BADISCHE LANDESBIBLIOTHEK, 410

15th c.; parchment; 255 × 190; 11 ff.; 27–32 lines.

   There are miniatures on six of these eleven leaves which were probably preserved for that reason. The leaves are mis-bound.[2]

1. Ff. 7, 4, 3, 8 and 1, [*Le Livre des Quatre Dames*].
   246 lines. Contains lines 1–102, 349–453, 3458–97. Lacks line 3464.
2. Fol. 6, [*Le Debat de Reveille Matin*].
   56 lines. Contains lines 155–210.

Nn was discussed by Kussmann in his study of the textual tradition of the *Livre des Quatre Dames*. A study of the two fragments which it contains suggests that *Nn* stands in the same tradition as *Qg*.

---

[1] *Catalogue of the Manuscripts at Ashburnham Place*, I, London, Hodgson, n.d., No. 124; G. de Bure, fils aîné, *Catalogue des livres de la bibliothèque de feu M. le duc de la Vallière, Première partie*, II, Paris, de Bure, 1783, No. 2807.

[2] See J. C. Laidlaw, 'An Unidentified Fragment of the *Livre messire Ode de Granson*', *Scriptorium*, XXIV, 1970, 53–4.

15th c.; parchment; 247 × 172; 40 ff., numbered (A), 1–38, (B); 35–45 lines.

No formed part of the library of the Marquis of Santillana.[1] It was probably copied by a 'Fraer Deffez', whose signature is found at the end of item 2. The manuscript is now mis-bound and one sheet (32/37) is upside-down.

1. Ff. 1r–6r, [*Le Debat de Reveille Matin*].
   358 lines. Lacks lines 17–24, 69, 317.

2. Ff. 6v–14v, 31, 33, 34, 37, [*La Belle Dame sans Mercy*].
   Fol. 34v, *Explicit la belle damme sans mercy par la main fraer Deffez*[2] *pour madamme l'amirale*.
   797 lines. Lacks lines 42–3, 601. Text with headings.

3. Ff. 15r–30v, [*Le Debat des Deux Fortunés d'Amours d'A.(?) Chartier*]. Title added later.
   1235 lines. Lacks lines 40–3, 255, 930, 1166.
   In the bottom margin of fol. 15r the scribe has written 'Ce sont la faculté et difficulté d'amours', apparently as an instruction to the rubricator.

4. Fol. 35r, *Copie des lectres envoyees par les dammes a Alain*.

5. Ff. 35r–v, *Copie de la requeste baillee aux dammes par aucuns contre ledit alain, laquelle copie estoit enclose dedans les lectres cy dessus escriptes*.

6. Ff. 32, 36r–38v, [*L'Excusacion aux Dames*].
   213 lines. Lacks lines 139–40, 179, 217–40. After stanza XIV there is the heading 'Response'.

No has not been listed or examined before. The text of the *Debat de Reveille Matin* includes many irregular lines and individual readings. When portions of the *Belle Dame sans Mercy* and the *Excusacion* were examined, they were found to have similar characteristics. None of the texts in *No* is complete.

c. 1430; paper; 180 ff.; contemporary binding.

The letters 'A.P.' are found on a number of leaves. On the verso of the fly-leaf they are accompanied by two unidentified coats of arms (d'or à la fasce de gueules chargée d'une étoile d'or; de gueules au chef emmanché de deux pièces et de deux demi-pièces d'or), and by the device 'Tant me dure'. On the recto of the same leaf the initials are combined with the following words in a contemporary hand: 'Je Jehan Devillers. Sine macula'.

Before passing to the Lausanne library, *Np* belonged to Arthur Piaget.[3]

4. Ff. 152r–157r, [*Le Lay de Paix*].
   270 = 271 lines. Lacks lines 11, 82, 101–2, 109, 120, 126, 226, 232–6. Lines 87–8 are written as one line.

---

1 M. Schiff, *La Bibliothèque du marquis de Santillane*, Paris, 1905, 371–2 (*Bibl. de l'EHE*, CLIII).
2 The name, almost illegible in microfilm, has been supplied from the description by Schiff.
3 The present description is based on that in Piaget, *Oton de Grandson*, 112–14.

7. Ff. 158r–175v, *La Belle dame Sans marcy* (sic).

   800 lines. Complete. At the end of the poem, almost as an *explicit*, is written 'Alain'.

8. Ff. 175v–180v, *La response*.

   240 lines. Complete.

Piaget did not include *Np* in his bibliography of the *Belle Dame sans Mercy*. The text of the *Lay de Paix* is closely related to that in *Fa*, also an early manuscript; both texts are incomplete, individual and of poor quality. When parts of the *Belle Dame sans Mercy* and the *Excusacion* were examined, they were found to contain a number of irregular lines and poor rhymes.

Nq +VATICAN, REGINA LAT. 1323

Late 15th c. (1475–80);[1] paper; 2°; 289 × 208; 261 ff.; 38–9 lines; table of contents.

   Nq was copied by 'Jehan Panier, marchant du palais' for his own use.

18. Fol. 225r, *Le Lay de paix fait par mestre alain chartier Notaire et secretaire du roy nostre sire.*

   Fol. 228v, *Cy fine le lay de paix fait par mestre alain chartier notaire et secretaire du roy nostre sire envoié au duc de bourgongne au traitié d'arras.*

   277 lines. Lacks lines 49–54, 126, 131, 206. Includes lines 123a, 260a. Lines 64–5 are inverted.

21. Fol. 229r, *Le breviaire des Nobles fait par mestre alain chartier.*

   Fol. 235r, *Explicit le breviaire des nobles fait par mestre alain chartier en son vivant notaire et secretaire du roy nostre sire.*

   447 = 444 plus 8 lines. Lacks lines 96 and 378. Lines 249–51 are repeated.

24. Fol. 241v, *Conplainte faite par mestre alain chartier quant sa dame fut morte.*

   Fol. 243v, *Explicit la conplainte faite par mestre alain chartier.*

   181 lines. Lacks lines 30, 159, 174. The order of stanzas is I–III, V–VII, IV, VIII–XII.

Nq was mentioned by Champion and was listed by Rice in his bibliography of the *Breviaire des Nobles*; it has not been examined before. None of the texts in *Nq* is complete and all three contain many individual readings. Where the *Lay de Paix* is concerned, *Nq* is closely related to *Po*. While the two manuscripts were assigned to different groups in the case of the *Complainte*, they nevertheless have a significant number of readings in common.

Nr +CLERMONT-FERRAND, ARCHIVES DU PUY-DE-DÔME, 28

15th c.; paper; 210 × 150; 59 ff.; c. 35 lines.

   The manuscript is badly damaged. The greatest part of what is now fol. 1 has disappeared; the bottom right-hand corner of ff. 2–12 has been eaten away and a small part of the texts on these pages is missing. The first item is not identified in the catalogue.[2]

---

[1] These dates are given by Langlois ('Notices des manuscrits français et provençaux de Rome antérieurs au XVIe siècle', 111). Although the rubric of item 18 and the *explicit* of item 21 suggest that the manuscript was copied before the death of Charles VII in 1461, Jehan Panier wrote in the *explicit* of items 1 and 6 that he finished copying these works in 1475 and 1476 respectively.

[2] *Catalogue général des manuscrits*, LI, Paris, Bibl. Nat., 1956, 312.

1. Fol. 1r, [*Le Debat des Deux Fortunés d'Amours*].

   Fol. 4v, ...*le debat dez deux... d...ours. Et sic finis.*

      All that can be read on fol. 1v are the last words of lines 1038, 1040, 1042, 1046 and 1049. The fragment really begins on fol. 2r with line 1052. Line 1206 is missing.

2. Fol. 5r, *Ci comanse Revelle matin.*

   Fol. 10r, *Explicit le debat du revelhe matim* (sic).

      359 lines. Lacks lines 17–24, 341.

3. Fol. 10r, *Cy comense la belle dame sans mercy.*

   Fol. 22r, *Explicit la belle dame sans mercy.*

      799 lines. Lacks line 458.

4. Fol. 22r, *Copie dez lettrez de la requeste envoiez par lez amans et serviteurs au* (sic) *damez contre alain.*

   Fol. 23r, *Cy finist la requeste dez servans contre alain.*

5. Fol. 23r, *Copie dez lettrez envoieez par lez damez alain* (sic).

6. Ff. 23r–27r, *La Responce faite aux damez par alain.*

      239 plus 4 lines. Lacks line 188.

7. Ff. 27r–29v, *Cy comence le lays de plaisance.*

      194 = 193 lines. Lacks lines 27, 32, 71. Line 165 is repeated.

8. Fol. 30r, *Incipit la plainte contre la mort.*

   Fol. 32v, *Explicit la conplainte contre la mort.*

      181 lines. Lacks lines 106, 117, 138, 173. Includes line 119a. Lines 146–7 are inverted. The order of stanzas is: I–III, V–VII, IV, VIII–XII.

Nr has never been listed or mentioned before. When the *Lay de Plaisance*, the *Debat de Reveille Matin* and the *Complainte* were edited, *Nr* was found to be related to *Nf* and *Nj* but to be inferior in quality to them. None of the texts in *Nr* is complete and those which were examined contain a large number of irregular lines.

Oa   PARIS, BIBL. NAT., F. FR. 1127

Mid 15th c.; parchment; 250 × 180 (170 × 120); 156 = 157 ff. (incl. fol. 121bis); 30 lines; signatures a–t, catchwords; collation 1–4^8, 5^{12}: 6–11^8, 12–13^{10}, 14–15^8: 16–18^8, 19^6 (sixth canc.); decorated initials and borders; space left for miniatures.

   On fol. 156v are written in near contemporary hands the name 'Charle de Saint George' and the tag 'Victorem a victo superari sepe videmus'.

1. Ff. 1r–31v, [*Le quadrilogue invectif fait par Me Alain Charretier. Prologue*]. Added by a later hand.

2. Ff. 32r–39v, [*Le Breviere des Nobles*]. Title added.

      434 plus 8 lines. Lacks lines 131, 140, 200-1, 308, 316–17, 346, 354–7. Line 315 has replaced line 308.

3. Fol. 40r, [*Le Lay de Paix*].

   Fol. 44v (ends quire 5), *Cy fine le livre de paix eureuse.*

      282 lines. Lacks lines 126, 135. Line 128 is copied between lines 131 and 132.

4. Fol. 45r (begins quire 6), [*Le Livre des Quatre Dames*].

   Fol. 103r, *Cy fine le livre des quatre dames.*

3484 lines. Lacks lines 415, 565, 891, 1336, 1362, 1379, 1657–75, 1715, 1828, 1953, 2072, 2306, 2405, 2522, 2582, 2643, 2652–5, 2851, 2938–9, 3158, 3302, 3386, 3453, 3455, 3464. Lines 1676–1708 and 1709–28 are transposed.

5. Fol. 103r, *Et cy apres s'ensuit le livre de reveille matin.*
   Fol. 109v, *Cy fine le debat resveille matin.*
   360 lines. Lacks lines 17–24.

6. Fol. 109v, *Et s'ensuit la belle dame sans mercy.*
   Fol. 122r, *Cy finist la belle dame Sans Mercy.*
   800 lines. Complete.

7. Ff. 122r–123v, *S'ensuivent les lectres closes que les dames envoierent a l'acteur. Et apres la supplicacion qui fut baillee aux dames contre l'acteur.*

8. Fol. 124r, [*L'Excusacion aux Dames*].
   Fol. 127v (ends quire 15), *Cy finist la response de l'acteur.*
   238 lines. Lacks lines 13, 72.

9. Fol. 128r, [*Le Lay de Plaisance*].
   Fol. 130v, *Cy fine le lay de plaisance.*
   176 lines. Lacks lines 161–80.

10. Ff. 130v–133v, *Et apres s'ensuit la complainte que fist l'acteur contre la mort.*
    180 lines. Lacks lines 31, 70, 83, 147.

11. Ff. 134r–154v, [*Le debat des deux fortunés*]. Title added later.
    1239 plus 4 lines. Lacks lines 90, 471, 623.

12. Ff. 154v–155r, *Balades* (sic).
    Incipit: Aucunes gens m'ont huy araisonné...
    30 lines. Only the first four words of the envoy are given.

13. Ff. 155r–156r, *Autre balade.*
    Incipit: J'ay ung arbre de la plante d'amours...
    35 lines. Complete.

Oa was included in the earlier bibliographies of the *Livre des Quatre Dames*, the *Debat des Deux Fortunés d'Amours*, the *Belle Dame sans Mercy*, and the *Breviaire des Nobles*. The manuscript was also mentioned by Champion. Piaget used *Oa* as the base text for stanzas LXXXV to XC of his edition of the *Belle Dame sans Mercy*. J. E. White's edition is based on *Oa*, which contains all the poetical works except the *Debat du Herault*... and some lyrics.

When the four poems were edited, *Oa* was chosen as the best text of its group on each occasion despite the fact that it had certain defects. The manuscript gives the impression of being itself careless and unfinished or of belonging to a careless tradition. The works which it contains often lack rubrics and are as often incomplete. The omission or the insertion of single words is one reason why so many lines in *Oa* are irregular. The number is increased by the scribe's habit of writing *elle* where the metre demands *el* and *telle* (or *quelle*) for *tel* (or *quel*) [feminine]. Spellings like *depars* (BD 679), *comme* (BD 719) or *faicte* (PA 213) support the view that the manuscript has not been revised.

These criticisms notwithstanding, *Oa* is an important manuscript as the discussion of the tradition of the *Lay de Plaisance* and other works will indicate.[1] It is written in quite a

[1] See pp. 147–8 and 320–1.

legible and well-formed cursive hand. The division between words is not always clear; little distinction is made between *u* and *n*.

Ob PARIS, BIBL. NAT., F. FR. 1128

Late 15th c.; paper; 2°; 280 × 205 (190 × 115); 199 ff.; verse sometimes in double columns; 24–30 lines; collation 1¹² (first canc.), 2–3¹²: 4–11¹²: 12–13¹⁴: 14¹², 15–16¹⁴; headings in red, coloured initials; binding with arms of Philippe de Béthune (1561–1649).

Water-marks

(a) A unicorn, 100 mm long, across chain-lines 37 mm apart. Most like Briquet 10024 (1474–7).
(b) As (a) but 95 mm long.
(c) An ox-head, surmounted by a stalk, 70 mm long, between chain-lines 35 mm apart.

1. Ff. 1r–35v (quires 1–3), [*Le Quadrilogue Invectif*].[1]
2. Ff. 36r–48v (begins quire 4), *Dyalogus Familiaris Amici et Sodalis super deploratione galice calamitatis Ab alano aurige editus.*
3. Ff. 49r–128r (ends quire 11), [*Le Livre de l'Esperance*].
4. Fol. 132r (begins quire 12), [*Le Lay de Paix*].
   Fol. 135r, *Explicit de paix eureuse par Maistre Allain charetier.*
   282 = 283 lines. Lacks lines 38, 75, 96, 155, 273. Includes lines 77a, 88a, 151a, 275a. Lines 64–5 and 109–10 are inverted; lines 94–5 written as one line.
5. Ff. 136r–159r (ends quire 13), [*Le Debat des Deux Fortunés d'Amours*].
   1235 plus 4 lines. Lacks lines 11, 40–3, 96, 653.

Ob was mentioned by Champion and was included in the bibliography of the *Debat des Deux Fortunés d'Amours*; it was used by J. E. White and by F. Rouy in their respective editions of the poetical works and the *Livre de l'Esperance*. Both poems in *Ob*, although they are generally regular, include a number of individual readings and neither work is complete. So far as the *Lay de Paix* is concerned, *Ob* closely resembles *Fc*.

Oc PARIS, BIBL. NAT., F. FR. 1130

15th c.; paper; 2°; 290 × 200 (200–10 × 130–50); 1 plus 182 = 181 ff.;[2] 22–4 lines (prose), 26–30 lines (verse); d.c. (ff. 118v–end); collation A⁷(1): 1–15¹², 16⁷(1); catchwords.

Water-marks

(a) A wheel with five teeth, 17 mm in diameter, between chain-lines 45 mm apart.
(b) A wheel with six teeth, 25 mm in diameter, with an 'M' and a 'starting-handle' attached to it; 55 mm long over-all and between chain-lines 45 mm apart. Very like Briquet 13438 (1452).

---

[1] A later hand has copied on the fly-leaf opposite: 'Quadrilogue Inventif (*sic*) de Mᵉ Allain Chartier'. There is added, in a second hand, 'sur les abbuz du monde'.

[2] Ff. 133ᵇⁱˢ and 147 have been ignored: they are of smaller paper, have been inserted and contain notes in a hand much later than that of the manuscript.

(c) A five-toothed wheel, 18 mm in diameter, with a 'starting-handle' attached; 40 mm long over-all and between sewn chain-lines 43–5 mm apart. In design very like Briquet 13245 (1431–43).

(d) A coat of arms (within a plain bordure, a fesse wavy), approx. 22 × 25 mm. The sewn chain-lines are 47–8 mm apart and the mark is attached to one of them.

The name 'Ant. Lancelot' is written on fol. 1r.[1]

1. Fol. 1r, *Cy commence le livre des trois estaz Nommé Quardrilogue* (sic).
   Fol. 41v, *Explicit Quadrilogues* (sic).
5. Ff. 134a–137c, *Cy commence le breviere des nobles.*
   The text stops at line 364; lines 140, 212, 276, 325 and 352 are lacking.
6. Fol. 137c, *Le lay de paix.*
   Fol. 139d, *Explicit le lay de paix.*
   281 lines. Lacks lines 44, 59, 155.
7. Fol. 140a, *Le lay de plaisance.*
   Fol. 141c, *Explicit le lay de plaisance.*
   193 lines. Lacks lines 115–16, 151.
8. Fol. 141c, *Complainte.*
   Fol. 142c, *Explicit la conplainte.*
   133 lines. Lacks lines 35, 69, 111, 117, 121–36 (stanza IX), 153–84 (stanzas XI–XII). Includes line 119a. The order of stanzas is: I–III, V–VII, IV, VIII, X.
10. Ff. 146d–156d, a collection of thirty ballades; the fifteenth (ff. 151d–152a) begins:
    Il n'est dangier que de villain…
    28 lines. Complete.
11. Fol. 156d, [*Le Livre des Quatre Dames*].
    Fol. 182b, *Explicit le lyvre des quatre dames.*
    The text begins at line 417. 45 other lines are missing.

Oc was included in the bibliographies of the *Livre des Quatre Dames*, the ballade ('Il n'est dangier…'), and the *Breviaire des Nobles*; it was also mentioned by Champion. The manuscript was used by J. E. White in his edition of Chartier's poetical works.

When the *Lay de Plaisance*, the *Lay de Paix* and the *Complainte* were edited, *Oc* was found to contain a large number of individual readings and irregular lines; none of the poems in *Oc* is complete.

Od PARIS, BIBL. NAT., F. FR. 2263

Mid 15th c.; paper; 4°; 210 × 140 (140 × 90); 64 ff.; 24–6 lines; collation 1–3¹⁶, 4⁷(16); catchwords; space left for miniatures and initials.

Water-marks

(a) A hand, the cuff with four tails; chain-lines 45 mm apart, the mark being attached to one of them. Most like Briquet 11114 (1436).
(b) The letter 'R' between sewn chain-lines 47 mm apart. Similar to Briquet 8951 or 8952 (1430–42).

[1] See Delisle, *Le Cabinet des manuscrits*, I, 409–11 etc.

On fol. 1r is the signature Brodeau and the year 1633.[1] An earlier owner of *Od* was Guilliaume —— whose surname has been erased on the same folio; other inscriptions elsewhere in the manuscript have been scored out or are difficult to decipher. The name of 'maistre francoys duclaux(?)' is found on fol. 39r.

1. Fol. 1r, [*Le Quadrilogue de Alain Chartier*]. Added by a later hand.
   Fol. 49r, *Explicit quadriloque* (sic).
2. Fol. 49v, *Cy commense le Breviere des nobles.*
   Fol. 58v, *Cy fine le breviere des nobles.*
   441 plus 8 lines. Lacks lines 184–7, 282.
3. Fol. 59r, [*Le Lay de paix baillé à Monseigneur de Bourgoingne*]. Added by a later hand.
   Fol. 64v, *Cy fine le livre de paix eureuse.*
   283 lines. Lacks line 126.

Od has not been listed or examined before. In form and content it is very like *Oe* with which it is closely connected so far as the *Lay de Paix* is concerned. Both texts are linked with that in *Oa* which was preferred to them when the poem was edited. *Od* contains quite a good text of the *Lay de Paix*; its version of the *Breviaire des Nobles* is often irregular.

Oe POITIERS, BIBL. MUN., 214

15th c.; parchment; 230 × 155 (165 × 100); 58 ff.; 27–8 lines; collation A² (first canc.): 1⁷(8), 2–7⁸: B² (second canc.); catchwords; decorated border and initial, space for miniature at beginning of first item; flourished initials.

1. Fol. 3r, [*Le Quadrilogue Invectif*].
   Fol. 42v, *Explicit le quadriloque* (sic).
2. Fol. 43r, *Cy commence le breviaire des nobles.*
   Fol. 51v, *Cy fine le Breviaire des nobles.*
   443 plus 6 lines. Lacks lines 282, 346, 442.
3. Fol. 52r, [*Le Lay de Paix*].
   Fol. 57r, *Cy fine le livre de paix eureuse.*
   283 lines. Lacks line 126.

Rice included *Oe* in his bibliography of the *Breviaire des Nobles*, but the manuscript has not been examined before. *Oe* contains quite a good text of the *Lay de Paix* but its version of the *Breviaire des Nobles* is irregular. The relationship between *Oe*, *Od* and *Oa* is discussed in the description of *Od*.

Of +BERLIN, KUPFERSTICHKABINETT, 78 C 7 (HAMILTON 144)

15th c. (after 1461);[2] parchment; 285 × 210; d.c. 195 × 70; 141 ff.; 37 lines; miniatures, decorated initials.

1. Ff. 1–23, [*Le Quadrilogue Invectif*].
2. Ff. 24–74, [*Le Livre de l'Esperance*].

[1] See Delisle, *Le Cabinet des manuscrits*, I, 300, 365.
[2] Item 12 (ff. 136–41) is an *Exitedium sive lamencio* (sic) *karoli septimi victoriosissimi regis francorum.*

3. Ff. 75–84, [*Dialogus Familiaris Amici et Sodalis*...].
4. Ff. 84b–86b, [*Le Lay de Paix*].
   281 lines. Lacks lines 11, 76, 89. Lines 231–2 are inverted. Line 124 is copied between lines 126 and 127.
5. Ff. 87a–90c, [*Le Debat du Herault, du Vassault et du Villain*].
   440 lines.

Siegfried Lemm published a description of *Of* when he edited from it the *Debat du Herault*...;[1] the poem was re-edited by J. E. White who used Lemm's edition rather than the manuscript. *Of* was used by F. Rouy in his edition of the *Livre de l'Esperance*.

The version of the *Lay de Paix* in *Of* is individual and irregular; it closely resembles that in *Pf* and *Pj*. The text of the *Debat du Herault*... also contains irregular lines; no other copy of the poem being known, *Of* has been used in this edition.

Of is written in a clear, cursive hand. The texts are carefully laid out and punctuated. The scribe has corrected his text, using a sharper pen; such corrections are frequent after the decorated capitals which begin each stanza and for which he had left insufficient space. N and u, and sometimes s and f, are difficult to distinguish. In places the parchment is stained and the ink has faded.

Og   +ESCORIAL, O. I. 14

Mid 15th c.; parchment; 345×250 (215×178); 58 ff.; d.c.; 36 lines.

Og formed part of the library of the Conde Duque de Olivares (1587–1645).

2. Ff. 22c–25d, *Cy apres ensuit le breviaire aux nobles*.
   442 lines. Lacks lines 251, 321, 362, 386.
5. Ff. 34r–58v, [*Le Quadrilogue Invectif*].

Og was mentioned by A. Piaget in 1908;[2] it has not been examined before. The copy of the *Breviaire des Nobles* is incomplete and contains a number of irregular lines and poor rhymes.

Oh   LONDON, BRIT. MUS., HARLEY 4402

Oh includes the *Quadrilogue Invectif* and an abbreviated version of the *Breviaire des Nobles*; it contains none of the poems edited here.

Oj   MANCHESTER, CHETHAM'S LIBRARY, MUNIMENT A.6.91

Mid 15th c.; parchment; 260×195 (175×110: 200×105 [quire 9]); 104 ff.; 28 lines (33 lines [quire 9]); collation 1–8⁸: 9⁸: 10⁸: 11–13⁸; catchwords, except in quires 11–13; decorated capitals, decorated borders in item 1; headings in red (items 1 and 2); initials highlighted in yellow (quires 11–13); copied by Jeunesse.[3]

---

[1] S. Lemm, 'Aus einer Chartier-Handschrift des Kgl. Kupferstichkabinetts zu Berlin', *Archiv für das Studium der neueren Sprachen und Literaturen*, CXXXII, 1914, 131–8.

[2] A. Piaget, *Le Miroir aux dames*, Neuchâtel etc., 1908, 40 (*Académie de Neuchâtel, Fac. des Lettres, Travaux*, II).

[3] The name appears in the initial *S* of *Sensuit* on fol. 1r and at the end of items 4, 5 and 7.

The manuscript is probably in the same hand throughout. So far as layout and decoration are concerned, it falls into three sections: quires 1–8 and 10; quire 9; quires 11–13. In the last three quires the hand has a more cursive appearance.

Oj formed part of the library of the Duc de la Vallière.[1] It was bought by Chetham's Library in Liverpool in August 1816 at the sale of the library of William Roscoe.[2]

1. Ff. 1r–36v, *S'ensuit le quadrilogue fait par maistre Alain charretier.*
2. Fol. 37r, *Le debat des deux fortunés d'amours.*
   Fol. 59r, *Explicit le debat des deux fortunez d'amours.*
   1242 plus 4 lines. Complete.
3. Ff. 60r–64v (ends quire 8), [*Le Lay de Paix*].
   284 lines. Complete.
4. Ff. 65r–72v (quire 9), *S'ensuit le breviaire des nobles.*
   446 plus 8 lines. Complete.
7. Fol. 81r (begins quire 11), *La belle dame sans mercy.*
   Fol. 97v, *Explicit la belle dame sans mercy.*
   800 lines. Complete. Text with headings.
8. Fol. 98r, *Coppie des lettres envoiees par les dames a Alain.*
9. Ff. 98v–99r, *Copie de la requeste baillee aux dames contre Alain.*
10. Ff. 99v–104r, [*L'Excusacion aux Dames*].
    240 lines. Complete.

Oj was mentioned by Hoffman, but has not been examined in detail or used before. It contains complete and generally regular texts of the poetical works, and was used as base text in the edition of the *Lay de Paix*, the only one of the four poems which it contains.

Oj is written in a flowing hand, which is part bastard, part cursive. *N* and *u* are usually, but not always, differentiated and *i* is generally dotted. Certain letters or combinations of letters, *c, t, ct, cc, tt, sf* and *ff*, are hardly distinguishable; final *z* and *r* are easily confused. The divisions between words do not follow a consistent pattern. Here and there the ink has faded.

Oj has been corrected on two, perhaps three, occasions. The different series of corrections cannot always be clearly distinguished one from another; where only an erasure is involved, it is naturally impossible to be sure to which series it belongs. The corrections are few in number; of the texts edited here, they particularly affect the *Debat des Deux Fortunés d'Amours* and the *Belle Dame sans Mercy*.

During the first series, the usual revision carried out by the scribe, obvious errors have been corrected and omissions made good. Letters to be deleted are marked with a dot underneath, for example in DF 285 and DF 328. At this stage too, some spellings have been altered, perhaps by the scribe. These alterations affect certain words and letters above all: *onc* to *onq* (DF 882, BD 762); *donc* to *donq* (BD 403, BD 741); *ylec* to *yleq* (BD 47, BD 70); *oublia* to *oublya* (DF 722); *airer* to *ayrer* (BN 100); *aide* to *ayde* (BN 368,

---

[1] See L. E. Kastner, 'Concerning an Unknown Manuscript of Alain Chartier's Selected Works', *Modern Language Review*, XII, 1917, 45–58; G. de Bure, fils aîné, *Catalogue des livres de la bibliothèque de feu M. le duc de la Vallière, Première partie*, II, Paris, de Bure, 1783, No. 2791.

[2] This information was kindly given by the librarian.

BN 380); *sefforcoit* to *sefforsoit* (BD 89; cf. BD 91, BD 185, BD 187); *leesce* to *lyesce* (BN 89, BN 106); *-esce* to *-esse* (PA 183, PA 186).

A further series of corrections (*Oj²*) was effected by a second hand very shortly afterwards. Where the original has been altered, it can sometimes still be read; elsewhere the new version has been written in after the original had been erased. Some of the corrections have been made with the help of another manuscript, most probably akin to *Nf* or *Nj*;[1] others seem to be idiosyncratic.

The excellent series of headings in *Oj*, the clear divisions between stanzas and sections of stanzas, the indications where speeches begin and end in item 2, all these confirm that the manuscript was produced with care.[2] It is one of the two best collected manuscripts of Chartier's poetical works and is used here as base text for three poems, the *Debat des Deux Fortunés d'Amours*, the *Breviaire des Nobles* and the *Lay de Paix*. The corrections in *Oj* are discussed in detail in the introductions to those editions; they are also mentioned in the introduction to the *Belle Dame sans Mercy*.

Ok   +MUNICH, BAYERISCHE STAATSBIBLIOTHEK, COD. GALL. 10

16th c.; parchment; 126 ff.; d.c. (ff. 1v, 2r, 11v–end): triple cols. (ff. 2v–11r); 60–5 lines (item 1): 30–3 lines (items 2–6); decorated initials.

Ok is a copy of the collected edition published in 1526 by Galiot du Pré.[3]

1. Fol. 1c, *Cy commance le livre des quatre dames composé par maistre alain chartier.*
   Fol. 11b, *Cy finist le livre des quatre dames composé par maistre allain chartier.*
   3469 lines; 65 lines are missing. Some of the lines omitted, for example lines 1141–4 and 1629–68, are also omitted in *Pa*. *Ok* has the same additional lines as *Pa*.
2. Ff. 11d–86a, [*Le Livre de l'Esperance*].
3. Ff. 86a–92a, *Comme le curial fut faict et composé par maistre Alain chartier qui apprent a soy gouverner en court et monstre les trafiques les dissolucions...*
4. Fol. 92b, *Ensuit le quadrilogue faict par maistre alain charretier. Comment en ce present prologue est demonstré que tout ainsi que par l'ordonnance du supernel monarche...*
   Fol. 123a, *Explicit le Quadrilogue.*

Ok was included in the earlier bibliographies of the *Livre de l'Esperance* and the *Livre des Quatre Dames*, and was used by Heuckenkamp and Rouy in their respective editions.

Ol   OXFORD, BODLEIAN LIBRARY, E. D. CLARKE 34

15th c.; parchment; 225 × 165 (150 × 108: 150 × 102); 118 ff., numbered 2–119; 24 and 29 lines; collation 1–14⁸: 15⁶; catchwords; miniatures, decorated borders and initials.

Items 1 and 2 were copied by 'Lois Herlin'[4] whose signature is found on fol. 110r.

---

[1] See pp. 157, 331 and 394.   [2] See however the note to DF 96.
[3] Heuckenkamp, *Le Curial par Alain Chartier*, x–xi; Piaget, *Romania*, xxx, 1901, 45, n. 2 (46); Rouy, *Alain Chartier: Le Livre de l'esperance*, c. The conclusions of Heuckenkamp and Rouy, based on an examination of the texts of the *Curial* and the *Livre de l'Esperance* respectively, have been confirmed by a study of the text of the *Livre des Quatre Dames*.
[4] Two scribes, Jehan Herlin and Pierre Herlin, are mentioned in the accounts of Jeanne de Laval between 1456 and 1459 (Delisle, *Le Cabinet des manuscrits*, III, 1881, 338).

The other three items appear each to have been copied in a different hand.

1. Ff. 2r–100v, [*Le Livre de l'Esperance*].
2. Fol. 101v, [*Le Curial*].
   Fol. 110r, *Explicit le Curial, fait par Maistre Alain charretier.*
3. Fol. 110v, [*La Complainte*].
   Fol. 112v, *Explicit la complainte de maistre alain charretier.*
       181 lines. Lacks lines 83, 117, 147, 163, 173. Includes lines 119a, 174a. The order
       of stanzas is: I–IV, VII, V–VI, VIII, X, IX, XI–XII.
4. Fol. 113r, [*Ballade*].
   Incipit: Il n'est dangier que de villain...
       28 lines. Complete.
5. Ff. 114r–118v (quire 15), [*Le Lay de Paix*].
       281 = 282 lines. Lacks lines 193, 237. Lines 125–6 are inverted. Lines 34–5 are written
       as one line.

Ol was included by Droz and Piaget in their bibliography of the ballade and was used
by Rouy in his edition of the *Livre de l'Esperance*. The texts of the poems have not been
examined before: neither of them is complete and both contain a number of individual
readings and irregular lines. So far as the *Complainte* is concerned, *Ol* closely resembles
Gc and *Gg*.

Om +STOCKHOLM, ROYAL LIBRARY, V.U.22[1]

Late 15th c. (after 1477);[2] paper; 4°; 205 × 150; 272 ff.; *c.* 32 lines.
    The manuscript is in several hands.

4. Fol. 3r, [*Ballade*].
   Incipit: Il n'est dangier que de villain...
       28 lines. Complete.
76. Ff. 113r–119v (incl. fol. 114[bis]), *Le breviaire des nobles.*
       446 plus 7 lines. Complete.
77. Fol. 120r, *Cy commence le lay de paix.*
   Fol. 123[bis]v, *Explicit le lay de paix.*
       284 lines. Lacks line 155. Includes line 156a. Lines 225–6 are inverted.
78. Fol. 124r, *La Belle dame sans mercy.*
   Fol. 136r, *Explicit la Belle dame Sans mercy.*
       800 lines. Complete.
95. Fol. 141[bis]v, [*Rondeau*].
   Incipit: Ou mon souhait s'assouvira...
       12 lines. Lacks line 11.

---

[1] A full description of *Om* is given in A. Piaget et E. Droz, 'Recherches sur la tradition manuscrite
de Villon. I. Le manuscrit de Stockholm', *Romania*, LVIII, 1932, 238–54.

[2] Item 22 comprises part of the *Temple de Mars* by Jean Molinet; the poem was not written before
1476. Item 74 is dated 1477.
    Having established the years 1476–7 as a *terminus a quo*, Piaget and Droz go on to say (*op. cit.*,
239): 'Mais s'il est exact que plusieurs copistes y ont travaillé, il semble que ce soit en même
temps et peu avant 1480.' All that can be said with certainty is that the manuscript dates from the
last quarter of the fifteenth century.

96

120. Ff. 253r–272v, *Le Quadrilogue Invectif.*

Om was included in the bibliographies of the ballade, the rondeau, and the *Belle Dame sans Mercy.* Rice gave some variants from *Om* in his edition of the *Breviaire des Nobles.*

Om contains a good and complete text of the *Lay de Paix*; it closely resembles those in *Nf* and *Nj* which, having fewer peculiarities, were preferred to it. The other texts in *Om*, although they are a little more individual than the *Lay de Paix*, are generally complete and regular. *Om* was seriously considered for use in this edition; it was finally rejected in favour of *Nf* and *Nj*, related manuscripts which are of better quality and contain larger collections of poems.

On +VIENNA, NAT. BIBL., 3391

15th c.; paper; 2°; 581 ff.; *c.* 38 lines (prose), 25 lines (verse).

15. Fol. 134r, *S'enssuit les miseres de court.*
   Fol. 140v, *Cy fine l'epistre de maistre alain chartier* (sic) *en laquelle sont embrief descriptures* (sic) *les miseres de court qu'il envoya a son frere l'evesque de paris.*
38. Fol. 469v, *C'est le breviare* (sic) *des nobles.*
   Fol. 480r, *Explicit le breviaire des nobles.*
      446 plus 8 lines. Complete.
39. Ff. 480r–483v, [Collection of ballades].
   Ff. 481r–v, *Balade.*
   Incipit: Il n'est dangier que de villain...
      27 lines. Lacks line 14. The second and third stanzas have been largely rearranged.

On was included in the bibliographies of the *Breviaire des Nobles* and of the ballade. The text of the *Breviaire des Nobles* contains a large number of irregular lines and some poor rhymes.

Oo GENEVA, LIBRARY OF MLLE E. DROZ

15th c.; paper; 251 ff.; 25–30 lines; parchment binding with the arms of Jean-Christofle Virey.

Oo was bought by Mlle Droz in London in 1935 and had earlier belonged to F. Kirbet. Previously it had been lot 238 in the Libri sale of 28 March 1859.[1] A detailed description of *Oo* published by Mlle Droz shows that the present volume is made up of several originally separate manuscripts.[2]

1. *L'exil maistre Alain Chartier* (*Le Livre de l'Esperance*).
3. *Le Breviaire de Noblesse.*

The present volume also contains the *Amant Rendu Cordelier en l'Observance d'Amours* (item 5) and the only known copy of the *Renoncement d'Amours* (item 4), both of which are

---

[1] *Catalogue...First Day (28.iii.1859)*, Sotheby and Wilkinson, 55. It was listed under its Libri sale number in the list of manuscripts published in 1966 (see p. 43, n. 2).
[2] Eugénie Droz, 'Un recueil de manuscrits du XVe siècle de la bibliothèque de Claude-Enoch Virey', *Bulletin de l'Institut de Recherche et d'Histoire des Textes*, xv, 1967–8 (1969), 157–73.

imitations of the *Belle Dame sans Mercy*. Since these two works were originally separate from items 1 and 3, the manuscript is of type O rather than type Q.

Oo has not been examined.

Op BRUSSELS, BIBL. ROYALE, 21521–31

15th c. (after 1465);[1] parchment fly-leaves and paper; 2°; 285 × 205 (*c.* 190 × 125); single and double cols. (of 55 mm); 2 plus 229 plus 2 ff.; *c.* 35 lines; collation (part 3) 1²² (first canc.): 2¹⁴: 3²², 4²⁴, 5²⁸ (last two canc.); traces of signatures; decoration in red; binding of stamped leather on boards.

Water-marks (Part 3)

(a) A 'Y' surmounted by a cross, the tail ending in a trefoil, 62 mm long, between chain-lines 37 mm apart. Briquet 9184 (1483).

(b) A 'P' with a forked tail, surmounted by a fleuron, 67 mm long, between chain-lines 37 mm apart. Most like Briquet 8599 (1462–8).

(c) A pair of keys, 58 mm long, between chain-lines 37 mm apart. Very similar to Briquet 3818–19 (1452–86).

The three parts of the present volume (ff. 1–58; 59–122; 123–229)[2] were bound together in the sixteenth century; this description is chiefly concerned with the third part.

Op belonged to Philippe de Lannoy whose signature and device 'Souffriray je tousjour (*sic*)' are found on fol. 57r with the date 1 December 1552.

3. Ff. 123r–157r, *Coppie des lettres envoyés* (sic) *par Jehan seigneur de lannoy, A loys son filz.*

The letters include the *Curial*:

Ff. 144r–149r (begins quire 2), *S'ensyeult la Coppie des lettrez escriptes par maistre alain charetier, A son frere.*

8. Ff. 214v–220r, *Chy commence le breviaire des Nobles.*

437 plus 8 lines. Lacks lines 218–21, 286, 394–7. Line 252 is copied between lines 249 and 250. Ballades v, viii, x and the final rondeau are in double columns.

Op was used by Heuckenkamp in his edition of the *Curial*. The text of the *Breviaire des Nobles* has not been listed or examined before. Although it is generally regular, it is incomplete and includes a number of poor rhymes.

Oq PARIS, BIBL. NAT., ROTHSCHILD 2796 (1.1.9)[3]

Mid 15th c.; parchment; 285 × 185 (210 × 110); 132 ff.; 35 lines (prose), *c.* 33 lines (verse); collation 1–4⁸: 5–6⁸, 7⁴: 8–10⁸: 11–12⁸: 13–17⁸; catchwords, signatures; miniatures, decorated initials and borders, headings in red.

[1] The letters of Jehan de Lannoy (item 3) were completed on 3 May 1465; the date is given in the *explicit*. The date applies only to the third part of the present volume.

[2] Ff. 57, 122 and 229, that is the last, or last but one, leaves of each part, are also numbered 57, 63 and 107 respectively.

[3] *Catalogue des livres...de feu M. le baron James de Rothschild*, iv, Paris, Morgand, 1912, 93–9.

Oq formed part of the collection of the tenth Duke of Hamilton (No. 145). The collection was sold to the Prussian government in 1882. Part of it, including this volume, was resold in London, at Sotheby's, on 23 May 1889.

1. Ff. 1r–32r (quires 1–4), [*Le Quadrilogue Invectif*].
   Fol. 32r, *Explicit quadrilogus.*
4. Ff. 53r–57r (begins quire 8), *Lay de paix aux seigneurs de france.*
   283 lines. Lacks lines 82, 110. Includes line 173a. Lines 273–5 are copied in the order 274, 275, 273. Line 82 has been added in a second hand.
7. Ff. 69r–76v (ends quire 10), *Cy commence le breviaire des nobles.*
   441 = 446 plus 8 lines. Complete. Lines 256–7 are inverted. Lines 220–1, 228–9, 253–4, 258–9 and 313–14 are written as one line. The text has been corrected in a second hand.
29. Ff. 130v–131r, *Ballade.*
   Incipit: J'é maintes fois oy paler (*sic*) d'amours...
   36 lines. The envoy is lacking.

Oq was included by Rice in his bibliography of the *Breviaire des Nobles*. The manuscript has not been examined in detail before. The text of the *Lay de Paix* in *Oq* closely resembles that in *Pc* which was chosen as the best text of its group in preference to *Oq*. Comparison of the texts of the *Breviaire des Nobles* in *Oq* and *Pc* shows that they are related and that *Oq* is again a little more individual than *Pc*. *Oq* was considered for use in this edition but was excluded in favour of *Ql*, which is in the same tradition as *Oq* and *Pc* and is of similar quality to *Oq*; *Ql* contains the larger collection of poems.

Pa   PARIS, BIBL. NAT., F. FR. 833

Late 15th c., early 16th c.; parchment; 330 × 240 (225 × 140); 2 plus 195 ff.; single and double columns (of 65 mm); 34 lines; collation A^2 (first stuck down): $1-20^8$, 21^6, $22-4^8$, 25^6 (first canc., last stuck down); decorated initials, space for miniatures; contemporary binding of stamped leather on boards with traces of two clasps.

Title-page (fol. 1r): *Les Faicts Maistre Alain Charetier.*
   Underneath and on the verso are copied verses playing on the name Chartier.

1. Ff. 2r–61r, [*Le Livre de l'Esperance*].
2. Ff. 61v–65v, *Le curial fait par maistre Alain Charretier.*
3. Fol. 65v, *Ensuit le quadrilogue fait par Maistre Alain Charretier.*
   Fol. 89r, *Explicit le quadrilogue.*
6. Fol. 94r, [*Le Lay de Paix*].
   Fol. 98v, *Cy finist le petit libelle que ledit Maistre Alain envoia au Roy et a la seigneurie de france.*
      279 = 281 lines. Lacks lines 24–5, 148. Lines 15–16 are inverted; lines 87–8 and 95–6 are written as one line.
7. Fol. 98v, *Et commence le breviaire des nobles selon icelluy maistre Alain.*

Fol. 105v, *Finist le breviaire des nobles.*

> 444 lines. Lacks lines 25–8, 433. Ballade IV has an envoy of four lines and Ballade V an envoy of five lines.[1]

8. Fol. 105v, *Et commence le livre de reveille matin fait par maistre Alain. Le ve livre.*

Fol. 110v, *Cy finist le Debat de Reveille matin.*

> 352 lines. Lacks lines 17–24 and 345–52.

9. Fol. 110v, *Et commence le Septiesme livre Appellé La Belle Dame sans mercy.*

Fol. 123r, *Cy finist la Belle Dame sans mercy.*

> 799 lines. Lacks line 485. Text with headings.

10. Ff. 123r–v, *Complainte et supplicacion envoiee aux dames par les poursuivans et loiaulx serviteurs de la court amoureuse du dieu d'amours. Le viiie livre.*

11. Ff. 123v–124r, *Lettres closes envoiees a maistre alain de par les Dames de la Royne katherine marie et jehanne.*

12. Ff. 124r–128r, *Response faicte par maistre alain sur les lectres que les dames luy ont escriptes.*

> 240 plus 4 lines. Complete. There is the following heading between stanzas XIV and XV: 'Comment le Dieu d'amours tient l'arc entexé et la fleche en la corde oyant l'excusacion de maistre Alain. Le ixe livre.'

14. Fol. 134r, *Cy commence le tresgracieux livre des Quatre dames compilé et fait par maistre Alain L'an mil cccc xxxiii. Le xie livre.*

Fol. 162c,[2] *Cy finist le livre des quatre Dames fait et composé par Me Alain Charretier.*

> 3482 lines. Lacks lines 17, 1141–4, 1629–68, 1928, 1953, 2521, 2594, 3158, 3366, 3511. Includes lines 471a, 1606a, 3531a.

(15. Ff. 162d–172b, *Commence l'ospital d'amours fait et compilé par ledit Me Alain. Le xii livre.*)[3]

(16. Ff. 172b–174b, *Et commence la complainte de saint valentin gransson compilee par M^e alain charretier.*)[3]

20. Ff. 178b–179c, *Complainte trespiteuse.*

> 183 lines. Lacks lines 103, 117. Includes line 119a. The order of stanzas is: I–IV, VII, V–VI, VIII, X, IX, XI–XII.

24. Ff. 184d–186b, *Lay de plaisance.*

> 192 lines. Lacks lines 85, 115–16, 118. Lines 47–8 are inverted.

Pa was described in 1845 by Paulin Paris who noted the manuscript's similarity to the collected edition of 1529 published by Galiot du Pré; the same works appeared in the

---

1   Qui garde honneur on le doit honnorer.   (fol. 100v)
            Nobles hommes tenez en plus grant compte
            Que de tresor que de tresor (*sic*) que puissez procurer,
            Car c'est le bien qui les autres surmonte.

            Ne faisons par murmurer   (fol. 101r)
            Conjurer
            Contre nous en quelque endroit,
            Mais faisons pour plus durer
            A chascun son loial droit.

2   The manuscript is laid out in double columns from fol. 138v on.

3   Neither of these works is by Chartier. See J. C. Laidlaw, 'André du Chesne's Edition of Alain Chartier', *Modern Language Review*, LXIII, 1968, 569–74.

same order.[1] In 1892 Arthur Piaget showed that *Pa* had been copied from the second edition published by Pierre le Caron.[2] Piaget's findings were confirmed when *Pa* was used in the edition of the four poems. A similar conclusion was reached by F. Rouy in his edition of the *Livre de l'Esperance*.[3]

The imitations of the *Belle Dame sans Mercy* in *Pa* were discussed by Piaget and the manuscript was included in the bibliographies of the *Livre des Quatre Dames*, the *Belle Dame sans Mercy* and the *Breviaire des Nobles*.

The printed catalogue of the library contains no mention of items 11 and 12, nor of item 13 (*La Belle Dame qui eut Mercy*).[4]

Pb PARIS, BIBL. NAT., F. FR. 924

Late 15th c.; paper and parchment (sheet 1/18); 2°; 275 × 190 (200 × 100); 282 ff.;[5] 21–4 lines; collation 1^{18}: 2^8: 3^{14} (last canc.): 4^{12} (last canc.): 5^{20}: 6^{20} (first canc.): 7^{22}: 8^{14}, 9^{14} (last canc.): 10^{16}: 11^{18} (first canc.): 12^{14}, 13^{12}: 14^{24} (first canc.): 15^8: 16^8: 17^6: 18^4: 19^{16} (first canc.): 20^{10}: 21^{14} (first, and last three canc.; new leaf inserted at end); catchwords in items copied on more than one quire; decorated border and initial, space for miniature at beginning of first item; capitals in red.

Water-marks

(a) A barred 'P', surmounted by a fleuron and cross; 70 mm long, between chain-lines 33 mm apart. Briquet 8693 (1475).
(b) A unicorn 90 mm long over-all, across chain-lines 33 mm apart. Briquet 9994 (1467–70) is similar.
(c) A coat of arms (quarterly, 1 and 4, a fleur-de-lys; 2 and 3, a dolphin) crowned, 63 mm long, fixed to chain-lines 37 mm apart. Very like Briquet 1655 (1477–93).
(d) A pot surmounted by a cross, 80 mm long; chain-lines 33 mm apart. Very like Briquet 12482 (1474–80).
(e) An unidentified mark, perhaps a balance or a weather-vane, 30 mm long and fixed to a chain-line;[6] lines 23 mm apart.

There is the following inscription on fol. 1r: 'Ce present livre appartient A m^e Jaques Thiboust Notaire et secretaire du roy Esleu en Berry et s^r de Quantilly...'; a similar inscription is on fol. 282v.

Pb has been extensively corrected, especially the texts of items 1, 21 and 22; the titles

[1] P. Paris, *Les Manuscrits françois de la bibliothèque du roi*, VI, Paris, Techener, 1845, 386–7.
[2] A. Piaget, *Romania*, XXI, 1892, 429. Piaget did not say which of the two undated editions he considered to be the second; textually, these two editions are very similar. When he discussed Heuckenkamp's edition of the *Curial* in 1901, Piaget stated wrongly that *Pa* was copied from the first edition of 1489 [*I* in Heuckenkamp]. (*Romania*, XXX, 1901, 45, n. 2.)
[3] Rouy, *Alain Chartier: Le Livre de l'esperance*, c.
[4] *Bibliothèque Impériale: catalogue des manuscrits français, ancien fonds*, I, Paris, Firmin Didot, 1868, 92–3.
[5] The leaves are numbered in both Arabic and Roman. The Arabic numbering is continuous and is used here. There are errors in the Roman numbering, including a gap of ten between ff. 89 and 90, that is between quires 6 and 7; it is possible that a quire of ten leaves is missing.
[6] There is a similar water-mark in *Bc*.

of many works have been either added or expanded. Paulin Paris suggested that these corrections and additions might be in the hand of Alain Chartier himself.[1] The corrections were later examined by Arthur Piaget, who showed that they were the work of Jacques Thiboust; the titles, in particular, had been taken from an early collected edition.[2]

1. Ff. 1r–17v (quire 1), (*Le livre de la belle dame sans mercy*).[3]
    800 lines. Complete. Text with headings.
4. Ff. 40r–43v (begins quire 4), *La complainte et regretz maistre alain chartier* (*Contre la Mort qui luy a tollu sa maistresse*).
    180 lines. Lacks lines 26, 78, 103, 114.
5. Ff. 43v–44r, *Coppie des lectres envoiees par les dames a maistre alain chartier.*
6. Ff. 44r–45v, *Coppie de la requeste baillee aux dames.*
7. Ff. 45v–50v (ends quire 4), *Responce sur ladicte requeste par l'acteur baillee aux dames.*
    Fol. 46r, (*La Response baillee aux dames Par m^e alain chartier*).
    240 lines. Complete.
14. Ff. 172r–197v (quires 12–13), *Le debat des deux fortunez en amours* (*Autrement dict le Gras et le maigre*).
    Fol. 197v, *Explicit le debat des deux fortunez en amours autrement dit le gras et le maigre.*
    1235 lines. Lacks lines 97–100, 635, 653, 909.
17. Ff. 229r–236v (quire 16), *Reveille matin.*
    368 lines. Complete. Lines 316–17 are inverted. Sheet 230/235 has been wrongly inserted, giving the order of stanzas: I–VI, XXXVII–XLII, XIII–XXXVI, VII–XII, XLIII–XLVI.
18. Ff. 237r–242r (quire 17), *Le lay de paix.*
    Fol. 242r, *Explicit le lay de paix.*
    274 = 275 lines. Lacks lines 15, 44, 111, 120, 128–9, 150, 155, 225, 267. Includes line 156a. Lines 101–2 are written as one line.
19. Ff. 243r–246v (quire 18), *Le lay de plaisance.*
    Fol. 246v, *Explicit le lay de plaisance.*
    188 = 190 lines. Lacks lines 38, 54, 63, 114–16. Lines 82–3 are inverted; lines 51–2 and 61–2 written as one line.
21. Ff. 262r–271v (quire 20), *Le breviaire des Nobles.*
    443 plus 4 lines. Lacks lines 315–17.
22. Ff. 272r–282v (quire 21), *Le Curial maistre Alain.* (*Le Curial ou Courtisan de maistre Alain Chartier quand il vivoit Notere et Secretere du roy.*)
    Fol. 282v, (*Explicit le curial de m^e Alain chartier en son vivant notere et secretere du roy Charles vij^{me} de ce nom*).
    Fol. 282 has been inserted and is entirely in the hand of Jacques Thiboust.

The imitations of the *Belle Dame sans Mercy* in *Pb* were discussed by Piaget. *Pb* was included in the bibliographies of the *Debat des Deux Fortunés d'Amours*, the *Belle Dame sans Mercy* and the *Breviaire des Nobles*.

[1] Paris, *Les Manuscrits françois de la bibliothèque du roi*, VII, 1848, 251–5.
[2] A. Piaget, 'Un prétendu manuscrit autographe d'Alain Chartier', *Romania*, XXV, 1896, 312–15. Thiboust was born in 1492. He also owned Paris, Bibl. Nat., f.lat. 15427 and New York, Pierpont Morgan Library, 438 (*El*) (see Delisle, *Le Cabinet des manuscrits*, II, 418).
[3] Here and in later items, Thiboust's additions are given in round brackets.

Pb, which was used in the edition of each of the four poems, was found to be linked to *Ff*, so far as the *Lay de Paix* is concerned. Elsewhere it closely resembles *Qh* and *Qk*; the three manuscripts are laid out in similar fashion and were probably copied in the same scriptorium. They contain a large number of readings peculiar to themselves and not a few irregular lines. Many of the works which they contain are incomplete.

Pc   PARIS, BIBL. NAT., F. FR. 1131

Mid 15th c.; parchment; 290 × 205 (210 × 115); 208 ff.; 35 or 36 lines; collation 1–26⁸; some catchwords, traces of signatures; decorated initials, headings in red, space left for small miniatures.

1. Fol. 1r, *Cy commence le livre des quatre dames dont les maris furent a la bataille d'agincourt.*
   Fol. 50v, *Cy fine le livre des quatre dames.*
   3527 lines. Lacks lines 707, 1554, 1953, 3464.
2. Fol. 51r, [*Le Debat du gras et du maigre*].[1]
   Fol. 68v, *Explicit le debat du gras et du maigre.*
   1229 plus 4 lines. Lacks lines 635, 642–5, 653, 678, 821, 838, 886, 1074, 1126, 1129. Where a line is missing from a four-line stanza, the scribe has generally left a gap; on three occasions the gap is in the wrong place.
4. Ff. 73r–80r, *Cy commence le breviaire des nobles.*
   446 plus 8 lines. Complete.
5. Ff. 80r–84r, *Lay de paix aux seigneurs de france.*
   282 lines. Lacks lines 82, 110. Lines 273–5 are copied in the order 274, 275, 273.
7. Ff. 88r–90v, *Conplainte de la mort a la dame m. alain.*
   184 lines. Lacks line 117. Includes line 119a. Lines 34–5 and 177–8 are inverted. The order of stanzas is: I–IV, VII, V–VI, VIII, X, IX, XI–XII.
8. Ff. 91r–103v, [*La belle Dame sans mercy*].[1]
   800 lines. Complete.
9. Ff. 103v–104r, [*Complainte et supplication envoyée aux Dames par les poursuivans et loyaux serviteurs de la court amoureuse du Dieu d'amours*].[1]
10. Ff. 104r–v, [*Letres closes envoyées à Maistre Alain de par les Dames de la Royne, Katherine, Marie, et Jehanne*].[1]
11. Ff. 104v–108v, [*Response faite par Maistre Alain sur les letres que les Dames luy ont escrites*].[1]
    240 plus 4 lines. Complete. Between stanzas XIV and XV there has been added the heading: 'Comment le Dieu d'amours tient l'arc entexé et la flesche en la corde oyant l'excusation de Maistre Alain.'
16. Fol. 167r, [*Le Debat de Reveille matin*].[1]
    Fol. 172v, *Cy fine resveille matin.*
    368 lines. Complete.

The imitations of the *Belle Dame sans Mercy* in *Pc* were among those discussed by Piaget. *Pc* was listed in the bibliographies of the *Livre des Quatre Dames*, the *Debat des Deux*

<hr />

[1] Title added in a later hand.

103

Fortunés d'Amours, the *Belle Dame sans Mercy* and the *Breviaire des Nobles*. Champion also referred to *Pc*, and the manuscript was used by J. E. White in his edition. The published catalogue makes no mention of item 2.[1]

Pc contains copies of three of the four poems edited and was chosen on each occasion as one of the best texts of its group. It is written in quite a clear but compressed cursive hand. No consistent distinction is made between *n* and *u*; *i* is not always dotted. It is possible to confuse *b*, *l* and *h*: *chalenge* (BD 205) could be taken as *clalenge*; in BD 749, the fourth word could be read as *hunble* or *l'umble*; in EX 242, *beaulté* and *leaulté* are equally possible interpretations. *Pc* seems not to have been revised: there are few headings and no miniatures; omissions and irregular lines have not been corrected.

The texts in *Pc* contain some north-eastern forms, as do *Gf* and *Ql*, with which *Pc* is linked textually: *s'efforchoit* (BD 89), *s'enlachoit* (BD 94), *francise* (BD 104). *Peust* is often found in *Pc* where other manuscripts have *puet*; the form has not always been included as a variant.

Pd PARIS, BIBL. NAT., F. FR. 1642

Late 15th c., early 16th c.; paper; $2°$; 285×210 (*c.* 215×130); 2 plus $479 = 480$ ff. (includes fol. 339bis); 35–40 lines; collation[2] $A^?(4)$: 1^{16} (first lost), 2^{12}: 3^{14}, 4–8^{12}, 9^{14}, 10–14^{12}: 15–16^{12}: 17–21^{12}: 22^{12}: 23^{6}, 24^{6} (last canc.): 25^{12}: 26^{12}: 27^{12}, 28^{10}: 29–35^{12}: 36–7^{12}, 38^{10}, 39^{8}: 40^{12}: $41^{?}(12)$; signatures a–z, a–o (some quires unsigned); catchwords at right angles; contemporary table of contents; title-page; decorated border and initial at beginning of most items; coloured initials.

Water-marks

(a) and (b) Two unidentified marks.

(c) A six-toothed wheel, 20 mm in diameter, surmounted by a stalk bearing three five-petalled flowers; 54 mm long over-all, fixed to chain-lines 30 mm apart. Briquet 13364 (1490–1503).

(d) A six-toothed wheel, 18 mm in diameter, surmounted by a stalk bearing a five-petalled flower; 43 mm long over-all, fixed to chain-lines 30 mm apart. Briquet 13357 (1492–5).

(e) A six-toothed wheel, 19 mm in diameter. The mark incorporates a 'starting-handle', three flowers and two initials; 57 mm long over-all, fixed to chain-lines 22 mm apart. Briquet 13490 (1498–1513).

(f) A unicorn 95 mm long over-all, fixed to sewn chain-lines 29 mm apart.

(g) and (h) As (f) but 93 mm long, fixed to sewn chain-lines 27 mm apart.

---

[1] *Bibliothèque Impériale: catalogue des manuscrits français, ancien fonds*, 1, Paris, Firmin Didot, 1868, 191.

[2] Quire A, containing the table of contents and the title-page, has perhaps been added later; the position of the chain-lines in that quire suggests that the paper may be in-quarto. It is possible that quires 23 and 24, which are blank and the paper of which bears no water-mark, were added later. The paper in quire 41 likewise has no water-mark.

The manuscripts

(i) A six-toothed wheel, 18 mm in diameter, together with two stalks bearing heart-shaped flowers; 60 mm long over-all, between chain-lines 33 mm apart. Very like Briquet 13355 (1527–41).

Title-page: *Les faiz maistre allain charretier ou vivant du roy charles vij^e son notere et secretere.*

1. Fol. 3r, [*Le Curial*].
    Fol. 6v, *Explicit curiale magistri alani Chartier ipso vivente Caroli septimi regis secretarii.*
    The collation shows that the first leaf of the text is missing.
2. Fol. 7r, *S'ensuit la translacion d'ung dyalogue en latin que fist en son vivant feu maistre alain chartier*[1] *et fut translaté Par* (sic).
    Fol. 28r, *Explicit dyalogus magistri alani chartier.*
3. Fol. 30r (begins quire 3), *Le quatrilogue.*
    Fol. 52v, *Explicit Quatrilogus magistri Alani Chartier ipso vivente secretarii regis karoli Septimi.*
4. Fol. 54r, [*Le Livre de l'Esperance*].
    Fol. 116v, *Explicit l'exil autrement l'imparfait de maistre alain chartier.*
5. Fol. 117r, *Cy Commence le breviere des nobles.*
    Fol. 123v, *Explicit le breviaire des nobles fait et compillé par maistre alain chartier.*
    419 lines. Lacks lines 382–93, 413–27.
6. Fol. 124r, *Le Lay de paix.*
    Fol. 127v, *Cy finist le lay de paix que maistre Alain envoya au roy et a la seigneurie de france.*
    282 = 283 lines. Lacks lines 110, 232. Includes line 125a. Lines 41–2 are written as one line.
7. Fol. 128r, *Les quatre dames.*
    Fol. 177v (ends quire 14),[2] *Cy finist le tresgracieux livre des quatre dames.*
    3509 lines. Lacks lines 338, 479, 760, 1008, 1219, 1695, 1910–11, 1986–7, 2214, 2216, 2268–9, 2586, 2710, 2746–7, 3170, 3250–1, 3265. Space is left for some of the missing lines.
8. Fol. 178r (begins quire 15), *Cy Commence le debat des deux amans Autrement le gras et le maigre.*
    Fol. 195v, *Cy finist le debat des deux amans autrement le gras et le maigre.*
    1242 plus 4 lines. Lacks line 300. Includes line 1242a (Vueille parfaire).
9. Fol. 196r, *Cy Commence le reveille matin.*
    Fol. 201v (ends quire 16), *Cy finist le debat reveille matin.*
    368 lines. Complete.
10. Fol. 202r (begins quire 17), *Cy commence la Complainte maistre alain chartier.*
    Fol. 204v, *Cy finist la Complainte maistre alain Chartier.*
    184 lines. Complete.
12. Fol. 224r, *La Belle dame Sans mercy.*
    Fol. 235r, *Explicit la belle dame sans mercy.*
    800 lines. Complete. Text with headings.
13. Fol. 235v, *Coppie de la requeste faicte et baillee aux dames Contre maistre alain.*

[1] The apparently unique copy of a French translation of the *Dialogus Familiaris Amici et Sodalis.*
[2] Fol. 177v has two columns.

14. Fol. 236r, *Coppie des lettres envoyees de par les dames A maistre Alain.*
15. Ff. 236r–239v, [*L'Excusacion aux Dames*].

> 248 plus 4 lines. The text includes both versions of stanza XVII. Between stanzas XIV and XV there is the heading: 'Response faicte par maistre Alain chartier Au dieu d'amours en soy excusant de ce qu'il l'accusoit avoir escript et fait livres nouveaux contre ses droiz.'

The imitations of the *Belle Dame sans Mercy* in *Pd* were listed by Piaget. *Pd* was discussed by Kussmann in his study of the textual tradition of the *Livre des Quatre Dames*. The manuscript was mentioned by Champion, and was included in the bibliographies of the *Debat des Deux Fortunés d'Amours*, the *Belle Dame sans Mercy*, and the *Breviaire des Nobles*. It was consulted by J. E. White when he edited the poetical works, and used by F. Rouy in his edition of the *Livre de l'Esperance*.

The texts of the *Excusacion* and the *Lay de Paix* in *Pd* are contaminated: the first contains an additional stanza, the second an extra line. *Pd* includes three of the four poems edited and their texts have some connection with those in the first collected edition, *Xa*, and with related manuscripts such as *Pa* and *Pk*. The three texts which were examined contain a number of individual readings and some irregular lines.

Pe PARIS, BIBL. NAT., F. FR. 1727

Mid 15th c.; paper; 2°; 280 × 200 (*c.* 205 × 100); 189 ff.; 35–45 lines; collation 1–3^{16}, 4^{16} (fourth, fifth and sixth lost), 5–6^{16}: 7–12^{16}; signatures, catchwords (at right angles, quires 1–9).

Water-mark: A bunch of grapes within a border of branches and leaves, *c.* 65 × 50 mm; chain-lines 38 mm apart. The mark is the same as Briquet 13055 (1453), save that the chain-lines are in a different position.

Pe was described in 1894 by Arthur Piaget, who identified it as the Du Puy MS used by Du Chesne in his edition of Chartier's works. Piaget listed, but did not discuss the state of, the texts; nor did he mention the corrections found in some works.[1]

The manuscript has been rebound since Du Chesne used it, and the margins cut down.

1. Ff. 1r–5r, *Reveille matin.*
   > The text, as copied by the scribe, lacked lines 17–24, 125, 170–1 and 295–6. These lines have all been added in the margin in a second hand; in addition, the text has been extensively corrected.
2. Fol. 5v, *La belle dame sans mercy.*
   Fol. 15r, *Explicit La belle dame sans mercy.*
   > 797 lines. Lacks lines 213 (supplied in a second hand), 667–8. Text with headings. Before stanza XXV is the heading: 'Cy commance l'amant a parler a sa dame.' Another heading follows line 220: 'La dame commance sa responce.'
3. Ff. 15r–v, *Coppie de la requestee* (sic) *baillee aux dames contre maistre alain.*[2]
4. Ff. 15v–16r, *Coppie des lectres envoyees par les dames a maistre Alain.*

---

[1] A. Piaget, 'Notice sur le manuscrit 1727...', *Romania*, XXIII, 1894, 192–208. See also J. C. Laidlaw, 'André du Chesne's Edition of Alain Chartier', *Modern Language Review*, LXIII, 1968, 569–74.

[2] Part of the letter is missing because of a hole in the middle of the leaf.

5. Ff. 16r–19r, *Cy apres s'ensuit l'excusation de maistre Alain contre ceulx qui dient qu'il a parlé contre les dames en son livre nommé La belle dame sans mercy.*
   Excusation contre ceulx qui dient l'acteur avoit parlé contre les dames (sic).
   240 lines. Complete.

6. Ff. 19r–21r, *Complainte de maistre Alain Contre la mort qui lui oste sa dame.*
   181 lines. Lacked lines 16–18. The text has been corrected, and the missing lines added, by a second hand.

7. Ff. 21v–23r. *Le lay de plaisance.*
   175 = 176 lines. Lacks lines 161–80. Lines 61–2 are written as one line. The text has been corrected in a second hand.

8. Ff. 23v–26v, *Autre lay maistre alain baillé A monseigneur de bourgoigne.*
   283 = 284 lines. Lacks line 41. Includes line 275a. Lines 101–2 are written as one line.

9. Ff. 27r–41v, *Le debat des deux fortunés D'amours.*
   1231 plus 4 lines. Lacks lines 360, 635, 653, 729, 904–7, 986, 1160, 1216. Lines 635, 653 and 729 excepted, all the missing lines are written in the margin, in a second hand.

10. Ff. 42r–48r, *Cy commance le breviaire des nobles.*
    445 plus 8 lines. Lacks line 432, which has been added in a second hand.

11. Fol. 48v, *Cy commance le livre des quatre Dames Compilé par maistre alain charretier secretaire du roy.*[1]
    Fol. 85r, *Explicit le livre des quatre dames.*
    3222 lines. 309 lines are missing, including lines 309–584, as a result of the gap in quire 4. Where single lines, or groups of two or three, are omitted, they have generally been added in the margin in a second hand.

(14. Ff. 124v–130r, *Complaincte d'amours et Responce faicte par maistre alain charretier secretaire du roy. (La Belle Dame qui eut Mercy.)*)[2]

19. Fol. 146r, [*Le Quadrilogue Invectif*].
    Fol. 172v, *Cy finist ce present quadrilogue.*
    The text has been corrected in the same hand as have the other works.

20. Fol. 172v, *S'ensuit le Curial fait par maistre alain charretier.*
    Fol. 179r, *Explicit le curial fait par maistre alain charretier.*

The imitations of the *Belle Dame sans Mercy* in *Pe* were discussed by Piaget. Kussmann used *Pe* in his study of the *Livre des Quatre Dames*. The texts of the *Debat des Deux Fortunés d'Amours*, the *Belle Dame sans Mercy* and the *Breviaire des Nobles* have all been listed in earlier bibliographies. *Pe* was also mentioned by Champion.

A. Pagès chose *Pe* as the base for his edition of the *Belle Dame sans Mercy* published in 1936.[3] *Pe* was used by J. E. White in his edition of the poetical works.

Only one of the works in *Pe* is complete. The texts of the four poems which were edited

---

[1] A similar rubric is also copied on fol. 48r.

[2] The poem, also attributed to Chartier in *Qa*, further appears in all the collected editions of Chartier's works. It is not by him; see p. 106, n. 1.

[3] A. Pagès, 'La Belle Dame sans merci d'Alain Chartier: texte français et traduction catalane', *Romania*, LXII, 1936, 481–531.

were found to be of fair quality: while they contain relatively few individual readings, they include some irregular lines. Examination of part of the *Belle Dame sans Mercy* showed that it had similar characteristics. *Pe* is most closely related to *Qr*; its relationship to *Oa* is more remote. The manuscript contains an interesting series of rubrics. The corrections found in some works have been made with the help of a collected manuscript akin to *Pb*, *Qh* or *Qk*.

Pf PARIS, BIBL. NAT., F. FR. 2230

Mid 15th c. (after 1445); parchment; 210 × 155 (140 × 75); 2 fly-leaves and 248 ff.; 30 lines; collation A⁷(1): 1–15⁸: 16–31⁸: B⁷(1); catchwords, traces of signatures; miniature, decorated and coloured initials, decorated borders; coat of arms.

The coat of arms (Angoulême and Rohan impaled) is that of Marguerite de Rohan, wife of Jean d'Angoulême; they were married in 1445.[1] On the verso of the front fly-leaf are these signatures and devices: 'A mon premier'; 'Rien ne m'est plus, cleves'; 'Vostre rien, de bourbon'; 'Sejour de dueil, rochefoucault'; 'Fors vous seulle, thignonville'; 'perrete'; 'blossete'; 'Le chois d'onneur'; 'Sera je vostre, de la tremoylle'. More names are written on the back fly-leaf (fol. 249r): 'Jehanne de coulonges'; 'Yzabeau d'alebret'; 'Jehanne d'orleans'; 'Madame de coullonges'; 'Jehanot(?) de Monst(?)'.[2]

1. Fol. 1r, [*Le Lay de Paix*].

   Fol. 6v, *Explicit le lay de paix et d'amitié.*

   277 = 278 lines. Lacks lines 9–12, 71, 77. Lines 231–2 are inverted; lines 260–1 copied as one line. Line 124 is copied between lines 126 and 127, and line 138 between lines 127 and 128.

2. Fol. 6v, *Apres s'enssuit le debat du bien et du mal d'amours. (Le Debat des Deux Fortunés d'Amours.)*

   Fol. 27v, *Explicit le livre du debat du bien et du mal d'amours.*

   1229 plus 4 lines. Lacks lines 96, 231, 281, 393–6, 431, 635, 653, 969, 994, 1081.

5. Fol. 68r, [*Le Livre des Quatre Dames*].

   Fol. 120v (ends quire 15), *Cy finist le livre des quatre dames.*

   The introduction to the poem is largely complete but the narrative has been abridged from 841 stanzas to 730. In addition, some single lines are omitted. The text is very similar to that in *Pj*.

6. Ff. 121r–137v (begins quire 16), [*La Belle Dame sans Mercy*].

   800 lines. Complete. Text with headings.

7. Ff. 137v–138v, *Cy est la requeste baillee aux dames Contre maistre Alain chartier.*

8. Ff. 138v–139r, *Cy sont les lettres envoiees par Les dames Audit maistre Alain.*

9. Fol. 139r, *Cy apres est l'excusacion de maistre Alain contre ceulx qui dient qui la* (sic) *parle contre les dames sans mercy.*

   Fol. 144v, *Explicit livre* (sic) *de la belle dame sans mercy.*

   240 lines. Complete.

[1] Champion, *La Librairie de Charles d'Orléans*, 120.

[2] Some of these signatures and devices are also found in *Pj*; *Gc* contains the signature of Isabeau d'Albret. The same name is found in Paris, Bibl. Nat., f. fr. 17229 and 19121; the name 'Jeanne de Colonges' is written at the end of F. fr. 1501 (Delisle, *Le Cabinet des manuscrits*, II, 335 and 357).

10. Fol. 144v, *Apres s'ensuit la complainte maistre Alain Contre la mort, En disant ainsy.*
     Fol. 148r, *Explicit la complainte maistre Alain Chartier, contre la mort.*
     184 lines. Lacks line 117; includes line 119a. The order of stanzas is: I–III, V–VII, IV, VIII, X, IX, XI–XII.
13. Fol. 168r, *Apres s'enssuit le debat Reveille Matin de deux Amoureux.*
     Fol. 175r, *Explicit le debat Reveille matin de deux Amoureux.*
     327 lines. Lacks lines 17–24, 96, 303–34. Lines 335–6 are copied as the last two lines of stanza XXXVIII. Stanzas XXXI and XXXVII are transposed. Line 96 has been added in a second hand.
14. Ff. 175r–184v, *Cy apres s'enssuit le breviaire des nobles Que tous gentilz hommes doivent aprendre.*
     439 plus 8 lines. Lacks lines 140, 200–1, 308, 316–17, 346. In Ballade X line 315 has replaced line 308 and the ballade has no envoy.

The imitations of the *Belle Dame sans Mercy* in *Pf* were discussed by Piaget. The manuscript was listed in the bibliographies of the *Livre des Quatre Dames*, the *Debat des Deux Fortunés d'Amours* and the *Belle Dame sans Mercy*, but not in that of the *Breviaire des Nobles*. *Pf* was mentioned by Champion. The manuscript has not been examined in detail before.

Pf and *Pj* are in the same hand and contain almost identical copies of the works which they have in common. They include three of the four poems which were edited; the texts of these works contain many individual readings, irregular lines and poor rhymes.

Pg PARIS, BIBL. NAT., F. FR. 2264

15th c.; paper; 4°; 210 × 145 (140 × 75); 224 ff.; *c.* 24 lines; quires generally of twelve leaves;[1] catchwords, signatures; decoration in red.

Water-marks: An ox, between chain-lines 40 mm apart; three varieties. Akin to Briquet 2790–7 (1452–84).

The manuscript is incomplete and disarranged. From the gaps in the first and second items it appears that quire I lacks two outer sheets and part of a third; fol. 224, which contains stanzas XVI–XXI of the *Belle Dame sans Mercy*, must have formed part of the first quire.

The name of 'Guillaume lenffent escuyer Sr. de la tandoure(?)' occurs frequently. On fol. 157r is written 'Jacques du bonaiffiard(?)'. The name 'A. Lancelot', perhaps with the year (1)638, occurs on fol. 1r.

1. Fol. 1r, [*Le Debat de Reveille Matin*].
   Fol. 6r, *Cy finist le debat reveille matin.*
   264 lines. The text begins with stanza XIV.
2. Ff. 6r–19v, 224, *Cy commance la belle damme sans mercy.*
   Fol. 19v, *Cy finist la belle dame sans mercy.*
   704 lines. Lacks lines 25–120.

   [1] The tightness of the binding makes it difficult to work out the collation.

Piaget listed and discussed the imitations of the *Belle Dame sans Mercy* in *Pg* and included the manuscript in his bibliography of the poem itself. The text of the *Debat de Reveille Matin* in *Pg* resembles that in *Nf* or *Nj* but is more individual and contains more irregular lines. Examination of part of the *Belle Dame sans Mercy* showed that it has similar characteristics. Neither poem is complete.

Ph PARIS, BIBL. NAT., F. FR. 19139[1]

15th c.; paper; 2°; 270 × 185 (195 × 105); 482 = 486 pp.;[2] 26–30 lines; collation 1^{16} (first canc.), 2–3^{16}, 4^{12}: 5^{10}, 6–11^{16}, 12^{16} (last lost), 13–15^{16}, 16^{16} (last canc.); catchwords; decoration in red; space for miniatures.

Water-marks

(a) A stag, 85 mm long over-all, fixed to chain-lines 39 mm apart.
(b) As (a), but 77 mm long over-all, across chain-lines 38 mm apart.

A note on p. 481 states that 'ce present livre est escript de la main de Bonnefoy'; the scribe's name is also found elsewhere, for example at the end of items 8 and 13. On p. 482 is written in a contemporary hand: 'Ce livre est a colin lateignent qui le trovera Sy le rande Et il payera bon vin.'

2. Pp. 121–34 (begins quire 5), *Cy commence le debat de Reveille matin.*
   359 lines. Lacks lines 17–24, 35.

3. Pp. 135–246, *Cy commence le livre des quatre dames.*
   3513 lines. Lacks lines 20, 415, 565, 891, 1651, 1953, 2044, 2173, 2192, 2306, 2377, 2522, 2643, 2938–9, 2943, 3302, 3402, 3464. Includes line 567a.

4. P. 247, *Cy commence la Belle dame sans mercy.*
   P. 275, *Cy fine la Belle dame Sans mercy.*
   799 lines. Lacks line 699. Text without headings.

5. P. 276, *La Responce a la Belle dame sans mercy.*
   P. 284, *Cy fine la responce maistre alain.*
   238 lines. Lacks lines 77, 228.

6. Pp. 285–301, *Le Breviere des nobles.*
   442 lines plus rondeau. Lacks lines 120 (added later), 315–17.

7. Pp. 301–10, *Cy commence le lay de paix.*
   278 = 279 lines. Lacks lines 11, 87, 101, 116, 168. Lines 67–8 are inverted, lines 30–1 written as one line.

8. Pp. 311–17, *Cy commence la complainte maistre alain.*
   183 lines. Lacks lines 94, 117. Includes line 119a. The order of stanzas is: I–III, V–VII, IV, VIII, X, IX, XI–XII.

9. Pp. 318–58, *Cy commence le gras et le maigre.*
   1242 plus 4 lines. Line 96 has been scored out.

---

[1] See A. Piaget, 'Jean de Garencières', *Romania*, XXII, 1893, 422–81, esp. 425–7.
[2] The pagination in quire 8 runs 203–19, (–), 220, (–), 221–32; that in quire 15 runs 423–41, (–), 442, (–), 443–52.

110

11. Pp. 403–4, *Balade d'alain.*
    Incipit: Aucunes gens m'ont huy araisonné... 35 lines
12. Pp. 404–5, *Rondel de ce mesmes.*
    Incipit: Joye me fuit et desespoir me chace... 13 lines
13. P. 405, *Le lay de plaisance.*
    P. 412, *Cy fine le lay de plaisance.*
        194 lines. Lacks lines 115–16.

The imitations of the *Belle Dame sans Mercy* in *Ph* were discussed by Piaget. The manuscript was included in the bibliographies of the *Debat des Deux Fortunés d'Amours,* the *Belle Dame sans Mercy* and the *Breviaire des Nobles. Ph* was also mentioned by Champion, and was consulted by J. E. White when he edited the poetical works.

The large collection of works in *Ph* includes the four poems which were edited. When the textual tradition of each was examined, *Ph* was found to be of quite good, though not outstanding, quality; it was always among the best texts of its group. *Ph* contains a certain number of readings peculiar to itself and some irregular lines. Most of the texts in *Ph* are incomplete. As these criticisms indicate, *Ph* was not an automatic choice for use in this edition. It was chosen in order to represent a tradition which is of some quality and which would otherwise have been excluded.

Ph is written in a small and flowing hand which has a cursive appearance and is generally legible; *s* and *f* are easily confused, as are *ir* and *er*. The few corrections made by the scribe can usually be distinguished from a second and later series, which was made almost certainly with the help of an early collected edition. The sign *Ph²* is used for these corrections.

Pj PARIS, BIBL. NAT., F. FR. 20026

Mid 15th c. (after 1440);[1] parchment; 220 × 150 (135 × 70); 3 fly-leaves (–, A, B) plus 179 ff.; 30 lines; collation A⁴ (first canc.): 1–22⁸: B⁴ (first canc.); catchwords, traces of signatures; decorated initials and borders; coat of arms; binding of skin on boards.

The coat of arms of Marie de Clèves, wife of Charles d'Orléans (Orléans and Clèves impaled) appears on fol. 1r, together with her device 'Rien ne m'est plus'. The many signatures and devices on the fly-leaves have been listed and discussed by Pierre Champion.[2]

1. Ff. 1r–17v, [*La Belle Dame sans Mercy*].
    800 lines. Complete. Text with headings.
2. Ff. 17v–18v, *Cy est la requeste baillee aux* (sic) *Contre maistre Alain.*
3. Ff. 18v–19r, *Cy sont les letres envoiees par les dames Audit maistre Alain.*
4. Fol. 19r, *Cy apres est l'excusacion de maistre Alain contre ceulx qui dient qui la* (sic) *parle contre les dames sans mercy.*
    Fol. 24v, *Explicit le livre de la belle dame sans mercy.*
        240 lines. Complete.

[1] The date of the marriage of Charles d'Orléans to Marie de Clèves. See Champion, *Charles d'Orléans,* 319.
[2] P. Champion, 'Un *Liber Amicorum* du XVe siècle', *Revue des bibliothèques,* xx, 1910, 320–36; seven pages of *Pj* are reproduced. Several of these signatures and devices are also to be found on the fly-leaf of *Pf.*

5. Fol. 24v, *Apres s'ensuit la complainte maistre Alain Contre la mort, En disant ainsi.*

Fol. 27v, *Explicit la complainte maistre Alain chartier Contre la mort.*

184 lines. Lacks line 117. Includes line 119a. The order of stanzas is: I–III, V–VII, IV, VIII, X, IX, XI–XII.

8. Fol. 47v, *Apres s'ensuit le debat reveille matin de deux amoureux.*

Fol. 54v, *Explicit le debat reveille matin de deux amoureux.*

327 lines. Lacks lines 17–24, 96, 303–34. Lines 335–6 are copied as the last two lines of stanza XXXVIII. Stanzas XXXI and XXXVII are transposed.

9. Fol. 54v, *Apres s'enssuit le lay de paix d'amour et d'amitié.*

Fol. 60v, *Explicit le lay de paix et d'amitié.*

277 = 278 lines. Lacks lines 9–12, 71, 77. Lines 231–2 are inverted; lines 260–1 copied as one line. Line 124 is copied between lines 126 and 127, and line 138 between lines 127 and 128.

10. Fol. 60v, *Apres s'enssuit le debat du bien et du mal d'amours.* (*Le Debat des Deux Fortunés d'Amours.*)

Fol. 81r, *Explicit le livre du debat du bien et du mal d'amours.*

1229 plus 4 lines. Lacks lines 96, 231, 281, 393–6, 431, 635, 653, 969, 994, 1081.

13. Ff. 121v–174v, [*Le Livre des Quatre Dames*].

The introduction to the poem is largely complete but the narrative has been abridged from 841 stanzas to 730. Some single lines are omitted in addition. The text is very similar to that in *Pf.*

The imitations of the *Belle Dame sans Mercy* in *Pj* were listed and discussed by Piaget. The texts of the *Livre des Quatre Dames*, the *Debat des Deux Fortunés d'Amours* and the *Belle Dame sans Mercy* were listed in the earlier bibliographies. *Pj* was mentioned by Champion.

Pj and *Pf* are in the same hand and contain almost identical texts of the works which they have in common. An assessment of the quality of *Pj* is given in the description of *Pf.*

Pk PARIS, BIBL. NAT., F. FR. 24440

15th c.; parchment; 295 × 205 (190 × 115);[1] 2 plus 270 ff.; 32–6 lines; collation A²: 1–6⁸, 7⁶, 8–9⁸, 10⁴: 11⁸, 12⁶, 13–19⁸, 20⁶, 21–5⁸, 26⁶, 27–9⁸, 30¹⁰: 31–3⁸, 34⁸ (last repaired), 35⁸ (seventh lost or canc.): B⁷(1): signatures, catchwords; miniature, space left for others; decorated borders; decorated, flourished and coloured initials; headings in red; binding of leather on boards with traces of clasps.

On fol. 1r is the note 'Emptus fuit 7¹¹. F. Bourdon Bibliot. 1683'; Bourdon was librarian of the Abbey of Saint Victor.[2]

1. Ff. 1r–74v (quires 1–10), [*Le Livre de l'Espérance*].

Fol. 74v, *Cy fine la calamité de france.*

2. Fol. 75r, [*Le debat des deux fortunés d'amour*]. Title added in a later hand.

---

[1] The written area varies in size and is sometimes as small as 170 × 110. See also the note to item 20.

[2] Delisle, *Le Cabinet des manuscrits*, II, 233.

Fol. 94r, *Ci fine le gras et le maigre.*

1229 plus 4 lines. Lacks lines 236, 267, 635, 642–5, 653, 703, 713, 821, 838, 1074. Space has been left for line 821, but in the wrong place.

3. Ff. 94v–98v, *Ci commence le livre de paix eureuse.*

282 = 283 lines. Lacks line 20. Lines 15–16 are inverted; lines 95–6 written as one line.

4. Fol. 99r, *Ci commence le debat resveille matin.*

Fol. 104r, *Cy fine le debat resveille matin.*

352 lines. Lacks lines 17–24 and 345–52.

5. Fol. 104v, *Ci commence le livre de la belle dame sans mercy.*

Fol. 116v, *Cy fine la belle dame Sans mercy.*

797 lines. Lacks lines 575–6 and 624, for which space has been left.

6. Ff. 116v–117r, *Complainte et Supplicacion envoyees aux dames par les poursuivans et loyaulx serviteurs de la court amoureuse du dieu d'amours.*

7. Ff. 117r–v, *Lettres closes envoyees a maistre alain de par les dames de la royne katherine marie et jehanne.*

8. Ff. 117v–121r, *Response faitte par maistre alain sur les lettres que les dames lui ont escriptes.*

238 plus 4 lines. Lacks lines 119–20. Between stanzas XIV and XV is inserted the heading 'Comme le dieu d'amours tient l'arc entezé et la fleche en la corde oyant l'excusacion de maistre Alain'.

12. Ff. 157r–160r, [*Complainte contre la mort qui luy ôte sa Dame.*] Title added in a later hand.

183 lines. Lacks lines 103, 117. Includes line 119a. The order of stanzas is: I–IV, VII, V–VI, VIII, X, IX, XI–XII.

14. Fol. 165v, *Cy commance le livre des quatre dames.*

Fol. 215r, *Cy finent les quatre dames.*

3484 lines. 47 lines are omitted, in the main single lines. For several of them space has been left.

15. Ff. 215r–221r, *Cy commence le breviaire des nobles.*

425 lines. Lacks lines 82–4, 218–21, 270–9, 289, 315–17.

20. Ff. 231r–269r (quires 31–5),[1] *Ci commance ung notable et excellent traictié sur le fait de la guerre En corrigent et reprenant les escuiers chascun en l'endroit de soy lequel traictié est nommé quadriloghe pour ce que en quatre personnes fut comprise par deffunct venerable discret et saige maistre alain chartyer en son vivant docteur en decret et secretaire du roy nostre sire Charles le viime de ce nom.*

The imitations of the *Belle Dame sans Mercy* in *Pk* were listed by Piaget. *Pk* was included in the bibliographies of the *Livre des Quatre Dames*, the *Debat des Deux Fortunés d'Amours*, the *Belle Dame sans Mercy* and the *Breviaire des Nobles*. It was also consulted by J. E. White when he edited the poetical works, and by F. Rouy in his edition of the *Livre de l'Esperance.*

---

[1] Though the written area is similar in size to that in the rest of the manuscript, quires 31–5 have only 30 ruled lines per page. The hand has a more angular and finished appearance than in the preceding quires and is probably that of another scribe. Fol. 269, which contains the last five lines of the text, is in a different hand from the rest of item 20.

Pk includes three of the four poems chosen for detailed examination. So far as these texts are concerned, *Pk* is related to the earliest edition, *Xa*,[1] and to manuscripts associated with the collected editions, such as *Pa* and *Pd*. The few individual readings in *Pk* include some which are irregular.

Pl PARIS, BIBL. NAT., ROTHSCHILD 440 (1.4.31)

Mid 15th c.; parchment; 205 × 135 (135 × 80); 212 unnumbered ff.;[2] 26 lines; collation 1–17⁸, 18⁴: 19–27⁸; catchwords, some at right angles; traces of signatures; decorated borders and initials; space for miniature at the beginning of each item.

The following names can be read: 'Loyse de daillon' (fol. 1r); 'Renee de daillon' (fol. 211r); 'Loyse de savoisy' (fol. 209r); 'Marie de gras(s)ay' (ff. 209r and 210r); 'Loyse Despeaux(?)' (fol. 43r);[3] 'Madamoyselle du lude' (fol. 212r).

1. Fol. 1r, [*Le Quadrilogue Invectif*].
   Fol. 43r, *Cy finist le quadrilogue*.
2. Ff. 43v–52v, [*Le Breviaire des Nobles*].
   445 = 446 lines.[4] Complete.
3. Ff. 53r–58v, [*Le Lay de Paix*].
   277 lines. Lacks lines 20–1, 30–2, 38, 159.
5. Ff. 75v–82v, [*Le Debat de Reveille Matin*].
   360 lines. Lacks lines 17–24.
6. Ff. 83r–100r, [*La Belle Dame sans Mercy*].
   799 lines. Lacks line 475.
7. Ff. 100r–101r, [*La Requeste Baillee aux Dames contre Alain*].
8. Ff. 101r–v, [*Les Lettres des Dames a Alain*].
9. Ff. 102r–107r, [*L'Excusacion aux Dames*].
   240 plus 4 lines. Complete.
12. Ff. 141r–208v (quires 19–27), [*Le Livre des Quatre Dames*].
    3498 lines. 33 lines are omitted, in the main single lines.

Piaget discussed the imitations of the *Belle Dame sans Mercy* in *Pl* and included the manuscript in his bibliography of the poem itself. *Pl* has not been listed elsewhere.

The texts in *Pl* are of reasonable quality but seem not to have been revised. *Pl* resembles *Qr* where the *Lay de Paix* is concerned; it is difficult to relate the text of the *Debat de Reveille Matin* to any other text very closely. Readings peculiar to *Pl*, infrequent in the *Lay de Paix*, occur more frequently in the *Debat de Reveille Matin*. The latter poem includes a number of irregular lines, as do the *Belle Dame sans Mercy* and the *Breviaire des Nobles*.

[1] F. Rouy (*Alain Chartier: Le Livre de l'esperance*, c) came to a similar conclusion.
[2] The folios have been described here as though they were numbered.
[3] For notes on some of these persons see the description of *Pl* in *Catalogue des livres de M. le baron James de Rothschild*, I, Paris, Morgand, 1884, 244–6.
[4] The refrain is omitted from the first stanza of Ballade VII.

Pm PARIS, BIBL. NAT., F. FR. 1661

Late 15th c.;[1] paper and parchment (ff. 1 and 244); 2°; 290×205 (*c.* 210×110); 244 ff.; *c.* 35 lines; collation A$^?$(1): 1^{16}, 2^{20}, 3^{18}, 4–9^{16}: 10–12^{12}, 13^{14}, 14^{12} (last two canc.), 15–16^{12}: 17^8: B$^?$(1); catchwords; contemporary table of contents on fol. 1.

Water-marks: A hand making the sign of benediction, three varieties, all between sewn chain-lines 42–3 mm apart.

(a) 80 mm long, the cuff with seven tails. Nearest is Briquet 11494 (1463).
(b) 70 mm long, the cuff with seven tails.
(c) 65 mm long, with a heart motif on the cuff of five tails. Nearest is Briquet 11526 (1467).

   On fol. 2r is the unidentified device 'Outre mon cueur'.[2]

14. Fol. 158r, *Le breviaire des nobles.*
   Fol. 164v, *Explicit le breviaire des nobles.*
   444 lines. Lacks lines 315–17. Includes line 129a (Et dont adroit mesurer).

The imitations of the *Belle Dame sans Mercy* in *Pm* were discussed by Piaget. *Pm* was mentioned by Champion and was included by Rice in his bibliography of the *Breviaire des Nobles*. The text in *Pm* contains many irregular lines and some poor rhymes.

Pn PARIS, BIBL. DE L'ARSENAL, 3521

15th c.; paper; 2°; 280×195 (*c.* 170×90); 299 ff., numbered A–D, 1–57, 57, 58–294;[3] 30–4 lines; collation 1–3^{12}, 4^{10}: 5^{12}, 6^{10}, 7^{12}: 8^{12}: 9^{14}: 10–16^{12}: 17–19^{12}: 20–1^{12}: 22–3^{12}, 24^{14}: 25^{12} (last canc.); catchwords, signatures; table of contents (ff. Ar–Cr).

Water-marks

(a) A unicorn with its head lowered, 100 or 105 mm long over-all, fixed to chain-lines *c.* 26 mm apart.
(b) A unicorn with its head erect, 95 or 100 mm long over-all, across chain-lines 35 mm apart.
(c) An ox-head surmounted by a cross, between lightly sewn chain-lines 38 mm apart; 60 or 65 mm long over-all. Most like Briquet 14239 (1478–83).
(d) A coat of arms (quarterly, 1 and 4, a fleur-de-lys; 2 and 3, a dolphin), 40 mm long, between chain-lines 35 mm apart.

2. Ff. 30r–37v, *S'ensuit le Breviaire des nobles que fist maistre allain charretier.*
   446 plus 8 lines. Complete.
3. Ff. 38r–42v (ends quire 4), *Lay de paix fait par maistre Allain chartier.*
   275 lines. Lacks lines 79–84, 159, 194–5.

---

[1] *Le Martir d'Amours* (ff. 12v–27r) dates from 1464 (see A. Piaget, *Romania*, xxxiv, 1905, 585). On fol. 244r is a note of the birth, in 1505 and 1506, of two sons to 'Jehan d'auvergne'.

[2] A description of *Pm*, together with a reproduction of ff. 236r–240v, is contained in A. Jeanroy et E. Droz, *Deux manuscrits de François Villon: Bibl. Nat., f. fr. 1661 et 20041*, Paris, E. Droz, 1932, ix–xi (*Documents artistiques du XVe siècle*, VI).

[3] There are three foliations; the most recent, in pencil, has been followed.

8. Ff. 56v–58r, *Complainte de Maistre allain charretier.*
   183 lines. Lacks lines 80, 103, 112. Includes lines 83a, 115a.

9. Ff. 58v–70v, *S'ensieut la belle dame sans mercy.*
   752 lines. Lacks lines 337–84. Text with headings. The order of stanzas is: I–XXX, XXXVII–XLII, XXXI–XXXVI, XLIX–C.

10. Fol. 71r, [*Les Lettres des Dames a Alain*].

11. Ff. 71r–v, [*La Requeste Baillee aux Dames contre Alain*].

12. Ff. 72r–75v (ends quire 7), *S'ensuit l'excusacion de maistre Allain.*
    240 plus 4 lines. Complete.

18. Ff. 137r–142v, *S'ensuit le debat Resveille matin.*
    360 lines. Lacks lines 17–24.

19. Ff. 143r–146r, *Lay de plaisance.*
    196 lines. Complete. Lines 1–2 are inverted. Lines 127–9 and lines 132–4 are transposed.

24. Ff. 170r–185v (ends quire 16), *Le debat de deux Chevaliers Sur les plaisirs et dolleurs qui pevent estre en amours fait par maistre Allain charetier.*
    1238 plus 4 lines. Lacks lines 96, 635, 653, 970.

Piaget listed and discussed the imitations of the *Belle Dame sans Mercy* in *Pn*. The manuscript was mentioned by Champion and used by Rice as base text for his edition of the *Breviaire des Nobles*.

Pn includes copies of the four poems which were edited. Although the texts are of reasonable quality and contain relatively few individual readings, they include a number of irregular lines. Examination of part of the *Belle Dame sans Mercy* showed that it had similar characteristics. Where the *Debat de Reveille Matin* is concerned, *Pn* is very similar to *Qf*; in the case of the *Complainte*, *Pn* resembles *Qg* most nearly; the text of the *Lay de Paix* in *Pn* is akin to those of *Of*, *Pf* and *Pj*. *Pn* contains more attributions than are usually found in the collected manuscripts.

Po PARIS, BIBL. DE L'ARSENAL, 3523

15th c.; paper; 2°; 290 × 195 (210 × 100); 818 pp.; *c.* 30 lines; collation 1^8: 2^8: 3^{10} (first canc.): 4^{10}: 5^6: 6^8: 7^{12}: 8^{10} (last canc.): 9^{12}: 10^{12} (last canc.): 11^{16}: 12^{14}: 13^{18} (first canc.): 14^{20}: 15^{10} (first canc.): 16^{10}: 17^{16}: 18^{16} (first canc.): 19^8: 20^{12}: 21^8 (last canc.): 22^{12}, 23^{10}: 24–5^{12}, 26^{12} (last canc.): 27^{14}, 28^{16} (first canc.): 29–30^{14}, 31^{10} (last canc.): 32^8 (first canc.): 33^{12}: 34^{18} (last canc.): 35^{14} (last canc.).

Water-marks

(a) The arms of France surmounted by a crown, with a 'c' at the point of the shield; 73 mm long over-all, between chain-lines, perhaps sewn, 40 mm apart. Very like Briquet 1725 (1463–4).

(b) A coat of arms (a fleur-de-lys, a three-pointed label), surmounted by a passion cross; 62 mm long over-all, between chain-lines 40 mm apart. Briquet 1547 (1459–74).

(c) The arms of France, surmounted by a crown, in all 45 mm long, between chain-lines, perhaps sewn, 40 mm apart. Similar to Briquet 1684 (1458–65).

(d) The letter 'Y' surmounted by a fleuron, its tail ending in a trefoil; 60 or 68 mm long, between chain-lines, perhaps sewn, 40 mm apart.

(e) As type (c) but 48 mm long and attached to one chain-line.

(f) A fleur-de-lys, 55 mm long, fastened to chain-lines, perhaps sewn, 42 mm apart. Like Briquet 6909 (1445–52).

(g) As type (a), but with a small 't'; 85 mm long over-all, between chain-lines 40 mm apart. Briquet 1739 or 1740 (1458–80).

(h) A unicorn, 100 or 95 mm long over-all, across chain-lines 39 mm apart.

The manuscript is in many different hands. The names of 'Jehan Maciot', 'Glaude Maciot' and 'Gilbert Coquille' appear on page 818; none of them has been identified.

Po contains works by Villon and has frequently been discussed. Bijvanck considered that it had been copied about ten years after the Stockholm MS of Villon's works (*Om*), which in its turn was not earlier than 1480; Jeanroy and Droz agreed with Bijvanck's dating.[1] More recently, D. M. Stewart has suggested that *Po* was copied after 1483: in line 56 of Villon's *Testament* (...*loys*...*roy de France*), the scribe has scored out *loys* and written *charles*; Charles VIII acceded in 1483.[2] Stewart's point is not in itself conclusive. The water-marks suggest that the manuscript may be earlier.

1. Pp. 1–16 (quire 1), [*Le Breviaire des Nobles*].
    P. 16, *Explicit*.
        Le Breviaire des Nobles. (sic).
    445 plus 8 lines. Lacks line 340.
5. Pp. 71–82 (quire 5), *Reveille Matin*.
    350 lines. Lacks lines 17–24, 220, 299, 345–52. Line 299 has been added in another contemporary hand; there are a few corrections in the same hand.
9. Pp. 141–64 (quire 9), *La belle dame sans mercy*.
    800 lines. Complete. Text without headings.
20. Pp. 391–8 (begins quire 18), *La complainte Maistre alain charretier*.
    184 lines. Complete. Lines 20 and 22 are transposed. The order of stanzas is: I–III, VII, IV–VI, VIII, X, IX, XI–XII.
22. Pp. 411–19 (ends quire 18), [*Le Lay de Paix*].
    248 lines. Lacks lines 77, 82, 126, 131, 136, 153–80, 206, 221, 274–5. Includes line 123a. Lines 22–3 and 24–5 are transposed. Lines 64–5 and 271–2 are inverted.

Piaget discussed the imitations of the *Belle Dame sans Mercy* in *Po* and listed the manuscript in his bibliography of the poem itself. *Po* was used by Rice in his edition of the *Breviaire des Nobles*. The manuscript has not been examined before in detail.

There is no mention of item 22, *Le Lay de Paix*, in the Arsenal catalogue[3] or in the description published by Jeanroy and Droz.

[1] W. G. C. Bijvanck, *Spécimen d'un essai critique sur les œuvres de François Villon*, Leyde, 1882, quoted in Jeanroy et Droz, *Deux manuscrits de François Villon*, viii; Jeanroy and Droz give a detailed description of *Po* (pp. vii–ix).
[2] D. M. Stewart, 'The Status of the Versions of Villon's *Testament*', *Studies in Medieval French Presented to A. Ewert*, Oxford, Clarendon Press, 1961, 150–64, esp. 151.
[3] H. Martin, *Catalogue des manuscrits de la bibliothèque de l'Arsenal*, III, Paris, Plon, 1887, 415–17.

The text of the *Debat de Reveille Matin* in *Po* is most closely associated with those in *Xa*, the first collected edition, and in *Pk*, a related manuscript. *Po* is very similar to *Nq* in its text of the *Lay de Paix*; at the same time, each of the two texts contains many individual readings. A relationship, albeit a more distant one, also exists between *Po* and *Nq* in the case of the *Complainte*, where *Po* again contains many readings peculiar to itself. When part of the *Belle Dame sans Mercy* was examined, it was found to contain a number of irregular lines.

Pp PARIS, MUSÉE JACQUEMART-ANDRÉ, 11

15th c.; parchment; 285 × 155 (195 × 75); 314 pp., numbered 1–84, 85, 84, 85–310, (311–12); 37 lines; collation 1–8⁸, 9⁶, 10–16⁸, 17⁸ (second lost), 18⁸, 19⁶, 20⁸, 21²; catchwords, signatures; headings in red; contemporary table of contents; binding of stamped leather.

On fol. 1 is the signature 'de Brieux'. There are also two book-plates: on the front board 'Mre. Jean Philibert Peysson de Bacot, Procureur Général en la Cour des Monnoyes de lion'; on the back board 'Ex Museo D. Claudii Ruffier in Lugdunensi Praefecturâ Franciae Quaestoris'.

Pp was originally Lyons MS 653 and a description of it appeared in the catalogue of 1812;[1] it later disappeared. In 1878 it was No. 36 in the *Catalogue Didot* and two years later it was listed by Quaritch in their November catalogue.[2] The manuscript subsequently passed into the library of Madame Jacquemart-André which was bequeathed to the *Institut de France* in 1912. A description of *Pp* together with an account of its history was published in 1914.[3] *Pp* may also have belonged at one point to the Comtesse de Béhague.[4]

In the bibliography of his edition of the *Belle Dame sans Mercy*, A. Piaget listed *Pp* under its (Jacquemart-) André and its Lyons press-marks, thereby giving the impression that there were two manuscripts.[5]

2. Pp. 41–8, [*Aucunes ballades en amours*].[6]
   (v) Pp. 45–6, *Aultre balade*.
   Incipit: Il n'est dangier que de villain...
      28 lines. Complete.
3. Pp. 49–75, *La belle dame sans mercy*.[7]
      799 lines. Lacks line 213. Text with headings.
5. Pp. 85–93, *Cy ensuit le lay de paix*.
      284 lines. Complete.

1 A.-F. Delandine, *Manuscrits de la bibliothèque de Lyon*, 1, Paris, Lyon, 1812, 412–15.
2 Paris, Bibl. Nat., n. a. fr. 23211 (E. Picot, *Répertoire historique*), 86–7.
3 Anon., 'Chronique', *Romania*, XLIII, 1914, 471–2.
4 Droz and Piaget listed a manuscript belonging to her in their bibliography of the ballade 'Il n'est dangier que de vilain'; the entry read: 'Béhague MS, p. 45'. Elsewhere in their notes to the *Jardin de Plaisance* (II, 208–9) they stated that the Béhague MS contained the ballade 'Qui ses besongnes veult bien faire' but did not give a precise reference. Both these ballades are copied in *Pp*, the first on p. 45.
5 Piaget, *Alain Chartier: La Belle Dame sans mercy*, 63–4.
6 The title is taken from the table of contents.
7 Immediately after the poem, almost as a postscript, are copied the first four lines of the *Loyalle Dame en Amours*, an imitation of the *Belle Dame sans Mercy*.

6. Pp. 93–109, *Cy commence le breviaire des nobles.*
   445 plus 8 lines. Lacks line 405.
9. Pp. 151–63, *Cy commence le debat reveille matin.*
   368 lines. Complete. Text with headings.
10. Pp. 163–279, *Cy ensuit le livre des Quatre dames.*
   3464 lines. Lacks lines 17, 37–8, 1153 (line 1157 has been copied in its place), 1953, 2305, 2579–82, 2684–742. Includes lines 124a (Aux fuitifs fortresses et tours) and 1512a (Et tant de joyes m'amenoyent). The long gap in the text is the result of the loss of a leaf from quire 17.

The imitations of the *Belle Dame sans Mercy* in *Pp* were discussed by Piaget. *Pp* was listed in the bibliographies of that poem and of the *Breviaire des Nobles.*

The texts in *Pp* are complete and regular on the whole. Although it is not an outstanding manuscript, *Pp* was seriously considered for use in this edition because the tradition in which it stands has some quality and is not otherwise represented. It was finally rejected because of the large number of individual readings which it contains.

Qa +BESANÇON, BIBL. MUN., 554

15th c.; paper; 208 × 143; 214 ff., plus 2 parchment end-leaves; 21–30 lines (3 stanzas); collation 1–9¹², 10¹⁰, 11–18¹²; signatures, catchwords at right angles; contemporary binding of stamped leather on boards.

Qa was formerly in the library of the Capucin House in Besançon. The scribe has signed his name, 'Ja. de bosco', on fol. 214v.[1]

1. Ff. 1r–10v, *Le breviaire des nobles.*
   445 lines. Lacks line 140.
2. Ff. 11r–14r, *Complainte d'amours.*
   183 lines. Lacks line 47. Lines 142–3 and 146–7 are inverted.
3. Ff. 14r–31v, *La belle dame sans mercy.*
   800 lines. Complete.
6. Fol. 64r, [*Les Lettres des Dames a Alain*].
   Fol. 64v, *Cy finist la copie des lectres.*
7. Fol. 64v, *Copie des lectres des dames en rithme envoyees a maistre Alain.*
   Fol. 66v, *Cy finissent les lectres des dames par rithme envoyees a maistre Alain.*
   9 stanzas of 8 lines, followed by 1 stanza of 6 lines.
8. Ff. 66v–68r, *Copie de la requeste baillie aux dames par aucuns contre ledit maistre Alain. Laquelle copie estoit enclose dedans les lectres cy dessus transcriptes.*
9. Fol. 68r, *La copie de la lectre envoyee aux dames par rithme contre ledit maistre Alain en maniere de supplicacion.*
   Fol. 71r, *Cy finist la supplicacion faicte aux dames contre maistre Alain.*
   18 stanzas of 8 lines.

---

[1] Jo. de Bosco copied Paris, Bibl. de l'Arsenal MS 1042 in 1468 (Ch. Samaran et R. Marichal, *Catalogue des manuscrits en écriture latine...*, I, Paris, CNRS, 1959, 125). Leodegarius de Bosco copied Besançon, Bibl. Mun., MS 75 in the second half of the fifteenth century (*Catalogue général des manuscrits*, XXXII, 1897, 48–9).

10. Ff. 71v–76v, [*L'Excusacion aux Dames*].
(i) Ff. 71v–73v, *Cy s'ensuit le songe de maistre alain.*
(ii) Ff. 73v–76v, *Cy s'ensuit la responce que maistre Alain fist au dieu d'amours.*
    240 lines. Complete.
(12. Ff. 79v–87r, *Cy s'ensuit une complainte d'amours que l'on dit autrement la belle dame a mercy faicte par maistre Alain charretier.*)[1]
13. Ff. 87v–95r, *Cy s'ensuit le debat de reveille matin.*
    358 lines. Lacks lines 17–24, 261, 341. Stanzas XXIV and XXV are inverted.
15. Fol. 107r, *Balade.*
    Incipit: Il n'est dangier que de villain... 28 lines

The imitations of the *Belle Dame sans Mercy* in *Qa* were discussed by Piaget. *Qa* was included in the bibliographies of the ballade ('Il n'est dangier...'), and of the *Belle Dame sans Mercy*. Rice gave variants from *Qa* in his edition of the *Breviaire des Nobles*.

The text of the *Debat de Reveille Matin* in *Qa*, which bears some resemblance to that in *Qq*, contains a very large number of individual readings, many irregular. Numerous readings peculiar to *Qa* are found in the *Complainte*; the text of the *Breviaire des Nobles* contains a number of irregular lines and poor rhymes.

Qb CARPENTRAS, BIBL. MUN., 390

15th c.; paper; 2°; 305 × 220 (175 × 110); 79 ff., numbered 11–39, 41–90; 25 lines; collation 1–2¹⁰, 3¹⁰ (tenth lost), 4–8¹⁰; catchwords, signatures b–h, y; contemporary binding of calf.

Water-marks

(a) An ox-head, 60 mm long, between chain-lines 44 mm apart.
(b) As (a) but 63 mm long. Both marks are similar to the group 14329–40 (*c.* 1440–80) in Briquet.

The foliation, which is in Roman numerals in a contemporary hand, and the signatures show that a quire of 10 leaves, signed *a*, has been lost.[2]

The names of 'Rene de Castellane filz du seigneur d'Andon et de Mazaingnes' and other members of the same family (Francois, Gaspar, Henry) occur frequently. On the back board is the name of 'Pierre parent, bachelier en loys'.

3. Ff. 38r–55r, [*La Belle Dame sans Mercy*].
    750 lines. Lacks lines 101–50, following the loss of fol. 40. Text with headings.
4. Ff. 55v–60r, [*L'Excusacion aux Dames*].
    240 lines. Complete. Between stanzas XIV and XV there is copied the heading 'Response de l'acteur'.
7. Ff. 73r–80r, [*Le Debat de Reveille Matin*].
    359 lines. Lacks lines 17–24, 224.

---

[1] The poem is not by Chartier. See p. 107, n. 2.
[2] Since the first surviving item in *Qb* is the *Psaultier des Villains*, it may well be that the first item was originally the *Breviaire des Nobles*. As it stands, *Qb* is the only known manuscript of the *Psaultier* which does not also contain the *Breviaire* (see W. H. Rice, *Romania*, LXXII, 1951, 381 and 385).

The imitations of the *Belle Dame sans Mercy* in *Qb* were not listed by Piaget,[1] although he did include the manuscript in his later bibliography of the poem itself.

Qb, which has not been examined before, is a manuscript of quite good quality. So far as the *Debat de Reveille Matin* is concerned, it is linked with *Qd*; the text in *Qb* contains some irregular lines and a relatively large number of individual readings. Its text of the *Belle Dame sans Mercy* has similar characteristics.

Qc CHANTILLY, MUSÉE CONDÉ, 686

15th c.; paper and parchment (fly-leaves); 2°; 300 × 220 (*c.* 250 × 170); d.c. of 85 mm (verse); 2 plus 117 = 119 ff. (includes ff. 27bis, 42bis); *c.* 50 lines; collation 1^{16}: 2^{18}: 3^{16}: 4^{18}: 5^{16} (last canc.): 6^{20}: 7^{16}.

Water-marks

(a) An ox-head surmounted by a pole (?), 80 mm long, fixed to chain-lines 40 mm apart. Very like Briquet 14495 (1451).
(b) An anchor surmounted by a cross, between chain-lines 39 mm apart; 62, 65, 78, or 83 mm long (four varieties).
(c) A fleur-de-lys, 60 mm long, fixed to chain-lines 40 mm apart.
(d) As (c), but 62 mm long, between chain-lines 42 mm apart.

Qc previously formed part of the Standish library. The red morocco binding bears the arms of Cardinal Richelieu.

  3. Ff. 32a–c, 33c–d, *Complainte faicte par maistre alain charretier a sa dame.*
     183 lines. Lacks line 174. Lines 1–24, 45–88 and 121–84 are copied on ff. 32a–c. The remaining lines are copied on fol. 33c–d, perhaps in a different hand; lines 89–120 are followed by lines 25–44. Between the two parts of the *Complainte* come short pieces of verse.
  12. Ff. 67a–71a, *La belle dame sans mercy.*
     799 lines. Lacks line 264. Stanza XLII is copied between stanzas LI and LII. Text with headings.

Although *Qc* had been described by Piaget in 1909,[2] he did not include it in his bibliography of the *Belle Dame sans Mercy*. The second part of the *Complainte* is not identified in the catalogue;[3] the text is of poor quality, containing many readings peculiar to itself and numerous irregular lines, and bears some resemblance to those in *Pn* and *Qg*. The text of the *Belle Dame sans Mercy* is of similar quality.

Qd TOULOUSE, BIBL. MUN., 826

Early 15th c.; paper; 2°; 295–300 × 210 (200 × 120); 107 ff.; 34–6 lines (prose), 32 lines (verse); catchwords; collation 1^{16} (first canc.), 2–5^{16}, 6^{12}, 7^{16}; bound in limp parchment.

---

[1] Two such imitations, the *Hospital d'Amours* (ff. 21r–37v) and the *Belle Dame qui eut Mercy* (ff. 61r–68v), are included together with the *Pastourelle de Gransson* (ff. 69r–72v).
[2] A. Piaget, 'Le Songe de la barge', *Romania*, XXXVIII, 1909, 71–110, esp. 76–7.
[3] *Chantilly: Le Cabinet des livres: Manuscrits*, II, Paris, Plon-Nourrit, 1900, 409–14.

(a) An ox-head, 47 mm long, between chain-lines 45 mm apart. Similar to Briquet 14313 (1419–30).

(b) A gloved hand, 44 mm long, between chain-lines 53 mm apart. Similar to Briquet 11084 (1432).

(c) A paschal lamb, in a circle 39 mm in diameter, between chain-lines 50 mm apart. Most like Briquet 39 (1425–35); in 39 the head is more detailed.

1. Ff. 1r–32r, [*Le Quadrilogue Invectif*].
2. Ff. 33r–38v, *Reveille Matin.*
   366 lines. Lacks lines 259, 317.
3. Ff. 39r–51v, *La Belle dame sans mercy.*
   800 lines. Complete.
4. Fol. 52r, *Coppie des lectres envoyees par les dames a Alain.*
5. Ff. 52v–53r, *Coppie de la requeste baillee aux dames contre Alain.*
6. Ff. 53v–57r, *Aux Dames.* (*L'Excusacion aux Dames.*)
   240 plus 4 lines. Complete.
8. Ff. 64r–83r, *Le debat des deux fortunés d'amours.*
   1242 plus 4 lines. Complete. Lines 12–15 and 16–19 are transposed and lines 961–2 and 1193–4 are inverted.
9. Ff. 83v–86v, *Complainte.*
   184 lines. Complete.
10. Ff. 87r–91r, *Le lay de paix.*
    284 lines. Complete.
11. Ff. 92r–100r, *Le Breviaire des nobles.*
    445 plus 8 lines. Lacks line 169.
12. Ff. 100r–104r, *Rondeaulx.*

A. Pres de madame et loing de mon vouloir...	10 lines
B. Comme oseroit la bouche dire...	10 lines
C. Au pouvre prisonner ma dame...	10 lines
D. Ou mon desir s'assouvira...	13 lines
E. Triste plaisir et doloreuse joye...	10 lines
F. Mort sur les piez faingnant d'avoir plaisir...	10 lines
G. Riche d'espoir et pouvre d'autre bien...	10 lines
H. Je n'ay pouoir de vivre en joye...	10 lines
I. Helas ni courtoisie ennemie...	10 lines
J. De quoy me sert le regart de mes yeulx...	10 lines
K. Je vi le temps que je souloye...	10 lines
L. Deshors deshors il vous fault desloyer...	10 lines
M. Cuidez vous qu'il ait assez joye...	10 lines
N. La bonne volenté que j'ay...	10 lines
O. Belle qui si bon cuer avez...	13 lines
P. Puis qu'autre rien ne me puet plaire...	13 lines
Q. Joye me fuit et desespoir me chace...	13 lines

R.	Quant un jour suis sans que je voye...	10 lines
S.	Au feu au feu au feu qui mon cuer art...	13 lines
T.	S'oncques beaux yeulx orent celle puissance...	10 lines
U.	Loyaument et a tousjours (*sic*)	13 lines
V.	Ainsi que bon vous semblera...	13 lines

13. Ff. 104v–106r, *Balades.*

A.	Aucunes gens m'ont huy araisonné...	35 lines
B.	J'ay un arbre de la plante d'amours...	35 lines
C.	J'ay voulentiers oy parler d'amours...	41 lines

A brief mention of Q*d* made in 1885[1] escaped notice; the only critics to refer to Q*d* since then have been Hoffman and White. The manuscript has not been examined before.

Q*d* contains three of the four poems which were edited and was used as base manuscript in two of those editions. The manuscript is written in a rapid cursive hand and has been corrected by the scribe; while he normally scored out errors, the scribe occasionally put a dot under a letter which is to be ignored.[2] In interpreting Q*d*, it is important to pay attention to the *ductus* of the hand: *e* and *o* can be written in a very similar fashion;[3] *c* and *t* can easily be confused, as can *s* and *f*, especially when they are combined. The distinction between *n* and *u* is not made in a regular way, and the divisions between words are not indicated clearly or consistently. The texts contain a number of abbreviations; *voustre* is written thus in BD 91 and 141.

The poems in Q*d* contain a large number of small errors; some are unimportant but others make lines irregular. Two readings in the *Breviaire des Nobles*, at lines 95 and 315, suggest that the text may be contaminated. Although Q*d* has been copied carelessly and has not been fully revised, it is one of the two best collected manuscripts of Alain Chartier's poetical works.

Q*e* +VALENCIENNES, BIBL. MUN., 417

15th c.; paper; 276 × 196; 133 ff.; 23–5 lines.

Q*e* was formerly in the library of the Croy family.

1. Ff. 2r–12r, *Le breviaire des nobles.*[4]

> 445 = 446 plus 6 lines. Lacks lines 107, 152, 194. Ballade IV has an envoy of 4 lines, as has Ballade X.[5]

[1] P. Meyer, 'Chronique', *Romania*, XIV, 1885, 632.
[2] See the notes to BD 249, 251, 355 and 729.
[3] See the notes to BD 262 and 702.
[4] The rubric is written in large letters vertically from the bottom to the top of the page; the poem begins on folio 3r.
[5]
> (Fol. 5r) Nobles hommes tenés en plus grant compte
> Pour vostre honneur noblement maintenir
> Car c'est le bien qui les aultres seurmonte
> Affin que paix puissés entretenir.
>
> (Fol. 9r) Par necte plaisant coinctise
> D'ordure se contregarde
> Et maintient tousjours franchise
> Cellui ou tous prennent garde.

7. Ff. 125r–133v, *Le debat de reveille mattin.*[1]
   360 lines. Lacks lines 17–24. Text with headings.

The imitation of the *Belle Dame sans Mercy* in Qe was listed by Piaget. The manuscript was mentioned by Champion, and included by Rice in his bibliography of the *Breviaire des Nobles*. The text of the *Debat de Reveille Matin* in Qe closely resembles those in Qr and, to a lesser extent, Qq; although it is generally regular, it contains a number of readings peculiar to itself. Irregular lines and poor rhymes are quite frequent in the *Breviaire des Nobles* which, as has been mentioned, contains extra lines.

Qf BIBLIOTHEEK ARNHEM, 79

c. 1480; paper; 2°; 290 × 220 (*c.* 220 × 90); 1 plus 69 plus 1 ff.; 32 lines (4 stanzas); collation A⁷(3): 1¹⁶ (first two canc.): 2¹⁰: 3¹⁴: 4¹²: 5⁸ (last canc.): 6¹⁰; ink drawing before item 1.

Water-marks

(a) A coat of arms (1 and 4, a fleur-de-lys; 2 and 3, a dolphin) 40 mm long; chain-lines 37 mm apart.

(b) A forked 'P', 48 mm long, between chain-lines 40 mm apart. Most like Briquet 8531–5 (1481–1511).

(c) An ox-head surmounted by a stalk, 68 mm long, between chain-lines 35 mm apart. Very like Briquet 14237 (1470–4).

(d) The arms of France, crowned, with a 't' at the point of the shield; 85 mm long over-all, chain-lines 38 mm apart. Very like Briquet 1741 (1468–82).

(e) A forked 'P', 59 mm long, between chain-lines 37 mm apart.

(f) A mermaid, between chain-lines 38 mm apart. Very similar to Briquet 13859 (1468–76), except that the chain-lines go in a different direction.

(g) A unicorn, 95 or 100 mm long, across chain-lines 36 mm apart (two varieties). Briquet 10028 (1478–82) and 10026 (1477–8).

(h) A 'Y' surmounted by a cross, its tail ending in a trefoil; 67 or 72 mm long, between chain-lines 37 mm apart (two varieties). Very like Briquet 9183 (1472–6).

Qf is bound in a charter dated 1476. On the outside covers and on the fly-leaves there appear the following inscriptions in fifteenth-century hands: 'Hauweell'; 'Iste liber pertinet florencio hauweel'; 'Pignewe(a?)rt'; 'Charlot de cherysy'. The catalogue number 104 is also found.

Qf is in several hands.

1. Ff. 3r–15r (quire 1),[2] *S'ensieult la belle dame sans mercy.*
   Fol. 15r, *Explicit la belle dame sans mercy.*
     800 lines. Complete. Text with headings.
4. Fol. 41r (begins quire 4), *L'excusacion de maistre alain.*
   Fol. 44v, *Explicit l'excusacion de maistre alain.*
     240 plus 4 lines. Complete.

---

[1] The rubric is written in large letters vertically from the bottom to the top of the page; the poem begins on folio 126r.

[2] Several short poems of no great interest have been copied on ff. 15v–16v which were originally blank.

6. Fol. 47r, [*Resveille Matin*]. Title added in a contemporary hand.
   Fol. 52v (ends quire 4), *Explicit resveille matin*.
   360 lines. Lacks lines 17–24.

Q*f* has not been listed or examined before. For knowledge of its existence, I am indebted to the Institut de Recherche et d'Histoire des Textes. Q*f* closely resembles *Pn* in its text of the *Debat de Reveille Matin*; it contains as many individual readings as *Pn* but fewer irregular lines. The texts of the *Belle Dame sans Mercy* and the *Excusacion aux Dames* are generally regular and of quite good quality.

Q*g*   BRUSSELS, BIBL. ROYALE, 10961–70

Late 15th c.; paper; 2°; 280 × 200 (190 × 110 [quires 1–11, 13–17]: 185 × 115 [quire 12]: 170 × 135 [quires 18–22]); 1 plus 227 ff.; 25 lines (quires 1–17): *c*. 30 lines (quires 18–22); collation 1–8^{10}: 9–11^{10}, 12^{14}, 13^{10} (first three canc.: blank leaves of more modern paper stuck to second and third cancels form ff. 125–6): 14–15^{10}: 16–17^{10}: 18^{12} (first canc.), 19–21^{12}, 22^{8} (last canc.); space for miniatures and initials (quires 1–17); flourished initial, coloured initials (quires 18–22); eighteenth-century binding bearing the arms of France.

Water-marks

(a) A unicorn, 95 or 100 mm long over-all, across chain-lines 36 or 38 mm apart (two varieties). Very similar to Briquet 10019 and 10021 (1459–70).

(b) (Quire 12) A coat of arms, surmounted by a crown and fleuron, with a 'c' or 't' at the point of the shield; 80 mm long over-all, across chain-lines 25 mm apart. The shield is indistinct.

(c) (Quires 18–22) A 'P' with a forked tail, surmounted by a fleuron, 60 mm long, between chain-lines 23 mm apart. Most like Briquet 8627 (1491–1504).

The manuscript was removed to the Bibliothèque du Roi in Paris after the Peace of Brussels in 1746, and was rebound there before being returned in 1770. Q*g* is made up of two originally separate manuscripts. The second part (MS 10970: quires 18–22) differs from the first in paper, hand, layout and decoration. In the first part, quires 1–11 and 13–17 are in one hand; quire 12 is in a later hand and is differently laid out, as the description of item 5 will indicate.

MS 10970 belonged to Olivier de la Marche whose signature and device 'Tant a souffert' are on fol. 227r.

On the front fly-leaf there are earlier press-marks: 'du premier pepitre le ij^e' (late fifteenth or early sixteenth c.); 807; and 86. Another is illegible.

Q*g* (MSS 10961–9) has been described as an early sixteenth-century manuscript by L. Mourin.[1] The hand and such evidence as is given by the water-marks suggest rather that it was copied towards the end of the fifteenth century. Mourin stated that the manuscript was among those listed in the inventory of the belongings of Margaret of Austria drawn up in 1523. Although no trace of it has been found in that inventory,[2]

---

[1] L. Mourin, 'Le Débat des deux grands amis', *Scriptorium*, I, 1946–7, 151–4.

[2] [V.] Michelant, 'Inventaire des vaisselles...manuscrits etc., de Marguerite d'Autriche...Malines le 9 juillet 1523', *Compte rendu...Commission Royale d'Histoire*, 3e Série, XII, 1871, 5–78.

the early press-mark on the fly-leaf may indicate that the manuscript once formed part of her library.

1. (10961) Fol. 1r, [*Le Livre des Quatre Dames*].
   Fol. 72v, *Explicit le livre des quatre dames.*
   > 3525 lines. Lacks lines 495, 565, 891, 1180, 1226, 3464.
2. (10962) Ff. 73r–80r, [*Le Debat de Reveille Matin*].
   > 360 lines. Lacks lines 17–24.
3. Fol. 80v (ends quire 8), *Ballades.*[1] (*Rondeaux.*)
   Incipit: Cuidez vous qu'il ait assez joye...   10 lines
   Incipit: La bonne voulenté que j'ay...   10 lines
5. (10965) Ff. 112v–133v (ends quire 13), [*La Belle Dame sans Mercy*].
   > 100 stanzas. Lacks lines 484–7, for which space has been left, and line 685. Lines 488–528 are repeated.[2]
7. (10967) Fol. 141v, [*La Complainte*].
   Fol. 145r, *Cy fine la complainte Maistre Alain chartier, a cause de sa dame etc.*
   > 183 lines. Lacks line 155.

The imitations of the *Belle Dame sans Mercy* in Qg were discussed by Piaget, who also included Qg in his bibliography of the poem itself. Kussmann examined Qg in his study of the *Livre des Quatre Dames*. Variants from Qg were included by Pagès in his edition of the *Belle Dame sans Mercy*, published in 1936.

The text of the *Debat de Reveille Matin* in Qg contains a number of irregular lines and faulty rhymes; it has some similarity to those in Qe and Qr. Where the *Complainte* is concerned, Qg again resembles Qr (and Gh) but is more closely linked with Qc and, above all, Pn; the text in Qg contains a number of irregular readings peculiar to itself. Qg's text of the *Belle Dame sans Mercy* also includes irregular lines together with some poor rhymes.

Qh   +COPENHAGEN, ROYAL LIBRARY, NY KGL. SAML. 1768.2°

Late 15th c.; paper and parchment (sheet 1/–);[3] 2°; 308 ff.; 30–2 lines; decorated border, space for miniature at beginning of first item.

The manuscript is in at least three different hands. In layout it closely resembles Pb and Qk, to which it is related textually. Medium-sized works (e.g. item 1) are each copied on a quire of paper and one or two sides may be left blank at the beginning or end of the

---

[1] Mourin listed only the first rondeau.

[2] The poem is copied partly in quire 12 (ff. 111–24), partly in quire 13 (ff. 127–33). (Ff. 125–6 are blank and of more modern paper, and can be disregarded.) Quire 12 ends with line 528 and quire 13 begins with line 488, so that 41 lines are repeated.

> The unusual make-up of quire 13 has already been mentioned, as has the fact that quire 12 is larger than, and in a different hand from, the other quires of Qg. Quire 12 seems to replace an earlier quire. The first three leaves of quire 13 were cut out, having been replaced by the last leaves of the new quire 12. The fourth (fol. 127), containing lines 488–531, could not be removed without leaving a gap in the text. Fol. 127 is torn and the first words of some lines have been lost.

[3] A parchment leaf, conjoint with fol. 1 and following fol. 15, appears to have been lost.

quire.[1] Short works are copied together in a single quire; this is the case with items 5 to 8 and explains the title of item 5. Items 18 and 20, both long works, each occupy several quires.

Qh was formerly Barrois MS 355 in the library of the fourth Earl of Ashburnham.[2]

1. Ff. 1r–15v, *Cy commence la belle dame sans mercy.*
   763 lines. Lacks lines 285, 765–800.[3] Text with headings.

5. Fol. 48r, *Cy commence la complaincte maistre alain charretier et la responce baillee aux dames.*
   Fol. 50v, *Explicit la complaincte.*
   180 lines. Lacks lines 26, 103, 114, 146.

6. Fol. 51r, *Coppie des lectres envoyees par les dames a maistre alain.*

7. Ff. 51v–52r, *Coppie de la requeste baillee aux dames.*

8. Ff. 52v–55v, *Responce Sur ladicte Requeste par l'acteur baillee aux dames.*
   240 lines. Complete.

11. Ff. 88r–93r, *Cy commence le lay de paix fait par maistre Alain chartier.*
    276 = 277 lines. Lacks lines 11–14, 87, 168, 237. Lines 67–8 are inverted; lines 102–3 written as one line.

12. Fol. 95r, *Cy commence le lay de plaisance.*
    Fol. 98r, *Cy fine le lay de plaisance.*
    186 = 188 lines. Lacks lines 21, 38, 54, 58, 63, 114–16. Lines 82–3 are inverted; lines 51–2 and 61–2 written as one line.

13. Ff. 99r–118r, *Cy conmance le debat des deux fortunés d'amours.*
    1230 lines. Lacks lines 26, 97–100, 255, 292, 507, 539, 635, 653, 909. Lines 939–40 and part of line 941 are copied a second time between lines 969 and 970.

18. Fol. 188r, *Cy commencent les quatre dames Nommeez le Joieulx de espoir.*
    Fol. 250r, *Cy fine le livre des quatre dames aultrement nommé le Joyeulx de espoir.*
    3507 lines. Lacks lines 30, 239, 760, 888, 1197, 1220(?), 1632, 1953, 2025, 2069, 2305, 2324, 2328, 2356, 2406, 2522, 2579–82, 2665, 3067, 3086, 3255.

19. Fol. 252r, *Cy commence le Curial fait par maistre Alain chartier lequel il envoya a ung sien Compaignon qui avoit voulenté de venir a court.*
    Fol. 260v, *Explicit le Curial de maistre Alain chartier en son vivant notaire et secretaire du roy Charles vij.ᵉ de ce nom (Quand le miliau coroit M. CCCC Et quarente cinq.* Added in a later hand).

20. Fol. 261r, *C'est le quadrilogue fait par maistre Alain Chartier.*
    Fol. 308r, *Explicit le quadrilogue.*

Qh was not among the manuscripts containing imitations of the *Belle Dame sans Mercy* which were discussed by Piaget. Kussmann listed *Qh* in his bibliography of the *Livre des Quatre Dames*, giving its number in the Ashburnham sale catalogue (No. 103), since he was unable to trace it. *Qh* was described in the bibliography of the *Debat des Deux Fortunés d'Amours* as Copenhagen, Bibl. Royale (anc. Harrassowitz Cat. 341: 936).

[1] Some of these leaves have been used in order to add poems to the manuscript at a later date; these additional works have been disregarded in numbering the items.
[2] *Catalogue of the Manuscripts at Ashburnham Place*, II, London, Hodgson, n.d.
[3] See p. 126, n. 3.

It is doubtful whether Droz and Piaget realised that it was the Ashburnham MS; indeed, in his list of manuscripts containing the *Belle Dame sans Mercy*, Piaget referred to Q*h* by its Ashburnham sale number.

The manuscript has not been used or examined before. It contains three of the four poems which were edited and was found to resemble *Pb* and *Qk*. An assessment of the quality of Q*h* is given in the description of *Pb*.

Q*j* FRIBOURG (*Switzerland*), DIESBACH MS[1]

Mid 15th c.; paper; 212 × 146; 196 ff.

The volume, which is in two hands, seems to be composed of two originally separate manuscripts. The first twenty-two leaves have been lost, together with fol. 150; other leaves, which had been missing, have been replaced.[2]

Q*j* has not been traced.

1. Fol. 23r, [*Lettre envoyée par les dames à Alain Chartier*].
   Fol. 24v, *Explicit la lectre des dames envoyee a meistre* (sic) *Allain*.
   9 stanzas of 8 lines, followed by 1 stanza of 6 lines.
2. Fol. 24v, *Cy appres s'ensuit l'excusacion faicte par ledit maistre Alain sur ces presentes*.
   Fol. 29v, *Explicit l'excusacion de maistre Alain*.
4. Fol. 42r, [*Le Debat de Reveille Matin*].
   Fol. 44r, *Cy finist Resveille matin. Deo gratias*.
   Stanzas I–XXX are missing.
18. Ff. 109r–196v, *Cy appres s'ensuivent les complaintes deis* (sic) *quatre dames qui perdiront leurs amis et commence l'acteur*.

The imitations of the *Belle Dame sans Mercy* in Q*j* were listed and discussed by Piaget.

Q*k* THE HAGUE, ROYAL LIBRARY, 71 E 49

Late 15th c.; paper and parchment (sheet 9/22); 2°; 285 × 195 (c. 195 × 100); 340 plus 2 ff., also numbered in Roman to 361 (with errors);[3] 28–32 lines; collation 1^{10} (first stuck down, third canc.): 2^{14}: 3^6: 4^{10}: 5^{10}: 6^{16}: 7^{16}: 8^{24}: 9^{14}: 10^{10}: 11^6: 12^4: 13^6: 14^6: 15–16^{10}: 17–21^{12}, 22^4: 23^{10}: 24^{16}, 25^{14}: 26^{10}: 27^{10}: 28^{12}: 29^{12}: 30^{16}: 31^6: B^2; catchwords in items copied in more than one quire; miniature, decorated and coloured initials; contemporary table of contents, drawn up by 'Bodin';[4] coat of arms.

Q*k* was formerly 'Ex Bibliotheca G. J. Gerard, 1761' (fol. 9). Two other catalogue numbers can be read: '7. p. A premier' (fol. 1r); and '753' (fol. 9). The arms are those of Claude de Toulongeon, seigneur de la Bastie et de Senecey, husband of Guillemette

---

[1] This description is based on that of A. Piaget in *Romania*, XXXIV, 1905, 597–602.

[2] 'Les cent dix-huit premiers feuillets, le titre du *Livre des quatre dames* et les feuillets 146, 156, 169, 170, 187–91, qui manquaient au poème d'Alain Chartier et qui ont été ajoutés après coup, semblent avoir été copiés à Fribourg même. Le *Livre des quatre dames*, sauf le titre et les feuillets remplacés, est d'une autre main et semble avoir été copié en France' (Piaget, *op. cit.*, 602).

[3] A later pagination (1–650) begins at fol. 9 and continues to the end, omitting ff. 22–8.

[4] *Eb* was copied by 'Bodin'.

de Vergy: the arms of Vergy are painted in the second quarter. Toulongeon and his wife appeared together in a law-suit in 1476; Guillemette was still alive in 1504.[1]

Water-marks

(a) The arms of France crowned, 55, 60 or 62 mm long, fixed to chain-lines 39 mm apart (three varieties). Most like Briquet 1685 (1471–80) or 1697 (1472).

(b) A fleur-de-lys, 43 mm long, between sewn chain-lines 38 mm apart. Most like Briquet 6921 (1485–6).

1. Ff. 9r–21v (quire 2), [*La Belle Dame sans Mercy*].
   Fol. 21v, *Explicit la belle dame Sans mercy.*
   800 lines. Complete. Text with headings.

3. Ff. 39r–41v (begins quire 5), *Cy commancent les complaintes Et regretz maistre alain chartier et la responce baillee aux dames.*[2] (*La Complainte.*)
   180 lines. Lacks lines 26, 103, 114, 157.

4. Ff. 42r–v, *Coppie des lectres envoyees Par les dames a maistre Alain chartier.*

5. Ff. 42v–43v, *Coppie de la requeste baillee Aux dames.*

6. Ff. 43v–47v (ends quire 5), *Responce sur ladicte requeste Par l'acteur baillee aux dames.*
   240 lines. Complete.

9. Ff. 81r–103v (quire 8), *Cy commence le debat des deux fortunez d'amours.*[3]
   1235 lines. Lacks lines 97–100, 635, 653, 909.

11. Ff. 119r–127v (quire 10), *Cy commance le breviaire des nobles.*
    Fol. 127v, *Explicit le breviaire des nobles.*
    418 lines. Lacks lines 73–84, 107, 135–6, 151, 270–9, 336, 389.

12. Ff. 129r–134r (quire 11), *Cy commence le lay de paix fait par maistre alain chartier.*
    Fol. 134r, *Explicit le lay de paix.*
    276 = 277 lines. Lacks lines 11–14, 87, 168, 237. Lines 67–8 are inverted; lines 102–3 written as one line.

13. Ff. 135r–138v (quire 12), *Cy conmance le lay de plaisance.*
    Fol. 138v, *Cy fine le lay de plaisance.*
    188 = 190 lines. Lacks lines 38, 54, 63, 114–16. Lines 82–3 are inverted. Lines 51–2 and 61–2 are written as one line.

15. Ff. 145r–150v (quire 14), [*Le Debat de Reveille Matin*].
    Fol. 150v, *Explicit le debat du Reveille Matin.*
    367 lines. Lacks line 56. Lines 76–7 and 316–17 are inverted.

17. Ff. 171r–233v (quires 17–22), [*Le Livre des Quatre Dames*].
    Fol. 233v, *Explicit le livre des quatre dames Aultrement nommé le joyeulx de espoir.*[4]
    3515 lines. Lacks lines 760, 1953, 2025, 2216, 2291, 2305, 2324, 2334, 2522, 2579–82, 3086, 3299, 3464.

[1] Anselme, II, 870D; VII, 36D. Claude de Toulongeon also owned Paris, Bibl. Nat., f. fr. 1281 (Delisle, *Le Cabinet des manuscrits*, II, 418).
   Identification of the arms was made by Mme Pecqueur of the Institut de Recherche et d'Histoire des Textes.
[2] The title of item 3 is explained by the fact that items 3 to 6 are all copied in quire 5.
[3] 'Le debat des deux fortunés d'amours dit le gras et le maigre' (table of contents).
[4] 'Le debat des quatre dames' (table of contents).

18. Ff. 235r–244v (quire 23), [*Le Curial*].

    Fol. 244v, *Explicit le curial de maistre Alain chartier en son vivant notaire et secretaire du roy Charles vij^e de ce nom.*

The imitations of the *Belle Dame sans Mercy* in *Qk* were listed and discussed by Piaget, and its text of the *Livre des Quatre Dames* was examined by Kussmann. *Qk* was included in the bibliographies of the *Debat des Deux Fortunés d'Amours* and of the *Belle Dame sans Mercy*. The manuscript contains the four poems which were edited and was found to be closely related to *Pb* and *Qh*. An assessment of the quality of *Qk* is given in the description of *Pb*.

        Ql +LENINGRAD, SALTIKOV-SHCHEDRIN LIBRARY, FR. F. V.XIV.7[1]

15th c.; parchment; 178 ff.; 28 lines; contemporary table of contents.

    Ql formed part of the library of Peter Dubrovsky.

    1. Fol. 3r, *Le proces des quatre dames.*[2]
        Fol. 65v, *Explicit les iiij dames.*
        3530 lines. Lacks line 3464.
    2. Fol. 66r, *La Complainte maistre alain de la mort de sa dame.*
        Fol. 69r, *Explicit la complainte maistre alain.*
        183 lines. Lacks lines 117, 147. Includes line 119a. Lines 34–5 and 177–8 are inverted. The order of stanzas is: I–IV, VII, V–VI, VIII, X, IX, XI–XII.
    3. Fol. 69v, *La Belle dame sans mercy.*
        Fol. 85v, *Explicit le livre de la belle dame sans mercy.*
        800 lines. Complete.
    4. Ff. 85v–86v, *Coppie de la requeste faicte et baillee aux dames contre maistre alain.*[3]
    5. Ff. 86v–87r, *Coppie des lectres envoyees par les dames A maistre alain.*
    6. Ff. 87r–92r, *S'ensuit l'excusacion maistre alain aux dames.*
        240 lines. Complete.
    12. Ff. 144v–152v, *Le Breviaire des Nobles.*
        446 lines. Complete. The ballades have no headings.
    15. Fol. 169r, [*Le Debat de Reveille Matin*].
        Fol. 176r, *Explicit reveille matin.*
        368 lines. Complete.

Piaget listed and discussed the imitations of the *Belle Dame sans Mercy* in *Ql*, and included the manuscript in his bibliography of the poem itself. *Ql* closely resembles *Pc* (and *Gf*), but is more individual and contains some irregular lines. The readings given by *Ql* complement those in *Pc* and it is for that reason that *Ql* has been used in this edition of the poetical works.

    Ql is written in a clear and legible cursive hand. The texts contain some corrections in the hand of the scribe and a few in a second hand, *Ql*[2]. The manuscript includes some

---

[1] I.e. French Folio Vellum. For a description of *Ql*, previously numbered 565, see Comte A. de Laborde, *Les Principaux Manuscrits à peintures conservés dans l'ancienne bibliothèque impériale publique de Saint Pétersbourg*, II, Paris, 1938, 140–1.
[2] 'Le debat...' (table of contents).
[3] 'Les lettres de l'impetracion contre maistre alain' (table of contents).

north-eastern forms, for example *s'efforchoit* (BD 89), *s'enlachoit* (BD 94), *calenge* (BD 205). *Gf* and *Pc* contain similar forms.

Some parts of *Ql* are wrinkled and faded, and are difficult to read. Elsewhere the parchment is thin or absorbent and lines from the other side of the leaf may show through. The *Debat de Reveille Matin* and parts of the *Belle Dame sans Mercy* and the *Livre des Quatre Dames* are affected above all; the variants given from *Ql* in the editions of those poems may not be entirely correct.

Qm LONDON, BRIT. MUS., ROYAL 19 A iii

Late 15th c.; paper and parchment (sheet 1/16); 2°; 285 × 200 (*c.* 200 × 90); 83 ff.; *c.* 24 lines; collation 1^{16} (sheet lost); 2^{12}: 3^{14} (last canc.): 4^{10} (last lost): 5^6: 6^{12}: 7^8: 8^7(7).

Water-marks

(a) A 'Y', surmounted by a cross, the tail ending in a trefoil, 67 mm long, between chain-lines 38 mm apart. Briquet 9183 (1472–6).

(b) The arms of France, crowned, 60 mm long, fixed to chain-lines 39 mm apart. Like Briquet 1685 (1471–80).

(c) A mark similar to (b), but 55 mm long and with a bar across the shield; it is fixed to chain-lines 39 mm apart.

(d) A barred 'P' with a forked tail, surmounted by a fleuron, 60 mm long, between chain-lines 39 mm apart. Most like Briquet 8666 (1466–83).

(e) A dog, with head turned back, 45 mm over-all, between chain-lines 40 mm apart.

(f) A unicorn, 100 mm over-all, between chain-lines 42 mm apart. Briquet 10025 (1474–8).

1. Ff. 1r–15v (quire 1), [*La Belle Dame sans Mercy*].
   704 lines. Lines 129–76 and 657–704 are missing as the result of the loss of a sheet of paper from quire 1. Text with headings.

4. Ff. 42r–50v (quire 4), [*Le Breviaire des Nobles*].
   399 lines. Lacks lines 89, 178, 244–54, 315–17, 378, 417–46 (last leaf of quire lost).

An imitation of the *Belle Dame sans Mercy* in *Qm* was listed and discussed by Piaget.[1] *Qm* was included in the bibliographies of the *Belle Dame sans Mercy* and the *Breviaire des Nobles*. Neither text is complete and both contain a number of irregular lines and poor rhymes.

Qn LONDON, CLUMBER SALE (SOTHEBY'S, 6.XII.1937), 941

c. 1490; parchment; 311 × 210; 136 ff.; d.c.; 43 lines; miniatures, decorated borders, coloured initials, headings in red.

The manuscript was made for a lady whose initials AA, joined by a widow's girdle, appear in the borders. Sotheby's sale catalogue[2] identifies her with Anne de Beaujeu,

---

[1] Piaget gave, in error, the press-mark Royal A XIII.

[2] *The Clumber Library: Catalogue... Third Portion*, London, Sotheby and Co., 1937 (sale, 6 December), 231–2, lot 941. The description includes an account of the manuscript's provenance. Ff. 18r (in colour), 122v, and part of ff. 86r and 112r are reproduced.

This description is based on the catalogue. Use has also been made of the description in G. de

daughter of Louis XI and wife of Pierre de Bourbon, Dauphin d'Auvergne. In the eighteenth century the manuscript formed part of the libraries of Louis-Jean Gaignat and the Duc de la Vallière. At the sale in 1937 Maggs Brothers bought it on behalf of a M. Burrus of Strasbourg. Its present whereabouts are unknown.

1. Fol. 1, *Le Quadrilogue Invectif.*
2. Fol. 18, *Les Complaintes des Quatre Dames.*
3. Fol. 39, *Le Lay de Paix.*
4. Fol. 41, *Le Curial,* in prose and verse.[1]
[4a. *Le Breviaire des Nobles.*][2]
6. Fol. 91, *Reveille-matin.*
7. Fol. 93, *Lay fait le premier jour de l'an.*[3]
8. Fol. 94v, *La Belle Dame sans Mercy.*
9. Fol. 99v, *Coppie de la Requeste baillee aux dames contre l'acteur; Lettres envoyees par les dames a l'acteur,* in prose.
10. Fol. 100v, *Excusation envoyee aux dames par l'auteur.*
12. Fol. 104v, *Le Debat des Deux Fortunés d'Amour.*
13. Fol. 112, *Complainte de l'Amant contre la Mort,* followed by three rondeaux.

The last leaves of the manuscript contain a collection of ballades and rondeaux. *Qn* has not been listed before.

Qo +MILAN, BIBL. TRIVULZIANA, 971

15th c.; 47 ff.; 33 lines; d.c.; catchwords.

1. Fol. 1a, [*La Belle Dame sans Mercy*].
   Fol. 7b, *Cy finist la Belle dame sans mercy.*
   800 lines. Complete. Text with headings.
2. Fol. 7b, *Cy apres s'ensuit la response de la Belle dame sans mercy.*
   Fol. 9b, *Cy finist la response que fist Maistre Alain Charretier dessus la belle dame sans Mercy.*
   240 lines. Complete. Text with headings.
3. Fol. 9c, *Cy apres s'ensuit le lay de Paix que fist Maistre Alain Charretier.*
   Fol. 11c, *Cy finist le lay de paix qui fut envoyé au duc de bourgogne.*
   283 lines. Lacks lines 155, 212. Includes line 156a. Lines 164–5 and 225–6 are inverted.
4. Fol. 11d, *Cy apres s'ensuit ung lay de plaisance.*
   Fol. 13a, *Cy finist le lay de plaisance.*
   195 lines. Lacks line 38. Lines 1–2 are inverted.

Bure, fils aîné, *Catalogue des livres de la bibliothèque de feu M. le duc de la Vallière, Première Partie,* II, Paris, de Bure, 1783, No. 2790.

[1] According to Bure, the *Livre de l'Esperance* and the *Curial* are here combined as they are in the early collected editions.
[2] Included by Bure as item 5, but not mentioned in the sale catalogue.
[3] Probably a text of the *Lay de Plaisance,* so called in *Qq.*

5. Fol. 13b, *Complainte pour la mort de sa dame Maistre Alain Charretier*.
   Fol. 14c, *Cy finist la Complainte*.
   > 184 lines. Lacks line 117. Includes line 119a. The order of stanzas is: I–III, V–VII, IV, VIII–XII.

6. Ff. 14c–16c, *Cy apres s'ensuit le Breviere des Nobles M. A. Charretier*.
   > Only the first seven ballades (lines 1–221) are copied, the rest of fol. 16v being blank. Line 15 is lacking and space has been left. The third and fifth ballades are entitled *Justice* and *Raison* respectively. Each envoy has the heading *Prince*.

7. Ff. 17a–33a, *Cy apres s'ensuit le livre des quatre dames M. A. Charretier*.
   > The text stops at line 2132. The last sixteen lines, those on fol. 33a, seem to be in a different hand; ff. 33v–34v are blank. Lacks lines 8, 707, 1596, 1738, 1829. Lines 641–3, originally omitted, have been added in a different hand.

8. Fol. 35a, *Cy commence le Resveille matin*.
   Fol. 37c, *Explicit le Resveille matin*.
   > 352 lines. Lacks lines 17–24 and 361–8.

The imitations of the *Belle Dame sans Mercy* in Qo were listed and discussed by Piaget who also included Qo in his bibliography of the poem. Qo, which has not been examined in detail before, was used in the edition of the four poems. In three of them it was found to be in the same tradition as Nj and, particularly, Nf; in the case of the *Debat de Reveille Matin*, Qo resembled Oa and Qq. Nf and Nj (and Oa) were preferred to Qo which includes a large number of individual readings. Qo contains a valuable series of attributions.

Qp   TURIN, BIBL. NAZ. UNIV., L.II.12

16th c.; parchment; 174 ff.

Qp was badly damaged by fire in 1904 and has not yet been restored.[1] In a note on Qp, A. Piaget stated that the manuscript, like Ok, had been copied from the collected edition published by Galiot du Pré in 1526.[2] Qp resembles the early printed editions in the works which it contains, in their order and in the titles given to them. The *Debat des Deux Fortunés d'Amours*, here item 22, was first printed as part of a complete edition by Du Pré in 1526.

1. Fol. 1, *Le Curial de Maistre Alain Charretier*.[3]
2. Fol. 60, *Le Quadrilogue*.
4. Fol. 86, *Libelle de Paix*.
5. Fol. 88, *Le Breviaire des Nobles*.
6. Fol. 91 pag. 2, *Le livre de reveil le matin* (sic).
7. Fol. 94, *La Dame sans mercy*.

---

[1] A letter from the director of the library, dated April 1961, stated that the manuscript could not be microfilmed for that reason.
   See J. Pasinus, *Codices manuscripti bibliothecae regii taurinensis athenaei*, II, Taurini, Ex typ. regia, 1749, 473–4. In the description the manuscript is said to be of the fifteenth century.

[2] A. Piaget, *Romania*, XXX, 1901, 45, n. 2. Piaget did not enlarge on his statement.

[3] The *Livre de l'Esperance* and the *Curial* are frequently combined under this title in the printed editions.

8. Fol. 100, *Complaincte et supplication envoyee aux Dames par les poursuivans et loyaulx Serviteurs de la Court amoureuse du Dieu d'amours.*[1]
9. Fol. 106, *Le livre des quatres (sic) Dames compilé et faict par Maistre Alain l'an M.CCCC.XXXIII.*
14. Fol. 147, *Complaincte tres pieteuse (sic).*
18. Fol. 154, *Lay de Plaisance.*
22. Fol. 165, *Le debat du gras et du meigre.*

The imitations of the *Belle Dame sans Mercy* in Qp were listed and discussed by Piaget. Qp was also included in the bibliographies of the *Debat des Deux Fortunés d'Amours* and the *Belle Dame sans Mercy.*

Qq   +VATICAN, VAT. LAT. 4794

Mid 15th c.; paper; 300 × 210; 217 ff.; 32 lines; contemporary table of contents.

An inscription on fol. 216v reads: 'Ce livre est A m^e Bertran b(l?)...secretaire du roy qui l'achata A paris Au palays le vandredi cinq jour d'octobre M cccc lxiiij'. Maistre Bertran has not been identified; his surname has been erased.

1. Fol. 1r, [*La Belle Dame sans Mercy*].
   Fol. 13r, *Explicit la belle dame sans mercy.*
   803 = 800 lines. Stanza LXXVIII is misplaced and follows stanza LXXX. Three lines are repeated: line 171 between 178 and 179; 577 between 640 and 641; 707 between 714 and 715.
2. Ff. 13v–14r, [*La Requeste Baillee aux Dames contre Alain*].
3. Ff. 14r–v, [*Les Lettres des Dames a Alain*].
4. Ff. 15r–18v, [*L'Excusacion aux Dames*].
   240 = 238 lines. Lacks lines 1 and 17. Lines 5 and 14 are repeated. The stanzas are in the order: I–X, XII–XIII, XI, XIV–XX, XXV–XXVIII, XXI–XXIV, XXIX–XXX. Between stanzas XIV and XV is the heading 'Responce'.
5. Fol. 19r, [*Le Debat de Reveille Matin*].
   Fol. 24v, *Explicit le debat resveille matin.*
   359 lines. Lacks lines 1, 17–24.
10. Fol. 79r, [*Le Breviaire des Nobles*].
    Fol. 86r, *Explicit le breviaire des nobles.*
    431 lines. Lacks lines 1, 89, 126, 211, 230, 257, 315–17, 328–9, 340, 380, 392, 401.
11. Fol. 87r, [*La Complainte*].
    Fol. 89v, *Explicit le lay contre la mort.*
    182 lines. Lacks lines 1, 139.

---

[1] According to Piaget (*Romania*, XXXIII, 1904, 200–6), this item includes the *Belle Dame qui eut Mercy*. That poem precedes the *Livre des Quatre Dames* in the printed editions. Since the heading of this item in Qp is almost identical with that of one of the prose letters in Xa (q.v.), it is possible that item 8 comprises the two prose letters and the *Excusacion* in addition to the *Belle Dame qui eut Mercy*. In the collected editions these four works are printed between the *Belle Dame sans Mercy* and the *Livre des Quatre Dames*.

12. Fol. 90r, [*Le Lay de Plaisance*].

    Fol. 92v, *Explicit le lay fait le premier jour de l'an.*

    183 lines. Lacks lines 1, 6, 10, 73, 85, 92–5, 112, 150, 170, 193.

13. Fol. 93r, [*Le Lay de Paix*].

    Fol. 96v, *Explicit le lay de paix.*

    266 = 267 lines. Lacks lines 1, 11, 15, 44, 52–3, 56, 80, 89, 121, 143, 155, 169–70, 196, 227, 248, 257, 283. Includes lines 156a, 273a. Lines 63–4, 87–8 and 271–2 are inverted. Lines 94 and 101 have been transposed and lines 161–3 written as two lines.

14. Fol. 97r, [*Le Debat des Deux Fortunés d'Amours*].

    Fol. 115v, *Explicit le gras et le maigre.*

    1233 plus 4 lines. Lacks lines 443–4, 495, 624, 635, 653, 820, 1021, 1177.

15. Fol. 117r, [*Le Livre des Quatre Dames*].

    Fol. 166v, *Explicit les quatre dames.*

    3284 lines. 247 lines are omitted, including lines 1962–2133.

16. Ff. 167r–216v, *C'est le quadrilogue Maistre Alain Chartier.*[1]

The imitations of the *Belle Dame sans Mercy* in Qq were discussed by Piaget. The manuscript was also included in the bibliographies of the *Livre des Quatre Dames*, the *Debat des Deux Fortunés d'Amours*, the *Belle Dame sans Mercy* and the *Breviaire des Nobles*.

Qq was used in the edition of the four poems and was found to be individual and irregular. Only one of the texts in Qq is complete. In its text of the *Debat de Reveille Matin*, Qq resembles Oa and Qo. The other three texts which were examined were found to be in the same tradition as Nf and Nj but to be of much poorer quality. Where the *Complainte* and the *Lay de Paix* are concerned, Qq and Nb are very similar.

Qr +VIENNA, NAT. BIBL., 2619

Mid 15th c.;[2] parchment; *c.* 148 ff.; d.c.; 42 lines; catchwords; miniature, decorated border at beginning of first item; decorated initials.

1. Ff. 1a–21b, *Quadriloge invectif et comitif A la correpcion des meurs des francoys Fait par venerable homme Maistre Alain charetier secretaire du roy de France.*

2. Ff. 21c–23b, [*Le Lay de Paix*].

    276 lines. Lacks lines 33–7, 63, 159–60.

3. Ff. 24a–71d, *Aultre traictié Sur la deploracion de la calamité des francois fait par ledit maistre Alain.* (*Le Livre de l'Esperance.*)

(4. Ff. 72a–77a, *Ensuit le debat du cueur et de l'oeil fait par maistre charetier secretaire du roy de france nommé charles.*)[3]

[1] Item 16 is in a second hand. Since the work is included in the table of contents, it is likely that it formed part of the manuscript as it was planned. The foliation, being in a contemporary hand and continuous, supports this view.

[2] The *explicit* of items 7 and 8 and the rubric of item 8 suggest that Qr was copied in the reign of Charles VII, that is before 1461.

[3] Almost certainly by Michault Taillevent (A. Piaget, 'Pierre Michault et Michault Taillevent', *Romania*, XVIII, 1889, 439–52).

5. Ff. 77b–79c, [*Ballades et Rondeaux*].
   Fol. 77d, [*Rondeau*].
   Incipit: Pres de ma dame et loing de mon vouloir... 10 lines
   Fol. 77d, [*Rondeau*].
   Incipit: Comme oseroit la bouche dire...
      Only the first two lines are copied.
   Fol. 78a–b, [*Ballade*].
   Incipit: J'ay oy voulentiers parler d'amours... 41 lines
   Fol. 78d, [*Rondeau*].
   Incipit: Du tout ainsi qu'il vous plaira... 10 lines

7. Fol. 86a, *Cy commence le breviaire des nobles.*
   Fol. 88d, *Explicit le breviaire des nobles fait par maistre alain charretier secretaire du roy nostre sire en son temps.*
      445 lines. Lacks line 118.

8. Fol. 88d, *Sy commance le livre des quatre dames Compilé par maistre l(?) charretier secretaire du roy nostre sire.*
   Fol. 118c, *Explicit le debat des quatre dames fait par maistre Alain charretier secretaire du roy nostre sire.*
      3524 lines. Lacks lines 1953, 2791, 3168–71, 3265.

9. Fol. 118c, *Cy commance le debat du gras et du maigre fait par ledit maistre Alain.*
   Fol. 125c, *Eplicit* (sic) *le gras et le maigre.*
      1242 plus 4 lines. Complete.

10. Ff. 125c–126d, *Complainte de maistre Alain charretier.*
      183 lines. Lacks line 130. Lines 146–7 are inverted.

11. Fol. 126d, *Cy comance le debat de deux compaignons Nommé resveille matin fait par maistre Alain.*
    Fol. 129a, *Cy finist le debat resveille matin fait par maistre Alain charretier.*
      360 lines. Lacks lines 17–24. Text with headings.

12. Fol. 129a, *Cy commance la belle dame Sans mercy.*
    Fol. 133c, *Explicit la belle dame Sans mercy.*
      800 = 799 lines. Lacks line 255. Line 610 is copied twice.

13. Ff. 133c–134a, *Requeste faictes* (sic) *aux dames par les actendans la queste du don d'amoureuse mercy.*

14. Fol. 134a–b, *Coppie des lectres envoyees de par les dames Au maistre rimeur.*

15. Fol. 134b, *Responce et excusacion de l'acteur sur le cas.*
    Fol. 135c, *Explicit la belle dame sans mercy Et la responce.*
      240 lines. Complete.

17. Fol. 142d, *Cy commance le lay de plaisance.*
    Fol. 143d, *Cy finist le lay de plaisance.*
      173 lines. Lacks lines 69, 92, 161–80, 195.

The imitations of the *Belle Dame sans Mercy* in Qr were listed and discussed by Piaget. Qr was included in the bibliographies of the *Livre des Quatre Dames*, the *Debat des Deux Fortunés d'Amours*, the lyrics, the *Belle Dame sans Mercy*, and the *Breviaire des Nobles*; it was used by Rouy in his edition of the *Livre de l'Esperance*.

Qr, which was used in the edition of the four poems, has some kinship with *Pe* and, to a lesser extent, *Oa*. Links with other manuscripts also exist: in the case of the *Debat de Reveille Matin*, with *Qe*; in the *Lay de Paix*, with *Pl*; in the *Complainte*, with *Gh*. The texts in *Qr* contain quite a large number of irregular lines and some poor rhymes. The manuscript has an interesting series of attributions.

Ta PARIS, BIBL. NAT., F. FR. 1722

16th c.; paper; 2°; 245 × 155 (185 × 105); 6 plus 112 ff.; 25–30 lines.

The manuscript is entitled: 'Vers et poesies de Margueritte D'orleans Duchesse D'Alençon.'

Fol. 90v, [*Rondeau*].
Incipit: Mort sur les piez, faignant avoir plaisir...   10 lines

Ta was listed by Droz and Piaget in their bibliography of the lyrics.

Tb PARIS, BIBL. NAT., F. FR. 9346

16th c.; parchment; 310 × 220; 109 ff.

Tb is often called the 'Manuscrit de Bayeux'.

49. Fol. 51v, [*Rondeau*].
    Incipit: Au feu au feu au feu qui mon cueur art...   7 lines
       The text, which is set to music, has been much altered and abbreviated.
72. Ff. 74v–75r, [*Rondeau*].
    Incipit: Triste plaisir et doulloureuse joye...   10 lines
       The text has been adapted and is set to music.

Tb was listed by Droz and Piaget in their bibliography of the lyrics.

Tc +LYON, BIBL. MUN., 1235

15th c.; paper; 288 × 205; 174 ff.

5. Ff. 170v–174v, [*Ballades et Rondeaux*].
   A. Fol. 170v, *Balade.*
      Incipit: Il n'est dangier que de villain...   28 lines
   D. Ff. 171v–172r, *Rondinet.*
      Incipit: Belle qui si bon cueur avez...   13 lines
   E. Fol. 172r, [*Rondeau*].
      Incipit: Triste plaisir et doulereuse joye...   10 lines
   F. Fol. 172r, *Chançonnete.*
      Incipit: Riche d'espoir et povre d'autre bien...   10 lines
   G. Ff. 172r–v, *Rondinot* (sic).
      Incipit: Je n'ay pouvoir de vivre en joye...   10 lines
   H. Fol. 172v, *Rondelinet.*
      Incipit: Loyaument et a tousjours mais...   13 lines

I. Fol. 172v, *Rondel.*
   Incipit: Puis qu'autre rien ne me puet plaire...   13 lines
J. Ff. 172v–173r, *Rondelinet.*
   Incipit: Dehors dehors il vous fault deslogier...   10 lines
K. Fol. 173r, *Rondel.*
   Incipit: Cuidés vous qu'il est assez joye...   10 lines
L. Fol. 173r, *Chançonnete.*
   Incipit: Joye me fuit et desespoir me chasse...   12 lines
   Lacks line 8.
O. Fol. 174r, [*Rondeau*].
   Incipit: Au povre prisonnier ma dame...   10 lines
P. Fol. 174r, *Rondel.*[1]
   Incipit: Tel rit joyeulx qui puys de douleur plure (*sic*)...   9 lines
Q. Fol. 174r, *Rondelet.*
   Incipit: Aussi que ben vous semblera...   13 lines
R. Fol. 174v, *Rondel.*
   Incipit: Mort sur le pié faignant d'avoir playsir...   10 lines

The collection of lyrics in *Tc* was edited by L. Clédat in 1886.[2] *Tc* was included in the bibliographies of the lyrics and of the ballade, 'Il n'est dangier...'

The catalogue contains no mention of items E, J, and O; several of the first lines are incorrectly quoted.[3]

Td BERLIN, KUPFERSTICHKABINETT, 78 B 17

Late 15th c.; parchment; 160 × 100 (115 × 60); 215 ff.; 31 lines; contemporary table of contents; miniature, decorated border; decorated and coloured initials.

The manuscript, although copied for a member of the family of Malet de Graville,[4] is generally known as the 'Chansonnier du Cardinal de Rohan' after its eighteenth-century owner. After the Cardinal's death in 1749 it disappeared and was not rediscovered until 1914.[5] *Td* was published in full by M. Löpelmann in 1923.[6]

A partial list of the contents of *Td* was inserted during the eighteenth century at the end of a copy of the *Jardin de Plaisance*;[7] references to *Td* before 1914 are not to the manuscript but to that list.

---

[1] In fact the item comprises the last nine lines of the *Complainte.*
[2] L. Clédat, 'Ballades, chansonnettes et rondeaux', *Lyon-Revue*, déc. 1886, 307–20.
[3] *Catalogue général des manuscrits*, XXX: i, 1900, 309.
[4] The family's arms (de gueules à 3 roses d'or) are found on fol. 22r. The original owner was probably Louis Malet de Graville, amiral de France etc., who died in 1516. *Td* may then have passed to his daughter Anne, who composed a version in rondeaux of the *Belle Dame sans Mercy* (see *Gj*).
[5] S. Lemm, 'Das Manuskript des Kardinals de Rohan', *Archiv für das Studium der neueren Sprachen und Literaturen*, CXXXII, 1914, 151–3.
[6] M. Löpelmann, *Die Liederhandschrift des Cardinals de Rohan*, Göttingen, 1923 (*Gesellschaft für Romanische Literatur*, XLIV).
[7] Paris, Bibl. Nat., Réserve Ye 169.

The manuscripts

The table of contents is on ff. 4–21. The scribe left blank ff. 1r–3v, 46r–61v, and 205v–215v; other works have been added in a sixteenth-century hand on ff. 46r–48r.

A. Ff. 22r–45v, [*Ballades*].

1. J'ay ung arbre de la plante d'amours... Ff. 22r–v.	35 lines
7. Aucunnes gens m'ont huy arraisonné... Ff. 25v–26r.	35 lines
20. J'ay voulentiers oy parler d'amours... Ff. 31v–32v.	41 lines
35. Il n'est danger que de villain... Ff. 41r–v.	28 lines

B. Ff. 62r–205r, [*Rondeaux*].

60. Triste plaisir et doulloureuse joye... Fol. 65r.	10 lines
61. Je n'ay pouoir de vivre en joie... Fol. 65r.	10 lines
82. De quoy me sert le reguard de mes yeux... Fol. 70r.	10 lines
83. La bonne volenté que j'ay... Ff. 70r–v.	10 lines
84. Pour qu'autre bien ne me peust plaire... Fol. 70v.	13 lines
151. Mourant sur piés faignant d'avoir plaisir... Fol. 86r.	10 lines
152. Joie me fuit et desespoir me chasse... Fol. 86r.	13 lines
175. Du tout ainsi qu'il vous plaira... Fol. 91v.	10 lines
186. Pres de ma dame et loing de mon vouloir... Ff. 93v–94r.	10 lines
188. S'oncques beaux yeulx orent telle puissance... Ff. 94r–v.	10 lines
213. Ainsi que bon vous semblera... Fol. 100r.	13 lines
215. Au povre prisonnier ma dame... Fol. 100v.	10 lines
217. Cuidés vous qu'il ait assés joie... Fol. 101r.	10 lines
219. Dehors dehors il vous fault deslogier... Fol. 101v.	10 lines
220. Helas ma courtoise ennemye... Fol. 101v.	10 lines
221. Loyaument et a tosjours mays... Ff. 101v–102r.	13 lines

222. Comme oseroit la bouche dire...   10 lines
     Fol. 102r.
223. Ou mon desir s'assouvyra...   13 lines
     Ff. 102r–v.
224. Riche d'espoir et povre d'autre bien...   10 lines
     Fol. 102v.
226. Quant ung jour suys sans que je voie...   10 lines
     Fol. 103r.
227. Au feu au feu au feu qui mon cueur art... 13 lines
     Fol. 103r.

Td was listed by Droz and Piaget in their bibliography. Löpelmann's text was used by Hoffman in his edition of the lyrics.

Repeated efforts to obtain a microfilm of *Td* had only partial success; see p. 373, n. 1.

Te LONDON, BRIT. MUS., ROYAL 20 C viii

Early 15th c.; parchment; 395 × 275; 165 ff.

   Te contains the *Arbre des Batailles* and was probably made for Jean, duc de Berry. Two rondeaux have been copied on a fly-leaf (fol. 165r), in a fifteenth-century hand slightly later than that of the manuscript as a whole. Part of the second rondeau is found a second time on another fly-leaf (fol. 1r).

A. Fol. 165r, [*Rondeau*].
   Incipit: Je n'ay pouoir de vivre en joye...   10 lines
B. Fol. 165r, [*Rondeau*].
   Incipit: Triste playsir et douloureuse joye...   10 lines

Droz and Piaget listed *Te* in their bibliography of the lyrics.

Tf LONDON, BRIT. MUS., ADDITIONAL 34360

15th c.; paper; 2°; 270 × 195 (195 × 105); 116 ff.; 25–30 lines.

6. Fol. 22v, *Lo here begynneth a roundel made be my lord of Suthfolk whiles he was prisonner in fraunce.*
   Incipit: Lealement a tous jours mais...   13 lines

The roundel is in fact by Alain Chartier. *Tf* has not been listed or examined before.

Tg OXFORD, BODLEIAN LIBRARY, CANONICI MISC. 213

15th c.; paper; 2°; 290 × 215; 4 plus 140 ff.

Fol. 56v, [*Rondeau*].
Incipit: Tristre plaisir et douleureuse yoie (*sic*)...
   10 lines. The text is set to music by Binchois.
Fol. 108r, [*Ballade*].
Incipit: Il n'est dangier que de vilain...

The text is set to music. Only the first two stanzas (16 lines) are given.

Droz and Piaget included *Tg* in their bibliography of the lyrics and the ballade.

Th   +WASHINGTON, LIBRARY OF CONGRESS, M.2.1.L25

15th c.; parchment; 130 × 90; 168 ff.

Th is generally known as the 'Chansonnier de Laborde', having been acquired by the Laborde family in the nineteenth century.

14. Fol. 22r, [*Rondeau*].
   Incipit: Je n'ay pouoir de vivre...
   Part of the rondeau and its musical setting are missing.

Th was included by Droz and Piaget in their bibliography of the lyrics.

Tj   PARIS, BIBL. NAT., F.FR.1881

15th and 16th c.; paper; 4°; 220 × 145 (*c.* 160 × 100); 308 ff.; 20–30 lines.

Ff. 218r–v, [*Ballade*].
Incipit: Il n'est dangie (*sic*) que de villain...   28 lines
   Lines 12–13 are inverted.

Tj was listed by Droz and Piaget in their bibliography of manuscripts containing the ballade.

Tk   PARIS, BIBL. DE L'ARSENAL, 3059

A fifteenth-century manuscript on parchment containing a copy of *Le Jouvencel* by Jean de Bueil. An early sixteenth-century hand has copied a ballade on a front fly-leaf.

Fol. Br, Maistre Alain Chartier.
Incipit: Il n'est danger que de villain...   28 lines

Tk was listed by Droz and Piaget in their bibliography of the ballade. Lines 13 and 21 are transposed.

Tl   BRUSSELS, BIBL. ROYALE 11020–35

15th c.; paper; 2°; 2 plus 153 ff.; 290 × 215 (170 × 130); 22 lines.

Ff. 32r–v, *Balade*.
Incipit: Il n'est dangier que de villain...   28 lines

Tl was listed by Droz and Piaget in their bibliography of the ballade. Stanzas II and III are rearranged.

Tm   LONDON, BRIT. MUS., HARLEY 4397

15th c.; paper; 2°; 290 × 195 (180–90 × 115–20); 169 ff.; *c.* 30 lines; flourished capital; coloured initials, headings in red.

2. Fol. 82r, *Balade bien substancieuse.*
   Incipit: Il n'est dangier que de villain. . . 28 lines

Droz and Piaget included *Tm* in their bibliography of the ballade.

Tn LONDON, BRIT. MUS., HARLEY 4473

15th c.; paper; 2°; 270 × 195 (c. 200 × 110); 131 ff.; c. 25 lines.

2:c, Ff. 40v–41v, *Autre dictié.*
Incipit: Il n'est dangier que de villain. . . 28 lines

Tn was listed by Droz and Piaget in their bibliography of the ballade.

To LONDON, BRIT. MUS., LANSDOWNE 380

Early 16th c.; paper; 4°; 210 × 145 (150 × 80); 280 ff.; c. 30 lines; headings in red.

Ff. 220r–221r (218r–219r),[1] *Ballade faicte et composee par le doulx poete Maistre Alain charretier.*
Incipit: Il n'est dangier que de vilain. . . 28 lines

Droz and Piaget listed *To* in their bibliography of the ballade. *To* was wrongly included by Piaget in his list of manuscripts containing the *Belle Dame sans Mercy.*

Tp WOLFENBÜTTEL, HERZOG-AUGUST BIBLIOTHEK, 84.7.Aug.fol.

15th c.; parchment; 270 × 190; 90 ff.

Tp, which has not been examined, was included by Droz and Piaget in their bibliography of the ballade 'Il n'est dangier que de villain'. The library catalogue states that item 4 (ff. 87v–89v) consists of 'Trois balades'.[2]

Tq CAMBRIDGE, TRINITY COLLEGE, R.3.20

15th c.; paper; 2°; 290 × 215; 374 pp.; 33 lines.

8. P. 32, *Roundell made by my lord of Suffolk whylest he was prysonnier in Fraunce.*
   Incipit: Lealement a tous jours mais. . . 13 lines

Tq has not been listed or examined before. The roundel is in fact by Alain Chartier.

Xa THE COLLECTED EDITION OF PIERRE LE CARON, 5 SEPTEMBER 1489 (GKW 6557)

Xa is the earliest collected edition. The later fifteenth-century and sixteenth-century collected editions are so similar to *Xa* that they can almost be considered reprints

---

[1] There are two foliations.
[2] Dr O. von Heinemann, *Die Handschriften der Herzoglichen Bibliothek zu Wolfenbüttel: Die Augusteischen Handschriften*, IV, Wolfenbüttel, Zwissler, 1900, 80–1, No. 2873.

of it.[1] The *Debat des Deux Fortunés d'Amours* is not included in *Xa* and was first printed in a collected edition by Galiot du Pré in 1526.

The edition is divided into some twenty *livres*, details of which have been omitted from the description since the *livres* and the works in the edition do not always correspond.

Part 2: Quires A–L[2]

6. Fol. A.1.a,[3] [*Le Lay de Paix*].

    Fol. A.3.b, *Cy finist le petit libelle que ledit Maistre alain envoia au roy et a la seigneurie de france.*

    > 279=281 lines. Lacks lines 24–5, 148. Lines 15–16 are inverted; lines 87–8 and 95–6 printed as one line.

7. Fol. A.3.b, *Cy commance le breviaire des nobles selon Maistre alain.*

    Fol. A.6.d, *Cy finist le breviere des nobles.*

    > 426 lines. Lacks lines 25–8, 103–11, 255–9, 297–8, 324. Includes line 142a (Rendroit).

8. Fol. A.6.d, *Cy apres commence le livre de reveille matin fait par maistre Alain.*

    Fol. B.1.d, *Et fin du debat Reveille matin.*

    > 352 lines. Lacks lines 17–24 and 345–52.

9. Fol. B.2.a, [*La Belle Dame sans Mercy*].

    Fol. B.8.a, *Cy fine la belle dame sans mercy.*

    > 797 lines. Lacks lines 195–6, 559.

10. Ff. B.8.b–c, *Complainte et supplication envoyé aux dames par les poursuians* (sic) *et loyaulx serviteurs de la court amoureuse du dieu d'amours.*

11. Fol. B.8.d, *Lettres closes envoiees a maistre alain de par les dames de la royne katherine marie et jehane.*

12. Ff. B.8.d–c.3.a, *Responce faitte par maistre alain sur les lettres que les dames luy ont escriptes.*

    > 237 plus 4 lines. Lacks lines 18, 234–5. Between stanzas XIV and XV there is this heading: 'Comment le dieu d'amours tient l'arc entezé et la flesche en la corde oyant l'excusation de maistre alain.'

14. Fol. C.6.c, *Cy commence le tresgracieux livre des quatres* (sic) *dames compillé et fait par maistre alain. L'an mil iiii[c] trente troys.*

    Fol. G.1.c, *Cy finist le livre des quatre dames fait par maistre Alain chartier.*

    > 3524 lines. Lacks lines 655, 1142–4, 1953, 2521, 2594, 3158, 3265, 3366. Includes lines 471a, 1606a, 3531a.

(15. Ff. G.1.c–H.2.d, *Cy commence l'ospital d'amours fait et compilé par maistre Alain chartier.*)[4]

(16. Ff. H.2.d–H.5.a, *Complainte de saint valentin gransson compillee par maistre alain chartier.*)[4]

---

[1] For a list of the collected editions see Walravens, *Alain Chartier, études biographiques*, 223–9.

[2] The first part of the volume, quires a–k, contains five items: *Le Livre de l'Esperance*; *Le Curial*; *Le Quadrilogue Invectif*; *La Genealogie des Rois de France*; *La Description de Gaule.*

[3] The folios are signed, now with small letters, now with capital letters, and with Roman numerals. Here, capitals and Arabic numerals are used throughout.

[4] Neither of these works is by Chartier. See J. C. Laidlaw, 'André du Chesne's Edition of Alain Chartier', *Modern Language Review*, LXIII, 1968, 569–74.

20. Ff. J.4.c–J.5.d, *Complainte trespiteuse.*

      183 lines. Lacks lines 103, 117. Includes line 119a. The order of stanzas is: I–IV, VII, V–VI, VIII, X, IX, XI–XII.

24. Ff. K.3.c–K.4.d, *Lay de plaisance.*

      192 lines. Lacks lines 85, 115–16, 118. Lines 47–8 are inverted and lines 98 and 100 transposed.

No detailed description of *Xa* has been published before. Since it contains imitations of the *Belle Dame sans Mercy*, *Xa* is akin to the manuscripts of types *P* and *Q*. *Xa* was used in the edition of the four poems and was found to contain very few individual readings; none of the texts in *Xa* is complete. A large number of readings, some irregular, link *Xa* with *Pa* and, less closely, with *Pd Pk* and *Po*. *Ok* and *Qp* were copied from collected editions dependent on *Xa*.

    Xa was often found to be in agreement with *Pc* and *Ql*, themselves closely related. *Pc* and *Xa* both contain poems by Oton de Granson.[1] Copies of the *Dialogue d'un Amoureux et de sa Dame*, an imitation of the *Belle Dame sans Mercy*, are found only in *Pc* and *Xa*, and in manuscripts dependent on *Xa*.[2] However, *Xa* cannot depend solely on a manuscript in the tradition of *Pc*, for *Xa* often agrees with other manuscripts and contains works, for example the *Lay de Plaisance*, which are not found in *Pc* or kindred manuscripts. *Xa* is inferior in quality to *Pc* and *Ql*.

[1] The *Complainte de Saint Valentin* and the *Pastourelle* are found in *Pc* (ff. 69r–71r; ff. 192v–194v) and *Xa* (ff. H.2.d–J.1.c).

[2] It is found in *Pc* (ff. 195r–201r) and *Xa* (ff. J.8.a–K.3.b), and also in *Pa Po* and *Qp*. See A. Piaget, *Romania*, XXXIII, 1904, 206–8.

4

The Critical Editions

Vertu se parfait d'avoir paine.

Alain Chartier

The introduction to each poem begins with a list of the manuscripts and editions in which the poem is available. Reasons are then given why the poem has been accepted as authentic. The account of the textual tradition which follows is concerned only with the texts actually used in the edition. A limited number of readings is cited as evidence that texts are related; as a rule no more than the first ten are listed, whatever their importance.

Once a base text is chosen,[1] it is altered as little as possible. Obvious errors have been corrected. Where the base contains individual readings, they have not been rejected for that reason alone. Much depends on the characteristics of the base manuscript taken as a whole. More credence has been given to a manuscript which has been carefully copied and revised than to one known to contain scribal errors.

In punctuation and in the use of accents and capitals, normal editorial practice has been followed. All variants, except those of a purely orthographic nature, have been given; the descriptions of individual manuscripts should be consulted to see what peculiarities they may have in that respect. It is not always easy to decide what is or is not an orthographical variant, and any editor must make arbitrary decisions. Thus, alternatives of the type *fus/fu, fut/fu, dit/dist, franchise/francise*, which occur frequently, have been included only where they appear to affect meaning or rhyme.

The spelling of the base texts has been retained with the following exceptions. *V* has been substituted for consonant *u*, and *j* for consonant *i*. Among words which gave difficulty were *pouez, avra* and related forms. The spellings just used were chosen in the light of the rhymes at lines 2026–9 and 3396–9 of the *Livre des Quatre Dames* and in stanza XLII of the *Debat de Reveille Matin*.

In quoting variants, the spelling used is that of the first text listed. When a variant affects an entire line, it comes first and is separated from any shorter variants by a colon. Shorter variants are separated from each

[1] See pp. 52–8.

other by semicolons. If different variants, separated by a comma, occur between semicolons or between a semicolon and a full stop, they are of equivalent length in the texts from which they are cited. Passages quoted from the poem itself are given in an abbreviated form before a right-hand square bracket, and all the variants which follow are of equivalent length.

The love poems have been grouped together and arranged in the order which was suggested by the discussion in chapter 2. They are followed by the three political and moralising poems.

5

'Le Lay de Plaisance'

Seventeen Manuscripts: *Nf Nj Nr   Oa Oc   Pa Pb Pe Ph Pn   Qh Qk Qn Qo Qp Qq Qr*.
  Qn has not been traced and *Qp* has been damaged by fire. All the other manuscripts have been examined.

The poem was included in all the early collected editions and in the Du Chesne edition of 1617. The 1489 and 1617 editions have been consulted.

The *Lay de Plaisance* is so called in all the manuscripts except *Qn* and *Qq*, where it is entitled *Lay fait le premier jour de l'an*. The poem is attributed to Alain Chartier in *Pe*, but only indirectly;[1] in the other manuscripts and in the editions it is anonymous. The *Lay de Plaisance* has been edited here from four manuscripts: *Nf Nj Oa* and *Ph*.

Nf and *Nj* both contain complete texts of the poem. In *Ph* lines 115–16 are omitted, and in *Oa* the whole of stanza XI. The readings of *Nf* and *Nj* are often in opposition to those of *Oa* and *Ph*; the differences at lines 1–2, 28, 36, 99, 182 and 183 are particularly important. Each of the texts contains readings peculiar to itself. Such readings, rare in *Nj*, are quite frequent in *Nf Oa* and *Ph*. The text in *Nf* is technically irregular at line 111 and rhymes poorly at lines 28 and 194. *Nj* contains one irregular line (line 117) and three poor rhymes (lines 28, 176 and 194). Irregular lines are more numerous in *Oa* (lines 55, 60, 73, 75, 81, 104 and 155) and in *Ph* (lines 36, 55, 60, 65 and 188). *Ph* includes unsatisfactory rhymes at lines 15, 64, 137, 183 and 194.

The first stanza of the *Lay de Plaisance* is divided into four quarter-stanzas which, in *Oa* and *Ph*, rhyme as follows: *abab baab baab baab*. In *Nf* and *Nj*, on the other hand, the rhyme-scheme of the first quarter is exactly the same as that of the other three quarters. Although the version of the first stanza in *Nf* and *Nj* is apparently regular, the first stanza cannot be considered in isolation. Successive definitions of the *lay* given in fourteenth- and fifteenth-century manuals all state that the rhyme-schemes of the first and last stanzas must be identical.[2] The rhyme-scheme of the final stanza of the *Lay de Plaisance* is, in all the manuscripts, identical with that given for the first stanza by *Oa* and *Ph*. Their version must therefore be accepted; it also provides the more satisfactory first line.

At lines 9 and 27 the readings given by *Oa* are preferable: the alternative readings make poor sense in the first case, and in the second are out of tone with the rest of the poem. At lines 115–16, where the texts vary markedly, the version in *Oa* is more positive than the reprise offered by *Nf* and *Nj*. *Oa* also contains satisfactory readings at other points of disagreement, notably lines 28, 36, 99, 182 and 183.

Although *Oa* contains a better text of the *Lay de Plaisance* than do *Nf Nj* or *Ph*, it is

---

[1] In *Pe* the *Lay de Plaisance* is followed by the *Lay de Paix*, which is entitled *Autre lay maistre alain*.
[2] G. Lote, *Histoire du vers français*, II, Paris, Boivin, 1951, 253–9.

not entirely suitable as a base; it is incomplete and includes numerous irregular lines and individual readings. *Nj* must also be considered. The choice between the two is essentially a choice between the careful copy of an inferior tradition (*Nj*), and the rather careless copy of a good tradition (*Oa*). *Nj*, being complete and generally regular, has been chosen as the base for this edition. Where it is unsatisfactory, as at the lines discussed above, it has been corrected with the help of *Oa*.

LE LAY DE PLAISANCE   *Nj*, 47v

I   Pour commencer joyeusement l'annee
Et en signe de bien perseverer,
Est au jour d'uy mainte dame estrenee
4   De son amant qui la veult honnourer.

Et d'autre part, pour plus s'enamourer,
Dame qui est de servant assignee
A de long temps quelque chose ordonnee
8   Pour son amant courtoisement parer.

Mais aux amans ne me vueil comparer:
Sans dame suy; onc ne me fut donnee
Loyale amour jusqu'a celle journee,
12   Car je n'ay pas sens pour y labourer.

Ainsi me fault tout soulet demourer;
Dame qui soit ne sera huy penee
Pour m'estrener, ne moy pour dame nee.
16   Donc je doy bien piteusement plourer.

II   En ce point me desconforte,
Car Plaisance est en moy morte,
Sans qui riens ne vault.

20   Tristesce ne se deporte
De moy mener guerre forte;
Pensee m'assault.

Pour ce, amis, je vous enhorte   48r
24   Que tousjours tenez la sorte,
Sans faire deffault,

148

'Le Lay de Plaisance'

De Plaisance qui supporte
Cil qui en lui se deporte;
28 Riens plus ne vous fault.

III
Plaisance du tout maintient
Et detient
Cil qui se contient
32 Et tient gracïeusement:

Car tous biens elle entretient
Et contient;
A elle appartient
36 Et vient gay esbatement.

Ce qu'elle fait lui avient,
Et avient
Que, qui la retient,
40 Devient plaisant, doulz et gent.

Les vieux en vie soustient,
Contretient.
Cil cui en souvient
44 Parvient a honneur souvent.

IV
Plaisance fait maint tour faire,
Puis deffaire,
Puis refaire,
48 Puis l'un l'autre contrefaire,
En suivant porter devises.

48v

Sans nul grever, sans mal faire,
Son affaire
52 Veult parfaire;
Pour ce est elle neccessaire
A l'amant en maintes guises.

El fait ungs homs a tout plaire,
56 Et complaire
Sans desplaire;
Estre des bons essemplaire,
En moustrant ses grans franchises.

27 ou liz *NfPh*, ou lis *Nj*. 28 vault *NfNj*. 36 Sen v. g. e. *NfNj*, Et en v. g. e. *Ph*. 43 qui *OaPh*. 49 En fumant *NfPh*. 50 ne m. f. *Nf*. 55 Elle *OaPh*; tous *Ph*. 58 de vous *Oa*.

149

60 El scet les gens bel actraire,
　　Sans retraire
　　Ne detraire,
　　Car a nully n'est contraire,
64 Ains plaisant et sans faintises.

V　Fuyez donc Mirencolie
　　Qui toute douleur pourchace
　　Et Plaisance du tout chace;
68 Qui la reçoit fait folie,

　　Car Plaisance est plus jolie,
　　Qui dueil et soussi enchace,
　　Et n'est n'ingrate n'eschace,　　　　　　　　49r
72 Ains a Largesce se alie.

　　Et fait la pensee lie,
　　Et de doulceur l'entrelace;
　　Le cuer esjoie et soulace,
76 Et l'homme d'ennuy deslie.

　　Les haults princes humilie,
　　Et fait faire mainte chace
　　Et mainte bonne grimace,
80 Et maint dur cuer amolie.

VI　Et fait l'homme sage,
　　Plaisans en langage,
　　Courtois en courage,
84 Ainsi sur tous l'avantage;

　　Privé du sauvage,
　　Prouffit de dommage,
　　Ung seigneur d'un page,
88 Et faire a Amours hommage;

　　Aler en boscage,
　　Jouer en l'ombrage,
　　Passer maint passage,
92 Assembler ung mariage;

60 Elle *OaPh.*　61–2 Sans detraire / Ne retraire *Nf.*　64 faintise *Ph.*　65 doncques *Ph.*　71 ingrate
Nf, ne guicte *Oa*, mignocte *Ph.*　73 Et] Elle *Oa.*　74 sentrelace *Nf.*　75 esjoyst *Oa.*　81 Et]
Elle *Oa.*　82 Plaisant *NfOaPh.*　85 Prince *Ph.*　89 ou b. *Oa.*

Acroire sur gage,
Galer sans oultrage,
Mettre oyseaulx en cage: 49v
96   Riens n'est qui se y comparage.

VII   Homs jolis et cointe,
Qui de Plaisance s'acointe
Et qui vit en joie,

100   Sent d'Amours la pointe
Qui d'un doulz espoir est oingte,
Lequel la convoie.

A amer s'appointe:
104   La treuve a plaisir conjointe,
D'honneur la monjoie;

A lui est adjointe,
Et n'est nul qui l'en despointe
108   Par quelconque voie.

VIII   Plaisance est bien souverain
Et haultain,
Qui rent joie souveraine
112   Et haultaine;

Car, qui l'ensuit soir et main,
Main a main,
A fin loyale l'amaine   50r
116   Et amaine.

Donc est il huy que demain
Plus certain
De soy mettre en son demaine,
120   Car certaine

Est en cest estat mondain
Qui est vain;
C'est nostre adresce mondaine
124   Non pas vaine.

97 joly *Nf.* 99 vient *NfNj.* 100 Sens damours lapointe *Oa.* 101 Que *Ph.* 102 conjoie *Nf.*
104 c.] cointe *Oa.* 106 A lie *Oa.* 109 Plaisans *Oa.* 111 joye *repeated Nf.* 115–16 *Omitted Ph,* Cest
celle qui bien le maine / Et ramaine *NfNj.* 117 e. il h.] e. h. *Nj.*

IX

Et se Plaisance n'estoit,
Le pouoir d'Amours faudroit.
Qui seroit
128   Cellui qui plus dicteroit
Balades nouvelles?

Nul homme ne danseroit,
Ains aux cendres crouppiroit.
132   Qui riroit?
Qui seroit cil qui yroit
Prïer les pucelles?

Chascun oyseau se tairoit;
136   Le lus se reposeroit;
Si feroit
Cellui qui sonner saroit
Harpes et vïelles.

50v

140   Ainsi tout bien cesseroit
Et vivre nous desplairoit;
Et diroit
Chascun que mieulz ameroit
144   Mort que douleurs telles.

X

Qui vit en Plaisance,
Il a suffisance
Et de joie congnoissance;
148   Si lui doit suffire.

S'il a esperance
Et humble souffrance
Et a sa dame acointance,
152   Donc lui puet il dire,

S'il voit sa semblance,
Que Pitié s'avance
De mectre bonne alegance
156   En son dur martire.

Lors avra fïance
En sa contenance,

136 lux *Oa*, luz *Ph.* 137 Qui seroit *Ph.* 148 Qui *Nf.* 149 Il a *Oa.* 151 a.] cointance *Oa.*
155 De m. a. *Oa.*

152

D'avoir des biens abondance,
160 Lesquelz il desire.

XI   Plaisance honnorable
Est vie agrëable,
Au corps prouffitable,   51r
164 A l'ame sauvable,
Qui nully ne grieve;

A nully nuisable,
A tous prouffitable,
168 Joyeuse a la table,
Au repos aidable,
Quant on couche ou lieve.

Nully n'est notable
172 S'il n'est acointable,
Plaisant, amïable,
Joyeux, secourable;
C'est ce qui l'achieve.

176 Car Tristeur musable,
Aigreur detestable,
Chagrin redoubtable
Font homs miserable
180 Et sa vie brieve.

XII   Vueillez donques mectre cuer et pensee
A Plaisancë, et plaisamment ouvrer.
Ainsi sera en vous douleur cassee,
184 Et pourrez loz et honneur recouvrer

Et de soussi vous pourrez delivrer.
Tristeur sera de vous grever lassee,
Et la saison joyeusement passee,   51v
188 Car Plaisance sert de joye livrer.

Or servez donc, sans jamais dessevrer,
Amours, par qui grant joie ert amassee;
Et par ce avrez dame en qui compassee
192 Sera beauté qu'Amours scet preparer.

XI omitted Oa. 176 nuisable *Nj.* 182 A P.] A vo p. *NſNj.* 183 sera] si ert *NſNj*; a v. d. passee *Ph.*
188 l.] delivrer *Ph.* 190 est *NſPh.* 191 Par qui avrez d. *Nſ*; avras d. *Oa.*

Ainsi pourrez en tous lieux comparer
Et en amant passer mainte passee;
Et tant sera honneur en vous tassee
196 Que vous pourrez amoureux apparer.

194 pensee *NƒNjPh.* 195 en vous honneur *Oa*; taxee *Nƒ.* . . .le lay de plaisance *OaPh,* . . .le lay de paix (*sic*) *Nƒ.*

6

'Le Debat des Deux Fortunés d'Amours'

Twenty-seven Manuscripts: *Ga Gd   Nd Nf Nj Nl No Nr   Oa Ob Oj   Pb Pc Pd Pe Pf Ph Pj Pk Pn   Qd Qh Qk Qn Qp Qq Qr.*

Qn has not been traced; *Qp* has been damaged by fire. All the other manuscripts have been examined. There is an abridged version of the poem in Paris, Bibl. Nat., f.fr. 2152.

The *Debat des Deux Fortunés d'Amours* was printed in the *Jardin de Plaisance* about 1501 and in the later editions of that anthology. The debate was first included in a collected edition of Chartier's works by Galiot du Pré in 1526 and 1529; there is no separate early edition. The text of Du Chesne, published in 1617, was based partly on the *Jardin de Plaisance* and the Du Pré editions, partly on *Pe*. The texts in the *Jardin de Plaisance* and in the Du Chesne edition have been consulted.

A list of twenty manuscripts containing the poem was published by Droz and Piaget in 1925, in their notes to a facsimile edition of the *Jardin de Plaisance*.[1] The poem was edited in 1970 by Pascale Hemeryck in a thesis for the Ecole des Chartes;[2] use was made of all the manuscripts listed above except *Oj Qh Qn* and *Qp*.

The manuscripts are in greater disagreement about the title of the poem than they are about any other by Chartier; some of the manuscripts even offer alternative titles.[3] Although other titles are found,[4] *Le Gras et le Maigre*[5] and the *Debat des Deux Fortunés d'Amours*[6] occur most often. The latter has been chosen since it is given by *Oj* and *Qd*, which contain the best texts of the poem. *Fortunés* has been preferred to *Fortunes*, although certain critics have taken the contrary view: Middle French debates are generally between persons, real or otherwise, rather than about things; the spelling *fortunez*, found in several *incipits* or *explicits*,[7] points to the same interpretation. In almost all the manuscripts the poem is followed by, or rather signed with, a quatrain playing on the name 'Alain', which indicates that the *Debat* is by Alain Chartier.

The *Debat des Deux Fortunés d'Amours* has been edited here from seven manuscripts, *Nf Nj Oa Oj Pc Ph* and *Qd*. It is made up of 310 stanzas, in the main of four lines, with the rhyme-scheme $a^{10} a^{10} a^{10} b^4 b^{10} b^{10} b^{10} c^4$ etc.; the last stanza has only three lines. Four stanzas, stanzas 24, 159, 163 and 282, are found in some manuscripts with four lines, in others with five. The longer version of stanza 282 occurs only in *Ga*; the longer versions of the other three stanzas are found more often, and occur in four manuscripts, *Oa Oj Ph* and *Qd*, out of the seven used in this edition. In *Nf* and *Nj*, stanzas 24, 159 and 163

---

[1] E. Droz et A. Piaget, *Le Jardin de plaisance*, II, 1925, 263–4 (*SATF*).

[2] Pascale Hemeryck, *Alain Chartier, poète et penseur, d'après 'Le Debat des deux fortunes d'amour' et les œuvres latines*, Paris, 1970 (Thèse de l'Ecole Nationale des Chartes).

[3] *Nd Nf Nj Pb Pd* and *Qk*.

[4] *Nf Nj No Pd Pf Pj* and *Pn*.

[5] *Nd Nf Nj Pb Pc Pd Ph Pk Qk Qp Qq* and *Qr*.

[6] *Nd Nl Nr Oj Pb Pe Qd Qh Qk* and *Qn*.

[7] *Nd Oj Pb* and *Qk*.

contain four lines; in *Pc* stanza 24 is of five lines, stanzas 159 and 163 are each of four lines.

Some stanzas of five lines also occur in the *Livre des Quatre Dames*. Given that they exist in both of Chartier's long narrative poems and that they are copied in the best texts of the poems concerned, the stanzas of five lines have been retained. The extra lines can be considered emphatic; they may also result from contamination.

Readings at lines 286, 306, 307, 519, 538, 539, 635, 636, 648, 653 etc. are found only in *Nf Nj* and *Pc*. Readings peculiar to two out of the three texts are also found: to *Nf* and *Pc* at lines 255, 358 and 754; to *Nj* and *Pc* at lines 546 and 547; to *Nf* and *Nj* at lines 9, 21, 50, 58, 74, 96, 112, 131, 139, 145 etc. Each text contains individual and irregular readings: they are less frequent in *Nj* (lines 849, 884, 1076, 1148, 1185, 1189, 1229 etc.) than in *Nf* (lines 81, 200, 316, 378, 492, 575, 586 etc.); in *Pc* they occur frequently (lines 23, 160, 175, 211, 283, 350, 427 etc.). In *Nf* and *Nj* lines 567–8 are inverted. *Nf* lacked line 583, and a version of it has been added in a second hand. In *Pc*, lines 642–5, 678, 821, 838, 886, 1074, 1126 and 1129 are omitted.

Certain readings link these three texts now with *Ph* (lines 76, 207, 348, 479, 506–8, 511–12, 515 etc.), now with *Oj* (lines 30, 31, 79, 93, 306, 474, 476 etc.). Readings peculiar to two or more of the five texts are also found: to *Nf Nj* and *Ph* at lines 295, 357, 550, 611, 686, 930 etc.; to *Nf Nj* and *Oj* at lines 403, 446, 582, 712, 728, 905, 956 etc. (cf. lines 708, 921 and 935); to *Oj* and *Pc* at lines 208, 584, 641, 848, 907, 974 etc.; to *Pc* and *Ph* at lines 154, 180, 266, 387, 486, 682, 830 etc. The only reading peculiar to *Oj* and *Ph* occurs at line 79.

Oj and *Ph* are also related to *Oa* and *Qd*. Readings peculiar to *Oa* and *Oj* occur at lines 218, 507, 780, 930 and 1010; to *Oj* and *Qd* at lines 270, 357, 376, 471, 515, 641, 681 etc.; to *Oa* and *Ph* at lines 7, 63, 143, 147, 292, 443, 471 etc.; to *Ph* and *Qd* at lines 183, 574, 682, 894 and 988. *Oa* and *Qd* contain readings peculiar to themselves at lines 97, 203, 262, 306, 424, 841, 904 etc. Many of the lines already mentioned which contain readings peculiar to *Nf Nj* and *Pc*, with or without *Oj* or *Ph*, give *ipso facto* readings peculiar to *Oa Oj Ph* and *Qd*, or to *Oa Oj* and *Qd*, or to *Oa Ph* and *Qd*.

Oa, which lacks lines 90 and 623 in addition to line 471, contains many individual and irregular lines (lines 159, 221, 288, 350, 434, 504, 514 etc.), which often result from scribal carelessness. *Ph* includes many similar examples (lines 1, 31, 126, 148, 208, 258, 279 etc.). A small number of corrections in a second hand (*Ph²*) is found in the first quarter of the poem; they seem to have been made with the help of a text of the type *NfNjPc* (see lines 96, 108 and 210).

The text in *Oj* is complete and includes fewer individual readings than the other six texts; none the less *Oj* is irregular at lines 300, 398, 584, 597, 682, 862 and 1178. *Oj* has been corrected on two occasions; details of those corrections are given below. Although there are more readings peculiar to *Qd* than to *Oj*, their nature differs: in *Oj* they may be substantial; in *Qd* they are often trivial and the result of carelessness. *Qd* contains a complete text in which lines 12–15 and 16–19 are transposed and lines 961–2 and 1193–4 are inverted. Irregular readings peculiar to *Qd* are found at lines 29, 94, 155, 171, 195, 234, 352 etc.

Either *Oj* or *Qd* would have been suitable as a base text. On many occasions, for example at lines 270, 360, 471, 506–8 and 511–12, the two texts agree and offer better readings than most of the other texts. The choice between *Oj* and *Qd* is made more difficult because, where they differ, for example at lines 203, 218, 728, 961–2 and 988, both texts generally give acceptable versions. However, at lines 122, 306, 580 and 791, *Oj* makes better sense than *Qd*, while at lines 30–1 and 247 its version is better from a rhetorical point of view. *Qd* often gives a plural where a singular would be better or *vice versa*: lines 45, 574, 896, 904 and 1013. On the other hand, *Qd* can make better sense than *Oj*, as at line 476 (see note to lines 466–81). These occasions being relatively rare and *Oj* having fewer individual readings than *Qd*, *Oj* has been chosen as base text.

Corrections in Oj

The scribe has corrected some errors. In line 67 he has added *y*, and in line 184 he has inserted *et* in a space which he had left. In line 219 *qulconques* has been changed to *quiconques*. In line 962 he has added *le*.

Certain changes in spelling were mentioned earlier in the description of *Oj*.[1] Additional examples include: 286 *lyesce* to *leesce*; 471, 506 *Affin* to *A fin*; 701 *Autruy* to *Autry*; 1088 *courcant* to *coursant*; Explicit: *fortunes* to *fortunez*. It is not certain that these changes were made by the scribe. The same is true of the erasures in the text: *dont* has been altered to *don* in line 32; *Ne ilz* to *Nilz* in line 55; *des* to *de* twice in line 204. In line 312 *de* has been deleted between *recorde* and *sa*; *celle* has been changed to *elle* in line 408; *resourse* to *sourse* in line 611; *sa robe* to *robe* in line 808.

The further series of corrections (*Oj²*) affect thirty-four lines. In the list which follows, corrected letters are in Roman and oblique lines indicate that the correction is above the line: 11 et; 17 conce*voir*; 73 m*es*tre; 83 b*end*ent; 122 *qui* to *quil*; 130 a; 208 *aucune* to *aucun*; 244 rediray; 247 doy /je/ estre; 390 sadonne; 488 selle; 492 esmailleurs; 546 livres /ou/ en prose; 600 *Et* to *En*; 614 *Que des fames* nous; 689 haulouer; 748 *seellees* to *sellees*; 761 *neu* to *neuz*; 778 ce; 799 occupee; 804 scet /tour/ ne; 812 de fait; 848 en voie; 908 plus *que*; 909 aguetz; 951 sa; 969 ou; 988 ce; 1005 envyeux; 1022 *prie* to *crie*; 1062 maistre est repris; 1137 a; 1157 l*autre*; 1241 part*i*s. While certain corrections seem to be individual (lines 17, 247, 600, 614, 689, 804, 812 etc.), others were probably made with the help of a manuscript akin to *Nf* and *Nj* or perhaps *Pc* (lines 11, 122, 130, 208, 799, 988, 1157 and 1241).

While the first series of corrections in *Oj* is a normal part of the preparation of a manuscript, does the presence of a second series of emendations and of corrections (*Oj²*) make the text unsuitable for use as a base? The emendations raise again the problem of contamination, which was discussed earlier.[2] The cases listed above are clear examples of an operation which underlay the preparation of many a fifteenth-century manuscript. Evidence of contamination also exists in texts from other manuscripts, for example *Nj* and *Qd*, which have been used as base in the edition of other poems. In the case of *Nj* and *Qd*, however, the evidence is insufficient for the case to be proven.[3] Given that contamination is widespread, as was shown earlier, its presence in *Oj* does not of itself make the manuscript unsuitable for use as a base.

[1] See pp. 94–5.   [2] See pp. 52–4.
[3] See pp. 83 and 123.

The discussion of the texts of the *Debat des Deux Fortunés d'Amours*, in the course of which *Oj* was chosen as base text, considered the text as it exists today, that is *Oj* plus *Oj*². In other words, *Oj*, even with the corrections of *Oj*², contains the best text. It does not follow, however, that *Oj*² should be given the same credence as *Oj*, especially since *Oj*² is often idiosyncratic. In the edition which follows, the readings of *Oj*² have been accepted only if they have substantial support.

LE DEBAT DES DEUX FORTUNÉS D'AMOURS   *Oj*, 37r

Ung jour passé fu, namie granment,
En un chastel, assis moult plaisanment
Et bien duisant a tout esbatement,
4 Que maintes belles
Haultes dames et doulces damoiselles
Enrichissent par la grant bonté d'elles.
Si leur ouÿ compter maintes nouvelles
8 Lez une couche,
Et je fu loing, pensif, triste et farouche
Comme cellui que Dueil espoint et touche,
Sans yeulx mouvoir et sans ouvrir la bouche;
12 Et escoutoye
Në ou parler d'elles ne me boutoye,
Mais mon penser et ma langue arrestoye
Et de faillir a parler me doubtoye,
16 Ardant d'apprendre
Et d'aucun bien recevoir et comprendre
En si hault lieu ou Honneur se doit prendre,
Ou j'estoye le plus nice et le mendre.
20 Yleq estoient
Des chevaliers qui hault renon portoient.
Aprés disner vers elles s'esbatoient;
D'onneur, d'armes et d'amours quaquetoient.
24 Mains propos dirent

...le debat sur la quantite de fortune des biens et des maulz damours (...le traictie des biens et des maulz de fortune sur amours *Nj*) que aucuns nomment le gras et le mesgre *NfNj*. ...le gras et le maigre *Ph*, *No heading OaPc*.

1 fu n.] moult n. *Pc*, fu na pas *Ph*.   4 Quant *Ph*.   5 doulce *Nf*.   6 pour *Ph*.   7 Et *OaPh*; les o. *NfNjOaPcPhQd*.   9 Et je qui fu l. p. et f. *NfNj*.   10 qui *Pc*; espraint *Oa*.   11 ne *OaPcPh*.   12-15 *and* 16-19 *Transposed Qd*.   12 Si *Pc*.   13 Et en p. *Pc*.   14 parler *Pc*.   16 Ardans *Pc*.   17 r.] concevoir *Oj*².   19 Si fu de tous le p. n. et le m. *OaPhQd*.   21 De *NfNj*; honneur *Pc*.   23 D'o., d'a.] Donneurs da. *Oa*, Donneur et da. *Pc*.   24 Maint *Pc*.

Et mains bons mos dont les dames se rirent,
Et compterent comptes qui bien leur sirent.
Et en parlant a demander se mirent
28 Que c'est d'amours;
Et qu'il y a assez joye et doulours,   37v
Et jeux et ris, et puis lermes et plours,
Et joyeux chans et trestristes clamours;
32 Et don ce vient
Qu'en son dangier ainsi passer couvient –
Et tost ou tart chascun sa foys y vient
Dont l'un joyeux, l'autre triste devient –
36 Et qu'en une heure
Tel rit du cuer, qui aprés des yeulx pleure,
L'un est eureux et l'autre est au desseure,
L'un a plaisir, Dueil court a l'autre seure,
40 L'un rit et chante,
L'autre maudit sa fortune meschante,
L'autre est ravy en pensee plaisante,
L'un ne s'en plaint ne l'autre ne s'en vante.
44 Ainsi endurent
Leurs pensees tant comme elles leur durent,
Et desirent ce qu'oncques ne voulurent
Et deviennent tous autres qu'ilz ne furent
48 Pour cuider plaire:
Cil qui jangloit veult songier et soy taire,
Et le songeart du joyeux contrefaire,
Et si cuide chascun d'eulx le mieulx faire.
52 Si les gouverne
Et enyvre du vin de sa taverne
Amours qui clos les tient dedens son cerne,
N'ilz ne scevent huis, porte ne posterne
56 Par ou saillir.
Un jour les fait trembler et tressaillir,   38r
L'autre d'ardeur et cuer et corps faillir,

---

25 maint bon mot *Pc*.   26 b. len s. *Qd*; firent *Oa*.   27 parlent *Qd*.   29 Et qu'il] Quil *Qd*.   30 Et joyeux ris *OaPhQd*.   31 Tres plaisans chans *OaPhQd*; et t. c.] et tristes c. *Ph*.   35 t. d.] t. en d. *NfPcPh*.   36 Et en poy de h. *Pc*.   37 de c. *Oa*.   38 Lun au dessoubz et la. est au d. *Pc*.   40 Lun rit a lautre *Oa*.   41 meschance *Qd*.   42 plaisance *Oa*.   43 se p. *Pc*.   45 elle *PhQd*; leurs *Oa*.   46 En desirant ce que onc ne v. *Pc*.   49 quil j. voult *Qd*; et retaire *Pc*.   50 sonjant *NfNj*.   54 les t.] les a *Ph*.   58 dardent *Qd*; et corps et cuer *NfNj*.

Adés chierir et adés assaillir,
60   Puis mal, puis bien,
N'ilz n'ont pouoir ne franchise de rien.
Ou Amours est, il veult que tout soit sien
Et gouverne sens, vouloir et maintien
64   Par sa maistrise;
Et des qu'il a la pensee conquise
Et ou logeis sa droitte merche mise,
Il y veult faire aussi bien a sa guise
68   Qu'en sa maison.
Plus n'y a lieu le pouoir de raison;
Du chastïer n'est il mie saison;
Penser ailleurs, ce semble desraison.
72   Amours son estre
Prent es haulx cuers comme seignieur et mestre,
N'oncques n'eusmes ne pere në ancestre
Qui en son temps ne l'ait veu ainsi estre;
76   Dont fault il dire
Que son pouoir et son haultain empire
Est si puissant qu'on n'y scet contredire.
Roys par force ne clercs par livres lire
80   Ne s'en deffendent.
Ilz voient bien les laz qu'Amours leur tendent,
Maiz de leur gré dedens les laz se rendent.
Plaisir, Desir, ces deux les yeulx leur bendent,
84   Si font hommage
Et vont cerchant leur tresplaisant dommage,   38v
Vueillent ou non. Du gré de leur courage,
Par franchise, se mettent en servage.
88   Rien ne leur vault,
Leur ost armé ne leur grant palais hault.
Amours a qui de leur pouoir ne chault
Leur fait sentir un desir trop plus chault
92   Que feu de pailles,

59 A. cheoir *Pc*. 63 sans v. *OaPh*. 65 sa p. *Ph*. 66 au l. *Oa*, en l. *Pc*. 67 Il y v.] Il v. *NfOaPhQd*, En v. *Pc*, Il en v. *Nj*. 69 ne p. ne r. *Pc*. 70 Du ch.] Et de chanter *Pc*. 73 es] ex *Qd*. 74 Oncques *Ph*; ne parent ne a. *NfNj*. 75 Qui en son t.] Que en t. *Pc*. 76 il fault *NfNjPcPh*. 77 Qui *Ph*. 78 ne s. c. *Ph*. 79 pour l. *NfNjOaPcQd*; livre *OaPhQd*. 81 v. b.] v. *Nf*; leurs *Qd*. 82 Et *NfNjOaPcPhQd*. 85 Si *Ph*. 86 ou nom *Ph*. 89 Leurs host a. *Ph*, Leur armeure *Pc*; p.] parlens (*sic*) *Ph*. 90 *Omitted Oa*: Amour *Nj*.

Qui entre ou cuer et dedens les entrailles,
Parmy fossez et espesses murailles,
Tout au travers de l'ost et des batailles,
96 Et se lance par ces harnois de mailles
Ou plus profont,
Dont cuer et corps frit souvent et defont
Par tel party qu'ilz ne scevent qu'ilz font,
100 Car ce penser tous les autres confont.
Si fait valoir
Les cuers des bons et croistre leur vouloir
Et mettre paour et crainte en nonchaloir
104 Et de tous faiz honteux leur cuer douloir,
Et si leur donne
Le hardement et la voulenté bonne
Qui par honneur croist en eulx et foisonne.
108 Mais les gaiges dont il les guerredonne
A son loisir,
C'est de lever un jour, l'autre gesir,
Huy de joye, demain de desplaisir,
112 Adés d'espoir, adés d'ardant desir
Tout a son vueil;   39r
Un jour refus, un autre bel acueil,
Moitié confort, moitié soucy et dueil,
116 Parmy les gens rire la lerme a l'ueil,
Son semblant faindre,
Souffrir douleur et ne s'en oser plaindre,
Et ses souspirs estrangler et refraindre,
120 Et d'un regart a coup son mal estaindre
Et sa mesaise.
Se une dame monstre a un qu'il lui plaise,
Il est ce jour et plus riche et plus aise
124 Que s'il gaignoit tout l'or d'Auffrique et d'Aise.
Le cuer lui vole

---

93 en c. *Pc*; leurs (leur *Ph*) e. *OaPhQd*.   94 et e. m.] et esepesses m. *Qd*.   96 *Omitted NʃNj*, *Scored
out Ph²*(?): ses *Qd*; ces espesses m. *Oj*; maille *Ph*.   97 Au *OaQd*, En *Pc*, Du (?) *Ph²*.   98 f. s. et d.]
fiert s. et d. *Oa*, s. sentredeffont *Ph²*.   99 qui f. *Ph*.   100 tout *Pc*.   102 Le cuer *Ph*, Le cuerz *Ph²*.
103 Et m.] Mectre *Pc*; a n. *OaPcQd*.   104 les cuers *Oa*, leur cueurs *Pc*.   105 sil *Qd*.   107 Que *Pc*.
108 les reguerdonne *Nj*, les reguerredonne *Ph²*.   109 Et *Oa*.   110 de l.] l. *Ph*, de l. *Ph²*.   111 d. de d.]
lautre de d. *Oa*.   112 A. espoir a. ardant d. *Pc*: A. de joye *NʃNj*, A. espoir *Ph²*.   119 les s. *Nf*; e. et
r.] transgloutir et r. *Pc*.   120 estraindre *Qd*.   122 qui *NʃOjPcPhQd*.   124 gaignast *Pc*.

Et de joye pert maintien et parolle;
Et s'aucun scet son secret, il l'acolle.

128 En ce plaisir se murtrit et affole
Plus que devant,
Et se remet a penser plus avant.
Voue et jure d'estre loyal servant

132 A tousjours mais tant qu'il sera vivant,
Mais peu lui dure.
Il oyt aprés quelque response dure
Et voyt autry qui quiert son aventure,

136 Ou l'en lui dit quelque parolle obscure
Dont il se doubte;
Si pert a coup celle grant joye toute,
Se deult et plaint plus que s'il eust la goute.

140 Il va, il vient, il se couche, il s'accoute,
Il fuit les gens.   39ᵛ
Il vient a l'uis et puis rentre dedens,
Il dit qu'il a mal en teste ou en dens,

144 Au lit se met, puis envers, puis adens;
Si se tempeste
Et de veillier rompt son corps et sa teste,
Ne il n'a plaisir de joye ne de feste

148 Et fait tout seul sa plainte et sa requeste,
Pensif et mourne.
S'il est couchié d'un lez, sur l'autre tourne,
Puis se lieve, puis couchier s'en retourne;

152 Et lui tarde bien que le jour adjourne
Afin que d'elle
Il puist oïr ou rapport ou nouvelle
Et qu'elle dit et comme elle l'appelle;

156 Et lui mesmes croist sa plaie mortelle
Par telz ouvrages.
Puis envoie ses plus privez messages
Qui bien souvent ne sont mie trop sages,

126 p. m. et p.] p. et m. et p. *Ph.*   128 et saffole *Oa.*   130 en p. *PcPhQd.*   131 Puis jure et voue de.
l. s. *NfNj*: Voire et j. *Oa.*   132 Et *Oa.*   135 autre qui quier *Qd.*   138 Et *Pc*; c. pensee t. *Pc*, ceste joye
trestoute *Ph.*   139 que cil qui a g. *NfNj.*   141 fiert *Pc.*   143 et en d. *OaPh.*   145 Et *NfNj.*   146 Cil
de v. se rompt et c. et t. *NfNj.*   147 Nil na p. ne de j. ne de f. *OaPh.*   148 f. t. s.] f. sa t. s. *Nf*; sa
r.] sa queste *Ph.*   151 sen l. *NfNj*; se r. *NfOa.*   152 Puis se relieve et daller hors sa tourne *Pc*: j.
nadjourne *Ph.*   154 Il puisse o. *PcPh.*   155 Et quelle dit et c. elle sappelle *Ph*, Et quel dit et c. elle
appelle *Qd*, Et quelle dist et comment on la. *Pc.*   156 mesme *Nj.*   159 ne sonu (*sic*) *Oa.*

160 Et s'ilz portent quelque plaisans langages
 Qu'il leur demande,
 Ilz font tousjours la nouvelle plus grande
 Et dïent bien qu'elle se recommande
164 A lui cent foiz, et que par eulx lui mande
 Qu'il se conforte
 Et qu'en espoir s'esjouÿsse et deporte.
 Lors embrasse cellui qui lui rapporte
168 Et va passer trois fois devant la porte
 Pour veoir la preuve,   40r
 Et fait tantost faire une robe neufve,
 Ne de chanter n'est nul qui le desmeuve.
172 Et s'ainsi est qu'il la rencontre ou treuve
 En aucuns lieux
 Et el lui rit de la bouche ou des yeulx,
 Il est ravy trop plus hault qu'es tiers cieulx
176 Et prent pour soy tousjours la chose au mieulx;
 Et se tient cointe
 Et des prouchains de sa dame s'acointe,
 Ne de meschans n'a vouloir d'estre acointe,
180 Mais en doulceur tost adresse et appointe
 Du tout son fait,
 Et hait vergoigne et tout villain meffait
 Et lait parler qui son parleur deffait:
184 Il change meurs et en mieulx se parfait.
 Ainsi disoient
 Les chevaliers qui la se deduisoient;
 Comme savans, bien profont en lisoient
188 Et sur ces mos aux dames devisoient.
 Une y avoit
 Belle et bonne, qui bien parler savoit
 Comme il affiert et quant elle devoit,
192 Qui leurs vouloirs assez appercevoit;
 Et pour esbatre

160 Et silz rapportent quel que p. l. *Pc*: quelques *NʃNjOaPhQd*. 161 Qui *OaPcPh*. 164 que par luy luy m. *Pc*. 169 veir *Qd*; lespreuve *NʃOaPc*. 171 Et *NʃPhQd*; de ch. n'e. nul] de ch. nul *Qd*. 172 recontre *Pc*. 174 el lui rit] elle lui rit *OaPcPh*, elle rit *Ph²*; et des y. *Oa*. 175 que t. c. *Oa*, que es c. *Pc*, questre es c. *NʃNj*; tieulx *Ph*. 179 Et *Ph*; Ne des m. *NʃNjOaPcQd*. 180 tout a. *PcPh*. 182 hoit *Nj*. 183 lay p. *Nj*; son parler (parleur *Ph²*) d. *PhQd*. 184 ch. m.] ch. en mieulx *Pc*. 188 sus *Pc*. 191 Quant il (y *Oa*) a. *NʃNjOaPcPhQd*.

S'ala un peu en leur parler embatre
Et demanda a trois d'eulx ou a quatre,
196 Pour les faire joyeusement debatre
Entre les dames, 40v
Que lui deissent verité, sur leurs ames,
Sans en mentir pour hommes ne pour fames,
200 Si chier qu'ilz ont d'eschever honte et blasmes,
Comme loyaulx:
S'en amours a biens et plaisirs si haulx
Et d'autre part dueil et mortelx assaulx,
204 Duquel y a plus? De biens ou de maulx?
Un peu muserent;
L'un sur l'autre de parler s'excuserent.
Les uns prïent, les autres refuserent;
208 En telz honneurs aucun espace userent.
Mais un d'entr'eulx
Vy, qui n'estoit pas mourne ne songeux,
Maigre, palle ne melencolïeux,
212 Mais en bon point, sain, alegre et joyeulx
Sans point de soing;
Et son semblant lui monstroit bien tesmoing
Qu'il n'avoit pas de reconfort besoing,
216 Ainçois estoit de tous maulx assez loing.
Si dist adoncques:
'Quant vous autres n'en voulez dire doncques,
Parleray jë, et di devant quiconques
220 Qui bien aiment et qui amerent oncques,
Que en bien amer –
Dont nul ne doit le hault los entamer,
Qui que s'en loe ou s'en vueille blasmer –
224 Y a trop plus du doulx que de l'amer.
Je l'ose dire.' 41r
Adonq se print une dame a soubzrire

194 Sela *Ph*; esbatre *Pc*. 195 demande *Qd*. 198 Quilz lui d. *NfNjPcPhQd*, Quilz d. *Oa*. 199 p. homme ne p. femme *Oa*. 200 h.] hontes *Nf*; blasme *Oa*. 202 Si en a. a b. et p. h. *Oa*: bien *Ph*. 203 duelz *OaQd*; d. et mort et a. *Oj*. 204 de b.] ou de b. *Pc*. 205 penserent *Pc*. 207 prierent *NfNjPcPh*. 208 En t. oeuvres *NfNj*; aucune e. *NfNjOaOjPh²Qd*, aucune esperance *Ph*. 210 ne m. *NfNjPcPh²*. 211 M. ne p. ne m. *Pc*. 214 En son s. *Qd*; portoit *Nf Nj*, moustre *Oa*. 215 point *Pc*. 216 a. l.] au plus l. *NfNjOaPcPhQd*. 218 ne v. *NfNjPcPhQd*. 219 quelconques *NfOa*, quelzconques *NjPcPhQd*. 221 Bien a. *Oa*. 223 Que qui *NfNj*. 224 de d. que de la mer *Oa*. 226 A.] Et dont *Oa*.

Et en rïant lui a dit: 'Dea, beau sire,

228 Vostre parler ne nous puet pas souffire,

Et se a par vous

Amours vous est si courtois et si douls

Qu'il vous laisse sans paine et sans couroux,

232 Il ne fait pas puet estre ainsi a tous.

Trop de legier

Se pourroit mettre a autry fais jugier

Qui n'a esté en un pareil dangier;

236 Mais, s'il vous plaist, pour la chose abregier

Dittes comment,

Pour quel raison ne par quel mouvement

Vous maintenez a vostre entendement

240 Qu'il y a plus plaisance que tourment.'

'Je vous diray',

Dist il tantost, 'et ja n'en mentiray.

Et si sachiez que maint desplaisir ay,

244 Et maint ennuy que ja ne rediray,

Pour amours pris.

Si sçay trop mieulx qu'en doit valoir le pris

Ne d'en parler ne doy estre repris,

248 Car a chier coust l'ay a l'essay apris

Mainte sepmaine,

Et n'ay pas eu tousjours la teste saine.

Mais il n'est bien ne joye si haultaine

252 Que l'en prise se on l'a a peu de paine,

Ne ce n'est droit,   41v

Car se chascun avoit ce qu'il vouldroit,

Ne bien servir ne souffrir n'y vauldroit;

256 Ainsi Raison et Loyaulté fauldroit,

Et Crainte et Honte,

Ne on ne sçaroit plus qu'Honneur vault et monte

Car bien et mal seroit tout en un compte,

260 Ne Hault Vouloir qui tout vaint et seurmonte

---

227 dist *Pc.* 228 doibt *Pc.* 229 Et se par v. *Oa.* 231 plaise *Ph.* 234 m. a autres f. *NfNj,* m. autrui f. *Qd,* m. a (en *Pc*) autruy fait *OaPc,* m. a autrui sans *Ph.* 236–7 Or nous dictes (?) p. la ch. a. | Donques c. *Pc.* 238 Par *NfNjOaPcPhQd;* et par *Nj.* 239 en *Nf.* 244 ja ne jehiray *Pc.* 246 Et *Oa.* 247 nen doy *NfNjOaPhQd;* doy je e. *Oj²* (doye e. *Oj).* 248 a ch. c. en ay le. a. *Pc.* 251 b. que j. *Qd.* 252 Que on la p. *Pc.* 254 ce *Ph.* 255 A b. s. *Oa;* ne v. *NfPc.* 258 Ne ne s. *Oa;* s. p.] s. *Ph;* quamour *Qd.* 259 feroit *Oa;* s. t.] t. s. *NfNj;* a un c. *Ph.* 260 Ne vault valoir *Ph;* t. vault *Oa.*

Ne cerche guiere
A s'empeschier en basse euvre et legiere.
Mais qui acquiert en douleur chose chiere,
264　Plus a de bien et de joyeuse chiere
En sa comqueste (*sic*)
Et lui semble plus hault et plus honneste
Le bien qu'il a a paine et a requeste,
268　Et en maine plus de joye et de feste
Et mieulx le prise
Que s'il l'eust eu tout a sa belle guise,
Car Nature a en nous ceste loy mise
272　Que mieulx nous plaist chose a dangier conquise.
A ce propos,
Aprés travail nous plaist plus le repos
Et la grant soif fait boire enmy les pos,
276　Et es perilz acquiert on les grans los.
Assez tesmoingne
Nature en nous toute ceste besoigne
Quant nous voions qu'en son euvre elle adjoigne
280　Souvent au doulx quelque chose qui poigne,
Et les assemble.　　　　　　　　　　　　　　　42r
On le voit bien es rosiers, ce me semble;
Et la mousche de ce bien les ressemble,
284　Qui porte miel et aguillon ensemble.
Or je delesse
Celle raison et viens a la lëesce,
Ayse de cuer et haultaine richesce
288　Que un amant puet avoir de sa maistresse
Si largement;
Au bien aussi et a l'amendement
Que jeune cuer en son commencement
292　Reçoit d'Amours pour son avancement,
S'il a vouloir

261 Ne forche *Pc*; guerre *Oa*. 262 de b. e. *OaQd*. 263 en honneur *Pc*. 264 Mieulx la garde et plus fait bonne ch. *Pc*. 266 haulte *PcPh*. 270 sil eust *NfNjOaPh*; sil eust t. a sa b. devise *Pc*. 274 mieulx *Oa*. 275 Et g. s. f. b. a mesme les poz *NfNj*, Et la g. s. nous f. b. a plain pos *Pc*. 276 Appres reffus viennent souvent doulx motz *Pc*. 279 son e.] son envye *Ph*. 280 aux d. *Ph*. 282 es roses *NfNjOaPcPhQd*; se me s. *NjOaPcPhQd*. 283 m. en ce *Pc*. 284 Qui morte m. *Ph*. 286 Ceste *NfNjPc*, Telle *Ph*. 288 Que un a.] Demy a. *Oa*; peust *Pc*. 290 lentendement *NfOa*, lemmendement *Pc*. 291 entendement *Ph*. 292 damour *Nf*; par *OaPh*.

N'entencïon de jamais rien valoir.
Premierement il met a nonchaloir
296 Tout ce que cuer gentil ne doit vouloir.
Tout son cuer tire
A parvenir au hault bien qu'il desire;
Et pour savoir son euvre bien conduire,
300 Desir l'apprent a lire et a escripre
Pour mieulx entendre
Tout ce qui sert au fait ou il veult tendre.
Et le plaisir qu'Amours lui fait lors prendre
304 Lui donne cuer et volenté d'apprendre
Et de savoir;
Si veult rommans et nouveaux dis avoir,
Et met son sens, sa paine et son devoir
308 A les pouoir entendre et concevoir.   42v
Lit et relit,
Et ce qui fait a son propos eslit;
Un mot lui nuit, l'autre lui abelit.
312 Si recorde sa leçon en son lit,
Tresententis
Et d'en savoir du tout entalentis.
La est le lieu ou Amours le gentis
316 Tient son escole a tous ses apprentis
Sains et malades,
Dont les plusieurs portent leurs couleurs fades.
Or veult l'amant faire dis et balades,
320 Lettres closes, secretes ambaxades;
Et se retrait
Et s'enfermë en chambre ou en retrait
Pour escripre plus a l'aise et a trait,
324 Et met une heure a faire un tout seul trait
De lettre close.
Un peu escript, puis songe et se repose,
Puis efface pour mettre une autre chose,

295 en *NfNjPh*. 298 a h. b. *Nf*. 299 Et p. s. de soy oster toute yre *Pc*: condire *Nj*. 300 a l. et a e.] a l. et e. *Oj*, a lescrire et a lire *Oa*. 302 T. ce quil s. au f. il v. t. *Ph*. 304 donner *Oa*. 306 Il *Nf NjPc*, Sil *OaPhQd*; ou *OaPhQd*; savoir *OaQd*. 307 savoir *NfNjPc*. 308 De *NfNjOaPcPhQd*. 310 ce quil voist *Pc*. 311 mist *Ph*. 312 Se r. *Oj*. 313 Tresententif *Nf*. 314 entalentif *Nf*. 315 ly g. *NfNjOa*. 316 T. son e.] T. e. *Ph*; ses a.] se a. *Nf*. 318 D. a pl. en fait de c. f. *Pc*: les c. f. *Oa*. 319 vient *Oa*. 322 Et puis se. en ch. et en r. *NfNj*: et en r. *Oa*. 323 P. e. p. aise et actrait *Ph*.

328 Et volentiers mettroit plus, mais il n'ose;
Or prent courage
De adrecer bien sa lettre et son message.
Et s'il apprent de ces choses l'usage,

332 Il en devient en tous endrois plus sage
Au long aler,
Et en scet mieulx bien taire et bien parler,
Bien soy garder et bien dissimuler,

336 Querir son bien et sagement celer
Sans soy vanter.   43r
S'aucuns scevent ou dancer ou chanter,
Il les vouldra acointer et hanter

340 Et les chetifs delaisser et planter.
Ainsi s'avance
Et y aprent maniere et contenance,
Sens, hardement, maintien et ordonnance;

344 Et si acquiert des bons la congnoissance
Et est tenuz
Pour gracïeux et partout bien venuz,
Amé, aydé, chiery et soustenuz,

348 Et par honneur des gros et des menuz
Se fait priser.
Aprés met paine a songier et viser
De quelque habit tout nouvel adviser,

352 Et s'estudie a bien le deviser
Nouvellement,
Et le vestir et porter gentement,
Et d'assez peu soy tenir nettement,

356 Marchier a droit, chevaucher seurement
Sus fiers chevaulx,
Tourner en l'air son coursier les grans saulx,
Faire saillir le feu de ces quarreaulx

360 Et affuÿr les dames aux quarneaulx

330 De a. b.] De a. *OaPh*, De dicter b. *Pc*.   331 ses *Qd*.   332 d. plus abille et p. s. *NfNj*.   333 loing
Nf.   338 ou chanter ou dancer *Qd*.   339 I les vendra *Oj*, Il les veudra *Pc*.   340 delaissir et p. *Qd*,
delaisse et ahonter *Pc*.   342 a. savoir et c. *NfNj*, a. menniere et c. *Pc*.   343 S. h. maniere et o. *Nf*
Nj, S. et honneur m. et o. *Pc*.   344 de vous *Qd*.   346 Partout creus et p. b. v. *Pc*.   348 grans
NfNjPcPh.   350 A. me p. *Qd*; p. de s. *Pc*; v.] visiter *Oa*.   351 t. n.] de n. *Pc*.   352 se. de *Qd*.
354 porter et vestir *NfNj*; nectement *Nf*.   357 Se a f. ch. *Pc*: Sur *NfNjPh*, Sans *Oa*.   358 T. aler
(T. alaer *Nj*) son c. *NfNjPc*; a g. s. *NfNjOaPcPhQd*.   359 de ses *NfQd*.   360 Et raviser les d.
NfNj, Et a suir les d. *Oa*, Quant apperchoit les d. *Pc*, Et a veoir les d. *Ph*.

Dessus la voye.
Et s'il avient que sa dame le voye
Et que sans plus un regart lui envoye,
364 Il pensera que le cuer le convoye.
Or est repeu   43ᵛ
Et s'esjouït et contente de peu
Quant de long temps celle vëoir n'a peu,
368 Qui en passant l'a d'un seul regart peu
A chiere lie.
Lors Fol Cuider et Jeunesse et Folie
Et Souvenir qui la pensee lie,
372 Lui font oster toute melencolie,
Et cuide bien
Que la belle lui vueille assez de bien,
Et jure Dieu qu'il est et sera sien
376 N'autre qu'elle n'amera il pour rien.
Passe et rapasse,
Et de passer devant l'uys ne se lasse;
Et met a point ou sa robe ou sa tasse.
380 Et sur la nuyt va chantant a voix basse,
Et s'entretient
Par soubz les braz a quelque autre qui vient
Avecques lui, qui bien chante ou bien tient;
384 Et se sa dame a la fenestre vient
Soy monstrer goute
Ou se le vent une fenestre boute,
Dont il cuide que sa dame l'escoute,
388 S'il va couchier joieux, n'en faictes doubte.
Si arraisonne
Son compaignon a qui sa foy s'adonne,
Et toute nuit la teste lui estonne
392 De lui compter comme elle est belle et bonne,
Et du semblant   44ʳ
Qu'el lui a fait, comme il cuide, en emblant,

364 Or p. *NfNj*. 366 Si *NfNj*; dun peu *Pc*. 367 ne peu *Pc*. 368 passent *Qd*. 371 sa p. *NfNj*, a
p. *Pc*. 373 cuider *Oj*. 376 nam. jour p. r. *NfNjOaPcPh*. 377 Et passe et r. *Ph*. 378 Et de p. d.]
Et d. *Nf*; se passe *Pc*. 380 sus *Pc*; va et chante a v. b. *Oa*. 382 le bras *OaPcQd*, les mains *NfNj*;
aqulque (*sic*) *Qd*. 383 Mieulx son prive et qui plus luy revient *Pc*: et *Ph*. 387 D. il c.] Adonc c.
NfNj, Adont il c. *PcPh*. 388 Sen va *NfNjPhQd*, Cil va *Oa*, Si va *Pc*; ne f. d. *Oa*, nen fay (fait *Nj*)
pas d. *NfNj*.

Et qu'el müa sa couleur en tremblant;
396 Et demande qu'il lui en va semblant.
Et le compains
Qui congnoist bien comment il est attains,
Pour lui plaire ne lui en dit pas mains;
400 Ains le scet bien de ses plaisirs haultains
Lors blasonner.
Et au matin, a la messe sonner,
L'amant s'en va l'eglise environner
404 Et l'eaue benoiste a sa dame donner,
Et la paix prendre
Tout volentiers pour lui porter et tendre,
Car c'est le bien ou il veult lors entendre
408 Qu'aprés elle baisier sans plus attendre.
Et cerche festes,
Nopces, esbaz et autres lieux honnestes
Ou les amans quierent leurs droittes questes;
412 Et la fait il, quant il puet, ses requestes,
S'il est savant.
Il chante, il dance, il est humble et servant;
S'il scet du bien, il met tout en avant.
416 A festoier jusqu'a soleil levant
Amours le porte.
Desir le maine et Espoir le conforte,
Et Plaisance le soustient et supporte;
420 Et le desir de sa dame l'enhorte
A s'esjouÿr,   44v
A chacer Dueil et Tristesce fouÿr,
A soy faire regarder et ouÿr
424 Et les autres de le veoir s'esjouÿr
Par grant plaisance.
Et se ainsi est que Fortune l'avance
Tant qu'il tieigne par la main a la dance

396 que lui *NjOa*, qui lui *Ph*.   398 congnois *Qd*; comme il en (comme il *Oj*) est a. *NfNjOj*.   399 luie en d. (*sic*) *Qd*.   403 le. avironner *PcPhQd*, a le. annonner *Oa*.   404 Et l'e.] Le. *Pc*.   407 attendre *Pc*.   408 Quelle veoir sans a quelque aultre entendre *Pc*: baise *Oa*.   409 Or *NfNjOaPcPhQd*; cerches *Qd*.   411 leurs a. *Ph*; droite *Qd*.   412 peust *Pc*; r.] reques (*sic*) *Qd*.   414 h. et s.] h. s. *NfNj*, h. et savant *Ph*.   415 met la t. a. *NfNjOaPcPhQd*.   418 D. le m. es. le reconforte *Nf*.   420 le regart *NfNjOa PcPhQd*.   421 Et sesjoyst *Oa*.   422 Et ch. *NfNjPcPhQd*, Et chanter *Oa*.   423 Et *NfNjOaPcPhQd*; fouir *Ph*.   424 de le (lee (?) *Nf*) v. esjoir *NfPcPh*, de le v. essouyr *Nj*, de le v. resjoir *OaQd*. 427 qu'il t.] quil se t. *Pc*; en la d. *Nf*.

428 Sa maistresse par droitte bienwueillance,
Et qu'elle vueille
Monstrer semblant que bien en gré recueille
Ses fais et dis et doulcement l'accueille,

432 Il ne croit pas que jamais il se dueille;
Mais lui souffist
Son bon eür plus qu'oncques mais ne fist,
N'il n'est couroux qui alors lui meffist

436 Ne il ne sera ja ce jour desconfist.
Et cerche et quiert,
Et ce qui plus plaist a sa dame enquiert,
Et de savoir son plaisir la requiert,

440 Et si fait tant que l'acointance acquiert
De ceulx qui sont
D'elle prouchains, ou qui vers elle vont,
Et qui sa grace et sa priveté ont,

444 Et qu'elle hante ou qui plaisir lui font;
Ceulx il festoie.
Pour estre entr'eulx mieulx venu se cointoie
Et devant eulx a la table nettoie,

448 Et par ville les maine et les costoie;
Et tant les sert   45r
Que par son sens leur bonne amour desert
Et a l'amer les contraint et assert.

452 Ceulx le loent devant elle en appert
Et le blasonnent,
Et de ses faiz lui parlent et raisonnent,
Et sans savoir a quoy leurs mos s'adonnent

456 Devers elle bonne entree lui donnent.
Et avec eulx
Maintenant l'un ou maintenant les deux
Le mainent la ou il n'ose aler seulx,

460 Et il y va dessoubz l'ombre de ceulx
Qui pas n'entendent

428 par tres grant b. *Nf.* 430 b. elle r. *Pc.* 431 Ses f. ses diz *Pc.* 434 bon cuer *Oa*; p. que jamais ne f. *Nf.* 435 Il *NfNjOa*; qui james luy m. *Pc.* 436 Il ne (ny *Nj*) s. *NfNj*; desconfiz *Oa.* 437 Or *NfNjOaPcPhQd.* 438 Ce qui plaist plus a sa d. senquiert *Oj.* 443 ou *Pc*; sa priere *OaPh.* 444 Ou *NfNjOaPcPhQd.* 446 P. es. o eulx *Pc*; sacointoye *OaPcPhQd.* 448 Et par la v. les m. et c. *Ph*: par v.] par la v. *Pc*; et les c.] et c. *Oa.* 449 le *Qd.* 451 Car *Ph.* 458 et *NfNjQd*; le d. *Qd.* 459 Les maine *Ph.* 460 desombz (*sic*) *Qd.* 461 netendent (*sic*) *Qd.*

A quelle fin toutes ses euvres tendent.

Neantmoins ce bien pour les servir lui rendent

464 Qu'ilz le mainent, conduisent et attendent

En la maison.

Et s'il treuve quelque fois sa saison

Que Bel Accueil lui donne l'achaison

468 D'oser compter et dire sa raison

En tresgrant crainte,

Et de fairë a la belle sa plainte

Afin de mieulx venir a son attainte,

472 Tant qu'elle voit que ce n'est mie fainte

De ce qu'il dit,

Et el lui donne un courtois escondit

Meslé d'espoir que refus contredit

476 Et d'un regart qui sa durté desdit

A longue attente,   45v

Et il le prent pour soy a son entente,

Il n'est joye que a celle heure il ne sente

480 N'il n'est douleur qui ce jour le tourmente

Ne qui l'esmeuve.

Or prent devise ou brouderie neuve

De quelque mot, fueille ou lettre qu'il treuve,

484 Et la porte, sans que nul l'en desmeuve,

Faitte de point

Ou sur sa robe ou dessus son pourpoint,

Ou en aneaulx s'il ne se broude point,

488 Ou quelque part, s'elle y siet bien a point,

Sur lui ailleurs.

Or fait venir et drapiers et tailleurs,

Broudeurs, ouvriers et bons entretailleurs,

492 Et jouëlliers, orfevres, esmailleurs;

462 quelles fins *Oa*.   463 Et aucun bien pour deservir luy r. *Pc*.   464 la m. *Qd*; m. c.] m. et c. *Ph*.
467 Que bel lui d. la. *Ph*.   470 Et de f.] Et puis de f. *NſNj*.   471 *Omitted OaPh*, Adonc lui fait
inquisicion mainte *NſNj*, Doubteusement ainsy que par contrainte *Pc*.   472 v.] voye *Pc*.   472a La
voulente nest pas de grant contrainte *Ph*.   473 A *Qd*.   474 el] elle *OaPhQd*.   475 Mais le de. *Ph*;
qui *OaQd*.   476 Une autre foiz ung bon mot lui redit *NſNjOjPc*: que sa dame d. *Ph*.   477 longe *Qd*.
478 en son e. *Qd*.   479 tele h. *Ph*; h. il ne s.] h. ne s. *NſNjPcPh*.   480 Il *Oa*.   481 Ne] Le *Nj*;
meuve *Pc*.   482 brodeure *Ph*.   483 De qu. mot ou de feulle quil t. *Pc*.   484 sens *Qd*.   486 sur (sus
PcPh) la r. *NſNjOaPcPhQd*.   488 quelle p. *Qd*; sel lui s. b. a p. *Ph*, sel lui s. mieulx a p. *NſNj*,
selle luy sciet appoint *Pc*.   489 Sus *Pc*; soy *NſNj*.   490 Ou *OaPcPh*; ou brouders ou t. *Pc*.
491 Drappiers o. *Pc*; bon e. *Qd*.   492 joueilleurs *Oa*; orfevre *Nſ*.

Tous embesoigne
Et chascun met en euvre et en besoigne.
En ce faisant d'oisiveté s'esloigne,
496 De tout apprent et de tout pense et soigne
En amendant;
Et en devient plus caut et entendant
Le jeune temps de son aage pendant,
500 Car tout ce qu'est a son desir tendant
Va exploittant
Et s'enjouant o elle et s'esbatant.
Verge ou anel lui offre et si fait tant
504 Qu'elle le prent et lui redonne autant.
Assez lui tarde   46r
Qu'il soit tout seul afin qu'il le regarde
Et qu'il le baise; et chierement le garde
508 Et se prent plus de non le perdre garde
Que cent marcs d'or;
C'est son espargne et son riche tresor.
Et s'il l'a veu et remiré, tresor
512 Il le reprent et le veult veoir encor
Et du doy traire,
Car quantque vient d'elle souëf lui flaire.
Ainsi en fait comme reliquïaire
516 En memoire du gracïeux vïaire
Qui lui plaist si
Qu'il lui semble pour vray qu'il soit ainsi
Qu'oncques d'elle rien ne vint në yssi,
520 Qui ne doie plaire a chascun aussi.
Et s'il avient
Que si a point de ses amours lui vient
Que a sa dame quelque peu en souvient,

---

493 Tout e. *Pc.*   494 ou en b. *Qd.*   495 En ce f. foles oeuvres esloigne *NfNjOaPcPhQd.*   496 Et *Ph*;
de t. poyse *Pc.*   498 p. chault en attendant *Pc.*   499 perdant *Pc.*   500 en son d. *Qd.*   502 Ou (O
Nj) elle va j. et esbatant *NfNj*: Et va j. *Pc*; et (ou *Ph*) esbatant *OaPcPhQd.*   503 a. (anel anel (?)
Qd) du sien lui plaisent t. *NfNjOaPhQd,* a. du sien luy presentant *Pc.*   504 Selle *Pc*; le p.] p. *Qd*;
et] el *Pc*; lui r. a.] lui en donne a. *NfPh,* lui en r. a. *Oa.*   506 la *NfNjPcPh.*   507 la b. *NfNjPcPhQd*;
la g. *NfNjPcPh.*   508 la p. *NfNjPcPh.*   510 cest son r. t. *Pc.*   511 Et sil la veue et remiree (remire (?)
Ph) t. *NfNjPcPh*: Et sil a veu *Oa.*   512 la r. et la v. (et v. *Ph*) *NfNjPcPh*; et v. avoir e. *Oa,* et le remire
e. *Oj.*   514 quanquil v. *Pc*; s. le f. *Qd,* s. f. *Oa.*   515 Quainsi *Ph*; com dun r. *NfNjPcPh,* comme
de r. *Oa.*   516 Et *Ph.*   517 Ou *Ph.*   518 par *Oa*; est a. *NfNJ.*   519 Qu'o.] Car oncques *Ph*; ne nyssi
NfNjPc.   520 Que *NfNj*; p. a] p. et a *Pc*; a.] autressi *OaPh.*   523 poy *Pc.*

524 Ou qu'el lui veult aucun bien, se devient,
    Et il perçoit
    Que le semblant d'elle ne le deçoit
    Mais qu'en bon gré son service reçoit,
528 Et qu'elle veult le faire tel qu'il soit
    Si bon qu'il vaille
    D'avoir honneur en quelque lieu qu'il aille,
    Soit en armes, en presse ou en bataille,
532 Et que tousjours d'avoir renon lui chaille
    Sans nul meffait,   46v
    Il prent courage et s'efforce de fait;
    Et s'il n'a cuer, Amours tout neuf lui fait
536 Et l'enhardit ainsi et le parfait
    D'estre vaillant,
    Entrepreneur, prest, legier et saillant,
    Soit a deffendre ou soit en assaillant.
540 Ja ne sera au premier hurt faillant
    Jusqu'a la mort,
    Ne il n'a jamais a celle heure recort
    Fors de penser qu'a droit, non pas a tort,
544 Sa dame puist en ouÿr bon rapport.
    Et s'il est clercs,
    Il fait livres en rimes ou en vers,
    Ou beaux motez a chants doulx et divers
548 Ne il ne sera cauteleux ne pervers.
    Et se par lettre
    Ou messaige qu'el lui vueille transmettre,
    Elle lui veult quelque hault fait commettre,
552 Cela lui fait le courage ou cuer mettre
    Et maintenir.
    Ainsi Amours fait honneur soustenir
    Et les couärs a prouesse advenir

---

524 qu'el] quelle *OaPh*.   525 Et il aparcoit *Oa*.   527 M. en bon gre *OaPhQd*.   528 Et quel le v. *Ph*; v. le fait tel et quil s. *NſNj*; tel qui s. *Pc*.   531 en p.] en jouste (joustes *Ph*) *NſNjOaPcPhQd*.   534 p. congie *Ph*.   535 na cure a. t. n. le f. *Pc*.   536 Qui *NſNj*.   537 De faire v. *Oa*.   538 Entreprenant *NſNjPc*; l. assaillant *Ph*.   539 en d. *NſNjPc*; aissaillant *Qd*.   540 au p. (aux premiers *Nj*) huis *NſNj*, aux premiers hurs (hus *Pc*) *OaPcPhQd*; faillans *Ph*.   542 Nil nest j. *NſNjOaPcPhQd*; a c. h.] telle h. *Oa*.   543 F. que *Pc*; p. a d. *OaPcPh*.   544 Sa d. en p. o. tout b. r. *Pc*: p.] en p. *Ph*, puit *NſNjQd*.   546 Il f. r. en l. ou en v. *Oa*: en r.] ou en prose *Oj²Ph*; et *NjPc*.   547 Et *Nſ*, En *NjPc*; a haulx d. et d. *Ph*.   550 Ou par m. que luy v. t. *Pc*: qu'el] quil *NſNjPh*, quelle *Oa*.   552 Et la lui f. *Oa*, Ce la luy f. *Pc*; en c. *Pc*, au c. *Qd*.   555 a p. a.] a p. venir *NſNjOa*, a prouce a. *Qd*.

556 Et les tresbons meilleurs en devenir
   De leurs personnes,
   Quant ilz servent a belles et a bonnes
   Qui d'eulx chacent toutes euvres felonnes
560 Sans trespasser de loyauté les bonnes.
   Tantost li homs   47^r
   En amende de ses condicïons
   Et prent a cuer haultes entencïons,
564 Doulx en parler et en armes lÿons
   Et cler vëant,
   A mieulx faire que tous autres bëant
   Et ce qu'il fait lui estre mieulx sëant,
568 Villenies et mauparler hëant.
   Si le conduit
   Ardant Desir et a bonté le duit,
   Si qu'en doulceur devient parfait et duit.
572 Comme le sucre a la chaleur recuit,
   Quant il est prest
   Par recuittes et maint divers apprest,
   Quel part qu'il soit, ou en don ou en prest,
576 Jamais ne fait si non bien ou il est:
   Doncques l'ardure
   De Jennesse, qui soy mesmes n'endure
   Et qui tant est a passer forte et dure,
580 Est par Amour amenee a mesure
   Et bien passee
   Et de mainte grant foleur respassee;
   Et la cuidance oultrageuse cassee,
584 Dont Jeunesse ne scet estre lassee,
   En jeunes gens
   Qui veulent estre oyseux et negligens,
   Qu'Amours fait puis soigneux et diligens,
588 Prests de servir, rassis, courtois et gens
   En son service.   47^v

556 Et puis les b. *NfNj*. 560 trepassez *Qd*. 563 au c. *Ph*; autres e. *Oa*. 564 l.] li l. *Ph*. 566 veant *Oa*, veans *Ph*. 567 ce qui *Ph*; e. m.] m. e. *Oa*. 567–8 *Inverted NfNj*. 568 V.] Villennie *Oa*; lait parler *Nf*. 572 C. lor fin *Pc*. 574 et mains d. a. *PhQd*, et par d. a. *Oa*. 575 Qu. p. qu'il s.] Quelpar quil en s. *Nf*, Quelque part quil s. *Ph*. 576 f. que tout b. *Pc*. 577 Adoncq *Ph*. 578 mesme *NjOa*; nenduire *Qd*. 579 force *Qd*. 580 Et *NfNjPhQd*; ramenee *NfNjOaPcPhQd*. 582 rapassee *OaPhQd*, sest passee *Pc*. 583 A face maigre et coleur effassee *Nf* (*added by second hand in space left blank*): o. pensee *Pc*. 584 D.] Et d. *OjPc*; ne doit *NfNjPc*. 586 n.] neglgens (*sic*) *Nf*. 588 r. c.] c. r. *Pc*.

175

Et tient sur eulx sa court et sa justice
Et leur oste la bejaunie nice,
592   Et les retrait de maint oultrageux vice
Et de diffame.
Si les muë, amaigrit et affame,
Puis au loirre les affaicte et reclame
596   A obeïr au vouloir de leur dame.
Et se ilz y veillent
Et pour avoir un si hault bien traveillent,
Dont cuer et corps et Vertu se resveillent,
600   Et valent mieulx, ja nulz ne s'en merveillent;
Car quant bien quis
A tous les biens qu'ou monde sont conquis,
En vain n'a pas travaillé ne requis
604   Qui a un cuer de belle dame acquis,
Qui bien lui veult
Et a vertu et bon renon l'esmeut,
Son preu desire et de son mal se deult
608   Et lui donne le confort qu'elle peut.
Et pour certain,
C'est le plaisir qui nous est plus prouchain
Et la sourse du reconfort humain
612   Et le parfait de tout desir mondain.
Se nous tenons
Que de fame nous naissons et venons
Et par elles noz joyes maintenons,
616   Grans et nourris et bons en devenons,
Et que Nature   48r
Nous en donne naissance et nourreture,
Amendement, joye et bonne aventure,
620   Dont devons nous les amer par droitture;
Et sommes faulx,
Desnaturez, vilains et desloyaulx
Desvergondez, mauvais et bestïaulx

591 b.] bejaune *Oa*.   594 Si] Et si *NfNj*.   595 P.] Et p. *Pc*; en leure *NfNjOaPh*(?), au leurre *Pc*; les reffaite *Oa*.   597 Et cilz *NfNj*; y v.] v. *Oj*.   598 si grant *Ph*.   599 D. ce (se *Nj*) cuer corps et v. se r. *NfNj*: vertus *PcQd*.   600 En *Oj*² (Et *Oj*).   602 Avront les b. *NfPcPh*, Avrons les b. *NjOaQd*; quau m. *Pc*, qui ou m. *Oa*; acquis *Ph*.   608 peust *Pc*.   611 de r. *NfNjPh*.   613 Et *Qd*.   614 des fames *Oj*², de femmes *Pc*.   616 Gras *Nf*.   618 a d. *Nf*.   621 somme *Ph*.   622 D. mauvaiz et bestiaulx *Oa*: Desnaturelz *Ph*.   623 *Omitted Oa*: et desloyaulx (*sic*) *Ph*.

624 S'en fait n'en dit nous pourchassons leurs maulx.
    Ceulx qui s'en rusent,
    A jeu de dez, ou pis, souvent s'amusent
    Ou a suÿr quoquars qui les abusent,
628 Ou a chacer corps, temps et robes usent.
    Le corps leur sue
    D'aler aprés la povre beste mue;
    L'un crie et brait, l'autre l'espieu lui rue,
632 Et la fin est que en un laz on la tue,
    Ou el s'enlace.
    Quant est de moy, qui peut chacer si chace,
    Ou pour voler faucon haquart pourchace;
636 Mais oncq ne fut si gracïeuse chace
    Que du deduit qui parle face a face,
    Bel comme un ange.
    L'oyseau s'essore et le cerf va au change,
640 Le chien se pert, le fauconnier s'enfange,
    Le senglier rompt des dens corps, linge ou lange.
    Leur saison cesse:
    Oyseaulx muent et cerfs perdent leur gresse,
644 Les chiens ullent et font ennuy et presse.
    Mais le deduit amoureux ne se lesse;   48v
    Tant est plaisant
    Qu'il se maine par semblans en taisant,
648 Non pas en bruit et en noise faisant.
    Qui eur y a, il n'est rien si aysant;
    Je ne vous mens.
    Amours trouva premier haulx instrumens,
652 Chançons, dances, festes, esbatemens,
    Chappeaulx de fleurs, jolis habillemens,
    Joustes, essais, bouhours, tournoiemens,

624 Se endroit nous pourchassions l. m. *Pc*: Sen faiz nen diz *Oa*.   626 geuz *NfNjPcPh*; des dez *Oa*.
627 suivir *NfNjQd*; ququars *Ph*.   628 Ou achater *Qd*; c. t. et r.] t. c. et r. *NfNj*, ou c. t. r. *Pc*.
629 leurs *Qd*.   630 prouve b. *Qd*.   631 l'e. lui ruc] lespie lui rue *NfOaPh*, ung espieu luy r. *Pc*, le.
lui rut rue *Qd*.   632 En *Pc*; le t. *Nf*, les t. *Oa*.   633 Ou elle se. *Oa*, Ou el sen lasche *Pc*.   634 Q. est
de moy] Q. de moy *PcQd*; peust *Pc*.   635 *Omitted NfNjPc*.   636 Onques ne fut *NfNjPc*, Mais
oncques ne fu *Oa*.   637 Comme d. *Pc*.   638 c. lange *NfNjOaPcPhQd*.   641 r. dedens *NfNjOa*, r.
dessuz *Pc*, r. de dent *Ph*; et *NfNjOaPhQd*; large *Oa*.   642-5 *Omitted Pc*.   645 lasse *Oa*.   646 Amours
plaist tant *Pc*.   647 Qui se m. *Pc*, Quil m. *Oa*; semblant *Pc*.   648 Sans cor sans cry et sans n. f.
Qd: ne en *NfNj*; noises *NfNjPc*.   649 n'e. r. si a.] nest si plaisant *Pc*.   651 premiers *Ph*.   652 d. f.]
f. d. *Oa*.   653 *Omitted NfNjPc*: j. h.] j. a h. *Qd*.

Prëaulx et treilles,
656 Et tonnelles a courtine de fueilles;
Et fist faire les gales et les veilles,
Les jeux, les ris et les autres merveilles
Dont joye sourt.
660 Amours refait les nices et resourt,
Ne il n'est si sot, si simple ne si lourt
Qui n'amende de venir a sa court;
Et quant fauldroit
664 Que sa grant court et son pouoir fauldroit,
Ja plus a nul de joye ne chaudroit
Ne on ne sçaroit que Plaisance vauldroit,
Dont la valeur
668 Maintient le corps, la vie et la couleur.

Conclusion   Pour ce soustien, a droit et sans foleur,
Qu'en amours a plus joye que douleur.'
Quant il ot ditte
672 L'oppinïon qu'aprés lui je recite,
Et sa raison bien longuement deduite,   49r
Elle lui fut prestement contreditte
D'un chevalier
676 Vestu de noir, assez sus l'escolier,
Sans broudeure, sans chayne et sans colier,
Qui se sëoit au costé d'un pillier,
Pensif et pale.
680 Et ne menoit ris ne feste ne gale,
Mais bien sembloit sa douleur dure et male
Car chascun jour tournoioit par la sale,
Pensant toudis;
684 Et si sembloit porter cuer maladis,
Car rien n'estoit dont il fust resbaudis.
Si dist alors: 'Sire, voz plaisans dis
Font a louer

656 tournelles *NfNjPcPh*; a courtines *NfNjOaQd*, encourtinees *Pc*, a couvertures *Ph*. 658 Le j. *Qd*; les ris et] et ris et *Nf*, les et (*sic*) *Oa*. 661 si fol si nice ne si l. *Pc*. 662 n'a. de v.] na mande v. *Ph*. 664 Que son p. et sa g. c. f. *NfNj*, Que sa c. et son p. f. *Ph*. 666 P.] plaisir *Nf*, puissance *Pc*. 669 soustient *Nf*. 674 p.] en (de *Pc*) present *NfNjOaPcPhQd*. 676 sur *NfNjPhQd*. 677 et s. c.] s. c. *Ph*, et s. colies *Pc*. 678 *Omitted and space left Pc*: du p. *Qd*. 680 ris ne f.] f. ne ris *Pc*. 681 b. s.] s. b. *NfNjOaPcPh*; d. et m.] triste et m. *Pc*. 682 Et *PhQd*; t.] tournoit *Oj*, tournyoit *PcPh*. 684 Et si s.] Et s. bien *NfNjPcPhQd*, Et s. *Oa*. 685 Car r. n'e.] Et ne. r. *NfNjOaPcPhQd*. 686 Et *NfNjPh*; vous p. dis *Qd*, voz plaisirs diz *Ph*.

688 Pour passer temps et esbatre et jouer,
    Mais bien ne siet de rien trop deslouer;
    Ne de la fin ne vous puis je advouer
    Ou vous tendez,
692 Ne je ne sçay comme vous entendez
    L'oppinïon que de ce cas rendez,
    Ne les raisons dont vous la deffendez
    Si non que aiez
696 Les maulx d'amours trop petit essaiez
    Quant si tresbien en estes appaiez
    Que desja sont de voz comptes raiez
    Et oublïez.
700 Je croy au fort qu'en esbat le dïez;
    Autry s'en deult et vous vous en rïez.   49v
    Mais puet estre que oncq n'y fustes lïez
    A droittes certes,
704 Si n'en plaigniez les douleurs ne les pertes
    Ne les ennuis qu'on y a sans desertes,
    Et bien pouez par parolles appertes
    En dire assez,
708 Car voz maulx sont, Dieu mercy, beau passez
    Et en bon point en estes respassez,
    Et mains autres en sont mors, trespassez
    Par tel esbat.
712 Mais puis que vient a entrer ou debat
    De ce propos qui entre nous s'embat,
    Tel compte hault qui depuis en rabat.
    Vous racontez
716 Les haulx plaisirs, la joye et les bontez
    Ou jeune cuer est par Amours montez,
    Mais les douleurs ne les maulx ne comptez
    Dont tant y a
720 Que oncq homme qui en amours se lïa,
    Et qui souffert a certes les y a,

689 Car *NfNjOaPcPhQd*; ne sert *Ph*; t. haulouer *Oj*[2], t. fort louer *Pc*.   690 Mais *NfNjOaPcPhQd*; p. je a.] p. a. *NfNj*.   692 comment *Oa*.   694 Et *Oa*.   701 d.] deulx d. *Qd*.   702 peust *Pc*; que o.] quonques *NjOa*.   703 A droicte c. *Nj*.   704 plaignez *NjOaPhQd*.   708 vous m. *Qd*; bien p. *NfOaPhQd*.   709 rapassez *NfPh*.   711 estat *NfNjPc*.   712 M. p. quil v. rentrer au d. *Oa*: en d. *Pc*, au d. *PhQd*.   714 d. en r.] apres en (apres *Oa*) r. *NfNjOaPcPhQd*.   716 la j. et les b.] les joyes (les j. et *Oa*) les b. *NfNjOa*.   718 et *OaPhQd*.   720 Que oncques a. quen h. se lia *Pc*, Que oncques homs quen a. se lia *PhQd*, Quonques h. quen amer se lia *NfNj*: o.] oncques *Oa*.   721 s. tant a c. y a *Pc*.

En sa vie puis ne les oublÿa;
Et si sont teles

724 Qu'il en y a plus des trois pars morteles
Pour enragier et troubler les cerveles
Des plus sages o toutes leurs cauteles,
Et pour perchier

728 Jusques au cuer et jusqu'au sens fichier;
Et qui va la sa plaisance cerchier,   50r
Le bien qu'il a lui est vendu trop chier.
Je ne di pas

732 Que ceulx qui font d'amours un droit trespas
Et y passent en prenant leurs repas,
Sans arrester en ce perilleux pas
Et hault larris,

736 Doient vivre ne dolens ne marris,
Mais passent temps en esbas et en ris
Et s'en tournent gras, gros et bien nourris,
Quoy qu'ilz promettent.

740 Mais ceulx qui cuer, corps et pensee mettent
A une seule a qui ilz se soubzmettent,
Et du tout hors de liberté se mettent
Et joye quierent,

744 Souvent en dueil et angoisse se fierent
Au droit rebours de tout ce qu'ilz requierent,
Et cent douleurs contre un plaisir acquierent,
Longues et lees

748 Qui sont es cuers empraintes et seellees;
Et s'ilz en ont quelques joyes celees
Tousjours sont ilz de tristesce meslees
Et dangereuses,

752 Ou pour crainte de malparler doubteuses,
Ou a l'onneur de tous deulx perilleuses,
Ou trop courtes ou trop souspeçonneuses.
Pour moy le di

---

722 plus *Pc.*   723 Et si tous celles *Oa.*   724 de t. *Pc.*   725 P. esrachier et t. les entreilles *Pc.*   726 a *NfNjOaPcPh*; leur c. *Oj.*   728 j.] jusques au *OaPh*; sang *OaPcPhQd.*   732 bien d. t. *Ph.*   733 y pensent *Ph*; et prennent *Nf*; leur r. *NfNjOaQd.*   735 haulx l. *Pc.*   737 esbat *Ph.*   738 gros gras *NfNjPc.* 740 corps cueur *Pc*; p. m.] p. y m. *NfNjPc.*   741 a quoy *Oj*; il *Pc.*   744 en a. *Pc.*   745 du t. *Qd*; t. ce qu'ilz] ce quilz *NfNj*, ce quilz ont *Pc.*   748 sellees *Oj*[2] (seellees *Oj*).   749 Et si en ont *Oa*; qu. j.] quelque j. *Oj*, qu. joys *Qd*, quelxconques *Ph.*   750 tristesses *Ph.*   752 Et *Ph.*   753 t. d.] toutes d. *Qd.* 754 craintes *NfPc*, cointes *Nj*.

756   Qui de pieça en amours entendi
      Et a une de mon cuer m'attendi,   50v
      Qui guerredon oncques ne m'en rendi
      Tant que j'en suis
760   En tel parti qu'avoir santé ne puis.
      J'en meur sur bout, ne n'euz oncques depuis
      Ayse de cuer, bon jour ne bonnes nuis.
      Mais je me tais
764   De tout mon fait, et le delesse en paix.
      S'il m'est mal pris, autres n'en pevent mais;
      En ce qu'est fait n'a remede jamais.
      D'autres parlons
768   Et se attaindre verité en voulons,
      Comptons les biens et les maulx ne celons,
      Ou les dolens pour qui nous nous meslons
      Sont demenez,
772   Chacez, attains, assailliz, pourmenez,
      Et longuement travaillez et penez,
      Plus que le cerf qui des chiens est venez.
      Premierement
776   Amours ravit les cuers soubtivement,
      Et est on prins, et sans savoir comment.
      Et au premier ce semble esbatement
      Assez legier,
780   Et cuide on bien s'en pouoir estrangier;
      Mais qui cuide mieulx le chemin songier
      De s'en saillir, plus se treuve engregier.
      Et vous promett
784   Que quant plus fort d'y penser s'entremett,
      La penseë, a quoy il se soubzmect,   51r
      Pour s'en gecter, bien souvent l'y remect.
      Ainsi labeurent
788   Comme perdrix qu'en la tonnelle queurent:
      Jouans y vont et tristes y demeurent;

---

758 me r. *Pc.*   761 Et meurs *Pc,* Je muir *Ph*; et *NfNjOaPcPhQd.*   762 bons jours *Qd.*   765 Il *Ph*; aultre si nen peust m. *Pc*; puent m. *Qd.*   767 Dautre *Nf.*   768 se entendre *Pc.*   770 les douleurs *OaPc.* 772 Saichiez *Ph.*   772–3 *Inverted NfNjPc.*   774 de *Pc.*   776 subtilement *Nf.*   777 et s. s.] s. s. *Oa.* 778 se *Ph.*   780 son p. *NfNjPcPh,* sen cuider *Qd.*   781 jugier *Pc.*   782 Et *Pc*; p. se t. e.] se t. p. e. *Oa.* 783 Et v. prenent *Oa.*   784 sentremectent *Oa.*   785 La p.] Et la p. *NfNj*; ilz se soubzmectent *Oa.* 786 son g. *Qd*; lui r. *NfNjPcPh,* lui remectent *Oa.*   788 C.] Com les p. *Pc.*   789 Jouant *NfNjOaPcPhQd.*

Leur mal leur plaist, puis de leur joye pleurent.
Le cuer fremie

792 Souvent a tel qui de douleur lermie
Pour une amer comme dame et amie,
Qui ne l'aime ne ne l'amera mie.
Or ne repose

796 Le douloureux qui en son cuer propose
Qu'il lui dira, mais dire ne lui ose;
Et puet estre qu'el pense a autre chose.
La acoupee

800 Est sa raison et sa bouche estoupee;
Langue n'y sert plus que s'el feust coupee.
Et sa pensee est si envelopee
Et si en serre

804 Qu'il n'y scet bout ne fin ne moien querre,
S'il est es cieulx ou s'il est en la terre;
Si porte en cuer sa frontiere et sa guerre
En soy couverte,

808 Et cuer nercy souvent soubz robe verte.
Plaisir l'attrait et Dangier le deserte,
Accueil l'aleche et Durté veult sa perte.
Amours le triche

812 Et lui est large en offre, et en fait chiche;
Car il le met de tous poins et affiche   51v
A celle amer qui l'en tient sot et niche.
C'est bien joué

816 De lui offrir ce qu'est ailleurs voué!
Un tel seignieur doit bien estre loué,
Qui de son don est tost desadvoué!
Quel divers hoste

820 Qui offre assez et promet, et puis oste;
Et qui appelle et puis bannist de coste,
Faint d'approucher et puis tourne la voste!
Mais prenons ore

791 Leur *NfNjQd.* 793 Par *Nf.* 798 Et peust e. quelle p. a. ch. *Pc.* 799 La occupee *NfOj²Pc*,
Lacouppee *Ph*, La assouppee *Qd.* 800 sayson *Pc.* 801 s'el] selle *OaPc.* 804 ne s. *NfNjPcPh*; s. b.]
s. *Oj*, s. tour *Oj²*; ne f. ne m. qu.] f. ne m. enquerre *Pc.* 806 ou c. *NfNj.* 808 noiry *Oa.* 809 desir
NfNjPc. 810 A. le laist *Pc*; dangier *Oj.* 812 en o.] en offrant *Ph*; en o. le fait riche *Pc*; de f. *Oj².*
814 telle *NfNj*; que len (que on *Pc*) t. sote et n. *OaPcPh*; nice *OaQd.* 816 Et *Pc.* 817 b. e.] e. b. *Ph.*
821 *Omitted and space left Pc.* 822 Fait da. *Nf*, Femme da. *Oa.*

824   Qu'el ait de lui quelque peu de memoire.
       Il prendra tost en ses semblans sa gloire
       Et l'endemain retournera encore
       En son hostel,
828   Ou l'ira veoir en ville ou en chastel,
       Ou son semblant ne sera pas autel.
       Vez sa joye tourner en dueil mortel
       Et ravalee,
832   Et sa chiere devenir adoulee,
       Gresse et couleur en trois jours escoulee,
       Ses yeulx moilliez et sa face foulee.
       Or pense et songe,
836   Ses mains detort et ses levres deronge,
       Et ne choisist le voir de la mensonge.
       Toute nuit veille en fantosme et en songe,
       Tant soit el grande;
840   Et ne respond a rien qu'on lui demande,
       Ne il ne lui chault qui prie ou qui commande.   52r
       Ne il n'a saveur en vin në en vïande:
       Mengut sans fain;
844   S'il quiert le boire, il va prendre le pain.
       Le front lui sue et lui tremble la main;
       Il va et vient, et se travaille en vain.
       Vers elle envoye,
848   Lettres escript, met messagiers en voie;
       Il charge a l'un, quoy que soit, qu'il la voye –
       Et qui y est, qui la sert ou convoie,
       S'el est songeuse
852   Ou se sa chiere est melencolieuse,
       A qui el parle ou s'el est bien joieuse.
       L'un revendra, qui fait chiere piteuse,
       Le traire a part;
856   Dit qu'il n'a peu y parler fors a tart,

824 Quelle *NfNjPcPhQd*; qu. bonne m. *Ph.* 825 et ses s. *Ph*, en son semblant *Pc.* 828 On *Oa*, Et *Pc.* 830 Veez *NfNjOaPcPhQd*; tournee en (et *Pc*) *PcPh.* 833 e.] est coulee *Oa.* 834 moulez *Oa.* 837 choisir *Nf.* 838 *Omitted and wrong space left Pc.* 839 el] elle *Oa.* 840 en r. *Oa.* 841 Ne il ne] Ne ne *OaQd*, Et ne *Ph.* 842 en vim *Qd*, ne en vin *Oa*; ny en viande *Pc.* 843 M.] Mengue *NfQd*, Mengeust *Pc*; fin *Ph.* 844 le voirre *OaPh*, le vin *Pc.* 846 Or va *NfNj*, Et va *OaPcPh*; il vient *Qd.* 848 met m.] et m. *Oj*, met messages *NfNjOaPhQd.* 849 Et *NfNjOaPcQd*, Si *Ph*; quoy quil s. *Oa*, quoy s. *Nj.* 851 Selle *NfNjOaPcPhQd.* 853 el] elle *OaPh*; et *Qd*; selle *NfNjOaPcPhQd*. 856 Dist *Pc*; peu y p.] peu p. *Oa*; f. que a t. *Pc.*

Car la estoit quelque autre bien gaillart,
Et qu'il est fol que brief ne s'en depart.
Lors Fantasie,
860 Rage de Cuer, Souspeçon, Frenesie
Le seurprennent avecques Jalousie;
Si fault en lui Doulceur et Courtoisie
A celle fois
864 Qui lui dure puet estre tout le mois.
Et va rompant ses cheveulx a bons dois –
Et ses souspirs entrecouppent sa voix –
Tout forsené;
868 N'il ne semble ne sage ne sené,
Tant se demaine et tant est malmené.
Et se clame d'Amours mal assené
Et baraté,
872 Et se complaint de sa grant loyauté;
Ou il maudit sa dame et sa beauté,
Et la blasme de sa desloyauté
Mal advenant.
876 Et se soucie et va entreprenant
La ou il n'a ne foy ne couvenant,
Ottroy, seurté, droit ne le remenant,
N'oncq n'y advint.
880 Et croit de vray ce qui oncques n'avint
Et jure Dieu des fois ou quinze ou vint
Qu'el ayme tel dont onq ne lui souvint.
Or devient maigre,
884 Chagrin, felon, et rïoteux et aigre;
Chascun lui nuit, rien ne lui est alegre.
Tout lui messiet et reconfort l'enaigre,
Car si mal nee,
888 Venimeuse, dangereuse et dampnee
Est de nature – et si desordonnee –
Jalousie la felle et forsenee,

52v

857 queque a. *Nj.* 859 sanrafie (*sic*) *Oa.* 861 Leur prenent a. j. *Ph.* 862 D. et C.] d. c. *Oj.* 864 peust *Pc.* 866 les s. *NfNjOaPcPhQd*; entrerompent *NfNjOaPcQd*, entrerompre *Ph.* 868 ne se.] ne secre *Oa.* 872 se c.] c. *Qd.* 874 se b. *Ph.* 878 O. s. ne le r. *Oa.* 880 qui o.] que o. *PcPh.* 882 Que telle laime a qui onq nen s. *NfNj*: Quelle *Qd*, Quil *Pc*; tel] telle *Pc*; onq] oncques *Oa.* 883 Et *Pc.* 884 et r.] fier r. *NfNj*; et a.] et a esgre *Nj*, et maigre *Oa.* 886 *Omitted and wrong space left Pc*; meffait *Qd.* 887 sil *Qd*; ma nee *Ph.* 888 V. rioteuse et d. *Pc.*

Que des qu'elle entre
892   Dedens le cuer qui nous est le droit centre
Et le milieu, et du corps et du ventre,
Tout bien s'enfuit, s'il en a point dedentre,
Sans nulz respis;
896   N'il n'est venin de serpent ou de aspis,
Ne de dragon, tant soit lais et despis,
Qui peust au cuer në au corps faire pis
Ne plus d'aÿr.
900   Qui est jaloux veult ses amis haÿr,
Tous estrangier, courroucer, envaÿr,
Et de chascun croist qu'il le veult traÿr;
Et ses leçons
904   Sont de noises, d'argus et de tençons,
De reprouches et de malefaçons.
Et croit rappors et forge souspeçons
Sus tous et toutes,
908   N'il n'a repos ne que s'il eust les goutes.
Or met aguetz, espïes et escoutes,
Et lui croissent tousjours nouvelles doubtes;
Si veult rouver
912   Et cerchier ce qu'il ne veult pas trouver,
Et son meschief acroistre et esprouver,
Et traÿsons et mauvaistiez couver,
Car sans faillir,
916   Jalousie, qui s'en laisse assaillir,
Fait en homme tout honneur defaillir,
Ne d'ou el est ne puet nul bien saillir.
Dieu la confonde
920   Et ou parfont de la terre l'affonde,
Car el porte son enfer en ce monde
Dedens son cuer ou mauvaistié habonde!
Et la dolente

53r

892 d. gentre *Oa*.   893 et du c.] du (et du *Pc*) cuer *OaPc*.   894 sensuit *PhQd*; en a p.] en ya *NfPh*, nya p. *Oa*.   895 nul *Nf*.   896 venins *Pc*; serpens *NfNjPcQd*; ne *NfNjOaPc*.   897 Ne de] De *Oa*; lait *OaPc*; ne *NfNjPcPh*.   901 estranges *Pc*; courrocor *Qd*; enhair *Oa*.   902 qui *Ph*; le doit *Nf*.   904 Soit *Ph*; noise *OaQd*.   905 de males facons *OaPcPhQd*.   906 songe s. *Oj*, forges s. *Ph*.   907 Sur *NfNjOaPhQd*.   908 ne que] plus que *Oj²*.   909 Et *Pc*.   911 Or *NfNjOaPcPhQd*.   912 Et cerche ce quil ne ne vouldroit pas t. *Ph*.   913 approuver *Pc*.   916 qui en laissie a. *Qd*, qui laisse scens faillir *Pc*.   918 dont *PcPh*; elle *NfNjOaPcPhQd*; nen p. *Oa*, ne peust *Pc*.   920 au p. *NfNj*, en p. *Pc*. 921 el] elle *NfOaPcPhQd*.   922 mauvaite *Qd*.

924 D'autry plaisir se murtrit et tourmente,
Et a le mal qui que la joye en sente;
Et veult faire d'autry bien propre rente
Comme en reserve,

928 Et Franchise tenir esclave et serve,
Et que l'autry plaisir au sien s'asserve
Et qu'on l'ayme, sans qu'elle le deserve,
Par droitte force.

932 Et il n'est rien qui Franc Vouloir efforce
Fors Beau Parler qui la lengue n'escorche,
Et Doulx Prïer; autre rien n'y vault fors ce.
Si meurt tout vis

936 Homme jaloux comme en enfer havis,
Quant voit qu'esbas ou festes ou convis
S'entreprennent si non a son devis.
Les gens le fuyent,

940 Ses dis mordent, ses parolles ennuyent;
Tous s'en farsent et le moquent et huyent.
Ceulx qui veulent mesdire, a lui affuyent
Et lui sacoutent,

944 Car teles gens croyent tost et escoutent;
De mal en pis le nourrissent et boutent.
Ainsi de lui s'acointent et arroutent,
De son vin boivent,

948 Ou autre preu, s'ilz pevent, en reçoivent.
Quant son vouloir d'enquerir apperçoivent,
A ses despens le courcent et deçoivent.
La court sa chance

952 Et si lui couste a savoir sa meschance.
D'eulx se fie pour sa grant deffiance,
Tout deffié de parfaitte fïance.
Et sachiez brief:

956 Quant il cuide bien garir son meschief

925 lo j. *Qd*; en s.] s. *Pc*.   926 droicte r. *OaPh*.   930 s. ce quelle d. *NfNjPh*, s. ce quel (quil *Pc*) le d. *PcQd*.   932 que *OaPcPh*.   934 a. ny v. r. f. ce *Oa*; a. bien *Ph*; ne veult *Pc*.   935 tous v. *NfOaPhQd*.   936 H. j. c.] Et h. j. c. *Oa*, Homs j. est c. *NfNj*; ravis *NfNjOaPcPhQd*.   937 Sil *NfNjOaPcPh*.   941 T. sen m. et sen f. et h. *Pc*.   942 v. m.] v. du sien *NfNj*, v. jengler *Pc*.   943 A luy saroutent *Pc*: cacoutent *Oj*.   944 Car tieulx g. c. tout ce que ilz c. *Pc*: celles *NfNj*; c. tout *Nf*. 945 le mectent et le b. *Pc*.   948 a. peu *Nj*.   950 c.] courroucent *Oa*.   951 La c. saichante *Ph*. 952 meschante *Ph*.   953 se fie p.] se deffuit p. (par *Nf*) *NfNj*, se fait hayr par *Pc*, se deffie par *Ph*; deffiante *Ph*.   954 Tous *NfNjPc*.   956 Que quant il c. plus couvrir (*sic*) *Pc*; c. plus *OaPhQd*; so m. *Nf*.

Par enquerir du fait de chief en chief,
Il y entre plus avant derechief.
Mais hault cuer d'omme,

960 Que Courtoisie et Loyauté renomme,
Puet bien avoir soing et pensee comme –
Sans que jaloux on l'appelle ou le nomme –
Il gardera

964 La bonne amour de ce qu'il amera.
Et plus craindra et perdre doubtera
Ce qu'il ayme, plus son devoir fera
Sans rien mesprendre

968 Et sans blasmer, attayner ne reprendre,
Ne seignieurie et maistrise entreprendre,
Në espïer, escouter ou seurprendre
Ne pres ne loing;

972 Et ce penser s'appelle Amoureux Soing,
Ou cuer empraint comme monnoie en coing,
Et si siet bien et sert fort au besoing.
Mais retournons

976 Au droit propos qu'a present demenons
Pour les partis que nous deux soustenons
De l'amoureux tourmenté, et prenons
Que ainsi advieigne

980 Que hors du cuer Jalousie revieigne
Et quelque bien ou reconfort lui vieigne   54v
Par quoy du mal passé ne lui souvieigne.
Or revendra

984 Veïr sa damë, et ja ne s'en tendra,
Toutes les foiz qu'il lui en souvendra,
Ne temps ne lieu par raison n'attendra.
La penseront

988 Ungs et autres qui ce regarderont.
Et s'il s'en tient, le cuer ou corps lui rompt;

957 Pour *NſNj*. 958 Il y e.] Il e. *Oa*. 961 Peust *Pc*. 961–2 *Inverted Qd*. 962 S. ce que j. on le n. *Pc*; on l'a.] on (?) lon la. *Qd*, on len appelle *Oa*; ou le n.] ne n. *NſNj*, ou n. *Ph*. 965 Et que (Et *Pc*) p. craindre a p. d. *NſNjPc*. 968 attaigner *Nj*, entamer *Pc*. 969 s. ne m. *NſNjPc*, s. ou m. *Oj²*. 970 Ne escouter espier ou s. *Oa*. 972 Ce p. cy sa. a. s. *Pc*: ce p.] p. *Qd*. 973 Que *NſNj*; c. mouque ou c. *Oa*, c. monnoir ou c. *Pc*. 974 et si s. (si siert *Oa*, si fert *Qd*) au b. *NſNjOaPhQd*. 976 qua presens *Qd*. 977 p.] parties *Pc*. 978 tourmenter *Pc*: prions *Nſ*. 980 corps *Oa*. 981 b. pour r. *Oj*. 982 passer *Oa*. 984 et ja] ne ja *Ph*. 985 que lui *Oa*, qui luy *PcPh*. 986 l. ne r. *Pc*. 988 le r. *Pc*, se r. *PhQd*. 989 en c. *Pc*; lui font *NſNj*.

Et s'il y va, les gens en parleront.
L'un mouvera
992 Les parolles ou les controuvera,
Ou qui que soit son fait descouvrera.
Lettres cherront en quoy on trouvera
Dedens enclos
996 Noms ou signes dont tout sera desclos
Ce qu'il tenoit secret, couvert et clos.
Adonq sera le compaignon forclos
D'en approuchier,
1000 Ne la porte regarder ne toucher,
Quant il s'orra telz choses reprouchier,
Et s'en yra de fin despit couchier.
Lors mesdisans
1004 En parleront et seront voir disans;
Et envÿeux lui reseront nuysans,
Qui en diront mos aigres et cuisans
Pour l'esloignier,
1008 Et saront bien contre lui tesmoigner.
Si a de neuf assez a besoignier   55r
Et mal foison pour son cuer engaignier,
Triste et malmis.
1012 Or le fault estre en doubte des amis,
De bruit de gens, de rapport d'ennemis,
Obeïssant, triste, coy et remis,
Son cuer mater,
1016 Dangier cherir et envïeux flater
Qu'ilz ne puissent de lui mal relater
Et la grace Male Bouche achater
Par quelque don,
1020 Dont ja n'ara bienfait ne guerredon.
Et d'autre part, se bien y regardon,
Il fault qu'il prie a sa dame pardon,

991 Lors m. *Pc*, Lun nommera *Ph*.   992 et *NfNj*.   993 A *NfNjPcQd*; quoy quil s. *Oa*.   994 Lectre
Ph.   996 N. et s. *Nf*, Moins s. *Ph*.   997 Et *Ph*.   998 forchos *Qd*.   1000 Et de la p. r. ne t. *Pc*: ou *OaPh*
Qd.   1001 orra tieulx ch. *Pc*.   1002 Il *NfOaPcPh*.   1004 veoir *Qd*; disant *Oa*.   1005 r.] seront
Oa.   1009 a. que b. *OaPh*.   1010 friczon *NfNjPcPh*, saison *Qd*; enseignier *NfNjPhQd*, ensoingner
OaPc.   1013 rappors *NfQd*.   1014 t.] simple *NfNjOaPcPhQd*; submis *Pc*.   1016 D. cheoir *Oa*, D.
fuyr *Oj*.   1017 Quil *Qd*.   1020 D. il na. ja bien ne g. (ja bienfait ne guerdon *Nj*) *NfNjPc*.
1022 crie *Oj²* (prie *Oj*).

Qui pensera
1024 Que ce meschief par sa faulte sera,
Et desormais de lui se passera
Ou puet estre jamais ne l'amera.
Ou s'elle a cuer
1028 De non vouloir l'enhaÿr pour nul feur,
Pour tout oster le bruit et la rumeur
Loing s'en yra ou devers frere ou seur,
Et le meschant,
1032 Que sa foleur va ainsi empeschant,
Yra aprés secretement cerchant,
Soit en guise de moine ou de marchant.
Se mucera
1036 Et en buissons de jour s'embuchera –
Visage et nez et mains enronchera –
Ou en fossez de nuit trebuchera.
Ou escherra
1040 Que d'uns carneaulx ou d'un hault mur cherra
Et au chëoir du corps lui mescherra,
Dont le renom de tous deux decherra
Et descroistra.
1044 Ou en alant aucun le congnoistra,
Qui grant desir de le recongnoistre a,
Dont le meschief et la rumeur croistra.
Et sera lors
1048 En grief peril et d'onneur et de corps,
Car moult d'autres aussi bons en sont mors
Par telz essais et perilleux effors;
Si retourra
1052 Ne jamais d'elle approucher ne pourra.
Ou cependant sa dame se mourra,
Dont tousjours seul douloureux demourra.
Ce sont les gages,
1056 Les haulx plaisirs, les dons, les hostellages

55v

1024 Que ce] Que *Oa*, Que cest *Pc*, Ce que *Ph*.   1026 peust *Pc*.   1027 celle *Ph*.   1028 l'e.] enhair
Oa; par *NfNj*, a *Pc*.   1029 rimeur *NfNjOa*.   1030 sueur *Ph*.   1032 Qui *OaPcPh*.   1034 en abit *Pc*.
1036 jours *Oa*.   1037 mains et nes *Oa*; senroncera *NfNj*, enrochera *Oa*, esronchera *Pc*, enruchera *Ph*,
en roncera *Qd*.   1040 Que dun h. mur ou dun carneau ch. *Ph*: dung carneau *NfPc*; d'un h. mur]
dun mur *Oa*.   1041 a ch. *Qd*.   1043 Ou *Ph*.   1044 Et *Oa*.   1045 r.] congnoistre *OaPh*.   1046 rimeur
NfOa.   1048 grant *Ph*; et de c.] et du c. *OaQd*, de c. *Ph*.   1049 a. bien *Pc*.   1051 recourra *Oa*.
1054 s. d.] d. *Nf*.

Que ont les amans qui pour tous avantages
Y entrent folz et s'en retournent sages
Et bien apris.

1060 C'est la chace dont le veneur est pris;
C'est le beau los qui retourne en mespris;
C'est le mestier dont le maistre est repris.
C'est ly esbas

1064 Dont sourt discors, rïotes et debas,
Dechié de corps et de chatel rabas,   56r
Et qui a mis mainte cité au bas
Sans retourner;

1068 Car Amours fait cuer d'amant bestourner
Et de son droit estat le destourner,
Et en homme par son pouoir tourner
Sens insensible,

1072 Et ce qui doit ayder estre nuysible,
Et puissance devenir impossible,
Et ce qu'on voit apparoir invisible,
Seurté doubter

1076 Et en doubte seurement se bouter,
A son preu sourt, son contraire escouter,
Volenté croire et raison rebouter.
C'est bien grevable,

1080 Mal deliteux, fermeté varïable,
Arrest mouvant, legiereté estable,
Dolent confort, fëauté decevable,
Joye esplouree,

1084 Los reprouchié, honneur pou honnouree,
Aigre doulceur, beauté descoulouree,
Hayneuse paix et guerre enamouree,
Eur envïeux,

1088 Coursant esbat, jeu melencolïeux,
Repos penible et tourment gracïeux,
Plaisant ennuy et plaisir ennuyeux,

1058 sotz *NfNjPcPh*; et en r. *OaPhQd*. 1061 au m. *Nf*, a m. *NjPcPh*. 1062 Et *NfNjOaPcPhQd*; est r.] r. *Nf*. 1064 descort *Oj*; r.] riotes riotes (*sic*) *Ph*. 1065 Dechief *Nf*, De chief *OaQd*, De chie *NjPc*, Dechiet *Ph*. 1066 maintes cytes *Pc*. 1068 destourner *Ph*. 1069 retourner *Pc*. 1070 Et en (Et son *Pc*) honneur *NfNjPcPh*; povoit (?) *Ph*. 1072 Et de ce qui a. *Oa*; quil *Qd*; a. et n. *Ph*. 1074 *Omitted and wrong space left Pc*. 1076 s.] souvent *Nj*; soy b. *NfNjPc*. 1077 Et a son p. son c. e. *PcPh*, A son prouffit son c. e. *NfNj*: soult *Oa*. 1078 Volentiers c. *Nj*; debouter *Pc*. 1084 Lo *Qd*. 1086 et crainte e. *NfNj*. 1087 Cui *Nf*, Cuer *NjPc*; ennuyeulx *PcPh*. 1088 C.] Courroussant *Oa*.

'Le Debat des Deux Fortunés d'Amours'

Fiel emmielé,
1092 Chaude friçon, eaue ardant, feu gelé,
Certain espoir de souspeçon meslé,
Taisible bruit et secret descelé,
Coup sans sentir
1096 Et penitance avant que repentir,
Et vray cuider qui se lesse mentir,
Vouloir sans vueil et sans gré consentir,
Crainte hastive,
1100 Seure päour, hardïesce craintive,
Desir forcé et force volentive,
Advis musart, muserie soubtive,
Clarté obscure,
1104 Loyal meschief, desloyale droitture,
Conseil ouvert, descouvrant couverture,
Temps sans exploit et paine a l'aventure.
Pour ce maintien,

Conclusion L'onneur gardant que des dames je tien,
Et pour esbatre, a ceste fois soustien
Qu'en amours a plus de mal que de bien.'
Adonq se teut,
1112 Car tout le cuer serré et dolent eut
Ne ses lermes contretenir ne peut.
Lors le premier ses raisons ramenteut
Sans y muser,
1116 Et va dire pour sa part excuser:
'Frere, cellui se doit d'Amours ruser
Qui de ses biens ne scet a droit user,
Et qui en use
1120 Si folement que sans joye s'y use
Et soy mesmes se destourbe et encuse.
Se bien le fuit et Amours le refuse
Par sa folie,
1124 C'est tout par lui s'il a melencolie;
Mais quant d'Amours qui les cuers amolie

56v
57r

1091 enmelle *Oa.* 1097 le l. *Nſ.* 1098 s. gré c.] s. c. *Oa.* 1100 S. p. et h. c. *Oa.* 1101 D. forte *Ph*; et f.] et force et force *Pc.* 1102 musant *NſNjPh*; m. sensive *Pc.* 1105 couvert *Oj*; descouvert *Pc.* 1108 gardent *Qd.* 1108–9 *Inverted NſNjOaPcPh.* 1117 da. gruiser *Oa.* 1121 mesme *NjOa.* 1122 Et (Ce *Ph*) b. le f. et bon eur le r. *NſNjPh*, Et le b. f. et le bon eur r. *Pc*; lui f. *Qd*; et bon eur r. *OaQd.* 1125 qu. amours *NſNjPcPh.*

191

Et fait entrer en pensee jolie,
Com j'ay compté,

1128 Par qui maint cuer est a vertu dompté,
Ja pour chose que vous aiez compté
N'amendrirez son los ne sa bonté,
Ne sa value

1132 Ne doit estre foulee ne pollue.
Pourtant s'aucuns s'en sont joye tollue
Par conduite meschante et dissolue,
S'ilz se deçoivent

1136 Par en user autrement qu'ilz ne doivent
Et maulouyer en la fin en reçoivent –
Ilz l'ont brassé, c'est raison qu'ilz le boivent.
Et nëantmoins

1140 En ceste foy je demeure et remains
Que sages cuers atrempez et humains
Pour bonne amour ne pevent valoir mains,
Tant est courtoise,

1144 Car quelque ennuy qui leur en vieigne ou voise –
De quoy souvent aux fins amoureux poise –
Une joye contre mille maulx poise.'
Cy duppliqua

1148 Le douloureux qu'ouÿ la replique a,
Et son propos de tous poins appliqua   57v
Sur un seul mot que lors il descliqua,
Et dist sans plus:

1152 'Quelque chose que dïez au seurplus,
Dueil est tousjours la fin, l'issue et l'us
Ou tous les faiz amoureux sont conclus;
Et plus n'en di.'

1156 Lors quant chascun leur debat entendi
Et ce qu'un dist et autre deffendi

1126 *Omitted and space left* (?) *Pc*: Et f.] Reffait *NfNj*, Elle f. *Ph*.   1128 Par qui c. a verite est
d. *Pc*: donne *Oa*.   1129 *Omitted and space left Pc*: Ja p. ch. quayez v. raconte *NfNj*: que v. a.] que
a. *Qd*.   1130 Namenderies *PcPh*.   1133 sa. en ont j. t. *Ph*.   1134 c. meschant *Pc*.   1135 Si *NfPh*.
1136 Pour en u. *Ph*, Par u. *Oa*.   1137 m. a *Oj²*.   1138 Silz *Oj*; quil *Pc*; en b. *Oa*.   1140 remens *Ph*.
1142 Par *NfPhQd*; puent *Qd*.   1144 Et *OaPh*; Car pour e. *NfNjPc*; que *NjOaPh*.   1145 Dont bien
s. *NfNjOaPcPh*.   1147 Si *NfNjOaPcPhQd*; supplia *Oa*.   1148 qui oy r. a *Nf*, qui oy la r. a *Nj*, qui
ouye la r. a *Pc*, qui la r. a *Ph*.   1149 a.] applique a *Ph*.   1150 Sus *Pc*; que l. il d.] que illec (que
illeques *Nj*) d. *NfNj*, qualors il (que alors *Pc*) d. *OaPcPhQd*.   1152 que dici (?) au s. *Nf*; ou s. *Nj*.
1153 l'i.] lentree *Pc*.   1154 Or *Oa*; s. c.] c. *Pc*.   1155 ne dy *Ph*.   1156 Et *NfNjOaPcPh*.   1157 Ce
que lun d. et lautre (d. li autre *Nj*, d. lautre le *Pc*) de. *NfNjPc*: et a.] li a. *Ph*, et lautre *Oj²* (et a *Oj*).

Et que nulz d'eulx pour mat ne se rendi,
Les ungs en dirent
1160 A leur plaisir, les autres contredirent.
Mais les dames le parler deffendirent
Ne plus alors enquerir n'en souffrirent,
Fors qui seroit
1164 Cellui qui bien du debat jugeroit
Et a tous deulx loyal droit en feroit;
Et chascun dist que l'en y penseroit.
Assez penserent
1168 Et longuement de parler se cesserent,
Puis leur parler aprés recommencerent
Et leur advis dirent et remonstrerent.
Plusieurs nommoient
1172 Divers princes que sages renommoient,
Qui avoient amé et qui amoient,
Et leurs vertuz et leurs bons sens sommoient,
Et vraies fois,
1176 En les nommant sans gabe et sans truffois.
Une dame, quant ce vint a sa fois,   58r
Ala nommer le bon conte de Foix
Sage et entier,
1180 Noble Jehan, de Phebus heritier,
Et qui porte son escu en quartier
Et de tousjours suit l'amoureux mestier.
Quant on l'ouÿ
1184 Ainsi nommer, chascun s'en esjouÿ
Comme de cil qui d'onneur a jouÿ;
N'oncques nul d'eulx sa court ne defouÿ,
Ains se soubmistrent
1188 En son decret et ainsi le promistrent
Et devant lui en jugement se mistrent,
Et les dames leur pouoir lui commistrent

1158 Si *Nf*; nul *NfNjOaQd*, lun *Ph*; p. mal *Ph*.   1160 leurs plaisirs *NfNjOaPcPhQd*.   1161 les p. *Nf*, de p. *Ph*; d.] deffendent *Qd*.   1162 Le *Ph*.   1165 seroit *Qd*.   1166 lon *Qd*.   1168 de penser ne c. *OaPhQd*.   1169 P. lui p. *Qd*.   1170 leurs a. *NjPcQd*; et anuncerent *NfNjOaPcQd*, et denoncerent *Ph*. 1173 av. amé] av. dame *Oa*; qui am.] qui encor am. *Nf*.   1174 leur bon sens *NfNj*; louoyent *Pc*. 1175 Et vrays f. *Qd*.   1176 s. gale *Oa*; et s. t.] s. t. *Of*.   1178 n.] nommee *Oj*.   1180 N. J.] Le n. j. *Pc*, Lequel estoit *Oj*.   1182 des t. *Oa*, qui t. *Qd*; fist *Pc*.   1184 sen resjoy *NfNj*.   1185 C. de cil] Com (Comme *Nj*) de cellui *NfNjOaPcPhQd*.   1186 nulz *PcPhQd*.   1188 Et *Oa*.   1189 se m.] m. *Nj*.

En son abscence.

1192   Toutes dirent qu'il a sens et scïence
Et de chascun escouter pacïence,
Et en amours bien grant experïence
Et grant savoir,

1196   Valeur, bonté, hault cuer et bon devoir,
Et droit advis pour congnoistre le voir
Et qu'il vault bien a belle dame avoir.
Aussi son port

1200   En fait assez tesmoignage et rapport
Car il portë en son mot par deport,
Comme cellui qu'Amours maine a bon port,
'J'ay belle dame',

1204   Qui sans paine n'avint oncques a ame
Et sans sentir le mal et l'ardant flame
Qu'a la gaigner cuer amoureux enflame.
Or l'a il belle,

                                                                                  58v

1208   Si doit savoir qu'est l'ardant estincelle
Et congnoistre le plaisir que l'en cele,
Et bien jugier sans que nul en appelle.
Ainsi conclurent

1212   Et d'un accort dames et servans furent.
Aussi les deux de bon cuer le volurent,
Et bien firent quant si bon juge eslurent
Sans respiter,

1216   Qui en haulx fais se scet bien delitter
Et en honneur loyauté acquiter,
Et a Phebus de vertu heriter,
Qui tant fut preux

1220   Et tant haÿ chietifs faiz et honteux
Et tant ama les deduis deliteux,
Tresdur aux fiers et aux folez piteux,
Comme je sent.

1224   Or fu alors le noble conte absent
En ost armé comme Honneur le consent.

1191 leur *Pc.* 1193-4 *Inverted Qd.* 1194 tres g. *NſNjPc.* 1197 veoir *Qd.* 1200 aussi *OaPh.* 1201 Car en son mot il porte *NſNj.* 1202 celle *Ph.* 1206 Qui enbrase c. *Pc*; c. damoureux *NſNjOaPcPhQd.* 1210 len en a. *Oj.* 1212 attort *Oj.* 1213 Ainsi *OaPh*; le d. *Qd.* 1217 par h. *NſNjOaPcPh.* 1218 Apres ph. *Pc*; vertus *NſNjPcPh.* 1220 chastiz *Qd.* 1221 deliz *Qd.* 1222 aux fiebles p. *Pc.* 1223 Comment je sens *Pc.* 1224 absens *Pc.* 1225 Et ilz len chargent comme h. le consens *Pc.*

Pour ce furent tous d'un commun assent
Que on escriproit

1228   Tout ce debat, ou tant qu'il souffiroit,
Et qu'au retour le hoir Phebus le liroit
Et s'il lui plaist, son advis en diroit.
Et je qui yere

1232   Seul clerc present, escoutant par derriere
Tout le debat, les poins et la maniere,   59r
Fu lors requis par courtoise prïere
Que je l'escripve.

1236   Et Dieu me gart que, tant comme je vive,
Contre le gré de telz dames j'estrive;
Si l'ay escript de pensee ententive.
Pour ce supplie,

1240   Se je n'ay bien ceste chose acomplie
Et des raisons des deux partis emplie,
Qui mieulx sçaira, le demourant supplie.

Ce livret voult ditter et faire escripre,
1244   Pour passer temps sans courage vilain,
Un simple clerc que l'en appelle Alain
Qui parle ainsi d'amours par ouïr dire.

Explicit le Debat des Deux Fortunez
d'Amours.

1226 tout *Pc*; absent *OaPc*.   1228 le d. *NfNjPc*.   1229 Et au r. *Pc*, Et qua r. *Ph*; le h. ph.] lhoir *Nj*, leir (?) ph. *Pc*.   1232 S. c. p.] S. c. *Oa*.   1233 le point *Oa*, le p. *Qd*.   1234 c. p.] courtoisie prierere (*sic*) *Ph*.   1236 Et diu *Qd*.   1237 j'e.] estrive *NfNjOaPhQd*, nestrive *Pc*.   1240 je n'ay] ne ay *Nj*; celle *NfNjPc*; a.] complie *Oa*.   1241 p.] parties *OaQd*.   *After* 1242...la fin du gras et du maigre Finis *Nf*. 1243 livre *Oa*.   1244 oultrage *NfNjPh*, ouvrage *OaQd*.   1245 que l'en] que on *Pc*.   1246 pour *Qd* No explicit *NjOaPhQd*, Finis *Nf*, ...le debat du gras et du maigre *Pc*.

7

'Le Livre des Quatre Dames'

Thirty-two Manuscripts: *Da Db Dc Dd De Df   Nc Nd Nn   Oa Oc Ok   Pa Pc Pd Pe Pf Ph Pj Pk Pl Pp   Qg Qh Qj Qk Ql Qn Qo Qp Qq Qr.*

Qj and *Qn* have not been traced; *Qp* has been damaged by fire. All the other manuscripts have been examined. *De Pf* and *Pj* contain an abbreviated version of the poem.

The *Livre des Quatre Dames* was included in all the early collected editions. No separate early edition has been traced.[1] Du Chesne's text is based on the collected editions and on *Pe*. The 1489 and 1617 editions have been consulted, but a more modern edition, published by Vallet de Viriville in 1858, has not been examined.[2]

The poem is entitled *Les Quatre Dames*[3] or more frequently *Le Livre des Quatre Dames*.[4] In some manuscripts it is not 'le livre' but 'le debat' or 'le procés' or 'les complaintes'.[5] Three related manuscripts, *Da Qh* and *Qk*, add the subsidiary title *Le Joyeulx de Espoir*. The *Livre des Quatre Dames* is attributed to Alain Chartier in seven manuscripts but, since three of them, *Ok Pa* and *Qp*, are copied from printed editions, it is effectively attributed to Chartier in only four: *Df Pe Qo* and *Qr*; the attribution in *Df* is indirect and results from a quatrain playing on the name 'Allain', copied at the end of the poem. In all the other manuscripts the poem is anonymous.

The *Livre des Quatre Dames* has been edited here from eight manuscripts: *Db Dc Dd Df Oa Pc Ph* and *Ql*. The introduction to the poem is made up of 164 octosyllabic lines, arranged in twelve stanzas of twelve or sixteen lines, rhyming *aa(a)baa(a)bbb(b)cbb(b)c*. The narrative comprises 841 stanzas,[6] in the main of four lines, with the rhyme-scheme $a^8a^8a^8b^4b^8b^8b^8c^4$ etc. The final stanza is of only three lines.[7] Seven stanzas, 77, 136, 337, 361, 447, 535 and 619 are found in some manuscripts with four lines, in others with five. The longer version of stanza 337 occurs only in *Pp*; that text also contains an extra line in stanza 10 of the introduction. The 1489 edition, together with *Pa* and *Ok*, manuscripts associated with it, have an extra line in stanza 361. Stanza 77 has an extra line in those three texts, and also in *Pk*. The longer versions of stanzas 136, 447, 535 and 619 occur in four manuscripts, *Db Dd Df* and *Ql*, out of the eight used here. *Pc* contains two long stanzas, 535 and 619; *Dc Oa* and *Ph* have only one five-line stanza, 136. The problem of these long stanzas is discussed in the introduction to the *Debat des Deux Fortunés d'Amours*.

Readings at lines 43, 113, 227, 237, 254, 314, 337, 425, 633, 751 and 896 show that the

---

[1] A separate edition is mentioned by J. C. Brunet, *Manuel du libraire...*, I, Paris, Didot, 1860, 1814.

[2] Vallet de Viriville, *Le Livre des quatre dames*, Paris, 1858 (limited edition).

[3] *Da Nc Nd Pd Pk Ql Qq.*

[4] *De Oa Oc Ok Pa Pc Pd Pe Pf Ph Pk Pp Qg Qh Qk Qo Qp Qr.*

[5] *Db (Qk), Qr; Ql; Qj Qn.*

[6] So far it has not been possible to decide whether it is fortuitous that the number of stanzas is the square of 29.   [7] It has an extra line in Dc^2 and Dd^2, and in *Ok Pa* and *Xa*.

texts can be divided into two groups: *Db Dd* and *Df*; *Dc Oa Pc Ph* and *Ql*.[1] The division is not absolute: *Dc*, for example, occupies almost an intermediate position between the two groups.

Of the texts in the second group, *Oa Pc Ph* and *Ql* have readings in common at lines 132, 159, 160, 277, 295, 334, 382, 419, 454, 932 and 979. *Oa* and *Ph* are closely related (lines 2, 34–6, 48, 61, 73, 84, 104–5, 108, 121, 151 etc.). Irregular readings peculiar to *Oa* are found at lines 9, 11, 66, 96, 162, 198, 299, 301, 347, 471 etc. Readings of the same type occur in *Ph* at lines 38, 62, 70, 71, 87, 154, 177, 261, 393, 396 etc.

Like *Oa* and *Ph*, *Pc* and *Ql* resemble one another closely (lines 9, 108, 116, 120–1, 156–7, 165, 172, 198, 202, 271 etc.). Irregular readings peculiar to *Pc* occur at lines 136, 194, 267, 401, 443, 552, 642 and 801; readings at lines 16 (17a), 18, 25, 34, 44, 63, 77, 78, 81, 111 etc. are found only in *Ql*.

Dc contains readings which link it now with *Oa* and *Ph* (lines 4, 76, 178, 193, 269, 275, 349, 388, 461, 495 etc.), now with *Pc* and *Ql* (lines 19, 174, 177, 338, 346, 371, 471–2, 482, 510, 530 etc.) and particularly with *Ql* (lines 15, 57, 319, 534, 712 and 759). Readings which are peculiar to *Dc* are found at lines 27, 31, 36, 39, 42, 50, 67, 71, 82, 83, 84 etc. The text contains some corrections in a second hand (*Dc*[2]), for example at lines 12, 127, 732 and 746. *Dc* has some connection with texts of the first group, particularly *Df* (lines 127, 266, 453, 598, 704 and 858), as is also suggested by many of the readings cited above to show that *Oa Pc Ph* and *Ql* are related.

Db Dd and *Df*, the texts of the first group, are linked by readings at lines 349, 374, 515 and 582, in addition to those listed earlier. *Db* and *Dd* contain readings peculiar to themselves at lines 46, 101, 104, 425, 449, 459, 541, 554, 565, 766 etc., as do *Db* and *Df* (lines 201, 293, 387, 402, 506 and 985) and *Dd* and *Df* (lines 65, 702, 844 and 898). Individual readings are quite frequent in *Db* (lines 27, 36, 62, 101, 109, 114, 121, 142 etc.) and in *Df* (lines 12, 36, 52, 58, 78, 102, 111, 121, 147, 178 etc.); they occur much less often in *Dd* (lines 3, 153, 185, 219, 225, 300, 302, 320, 378, 407 etc.).

Texts of the second group have readings in common with *Db* and *Df* (lines 57, 58, 72, 177, 637 and 775); or with *Db* (lines 54, 77, 251, 339, 573, 642, 681, 693, 705, 738 etc.), or with *Df* (lines 49, 78, 173, 619, 640, 661, 662, 666, 689, 698 etc.). There is some link between *Df* and *OaPh*, particularly *Oa*: lines 7–8, 56, 225, 305, 401, 520, 565, 617, 784, 793 etc.

Dd has many fewer individual readings than the other texts. It has been carefully copied and corrected. Notable features of the text are the clear punctuation and the care which the scribe has taken with the rhymes.[2] Although it lacks lines 747, 2402 and 3386, *Dd* is more nearly complete than any of the other texts. Where they differ widely, for example at lines 495, 891, 2591–4, 2934–6 and 3464, *Dd* provides a good reading. Elsewhere, for example at lines 565–7, 734, 842–6, 1318, 1320, 2192, 2974, 3033, 3242 and 3264–9, some of which are discussed in notes, its readings are as good or better than the alternatives. It makes an excellent base text. Where necessary, it has been corrected with the help of *Df* and occasionally *Db*: see the notes to lines 1767 and 2523–4. The missing lines have been supplied from *Df*.

[1] The readings cited in this discussion are taken from lines 1–1000.
[2] See the notes to lines 879–80, 1709–16, 3158; 2535–8, 2768, 2776, 2777, 3180 etc.

LE LIVRE DES QUATRE DAMES

Pour oublïer melencolie   *Dd*, 1r
Et pour faire chiere plus lie,
Un doulz matin es champs yssy,
4   Ou premier jour qu'Amours ralie
Les cuers et la saison jolie
Fait cesser ennuy et soulcy.
Si alay tout seulet, ainsy
8   Que l'ay de coustume, et aussy
Marchay l'erbe poignant menue
Qui toute la terre tissy
Des estranges couleurs dont sy
12   Long temps l'yver ot esté nue.

Tout autour oyseaulx voletoient   1v
Et si tresdoulcement chantoient
Qu'il n'est cuer qui n'en fust joieux.
16   Et en chantant en l'air montoient,
Et puis l'un l'autre seurmontoient
A l'estrivee, a qui mieulx mieulx.
Le temps n'estoit mie nuyeux:
20   De bleu se vestoient les cieulx,
Et le beau soleil cler luisoit.
Vïolete croissoit par lieux,
Et tout faisoit ses devoirs tieulx
24   Comme Nature le duisoit.

En buissons oyseaulx s'assembloient.
L'un chantoit, les autres doubloient
De leurs gorgetes qui verbloient
28   Le chant que Nature a apris;
Et puis l'un de l'autre s'embloient.

...le l. des qu. d. dont les maris furent a la bataille dagincourt *Pc*, le proces des qu. d. *Ql, No heading DbDcDdDfOa.* 2 ch. p. lie] p. ch. lie *OaPh.* 3 aux ch. *DbDcDfOaPcPhQl.* 4 Au *DcOaPh.* 7 aussi *DfOaPh.* 8 ainsi *DfOaPh.* 9 Marche *PcQl;* l'e.] lerbecte *Oa.* 11 Des e. c.] Destranges c. *Oa.* 12 l'y.] por li. *Dc²;* ont *Df.* 15 Qui *DcQl.* 16 *Omitted Ql.* 17a Sans cesser ainsi quilz voloient *Ql.* 18 a qui] qui *Ql.* 19 mie (pas *Pc*) ennuieux *DcPcQl,* mie nueux *OaPh.* 20 *Omitted Ph,* De b. se vestoit li c. *Oa.* 22 Violetes (Fleurettes *Ql*) croissoient par l. *DcOaPhQl.* 24 C. n. (n. le *Ph*) devisoit *DcPh,* Com n. le devisoit *OaQl;* luy d. *Pc.* 25 voletoient *Ql.* 27 L. g. qui verboient *Dc,* L. g. qui verbeoient (verbectoient *Ph*) *OaPhQl,* De l. g. verbeoient *Pc:* verboient *Db.*

Et point ne s'entreressembloient;
Tant en y ot qu'ilz me sembloient
32 Fors a estre en nombre compris.
Si m'arrestay en un pourpris
D'arbres, en pensant au hault pris
De Nature qui entrepris
36 Ot a les faire ainsi harper;
Mais de joie les vy seurpris
Et d'amour nouvelle entrepris,
Et un chascun avoit ja pris
40 Et choisy un seul loyal per.

En ce chemin retentissant
De doulz accors, alay pensant
A ma maleuree fortune,   21
44 En moy mesmes m'esbahissant
Comme Amour, qui est si puissant,
Est large de joies fors d'une
Que je ne puis par voie aucune
48 Recouvrer, combien que nesune
Autre grace en Amours ne vueil.
C'est mal eür ou infortune;
Autres par maniere commune
52 Ont les biens, dont je n'ay que dueil.

Les arbres regarday flourir
Et lievres et connins courir;
Du printemps tout s'esjoÿssoit.
56 La sembloit Amours seigniourir:
Nul n'y puet vieillir ou mourir,
Ce me semble, tant qu'il y soit.
Des herbes un doulz flair yssoit,
60 Qui l'air sery adoulcissoit;
Et en bruyant par la valee

31 qui me *Ph*; ne s. *Dc*. 33 Je ma. *Pc*. 34 a h. p. *OaPh*; aux haulz p. *Ql*. 35 qui e.] qui a e. *OaPh*. 36 Ot a] A a *Dc*, Ont a *Df*, A *OaPh*; Oult ale f. *Db*. 38 damours nouvelles *Ph*. 39 Car *Dc*; a. aprins *Oa*. 42 deulx a. *Dc*; a. p.] a lui p. *Ph*. 43 maleureuse *DcOaPcPhQl*. 44 A moy *Ql*. 45 amours *PcQl*. 46 Et *Ph*; joye *DcDfOaPcPhQl*. 48 que nest une *OaPh*. 49 amour *DcDfOa*, amer *Pc*. 50 C'e. m.] Cest bien m. *Dc*, Soit m. *Pc*. 52 On *Ph*; que d.] d. *Df*. 54 counnilz *DbDcOaPh*. 56 amour *DfOa*. 57 ne p. *OaPh*, ny peust *DbDfPcQl*; ne m. *DcQl*. 58 Se *DbDfOaPh*; t. com y s. *Df*. 59 *Omitted Db*. 60 s. et doulcissoit *Ph*. 61 venant *OaPh*.

Un petit ruisselet passoit,
Qui le païs amoistissoit,
64 Dont l'eaue n'estoit pas salee.

La bevoient les oyseillons
Aprés ce que des gresillons,
Des mouschetes, des papillons
68 Ilz avoient prins leur pasture.
Lasniers, autouers, esmerillons
Vy, et mousches aux aguillons,
Qui de miel nouveaulx paveillons   2v
72 Firent es arbres par mesure.
De l'autre part fut la closture
D'un pré gracïeux ou Nature
Sema les fleurs sur la verdure,
76 Blanches, jaunes, rouges et perses.
D'arbres flouriz fut la ceincture,
Aussi blans com se neige pure
Les couvroit; ce sembloit paincture,
80 Tant y ot de couleurs diverses.

Le ruissel d'une sourse vive
Descendoit de roche naÿve,
Larget d'environ une toise;
84 Si couroit par l'erbue rive
Et au gravier, qui lui estrive,
Menoit une tresplaisant noise.
Maint poissonnet, mainte vendoise
88 Vy la nagier, qui se degoise
En l'eaue clere, nete et fine;
Si n'ay garde que je m'en voise
De la, maiz largement me poise
92 Qu'il faille que si beau jour fine.

---

62 r.] russet *Db*, ruissel *Ph*. 63 Qui le p. raverdissoit *Ql*, Qui le pourpris enbelissoit *Pc*.
65 venoient *DbDcOaPcPhQl*. 66 A. ce que] A. ce *Oa*, Et a. ce *Ph*. 67 m. et p. *Dc*. 68 leurs
pastures *Ph*. 69 autour *Ph*. 70 m.] mouchectes *Ph*. 71 Qui de beau m. leurs p. *Pc*: m. n. p.] m.
nouveau p. *Dc*, m. nouvel aux p. *Ph*. 72 aux *DbDcDfOaPh*. 73 fist *OaPh*. 75 sus *Pc*. 76 j. r.]
r. j. *DcOaPh*. 77 sur la c. *DbOa*, sus la c. *Ql*, sur la tainture *Ph*. 78 Ainsi b. *Ql*; que se (si *Df*)
DcDfOaPh. 79 couvrist *Db*; se s. *Ph*. 81 roche *Ql*. 82 Descendant *Dc*; dune r. *OaPh*. 83 Large
Dc. 84 par long dune r. *Dc*, par lerbe une r. *OaPh*, par les une r. *Pc*. 87 m. poisson et *DcOa*, m.
poisson *Ph*. 89 c. n.] c. et n. *Oa*, n. c. *Pc*. 92 que] qung *DcOaPhQl*.

Tout au plus pres, sur le pendant
De la montaigne en descendant,
Fut assiz un joieux boscage
96 Qui au ruissel s'aloit rendant
Et vertes courtines tendant
De ses branches sur le rivage.
La hante maint oisel sauvage –
100 L'un vole, l'autre ou ruissel nage –
Cannes, ramiers, herons, faisant;
Les cerfz passoient par l'ombrage
Et, ces oiseillons hors de cage,
104 Dieu scet s'ilz estoient taisant.

Ainsi un pou m'esjoÿssoie
Quant a celle doulceur pensoie,
Et hors de la tristour yssoie,
108 Que je porte celeement.
Et puis a moy mesmes tensoie
Et de chanter je m'efforçoie,
Maiz se de ce bien joÿssoie,
112 Il ne duroit pas longuement.
Ains rentroie soubdainement
Ou penser ou premierement
J'estoie, dont si durement
116 Suis, et de long temps, assailly.
Ce bien accroissoit mon tourment,
En voiant l'esjoÿssement,
Dont il m'estoit tout autrement,
120 Car Espoir m'estoit deffailly.

Si disoie: 'Ha, Amours, Amours,
Pourquoy me faiz tu vivre en plours
Et passer tristement mes jours,

3r

---

93 au pl. pr.] au pl. *DdPh*; sus *Pc.* 96 r.] ruissellet *Oa.* 98 Et *Ph*; sus *Pc.* 99 chante *Oa.* 100 en r. *DbPc.* 101 Quennes *Db*; heron *Db*; faisans *DcDfOaPcPhQl.* 102 payssoient *Df.* 103 ses *Ph.* 104 Dieux *Ql*; soit *Pc*; quilz *OaPh*; taisans *DcDfOaPcPhQl.* 105 Aussi *OaPh.* 106 douleur *Oa.* 108 Que porte avoie c. *Dc*, Que jay porte (portee *Ph*) c. *OaPh*, Que lors portay c. *PcQl.* 109 en moy *Oa*; tenoye *Db.* 111 M. se de ce mesjouyssoye *Ql*: si *Df.* 113 r.] retournoie *DcOaPcPhQl.* 114 Eu *Db*, Au *DcOaPh*; pense *Ql.* 116 de l. t.] de si l. t. *PcQl.* 118 venant *Ph*; leffroyssement *Oa.* 119 mectoit *Oa.* 120 me. ja failly *PcQl.* 121 Ha A. A.] haa a. a. *Db*, ha a a. a. *Df*, a. a. *Oa Ph*, a a. a. *PcQl.*

124 Et tu donnes partout plaisance?
    Tien suis a durer a tousjours,
    Et je treuve toutes rigours,
    Plus de durté, moins de secours
128 Que ceulx qui ayment Decevance.
    J'ay prins en gré ma penitance,
    Actendant la bonne ordonnance
    De la belle qui a puissance   3v
132 De moy mectre en meillieur party;
    Maiz je voy que Faintise avance
    Ceulx qui ont des biens habondance,
    Dont j'ay failly a l'esperance.
136 Ce n'est pas loyalment party.'

    Ainsi mon cuer se guermentoit
    De la grant douleur qu'il sentoit
    En ce plaisant lieu solitaire,
140 Ou un doulz ventelet ventoit,
    Si sery que on ne le sentoit
    Fors que l'erbete mieulz en flaire.
    La fut le gracïeux repaire
144 De ce que Nature puet faire
    De bel et joieux en esté.
    La n'avoit il riens a refaire
    De tout ce qui me pourroit plaire,
148 Maiz que ma dame y eust esté.

    En une sente me vins rendre,
    Longue et estroicte, ou l'erbe tendre
    Croissoit tresdrue et un pou mendre
152 Que celle qui fut tout autour.
    La me vint un acez seurprendre
    De Desir qui me fist esprendre;
    Et en alant sans garde prendre
156 Ne sans penser a mon retour,

127 durtez *Dc²OaPcPhQl.*   132 me m. *OaPcPhQl.*   134 qui des b. ont *Ph.*   136 pas l.] l. *Pc.*
138 qui s. *Ql.*   142 leberte *Db.*   144 peust *Pc.*   146 na. de rien (riens *DcDfOaPh*) *DbDcDfOaPc PhQl.*   147 ce que me povoit p. *Dc,* ce quamours pourroit faire *Pc;* quil *Df.*   148 eult *Ql.*
151 tresdure *Db;* tresdoulce ung peu m. *OaPh.*   153 une a. *Dd,* en un lieu *Ph.*   154 De] Et de *Ph;* emprendre *Ph.*   155 Et en a.] En a. *Db;* s. g. y p. *Dc.*   156 Ne sceuz p. *PcQl.*

Me trouvay loing en un destour.
La me fist Desir dur estour
Ne je ne savoie plus tour,
160 Quant vy de pres s'entrebaisier
Une pastoure et un pastour,
Et de loing yssir d'une tour
Quatre dames en noble atour;
164 Cela fist mon mal appaisier.

4r

Quant ces dames choisy a l'oeil,
Un pou entr'oublïay mon doeil,
Dont j'ay trop plus que je ne soeil,
168 Qui cessera
Au fort quant a Amours plaira
Ou Mort du tout l'abbregera;
Un de ces deux le m'ostera.
172 Autre n'y puet
Fors celle que mon cuer ne veult,
Qui en sache plus qu'elle seult,
Combien que par elle se deult
176 Le povre cuer
Qui tant en a de la douleur
Que j'en pers et chiere et couleur;
Maiz ou soit sens ou soit foleur,
180 Quoy qu'il advieigne,
Il couvient que tousjours s'y tieigne
Sans que jamaiz autre devieigne,
Combien que pas ne m'appartieigne
184 Grace avoir tele
Comme estre amé de la plus belle.
Ce m'est assez bien, que pour elle

157 Si me t. en ung d. *PcQl.* 159 Ne je ny s. *OaPcPhQl,* Si que ny s. *Dc.* 160 de p. vy *Db DcDf*; de p. vit (vis *Ph*) entrebaiser *OaPcPhQl.* 161 un p.] une p. *Db.* 162 y.] yssirent *Oa.* 163 de n. a. *PcQl.* 164 C. f.] Ce me f. *OaPcPhQl,* Ce la me f. *Db.* 165 les d. *PcQl.* 166 Ung bien peu en troublay mon d. *Oa.* 167 ne vueil *Ph.* 171 Lun *Db*; ses *Ph*; moustera *Ql.* 172 ny peust *PcQl.* 173 qui *DcDfOaPcPhQl.* 174 Guerir neant p. que. s. *DcPcQl*: s.] ne s. *Ph.* 177 Qui a souffert tant de d. *DcPcQl*: en a tant *DbDfOaPh*; de la d.] de d. *Ph.* 178 Quil en pert ch. (et ch. *Oa*) et c. *DcOaPh*: et ch.] ch. *Df.* 179 M. au fort soit sens ou f. *Dc,* M. ou soit (M. soit *Oa*) ou sens ou f. *OaPcQl*: ou s. f.] ou f. *Ph.* 181 qua t. *Df*; que sien je me t. *Dc*; se t. *OaPhQl.* 185 *Repeated Ql*: la tres b. *DbDcDfOaPcPhQl.*

J'aye du mal que mon cuer cele,   4v
188 Et que je l'ayme
Sans plus par penser, en moy meisme,
Et que seule dame la clayme
Et en mes douleurs la reclaime,
192 Quant autre chose
Faire n'en puis, et que je n'ose
Pas sans plus penser que desclose
Lui soit l'ardeur que je tien close,
196 Car se le dire
Actraioit a soy l'escondire,
Il n'y aroit plus de quoy rire;
Si me vault mieulx ce mal que pire
200 Et un que deux.
Ainsi estoie es champs tous seulx,
Et entre les pastours vy ceulx
Qui s'amerent et autour d'eulx
204 Leurs brebïetes.
Si firent par leurs amouretes
Tant de gracïeuses chosetes,
Et s'entredonnoient fleuretes
208 Et chappeaulx vers;
Et puis dançoient au travers,
Tous de fleurs estranges couvers,
Et faisoient mains tours divers.
212 Moult eu envie
De leur tresgracïeuse vie
Qui en joie sembloit ravie
Et de suffisance assouvie.   5r
216 Et par mon ame,
S'Amours consentoit que ma dame,
Celle qui si mon cuer enflame,
Si fust comme une basse fame,
220 Aux champs bergiere,

187 Jay du mal que mon c. ne c. *Ph*: le mal *Dc*.   188 Et que il ayme *Db*.   189 S. y plus pe. *Dc*,
S. pl. pour pe. *Pc*, S. pl. pe. *Db*; a *DcPcPhQl*; mesmes *Oa*.   193 ne p. *DcOaPh*.   194 s. p. pe.] s.
pe. *Pc*; que de chose *OaPh*.   196 si *Df*.   197 Atrairoit *Db*, Attrayent *Ql*.   198 a. ja p. que r. *Dc*, a.
p. que de r. *Df*, a. p. que r. *Oa*, a. maiz point du (de *Ql*) r. *PcQl*, a. p. que redire *Ph*.   201 aux
DbDcDfOaPcQl; tout *DbDf*.   202 Entre les pastoureaux oyseux *PcQl*.   203 semerent *Db*.   211 grans
t.(?) *Ql*, maint t. *Dc*.   212 ay *PhQl*.   213 leurs *Db*.   219 Estoit c. *DbDcDfOaPcPhQl*.

Bien sçay qu'il ne demourroit guiere,
Toutes choses mises arriere,
Que de ma volenté plenniere
224   Je ne gardasse
Brebiz es champs; si ne pensasse
Plus en douleur, et mieulx osasse
Lui dire le mal qui me lasse,
228   Quoy que ja las
Je ne seray d'estre en ses las,
Pour plaindre ne pour dire 'halas'.
Plus vueil son gré que mon soulas;
232   C'est mon desir,
Soit au lever, soit au gesir.
Je souhaide temps et loisir,
Ou quelque chose a son plaisir
236   Faire peüsse,
Et que ainsi faire le sceüsse
Comme le vouloir en eüsse,
Non pas si bien que je deüsse
240   Et qu'elle vault.
Maiz ou la puissance deffaut,
A la fin bon vouloir ne faut;
Se mon cuer a choisy trop hault,   5v
244   Je ne l'en prise
Que mieulx, quant il a entreprise
Une si gracïeuse emprise.
Ma dame en fera a sa guise
248   Quant vient au fort;
Et si m'est un grant reconfort –
Et en deusse prendre la mort –
Que nul ne puet dire, 'Il a tort
252   De celle amer',
Ne je n'oseroie blasmer
Desir qui m'en fait enflamer

---

221 que ne *Dc*; demouroit *PhQl*, demouroie *Dc*; guerre *Dc*, guier *Ql*.   225 aux *DbDcDfOaPcPhQl*; se *DfOa*, et *Pc*, je *Ph*.   226 douleurs *Oa*.   227 quil *Ph*; casse *DcOaPcPhQl*.   229 *Omitted Ql*.   230 et *Dc*.   233 ou au g. *Dc*.   235 Que *PcQl*.   236 F. je p. *DcPcPhQl*, F. y p. *Oa*.   237 aussi *DcOaPcPhQl*.   238 C. bien le v. en e. *Dc*.   239 que] comme *Dc*.   241 plaisance *Ph*.   242 foiz *Df*; me f. *OaPh*.   243 Si *Df*.   245 entreprinse *Ql*.   249 ce me. *Dc*; desconfort *OaPh*.   250 Et en deusses je p. m. *Db*.   251 peust *DbPcQl*.   253 Ne je nen o. b. *Dc*.   254 me f. *DcOaPcPhQl*.

Et par qui j'ay tant de l'amer.
256   Cellui seroit
Sans cuer, qui bien aviseroit
Au bien d'elle et y penseroit,
Quant volentiers ne l'ameroit.
260   Aussi pour voir
Je croy, et le cuide savoir,
Que plusieurs desirent avoir
Sa grace et en font tout devoir,
264   Desquelz le mendre
Je suy, qu'Amours fait entreprendre,
Et a quoy je ne m'ose actendre;
Et ja pour doubte de mesprendre,
268   Riens n'en sara.
Au moins la bouche le taira,
Et le semblant faire laira
Par lequel puet estre elle ara   6r
272   Appercevance
Que je n'ay si non desplaisance;
Et de tous ceulx qui sont en France
N'en a un, d'Amours a oultrance
276   Plus assailly.
Maiz s'Espoir m'estoit defailly
Et j'estoie plus mal bailly,
Au moins n'ay je mie failly
280   A choisir bien,
Car a mon gré ainsi le tien
De doulceur et de beau maintien;
Fors tout parfait n'y a il rien
284   En la tresbelle.
Et se j'eusse une grace tele
Que sans plus je fusse bien d'elle
Ou que aucune bonne nouvelle
288   J'en peusse ouÿr,
Oncques nul ne vit esjouÿr

259 Qui *OaPh*. 261 Je c. et c. s. *Ph*. 262 savoir *Ph*. 263 leur d. *Db*, tous d. *Dc*. 266 Et a qu.] Ce a qu. *DcDf*; je ne m'o.] je mo. *OaQl*; entendre *Ph*. 267 ja p.] p. *Pc*, ja par *Ql*. 268 Rien *PcQl*; ne s. *Ph*, nen sera *Dc*. 269 sa b. *Ph*; se t. *DcOaPh*. 271 peust *PcQl*; ayra *Df*. 272 Appartenance *Db*. 275 Nen a da. ung (une *Ph*) a o. *DcOaPh*. 277 M. espoir *OaPcPhQl*. 278 Dont *Ql*; p. merveilly *OaPh*. 281 la t. *Oa*. 285 si *Df*. 287 Ou a. b. n. *PcQl*. 288 Je p. *Dc*, Je peuse *Ph*. 289 nulz *PcQl*.

Amant – et deüst il jouÿr –
Ne ainsi toute douleur fouÿr
292 Que on me verroit.
Maiz cela estre ne pourroit:
Ma fortune ne le vourroit,
N'en mon courage ne cherroit
296 Qu'il advenist
Que se de moy lui souvenist
Ne qu'a servant me retenist,
Car de riens ne m'appartenist
300 Tant amoureuse
Pensee ne si gracïeuse,
Tant haulte ne si eüreuse,
Ne de joie tant planteureuse,
304 Veu que je suis
Cellui qui a moy mesmes nuys
Par mon mal eur; n'oncques depuis
Mon enfance n'eu fors ennuis,
308 Et en amours
Courte joie et longues doulours.
J'ay pour loyauté le rebours
De ceulx qui usent des faulx tours,
312 Et bien leur vient.
Ce meschief porter m'escouvient
Quant de tout si tresmal m'avient.
Au fort se droit a droit revient,
316 Un temps vendra
Qu'Amours grant pitié en prendra
Et a celle mon cuer rendra
Que, s'il lui plaist, le retendra.
320 Je l'y ay mis

6v

290 et d.] et en d. *Dc*, et deult *Ql*. 291 t. doulceur *Db*, toutes douleurs *DcOaPcPh*. 292 Comme v. *Oa*, Com me v. *PcQl*, Quomme v. *Ph*. 293 cela *DbDf*. 295 Na mon c. *OaPcPhQl*; nescherroit *OaPcQl*, ne chauldroit *Ph*. 296 Quil en a. *Ph*, Quil en advint *Oa*. 297 Que ja *DfPc*, Car si *Dc*. 298 Et *Dc*. 299 Car de r.] Car r. *Oa*, Car en r. *PcQl*, Combien quil *Dc*, Et que r. *Ph*. 300 Si *DbDcDfOaPcPhQl*. 301 P. si g. *Oa*. 302 Si *DbDcDfOaPcPhQl*; si e.] si tres e. *Dc*. 305 mists *Db*, mis *DfOa*. 306 Par mon (moy *Ph*) mal ou oncques d. *OaPh*: mon m. e.] m. e. *PcQl*. 307 n'eu] nuz *Ph*; f. enuays *Db*. 309 C. j. et] C. j. *Pc*, Courtes joyes et *Oa*, Courtes joyes *Ql*; longue *PcPh*. 310 par *Oa*. 311 de f. t. *DcPc*. 313 me couvient *DcDfOaPhQl*. 314 du t. *DcOaPcPhQl*; me vient *DcOaPcPh*. 314–15 Inverted *Pc*. 315 si *Df*, ce *Ph*; au d. *OaPh*. 317 Quamour *Df*. 319 Que si *DcQl*, Et si *Ph*. 320 lui ay *DbDfOaPcPhQl*.

Puis deux mois et m'en suy desmis,
Et si ay a Amours promis
Lui quicter, et m'en suy soubmis
324 A son bon vueil,
Lui prïant qu'il change le dueil
Que passé a deux ans recueil,
Qui appert au doy et a l'oeil,
328 Par le refuz
De celle a qui servant je fuz,
Qui mist en mon cuer fers et fustz
D'un dart amoureux dont confuz
332 Je me rendi.
Par deux ans sa grace actendi:
S'el commanda ou deffendi,
Je le fiz, maiz elle entendi
336 Bien autre part;
Si vins puet estre un peu trop tart
Et elle ot au meillieur regart.
Maiz je pry a Dieu qu'Il la gart
340 Et lui en doint
Tel joie qu'il ne faille point
Qu'elle essaie com Amours point
Ceulx a qui n'en va pas a point,
344 Comme je l'ay
Essaié. Ainsi m'en alay
En penser que jamaiz ne lay,
Et en un val ou j'avallay
348 Apperceü
Les dames qu'eu premier veü;
Et a l'approuchier congneü
Que moult de dueil orent eü.
352 Ainsi aloient
Comme celles qui se douloient

Et riens fors penser ne vouloient,
Ne point ensemble ne parloient;
356   Maiz par l'erbete
Chascune aloit toute seulete.
Oncques ne distrent chançonnete,   7v
Ne de cueillir la vïolete
360   Ne leur tenoit;
Maiz chascune son dueil menoit,
De quoy tousjours lui souvenoit,
Et l'une aprés l'autre venoit.
364   Moult loing derriere
Furent leurs gens, si firent chiere
Tant mate et si triste maniere,
Ne leurs habiz ne furent guiere
368   De trop grant monstre.
Je prins a aler a l'encontre
Par un chemin qui le me monstre,
Löant Amours que tel encontre
372   M'est advenuz;
Si alerent les pas menuz
De leurs beaulx, blans, petis piez nuz,
Et les yeulx vers terre ont tenuz.
376   Tant recevoient
De douleurs qu'elles ne savoient
Par quelz lieux ja passé avoient,
Ne moy mesmes n'appercevoient
380   Jusques aprez
Que je fuz d'elles au plus prez,
Dessus la coste d'un vert prez,
Trop mieulx odorant que cyprez.
384   Si dis alors:
'Joie de cuer, ayse de corps,
Mes dames, et bons reconfors,
Meillieurs qu'ilz n'appairent dehors,   8r

354 rien *Ql.* 358 Noncques *DcPcQl;* ny d. *Df.* 365 gent *PcQl.* 366 Si *DbDcDfOaPcPhQl;* male *Oa.* 369 Si p. *Dc;* a l'e.] en le. *Pc,* a la route *Db.* 371 qui *Oa;* telle e. *DcPcQl,* tel rencontre *Df.* 374 b. p. p. n.] piez b. et tous n. *Dc,* piez petiz (petiz piez *Ph*) menuz (tous nuz *Ql*) *OaPcPhQl.* 375 Les y. v. la t. ont t. *Dc:* t. ont t.] t. t. *PcQl.* 378 quel lieu *DbDcDfOaPcPhQl.* 379 n'a.] apparcevoient *Ph.* 382 le c. *OaPcPhQl;* dun v. p.] dun p. *Db.* 383 adorant *Ph.* 386 bon r. *Df,* bons reconfortez *Ql.* 387 quilz ne pairent d. *DbDf,* quil nappert par d. *Dc.*

388   Vous octroit Dieux!'
       Lors en hault leverent les yeulx
       Et une ou il n'a riz ne gieux
       M'a dit: 'Dieu doint qu'il vous soit mieulx,
392   Sire, qu'a nous,
       Et n'aiez ennuy se sans vous
       Salüer passïons, car tous
       Noz cuers sont si plains de courroux
396   Et de tristesce,
       Dont ilz sont encloz en destresce,
       Et assegiez par tele aspresce
       Qu'il n'est en ce monde lëesce
400   Qu'ilz receüssent
       Ne que pour rien vëoir peüssent,
       Sans que leurs douleurs en creüssent
       Et que leurs maulx ne s'esmeüssent
404   Contre plaisance;
       Car en nous a tele habondance
       De dueil et de desesperance
       Qu'il n'est pas en nostre puissance
408   De savoir faindre,
       Ains a paine nous puet contraindre
       Raison, et noz bouches refraindre
       De crïer haultement et plaindre,
412   Car noz cuers sont
       Si plains du desplaisir qu'ilz ont
       Que je ne sçay qu'il ne les rompt;
       A peu que chascun d'eulx ne font
416   Et qu'ilz ne fendent.   8v
       Riens plus noz volentez n'actendent
       Fors que noz corps les ames rendent
       Et par Mort noz vies amendent
420   En brief termine.
       Elle en est seule medecine,

---

388 o.] octroye *DcOaPh*. 390 Et une ou na ne ris ne g. *PcQl*, Et ou il na ne riz ne g. *Ph*. 391 Me dist *Dc*. 393 s. v.] savez v. *Ph*. 395 de c.] de douleurs *OaPh*. 396 Et de t.] Et t. *Ph*. 397 en lestresse *OaPhQl*. 399 Qui *Ql*; cest m. *Ql*. 400 Quilz ne r. *Db*. 401 Ne p. r. que v. p. *Dc*: Et *OaPh*; qui *Db*; p. r. v.] p. v. *Pc*; riens *DfOaPh*. 402 S. que] S. ce que *OaPh*; nen c. *DbDf*. 403 m. en esmeussent *Pc*. 407 Qui *Dd*; pas en] pas a *Dc*. 409 peust *PcQl*. 411 De c. et h. p. *Dc*. 412 Et *Db*. 413 de *Dc*. 414 quilz *Pc*, qui *Ql*. 415 *Omitted OaPh*, Ou que ch. par soy ne f. *DcPc*. 416 Ou *Pc*. 417 Rien *DcPc*. 418 cuers *Oa*. 419 les v. *OaPcPhQl*.

Si lui requier que je define
Et qu'ensemble vie et dueil fine,
424 Car enhaÿs
Ay je du tout terre et païs;
Tout m'ennuit. Mon cuer envaÿs
Est du tout; Espoir l'a traÿs,
428 Dont je lamente,
Car je suy la triste et dolente
Qui faut a toute son entente.
J'ay perdu de joie la rente
432 Qui soustenoit
Mon cuer et en joie tenoit,
Et bien a mon gré revenoit
Tout ainsi qu'il appartenoit;
436 Or me default.'
Lors fist elle un souspir si hault
Et s'assist, car le cuer lui fault;
Pasmee fut, ou autant vault.
440 Si l'escoutoie
Et ainsi courcié que j'estoie,
Toutesfoiz je la confortoie;
Maiz ja soit ce que je doubtoie
444 A enquerir
De son mal et l'en seurquerir,
Si osay ge bien requerir
Que vers elle peusse acquerir
448 Si privé bien
Qu'il lui pleüst, sans doubter rien,
Me dire quel mal est le sien,
Et que je le celeroie bien,
452 S'il le faloit;
Et se commander me vouloit
Aucune chose quë il loit,

9r

424 Car tu hays *Ph.* 425 Lerray du t. *DcOaPcPhQl*, Les ay du t. *Df.* 426 Dont *Db*, Tant *Dc*; m'e.]
mennuye *Dc*, mennuy et *Ph.* 427 Car du t. e. la venus *Dc*: Et *OaPh*; ma t. *Ph.* 429 la t.] t. *OaPh*;
t. et d.] t. d. *Pc.* 430 Qui fail a t. mon e. *Ql.* 431 Jay p. la j. et la r. *Oa.* 433 Mon c. en j. t. *Db.*
437 f. el *Df.* 441 c. que je.] courouce que je. *Db*, courrouce que estoye *DcOaPh.* 442 lui c. *Oa.*
443 que je d.] que me d. *Dc*, que d. *Pc.* 445 secourir *OaPcPh.* 447 elles *Pc.* 449 Qui *Ql*; d. r.] d.
de r. *DcDfOaPcPhQl.* 450 Moy *DbDcDfOaPcPhQl.* 451 je le c.] je c. *Ph.* 452 Si le faisoit *Oa*:
failloit *DbDc.* 453 si *DcDf.* 454 que il l.] que y l. *Df*, qui lui l. *OaPcPhQl*, quelque soit *Dc.*

Ou se mon service y valoit,
456   Y emploieroie
Cuer et corps et ce que j'aroie,
Et si volentiers le feroie
Comme faire je le pourroie.
460   Lors la tressage
Tourna vers moy son doulz visage
Qui tout en grosses lermes nage
Et bien porte au cuer tesmoignage
464   De dueil tresgrief;
Et en souspirant de rechief
Mist ses deux mains contre son chief
Et dist: 'Quel douleur, quel meschief!
468   Et quele perte!
Jamaiz ne sera recouverte.
Ha, Mort! Or m'as tu bien deserte
Et courcié le cuer sans deserte,
472   Qui en mourra
Maugré toy si tost qu'il pourra,
Et non pas si tost qu'il vourra.
Maiz ja nul ne l'en secourra
476   Qu'il ne trespasse,
Car ma dolente vie lasse,
Qui a duré trop long espace
Et qui en durté la mort passe
480   Et tant me livre
De douleur, m'en fera delivre.
En desirant mon cuer ensuivre,
Je mourray par ennuy de vivre.
484   Ainsi yra,
Car quant la mort plus me fuira,
Ma vie mesmes m'occira
Et plus tost me desconfira

9v

455 si *Df*; y v.] vouloit *OaPh*. 456 Y emploieroie *Dc*, Y empleroye *Pc*. 457 ce que] que *Ph*; et tant que javoie *Dc*. 458 v. la f. *Db*. 459 savroie *DcDfOaPcPhQl*. 461 T. devers moy son v. *DcOaPh*. 464 Du d. *PcQl*. 466 ces *Dc*; mon ch. *Ph*. 469 Qui ja ne sera r. *Db*. 470 Ha] Haa *DbDcPc*, Ha a *Df*. 471 Et courroucee s. d. *DcPcQl*: c.] courrouce *Oa*. 472 Mon cueur m. *DcPcQl*. 473 qui *Ph*. 475 ne le s. *DcPcPhQl*, ne me s. *Oa*; secoura *Db*. 478 longue e. *DbDcPcPhQl*. 481 De d. que sera d. *Dc*, De douleurs quil sera d. *PcQl*. 482 De mon cueur qui de plours (pleur *Dc*) sen yvre *DcPcQl*: c. en muyre *Oa*, c. en yvre *Ph*. 483 Que *Dc*. 485 la m. p.] p. la m. *PcQl*; puis *Ph*; suivra (?) *Oa*. 486 m'o.] se o. *Pc*.

488   Que Mort qui targe
      A m'occire; et si ne vueil targe
      Vers elle, maiz l'en prie et charge.
      Et elle est a iceulx plus large
492   Qui la defuyent
      Qu'a ceulx qui envers elle affuyent
      Et a qui leurs vies ennuyent,
      Tant qu'ilz l'appellent et poursuyent;
496   C'est contre droit.'
      La parole prins cy endroit
      Et diz qu'en couroux trop perdroit,
      Et cuer et corps piz en vauldroit.
500   Si lui präay
      A genoulz – et me humilïay
      Pour la pitié que de ly ay,
      Et pas a dire n'oublïay   10r
504   Que de l'ennuy
      Avoie aussi, tel que je suy
      Autant comment homme nulluy –
      Qu'el me deïst du bien de luy,
508   Don ce lui vient
      Que tant douloir il la couvient
      Et qu'a tel destresce devient;
      Et je lui diray qu'il m'avient,
512   Car bien m'avise
      Que pensee de dueil seurprise
      Son mal maintes foiz amenuyse
      Et descroist, quoy qu'on en devise,
516   Car Dueil destraint
      Et muce le cuer trop contraint
      Quant la bouche fort se refraint.
      Si n'est pourtant secret enfraint
520   Se on s'en desclot

489 A martire *OaPh*.   492 desuient *Ph*.   492 a Et a vains remedes sappuient *Db*, Et qui pour luy fuyr sen fuyent *PcQl*.   493 e. luy a. *PcQl*.   495 *Omitted DbDfPcQl*, Et qui contre lui (elle *Dc*) point ne fuient *DcOaPh*.   498 dist *Db*; perdoit *Df*.   502 delle jay *Dc*, de lui ay *DbDfOaPcPh*. 506 A. comme h. priant luy *DcOaPh*, Puis la priay tant com je puy *PcQl*: c. h.] comme h. *DbDf*. 507 Quelle me dist *DcOaPh*.   510 Et qua telle d. vient *DcPcQl*.   511 je lui d.] lui d. *OaPh*; qui ma. *Dc*, dont ce lui vient *Ph*.   514 maintefoiz *Df*.   515 Et d. (destruit *Oa*) quant on en d. *DcOaPcQl*, Et destruit quanque on en d. *Ph*.   516 estraint *Pc*.   518 le r. *Pc*, le restraint *Db*.   519 Et *Ph*; pour quant *Oa*. 520 Son sens d. *DfOa*.

A aucun qui volentiers l'ot
Et qui n'est mal parlant ne sot,
Et que jamaiz un tout seul mot
524 N'en soit redit.
Et quant icelle m'entendit,
Bien doulcement me respondit:
'Je ne mect point de contredit
528 Que ne soiez
Si secret comme estre doiez.
Je suis ou point que vous voiez.
Puis qu'ouÿr voulez, or oyez,
532 Car il me semble   10v
Que mon mal a nul ne ressemble,
Et s'Amours vostre cuer vous emble,
De tant pöons nous mieulx ensemble
536 Comme tresfermes.'
Lors dist en beaulx et piteux termes,
Aiant aux rïans yeulx les lermes,
Qui de plorer furent enfermes:
540 'Haa, Destinee
Tresdure, et maudicte journee
Douloureuse, mal fortunee
Qui toute ma joie as tournee
544 En desconfort!
Helaz! Cellui y print la mort,
Que j'amoie tant et si fort
Que oncques cuers d'amans si d'accort
548 Et loyaument
Ne s'amerent si longuement.
Or est mort – honnourablement
Pour lui, et douloureusement
552 Pour moy. Hemy!
Haa, cuer de tresloyal amy,
J'ay eu par toy et tu par my
Tant de plaisir! Or en gemy

521 A a.] A. *Oa.* 522 quil *Oa*; nest pas *Ph.* 527 ny m. *DcOa.* 530 au p. *DcPcQl*; en p. *Ph*; ou v. v. *PcQl.* 531 P. que v. oir or o. *Oa.* 534 samour *DcQl*; c. dessemble *Dc.* 537 d. on *Db*; et petis t. *OaPh.* 538 riens *Ph.* 540 Ha a d. *DfPhQl.* 541 T. m. j. *DcDfOaPcPhQl.* 543 as t.] a destournee *Oa.* 544 A d. *Dc.* 547 Que o. c.] O. c. *Ph.* 552 P. h. *Pc.* 553 Ha a c. *Df.* 554 pour...pour *DcOaPcQl*; et toy *DcDfOaPcPhQl*; pour my *Ph.* 555 T. desplaisir *Dc,* T. de plaisirs *OaPcQl.*

556 Quant separee
Suis de toy, seule et esgaree,
De tout plaisir desemparee.
La doulceur m'est chier comparee,
560 Dont je mendie.
Mort, dure Mort, Dieu te maudie!   11r
Et comment es tu si hardie
Que noz deux cuers a l'estourdie
564 As departy
Et l'un loing de l'autre esparty,
Quant point n'assemblerent par ty
Ce qui estoit un seul party?
568 Las! Il n'a pas
En un mesme cuer deux repas,
Maiz une vie et un trespas;
Et doit passer un mesme pas
572 Ce qui est un.
Joie ou deul, tout est a commun;
Une mort a l'autre et a l'un,
Une seule vie a chascun.
576 Tu as ce fait
De volenté plus que de fait,
Quant par ton douloureux meffait
Tu as departi et deffait
580 Si loyal sorte.
Maiz – c'est ce qui me desconforte –
Pourquoy ne m'as aussi tost morte,
Qui ne suis mie la plus forte,
584 Que mon doulz per?
Ne comment te puis je eschapper?
Que ton dart ne me vient frapper,
Ou brief ne tens a m'atrapper
588 Sans tel langueur?

560 maudie *OaPh.*   561 M. dieu m. *Ph.*   563 Qui *OaPh.*   565 *Omitted DfOaPh*: As si lun de la. *DcPcQl.*   565 *Follows* 567 *DbDcPcQl.*   566a Com oses tu avoir parti *Df.*   567 Et qui *DcOaPh*; ung sans p. *Df.*   567a Cellui est de moy departy *Ph.*   569 mesmes *DbDcPcQl.*   571 mesmes *DbDcPc.*   572 Et qui *Db*; que est *Df.*   573 Pied ou d. *Db*; t. leur est c. *Dc*, t. est c. *DbOaPhQl.* 574 ou *Dc.*   575 voye *Dc.*   577 De v. aussi de f. *Db*, Et de v. et de f. *Df*; que deffait *Pc.*   582 ne m'as] ne suis je *DcOaPh*, ne fus je *PcQl*; a. t. m.] a. m. *OaPh.*   583 Que *Df.*   585 p. je e.] p. e. *Oa.*   586 veult f. *OaPh.*   587 Ou b. ne me t. a happer *PcQl.*   588 quel *Ph.*

Maiz son ennuyeuse longueur
Lui abregera sa vigueur
En despit de ta grant rigueur
592 Qui entreprent
Contre moy que Douleur esprent,
De quoy tresgrandement mesprent.
Quant tout ne lesse ou tout ne prent,
596 C'est desraison.
Il estoit en fleur de saison
Et nez de si noble maison;
Et tu l'as prins contre raison,
600 Ou prejudice
De moy, dont tu as fait que nice
Et mal usé de ton office,
Car il estoit en mon service
604 Et si m'amoit –
De quoy nully ne le blasmoit –
Et pour sa dame me clamoit
N'aultre nul droit n'y reclamoit.
608 Et tu le prens,
Qui n'y as riens, dont tu mesprens,
Et de soulcy toute m'esprens
Quant a un seul coup ne comprens
612 Dame et servant.
Haa, pourquoy fut il si avant,
Ne pourquoy ala il devant
En ses ennemis recevant,
616 Quant par vaillance
Il fist tant de hache et de lance
Que chascun doubtoit sa puissance,
Dont il fist grant honneur a France?
620 Et se Fortune
Eust voulu que par voie aucune
Fust prisonnier, je fusse l'une
Des plus ayses desoubz la lune.

589 ton *DcPcQl*; langueur *OaPh*, rimour *Ql*. 590 Si mabregera ma v. *DcPcQl*. 597 en f.] en point f. *Ql*. 598 Et ne *DcDf*, Et nay *PcQl*. 600 Au *DfOaPcPhQl*. 605 nulle *Ph*. 607 Ne aultre d. ny r. *PcQl*. 609 Et *Df*; rien *Db*. 611 me c. *Ph*. 613 Haa p.] Ha p. *DfPc*. 614 alloit *Dc*. 616 Tant *Dc*; de v. *DbDcDfOaPcPhQl*. 617 Y f. *Dc*; t. de h.] et de h. *DcQl*, de h. *DfOaPh*; et de l.] de l. *Dc*. 619 en f. *DcDfOaPh*. 620 si *Df*.

624   Quant on diroit
     L'onneur de lui qui flouriroit,
     Et que chascun le chieriroit,
     Lors mon cuer tant s'esjouÿroit.

628   Maiz autrement
     M'en est: je pers entierement
     Ceste joie premierement
     Et les autres semblablement,

632   Pourquoy j'estrive
     A la mort qu'en douleur hastive
     De cent mille joies me prive,
     Et veult qu'aprés maugré moy vive,

636   Comme qu'il soit.
     Et el m'oste ce dont yssoit
     Ma joie, et qui me nourrissoit
     En plaisir qui n'amenrissoit

640   Tant soit peu oncques.
     Pourquoy ne me prent elle doncques,
     Ou qu'el ne me print des adonques,
     Sans departir pour rien quelconques

644   Nostre joincture?
     Fust victoire ou desconfiture,
     Santé, vie, mort, sepulture,
     Tout fust une mesme aventure;

648   Et je pensasse   12v
     Qu'aprés lui point ne demourasse.
     Au fort se Dieu ne redoubtasse,
     De la mort par mort me venjasse.

652   Bien le vouldroie,
     Et compaignie lui tendroie
     Vive et morte; maiz g'y perdroie
     L'ame, et a la sienne touldroie

656   Le bien de grace.
     Or je pry a Dieu qu'Il efface

---

626 Et que ch. ch. *Ph.*   627 fort se. *Db.*   628 Ne a. *Db.*   629 Nen est *Db*; je prins e. *Ph.*   631 le a. *Dc.*   632 P. estrive *OaPh.*   633 quant *DcOaPcPhQl.*   634 m.] mil *Oa*; joye *Ph.*   636 Comment *DcOaPh.*   637 el] elle *DbDfOaPh.*   639 qui ja meurissoit *Db*, qui amenrissoit *Oa.*   640 Pour riens (rien *Dc*) quelconques (quelzconques *DcPh*) *DcDfOaPhQl.*   642 qu'el] quelle *DbOaPcPh*; prent (?) *Df*; des a.] a. *Oa.*   643 par *Db*; riens qu. *Oa*, riens quelxconques *DfPh.*   645 et d. *Ql.*   650 si d. *Df*, se je *Ph.*   651 men v. *Oa.*   654 je p. *OaPcQl.*   657 Or je prie *DcOa*, Or prie je *PcQl.*

Ses meffaiz et mercy lui face,
Et qu'en brief de son gré defface
660   D'avec le corps
M'ame qui vouldroit estre hors
Et qui ne desire rien fors
Que d'un seul coup fussons deux mors
664   En ceste guerre,
Et les corps tous ensemble en terre,
Tous en un cerqueil bien en serre,
Et peussons paradis acquerre.
668   Si doubleray
Tousjours mon dueil, et m'embleray
Des autres. Si ressembleray
La turtre: a nul n'assembleray,
672   Car tel estoit
Qu'en tout bien vers moy se portoit,
Tant me honnouroit et redoubtoit,
Et en mes maulx me confortoit.
676   Or est extaint,
Dont mon cuer est paly et taint,
Et de toute douleur actaint,
Qui ma couleur a ja destaint.
680   Desir demeure
Et est en mon cuer a toute heure,
Qui en vain et pour nient labeure.
Espoir faut quant Desir court seure,
684   Et se depart
De moy qui de dueil ay tel part
Qu'a bien pou que mon cuer ne part
Dehors, et qu'en deux ne se part,
688   Quant Souvenir
Me fait en pensee tenir
Comme il souloit vers moy venir,
Et son gracïeux maintenir,
692   Et les doulz mos

13r

---

658 pardon ly f. *Dc.* 659 son grief *Oa.* 660 Davecques le c. *Oa.* 661 Lame *DcDfOaPcPhQl.*
662 quil *Oa*; riens *DcDfOaPh.* 663 feussiez *Oa.* 665 tout *OaPh.* 666 En ung sarqueul tous b.
en s. *Ql*: Tout *DfOaPc.* 667 puissons *DcOaPh.* 669 Mon cuer de d. *Ph.* 670 et r. *OaPcQl*, et si
r. *Ph.* 674 Moult *Db.* 681 esta *DbOa*, est *Ph.* 682 et p.] p. *Dc.* 685 de d. telle p. *Oa.* 689 et
p. *DcOaPcPhQl*; venir *DcDfOaPcPhQl.* 690 com se s. *Df.*

Qu'il me disoit a tous propos;
Car il avoit, bien dire l'os,
De tous les gracïeux le los.
696   Moult lui sëoit
Son parler et bien l'assëoit,
Car trestout deshonneur hëoit,
Et doulcement me festëoit
700   Quant il venoit;
Maiz pas long temps ne s'en tenoit –
Desir souvent l'y admenoit.
Ris et gieux, tout lui advenoit.
704   Dieux, quel dommage!
Lessiee m'a le bel et sage,
De hault sang et royal lignage,   13v
Maiz plus noble quant du courage,
708   Qui avoit a droit heritage
M'amour acquise,
Dont par long temps m'avoit requise
Et si doulcement mercy quise.
712   Maiz sa valour m'avoit conquise,
Et si l'avoie
Essaié que son cuer savoie
Estre si mien et par tel voie
716   Que de lui doubter ne devoie;
La affermee
Yert ma volenté et fermee,
Qu'Amours a depuis confermee.
720   Maiz ceste douloureuse armee
Aventuree
Et Fortune desmesuree
Ne me puet avoir enduree
724   Ma seule joie avoir duree
Saison demie.

---

693 Quel *Db*; a tout p. *DbOa*.   695 Par devant tous et pris le los *Dc*.   697 et bel la. *OaPh*.
698 Car tout d. il h. *Dc*, Car toute d. h. (haioit *OaPc*) *DfOaPcPhQl*.   699 festioit *OaQl*.   702 lui
a. *DbDcOaPcPhQl*.   704 Dieu *DcDf*.   705 Laissie (Lessiee *DdOa*, Laisse *Ph*) ma le bel et le s.
DbDdOaPh, Laissee ma le bel le s. *DcPcQl*.   706 De h. sens et de loyal l. *Ph*.   707 *Omitted Pc*: au
c. *Dc*, de c. *OaPh*.   708 en *DcOaPh*; leritaige *Db*.   710 l. t.] l. *Db*.   712 A sa v. *OaPh*, Et sa v. *Pc*,
Qua (A *Ql*) son vouloir *DcQl*.   713 tant *Db*.   714 car *Dc*.   715 par telle v. *OaPh*.   718 Estoit ma
v. f. *Dc*, Yert ma v. f. *OaPh*.   723 peust *PcQl*.

Las, Fortune m'est ennemie,
Qui est aux desloiaulx amie,
728 Quant lessier ne me pouoit mie –
Dieu la confonde –
Une seule joie en cest monde,
Qui en mal a nul ne redonde.
732 Et el seuffre que maint habonde,
Tout a son ayse,
En quelque chose qui lui plaise,
Sans ce qu'a elle en riens desplaise
736 Et sans congnoistre qu'est mesaise,
Qui deservy
N'a pas estre des biens servy
Qu'Amours depart, car asservy
740 N'est pas son cuer, maiz desservy;
Et debouté
En doit estre, quant redoubté
N'a sa dame, ains s'est arrouté
744 A Faintise qui l'a bouté
En tel haultesce
Qu'il est, par faulse subtilesce
Et decepvance qui l'adresce,
748 Larron d'amoureuse richesce
Qu'il a emblee
Et de plusieurs lieux assemblee,
Dont la joie n'est point doublee,
752 Et mainte dame en est troublee.
Maiz il eschiet
Que une foiz, qui bien a point chiet,
L'onneur des faulx amans dechiet
756 Et qu'en la fin il leur meschiet,
Quant volentiers
Ont tenu les mauvaiz sentiers

141

726 Helas mest f. e. *DcDfOaPhQl*. 730 ce m. *DbDcDfOaPcPhQl*. 731 Qui en ennuy ne me r. *PcQl*: a mal *OaPh*; a nul a mal *Db*. 732 el] elle *OaPh*; quen moy h. *Dc²*. 733 Dont *Db*. 734 Et *DcDfOaPcPh*; quil luy *Db*, que en luy *Dc*. 735 S. qua elle r. en d. (r. d. *Ph*) *OaPh*, S. ce quen r. elle d. *PcQl*: en r.] r. *Dc*, en rien *Db*. 738 Na pas destre *DbDcPc*, Na pas este *OaPh*; de bien s. *DcOaPh*. 739 na a. *Ql*. 740 Na pas *Dc*. 741 de bonte *Dc*. 742 Doit il e. *Dc*. 743 a. est a. *Dc*, a. cest a. *Ph*. 744 En f. *PcQl*. 746 Qui *DcPcPhQl*; par faulsete et rudesse *Dc²*. 747 Omitted *Dd*. 749 Qui a *PcQl*, Qui la *Ph*. 751 sa j. *DcOaPcPhQl*; pas *Ph*. 752 d. en est] d. est *Ph*. 756 il l. m.] l. en m. *DcPc*.

Et qu'ilz n'ont point esté entiers
760 En amours qui ne passe en tiers.
De telz assez
En est, trop plus que es temps passez,
Qui tant de sermens ont cassez
764 Et n'en pevent estre lassez.
Leur bouche nomme   14v
Souvent mainte qu'a tort renomme.
Toutesfois scevent ilz bien comme
768 Nature un seul cuer a un homme
A ordonné;
Si ne doit estre abandonné
Ailleurs depuis qu'il l'a donné,
772 N'estre ne lui doit pardonné,
Car ordonner
Veult Amours, pour guerredonner
Les bons, qu'autel bien puist donner
776 Une com cent et foisonner,
Et si rassis
Est Amours qu'autant a assis
De pouoir en une qu'en six.
780 Plus lui plaist et mieulx lui a sis
En une mectre
Son cuer, que partout s'entremectre
De servir, soffrir et soubmectre,
784 Rien tenir et foison promectre.
Telz ne pourroient
Savoir qu'est bien. Pou s'en dourroient
Garde que telz gens secourroient,
788 Quant ilz diroient qu'ilz mourroient
Pour amours fines,
Et feroient si tristes signes,

759 qui *DcQl*. 762–3 *Inverted Ql*. 762 En est t. qui au t. p. *Dc*: Dont t. p. est *Ql*; quou t. p.
OaPh; passe *Ql*. 763 Ont t. de faulx s. c. *Dc*, Qui t. ont de seremens c. *Ph*: s.] seremens *DdDfOa*.
766 maintes *Dc*; que t. *DbDd*. 767 T.] Toutesvoies *DbDdOaPhQl*, Toutevoyes *Df*; servent *OaPh*.
768 N. ung c. a ung s. h. *Pc*. 771 quil a d. *DcOaPcQl*, qui la d. *Ph*. 774 V. oultre a. par guerdonner
Dc: g.] guerdonner *Db*, guerredonne *Ph*. 775 quautes biens *Oa*, quant tel (il *Ql*) b. *PcQl*; peult
DbDcDfOa, peust *PcQl*, veult *Ph*. 776 Une que c. *DcDfOaPcPh*. 778 Est A.] Est a a. *Db*; amour
Ph; est a. *Ql*. 779 pover *PcQl*, plaisir *Ph*; qua six *Df*. 780 luy assis *DcOaPh*. 781 En ung m. *Ph*.
782 p. entremettre *Dc*. 783 Desservir *Ph*. 784 Riens *DfOa*. 786 S. quelx biens *Oa*; Pou] sy *Ql*;
devroient *DcQl*. 787 Garder *DcQl* (?); qui *OaPcQl*. 788 d.] diront *Oa*. 789 Par *PcPhQl*. 790 f.]
feront *Oa*.

Manieres humbles et benignes,
792 Pour rober ce dont ne sont dignes.
Et se jouÿ
N'en avoient, comme esjouÿ   15r
Ilz se vanteroient qu'ouÿ.
796 Helaz, mon cuer a tant fouÿ
D'eulx les paroles
Et leurs grans loberies foles,
Leurs decevans blandices moles!
800 Moult ay desprisié telz frivoles.
Maiz tant rouvay
Que un tel qui me plaisoit trouvay,
Que bon et loyal esprouvay,
804 De qui tous les faiz approuvay.
La m'arrestay,
Et a l'amer tout apprestay
Le cuer que de fendre prest ay,
808 Que je lui donnay et prestay;
Et en eschange
Prins le sien par amoureux change.
Or pers tous deux par voie estrange
812 Dont je vois, nuz piez et en lange,
Prïer la Vierge
Qui des cieulx est vraie concierge,
Lui presentant un ardant cierge
816 Afin que par sa grace acquierge
Grace et pardon,
Et a nous deux vueille par don
Octroier qu'ainsi ne tardon
820 L'un aprés l'autre, ainçois gardon
Par sa pitié,
Vifz et mors, la nostre amictié.
Bien a cil sa foy acquictié,   15v
824 Dont mainte cronique et dictié

793 si *DfOa*. 794 c. ay je ouy *Ph*. 795 sen v. *Oa*. 798 leur grant l. f. *Pc*. 799 d.] decevances *Oa*, decevance (?) *Ph*. 800 leur f. *Dc*. 801 M. r. *Pc*, M. t. tournay *DcOaPh*. 802–3 *Inverted Db*. 802 Que un] Ung *Db*; que *Ql*; p.] desplaisoit *Ph*. 803 b. et l.] l. et b. *DbDcDfOaPcPhQl*. 804 Nonq de mal ne fu repprouvay *PcQl*: Du quel *Dc*; esprouvay *OaPh*. 806 t. (tant *Ph*) maprestay *DcOaPh*. 807 qui *OaQl*; deffendre *DbDcDfOaPh*. 808 d. et p.] p. et d. *Ql*. 809 Et en change *Ph*. 812 nulz p. *Ql*. 814 v. c.] vray c. *Db*. 815 presenter *Dc*. 816 acquiere *Ph*. 823 a seul la (sa *Ql*) foy *OaPhQl*.

Ja composé
Deust estre, car tant a osé
Qu'il a corps et vie exposé,
828 Sans estre lasche ou reposé,
Comme vaillant,
Encontre ceulx qui assaillant
Venoient France, en leur baillant
832 De courage non defaillant
Assez affaire.
Et se chascun eust voulu faire
Pareillement sans soy deffaire,
836 Anglois n'eüssent peu parfaire,
Maiz empoi tassent
Noz maulx et s'en desconfortassent,
Et autre part se transportassent;
840 Et desormaiz se deportassent
De nous grever.
Bien pevent envïeux crever:
Sa mort fait son honneur lever
844 Contre qui vouldrent eslever
Mauvaiz renon.
Or n'ont ilz veu en lui se non
Loyauté dont il a le nom,
848 Puis que ceulx pour loyaulx tenon
Qui se maintiennent
Si bien que foy et devoir tiennent
Vers leur seignieur et le soustiennent
852 Jusqu'au mourir, et entretiennent   16r
Leur loyauté
Au besoing, et la fëauté
De leur dame et de sa beauté,
856 Sans penser mal ne crüauté
N'aguetz subtiz.
Telz sont les meurs des cuers gentiz
A quoy doivent estre ententifz

---

825 Jay c. *OaPh*.   826 Deubt *Pc*; quant t. *DcPcQl*, quant tout *OaPh*.   827 c. et vie] vie et c. *PcQl*.
830 assaillent *Db*.   833 A. a faire *Db*.   834 si *Df*.   836 A. n'e.] A. ne. pas *Dc*, A. si ne. *Pc*.   842
puent *Dc*, pueent *Df*, peussent *Ph*.   844 vouldroit *DbDcOaPcPhQl*.   846 n'ont ilz] nont il
DcPh; veuz *Oa*; sy non *DbDcPc*.   848 telx *Dc*; loyal *Df*.   851 seigneurs *Pc*.   854 leur f. *Dc*.
855 et de] et *Dc*.   857 Naguet *DfOaPh*.   858 de c. g. *DfPcPhQl*, de cuer g. *DbOa*.   859 d.] il doit
DbDcDfOaPcPhQl.

223

860 D'armes ne d'amours apprentifz:
　　Humbles, piteux,
　　Et d'onneur sans plus couvoiteux;
　　N'estre ne doivent cremeteux
864 De rien si non de faiz honteux.
　　Et tel estoit
　　Cellui ou mon cuer s'arrestoit,
　　Qui tant de joie m'apprestoit
868 Et doulcement m'amonnestoit
　　Que lie et cointe
　　Me tenisse et que sans racointe
　　Son cuer estoit du mien acointe,
872 Une joie en deux cuers adjoincte;
　　Et tant jurer
　　M'en souloit sans soy parjurer.
　　Pourquoy ne m'a il peu durer?
876 A quoy s'ala aventurer?
　　Tant honnouree
　　Fusse, se me fust demouree
　　Celle joie. Or suis esplouree
880 Sans ja vëoir, en amouree
　　Plaine d'angoisse
　　Et de vain desir qui me froisse,
　　Dont je n'ay membre qui ne croisse
884 Ne sens que ne me descongnoisse.
　　Haa, peu loyaulx,
　　Fuitifz, lasches et desloyaulx,
　　Qui n'amez qu'estaz et joiaulx!
888 Vous lessastes tous les royaulx,
　　Et leur tournastes
　　Les dos et vous en retournastes,
　　Que tant soit pou n'y sejournastes,
892 Car alors les abandonnastes,

16v

860 D'ar. ne d'am.] Dam. et dar. *Oa*; et *DcPcPhQl*.　861 Humble et p. *DbDfOaPcPhQl*, Humble p. *Dc*.
863 Nul si ne doit estre doubteux *Dc*: Nil (Nul *Db*) ne doit estre *DbOaPcPhQl*, Il nen doit estre *Df*;
commetteux *Oa*.　864 se non *OaQl*.　865 Car *OaPh*; celle *Ph*.　869 Que lies et c. *Db*: l.] liee
DdOaPh.　870 et que] que *Ph*.　872 a joincte *Ph*.　874 Nen s. *Db*, Me s. *DcOaPh*.　876 Pourquoy
DbDcDfOaPcPhQl; a.] il a. *OaPcQl*.　879 s. je e. *Ph*.　880 S. ja v.] S. ne me v. *Dc*, S. me v. *PcQl*.
882 Et en *Dc*.　883 me c. *Ph*.　884 sans que *Df*; qui *DbDcOaPcPhQl*; ne se d. *Ql*.　885 Ha a peu l.
DfOaPcPhQl.　887 navez *DbDd*.　890 Le dos *Ph*.　891 *Omitted DfOaPh*, Du champ ou point ne s.
Db, Dont a plusieurs (a plusuers *Pc*) la mort donnastes *DcPcQl*.　892 Et *Df*.

Tous mescreüz

De traÿson et recreüz,

Dont le nombre fut descreüz

896 Et les cuers des Anglois creüz,

Car par troppeaulx,

Non obstans les cris et rappeaulx

Des bons, couvristes les cruppeaulx

900 Des hëaumes. Que de voz peaulx

Vifz escorchiez

Soiez vous, et si bien torchiez

Que jamaiz ne vous renforchiez!

904 Telz gens deussent estre porchiez,

Ou faisans viles

Oeuvres par citez et par villes,

Quant aux armes sont inutiles;

908 Et veulent avoir cens et milles

Pour leur bobant,

Et vont les povres gens robant,   17r

Decevant le monde et lobant!

912 Ilz sont bons en ne soy hobant

Soubz cheminees,

Quant leurs bouches sont avinees

Et ilz ont les bonnes vinees.

916 Lors comptent de leurs destinees

Les quoquars foulx;

Alors se vantent des gros coupx

Et font gras despens et grans coustx.

920 Et qui que soit prins ou rescoux,

Nul d'eulx n'y pense;

Prestz seroient a la despense,

Maiz trestardifz a la deffense.

924 L'un maugree Dieu; l'autre tense

Par grant yvresce,

Puis dort jusqu'a dix par paresce,

---

893 Tout *Ph.*   894 et r.] r. *Ph.*   896 le cueur *DcOaPcPhQl*; c.] acreuz *Dc.*   897 Et *Ph.*   898 obstant
DbDcOaPcPhQl; et r.] et les r. *Ql.*   899 cruvoictes (?) *Ph*; coppeaulx *DcDfOaPcQl.*   903 renforciez
Ph, ressourciez *Dc.*   904 porchiers *Df.*   905 En faisant v. *Ql*: En *Dc.*   909 Par *DbPcQl.*
910 *Omitted Db.*   912 en ne soy] en non soy *Df*, en soy *DbDc.*   914 b.] gorges *Dc*, gorgectes
Ph; enyvrees *DcOaPh.*   915 Et ont beu les b. v. *PcQl.*   917 solz *Ph.*   918 de *DbDcPh*; grans
DcOaPcPhQl.   919 grans d. *DbDcDfPcPhQl*, mains d. *Oa.*   922 Prest *Ph.*   924 maugrere (*sic*) *Ql.*
926 j. dix] dix (j. dix *Oa*) heures *OaPh.*

Maiz d'une bataille en aspresce
928 Scet bien tirer son cul de presse
Et son hëaume
Gecter au besoing du royaume.
Plus scet aux dez ou a la paulme;
932 Mieulx dort en lict que sus du chaume.
Dieux, quel rousee!
Tendres sont comme une espousee,
Tremblans comme brebiz tousee.
936 De fievre quartaine espousee
Soit tel merdaille!
Et ja povreté ne leur faille
Tant que chetifz mourir les faille
940 De fain, mis sus un pou de paille
Et delessiez.
Quant au besoing vous ont lessiez,
Princes royaulx qui les paissiez,
944 Leurs lignages ont abessiez
Et diffamez.
Moult ont leurs honneurs entamez,
Que leurs peres ont tant amez
948 Qu'ilz en furent nobles clamez,
Don sont venuz
Iceulx qui n'ont pas maintenuz
Leurs bons faiz ne bien retenuz,
952 Quant a honte sont revenuz;
Dont tant me dueil
Que vëoir n'en puis de bon oeil
Un tout seul, ne bien ne leur vueil,
956 Car ilz sont cause de mon dueil.
J'ay acheté
Leur recrëant escharceté:
Mort est cil par leur lascheté,
960 Qui ne puet estre racheté.
Dieu en ait l'ame!

17v

927 en la presse *Dc.* 928 S. b. son cul t. *PcQl.* 932 sur du ch. *DbDcDf,* sur (sus *Pc*) dur ch. *OaPcPhQl*(?). 933 Dieu *DcDfOa.* 937 S. telle m. *Ph.* 939 *Omitted Db*: leur f. *Oa.* 940 De f. nudz *DcPh,* De f. nulz *PcQl*; sur *DbDcDfOaPhQl.* 943 paissez *DcOaPcQl.* 946 leur honneur *DcOaPh.* 948 Qui en f. *OaPh.* 949 Dont *DbDcDfOaPcPhQl.* 950 point *Pc.* 951 biens f. *Ql.* 954 ne p. *DcOaPh.* 956 causes *OaPcQl.* 958 L. r. et laschecte *Ph.* 960 peust *PcQl.* 961 Dieux *DbDfPh.*

226

Leur fuite est cause, a leur grant blasme,
De la perte et de leur diffame.
964   L'eusse je fait, moy qui suy fame,
Ou le feroie,
S'il m'afferoit? Mieulx ameroie
Mourir, et plus aise en seroie,
968   Car honneur ainsi garderoie   18r
A heritage;
Et c'est trop plus grant avantage
Mourir par honneur en ostage,
972   Qu'aloignier sa vie a hontage.
Mieulx vault oultrer
Le corps, que soy faire moustrer
Au doy sans oser encontrer
976   Les bons n'en compaignie entrer.
Doncques pour voir,
Plus me plaist le loyal devoir
De cil que j'aym sans decevoir,
980   Et moins en gré doy recevoir
Qu'en la durté
De bataille ou s'est ahurté,
A trouvé moins de la seurté
984   Que ceulx qui onq n'y ont hurté.
J'ay grans remors,
Dure Mort, dont plus tost ne mors
Ceulx qu'a riens valoir sont amors
988   Et autant servent vifz que mors.
Moins aggrëable
M'est sa mort, combien que honnourable
Soit, car present plus delectable
992   Me fust sa vie et prouffitable.
Or est noiant,
Dont ma vie m'est ennoiant

---

962 faucte *Dd*; et c. *Pc*; et l. g. b. *Pc*, de l. b. *Ph*.   963 leur p. *Dc*.   964 Et le. f. *Ph*.   966 Si ma. *Ph*.   972 Qualonger *DcOaPc*, Queloingnier *Df*, Qualongnier *Ql*, Qua langourer *Db*; en h. *DbPcPh*, en heritage *Oa*.   975 aouser *Db*; rencontrer *Dc*.   978 p. deloyal d. *Ph*.   979 De ceulx *OaPcPhQl*; que ja.] quayme *Dc*, que jaime *Ql*.   980 mieulx *Dc*.   982 De b.] De la b. *OaQl*, A la b. *Ph*; cest a. *Dc*, sest heurte *Ql*.   983 de la s.] de s. *Dc*.   984 quoncques *Df*; ot h. *Ph*.   985 grant *DbDf*, grief *DcOaPcQl*, griefz *Ph*.   986 ne m.] ne remors *Oa*.   987 qua rien *Db*, qui rien *Dc*, qui a riens *OaPh*.   989 agreables *Ph*.   991 pr.] trop *DcPcQl*, prise *OaPh*.   992 et p.] plus p. *Ph*.

Sans la sienne, car plus aiant

996   Fust de bien, et mieulx fust soiant.

Si suy contrainte   18v

De douleur trop plus qu'autre mainte,

Car des bons ne puet estre rainte

1000   La mort, ne trop plouree ou plaincte;

Maiz des meschans,

Qui les autres sont empeschans

Et ne valent n'en bois n'en champs,

1004   Deust estre la mort despeschans,

Car eüreuse

N'en est la vie päoureuse,

Maiz faillie et pou vertüeuse;

1008   Si n'est point tele mort piteuse.

Maiz bien plourer

Doy d'aprés la mort demourer

De cil qui pour s'enamourer

1012   De moy s'est fait tant honnourer;

Si suy donnee

A Desconfort et adonnee.

Si m'a Amours guerredonnee

1016   Qu'Espoir m'a toute abandonnee,

Et plus ne voient

Mes yeulx un seul bien qu'ilz avoient,

Qu'il couvient que plus ne revoient.

1020   Pou perdroie s'ilz me crevoient,

Car tout de vray

Jamaiz par eulx n'appercevray

Chose dont joie recevray;

1024   Ains mourray quant mourir devray,

De joie nue,

Sans estre a Fortune tenue   19r

N'a Amours, qui d'une venue

---

995 S. la s. p. agreant *Dc.* 996 F. b. et m. me f. s. *Dc*: plus *Pc*; seant *DbOaPh.* 998 douloures *PcQl*; quautres m. *Ql.* 999 de b. *Dc*; peust *PcQl.* 1000 plourer *DcOa.* 1005 Car peu e. *Dc.* 1006 N'en] Si en *Dc*; p.] ne seureuse *Df*, peu (et peu *Ph*) eureuse *OaPh.* 1007 Et *Dc*; ou *Oa*; et p.] p. *Ph.* 1011 qui p.] par qui *DcDfOaPcPhQl*; son (feus *Dc*) amourer *DbDcOaPcPhQl.* 1012 f. t.] t. f. *Db.* 1013 Et *PcQl.* 1014 ordonnee *Dc.* 1015 *Omitted OaPh*, Si (Ainsi *Dc*) ma a. guerdonnee *DbDc.* 1016a Dont ma vie (vie point *Ph*) ne magree *OaPh.* 1018 quil *Ql.* 1020 Pou] Que peu *Ph*; sil me c. *PcQl*, si me c. *Ph*, silz me craingnoient *Oa.* 1021 t. pour v. *DcPcPhQl*, pour t. v. *Oa.* 1027 que *DcOaPcPhQl.*

228

1028   Pas une esperance menue
       Ne me delaissent,
       Car en toute douleur me laissent,
       Dont leur pris grandement abaissent,
1032   Car du premier desir me paissent
       Tousjours autel.
       Au fort, puis qu'il estoit mortel,
       Me demourra pour tout chatel
1036   Le loz d'avoir amé un tel.
       Ainsi s'acquicte
       Mon triste cuer que Mort despite.
       Si pry Dieu qu'Il me desherite
1040   De ma meschant vie maudicte
       Qui tant me greve
       Et qui a la mort a prins treve
       A celle fin qu'el ne l'aggreve;
1044   Si sera ma vie plus breve,
       Car plus n'en puis.'
       A tant elle se teut; et puis
       Du profont du cuer et du puis
1048   Tant gecta de souspirs depuis
       Et tant de plains,
       Et les yeulx de lermes si plains
       Avoit en faisant ses complains
1052   Qu'en moy mesme en plourant la plaings,
       Ne rimoier
       Ne puis le cas sans lermoier,
       Sans douloir et sans esmoier.   19v
1056   Moult y pensay a par moy hier
       Et me merveille,
       Veu le dueil qu'elle s'appareille,
       Que sa grant beauté non pareille
1060   Et sa couleur fresche et vermeille
       Puet demourer;

1028 Pas] Par *Dc*, Et par *Ph*.   1031 leurs p. *DcPcPh*.   1032 Et *Ph*.   1035 demoura *DfQl*; chastel *Dc*.   1037 Atant sa. *Ph*.   1038 t. c.] c. t. *DcDfOaPcPhQl*; qui *Db*.   1039 pry] prie *DfOa*; qui *Ql*.   1040 m.] meschante *DcPh*.   1042 Et a qui la m. *Dc*.   1043 qu'el] quil *Db*, que elle *OaPh*; ne me grief-ve *Pc*.   1046 celle se t. *DbDcDfPcQl*, se t. celle *Oa*, se t. elle *Ph*; et p.] et depuis *Ph*.   1047 et du p.] du p. *Df*; du pis *DcOaPcPhQl*.   1052 Que moy *DcDfOaPcPhQl*; m. en p.] meismes p. *DcOaPcPhQl*; le p. *Oa*, les p. *Ph*.   1055 douleur *OaPhQl*.   1057 Et mer. *OaPh*.   1061 Peust *PcQl*.

Maiz onq ne vy descoulourer
Son vis que deul fait esplourer,
1064 Ains plus lui sëoit a plourer
Que rire a maintes.
Lors lui diz: 'Bien voy que voz plainctes,
Ma dame, si ne sont pas fainctes
1068 Maiz d'angoisse toutes contraintes;
Maiz reprenez
Courage, et souffrir apprenez,
Car trop grandement mesprenez,
1072 Se a vous mesme guerre prenez.
Qui son dueil coeuvre
Trop fort, double mal en recoeuvre,
Car tristour est d'une tel oeuvre
1076 Qu'elle descroist, qui la descoeuvre
Ou il affiert,
Et qui trop la coeuvre, elle fiert
Le cuer et dedens se refiert;
1080 Maiz plus s'espart, et plus brief yert
Triste penser.
Mectez paine d'ailleurs penser
Pour voz douleurs recompenser;
1084 Et en vous gardant d'offenser,   20r
Vous avisez.
Avec ces dames devisez
Et ensemble a confort visez.
1088 Croiez moy et vous ravisez.'
Ainsi disoie
A la dame que moult prisoie,
A qui de son bien devisoie;
1092 Et les trois autres avisoie
Pareillement
Qu'elles voulsissent telement
La conforter, qu'allegement

1066 L. dis b. voy je que voz p. *Df*: Alors dis *DcPcQl*, Adonc dis *OaPh*.   1067 Ma d. ne s. mye f.
DbDcDfOaPcPhQl.   1068 dangoisses *Ql*.   1072 mesmes *DbDcDfOaPcPhQl*.   1074 r.] recoueuvre
Db.   1075 telle o. *DbOaPh*, tel preuve *PcQl*.   1076 desceoit *Dc*, decoipt *OaPh*.   1079 Le c. d. et si
r. *Oa*.   1080 briefve y. *Ph*.   1082–3 *Inverted Pc*.   1086 ses d. *DcDfPh*; d.] et d. *Ph*.   1087 Et e.] E.
et *Dc*.   1088 advisez *OaQl*.   1090 qui tant p. *Dc*.   1092 *follows* 1093 *and is written on same line Dc*.
1094 Quelle v. *Dc*.

1096   Prenist pou a pou bellement,
       Quant une d'elles
       Respondit: 'Las, je suy de celles,   20v
       Qui tant ay de douleurs mortelles
1100   Que nulle autre ne les a teles;
       Si suy bien loing
       D'avoir de conforter le soing,
       Quant j'ay de confort mieulx besoing
1104   Qu'elle n'a, et que plus ressoing
       Mon mal eür
       Qui ne me lesse estre asseür,
       Ne pour rien je ne m'asseür:
1108   Et elle est hors de la peür
       Et de la crainte,
       Dont je suy durement estrainte
       Et en cuer et en corps contrainte
1112   Et de toute joie restrainte.
       Si vous diray
       Mon fait, et ja n'en mentiray,
       De l'amour dont ne partiray
1116   Jamaiz, quoy que maint souspir ay
       Pour ce porté,
       Dont mon cuer n'est pas conforté,
       Qui de vraie amour enhorté,
1120   S'est a un tout seul assorté,
       Et se lÿa
       A cil qui tant s'umilïa
       Qu'a moy bien amer s'allÿa –
1124   Et tant de graces en ly a.
       Maiz tant avint,
       Ains que d'ans eüst jusqu'a vingt,
       Qu'a tort souvent lui mesavint   21r
1128   Par Fortune; et jusques la vint
       Puis que dix ans

1096 Prinst pou a pou tout b. *Ph*: Prensist *Dc*, Preist *OaPcQl*.　1100 Que nul a. *DbDcOaPc*, Et que nulle a. *Ph*.　1102 de c.] de confort *Ph*; le s.] besoing *PcPh*.　1103 Qu. de c. m. ay b. *Ph*: de c. m. b.] de c. b. *Dc*, de conforter m. b. *Db*.　1104 mieulx r. *OaPh*.　1105 Mon grant mal eur *Dc*.　1109 De la c. *Oa*.　1112 estainte *Dc*.　1116 moins souspirs *Dc*.　1119 vray *Db*.　1120 Cest *PhQl*.　1121 luia *Oa*.　1124 g.] grace *Dc*; luy *DbDcDfOaPcPhQl*.　1126 d'a.] des ans *DcDfPc*; j. v.] jusques a v. *Ph*.　1127 s.] il *Ph*.　1128 Par f. j. a v. *Ph*.

Ot que par mauvaiz mesdisans,
A verité contredisans,
1132 De lui et des siens maldisans,
Fut moult blechié
Son honneur, dont ce fut pechié,
Car il est si bien entechié

1136 Et a tout honneur adrechié
Qu'il est loué
De tous les bons et advoué
De vertus largement doué.

1140 Mais Fortune a son mal voué,
Comme il appert –
Mon cuer ce que plus chier a, pert
Et on le voit tout en appert –

1144 Combien qu'il soit sage et appert.
Maiz pour entendre
Son fait: depuis s'enfance tendre,
Qu'il pot le pié en l'estrief tendre,

1148 Fortune ne voult plus actendre
A l'assaillir;
Et depuis ne lui pot faillir
Dueil et Couroux qui tressaillir

1152 L'a fait souvent et mal baillir.
Maiz quant passé
A un ennuy qui l'a lassé,
Fortune a tantost compassé

1156 Un mal tout nouvel et brassé,   21v
Que on n'y prent garde.
Je croy que Dieu les bons regarde
Et qu'aprés dueil joie leur garde,

1160 Maiz trop demeure et trop me tarde;
Et moult sejourne
Fortune qu'el ne se retourne,

1130 Et que *Db*, Eust que *Pc*, Eust *OaPhQl*; ma.] maulx *Pc*.   1132 mesdisans *DcDfOaPcPhQl*.
1133 blecie *DbDcOaPcPh*.   1135 entachie *DcOa*.   1136 toute h. *Oa*; adrecie *DcPh*.   1137 Qui *Oa*.
1139 longuement *Ql*.   1142 Car ce plus en cueur en appert (en c. a. *DfOa*) *DcDfOa*, Car ce qui
plus en cuer appert *Ph*: appert *DbQl*.   1144 viste et expert *Oa*.   1146 lenfance *DfOaPhQl*, sen
faulte *Db*.   1147 peult *DbDfPhQl*, peust *DcOaPc*.   1148 veult *DbDfPc*.   1150 peult *DbDfOaQl*,
peust *DcPc*.   1151 que *OaPh*.   1152 Le f. *DbDcDfOaPcPhQl*; s. tres mal *OaPh*.   1154 En *DcPh*.
1156 tant *Dc*.   1158 dieux *Oa*.   1160 d.] me dure *Ph*.   1162 qu'el] quelle *DbDcDfOaPcPhQl*; r.]
tourne *DbDcOaPh*.

232

Qui de le vëoir me destourne,
1164 Dont je remains pensive et mourne.
Et si sachiez:
Mon cuer y est si atachiez
Et mes pensés tant enlachiez,
1168 Noz biens, noz maulx entrelachiez
Que, sans mentir
Et sans jamaiz s'en repentir,
Bonne amour me fait consentir
1172 A pareilz maulx ou biens sentir
Que sont les siens,
Et puis que tout mien je le tiens,
Je les reçoy comme les miens
1176 A butin, noz maulx et noz biens;
Ne sa diverse
Fortune n'ara ja tele erse
Sus nostre amour qu'elle renverse
1180 Noz volentez a la reverse,
Et quant vourroit
Faire du pis qu'elle pourroit,
Nostre amour tousjours demourroit
1184 Ou chascun de nous deux mourroit.
Quant plus s'efforce   22r
De nous nuyre, l'amour s'enforce,
Ne je n'y voy rien de bien fors ce
1188 Que Fortune en amour n'a force.
Si ne tien compte
Qu'elle face a nostre amour honte;
Jamaiz Fortune ne seurmonte
1192 Amours qui les treshaulx cuers monte
Que moult prison.
Maiz onq ainsi ne fut pris hom

1163 de leur v. *Db*; ne d. *Oa*.   1164 remais *Oa*, remens *Ph*; pasive *Oa*, pesive *Ph*.   1166 si est *Oa*.
1167 pencees *DcOa*; si *DcDfOaPcPhQl*; enlacez *Oa*.   1168 b. et m. *Db*; entrelacez *Oa*.   1170
j. en r. *Pc*, j. sans r. *Ph*.   1171 Bon a. *Dc*; font *Df*.   1172 m. ou b.] m. en b. *Db*, m. et b.
Pc, b. ou m. *Dc*; bien s. *OaPh*.   1173 font *Dc*, fait *OaPh*.   1175 le r. *Oa*.   1177 si *Ql*.   1178 ja
tant derse *Db*.   1179 Sur *DbDcDfOaPhQl*; quelle reverse *OaPh*, tant quelle verse *Dc*.   1180 v.]
voluntees *Dc*; renverse *OaQl*.   1184 noz d. *DbQl*.   1185 Tant *Dc*, Car *DfOaPhQl*.   1187 Mais
OaPh; ne voy *Db*; r. de b.] r. b. *DbDdPcQl*, r. bon *Dc*, r. *OaPh*.   1188 amours *DcOaPcPhQl*.
1189 nen t. c. *Db*, nen est c. *DcOaPh*, nest en c. *Df*, nen faiz c. *PcQl*.   1190 noz amours *Ql*.
1192 Amour *Df*; que *Ph*; les c. treshault m. *Dc*; donte *Df*.

233

De durtez, car sans mesprison,
1196 Mort d'amis, guerres et prison,
Couroux et pertes,
Blasmes par mensonges appertes,
Traÿsons, mauvaistiez couvertes
1200 A essaiees et expertes,
En soy taisant
Et bien contre le mal faisant,
Doulcement son cuer appaisant,
1204 Qui n'ot onq un seul jour plaisant;
Maiz envaÿ
A esté de maint et haÿ,
Qui volentiers l'eussent traÿ,
1208 Ce que pas deservy n'a y.
Point ne saroit
Estre autre que doulz, et n'aroit
Jamaiz cuer que rien lui plairoit
1212 Qu'il sceust qu'a autre desplairoit,
Car raisonnable
Est, courtois, doulz et amïable,
Pacïent, piteux et traictable;   22v
1216 Et veult estre a tous aggrëable
Sans que on perçoive
Qu'il blasme autre, grieve, ou deçoive,
Maiz chascun doulcement reçoive.
1220 Si ay dueil que nully conçoive
Blasme ou reprouche,
Ne que Fortune tant approuche
Sur cil qui plus au cuer me touche,
1224 Quant oncques n'yssit de sa bouche
Mot deshonneste;
Ains fait a chascun chiere et feste,
Prest d'octroier toute requeste,
1228 Sans nul blecier ne que sa teste;
N'oncques haitié

1195 De durte *Dc*, Ne hurtez *OaPcQl*, Ne hurte *Ph.* 1196 g.] guerre *DcOa.* 1198 pour *Dc.*
1200 es.] essayes *PcQl*; et e.] tres e. *Oa.* 1203 mal a. *Ql.* 1204 Quil neust onc *DcPh*, Oncques not *Ql.*
1208 Et *PhQl*; par desservir *Df*; d. nay *DcOaPhQl.* 1211 J. c. r. ne lui p. *Ql*: qui r. *DcOaPcPh.*
1212 autres *DcQl.* 1216 e. a t.] a t. e. *Dc.* 1218 aultruy *Db.* 1220 nul lui c. *Oa*, nul y c. *Ql*,
nullui en coive *Ph.* 1223 Sus *Pc.* 1228 queste *Ql.*

234

Ne fut que on pensast mauvaitié.
Ne il n'est deceveur affaitié,
1232 Maiz prest a tout loyal traictié,
Bien entendant;
Tousjours a bonne fin tendant
Va sa jennesce en amendant.
1236 Or est prins en soy deffendant
Des adversaires
Qui sont a son prince contraires,
Aprés tous ses autres affaires
1240 Et des meschiefz plus de cent paires
Qui l'ont grevé,
Dont encor n'est pas relevé.
Si est mon cuer tant abrevé   23r
1244 De douleur qu'a pou n'est crevé,
Quant si planté
Se sent de sa joie, en planté
De tristour ou tant a hanté;
1248 Et mal sus mal n'est pas santé
Maiz grief dangier.
Dont se veult Fortune estrangier
De soy mesmes, quant plus changier
1252 Ne scet son faulx tour estrangier
Et qu'elle maint
Tousjours vers lui dure, et remaint
A lui pire qu'a autre maint.
1256 Si pry Dieu qu'Il le me ramaint
Par sa benigne
Pitié, car pour ce je chemine
Comme piteuse pelerine,
1260 Lui prïant, quoy que n'en suy digne,
Qu'adez garder
Le vueille et a lui regarder.
Fortune fait son bien tarder,
1264 Dont fort est soy contregarder:

1230 p. m.] p. a m. *Ph.* 1231 Ny nest nul de cuer a. *Oa.* 1233 actendant *OaPh.* 1240 paire *Oa.*
1242 D. autour *Db.* 1244 douleurs *Dc.* 1245 surplante *Dc*, suplante *Ql.* 1246 la j. *Ph*; a p. *Dc.*
1248 sur *DbDcDfOaPhQl.* 1251 car *Dc.* 1255 prie *DbPc*; que a. *Ph.* 1256 Si prie (Si pry *Db*)
d. quil (d. qui *Ph*) le remaint *DbOaPh*: qui *DfQl*; le ma remaint *Df.* 1260 ne suis *Dc.* 1262 et
a] a *Ph.* 1263 garder *Ph.*

A coup adviennent
Ses tours qui d'ordre point ne tiennent,
Maiz si au rebours se maintiennent

1268 Que aux bons les adversitez viennent,
Et sont foulez
Et par Fortune triboulez,
Dont mains cuers en sont adoulez,

1272 Quant bien sont en amours coulez.   23ᵛ
Et quant ilz voient
Le seul bien qu'en ce monde avoient –
Dont tant de joie recevoient,

1276 Ou tous leurs souhaiz achevoient –
Si costoier
Par Infortune et guerroier,
Peser leur doit et ennoier,

1280 Car cuer amant est moitoier
A part equale
De s'amour seule et principale,
Soit l'aventure bonne ou male,

1284 Rire, plourer, couroux ou gale;
Dont raison yere
Qu'en terre estrange et maronniere
De cuer soie o lui prisonniere

1288 Et de sa prison parçonniere,
Sans y clamer
Franchise ou le droit entamer
D'Amours qui me fait affamer,

1292 En souspirant dela la mer,
Ou mon cuer vire
Et passe plus tost que une vire
Sans batel ou autre navire.

1296 Et le corps, palle comme yvire,
Remaint deça
Sans cuer et sans joie pieça,

1265 Au c. *Dc.* 1266 cours *Ph*; d'o. p.] p. do. *DcOaPcPhQl.* 1267 a r. *Ph.* 1268 Quau bons *Oa*, Quans vous *Ph*; a.] adversitees *Dc.* 1271 maint cuers *PhQl*; se s. *DbPcQl.* 1273 Et qu. veoient *Oa.* 1276 eschevoient *DcPh*, seschevoient *Oa.* 1277 coctoyer *Df*, coitoier *Oa*, toytoier *Ph.* 1278 I.] fortune *Ph.* 1279 droit *Ph*; envoyer *Db*, ennuyer *Df.* 1280 damant *DcPcPhQl*; mettoier *DbPcPhQl*, moityer *DfOa.* 1283 b.] ou b. *Db.* 1286 ou m. *DcPc.* 1287 soit *Dc.* 1287–8 *Inverted Oa.* 1291 f. tant amer *Dc*, f. enflamer *OaPcPhQl.* 1293 tyre *Dc.* 1294 que une v.] que vire v. *Db.*

Qui puis vers moy ne s'adreça
1300 Que Fortune tant le bleça.
Si suis alee,   24r
En toute joie tresalee,
De cuer dela la mer salee;
1304 Maiz, quoy que la grandeur a lee
Si qu'esgarer
S'y puet on sans terre apparer,
Jamaiz ne pourra separer
1308 Noz cuers qu'Amours fait reparer
Ensemble et joindre
En un seul vouloir que conjoindre
Les fait, et comme egaulx adjoindre
1312 Sans qu'il y ait greignieur ne maindre.
Amours oblige
Noz deux cuers en un, ainsi di ge
Comme deux raims en une tige.
1316 Il se dit mon vray servant lige
Et je suy sienne;
Mot n'y a si non "tien" et "tienne".
Se maistrise y a, elle est mienne
1320 Par la loy d'Amours ancïenne,
Qui l'ordonna
Pour les dames et leur donna
Maistrise, ou moult noble don a,
1324 Et par ce leur guerredonna
Les biens qui yssent
De leur grace quant s'eslargissent
En pitié vers ceulx qui languissent
1328 D'amours dont les cuers amaigrissent
Des plus puissans
Qu'Amours fait vrays obeïssans   24v
Par hommage, et recongnoissans

1299 plus *Oa*; v. moy] v. *Ph*.   1301 Et *Oa*.   1302 tressallee *Dc*; alee
DbDfOaPhQl, allee *DcPc*.   1306 peust *PcQl*; san *Dc*; apparoir *Db*.   1308 fist *DcDfOaPcPhQl*;
repairer *DbDd*, emparer *Dc*.   1310 qui *DbDcPcQl*.   1311 fist *Ph*.   1312 ou *PcQl*.   1314 Noz d.
c.] Noz c. *DbDcDfPh*; en un] et unit *DbDcDfPh*, et vint *Oa*.   1315 r.] ramis *Db*.   1316 se dit]
se dist *Pc*, est *OaQl*, en est *Ph*; l.] et l. *Ql*.   1318 *copied after* 1320 *Ql*.   1318 Motz *Db*; se *Oa*; mien
et (m. ou *Dc*) t. *DbDcOaPcPhQl*.   1319 Si *Df*; el *Df*.   1320 Par la foy *Db*, Fors par loy *DcDfOaPc*
PhQl.   1322 et lordonna *Oa*.   1323 m. n.] n. *Oa*.   1324 l. g.] l. (fort l. *Dc*) guerdonna *DbDc*.
1326 qu. eslargissent *DcOaPh*, qu. leslargissent *Pc*.   1328 corps *Pc*.   1331 Par hommages r. *OaPh*.

1332   Celles dont leurs biens sont yssans
        Comme maistresses
        Et treshonnourables princesses,
        Qui des amoureuses richesces
1336   Font escharcetez ou largesces
        Si qu'elles veulent,
        Dont quant l'un chante, autres s'en deulent.
        Maiz les folz s'arrester n'y seulent,
1340   Ne que moulins qu'a tous vens meulent;
        Puis quant batie
        Ont leur faintise, Amour atie
        Prent encontre eulx et les chatie,
1344   Dont ilz portent chiere amatie
        Et souvent plourent.
        Si s'en venge Amours qu'ilz s'amourent
        De teles qui ne les secourent
1348   Pour les mauvaiz noms qui d'eulx courent,
        Dont ilz reçoivent
        Tel guerredon qu'ilz se deçoivent
        Quant les autres decevoir doivent.
1352   Et tel qu'ilz l'ont brassé, le boivent
        Sans viser y,
        Car tost ou tart, aspre ou sery,
        Bienfait n'est en amours pery,
1356   Ne mal qui ne soit remery
        Quoy qu'on actende,
        Car Amours qui les cuers amende
        Veult des meffaiz avoir l'amende   25r
1360   Et qu'a chascun son louyer rende
        Comme vray juge
        Qui des amoureux debaz juge.
        Maiz pour plaindre, a lui a refuge
1364   Ne fut onq m'amour; si ne fuz ge,

1332 les b. *Db*.   1336 *Omitted Oa*: e.] escharcetees *Dc*.   1338 D. lun ch. lautre sen d. *OaPh*, D. lun ch. et a. sen d. *PcQl*, D. ungs chantent a. se d. *Dc*: D. qu. ung ch. *Db*, D. lune ch. *Df*.   1339 f. arrester *DbPcQl*; veullent *DcPh*.   1340 m. a t. v. *Db*.   1341 quen *Dc*.   1342 amours *Db*.   1344 il p. *Ql*.   1346 Tant *Db*; vante *Df*; qui sa. *DcQl*, qui seuvrent *Ph*.   1347 celles *DcDfOaPcPhQl*.   1348 Par *OaPcPhQl*; leurs *Dc*; que *OaPh*.   1350 g.] guerdon *DbDcPh*.   1352 telx *OaPh*; quil *Pc*, qui *Ql*; l'o.] ont *DcOaPcPh*; les b. *Dc*.   1354 ou s.] s. *Dc*.   1355 n'est] est *Dc*, nen *Ph*; amour *Df*.   1356 quil *Ph*.   1360 que ch. *DcPh*.   1362 *Omitted Oa*.   1363 au r. *DcDfOaPcPh*.   1364 onq] oncques *Oa*; si ne fuz ge] si ne suis je *Oa*, non fu je *Ph*, sienne suis je *Ql*.

Car tous adjoins
Deux cuers en un vouloir conjoings
Avons, d'un mesme desir poins.
1368 Et se m'aist Dieu a mes besoings,
Que tant l'amoie
Et aime que je le nommoie
"Tout mien", et lui moy "toute moie".
1372 J'en ay chanté: or en lermoie,
De cuer marrie.
Or est bien la joie amenrie
Que doulce amour avoit nourrie,
1376 Sans que jamaiz je chante ou rie,
Se Dieu n'y oeuvre
Et que le mal qu'a paine coeuvre
Cesse, par si que le recoeuvre,
1380 Car fors enviz mon oeil ne s'oeuvre
Ne n'ouvrera,
N'en rien plaisir ne trouvera,
A tant qu'il le recouvrera
1384 Et que Dieu plus y ouvrera
Par abbregié,
Ainsi qu'il puisse estre allegié
Des maulx dont il est assegié,
1388 Qui tousjours lui ont aggregié.   25v
Comme esmaié,
Tous maulx fors mort a essaié;
Le deu de Fortune a paié,
1392 Si deust du compte estre raié,
Car sans doubter
El l'a tant voulu debouter
Que plus n'y savoit que bouter

1366 D. en un v. (v. tous *Ph*) c. *OaPh*.   1367 mesmes *DbPcPhQl*; joints *DcQl*.   1368 Et si *DfOaPcQl*,
Ainsi *Dc*; dieux *DbOaPcPhQl*; mes] cestz *Df*, ces *Oa*, cest *Pc*, ce *Ph*.   1370 Et layme que *Db*, Et
comme amy *DcQl*.   1371 et a lui t. m. *Dc*.   1374 la j.] la cuer (*sic*) *Oa*.   1377 Sy *DcDf*.   1378 mal
a p. c. *Db*, mal a p. en euvre *Oa*.   1379 *Omitted Oa*: par ce quelle r. *Dc*, par ce que le r. *Ph*.
1380 Car f. ennuys *OaPcPh*, Car fort envis *Db*, Car fort ennuy *Dc*, Fors danuis *Ql*; cueur *DcOaPc*
PhQl; ne seuffre *OaPh*, abeuvre *Dc*, ne meuvre *Pc*, ne secoeuvre *Ql*.   1381 Et souffrira *Dc*, Ne naura
Oa, Ne mouvrira *Pc*, Ne navera *Ph*, Ne mouverra *Ql*.   1382 Ne nul p. *Ph*; plaisirs *Oa*.   1383 Jusques
a ce quil le r. *Dc*: qui *Oa*; se r. *Ph*.   1386 Et tant quil p. *Dc*; abregie *Db*.   1388 sont *DcOaPhQl*;
engregie *DcDfPcQl*, allegie *Ph*.   1390 fort *Ph*, sans *Pc*.   1391 dieu *OaPcQl*.   1392 doit *DbDcDfOa*
PcPhQl.   1394 Elle a *DcOaPhQl*, El a *Df*; t. v.] v. t. *PcQl*.

239

1396 De mal sans la mort adjouxter.
Maiz il me semble,
Quoy qu'Amours noz deux cuers assemble,
Mal fait que toute joie m'emble,
1400 En prenant guerre a deux ensemble.
Si lui suffise
S'elle me greve en mainte guise,
Sans ce qu'elle me desconfise
1404 En m'ostant la doulce franchise
De ce vëoir
Qui tant doit a mon cuer sëoir
Que mieulx ne le puis assëoir;
1408 Si l'aym d'amour sans dechëoir.
Foible et malade
Vint au dur jour a couleur fade,
Aprés que ot fait mainte balade
1412 Au lict, ou rien ne lui fut sade
Ne savoureux
Fors ses seulx pensers amoureux;
Maiz en ses acez rigoureux
1416 N'y lessa a penser pour eulx.
Maiz quant passee   26r
Fut la fievre ou corps ou cessee,
Si estoit l'autre en la pensee,
1420 Qui la tenoit entrelacee.
Si ne durast
Neantmoins, ne jamaiz n'endurast
Que ou dur champ ne s'aventurast
1424 Afin que nul n'en murmurast
Contre raison,
Si que on a fait sans achoison.
Maiz or a chascun mauvaiz hom
1428 De s'aviser belle saison;

1396 fors *DcDſOaPcPhQl*. 1399 qui *Dc*; nemble *OaPh*. 1403 S. ce qu'e.] S. que elle *OaPh*. 1404 En m'o.] Et mo. *Dſ*, En monstrant *DcOaPcPhQl*. 1407 ne le peut *DcPh*, ne le peust *OaPc*, ny pouoit *Ql*. 1408 damours *DſOaPhQl*; decevoir *Ph*. 1410 la c. *DbPcQl*. 1411 A. queust f. *Dc*, A. ce f. *OaPh*. 1414 telx s. p. *Oa*, les fins p. *Db*. 1415 actes *DcPh*, acees *Dſ*, asses *Ql*. 1416 l. dy p.*Db*. 1418 au c. *Dc*, en c. *Pc*; et ce. *DcDſ*. 1422 N.] Neant *OaPh*; j.] ja *Dc*; j. ne durast *Db*. 1423 Quaux champs hors ne sa. *Dc*: Que en *Pc*, Que au *Ql*. 1424 ne m. *DcOa*. 1426 Si comme (Si com *Oa*) a (c. on *Ph*) f. *DcOaPhQl*.

Et s'ilz ne daignent
Pour l'orgueil en quoy ilz se baignent,
Au moins les oeuvres vous enseignent
1432 Qu'a lui mal vouloir ilz mespreignent.
A Dieu pleüst
Que mon cuer pour le sien peüst
Estre hostage, et nul n'en sceüst
1436 Rien dont blasme venir deüst;
Si changisson,
Car j'aroie sa marrisson
Et il saroit quele frisson
1440 C'est de penser a ce que son
Cuer lui ravit
Et que de treslong temps ne vit.
En douloureuse prison vit
1444 Et ne sçay comme il s'en chevit.
Bien me venist
Se ainsi fust ou s'il advenist,   26v
Car quoy que le corps devenist,
1448 De m'amour au cuer souvenist;
Si me fauldroit
Son ennuy, et ne me chauldroit
De la douleur qui m'assaudroit.
1452 Son aise un plaisir me vauldroit,
Car plus me bleschent,
Le cuer courcent et le corps seichent
Ses tresgriefz maulx qui s'entreveschent
1456 Aux miens et ma pensee empeschent,
Et me deffont
Plus que mes propres griefz ne font,
Dont tout mon corps en lermes font

1429 si ne d. *DcOaPcPhQl*.   1430 Pour lo. grant ou il se b. *Dc*: Par orgueil *OaPcPhQl*.   1431 ses o. *Db*; les e. *Db*, leur e. *Dc*, v. apprennent *Ql*.   1432 mesprennent *DcPcQl*.   1435 E. h.] E. en h. *DcOa PcPhQl*; ne s. *OaPh*.   1437 Seschangisson *Pc*, Si eschangisson *Ql*.   1439 Et si savroie qu. f. *Dc*.   1440 Cest de pense que ce qui son *Df*: p. a] p. *Oa*, p. que *Ph*.   1442 que de] de *Db*, que *Oa*; si long *Dc*.   1443 d.] si d. *Dc*.   1444 comment sen ch. *Dc*.   1446–7 *Inverted Db*.   1446 et *Ph*; sil mavenist *Dc*.   1448 De samour au c. il s. *Ph*, De moy au moins lui s. *Ql*.   1449 Si deffauldroit *DcQl*.   1450 et ne me ch.] ne me ch. *Df*, ne ne men (me *Ph*) ch. *OaPh*.   1451 ma *Pc*.   1453 Car p. b. *Oa*.   1454 c. et] courroucent *Dc*, courcant et *OaPh*; serchent *Db*, pechent *OaPh*.   1455 Des *Ph*; quilz *Dc*.   1456 Au m. *Pc*; sa *Ql*.   1458 Trop plus que p. g. *OaPh*; maulx *Db*; sont *Ph*.   1459 t. mon cuer *DcPc*, mon cuer t. *Ql*.

1460 Et j'en souspir de cuer profont.
Plus que on ne cuide,
Mon mal fait place aux siens et wide,
Et le sien est des miens la guide,
1464 De dueil plaine et de lermes wide.
A brief compter,
Mon mal, qui le veult raconter,
Puet toutes lermes seurmonter
1468 Ne pleurs n'y pevent riens monter.
Tant ay plouré
Qu'il ne m'en est plus demouré,
Dont j'ay le cuer alangouré
1472 Et le vis tout descoulouré
Et arrousé.
De nuit mes yeulx n'ont reposé,
Car de jour moustrer n'ay osé   27r
1476 Cuer triste en corps mal disposé,
Foible et tremblant.
J'ay fait mes regraiz en emblant
Et pour estre aux gens ressemblant,
1480 De cuer courcié, joieux semblant.
Et se je dance,
Ce ne fait pas faire habondance
De joie në oultrecuidance,
1484 Maiz n'y a en toute la dance,
J'en suy certaine,
Pensee de douleur plus plaine.
Ce me fut plaisir: or est paine;
1488 Ne il n'est harpe, orgue ne doulçaine,
Luz n'eschequier,
N'instrument que on sceust appliquier,
Que desormaiz ouÿr requier
1492 Puis que je n'ay ce que je quier.
Las! Je souloie,

1460 Et en s. *OaPh*, Et je en soupire *Ql*, Et en souspirs *Dc*.   1463 et du mien *Ql*.   1464 p.] plain *Db*.
1465 bien *DfOaPcPhQl*.   1466 quil *Ph*.   1467 Peust *PcQl*.   1468 p. seurmonter *Oa*.   1469 a *Dc*.
1470 Qui *Ql*.   1471 enlangoure *DcOaPcPhQl*.   1472 tant *DbOaPh*.   1474 non r. *Dc*.   1478 Je fais
OaPh; regars *Oa*.   1479 P. e. aux autre r. *Dc*.   1481 si *Df*.   1483 De j. ou o. *Dc*.   1486 douleurs
si p. *Dc*.   1487 me fut] mest *Ph*; or mest p. *DbOaPcPhQl*.   1488 o. ne d.] o. d. *Ph*.   1489 Lut
Db.   1490 Ny instrument quon seult a. *Ph*: Nistrument *Pc*.   1491 r.] ne quier *DcOaPcPhQl*.

Lors que de riens ne me douloie,
Les amer; et tant les vouloie
1496 Que au son sembloit que je voloie,
Toute empennee
De joie, ne toute une annee
Ne fusse de dancer tennee,
1500 Lasse, mate në enhennee.
Si m'enhortoit
Amours et tant me supportoit
Par les joies qu'il m'apportoit
1504 Que le cuer le seurplus portoit.   27v
Tout y aloit
Et rien pour rien ne me faloit,
Car j'amoie qui tant valoit
1508 Qu'a mon cuer d'autre ne chaloit.
Tant habondoient
Mes plaisirs, qui d'un seul sourdoient
Et en un mesmes redondoient,
1512 Que tous les ennuis confondoient;
Ainsi resourse
Estoie et en lëesce sourse.
Deux ruisseaulx d'amoureuse sourse,
1516 Penser et Souvenir, leur course
Vers moy prenoient.
Lors de moy plaire se penoient
Et tant de joies m'amenoient,
1520 Qui toutes d'une main venoient;
Maiz la misere
De Fortune, diverse mere,
A si troublé la sourse clere
1524 Que je n'y truys savour qu'amere,
Tant a meslez
Les ruisseaulx du long et des lez,

1496 Quau somp s. *Ph.* 1498 De j. et de t. *Dc.* 1500 L.] Lassee *Dc*; m.] matee *OaPcPh*; ne e.] nenhannee *DcPh*, ne ahannee *Df*, nahennee *Oa*, ny enhannee *Ql.* 1502 surportoit *Dc.* 1503 Pour *Dc.* 1504 Que le c.] Le c. *Dc.* 1505 T. et a. *Oa.* 1506 r. plus *Pc*; p. lors *DcDf*; failloit *DbQl*, sembloit *OaPh.* 1507 javoye *OaPh.* 1510 Maiz *Pc*; que *DfOa.* 1511 mesme *DcOaPh.* 1512 e.] ennemis *Dc.* 1514 Estoient en l. et s. *Dc*: en liee s. *Oa.* 1515 D. rainseaux dedens une s. *Ql*: Des r. *Ph.* 1516 Pencee et *DbDcDfPcPhQl.* 1519 joye *DcDfPhQl.* 1520 *At first omitted, then added (twice) Ql*: Que *Dc*; dune me v. *DfOaPhQl.* 1523 tant *Db.* 1526 Li r. *Oa*, Li ruisseau *Ph*; du lez *DcOaPcPhQl.*

243

De Melencolie reslez

1528 Et de Tristece entremeslez.

Haa, dure Guerre,

Pourquoy veulx sur moy tant conquerre,

Sans deffïer, que d'une serre

1532 M'ostes mon paradis en terre,

Ma lie chiere

Et la joie que j'ay plus chiere,

Sans acomte ne sans enchiere?

1536 Bien m'est Fortune estrange archiere

Et ennuyeuse,

Si semble qu'el soit envïeuse

Que j'aie ja vie joieuse

1540 Pour plaisance delicïeuse,

Doulce et privee,

Qu'elle a de moy a tort privee

Comme oultrageuse desrivee;

1544 Et prent contre moy l'estrivee

Par dures sortes.

Helaz, Amours, pourquoy m'apportes

En foible cuer cent douleurs fortes,

1548 Dont cent devroient estre mortes?

Neantmoins je vifs,

Trop piz que morte a mon avis.

Onq en corps vif telz maulx ne vis.

1552 Je ne sçay comme j'en chevis,

Maiz plus ressoigne

Ce qu'Espoir me fuit et esloigne,

Qui deust entendre a ma besoigne

1556 Comme cil qui des amans soigne

Et doit vouloir

Que par lui puissent mieulx valoir.

Amours l'a fait pour moins douloir

28r

1527 r.] reellez *DbDc*. 1529 Ha a d. g. *DcDſOaPcPhQl*. 1530 v. tu sur moy c. *OaPh*. 1532 Me ostez *DbOa*. 1533 Ma liee ch. *DbDdPh*. 1534 la chose *DbDcDſOaPcPhQl*. 1535 acointer *Dc*, acointe *Pc*. 1538 sembloit *OaPh*; quel] quelle *DbDcOaPhQl*; fust *OaPh*. 1539 De ce que javoye v. j. *Ph*: la vie *Dc*, sa vie *Oa*. 1541 D. p. *Dc*. 1542 *Repeated Ql*: Quel *Dſ*. 1543 o. d.] o. et d. *DcDſ*, o. destinee *OaPcPhQl*. 1546 mapportez *Db*, massortes *Dc*. 1547 En f. cueur d. si f. *Dc*: foibles cuers *Oa*; tant *OaPhQl*; douleur *Ql*; sotes *Oa*. 1548 D. deveroient e. m. *Ph*. 1549 Au moins *OaPh*. 1550 a mon divis *DſOaPhQl*. 1551 Quonc *Dc*; c. vifs *DbDſ*; tel mal *Ql*. 1552 comment *Pc*. 1554 *Omitted Pc*: fait *Ph*; on aloigne *Dſ*. 1555 Que *Pc*. 1558 puisse *Dc*. 1559 le f. *DcOaPcPhQl*.

244

1560 Capitaine de mon vouloir,
 Il s'en yroit
 Souvent et se departiroit –
 Et Ennuy le consentiroit –
1564 Se Regret ne le ratiroit.
 Souvent ouvert   28v
 Lui a l'uiz tout a descouvert
 Empirement de mal couvert,
1568 Maiz Souvenir l'a recouvert
 Et ramené.
 En ce point se sent pourmené
 Mon povre cuer et demené
1572 Pour cil que j'aym plus que homme né,
 Se Dieu m'aÿe;
 Maiz seule suis et esbahie,
 Car mon cuer tout d'une envaÿe
1576 M'a pour le bien amer haÿe
 Et deguerpie.
 Si porte en lieu de cuer, tapie,
 Pensee qui m'est dure espie
1580 Et n'en puis estre descherpie;
 Ains me presente
 Tous les jours ainsi que de rente
 Son doulz semblant qui represente
1584 Sa personne comme presente.
 Lors assaillie
 Suis de Penser qui m'a baillie
 Sa doulce ymage et entaillie
1588 En ma pensee travaillie
 Et que tollir
 Ne l'en puet nul, në abolir,
 Oster, effacer, ne polir   29r
1592 Sans corps et vouloir demollir,
 Car departie

1562 Comment *Db*; sen d. *Ph*. 1564 Et *Ph*; regart *DbOa*; retiroit *DbDcOaPh*. 1566 Lui a] Lui a a *Ph*; t. a d.] a d. *OaPh*, et a d. *Ql*. 1567 E.] En prenant *OaPh*. 1570 si (cy *Ql*) est p. *DcQl*. 1572 que j'aym] quayme *Dc*, que jame *Oa*; h.] hom *Oa*, homs *Ph*. 1573 Si *Df*; dieux *Ph*. 1575 Car joye t. *Ql*; tant *OaPh*. 1576 Ma p. b. a. enhaye *Dc*: Na *Oa*; le mien *Oa*, le sien *Ph*; traye *Db*. 1578 de luy t. *DcQl*. 1581 Puis *Ph*. 1582 le j. *Ph*. 1586 p.] pensee *DcOaPh*; qui] et *Db*. 1587 d. amour *OaPh*; entaillee *DbDc*. 1588 travaillee *DbDc*. 1590 peust *PcQl*; nulz *OaPcPhQl*. 1592 Son *DcPhQl*; amollir *Oa*.

N'en sera, quant de ma partie,

Tant que l'ame soit hors partie.

1596 Tout sera une departie

Quant l'un mourra

Et que plus amer ne pourra.

L'autre au besoing lui secourra;

1600 Toute l'amour lui demourra

Pour tous les deux,

Car s'il se deult et je me deulx,

Le derrenier mort d'ambedeux

1604 Ara les couroux et les deulx

Que l'autre tient;

C'est droit puis que l'amour se tient.

Com hoir prochain lui appartient,

1608 Car qui le plus vit, le tout tient.

Amours ses les,

Ses testamens et ses delés,

Ne fait mie de chappellés;

1612 Qui ne le scet, essaie les.

Maiz ja muser

N'y doit aucun ou s'abuser,

S'il veult grans douleurs refuser

1616 Ou de grans biens ne scet user.

Bien s'en rigole

Tel qui n'en scet fors par parole,

Maiz oiseau bien pris ne s'en vole.

1620 Point ne faut aler a l'escole   29v

Pour estre sage

D'Amours et de son fort ouvrage.

Clercz n'y treuvent point d'avantage;

1624 Plus apprent l'essay que lengage.

De ce me vant,

Que les faiz vont trop plus avant

1599 Lun la. au b. s. *OaPh.*   1600 T. la. de lui mourra *Ph.*   1602 se d. et] se d. *Ql,* se deust et *DbPh.*   1603 Le d. m. (Le derrier m. *Dc*) dentre nous deux *DcPh.*   1604 le c. *OaPh.*   1605 Que autre t. *OaPh.*   1606 la mort *DcPhQl;* ce t. *Oa,* maintient *Dc.*   1608 Car cil (Car sil *Ph*) qui p. vit *OaPh,* Car qui p. vit *Dc;* le t. t.] le tres tout t. *Dc,* tout maintient *Pc.*   1610 debez *Oa.*   1611 des ch. *DbDcPh,* ch. *Oa.*   1612 les s. *Pc,* les sert *Db.*   1614 Ne d. *OaPh;* ne sa. *DcPcPhQl,* ne abuser *Oa.*   1615 Si v. *Df.*   1616 des g. b. *Ql;* ne s. u.] ne (il *Ql*) veult u. *DcQl.*   1617 se r. *Dc.*   1618 Telx *Oa;* quil *Ph;* ne s. *DcPh,* nen soit *Ql;* que par p. *Db.*   1619 pres *Df.*   1623 Clerc *Ph.*   1625 vault *Db.*   1626 t. p.] p. *Oa.*

Que ce que on pense par avant.
1628   Je parle en ce comme savant,
Non que je vueille
Dire que je m'en plaigne ou dueille;
Il me suffit qu'Amours m'accueille,
1632   Quelque douleur que j'en recueille,
Entre ses sers.
Pour prendre un seul servant, je sers
Amours, et servie m'assers,
1636   Dont j'ay piz que je ne desers
Pour louyer, mez
Amours a qui je me soubmez
Livre a sa court entre les mez
1640   Tousjours Douleur pour entremez:
Trop s'empliroient,
Saouleroient et rempliroient
Ses servans, si n'acompliroient
1644   Leur service et s'en partiroient,
Comme j'entens,
En trouvant cause de contens,
Car pou de servans sont contens
1648   D'endurer grant aise long temps;   30r
Amours se gardent
Quant les joies plus se retardent.
Se amans aux biens passez regardent,
1652   Tant moins en ont et plus en ardent,
Car Amours loirre
Les cuers comme faucon au loirre,
A qui l'en fait souvent a croirre
1656   De donner ce qu'on veult accroirre.
Jeuns, les atachent
Aux perches ou leurs giez se lachent,
Afin qu'aprés par fain pourcachent

1627 devant *Ph.*   1630 je men p.] je me p. *Dc,* je p. *Ph.*   1632 je r. *Dc.*   1635 et s.] et ferme *DbDc,* et a servir *Ql.*   1639 a secours *Ph;* ses *DbQl.*   1640 douleurs *DcPc.*   1642 r.] se r. *Dc.* 1643 Sers *Oa;* silz na. *Dc.*   1644 Son s. *Ql;* et] ains *Db;* nen p. *Pc.*   1646 causes *Dc;* de tout temps *Ph.*   1648 g. joye *DfOaPcPhQl.*   1650 en r. *Oa,* regardent *Ph.*   1651 *Omitted Ph.*   1654 faucons *OaPh;* en l. *OaPcPhQl.*   1655 on f. *DcDfOaPcPhQl;* bien s. c. *DcDfOaPhQl.*   1656 sceut *Db;* avoire *Df.*   1657–75 *Omitted Oa.*   1657 Si les a. *Dc.*   1658 grez *Db,* gitz *Df,* getz *Ql.* 1659 que puis *Pc;* pour *Dc;* pourcachent *DbDcDfPcPhQl.*

1660 Mieulx la proie qu'a prendre tachent
Sans y baster.
Puis leur donnent pour soy haster
Un pou de la proie a taster.

1664 On ne puet l'oiseau mieulx gaster
Que le repestre
Si que säoul il en puist estre:
Lors s'essore et lesse son mestre

1668 Et se va rendre en un autre estre.
En ce ne blasme
Jamaiz Amours, homme ne fame
S'aprés joie, de dueil m'enflame;

1672 Fors a moy ne m'en pren a ame.
Maiz plus me poise
Car mon cuer est, quel part qu'il voise,
En un, que onq de terre françoise

1676 N'issit personne plus courtoise.
Et si me face
Dieu pardon, qu'a paine cuidasse   30v
Que Nature en si pou d'espace

1680 Eust mis tant de bien et de grace,
Qu'en un seul homme
Fust le bien de tous mis en somme.
Son nom, qui il est, quoy ne comme,

1684 La voix le taist; le cuer le nomme.
Desir enquiert
De lui, Souvenir le requiert,
Espoir l'actent, Regret le quiert

1688 Et Loyauté mon cuer seurquiert.
Mes regars tendent
Ou il est, mes pensés l'actendent;
Mes oreilles ailleurs n'entendent

1692 Fors ouÿr que ses griefz amendent.

1660 chassent *DcDfPcPhQl*. 1662 donne *Ph*; eulx h. *Dc*. 1664 peust *Pc*; l'o. m.] m. oyseau *Dc*. 1666 saule *Dc*, saoule *DfPcQl*; puet *Ph*. 1667 sessaye *Db*. 1668 sen va *DbDc*. 1669 me b. *Db*. 1670 h.] ne h. *Ql*. 1671 nenflamme *Df*. 1674 est qu. p.] est qu. *Ph*, quelque p. *Dc*. 1675 En lieu de la t. f. *Dc*: un que onq] un qui onq *Db*, un pou *Ph*. 1676–1708 *and* 1709–1728 *Transposed Oa*. 1676 Verra p. *Dc*. 1677 Ainsi me f. *DcOaPcPhQl*. 1681 Que un s. h. *Ph*. 1683 quel il est *DcOaPhQl*; et c. *Ph*. 1684 La v. le scet *OaPh*. 1686 De lui et souvent le r. *Dc*. 1687 R.] desir *Oa*; le qu.] requiert *Ph*. 1688 loyaument *Oa*. 1689 Mais *Ql*. 1690 mais *Db*; pencees *DcOaPh* 1691 Maiz *Pc*.

Tout y travaille
Et mesmes, dont je me merveille,
La douleur qui si me resveille
1696 Pour moy faire plus veillier, veille
D'aguet. En tant
Me vont d'un accort tourmentant,
Dont mon vouloir est consentant,
1700 Et mon cuer n'en est repentant.
J'ay bien puissance
De confesser ma desplaisance,
Maiz quoy que je faiz ma penance,
1704 Je n'ay goute de repentance.
Plus tourmenté
Je sens mon cuer, plus est tempté
Et prent plaisir en orfenté   311
1708 Maugré moy, par ma volenté.
Trop argüer
Me fait Penser et tressüer:
Que l'amant sans amer, müer
1712 Puet, esjoïr et puis tüer,
Pour moy le sçay;
J'ay de tous deus fait long essay.
Puis qu'a amer pris, ne cessay,
1716 N'oncques puis Penser ne lessay,
Qui son couvent
Ne tient, maiz le tourne souvent,
Ainsi que le cochet au vent;
1720 Donne joie et puis chier la vent.
Maiz trop plus greve
Le mal et la pensee greve
Qui viennent aprés joie breve
1724 Qui commence sans qu'elle acheve
Et vient a bout.

1694 mesme *Dc*; mesme (mes me *Ph*) dueil je (dueil et *Ph*) me m. *OaPh*. 1695 que *Dc*. 1697 Dangier *DcOaPcPhQl*. 1698 Me bout *Db*. 1703 je f. ma p.] je f. ma (f. ma *Dc*, je f. *Ph*) penitance *DbDcPh*. 1706 Se sent *DcDfOaPhQl*; et t. *Pc*. 1711 amour *DcDfQl*, amours *OaPcPh*. 1712 Peust *PcQl*. 1714 ung e. *Dc*. 1715 *Omitted Oa*, P. quamer prins je ne c. *Dc*, Prins qua a. puis ne c. *Ph*: pres *DbDd*. 1716 No. depuis je ne l. *Dc*, Nonc puis pensee nen l. *Oa*, No. (Non puis *Ph*) pensee ne l. *PhQl*: P.] pensee *Df*. 1718 se t. *Oa*. 1719 que le c.] que c. *Ph*, comme c. *Ql*. 1720 D. j.] J. d. *DcDfOaPcPhQl*; le v. *Oa*. 1722 la p.] p. *Dc*. 1723 *Omitted Df*: Qui v.] Quilz ne v. *Dc*, Qui me v. *OaPhQl*, Qui me vient *Pc*. 1724 Quil *Ql*; s. quil a. *PcQl*, a ce (ce *Ph*) quil a. *OaPh*. 1725 Ne viegne a b. *Db*: au b. *PcPhQl*.

Au fort, qui a joie du tout,
Il ne scet quel en est le goust,
1728 Car nul bien n'est prisié sans coust;
Dont je regraite
De tant plus la tresdoulce actraitte
De joie que Dueil m'a fortraicte,
1732 Quant pour la perte ay paine traicte.
Si puis viser
Que plus ne se puet desguiser
Amours vers moy, sans l'aviser,
1736 Car tel que on le puet deviser,   31v
S'est remoustrez
Et ses divers tours m'a moustrez,
Biens et maulx ensemble acoustrez,
1740 Non pas petiz maiz tous oultrez.
Si estendue
A sa force a moy, sa rendue,
Que joie long temps actendue
1744 M'a donnee et puis revendue
Si chierement
Qu'il me va par empirement,
Car Douleur m'assault fierement
1748 Quant Espoir faut entierement
Sans moy promectre
Retour et sans s'en entremectre.
Encor se vient entre nous mectre
1752 La mer, si que une povre lectre
Ne vient en voie,
N'il n'est nouvelle qu'il m'envoie.
Puis qu'il faut que point ne le voie,
1756 Au moins se lectres recevoie,
Qui presentassent
Reconfort et se guermentassent

1728 nul b. n'e.] nully ne. *Dc*, nul ne. riens *OaPh*.   1730 sa *DbDd*.   1731 dieu *OaPh*; forfaicte *DbPh*.
1732 la joye *OaPcPhQl*.   1734 Que nul *Oa*; peust *Pc*.   1736 com le p. *DcPh*, con le peust *PcQl*.
1737 Cest *Oa*, demonstrez *DcQl*.   1739 Bien *Ph*.   1740 tres o. *Dc*.   1742 Et *Ph*; a moy sa r.] avray
sa r. *Db*, et a moy r. *Dc*; sest r. *OaPh*, et r. *Ql*.   1743 Que j.] Joye quay *Dc*, Que javoye *Ph*.
1744 d.] donne *DcDfOa*; r.] rendue *Oa*.   1746 Qui *PcQl*.   1747 doulceur *Ph*.   1750 Restor *Pc*; s'en
e.] soy e. *DcPc*, e. *Oa*.   1751 Quencor se vueille *Dc*.   1752 Lamour *Dc*.   1753 Venist en v. *Dc*.
1754 Mais nest *Dc*.   1755 P. f. que plus ne les v. *Oa*: p.] plus je *Ph*.   1756 si *Df*; l. r.] l. en r. *Oa*, lectre en r. *Ph*, l. en avoye *Ql*.

Des maulx que noz deux cuers entassent,
1760 Son doulz parler representassent,
Humble et humain,
Au moins congneusse je la main
Qui tant m'a escript soir et main
1764 Doulz mos de demain en demain,
Si les baisasse   32r
Et quoy que trop ne m'en aisasse
N'en cuer du tout ne m'envoysasse,
1768 Entretant un pou m'appaisasse
En regardant
Ses lectres et bien les gardant.
Ce petit bien va retardant
1772 Fortune, et j'ay desir ardant,
Ou je remains,
Qui me fait vouloir soirs et mains
Et requerir a joinctes mains
1776 Ce dont je puis finer le mains.
Si m'en desvoy,
Car plus le desir, moins le voy,
Quoy que de cuer lui faiz convoy
1780 Et mes pensees lui envoy.
Et par cela,
Puis que son mal renouvela,
Qui de mon regart osté l'a,
1784 J'ay trop moins deça que dela:
Cuer et vouloir
Sont hors, et quanqu'il puet valoir;
J'ay le corps dont ne puet chaloir,
1788 Et le mal qui me fait douloir
M'est remanant.
Le seurplus est dela manant,
Et ce que j'ay me va tennant;

1759 que] qui de *Db*; amassent *Dc*.   1762 c. je] je c. *DcOaPcPhQl*, congnoisse je *Db*.   1763 Que *Ph*;
ma (me *Oa*) rescrit *DcOaPhQl*.   1764 Dueilz mais *Db*.   1765 baissasse *Dc*.   1766 Et croy *OaPhQl*;
lassasse *Ph*.   1767 Nencor *DcQl*; menvoyasse *DbDcDdOaPcPhQl*.   1770 et les b. g. *DbDcDfPcQl*, et
les b. regardant *OaPh*.   1771 Si *Ph*; regardant *OaPh*.   1772 d. si grant *Dc*.   1774 douloir *Dc*, valoir
Oa; soir *DcDfOaPcPh*; maints *Db*.   1777 esmay *Dc*.   1779 du c. *OaPcPhQl*.   1780 pensee *Ph*; lui
e.] je lui e. *OaPh*.   1781 ce la *Df*.   1786 Tout *Ph*; h. de *Dc*; quanquel *Df*; quanquilz pevent *DbDd*;
peust *Pc*; avoir *Dc*.   1787 peust *Pc*.   1788 quil *Ph*.

251

1792 C'est bien douloureux remanant.
    Qui n'a pitié
    Du point ou mon cuer est traictié   32v
    Et que Desir tient deshaitié,
1796 Il n'ot oncques point d'amitié.
    Pour ce requerre
    Voulsisse aux dames d'Angleterre
    Que pour loz de pitié acquerre,
1800 Pour moy de lui vueillent enquerre
    Et demander
    Et son estat recommander,
    Car aucune puet commander
1804 A tel le puet bien amender.
    Par vray, semblable
    N'est que noblesce si notable
    N'ait mainte pensee honnourable
1808 En dame crainte et aggrëable;
    Si pevent mont
    Toutes les dames en un mont,
    Et leur doulceur les y cemont,
1812 Car ce qu'avenir veü m'ont
    En combatant,
    Se la guerre ne cesse a tant,
    Leur puet venir en rabatant
1816 (On chiet bien de tout son estant),
    S'il leur chëoit
    Si mal que leur fait dechëoit
    Et autres foiz leur meschëoit,
1820 Tant pour tant s'il nous eschëoit
    A seigniourir.
    Qu'a elles ne sçay recourir,
    Qui mieulx me puisse secourir.   33r
1824 Si suis entre vivre et mourir,
    Triste et plourant,

1792 trop d. *Db.* 1796 neust *Oa,* nest *Ql.* 1800 veulent *Ql.* 1803 Et *Oa;* veult *Pc,* peust *Ql.* 1804 A telle qui peust a. *Ql:* A celle p. *Ph;* peust *Pc.* 1805 Pour *OaPh.* 1806 quen n. *DcPhQl*(?). 1808 Et *DbDc;* cointe *Dc.* 1809 moult *DbDdDfOaPcPhQl.* 1810 moult *Ph.* 1811 y serront *Oa.* 1812 Car de ce que advenir mont *Dc:* nont *Ql,* ont *Pc.* 1814 Si *Df;* au t. *Dc.* 1815 peust *PcQl.* 1816 Lon ch. *Dc,* On (Et *Ph*) scet *OaPh;* b. du t. *OaPh,* de dessus *Db.* 1817 Et sil escheoit *Dc:* Si *DbDfOaPcQl.* 1818 qui *Db.* 1819 aultrefois *Pc.* 1820 si *PcQl.* 1822 Quant *Oa.* 1823 puissent *Oa,* peussent *Ph.* 1824 Je *OaPcPhQl.*

Desirant la mort en mourant,

Qui longuement est demourant

1828 Quant je n'ay autre demourant

D'Amours qui mate

Me rent sans que je le debate,

Car droit n'est qu'a lui me combate

1832 Et riens n'y vault se je le flate.

Ces maulx hastiz

M'a Fortune a durer bastiz,

Et Desir tient tout a pastiz

1836 Mon vouloir qui est amatiz,

Dont il se venge.

Quant Espoir au desir se renge,

Trop plus aspre en est la meslenge

1840 Quë Espoir faut; ainsi le sens ge,

Dont puis je dire

Que mon mal est plus long et pire.

Desir me chace, Espoir me tire;

1844 L'un ne puis vaincre ou l'autre fuire.

Mise la m'a

Fortune qui de ce blasme a,

N'onq mieulx nulle ne se clama

1848 La plus triste qui onq ama.'

A tant se teut

Celle qui le cuer dolent eut,

Ainsi que bien le ramentut,

1852 Maiz alors plus parler ne peut;   33v

Ains lui faillirent

Lengue et voix, car du cuer saillirent

Griefz souspirs qui si l'assaillirent

1856 Que cuer et corps en tressaillirent.

Si la frappoient

Ses maulx que sa bouche estouppoient,

1828 *Omitted Oa.* 1830 rens *OaPh.* 1831 Quadroit *Oa*; combatre *Ph.* 1832 ne v. *OaPh*; v. ce que ʳe f. *Dc.* 1833 Ses *OaPhQl*, Es *Pc*; bastis *Ql.* 1834 f. adverse b. *Dc.* 1835 tout] son *Pc.* 1836 a.] tout a. *Db*, amortis *Oa.* 1838 ou d. *OaPh.* 1839 Tant *OaPh.* 1840 Que E.] Quespoir *DbDd*, Quespoir qui *Dc*, Que sespoir *Df*, Quant (Ou *Ql*) espoir *PhQl*; fait *Db*; le senge *Ql.* 1843 Car d. ch. *Dc.* 1844 et *DcOaPcPhQl*; suivre *DcPh*, suire *Oa.* 1847 Noncquez m. n. se c. *Db.* 1851 que le b. r. *Dc.* 1852 nen p. *OaPh*; peult *Db.* 1853 saillirent *Ph.* 1854 dun c. *Oa.* 1856 corps et cuer *Df*; entre saillirent *Ql.* 1857 Tant *Db.* 1858 Des m. *Ph*, Ces motz *Oa*; qui *DcDfOaPcPhQl.*

Et les souspirs qui la rompoient,
1860 Son doulz parler entrerompoient.
Ses mains tortant,
Ça et la son chief transportant,
S'aloit si tresdesconfortant
1864 Que onq ne vy de desconfort tant
Qu'elle menoit.
Si durement se demenoit
Son cuer, et son corps tant penoit
1868 Que pasmee lors devenoit.
Pallie et maigre
Fut sa façon gente et allegre,
Tant lui fut la pasmoison aigre.
1872 Or n'avoie odeur ne vinaigre;
Endementier
Regarday au long d'un sentier,
Si cueilly un raym d'esglentier
1876 Et pres du nez lui mis entier,
Trestout joignant.
Et quant l'odeur l'ala poignant
Au cuer, elle ala empoignant
1880 Le raym qui tant estoit poignant,
Et se sourdi
Ainsi comme un homme assourdi
De pasmoisons, a l'estourdi.
1884 Adoncques a toutes lour di,
Et m'en souvint,
Ainsi qu'a la bouche me vint
Pour le cas qui alors avint
1888 De l'esglentier, dont el revint,
Que c'est droicture
Qu'en amours ait joie et ardure,
Car oncques Raison ne Nature
1892 Ne firent doulceur sans pointure

34r

1862 tremportant *Oa*. 1863 Sa. et si desconfortant *DcOaPh*. 1864 Quoncquez ne vi des. t. *DcOaPcPhQl*: onq] oncques *Db*. 1866 si *Dc*. 1869 Pale et m. *OaPh*. 1870 la *Ph*. 1871 sa *OaPh*. 1872 navoit *DbDc*. 1873 Et demantier *Oa*. 1877 Trestant *Oa*. 1879 el ala *Df*. 1882 Aussi *DbDf*; alourdy *Db*, estoudy *OaPcPhQl*. 1883 pasmoison *DbDcOaPcPhQl*. 1884 A.] Lors a. *DcOa*, Lors adonc *DfPcQl*, Lors doncques *Ph*; l. di] dy *Dc*. 1885 me s. *OaPhQl*. 1887 a. madvint *Pc*. 1888 el] elle *DbOaPh*. 1889 Queir(?) *Pc*, Car *Ph*. 1890 droicture *OaPh*. 1892 douleur *Ph*.

254

Et tous le voient:
'Rosiers qui des roses pourvoient
Ont piquans, et jadis avoient,
1896 Par quoy le cueillir nous devoient
Sans bleceüre;
N'en cueillant n'est la main seüre
Car la doubte nous espeüre,
1900 Soit neffle ou chastaigne meüre.
Amours refourme
Ses servans par semblable fourme
De la mousche qui le miel fourme
1904 En un creux d'un chesne ou d'un ourme.
La embuschiee
Est la grant doulceur et muchiee,
Du doulz miel estroit enruchiee,
1908 Maiz a dangier est desbuschiee
Pour les destroiz
Et la force des lieux estroiz.
On y faut des foiz plus de troiz
1912 Ains que on y ait tous ses octroiz.
Et s'escueillir
Se vient aucun du miel cueillir,
La mousche le vient accueillir
1916 Si que retraire ou recueillir
Ne s'en pourra,
Car la mousche vers lui courra,
Dont l'aguillon lui demourra,
1920 De quoy garde ne se dourra.
Lors recevra
La pointe qu'il n'appercevra.
Sans le savoir, s'en decevra
1924 A tant que douloir s'en devra.
Au partement

34v

1894 de r. *DbDcOaPcPhQl*. 1895 picquant *Db*. 1896 les c. *DcOa*, les cuers *Ph*; non d. *DcPh*. 1897 S. blessure *Dc*. 1898 Nen c.] En les c. *Dc*; n'est] est *Oa*. 1899 n. e.] si n. e. *Dc*. 1900 ch. m.] ch. ou m. *Ql*. 1903 bouche *Ph*. 1905 embuschie *Pc*, embrunchee *OaPh*, embrunchie *Ql*. 1906 et (est *Oa*) mucee *DcDfOa*, et muchie *PcQl*. 1907 estoit e. *DfPh*, et est enruchie *Ql*; en ruchie *Pc*. 1908 desbuchie *PcQl*. 1910 extraits *Db*. 1911 Ou il (Ou on *Ql*) f. *DcOaPcPhQl*. 1912 les o. *DcQl*, les actroiz *OaPh*. 1913 se cueillir *OaPh*. 1914 Se vant *Oa*; autrui *Ph*; pour m. c. *Dc*, de m. c. *Oa*. 1915 lui v. *Oa*. 1916 et r. *Ql*. 1920 sen *Ph*; douura *Dc*, donra *OaPh*. 1921 recourra *Db*. 1923 se d. *DcOaPh*. 1924 se d. *Dc*.

Feru sera appertement
De l'aguillon couvertement,
1928 Que puis verra ouvertement;
Car tant est digne
Nature que mort, medecine,
Doulz et aspre, tous d'une mine
1932 Naiscent, ou tous d'une racine.
L'un acompaigne
L'autre a la fin que plus en preigne
Aux cuers, et que mieulx les seurpreigne;
1936 L'un adoulcist, l'autre mehaigne.
Et brievement:
Plaisir est doulz, craintivement;
L'aguillon qui point vivement,   35r
1940 C'est Desir, trait soubtivement.
Amours consent
Que cil qui de ses plaisirs sent
Et qui a lui servir s'assent,
1944 Ait biens et maulx ensemble cent.
Pour cuers actraire,
Baille du doulz puis du contraire
Par Desir, dont il scet bien traire,
1948 Pour les garder de soy retraire
De son servage,
Car Amours par son droit usage
Est la prison de Franc Courage,
1952 Ou Bon Vouloir le met en gage
Afin qu'il ne soit pas volage.
Et le sergeant
Plaisir les va la hebergeant,
1956 Maiz Loyauté se va chargeant
Qu'eslargi soit, en le plegeant.
Celle gëole

1927 lesguillon *Dc.* 1929 Que *Dc.* 1931 tout *DcDfOaPcPhQl.* 1932 tout *Df.* 1933 Lune a. *Dc OaPcPhQl.* 1934 p.] le p. *Oa*; nen p. *Ph*, espraigne *Dc.* 1935 Au cuers que m. les s. *Oa*: leur s. *Db.* 1937 Et briefment *DbDcPh.* 1938 P. et tres d. craintement *Dc*: et d. *Oa.* 1939 Lesguillon *DcQl.* 1942 prent *Dc*, sont *Dd.* 1943 fussent *Db.* 1944 Et b. *Oa*, Et bien *DcPh*; sent *OaPh.* 1946 Saille *Db*; le c. *Ql.* 1950 de *Dc.* 1951 Et *Db*; du *DcOa.* 1953 *Omitted DcOaPcPh.* 1955 P. qui les va h. *Ql*: le va *Df.* 1956 sen va *Db*; les va sachant *Dc.* 1957 Queslargis *OaPh.* 1958 De le g. *Ph*, De le garole *Oa.*

Garde Desir qui pou parole,
1960 Quoy qu'en cuer soit de chaulde cole.
Cestuy rompt le cuer et affole,
Et ne le lesse
Yssir pour don ne pour promesse,
1964 Car lÿé le tient en la lesse
De Regart qui a paine cesse
Et le pourmaine,
Jour a jour, sepmaine a sepmaine,
1968 Tant qu'il le tient soubz son dommaine.   35ᵛ
Et puis devant Craintc le maine,
Qui a l'office
De faire en Amours la justice;
1972 Cellui maintient la grant police
D'Amours comme le plus propice.
La gehiné
Est par long ennuy l'obstiné
1976 Et devant Crainte examiné
De ce que penser n'a finé;
Si faut qu'il die
Par long ennuy sa maladie,
1980 Maiz quoy qu'a dire s'estudie,
Il n'a sur lui char si hardie
Qui ne fremisse.
Droiz est que le juge cremisse,
1984 N'en lui n'est qu'a droit dire puisse
Sans que cent foiz d'un propos ysse,
Quoy que ou registre
De Souvenir, tout enregistre.
1988 Maiz quant l'oeil la joie administre,
En entrant, elle empesche d'istre
Ce qui sejourne
En la triste pensee mourne;
1992 Passer ne puct, car tout a ourne

1959 Car de d. *Oa*.   1960 Quoy quen cuer soit (*sic*) *Ph*: de ch. c.] la ch. c. *PcQl*.   1964 le.]
leesse *Oa*.   1965 regret *DcDf*.   1968 sur *Db*.   1969 la m. *Df*.   1971 la j.] j. *Df*.   1972 Cestui
DbDcDfOaPcPhQl.   1974 La gehaine *DcOa*, La gehemine *Ph*.   1975 Et *DcDfOaPcPh*; pour *Oa*.
1976 e.] lexamine *Dc*.   1977 De cela que p. ne f. *Dc*.   1978 Sil *DbDcPh*.   1980 que d. *OaPcPhQl*.
1983 Droit *DcOaPcPhQl*.   1985 S. que] S. ce que *Ph*; du p. *Ql*.   1986 Quoy quen r. *DcOa*, Quoy r.
Ph.   1987 qui e. *Df*.   1989 Entretant *OaPcPhQl*; el *Df*.   1990 Et *DbDc*.   1992 peust *PcQl*.

Prins sont les pas, si s'en retourne
Vers le courage
Ou demeure, enmy le voiage,
1996 Sans point acomplir son message,
Dont par aprés de dueil errage.   36r
Ainsi seron
Tant que par amours ameron,
2000 Car de Desir n'eschapperon.
Cil est l'amoureux esperon
Qui l'amant chace
Batant vers grace qu'il pourchace,
2004 Et lui fait avancer sa chace,
Dont plus va avant, moins se lasse.
Ainsi m'en est
Car je n'ay cessé në arrest
2008 De pourchacer ce qui me plest,
Que d'avoir je suy tresmal prest
Et pou scïent
Pour souffrir inconvenïent.
2012 Maiz qui aime a droit escïent,
Cuer lui faut fort et pacïent;
A ce tendez.'
Lors dist la tierce: 'Or m'entendez.   36v
2016 Pour les plus tristes vous rendez
Et voz partis bien deffendez.
Je ne me plaing
De ce, ne ne l'ay en desdaing;
2020 Chascun blecié plaint son mehaing
Et congnoist son fait et son saing.
Maiz d'autry faiz
Ne scet nul le pois ne le faiz
2024 Ne n'a jugemens si parfaiz
Comme cellui qui les a faiz.

1993 ses *Dc*. 1994 Lors *Db*. 1995 ennuy (?) *Ph*. 1997 en raige *Dc*, esrage *Pc*. 2001 Cilz est *OaPhQl*, Celluy *Dc*; amoureux *DcPh*; lesperon *Df*. 2002 Que *Dc*. 2006 met est *Oa*. 2007 ne c. *OaPcPhQl*; ny a. *DbPc*. 2008 que *Df*, quil *DbOaPh*. 2009 Car *Ph*; da. je suy] je suys da. *DbDcDfPcQl*, je suis damours *OaPh*. 2011 De *DcOaPcPhQl*. 2013 fault avoir p. *Ql*. 2014 Ad ce entendez *Db*. 2015 Or *OaPhQl*; or entendez *DcOaPhQl*, or actendes *Pc*. 2017 Et se vos p. d. *Dc*, Et voz parties (parties bien *Ph*) d. *OaPh*. 2022 dautres f. *OaPh*. 2023 nulz *OaPcPh*; ne p. *Pc* le poix *Ql*. 2024 ja j. *Db*, na jugement *DcDfOa*. 2025 les a] le a *Df*.

Trop bien pouez
Parler, ou plaigniez ou louez,
2028 Du mal que pour vostre advouez;
Maiz a autry ne vous jouez.
Vous recevez
Voz maulx: les miens n'appercevez,
2032 Dont comparer ne les devez,
Et en le faisant me grevez.
Maiz puis que sommes
A comparer les dures sommes
2036 Dont nous perdons repoz et sommes
Pour quatre amans et pour quatre hommes,
Je ne refuse
Point; et n'est droit que je m'excuse
2040 De dire la douleur qui use
Mon cuer que Vain Espoir abuse
Et ou repaire
De desplaisirs plus de cent paire,
2044 Sans que un tout seul bien y appaire.
Puis que mal a mal se compaire,
Des maintenant
J'ose bien dire, en maintenant
2048 Ma part et raison soustenant,
Que le mal qui me va tenant
Et qui n'est que un,
Est aux vostres deux seul commun,
2052 Pire qu'eulx deux et que chascun;
J'ay les voz tous, non pas aucun.
Ainsi me vante,
Se vantance est d'estre meschante,
2056 Que ma tristece est plus pesante
Et suis plus douloureuse amante
Trop, que nesune

2027 ou pl.] ou plaignez *Db*, ou plaines *Df*, ou plaindre *OaPh*, estre plains *Dc*.   2032 comparez *Ph*.
2035 comparez *Db*, comparoir *Df*.   2037 ne *PcQl*.   2040 cuse *OaPh*.   2041 que] qui *Oa*, qui en *Ph*.
2043 De d.] Des d. *Df*, Des plaisirs *Ph*.   2044 *Omitted Ph*, S. (S. ce *Dc*) qung s. b. y a. *DcOaQl*.
2045 Plus *OaPh*.   2047 Ose *Dc*; d. en m.] d. m. *Oa*.   2048 Ma perte *Dc*.   2050 Et quil est qun *Oa*.
2051 Et *DcOaPh*; aux v.] les v. *Ph*, vostre *Oa*; seulx *Ql*.   2052 Pires *Ph*; ne *Ph*.   2053 voz] bons
OaPh: t. deux non a. *Dc*, nom pas a. *Db*, t. et (t. deux *Ql*) non pas ung *PcQl*.   2055 Que ma voulente
est de m. *Oa*, Ma voulente de. m. *Ph*, De ma voulente m. *Ql*: Ma v. *Pc*.   2058 nest une *Oa*.

De vous. Son ami mort plaint l'une;
2060 L'autre la prise et la fortune
Du sien que Adversité fortune,
Et sans deserte.
La premiere ploure la perte
2064 D'Espoir, comme a tousjours deserte.
L'autre dit: "Desir m'a deserte
Et recreüe,
Sans Desperance mescreüe;
2068 Plus l'ay par mon desir creüe,
Plus m'est doubte et douleur creüe".
A grans loisirs
L'une plaint les passez plaisirs.
2072 L'autre n'a rien fors desplaisirs,
Et lui croissent aprés desirs
Par mains assaulx.
Quoy que l'une a de griefz travaulx,
2076 Elle a eu a coup tous ses maulx;
L'autre les a tousjours nouveaulx.
Maiz la premiere
Dit qu'elle a de dueil plus matiere,
2080 Car el pert esperance entiere
Et elle n'est point si legiere
Qu'elle peüst
Autre amer, quel bien qu'en soy eust,
2084 Car oncques ne fut que rien sceust
De change ne qu'il lui pleüst.
Quoy que songeur
Soit son cuer, d'Ennuy hebergeur
2088 Et de son soulcy le forgeur,
Au moins n'est il mie changeur.
Or n'est possible

38r

2059 p.] plaine *Oa.* 2061 Du s. quaversaire f. *DcPcQl*, Du s. quant (quant la *Ph*) soue f. *OaPh*. 2062 Est *Oa.* 2062 a Dont chascune a douleur soufferte *Db*. 2064 quon a *DbDc*, qui ma *OaPh*. 2064-5 *Inverted Dc.* 2065 *Omitted Db*, La. de. si ma (de. me *Ph*) d. *OaPh*: me d. *DfPcQl*. 2066 Et je r. *Dc*, Et je creue *OaPhQl*. 2067 D.] desesperance *DbOaPh*, esperance *Dc*; me creue *Ph*. 2068 Puis *Df*; par my d. *DfOaPcPhQl*. 2069 P.] Et p. *Dc*; douleur et doubte *OaPh*, dure et douleur *Dc*. 2070 De *OaPhQl*. 2071 ses *DcPh*. 2072 *Omitted Oa.* 2074 moins *Dc*. 2075 des *Dc*. 2080 Car **es. la** pert en. *Oa*: el] elle *DbPh*. 2083 qu'en soy e.] quen e. *Pc.* 2084 o.] onc *Df* ;ne sceut *Dc*; qui *PcQl*; feust *Dc*. 2085 De changer ne qui point lui p. *Dc*: qui *Ql.* 2086 Quo que *Oa.* 2088 Et de son sens (son *Ph*) reforgeur *OaPh*. 2089 Amours *OaPh*.

Qu'elle face autre, ou plus sensible:
2092   Prendre autre cuer est impossible;
Faire contre cuer n'est loisible.
Amer la faut,
Quoy que sa partie lui faut
2096   Et n'a ami, ne qui le vault,
Car de nul autre ne lui chault.
L'autre debat
Qu'elle est plus triste et hors d'estat
2100   Car Doubte et Päour la combat,
Et Desir en elle s'embat.
Espoir nuysant
Lui est dessus tout et cuisant;
2104   C'est l'affilouere reluisant
Ou Desir se va aguisant.
Espoir par haste
Aguise Desir et le haste,
2108   Qui le point asprement et taste.
Et Desir Espoir use et gaste
Au long aler
Sans y lessier que regaler,
2112   Tant qu'il le fait tout tresaler;
C'est dur morsel a avaler.
Quel tour est mise   38v
En pire point et plus seurprise:
2116   Ou celle qui est pieça prise;
Ou l'autre, en tous costez assise
Et que on assault,
Dont au secours nully ne sault,
2120   Et n'a ne souldart ne vassault
Qui a reschapper sache sault?
Gemissemens
Y sont, cris, pleurs, hericemens

2091 Que le f. *Df*.   2092 est] il est *Ph*.   2094 le f. *Dc*, lassault *OaPh*.   2095 Quoy que] Combien que *DbDcDd*.   2099 Qu'e.] Quel *Df*; desbat *DfOaPcPhQl*.   2100 D. et P.] p. et d. *DcDfQl*, p. d. *OaPh*. 2103 est *Oa*; tous *PcQl*.   2104 la filouere *DbDc*, la cicoree *Oa*, lacitoree *Ph*; r.] luisant *OaQl*, lui sant *Ph*.   2105 esguisant *Df*.   2108 Qui la *DbDfOaPcPh*, Quil a *Ql*.   2112 quilz le font *Oa*, quilz se sont *Ph*; tous *Ph*.   2114 Car *Pc*.   2115 Empire *Oa*.   2116 Que *DcOaPcPh*.   2117 Et *Db*.   2119 ne fault *DbDcOaPh*.   2120 ne s.] s. *Db*.   2121 face *DbDcQl*.   2122 Gemissement *Ql*.   2123 plains *Ph*; aoursemens *OaPh*.

2124 Et crüelz amortissemens
De cuer; pensez se de ce mens.
L'autre tour toutes
A passé ces estranges doubtes,
2128 Quoy que ses portes soient rouptes;
Plus ne lui faut guet në escoutes.
"Ainsi, par m'ame,"
Dist la seconde, "Est il de dame
2132 Dont l'amant gist mort soubz la lame.
Dieu lui face pardon a l'ame!"
Quoy que amassee
A grant douleur et entassee
2136 Pour s'amour pieça trespassee,
La presse en est tantost passee.
Ma destinee
Est autre, et moins determinee.
2140 Je suy comme la tour minee,
Dont la prise n'est pas finee
De longue piece,
Et de qui on doubte qu'el chiece
2144 Ou qu'a ceulx de dedens meschiece;
Je craing que tout ne se despiece.
Maiz tant plus durs,
Ennuyeux, tresaigres et surs,
2148 Me sont mes maulx longs et obscurs,
Car mon mal vient par divers hurs,
Non pas confit
En un; et par Dieu qui nous fit,
2152 J'en ay cent, dont chascun suffit
A rendre un fort cuer desconfit.
En devisant
S'en vont ces deux, contredisant
2156 Et a leurs desplaisirs visant;

39r

2124 De c. *DcOaPhQl*, Deceveur *Df*. 2125 De c. pensees *Oa*, De c. pensees decepvemens *DcPh*: cueurs *Pc*. 2126 tres t. *DcQl*. 2127 p.] passees *Dc*; ses *DbDfPcQl*, les *DcOaPh*. 2128 qui *Db*; tes *Ph*. 2129 guaiz *OaPcPhQl*; ny e. *DbPc*. 2132 g. m.] g. *Oa*, m. g. *Ph*, g. hors *Df*; sur *Oa*. 2136 sa mort *OaPcPhQl*. 2137 Laspresse *DbDcDf*. 2141 point *DbQl*. 2143 de qui] dont *Dc*; ont *Ph*; qu'el] quil *Df*, quelle *DbDcOaPh*. 2144 c. de d. m.] c. d. ne m. *PcQl*, c. d. m. *Ph*. 2145 si se d. *Dd*. 2148 les *PcQl*. 2150 quon fist *Dc*. 2151 me fist *Db*. 2153 prandre *Oa*; corps *Db*. 2155 Se v. *DcDfOaPcPhQl*.

Chascune se tient voir disant.
Maiz quant cerchié
Aront leurs droiz et reverchié,
2160 Mon cuer de dueil est mieulx merchié,
Navré plus oultre et tresperchié.
Et sans debatre,
Pour leurs raisons toutes abatre,
2164 En mon cuer se viennent embatre
Plaies, dont j'ay contre une quatre.
Las! congnoissance
N'ay se m'amour et ma fïance
2168 Est mort, prins ou mis a finance.
Entre espoir et desesperance
Ainsi chancelle,
Plaine de doubtes, comme celle
2172 Qui a douleur et ne scet quele.   39v
Je ne sçay quel nom je m'appelle:
Ou d'amours veufve,
Ou prisonniere. Et si ne treuve
2176 De ce que j'aym tesmoing ne preuve
Ou vive ou non; c'est douleur neuve.
Tant me doubtoie,
Mes douleurs en moy racontoie,
2180 Quant la bataille redoubtoie:
Or suy moins seure que n'estoie
Et moins certaine!
Se j'ay esperance, elle est vaine
2184 Et ne puis perdre espoir sans paine,
Ne je ne sçay quel dueil je maine.
Bien souvent songe
Sa mort que mon cuer de dueil ronge,
2188 Puis faiz de la prison mon songe,
Et ne sçay lequel est mensonge.
Ce qui l'empesche

2157 Ch.] Chascun *Ph.* 2158 chercie *Ql.* 2160 Mon c. est de d. plus m. *Db.* 2161 N.] Nature *Ph*; trespercie *Dc.* 2163 t. a.] toute a. *Ql.* 2164 esbatre *Ql.* 2165 Paies *Db.* 2166 La c. *Dc.* 2167 ou *Ql.* 2168 mors *Df.* 2169 En e. *Oa.* 2171 doubte *OaPcPhQl.* 2173 *Omitted Ph.* 2179 a *DcQl*; r.] et acomptoye *Dc.* 2179–80 *Inverted OaPh.* 2180 Que *Oa.* 2181 Et *Db*; maint s. *Dc.* 2183 Si *Df*; el *Df.* 2184 Et ne perdray (ne prendray *Ph*) e. s. p. *OaPh.* 2185 dieu *Ql.* 2187 qui *DcOaPcPhQl*; de d. mon c. *Oa*; runge *Dd.* 2188 sa *DbDcDfOaPcPhQl*; mensonge *DdOaQl.* 2189 menchonge *Pc.* 2190 Et *Dc*; que *DfPcPhQl.*

Est mort ou prison trop grïesche;
2192 Ce sçay je bien, l'un des deux est che.
Maiz grief m'est que ne me despesche,
Sans plus remaindre
Pressee de maulx pour estaindre,
2196 De tost la verité actaindre
De ce dont plus je me doy plaindre
Et largement,
Car avoir certain jugement
2200 De son mal est l'abbregement
Des douleurs et l'alegement.

Nul ne saroit
Conforter, quoy qu'il lui plairoit,
2204 Cil qui ne saroit qu'il aroit,
S'a lui plus ne se declaroit
Que Dueil fendant
Va le cuer qui est actendant
2208 Son mal et tresbien entendant
Qu'aler ne puet en amendant.
Quant bien marchié
Avray et d'enquerre encerchié
2212 Ou l'en s'en sera descarchié,
Je n'en puis avoir bon marchié;
Maiz forte amour
Qui ne veult qu'en ce point demour
2216 Me fait enquerre sans demour
Ce que j'ay de savoir cremour.
Pour esprouver
Les cuers ou n'a que reprouver,
2220 Amours fait querir et rouver
Ce qu'on ne vouldroit pas trouver.
En ceste doubte
S'arreste ma pensee toute.

40r

2191 Cest *DcDfOaPcPhQl*.   2192 *Omitted Ph*: Si *DbDcOa*, Se *PcQl*; s. je b.] jay b. *Pc*, say b. *Ql*; l'un]
quun *Dc*, ung *Oa*; ce *DbDcDfOaPcQl*.   2193 g. est *DbDcOaPh*; qui *Dc*, quil *Oa*.   2195 P.] Presse
Oa; des *DcOa*; estraindre *Pc*.   2196 tout la v. *Pc*, toute v. *OaPhQl*.   2197 men doy *Ph*.   2200 et la.
PcQl, est abregement *Db*.   2201 est *DcOa*.   2203 qui *DfPc*, que *OaPh*.   2204 quil *DbPh*; savoit *Db*.
2206 Car *Db*, Quel *DcDfPh*.   2207 entendant *Dc*.   2208 est *OaPhQl*.   2209 peust *PcQl*.
2211 Avront *Dc*, Avre *Db*; de. serchie *Dc*.   2212 Ou on *DfOaPhQl*; descachie *Db*, deschargie *Pc*.
2213 ne p. *Dc*.   2215 v. quon en p. *Oa*, v. que en p. *Ph*.   2216 *Omitted Ph*.   2217 Et que (Ce dont *Ql*) je
dois avoir c. *OaPcPhQl*: Et que *Df*.   2217a Des amentes en tout honnour *Ph*.   2223 S'a.] Sa. en *Oa*.

2224 Sa mort plaing; la prison redoubte.
Se l'un fuy, l'autre me deboute.
Si enserré
Est, et de deux dars enferré,
2228 Mon cuer entre deux maulx serré
Que mieulx lui fust d'estre enterré;
Dont je maintien
Que suis la plus triste et m'y tien.
2232 Et s'on dit, "Quel mal est le tien?"
Les deux d'elles, je les soustien.
L'adversité
Court si que par necessité
2236 J'ay l'un des maulx en verité,
L'autre en doubte et craintiveté.
Je souspeçonne
Les deux; nulle part ne m'est bonne.
2240 Souspeçon tousjours me foisonne;
C'est dangier pour toute personne.
Ainsi debatent
Deux maulx qui en moy se combatent
2244 Et pour mon cuer gaignier s'embatent,
A celle fin qu'ilz s'entrematent
Comme haussaires,
Pillars de joie et adversaires,
2248 Et de ma mort les commissaires.
Maiz tous deux ne sont point faulsaires:
Si rescourray
A l'un mon cuer quant je pourray;
2252 Neantmoins a l'autre demourray,
Et triste vivray et mourray
Tresloing en l'ombre
D'Espoir dont j'ay en petit nombre.

40v

2224 sa *DcDfQl.* 2225 Sen lun *DcPcPhQl*; suy *Db*; la. me reboute *DcOaPhQl*, la. redoubte *Df*. 2227 Et de d. d. sy e. *Dc*, Est des d. d. et en ferre *Ph*: Est et] Est *DbOa*; des *Oa*; enserre *OaQl.* 2228 ferre *Df*, enserre *Oa.* 2229 f. estre *Pc*; enferre *Oa.* 2231 Destre la p. t. *DbDc DfOaPcPhQl*; me t. *Dc.* 2232 Et sont *Ql*; quel mal] que le mal *Db.* 2233 delle *Oa*; la *Dc*, le *OaPh.* 2234 Adversite *Dc.* 2237 et en craintite *Ph.* 2238 Je souspechonne *PcQl.* 2239 lune p. *PhQl.* 2240 Souspcon t. si me f. *Dc.* 2244 se batent *Pc.* 2245 qui se. *Pc*, quilz sentrebatent *Ql.* 2247 P. et de j. a. *PcQl*: Pillart *Db.* 2250 retourray *DcOa*, retournay *Ph.* 2251 Mon c. a lun *DcOaPcPhQl*; qu. je p.] je p. *Dd.* 2253 vivre et m. *Df*; ou *Pc.* 2254 a *Db.* 2255 bien p. *DcOa PhQl.*

2256 Maiz cuer qu'Ardant Desir encombre
Temps, jours, et nuiz, et heures nombre;
Tant me sont lees
Les nuis d'ennuy entremeslees,   41r
2260 Puis qu'en baisant furent seellees
Noz voix et noz lermes meslees,
Quant print congié
Cellui qu'ay tant depuis songié,
2264 Que j'aym par Dieu autant com gé;
Or est mort, ou trop eslongié.
Las! qui cuidast
Qu'alors tel congié demandast
2268 Et qu'a moy se recommandast,
Sans que jamaiz m'en amendast,
En descroissant
Les joies? Cuer n'est congnoissant
2272 Jamaiz qu'Amours soit si puissant
Comme quant maulx le vont froissant.
Or recongnoiz
Amours; plus ne le descongnoiz,
2276 Car en mon cuer fait ses tournoiz
Et m'apprent que ce sont qu'ennoiz.
Des lors senti
Ses cours que je me consenti
2280 A son service et assenti,
Maiz oncques foy ne lui menti.
Qui tient en fieu
De tel seignieur, ce n'est pas gieu.
2284 Je n'en tien qu'un cuer; et par Dieu
Aussi n'est il mis qu'en un lieu,
Ne ne mectray.
Ja plus ne m'en entremectray
2288 Maiz a Amours m'en soubmectray;   41v

2257 Tousjours y mis et heure et nombre *Ph*: Tant j. y n. *Oa*; et n.] n. *Db*; et h.] h. et *Dc*.
2259 dennuyz *Dc*; sentremeslees *Df*. 2260 celees *OaPh*. 2263 t. d.] d. t. *PcPhQl*. 2264 D. a.] d. *Db*.
2267 Que lors *Ql*. 2269 j. en a. *DcPh*. 2270 accroissant *DbDfOaPcPhQl*. 2271 Les j. donc c. nest
c. *Pc*: c.] tant c. *DbDd*. 2272 s. si] s. *Pc*, fust si *OaPh*. 2273 Comment quen m. se voit f. *Dc*:
Comment *DfPc*. 2275 pas ne les d. *Db*. 2276 Car amours fait ses faiz courtois *Oa*: Et *Db*. 2277 ce
s.] se s. *Db*, ce ne s. *Ql*. 2279 tours *DcOaPcPhQl*, coups *Db*. 2281 o.] onc *Ph*. 2282 Que *Df*.
2284 ny t. *Oa*, nen ay *Db*; que c. *Dc*. 2285 fors en ung l. *Dc*. 2288 me s. *OaPh*.

266

J'ay promis, plus ne promectray.
Si suis lÿee
Des giez d'Amours et allïee,
2292 Et ne me tien point oublïee
Se Mort ne s'y est emploiee.
Amours ravit
Les cuers, et pas ne s'assouvit.
2296 C'est un oisel qui de cuer vit;
Oncques nul tel oisel ne vit.
Maiz plus honneste
Est il de tant comme il acqueste
2300 Pour sa proie et pour sa conqueste
Le plus noble desus la beste,
Quel part qu'il gise.
Amours est de pareille guise
2304 A cil que on loge par franchise,
Qui puis veult avoir la maistrise
Du logeis et de la pourprise,
Quant est logiez;
2308 Et tient son hoste plus subgiez
Tandiz que la est hebergiez,
Que s'il fust en fers ou en giez,
Son deul faisant.
2312 Car amours est paine plaisant
Et un grant aise meffaisant;
C'est une guerre en appaisant,
Targe pour traire
2316 Encontre, et retrait pour actraire.
Amours efface pour pourtraire.
C'est un mal qui quiert son contraire:
Doulce rigueur,
2320 Courtois dangier, saine langueur,
Mortel plaisir, foible vigueur.
C'est une largesce de cuer,
Crainte hardie,

42r

2289 nen p. *Db.* 2291 gitz *Db*, getz *Pc*, jeux *DcOaQl*, deux *Ph.* 2292 men t. *Dc*, me tient *Ph.* 2293 Si *Df*; empliee *PcQl.* 2295 et point *Dc*, ne pas *Pc.* 2296 visel *Oa*; cueurs *DcOaPcQl.* 2297 O. nul] O. *Db.* 2300 sa c.] c. *OaPh.* 2301 de sus *Dd.* 2305 plus *DbDc*; par m. *Dc*, sa m. *Ph.* 2306 *Omitted DcOaPh.* 2308 subgitz *Db.* 2310 cil *DcOa*; gitz *Db*, cepz *Dc.* 2312 amour *Dc.* 2313 mesaisant *DcD*, *PcQl.* 2316 et r.] r. *Ph*, le trait *Oa.* 2317 pour (par *Ph*) contraire *OaPh.* 2318 un mal] ung *Pc.*

267

2324 Tresarrestee quouärdie
Et seurté a craindre enhardie,
Embusche qui le cuer hardie
Et qui descoeuvre
2328 Le cuer et fiert, et puis recoeuvre
Et le clot, et par aprés l'oeuvre;
Amours est droit maistre de l'oeuvre.
Et qui pensee
2332 A sa vertu pou appensee,
C'est maladie de pensee,
Ou toute joie est despensee
En desirant;
2336 C'est le mal qui, plus va tirant
A santé, plus est empirant.
On le congnoist en souspirant,
Non pas au poulx,
2340 Si que on fait les autres maulx tous.
Joie et deul en sont les deux bous,
Maiz dueil est le bout de dessoubz,
Car amours finent
2344 En deul lors que leurs cours terminent:
Autres maladies declinent
En joie quant elles definent.
S'Amours allume
2348 Un cuer en son grant feu qui fume,
Tel le forge ou de tel volume
Qu'il veult, com fevre sus enclume,
Qui par feu mue
2352 Un glaive en un soq de charue
Et sa nature lui remue;
Le soq nourrit, le glaive tue.
Et ainsi moule
2356 Amours les cuers selon son moule:

42v

2324 Tresasseuree *DcQl*; couhardise *Oa*. 2325 Et s.] S. *DcQl*; a c.] a (et *DcPh*) crainte *DbDcPhQl*, crainte *Oa*; ou hardie *Ph*. 2328 et f.] refiert *Db*. 2329 *Omitted Dc*: puis a. *OaPcQl*. 2330 a Et le clerc puis apres clost leuvre *Dc*. 2332 A la v. pour a. *OaPh*: apposee *Dc*. 2333 m. dispensee *OaPcPhQl*. 2334 En *Ph*; dispensee *OaPh*, disposee *Ql*. 2336 disant *Oa*. 2339 aux p. *Oa*. 2340 Si com f. *DfPc PhQl*; aultre m. *Dc*; tout *DfQl*. 2344 cueurs *PcQl*, cueur *Dc*. 2346 joyes *Dc*; qu. e.] tant quelles *Pc*. 2347 Samour *Dc*. 2348 a *Dc*. 2349 Telle f. *Dc*, De tel f. *Ql*, Telle (De tel *Ph*) force *OaPh*; te v. *Dc*. 2350 Qui *DcOaPcQl*; quon fiere *Db*, quon forge *Dc*; sur *DbDcDfOaPhQl*; lenclume *DbDcOaPhQl*. 2352 En g. (En ung g. *Ql*) ung soc de ch. *OaPhQl*: Dun *Dc*; en son soq *Db*, et un soc *Dc*. 2353 Et se *Db*. 2356 *Omitted Df*: le m. *OaPh*.

268

Il les change, remue et croule,
Puis qu'il les a mis en son roule.
Maiz plus donnez
2360 S'est es cuers qui sont ordonnez
D'estre bien condicïonnez
Et aux haulx faiz abandonnez,
Ou hardement
2364 Est ou trescler entendement,
Et on en prent amendement;
Qui le contraire cuide, ment.
Amours manoir
2368 Desire en tresnoble manoir,
Soit soubz vert habit ou soubz noir;
Ailleurs ne saroit remanoir.
Tant enhardiz
2372 S'est qu'il avance les tardiz,
Enhardit les aquouärdiz
Et les vaillans fait plus hardiz,
Quant ilz sont tieulx   43 r
2376 Qu'ilz veulent choisir en bons lieux
Et mectent paine a valoir mieulx
Pour plaire a la belle aux beaulx yeulx.
Sans varïer,
2380 Entendent a droit charïer
Et deshonneur contrarïer
Pour soy a elle apparïer
Et de maniere,
2384 Car la coustume d'amours yere,
Qui ameroit une bergiere
Vouldroit porter la pennetiere
Et danceroit
2388 Au flajol. Tout beau lui seroit:

2357 Ilz (Il *Ph*) les ch. et mue et c. (et cole *Ph*) *OaPh*. 2358 P. quil la mis en son roole *Oa*, P. les a mis en son beau role *Ql*. 2360 Cest *Oa*; les c. *Ph*. 2362 es *Oa*. 2363 Ou hardiement *Oa*. 2365 ou on *PcPhQl*, ou len *Dc*, ou en *Oa*. 2366 c. m.] c. il m. *OaPcPhQl*. 2367 Amour *DcOa*. 2369 Qui *Df*; h.] arbre *Ph*. 2372 Fust quil *Dc*, Fut il *DfOaPcPhQl*; a.] a mentir *OaPh*; le t. *Oa*, bien t. *Ph*. 2373 E.] Et e. *Dc*, Enhardiz *OaPh*; les a.] les coardis *DbDc*. 2374 villains *Dd*; faiz *Ph*. 2375 il *Pc*. 2376 Qui v. *Ph*, Et v. *DcPcQl*; es *OaPh*; bois l. *Oa*. 2376 after 2378 *Ql*. 2376–7 *Inverted Pc*. 2377 *Omitted Ph*: Et m.] Ilz m. *DbDcDfPcQl*, Il ny actend *Oa*; a v.] pour v. *Dc*. 2378 p.] plaira *Ph*. 2380 E.] Entendans *Db*, Entend *Dc*, Entendant *Oa*, En tendant *Ph*. 2382 o *Ql*; appaisier *OaPh*. 2386 Pourroit *Dc*.

Ce qu'elle vouldroit, ameroit;
Ce qu'elle fuyroit, lesseroit.
Amours est lierres

2392 De cuers, ou au moins un changierres,
Aux bons bon, aux bouleurs boulierres.
C'est le cep d'or a riches pierres;
Qui s'y appuye,

2396 Prins est sans querir qu'il s'en fuye.
C'est un beau soleil et puis pluye;
Une foiz plaist et l'autre ennuye.
Amours compasse

2400 Ses faiz comme la dance basse:
Puis va avant et puis rappasse,
Puis retourne, puis oultrepasse.
La engagiee,

2404 Et de ses biens du tout gagiee,
Est la volenté erragiee
Qui a dueil et joie en dragiee;
Si se declaire

2408 Si que autry le sent, voit ou flaire,
Et prent a la flamme exemplaire,
Qui de soy se moustre et esclaire
Non deffumee,

2412 Car une fournaise allumee,
D'ardeur seurprise et enfumee,
Giecte tousjours flamme ou fumee.
L'amant se trompe,

2416 Qui voit sa dame en feste ou pompe,
Car ou il faut que le cuer rompe
Ou que le semblant se corrompe.
Amours requierent

2420 Tout le cuer en quoy ilz se fierent;

43ᵛ

2390 Et *Dc.* 2392 ou au m.] au m. *OaPh.* 2393 Au b. *Pc*; voleurs (vouliers *Ph*) volierres *DcPcPh*, broleurs brolerres *Ql.* 2394 Cest lanel dor a r. p. *Ql*: r. p.] r. *Oa*, r. p. *Oa²*. 2395 Qui sen a. *Ph*, Qui sur paine *Oa.* 2396 s. qu.] na garde *Ql*; qui *Pc*; reffuye *Dc*, sensuye *Oa.* 2398 et la.] la. *Db*, et autre *Df.* 2400 la dame brasse *Dc.* 2401 repasse *DbPcQl.* 2402 *Omitted Dd*: r. p.] r. et p. *Ph.* 2404 Cest *Dc*, Est *PcQl*; ses gens *OaPh.* 2405 *Omitted Oa*: Cest *DbDcPcPhQl*; de v. *Dc*; enragee *DbDcDfPcPhQl.* 2406 engendree *Dc.* 2407 Et *Pc.* 2408 que a.] qua a. *Oa*; s. v.] v. s. *PcPhQl*, vent s. *Dc*, boit s. *Oa.* 2409 Saprent *Ph*; femme *OaPcPhQl.* 2410 se m.] m. *Ph*; efflaire *OaPh.* 2411 defuuee *OaPh*(?). 2413 enflammee *Dc*, alumee *OaPh.* 2414 Gite *Df*; feu ou f. *OaPh*, flambe ou f. *PcQl.* 2417 Car il f. que le c. luy r. *Dc.* 2418 son s. *Dc.* 2419 Amour *Dc.*

Tous semblans, tous pensers qui yerent
En amant, en un se refierent,
Pareil voiens,
2424   Car ruisseaulx petiz et moiens
Vont en mer par divers moiens,
En descendant trestous loiens
Aprés leurs tours:
2428   Ainsi font en un leurs retours
Pensers d'amant; bien ont trestours,
Puis leurs tresmerveilleux estours.
Un cuer tremblant,
2432   Ou douleurs se vont assemblant,
Au maintien, aux faiz, au semblant
En depart ou lui vont emblant.   44r
Ainsi qu'en fuicte
2436   Quant Desir gouverne la luicte,
Se par lui la chose est conduicte,
Selon seignieur mesnie duicte:
Ainsi poursuivent
2440   Amans leur vouloir et desuivent,
Desir plus que Raison ensuivent;
Et mesmes leurs semblans les suivent,
En couvoiant,
2444   Par un droit chemin forvoiant
Sans estre a Dangier pourvoiant.
Desir n'est que devant voiant:
Derrier n'a dextre,
2448   Ainsi ne scet amant son estre,
Car qui n'est pas de son cuer mestre,
Du maintien ne le pourroit estre.
Or est encloz

2421 T. p. t. s. y. *Dc*: t. p.] et pensees *Db*, toutes pensees *OaPh*, toute pensee *Ql*; qui y.] y. *PhQl*, y erent *Oa*.   2422 lamant *DcDfOaPcPhQl*.   2423 Pareilz *Dc*.   2425 en cuer *OaPhQl*.   2426 En d.] Et d. *Dc*, Et (Et se *Oa*) descendent *DbDfOaPcQl*, Et se deffendent *Ph*; en tous l. *Dc*.   2427 cours *DcPcQl*.   2428 sont *DbOaPh*; recours *DcOaPcQl*.   2429 P. damans (*sic*) *Oa*: P.] Pensees *DbDc*, Penser *Ql*; damans *PcQl*; b. ont] ont b. *Pc*, b. ou *DfPhQl*; tristours *PcQl*, trestous *Ph*.   2430 les *Db*; tresmaleu- reux *DcQl*, maleureux *OaPh*; retours *Ph*.   2432 si v. *Df*.   2433 au fait *DcOaPh*.   2434 despart *OaPh*, deport *Pc*; va *Dc*.   2435 que f. *Oa*.   2437 Si *Dc*.   2438 m.] mesniee *Dd*.   2440 Amours *DfOaPh*; leurs vouloirs *DcPcQl*, leurs devoirs *OaPh*; deffuient *Ph*.   2441 Desirs *Oa*; en suyenet (*sic*) *Pc*.   2442 les s. *Dc*, leur semblant *OaPh*; s. ensuivent *Df*.   2447 D.] Desirer *Db*, Arrier *Dc*, Darrier *Oa*; ne *Oa*; estre *Ph*.   2448 Aussi *OaPh*; soit *Pc*; avant *OaPh*; maistre *Db*.   2449 il nest *Ql*. 2450 Au *Dc*.   2451 en clos *Pc*.

2452 Mon cuer en l'amoureux encloz,
De hayes d'espines tout cloz,
Par quoy le partir m'est forcloz.
C'est pour la pointe
2456 De Desir dont je suy si pointe,
Et s'a la demourer m'appointe,
De nul confort ne suis acointe.
Le departir
2460 M'est fort; dur est m'en departir.
Mon cuer n'a qui puisse partir
A ses maulx, si est seul martir.
Dont suis tiree   44v
2464 De deux douleurs et martiree,
Quant la joie qu'ay desiree
Le plus, m'est du tout empiree
Par doubte, voire
2468 Si fort que je ne sçay que croirre:
Ou se je doubte, ou se j'espoire.
Mort ou vif, je l'ay en memoire;
Entretenu
2472 Il a tout. Ce m'est advenu:
Je n'ay fors les maulx retenu;
Ne sçay que tout est devenu.
J'ay devisees
2476 Les durtez d'Amours desguisees;
Maiz qui bien les a avisees,
Aspres les ay et atisees.
Ainsi ouÿe
2480 M'avez, de desplaisir fouÿe.
Suy ge doncques moins esjouÿe
Dessus toutes? Dictes "Ouÿe".'
Un pou fuz lent
2484 De respondre au fait vïolent,

2452 aclos *DfOaPcPh*. 2453 d'e.] et de. *Dc*; tous *Pc*; c.] enclos *OaPh*. 2454 Pourquoy *Db*. 2456 suis espointe *Dc*. 2457 Et se alla d. ma pointe *Db*, Et ce las damours si ma poincte *Dc*: se la *PcPhQl*. 2458 De nul] De desir nul *Oa*. 2459 *Omitted Db*: La d. *OaPhQl*, De d. *Pc*. 2460 Mest fault *Ql*; dur mest den (mest le *Ql*) d. *DbQl*, dur mais men d. *OaPh*, et dur a mon partir *Dc*. 2461 que *OaPh*. 2463 tuee *Dc*. 2464 Des *OaPh*. 2465 que d. *OaPh*. 2467 Pour *Db*; droicte *OaPh*. 2468 fors que *OaPh*. 2469 si...si *Dc*. 2477 M. que b. les a deguisees *Ph*. 2478 Et apres les ay a. *Dc*: Apres *DbPh*; les a *Db*. 2480 desplaisirs *OaPcQl*, tout plaisir *Db*; fournye *DcOaPcPhQl*. 2481 d. m.] m. d. *Dc*. 2483 Un pou] Ung *Pc*; feust *Oa*, fut *Ph*. 2484 A *Dc*.

Maiz j'eu de dire grant talent
Que je ne suy pas seul dolent.
En ce descort
2488   Furent, d'autres choses d'accort
Et que je leurs raisons recort.
Ne suy mie de tout recort:
Ensemble dirent
2492   Les droiz qui pour leurs partiz firent,   45r
Et tant de raisons avant mirent
Que je ne sçay ou tant en prirent
Pour tel explet,
2496   Fors qu'Amours avoit si replet
Leurs cuers de son art tout complet
Que la bouche en tient si long plet
Et s'en guermente,
2500   Car selon que cuer se demente,
La bouche d'amant parlemente
De ce qu'il faut que le cuer sente;
Quant Amours forge
2504   Ses dars ou cuer comme en sa forge,
L'ardant fumee qui regorge
S'espart par la bouche et desgorge.
Lors a songier
2508   Prins a leur fait, car c'est dangier,
Faucte de sens, vouloir legier,
De tart entendre et tost jugier;
Et bien est lasche
2512   Le juge qui trop tost se lasche
Et avalle sans ce qu'il masche,
En jugeant des choses en tasche
Sans faire pause
2516   Et entendre chascune clause
Que on veult dire, et comme on se cause

2485 M. eu *Oa*, M. eut *Ph*.   2486 point *Ph*; seu d. *Df*.   2489 Et quant l. ra. je re. *Dc*: l. raison *Ph*. 2490 Ne suy] Je ne suis *Dc*; du t. *DcOaPhQl*.   2491 Ensembls *Ql*.   2492 que *Dc*; leur party *DcPcQl*, parties *OaPh*.   2494 ou ilz les p. *Ql*.   2495 Par tel exploiet (*sic*) *Dc*.   2496 si r.] r. *Db*.   2497 Les c. *Db*, Le cueur *DcOaPcPhQl*; arc *DbDcDfOaPhQl*; tant *Dc*, si *Pc*, son *Ph*.   2499 se g. *DcQl*. 2503 amour *Dc*.   2504 Ce d. *Oa*; eu c. *Pc*, au c. *Ph*, en c. *Ql*, es cueurs *Dc*; la f. *DcOaPcPhQl*, sa gorge *Db*.   2506 Se part *Db*; et d.] d. *Oa*.   2509 F. de s. et de v. (*sic*) *Oa*.   2512 qui si t. *Ql*. 2513 s. quil (s. qui *Ql*) le m. *DcQl*.   2514 entasche *Df*(?)*PcPhQl*.   2517 Que lon v. d. ou quon se c. *Dc*: Com v. d. *Db*; c. on] c. *Ql*, quon *OaPh*.

Des droiz des partis, et la cause.
Pour ce en doubtant,
2520 Leurs raisons ensemble adjouxtant,
Me taisoie en les escoutant   45ᵛ
Comme elles aloient comptant;
Et n'entendoye
2524 Qu'a penser que dire j'en doie.
Rien plus en ouÿr n'actendoie,
Maiz le penser ou je tendoie
Cessa, car la
2528 Quarte de ces dames parla
Et rompit mon propos par la.
L'estrif qui tant se pourparla
Recommença,
2532 Car la quarte depuis en ça
Nouvelles plainctes commença.
Par doulz moz aux autres tença,
Et lermëoit
2536 Si fort que ses beaulx yeulx nëoit
Tant en plours qu'a paine vëoit;
Maiz en courçant se hontëoit.
Ce qui la trouble
2540 Est Honte qui son mal redouble;
Et pour ce est son desplaisir double
Qu'au dire la honte le double,
En leur disant:
2544 'Mes dames, qu'alez vous disant?   46ʳ
Je suis a vous contredisant,
Non pas pour estre desprisant
Ou courouchier
2548 Voz cuers que je n'ay pas pou chier;

2518 Les d. *DbDcDfOaPhQl*, Les *Pc*; p.] parties *DbDcDdOaPhQl*; clause *Ph*.   2521 M. t. elles e. *Dc*.
2521–2 *Inverted Dc*.   2522 *Omitted OaPh*, Tout autre soucy hors boutant *Df*: C.] Commant *Dc*.
2523 Et ne pensoye *DcDdDfOaPcPhQl*.   2524 savoir *Df*; d. en pourroye *Dc*.   2525 R. p. a oyr
nantendroye (o. nentendoye *Oa*) *DcOaPh*, R. p. ouyr nen (o. ny *Ql*) actendoye *PcQl*.   2528 Quatre
Ql.   2530 que *OaPh*; pou parla *Ph*.   2533 N. p. (Nouvelle plainte *Ql*) encommenca *OaPhQl*.
2536 ses b. y.] b. y. *Pc*; nayoit *Oa*.   2537 Tout *Dc*; qua peu v. *OaPh*.   2538 Et *DcOa*
Ph; torchant *Db*; hontoiet (*sic*) *Dc*, hontoiant *Ql*.   2539 que *DfOaQl*.   2540 Cest *DcDfOaPc*
PhQl.   2541 p. ce est] p. ce *PcQl*.   2542 Qua au d. la h. d. *Df*: Quen d. *Db*, Car d. *OaPcPh*,
Le d. *Ql*; h. redouble *Dc*, h. lui comble *Ql*.   2544 Mes d. qui les vont d. *Ph*.   2546 despisant
Pc.

Maiz de ce qui me puet touchier
Et que je m'oy cy reprouchier,
Me faut respondre.
2552 Force de dueil me vient cemondre
De mon cas treshonteux expondre,
Qui me fait toute en lermes fondre;
Et tien moins compte
2556 Du desplaisir que de la honte.   46v
J'oy l'une de vous qui raconte
Que par moy sa douleur seurmonte
Ou par celluy
2560 Que j'ay cuidié meillieur que luy
Et l'ay amé plus que nulluy.
Vous ne parlastes de tel huy.
Or a fuÿ
2564 Laschement et s'est enfuÿ,
Dont il a honneur defuÿ.
Et dit on: "Pourquoy y fu y,
Et ses semblables,
2568 Quant leurs laschetez dommageables
Et leurs fuites deshonnourables
Ont fait mourir tant de notables,
Pres qu'a milliers,
2572 Et fait perdre les chevaliers
Qui de France estoient piliers,
Menez comme beufx en coliers
En vïolentes
2576 Prisons ou n'a que poulz et lentes?"
Ainsi leurs quouärdies lentes
Ont fait tant de dames dolentes
Et esplourees;
2580 Tant en ont de lermes plourees
Maintes grans dames honnourees
Qui en sont seules demourees,

2549 me p.] p. *Db*; me peust *PcQl*. 2550 Et que je me voy r. *Dc*: si *DbOaPcPhQl*; reprouchay *Db*. 2552 de d.] d. *Dd*. 2553 piteux *OaPh*. 2554 tout en l. *DcDfQl*, tous en l. *Ph*. 2555 tient *DfPh*; mains *PcQl*. 2557 Je oys de vous lune qui r. *PcPhQl*. 2558 pour *Ql*. 2560 je cuide *OaPh*; m. de *Pc*. 2561 la ame *Oa*, si layme *Ph*. 2564 sest affuy *Db*, sen est fouy *DcOaPcPhQl*. 2565 D. est a *OaPh*. 2566 dist *Pc*; y fouy *Db*, y fuy *Ph*, il fu y *Ql*. 2572 des *Dc*. 2574 beuf *Ph*. 2576 p.] pououlz (*sic*) *Dd*. 2577 couhardises *DcDfOaPcQl*, cornardises *Ph*. 2578 dame *Dc*. 2582 *Omitted Oa*.

Comme vous dictes.

2584 Ainsi vous ensemble maudictes
Les fuitifz pour leurs demerites, 47ʳ
Dont ilz ne seront jamaiz quictes,
Quant courouchié

2588 Ont les bons comme on a touchié,
Dont j'ay le cuer bien courouchié
Qu'il me puist estre reprouchié
D'avoir amé

2592 Un lasche fuitif diffamé
Et de tel deshonneur blasmé,
Qui tant a son bien entamé
Comme de fuire

2596 En tel place et aux autres nuire,
Faire son bacinet reluire
Et vestir harnoiz pour defuire!
Haa! Quel journee!

2600 Fole, et de sens mal äournee,
Suy je oncques a l'amer tournee?
Ne pourquoy fuz je ce jour nee
En tel erreur?

2604 Les yeulx qui m'ont fait la tristeur
En portent la paine et le pleur.
Las! Comme eu je si lasche cuer
Qui m'y fist traire?

2608 Je cuidasse que, pour retraire
Ou pour fuÿr ou pour actraire,
Un cuer son bien ou son contraire
Sentist ainchois

2612 Qu'il feist son eslite ou son chois;
Maiz tout le rebours apperchois
Quant par moy mesmes me dechois. 47ᵛ
Amours eslire

2584 Aussi *OaPh*. 2585 Leurs fuites *OaPh*; par *Dc*. 2590 Qui *OaPh*; peult *DcOaPh*, peust *Pc*. 2591 a Et pour serviteur (p. service *Oa*) reclame *DcDfOaPcPhQl*. 2592 fuitifz *Pc*. 2594 *Omitted DcDfOaPcPhQl*. 2598 destruire *Ph*. 2599 A a qu. j. *DfPc*, Ha quelle j. *Ql*. 2600 F. et] F. *Dc*; mal a.] mal ournee *Oa*, male a. *Ql*. 2601 Eux *Db*, Fus *Dc*; o.] donc *PcQl*; a (en *Dc*) la mer *DbDcDfOaPh*. 2602 Ne p. fus celle journee *Dc*, Ne p. jay sejournee *Ph*: ce j.] de ce j. *Dd*. 2605 Emportent *DfOaPcQl*, En portant *Ph*. 2606 C.] comment *Dc*; je] je onc *Pc*. 2607 Quil *Pc*; me f. *DcOaPcPhQl*; croire *Dc*. 2608 Que *DcOa*, Qui *Ph*. 2609 suir *DbOaPcQl*. 2610 Un c.] Ung *Pc*. 2612 eust *Dc*; et *PcPh*. 2614 pour *Df*; mesme *Dc*; deczois *DbDcOaPh*. 2615 Amour *Db*; eslite *Ph*.

276

2616 M'a fait ce qui m'estoit le pire:
Cellui qui d'avoir bien empire
Et pour guerredon me martire.
Si lui rendray,
2620 Quoy que vers lui le cuer tendre ay;
Par semblant compte n'en tendray.
Las! A qui doncques m'en prendray
Fors qu'a moy seule,
2624 Quant mon cuer fist dire a ma gueule
Ce dont il faut que je me deule,
Portant plus grief fez que une meule?
C'est la droicture,
2628 Car j'ay quiz ma male aventure;
Si n'en blasme Fortune obscure,
La mort ne la bataille dure.
Et n'en ay haine
2632 Fors au cuer qui seulement maine
Ma pensee decevant, vaine,
Querir plaisir et trouver paine.
J'ay eu fïance
2636 En Faulx Semblant par l'allïance
Faintise qui sans deffïance
Fiert, et puis met en oublïance
Comme devant.
2640 Haa! Faulx Lengage decevant!
Or suy ge bien appercevant
Que ta doulceur est plus grevant
Que beauté de soleil levant   48r
2644 Que vent couvoie.
Ta traÿson point ne savoie
Ne que tu te meisses en voie,
Si non quant le cuer t'y couvoie
2648 A longs espaces.

2616 Me f. *OaPh*, Me fist *Pc*; que *DcDfQl*. 2618 par *Db*; g.] guerdon *DbPh*, qui guerdon *Dc*. 2620 Q. que le c. v. lui t. ay *Db*: tendray *OaPh*. 2623 F. a moy s. *Dc*. 2626 P. p. griefz qune m. *Db*: Pour tant *Dc*. 2629 Si] Et si *Ph*. 2630 ou *Pc*. 2632 follement *DbDcPcQl*. 2633 d. v.] d. et v. *Dd*, deceue et v. *Df*, decepvable et v. *Db*, de ce vanter v. *Dc*. 2635 en *OaPh*. 2636 la liance *DcQl*. 2640 Haa] Ha a *Df*. 2642 douleur *DbPh*; mest *Db*. 2643 *Omitted DcOaPh*: clarte *Db*. 2644 veut *Dc*; que on voye *DcOaPh*. 2645 convoye (?) *Ql*. 2647 Se *DfOa*; lui c. *Dc*, ti envoye *DfOaPcQl*. 2648 A lonc e. *Dc*.

Qui cuidast que jamaiz osasses
Passer par la bouche ou tu passes
Sans que saulfconduit apportasses
2652   Au cuer escript?
Parler d'amant, par Jesus Crist,
C'est la copie sans escript
De ce qui est ou cuer descript
2656   Par passïon,
Dont a grant visitacïon
Verité fait collacïon
Et la bouche relacïon
2660   En la presence
De celle qui a pouoir en ce;
Si ne doit avoir difference
De ce qu'il dit a ce qu'il pense.
2664   Maiz de present
Mains font de lengage present,
En disant, "Mon cuer vous present",
Sans que le cuer s'y represent.
2668   Ainsi enchantent
Qui les croit; sans lëesce chantent,
Et s'ilz n'ont dames, ilz s'en vantent;
S'ilz les ont, sans cause les plantent,
2672   Ou par contreuve   48v
Les blasment, sans y savoir preuve.
Et tel y a, ou qu'il se treuve,
Qui chascun jour fait dame neuve;
2676   Ainsi le sçay ge.
Mentir, jurer au fuer l'emplaige
Scevent, et l'un pour l'autre est pleige.
Maiz teles amours sont de neige
2680   Tost eslacie,
Ou de glace d'une nuitie,
Qui rompt a coup par la moitie;

2651 que] ce *Ph.*   2652–5 *Omitted Oa.*   2653 pa *Pc.*   2655 au c. *DcPcPhQl*; escript *DfPh.*   2661 a p.] pourveu *Oa,* a pourveu *Ph.*   2663 dist *PcQl.*   2665 Moins *Db.*   2666 v. p.] p. *Oa.*   2667 S. ce que le c. r. *Dc*: leur c. *Ph*; se r. *PcQl.*   2668 en chantent *PcQl.*   2669 les c.] lez *Db.*   2671 les p.] ilz les p. *DcOaPhQl.*   2674 En *Df*; y a eu *Dc*; qui *Ph*; se breuve *Dc.*   2675 Fait en ch. j. d. n. *Ql*: Que *DcOa.*   2677 f. en plaige *Db.*   2678 l'a. est p.] la. p. *DcOaPhQl.*   2680 Tout *OaPhQl,* Toute *Pc*; esglacie *DcOaPcPhQl.*   2681 g. une moictie *Oa.*   2682 au c. *OaPhQl.*

S'y appuyer n'est que sotie.
2684 Et vraiement,
Leur hantise et leur voiement,
Quoy qu'ilz se habillent gaiement,
Tout est bourdes en paiement.
2688 Et se delictent
Quant les plus grans secrez recitent
Des lieux ou ilz vont et habitent.
A l'envy leurs gorges acquictent;
2692 Ja säoulees
Ne sont tant qu'ilz ont defoulees
Les dames par maises goulees
Qui sont trop de legier coulees.
2696 Tant s'esvertuent
Que d'onneur ilz les destituent;
Si sont pareulx a ceulx qui tuent,
Car jamaiz ilz ne restituent
2700 L'onneur qu'ilz tollent
Par leurs mos qui des bouches volent,   49r
Quant ainsi ensemble parolent
De leurs faiz et s'entrerigolent.
2704 Dieu me deffende
Que des bons ce parler entende!
Maiz les mauvaiz, Dieu les amende,
Ou se non leur louyer leur rende!
2708 Car ilz desirent
Que autres qui a ce mesmes tirent
Disent devant eulx qu'ilz les virent,
Ou ilz alerent et qu'ilz firent;
2712 Alors se baignent
D'aise, leur disant qu'ilz mespreignent,
Puis eulx mesmes tant en enseignent
De loing qu'il faut que tous l'appreignent.

2685 Leurs haultesses et bayement *Dc*: vaintise *Oa*, vantise *Ph*; bayement *DbDfOaPh*, beement *Ql*.
2686 qu'ilz] que *DcOaPh*; sabile *OaPh*.   2687 poyement *Pc*.   2688 si d. *Dc*.   2691 A l'e.] A lennuy
Db(?)*Qa*, A lenvie *Dc*, A leure *Ph*.   2693 ont d.] aient d. *Db*, ont (sont *Oa*) desollees *DcOaPh*, ont
descelees *Pc*.   2694 faulses *Db*, malles *DcDfPcQl*, mauvaises *OaPh*.   2695 si de l. *DfOaPcPhQl*, de
si l. *Dc*.   2697 il *Pc*.   2698 Et *Db*, Cilz *PcQl*; pareil *Df*.   2701 gueulles *Db*.   2704 men d. *DfPcPhQl*.
2705 Car de vous *Oa*; tel p. *OaPh*.   2706 des m. *Pc*.   2707 si *DbDcPh*.   2709 ces m. *Oa*, ce mesme *Dc*.
2710 Dient *Db*, Disant *OaPcQl*, Dirent *Ph*; ceulx *Ph*; qui le v. *Dc*, ilz les v. *Ql*.   2713 disans *DfPh*.
2715 la preignent *Dc*, lapprennent *Pc*.

2716 Tel est leur stile
Qu'ilz nomment la rue et la ville
Ou qu'ilz disent des signes mille,
Par quoy qui que soit y a qui le
2720 Fait tout entent,
Dont le diseur est bien content;
Car combien qu'il faint ou actent,
Si est ce la fin ou il tent.
2724 Haÿ, haÿ,
Bien a renommee enhaÿ
Qui son vent pour estre traÿ
Met es mains de telz y a y!
2728 Maiz quel vaillance
Ara homme en guerre a oultrance,
S'il ne puet avoir la constance
De tenir sa lengue en souffrance?
2732 Mal se tendroit
De fuire au peril qui vendroit,
Quant du bien qui lui advendroit
Sa lengue point ne retendroit
2736 Qu'il n'en parlast
Et que du beq ne lui volast,
Quoy que droit fust qu'il le celast
Ou que traÿtre on l'appellast.
2740 Or avison
Doncques comme une traÿson
Actrait l'autre, ainsi le dison.
Se les fuitifz bien eslison,
2744 Tantost prouvez
Seront leurs faiz mal approuvez,
Et seront ceulx fuitifz trouvez
Qui sont faulx amans esprouvez,
2748 Dont les derrois,

49v

2717 Qui n. *Pc.* 2718 Ou ilz *Dc*; dient *DbDcPcPhQl.* 2719 Par quoy qui ne scet qui le *Db*, Parquoy (Par qui *Ph*) que soit ja qui le (le guille *Oa²*) *OaPh*: qui que s.] qui s. *Pc.* 2720 tost *OaPh*; e.] en e. *Ph*, entendent *Db.* 2721 disant *Dc.* 2722 c.] bien *Ph*; fait *OaPh*; entend *Dc.* 2725 a r.] renommer *Ph.* 2726 son voit *Db*, souvent *DcDfOaPcPhQl.* 2727 tel *Df.* 2728 M. que *Oa.* 2729 a g. *Ql.* 2730 peust *PcQl.* 2731 A *Dc*; sa guerre *Oa.* 2732 Mais se deuldroit *OaPh.* 2733 a p. *OaQl.* 2735 La *OaPh.* 2736 Que *OaPh*, Qui *Pc.* 2738 qui *OaPhQl.* 2739 Et *Df*; triste *Oa.* 2743 Si *Db*; leurs fuictes *Dc*; f. b.] b. f. *Ql.* 2745 les *Db.* 2746 tous *Ql*; fainctifz *DcOa PhQl.* 2747 Et *Ql.*

Les pou arrestez desarrois,
Cuer mat soubz orgueilleux arrois,
Ont deceu et dames et roys.

2752 Et leurs pechiez,
Dont ilz sont si fort entechiez
Et aux delices allechiez,
Les ont a bien faire empeschiez,

2756 Car les delices,
Les grans oultrages et les vices,
Ou ilz sont nourriz comme nices,
Les destourbent des haulx services 50r

2760 Qui enhardissent.
Aux aises trop s'affetardissent,
Dont les cuers s'en aquouärdissent
Et les meurs en appaillardissent.

2764 Plus ne s'excercent
A voiagier ne ne conversent
Entre les bons, maiz se renversent
Par oiseuse, dont leurs faiz versent.

2768 Si di encoire
Que leur fuite laide et notoire
Aux ennemis donne victoire
Plus que la vaillance et la gloire

2772 De leurs meilleurs.
Les bons ancïens batailleurs,
Furent ilz mignoz, sommeilleurs,
Diffameurs, desloyaulx, pilleurs?

2776 Certes, nonny,
Ilz estoient bons tout onny;
Maiz pour ce est le monde honny –
Et sera encore – que on n'y

2780 A secouru,
Car Honneur a bien pou couru
Et n'y a l'en point recouru,

2749 arrester *Db.* 2750 sur *OaPh*; courroiz *Ph.* 2751 d. et d.] d. d. *Oa*, deceuz d. *Dc.* 2755 Les ont]
Les autres *OaPh.* 2758 niches *Ql.* 2759 de h. s. *Ph.* 2760 senhardissent *Db.* 2761 se festardissent
DcOa. 2762 s'en a.] se a. *OaPh.* 2763 sen a. *Ql.* 2764 ne excersent *Ql.* 2765 noiagier *Db.*
2766 reverssent *DbDc.* 2769 l. et n.] l. n. *Dc.* 2770 donnent *DcPc.* 2777 tous *DcPcPhQl.*
2778 est le m.] est tout le m. *Ql*, ce m. est *OaPh.* 2779 e. son ny *DcQl.* 2781 pour c. *Db.*
2782 a on *DcDfOaPhQl*, a non *Pc.*

Puis que le bon Bertran mouru.
2784 On a guenchié
Aux coupx, et de costé penchié.
Proufit a Honneur devanchié;
On n'a point les bons avanchié.
2788 Maiz Mignotise,   50v
Flaterie, Oultrage, Faintise,
Villain Cuer paré de cointise
Ont regné avec Couvoitise
2792 Qui a tiré,
Dont tout a esté desciré
Et le bien publique empiré.
Nully ne s'est aux faiz miré
2796 Des ancïens
Qui furent sages et scïens,
Fors, courageux et pacïens,
Pourveuz aux inconvenïens.
2800 Chascun se pare
Et veult aler a la tantare;
Si semblent buhoreaulx en mare,
Qui actendent que on leur dit "Gare"
2804 Et que on les preigne
Sans aviser que on entrepreigne
A les grever, et que on appreigne
Les tours par quoy on les souppreigne,
2808 Lÿant leurs eles.
Plusieurs dancent les sautereles,
Et pour gaaignier grosses mereles
Deffendent les faulses quereles,
2812 Et s'abandonnent
A servir ceulx qui plus leur donnent
Et qui a mal faire s'ordonnent;
Et puis les princes leur pardonnent
2816 Et mieulx venuz

2785 coulx *Df*, corps *Ph*; planche *Df*.   2789 O.] o. et *Ql*, oultragieuse *Ph*.   2791 rene *Dc*.   2792 atise *Oa*.   2795 cest *Dc*.   2798 Fort *Dc*.   2799 Pourveu *OaPh*.   2800 sen p. *Db*.   2801 Qui v. a. a lentare *Dc*.   2802 Et *DcOaPh*; semble *Ph*; bigoreux *Oa*, bouberiaux *Pc*, vitoreaux *Ph*, b teriaux (*sic*) *Ql*.   2803 dit] dire *Db*, die *DcOa*.   2804 Ou *Db*.   2806 ne *Dc*; que on] cous *Ql*.   2807 pour *DcOa* *PcPhQl*.   2808 Lient leurs (*sic*) *Pc*: Lient *DcOaPhQl*.   2809 Plusent *Db*; chanterelles *OaPh*.   2811 leurs *Dc*.   2814 se donnent *Oa*.   2815 les] leurs *DcOa*, leur *Ph*.

Sont que ceulx qui se sont tenuz
Loyaulx, et tousjours maintenuz
Les droiz qu'ilz ont bien soustenuz.
2820 Ainsi regente
Fortune sans chemin ne sente:
Puis d'un costé, puis d'autre vente;
Si a en telz faiz pou d'actente.
2824 Haa! Fleur de Lis
Ou Dieu mist pieça ses delis,
Ainsi comme en escript le lis,
Ton nom n'est pas ensevelis
2828 Ne n'es deffaicte
Par Deshonneur ou contrefaicte,
Car ceulx de ta maison te ont faicte
Honneur par vaillance parfaicte,
2832 Dont ja en cendres
Sont les uns. Ceulx que tu engendres,
Les haulx princes piteux et tendres,
S'y sont mieulx portez que les mendres,
2836 Car enferrez,
Navrez, batuz et aterrez,
Et des mors couvers et serrez,
Furent tous, prins ou enterrez.
2840 Chascun happa
Sa hache et oultre se frappa,
Maiz Fortune les atrappa:
Des royaulx nul n'en eschappa,
2844 Car sans tourner
Le doz afin de retourner,
Voulurent la tous sejourner   5ıv
Pour leurs hers d'onneur äourner;
2848 Si rencontrerent
Si mal que leur vie y oultrerent.
Haa, fuitifz! Ilz se demoustrerent
Si bons que vo honte moustrerent!

2820 Et r. Db.   2824 Haa] Ha a DfOaPcPhQl.   2828 nest Dc.   2829 ne DbDcOaPcPhQl.   2830 te ont]
dont Oa.   2832 encendrez Oa.   2836 en serrez Ph.   2837 N. b.] B. n. PcQl; enterrez Dc.   2838 de m. Dc
PcPhQl.   2839 et DcOaPhQl; atterres Dc.   2843 nulz Dc.   2844 Cart (?) Ph.   2845 Les dos DcOaPcQl.
2846 V. larrons s. Ph.   2848 encontrerent DcOaPcPhQl.   2849 leurs vies o. OaPh; ilz o. Ql.   2850 Haa
f.] Ha a f. DfOaPcQl, Ha ha fuitif Ph, Ha fuites Dc.   2851 Omitted Oa: leur h. Db, voz hontes DcPcPhQl.

283

2852 Or rougissiez
De honte et de jour hors n'yssiez,
Car certes se rien vaulsissiez,
Si bons princes ne lessissiez,
2856 Qui deffendirent
Le champ et bien chier se vendirent;
Maiz les failliz quouärs fendirent
Les rengs quant a fuite tendirent
2860 Au desplachier,
Sans oncques espee y sachier.
Si n'y avoit il qui cachier
Les peust a la pointe d'achier,
2864 Maiz ilz casserent
L'ordonnance et oultrepasserent;
Leur honneur derrier eulx lesserent
Et leurs lignages abesserent.
2868 Que leur feïssent,
Ou quele injure leur deïssent
Leurs ancesseurs s'ilz les veïssent
Ainsi fuÿr? Bien les haÿssent
2872 De mors ameres
Leurs notables aieulx et peres,
Dont les vaillances sont si cleres;
Et ceulx cy sont droictes commeres.   52r
2876 Nous ne croions
Jusques a ce que nous voions,
Maiz je doubt que bon eur n'aions
Tant que plains de pechié soions.
2880 Raison rompue
Est si par vie corrompue
Que qui a robe derompue,
Se on est bon, si pert il que on pue
2884 Entre les gens,

2852 rougisses *DcDfOaQl.* 2853 et h. de j. *OaPh,* et de j. point *Pc*; nyssez *DbDcDfOaQl.* 2854 si *Dc*; vaulsissez *Df.* 2855 Vos p. pas ne l. *Dc*: Voz *OaPh*; laississez *DfOaQl.* 2857 se y v. *Dc,* sen v. *Oa.* 2859 a fouir *Dc.* 2861 e.] espees *Oa.* 2862 a. y *Df*; que *Ph*; chacher *Ql.* 2863 Le p. *Df*; a lespee *Ql.* 2867 leur lignage *Oa.* 2868 Qui *OaPh.* 2869 Oncques i. *OaPh,* Ou quaucune i. *Dc.* 2870 a.] antecesseurs *Db*; sil *Pc,* se *Df.* 2872 mort *Ph.* 2874 chieres *OaPh.* 2878 M. je d.] M. je doubte *DcOaPh,* Je doubte *Df*; bon eur] bien *Dc.* 2879 T. com *Df*; plain *Pc*; pl. de p.] tous pl. nous (nous en *Ph*) *OaPh*; pechies *DbDcQl.* 2881 Et *Ph*; vie] voye *Ql,* voye et *Pc.* 2883 Sil est *DcOaPh*; p. il] p. *Dc,* p. il *Dc²*; quil pue *Dc,* com pire *Ph.*

Soient conseilliers ou regens,
Dont chascun est moins diligens
D'acquerir vertuz que habis gens.
2888 Ainsi despent
Uns homs trop plus qu'a lui n'appent
En robe et ce qui en deppent;
Si s'endebte et puis s'en repent.
2892 C'est la semille:
S'il a dame riche, il la pille
Et faut qu'el le veste et habille;
Cil s'en moque et elle s'exille.
2896 J'en sçay de tieulx
Qui ont dames en mains hostieulx,
Dont ilz tirent les grans chatieulx
Et leur sont ennemis mortieulx,
2900 En n'en tenant
Loyauté ne le remenant.
C'est des amans de maintenant,
Trop plus gengleurs qu'entreprenant.
2904 Parmy la rue   52v
Chevauchent la voie pierrue,
Chascun a chascune l'oeil rue;
Si font ensemble une charue
2908 Mal atelee
Et vont la teste escervelee.
Chascune est meschante appellee;
Ja n'y ara chose celee.
2912 S'ilz cheminoient
Par cent rues, toutes guignoient;
Et celles qui pas ne les haient
Ne croient mie qu'elles n'aient
2916 Leur cuer entier,
Dont toutes n'ont pas un quartier.

2885 courtilliers Oa.   2886 mains Pc.   2887 qua viz g. Oa, qua vie g. Ph.   2889 Uns h.] Ung h. Oa, Ungs Db.   2890 robes Dc; despent DcOaPc.   2891 p. semprent Df.   2893 Cil Db.   2894 Il Ph; qu'el le v.] quelle le v. DbOaQl, que le v. Df, quelle v. Ph.   2895 Il Df, Si OaPcQl, Sil Ph; celle Db.   2897 et OaPh; hostelz Db.   2898 tindrent Oa; chastelz Db, chastieux Oa.   2899 leurs DcDd; mortelz Db.   2900 Et DcPc; ne t. Db, non t. DcPc.   2902 les a. Ql.   2903 jangleur DfOaPh; que reprenant Oa.   2905 Chevauchant DcPh.   2907 Ilz Dc; sont Ph.   2909 asservellee Ph.   2910 marchande OaPh.   2912 Si ch. OaPh.   2913 g.] guigneroient DcPcPhQl.   2914 ne le h. Oa, ne hayoient Db.   2915 quelle na. Db, que tous na. Dc.

Helaz, l'onnourable mestier
D'armes n'a de telz gens mestier,
2920   Car tout tauxé
Oncques puis ne fut exaulcé
En France, suyvy ne haucé.
Que tant ont en amours faulsé
2924   Les deffaillans,
Car se hystoires ne sont faillans,
Vraie amour fait les cuers vaillans,
Entrepreneurs et assaillans
2928   Semblablement!
Ilz vivent veritablement
Et a tous aggrëablement,
S'ilz aiment honnourablement.
2932   Assez acquiert
Qui en a ce que honneur requiert;
Maiz de trop fier baston la fiert,
Qui de deshonneur la seurquiert
2936   En la servant.
C'est un service en desservant,
Et me semble que un tel servant
Est de tout perdre deservant
2940   Quant envaÿr
Veult l'onneur sa dame et traÿr.
Trop moins semble amer que haÿr;
Ce n'est pas amour maiz aÿr.
2944   Las on en use
Present ainsi que d'une ruse.
Pou voy qui s'y boute ou amuse
Fors s'il n'a que faire ou s'il muse.

53r

2918 honnourable *DbPc*, larronnable *OaPhQl*, le dames ja *Dc*. 2919 Nont de telz gens ne a besongner *Dc*. 2920 Quen toute cause *OaPh*: Quant *PcQl*. 2921 O. p.] O. depuis *OaPh*, Onq de puis *PcQl*; e.] en fause *Oa*, sause *Ph*. 2922 suuy *Db*, se il *OaPh*, suy *Ql*; ny h. *Dc*, neshauce *Dd*. 2923 Qui *DcOaPh*; ont leur amour *Dc*, ont leurs amours *Ql*, ont leur honneur hausse *OaPh*. 2925 se h.] si h. *Dc*, se les h. *Oa*, se histoire *Ph*. 2927 Entreprenans *DcOaPcPhQl*. 2928 semblalement *Pc*. 2931 Sil *Ql*. 2933 que h.] h. *Ph*. 2934 *Omitted DcOaPhQl*, Mais vers sa dame trop enquiert *Db*, Car foleur vers sa damme quiert *Df*, Et son enuy et honte quiert *Pc*. 2935 le s. *OaPcPh*. 2935a Sans coup ferir a mort se fiert *DcOaPh*, Sa desplaisance par droit quiert *Ql*. 2936 le *OaPh*. 2937 s. en d.] s. d. *OaPhQl*. 2938 que un tel] que tel *Dc*. 2938–9 *Omitted OaPh*. 2941 honneur *DcPcQl*; d. et t.] d. t. *Ql*. 2943 *Omitted Ph*: Cest nest *Df*; pas a.] a. *Dd*, pas amer *PcQl*. 2945 A p. comme dune r. *Dc*: aussy *Pc*. 2946 Pou voit *Db*, Pour veoir *Oa*, Pour vray *Ph*; sen b. *Dc*, se b. *OaPc Ql*; et a. *Oa*, ou abuse *Dc*. 2947 *Omitted Db*: F. s'il] F. qui *Dc*, F. que sil *Ph*; ou qui m. *Dc*.

2948 Comme qu'il voise,
Ilz veulent amer a leur aise
Et que on face ce qui leur plaise;
Et qui veult en ait la mesaise.

2952 Maiz s'ilz entendent
Bien qu'est amours quant ilz y tendent,
Les plaisans ennuis qu'amours rendent
Les cuers afferment et amendent.

2956 Cil qui y ferme
Son cuer, il le trempe et afferme,
Et a mieulx souffrir le conferme,
Dont il est en tous cas plus ferme

2960 Et asseuré,
Rassiz de meurs et meüré,
Ne trop baut ne trop espeuré,
Et en bataille bien euré;

2964 Et qui pener
Se scet a amours demener,
Trop mieulx en sara assener
A ses besoignes bien mener.

2968 Qui bien pourcache
D'amer, celer lui faut sa cache,
Parler et maintien faut qu'il sache;
Si ne puet qu'il ne se parfache,

2972 Dont bien amez
Doivent estre et tresrenommez,
D'onneur les vrais commans nommez,
Qu'en present sont si cler semez.

2976 Or ay cuidé
Qu'Amours eust bien mon cuer guidé
En un bon non oultrecuidé;
Et il est d'onneur tout widé.

53v

2950 quil *DbOa*. 2951 Qui que en doye avoir la m. *Dc*: le m. *DfPh*. 2953 amour *PcQl*; y t.] t. *Oa*. 2954 plaisirs *Oa*. 2955 Le cuer *Oa*. 2956 Cil qui a afferme *Oa*. 2957 il le t.] il t. *DcOa*, y t. *Ph*; latrempe *Df*. 2959 en t. cas] en t. *Oa*. 2961 et mesure *DcOaPhQl*. 2962 hault *DfOaPh*, chault *Pc*; espure *Ph*, mesure *Oa*. 2963 cure *Oa*. 2964 que *OaPh*; prener *Oa*. 2965 a a.] en a. *Dc*, a. *Oa*. 2967 Et *Ql*; b.] besoings et *OaPh*. 2969 Dame *DfPcPhQl*. 2970 maintien *Dc*; face *Dc*. 2971 Sil *Dc*, Cil *Oa*; si p. *Df*. 2973 t.] renommes *DcOaPh*. 2974 amans *DcDfOaPcPh*, amis *Ql*. 2975 Quant *DfOaPh*, Qua *PhQl*, Qui *Dc*; clers *DcDf*. 2976 Ore (Ore ny *Ph*) c. *OaPh*. 2977 Quamour eust lieu mon c. g. *Dc*, Quant amours e. b. g. *Oa*: b.] b. a *Ph*. 2978 Et *Oa*. 2979 tant *OaPh*.

2980 Point n'affermast
Mon cuer que tousjours ne l'amast?
Or est il, qui bien le nommast,
Le plus faulx qu'oncques Dieu fourmast.

2984 Souspirs gectoit
Au partir, et sa main mectoit
En la mienne, et me promectoit
Que de son cuer se desmectoit

2988 Et tant feroit
Pour moy que nouvelle en seroit
En bien, plus que on ne penseroit,
Ou jamaiz il ne cesseroit. 54r

2992 Et me disoit
Qu'a autre chose ne visoit
Qu'a moy plaire, et tant me prisoit
Qu'a son cuer garder m'eslisoit.

2996 Lors m'acola,
Maiz le mal gueres n'affola
Son cuer qui bien loing s'en vola.
Ainsi de moy se rigola,

3000 Qui effraiee
Fuz pour lui, triste et esmaiee,
Plaine de päour, desvoiee;
Et së il m'eust veü noiee,

3004 Ne l'eust chalu.
Or fuÿt quant ferir falu;
L'amour de moy riens n'y valu
Et son honneur fut nonchalu.

3008 Tout sain sans plaie
S'en revint, dont il faut que j'aie
Contrecuer et que plus je haie
Cellui que sur tous plus amoie.

3012 Et depuis l'ay ge
Veu souvent, dont mon mal aggreige,

2981 qua t. *DfPcPhQl*; mamast *DcDfOaPcPhQl*. 2982 b. ne mamast *Oa*. 2985 a sa m. *Ph*. 2987 me d. *Db*. 2990 Et *DcOaPcPhQl*. 2995 garde *Ph*. 2998 Son c. que (c. qui *Ph*) si b. sen v. *OaPh*. 3000 e.] effraye *Pc*, effacee *OaPh*. 3001 esmaye *Pc*. 3002 p.] p. et *PcPh*, plours et *Dc*, plour et *Ql*; desvaye *Pc*. 3003 veu n.] veue n. *DfOaPhQl*, veu toute n. *Dc*, veue naye *Pc*. 3004 Ne luy eust ch. *Dc*. 3005 Au fort qu. fuir (fuir a *Ph*) f. *OaPh*. 3010 p. se h. *Dc*, p. nen h. *Ph*, je p. h. *DbDf*. 3011 qui *DcQl*; sus *Pc*. 3012 laage *Oa*. 3013 engrege *DcDfOaPcPhQl*.

Car l'esloignier le cuer soulleige
Et le veÿr est une engreige.

3016 Ainsi di fy
De mon cuer et plus ne m'y fy,
Et de guerre a mort le deffy,
Quant par lui tel folie fy

3020 Que je l'amay
Le premier, ot deux ans en may;
De lors a amer entamay,
Car onq autre ami ne clamay.

3024 Or est escheu
Qu'il m'est au commencer mescheu,
Dont Amours qui si m'a decheu
Plus ne tendra mon cuer rencheu

3028 Pour l'empirer
Et le faire ainsi souspirer,
Se jamaiz l'en puis retirer.
Si me puis en mon fait mirer:

3032 Bien doit savoir
Qu'il fait, qui pour amie avoir
Fait de son cuer autry avoir;
Le fort est quant vient au ravoir

3036 Un cuer loié.
Pourquoy l'ay ge dont desploié
Pour se trouver si forvoié,
Quant je ne l'ay mieulx emploié?

3040 Assez me paine
D'oublïer tout pour estre saine,
Maiz je ne puis pour nulle paine
Oster ne l'amour ne la haine.

3044 L'amour assise
Y est de long temps fort esprise;
Son meffait y a haine mise:

54v

3014 folege *Oa*. 3015 le v. mest *DcOaPh*. 3016 diz sy *Ph*. 3017 ne me fy *OaQl*. 3019 telle f.
Db. 3020 Quant *Dc*. 3021 ot] et *Db*, ont (?) *Pc*; d. ans a moy *Ql*. 3022 Des *DcOaPcPhQl*; que a.
Db; lentamay *Dc*, mentamay *Oa*, enterinay (?) *Ql*. 3023 onq] oncques *Db*. 3027 c. r.] r. *DbDdDf*,
c. receu *Dc*, receu *OaPh*. 3031 men p. *Oa*; a *Dc*. 3033 que *OaPh*, quant *Dc*; amy *DbDcDfOaPcPh*
Ql. 3035 Leffort *Oa*. 3036 lye *Dc*. 3037 lay doncques d. *Ql*, lay je ainsy d. *Dc*; employe *OaPh*.
3038 ce t. *Oa*. 3039 Qu. je nay m. e. *Oa*. 3041 Doubler *Oa*. 3042 Dont je ne p. pas n. p. *Dc*.
3045 des *Ph*. 3046 paine *Oa*.

A les oster est la maistrise.

3048 S'amant s'esloigne
Ou qu'il meurt en haulte besoigne,   55r
L'onneur la loyauté tesmoigne;
Maiz je pers le mien en vergoigne

3052 Honteusement,
Villené treshideusement.
Les autres sont piteusement
Prins, ou mors vertüeusement

3056 Pour la couronne;
Et quoy qu'il soit de la personne,
Au moins la renommee bonne
Demeure, qui pour vie sonne.

3060 Maiz plus grevant
Est le mal que vois recevant:
Vif et sain, je pers mon servant
Et son honneur qui va devant,

3064 Car en ouvrant,
Son deshonneur est descouvrant
Par estre laschement ouvrant.
Je le pers en le recouvrant:

3068 La recouvrance
Honteuse en est la delivrance;
Recouvrer en est dessevrance,
Si suy de ma foy delivre en ce.

3072 Doncques n'a coulpe
Mort en mon deul – je l'en descoulpe.
Prison la voie ne m'estouppe
De le vëoir. Si n'en encoulpe

3076 Nul que moy lasse
Qui mieulx vëoir la mort amasse
Qu'il faillist que ainsi le blasmasse;   55v
Maiz tel le boit qui tel le brasse.

3048 Souvent *OaPh*; s'e.] eslongne *Oa*.   3049 quel *Ph*; m.] mourust *Db*.   3051 a v. *OaPhQl*, v. *Dd*. 3053 Et villenee hideusement *OaPh*; treshonteusement *Dd*.   3055 mort *Dc*.   3058 Amours *Ph*. 3059 que p. une s. *OaPh*.   3062 et serf *OaPh*.   3065 et *PhQl*.   3066 Pour *Dc*.   3070 Recouvert *Dc*, Retourner *OaPh*; decepvance *DcOaPcPhQl*.   3071 Fy fais *Ph*; delivrance *DfOaPh*.   3072 ma *Db DcPh*, nest *Oa*.   3074 me (ne *Dc*) descoulpe *DbDc*.   3075 si non en coulpe *Dc*, si nen eu coulpe *Df*.   3077 Que *Oa*, Car *Ph*; v. la m.] le v. m. *DcPc*, v. le m. *Ql*; lamasse *PcQl*.   3078 fausist *DcOa PcPhQl*.   3079 voit *DfQl*; qui ne le b. *Ph*.

3080 Si hay moy meismes
Et tous les mos que oncques deïsmes
Ou lieu ou premier nous veïsmes,
Et les cuers qu'en Amours meïsmes,

3084 Les souvenances,
Les pensers et les couvenances,
Les regars et les contenances,
Dont je porte les griefz penances,

3088 Se dire l'oz,
Quant depuis le temps qu'amé l'oz,
Ne m'en demeure part ne loz
D'onneur, de joie ne de loz.

3092 Dont sans faulx tour,
Qui pert en champ son servitour,
L'onneur, la bonté, la haultour
Qui demeure, abat la tristour.

3096 Or n'ay confort,
Ains le pers piz que s'il fust mort;
Si di que mon mal est plus fort
Et vueil jugement se j'ay tort.'

3100 'Or en jugiez',
M'a dit la tierce, 'et abregiez
Le debat, et vous en chargiez;
Maiz gardez bien que comprengiez

3104 Les droiz de toutes
Et laquele est en plus grans doubtes,
Qui sue sang a plus grans goutes,
Quant toutes voies lui sont rouptes.   56r

3108 Au renouvel,
La premiere en fin de l'anvel,
Pour recouvrer joie et revel,
Sans tort puet faire ami nouvel.

3112 La quarte peut

3080 Sy hes *Db*, Si ay *DcOaPh*; mesmes *DbDdOaPh*. 3081 maulx *Ph*; o.] onq *Pc*. 3082 Eu l. *Db*, Le l. *OaPcPhQl*; venismes *Ph*. 3083 qu'en] qui en *Dc*. 3085 p.] pencees *DbOaPh*; les c.] c. *Dc*, les contenances *DbPc*. 3086 couvenances *DbPc*. 3087 les g. p.] griefves p. *Db*. 3088 De *Ph*. 3089 los (?) *Ql*. 3090 me d. *Db*; pars *Df*. 3092 D. s. retour *DcQl*, D. soit fauteur *Df*, D. cest (D. fait *Ph*) faulseur *OaPh*, D. seyt (?) facteur *Pc*. 3093 son ch. *Oa*. 3096 Je *Db*. 3097 pert *Pc*. 3099 si *Dc*. 3101 Sa dit *Dc*, Ha dist *Dd*, A dit *Ph*; or a. *Db*. 3103 compaigniez *Ph*. 3105 p. grant d. *DcDfOa*, greigneurs d. *Db*. 3106 Qui sue le s. a g. g. *Df*: a grosses g. *DcOaPhQl*. 3109 en suis *OaPh*, est fui *Dc*; launel *Dc*. 3111 Et s. t. f. *DcOaPh*; peust *PcQl*. 3112 La qu. le p. *Db*: peust *PcQl*.

Le faire si tost qu'elle veult;
Et se la seconde se deult,
En espoir son vray dueil requeult.

3116 Maiz moy lassete,
Vif ou mort, mon las cuer regrete,
Dont puet estre j'aime seulete
Et si n'est droit qu'ailleurs le mecte.

3120 Sans rien celer,
Je ne me puis, a brief parler,
Ne d'amy pourveue appeller,
Ne changier ne renouveler.

3124 Pensez cela.'
Lors la premiere m'appella
Et ses raisons renouvela,
De la faucte d'espoir qu'elle a

3128 D'avoir jamaiz
Joie, plaisir, ayse ne paix,
Car trouver ne pourroit si vrais,
Tant noble, tel ne si parfaiz

3132 Que Mort lui oste,
Si a prins Desespoir pour hoste;
Les autres ont Espoir de coste.
Et si m'a priẽ que je note,

3136 Ains que je couche   56v
Sentence, qu'il n'est nul reprouche,
Prison ne perte si farouche
Que la mort trop plus ne courouche;

3140 Ce sont entroignes
D'y comparer autres besoignes
Ou il a conseil ou aloignes,
Car Mort n'a remede n'exoignes

3144 En nulz endroiz.

3113 F. si t. comme elle v. *Dc*: Le f.] F. *Db*; puet *Oa*. 3114 Et se] Et si *Dc*, Et *Oa*; sen d.
OaPh, se deust *Db*. 3115 requeust *Db*, receut *DfOa*. 3116 l.] la chacte *Oa*, la tierce *Ph*.
3117 doulx c. *DfOaPh*, c. le *Dc*, amy *Db*. 3118 peust *PcQl*; j'a.] samye *Db*. 3119 droitz *DcPhQl*.
3122 Ne dame p. mappeller *Db*: a parler *Df*. 3124 Penser *Oa*; ce la *DfPc*. 3127 Et *Ph*; feaulte
Oa. 3130 ny p. *Dc*. 3131 Si n. *DbDcDfOaPcPhQl*. 3134 ont E.] e. ont *Pc*; de c.] par de c. *OaPh*.
3135 Si ma priee que je n. *OaPh*. 3136 touche *DcOaPcPhQl*. 3137 S. que nulle nait r. *OaPh*: qui
DbDcDf; nait *DbDc*. 3139 Qua *Ph*; me c. *DcOaPh*. 3140 Et *Dc*. 3141 De c. *DcOaPcPhQl*.
3142 et *DcOaPh*; esloingnes *OaPcPh*. 3143 ne r. *Oa*; nexoynes *Db*, ne soingnes *DcDfOa*. 3144 nul
Df.

'Pour Dieu', dist el, 'Jugiez a droiz
Et soit vostre parler si droiz
Que gardez y soient mes droiz.'

3148 Ainsi avoie
Tant a ouÿr par mainte voie
Que ne sceu que faire devoie,
N'a qui entendre ne savoie.

3152 L'une parloit,
L'autre se plaignoit et douloit;
Des yeulx mainte lerme couloit.
Chascune respondre vouloit:

3156 Leurs faiz disoient
Et la bataille maudisoient
Toutes; les fuites desprisoient,
En löant ceulx qui mors gesoient

3160 Ou asserviz
Es prisons ou ilz sont serfz vifz,
Desquelz le roy fut bien serviz.
Ceulx ont les grans biens deserviz

3164 Et n'en joÿssent.
Tant dirent que se les ouÿssent
Les fuitifz, point ne s'esjouÿssent;
Et croy que jamaiz ne fouÿssent,

3168 Ains demandassent
Pardon, et leurs pouoirs mandassent
En tant que leurs faiz amendassent
Et aux bons se recommandassent.

3172 La blasonnez
Furent et leurs faiz hault sonnez
Ainsi que gens abandonnez
Ou a l'eschauffaut sermonnez.

3176 Et s'embuschié
En fust un auprés bien muchié,

57r

3145 P. D.] P. ce *Dc*, P. *Pc*; el] elle *DbOaPhQl*. 3146 si vrais *OaPh*. 3149 par] et par *Db*. 3150 nay s. *Dc*; s. quel part je d. *Ql*. 3153 p.] complaignoit *Oa*, complaint *Pc*. 3154 mainctes lermes *DcOa*. 3158 *Omitted Oa*, T. les fuitifz maudissoient *Ph*. 3161 En prison *DbOaPh*; ilz s.] ilz *Db*. 3162 fust *OaPcPh*. 3165 T. d.] T. (Et t. *Ph*) diceulx *OaPh*; si *Dc*, silz *Db*. 3169 l. amis *DcOaPh*, leur povair *Pc*. 3170 Et *DcPh*; leur fait *Oa*. 3173 l. haulx f. s. *OaPcPhQl*, l. meffaiz s. *Dc*. 3175 Et en *DcOaPcPhQl*; les chauffaux *Dc*. 3176 Et subverchie *OaPh*. 3177 Et *OaPh*; lun *Ql*; anpres *Pc*, empres *DfOaPh*; ou m. *Dc*, ung m. *OaPh*.

N'eust voulu pour une duchié
Qu'on l'eust apperceu ne huchié.
3180 Ains pouez crerre
Que pour honte de ceste guerre,
S'aler ne s'en peüst grant erre,
Se muchast volentiers en terre,
3184 Car l'une en dist
Que ce fust bien, qui les pendist,
Et l'autre que nul n'entendist
A eulx, et que on leur deffendist
3188 Les lieux honnestes,
Les cours, les jouxtes et les festes,
Et que jamaiz ne fussent prestes
Dames d'escouter leurs requestes,
3192 Maiz defuÿs
Fussent sans avoir nulz refuis,
Et de tous fussent ceulx fuÿs   57v
Qui s'en sont du champ enfuÿs
3196 Com negligent;
Et du roy de France regent
Ont ceulx comme refuz de gent
Grevé l'onneur et prins l'argent.
3200 Tantost me tire
La seconde en disant: 'Beau sire,
Entendez que je vous vueil dire.
Je croy que ce que je desire,
3204 Vous desirez
Et que je tire ou vous tirez.
Quant sentence pour moy direz,
Croiez que point ne mentirez.
3208 Vous savez bien
Et pour quel cas et puis combien
Nous n'eusmes en France nul bien.

3179 neust *Oa*; ou h. *Dc.*   3181 hoste *Oa.*   3182 S'a.] Si aler *Dc*; p.] puet *OaPh.*   3183 m.] mussassent *Oa.*   3185 Ce f. b. fait que on les p. *Dc*, Ce f. (Ce feust *Ph*) b. quon (b. que on *Pc*) les p. *OaPcPh*: con les p. *Ql.*   3186 nattendeist *Db*, ne tendist *OaPcPhQl.*   3187 A ceux *Dc*; mais quon *Db.*   3189 tours *Ph.*   3190 prestres *Ph.*   3193 nul r. *DbDc.*   3194 Car *OaPh*; furent *Oa*; c. f.] c. deffuiz *Ql.*   3195 Qui laschement sen s. fuys *Dc*: affuiz *Db.*   3196 Comme n. *Db.*   3198 Ou *OaPh.*   3199 Grevent *Oa*; honneur...argent *Dc*; et puis *Oa.*   3200 T.] Atant *DcOaPcPhQl*, Tant *Df.*   3202 E. ce que v. v. d. *DcDfOaPcPhQl.*   3205 je t.] t. *OaPcPh.*   3209 et pour c. *Df.*   3210 N. meismes *Ph.*

Chascun scet don ce vient, combien
3212 Que on dissimule
Et que on fuit au fait et recule;
Maiz joie n'arons, nul ne nulle,
Tant com France soit incredule
3216 Et tant que on voit
Ainsi qu'au premier on devoit.
Peuple croit, se on l'appercevoit,
Plus mensonges que ce que on voit;
3220 Ainsi deboutent
Verité, et droit ne redoubtent.
Les trouveurs des bourdes escoutent,
Qui en sediciön les boutent.   58r
3224 Lors amusez
Sont les simples et abusez
Par gens en mauvaistié rusez,
Et pour leurs delis refusez
3228 Occasiön
Leur donnent par decepciön
Et faulse machinaciön
De querir leur destructiön
3232 Et ledengier
Cil qui pour bien est en dangier,
Duquel, pour eulx a tort vengier,
Vouldroient bien le cuer mengier,
3236 En destruisant
L'innocent de vertuz luisant
Et en tout honneur reluisant,
Qui onq a nul ne fut nuisant;
3240 Maiz envaÿs
A esté par les faulx naÿs
Ou plas justiciers des païs,
Grevé a tort et puis haïs.

3211 dont *DbDcDfOaPcPhQl*.   3214 navons *Db*.   3215 T. que *DcDfOaPcPhQl*.   3218 P. c. sans apparcevoir *Oa*, P. sans aparcevoir c. *Ph*, Sans apparcevoir p. c. *Dc*: se on] sen *Pc*, si *Ql*.   3219 mensonge *OaPhQl*; se *Ph*.   3221 me r. *Ph*, ne deboutent *Db*.   3222 de b. *DbDcOaPcPhQl*.   3223 en sedicions le b. *Df*.   3226 a *DcDfOaPcPhQl*; mauvaisties *DcOaPhQl*.   3227 debaz *Oa*, deblatz *Ph*.   3229 *between* 3231 and 3232 *Db*.   3233 ou d. *OaPh*.   3235 V.] Vouldroit *Oa*.   3236 Et *Dc*.   3237 vertu *Dc*.   3238 toute h. *PcQl*.   3239 Qui onq] Que (Qui *Oa*) onques *DcOa*; luysant *Dc*.   3241 le f. n. *Ph*.   3242 plus *DbDcDfOaPcPhQl*; du pays *DcQl*.   3243 Grevant *Dc*, Grevez *Ph*.

3244 Et la l'a mis
Fortune a qui il est soubmis,
Qu'il n'a peu vivre o les amis.
Or est prins de ses ennemis;

3248 Si apperroit
Quë air et terre le herroit
Et Fortune sa mort querroit,
Quant vivre en paix ne le lerroit.

3252 Oncques ne sceut
Que fut joie ne point n'en eut;
Et se avoir la voult, il ne peut
Pour les nouveaulx maulx qu'il receut

3256 Et qu'il reçoit.
Ses maulx un chascun apperçoit,
Dont mon cuer tout autant reçoit;
Qui dit qu'il a piz, se deçoit.

3260 La mort neü
Nous a. Le cas est congneü;
Estre ne puet descongneü.
Onq en France tel cas n'a eu.

3264 Autres dommages:
Desloyauté, faucte d'ommages,
Perte d'amis et d'eritages,
Males paroles, faulx lengages,

3268 Blasmes tixus
Qu'a grand tort lui a l'en mis sus.
Or est en prison par dessus,
Dont encor n'est il pas yssus.

3272 Si vous souvieigne
De mon droit, et plus n'en couvieigne
Parler, car quoy que nul maintieigne,
J'ay le droit, si faut qu'il me vieigne.'

3245 cest s. *Dc*, a s. *Oa*, sest s. *Ph*.   3246 Qui *DcOaPh*; ses *DcDfOaPcPhQl*.   3248 Sil *Dc*; apperoit
DcOaPh.   3249 Que ciel et t. *Dc*; haroit *Oa*, hayoit *Ph*.   3250 la m. queroit *OaPh*.   3250–1 *Omitted*
Df.   3251 le l.] le lairoit *Oa*, lairoit *Ph*.   3253 ne joye neut *DbDcDfOaPcPhQl*.   3254 Et si savoir
v. *Dc*; le *OaPcQl*; veult *OaPh*.   3255 Par *PcQl*.   3257 Ses m. ch. bien a. *Db*.   3258 c. a. en r.
DcOaPh.   3259 dechoit *Ql*.   3260 veu *Ph*.   3261 et c. *DcOaPh*.   3262 peust *PcQl*.   3263 Onq]
Oncques *DbDcOaPh*; n'a eu] neu *DcDfOaPh*.   3265 faultes *Pc*.   3266 Pertes *PcPhQl*; et d'e.] de
heritaiges *Ph*.   3267 Faulses *DbDcDfOaPcPhQl*.   3269 De menconges (De menconge *Df*) lui courent
sus *DcDfOaPcPhQl*.   3271 D. encores (encore il *Pc*) nest pas y. *DcPc*: e.] encore *DbOa*.   3272 Et
Df.   3273 ne c. *Df*.   3274 car quoy] par quoy *Dc*, quoy *OaPh*.   3275 sil *OaPh*; qui *Ql*.

3276 Bien avisay
Son grant couroux et y visay,
Maiz la grant amour moult prisay
Qu'en ceste dame compris ay.

3280 Tant fut loyale
Que Fortune si dure et male
Ne puet amenrir son cuer pale
Vers s'amour tresespecïale.

3284 Et pour ce mentent
Ceulx qui dïent et qui consentent
Que quelque amour que dames sentent,
Tousjours de changier se dementent.

3288 Tel genglerie
Est contreuve par moquerie,
Car amour est sans menterie
Par hommes plus souvent perie,

3292 Et moins fëables
Y sont. Hommes tiennent leurs fables
De ce que femmes sont müables,
Maiz monstrez se sont varïables

3296 Trop plus que dames,
Et de conscïences et d'ames,
Puis dix ans dont ilz sont infames
Et trouvez moins fermes que fames

3300 En leur devoir.
On l'a peu en France savoir;
Tournez se sont avec l'avoir
Et n'ont pas ensuÿ le voir.

3304 Puis en bataille
S'en sont fuÿs comme peautraille,
Monstrans que d'onneur ne leur chaille
Et qu'en eulx loyauté deffaille.

3308 Or se teüssent

3277 et advisay *OaPh.*   3279 Quant *DcOa.*   3281 et m.] et si m. *DbOaPh.*   3282 peust *PcQl.*
3283 V. amours *OaPcPhQl.*   3285 et se c. *Dc.*   3286 Que qu.] Qu. *OaPh.*   3289 Est c.] Est (Et
Db) controuvee *DbPcQl*, Est tournee *OaPh*, Cest contre mont *Dc.*   3290 amours *DcOaPh.*
3291 homme *DcOa.*   3292 feable *Dc.*   3293 treuvent *DbOaPcQl*, tenans *Dc*, trouvez *Ph.*   3295 si
Dc.   3297 c. et d'a.] c. da. *Oa*, conscience et de ames *DcPh.*   3299 dames *Ql.*   3302 *Omitted OaPh:*
Trouves *Dc.*   3303 Ilz *Oa*; point *Pc.*   3304 de *Db.*   3305 fouy *Dc.*   3306 Moustrant *OaPcQl*;
damour *Oa.*

Ne blasme aux dames n'esmeüssent
De ce que deservy n'eüssent,
Se bien leurs fauctes congneüssent

3312 Et leur volage
Cuer qui passe temps en oultrage,
Don en honneur et bon courage
Pevent bien femmes l'avantage

3316 En emporter.
Ceste dame voulz conforter
Pour plus son couroux supporter,
Ne je ne m'en peu deporter.

3320 Pitié me fist
Que Fortune ainsi desconfit
Cil qui en tout bien se parfit
Et onq a autry ne meffit.

3324 Si diz: 'Aiez
Espoir, et ne vous esmaiez.
Ja Fortune trop ne haiez
Et de rien ne vous effraiez.

3328 Ne croiez point
Qu'adez soit Fortune en un point;
Et s'a present elle vous point,
Elle remectra tout a point.

3332 Et mesmement
Je tien, selon vray jugement,
Que un doulereux commencement
Monstre signe d'exaulcement;

3336 Grant grief ou perte
Sans cause est voie en bien ouverte.
Dieu ne fait souffrir sans deserte
Paine qui ne soit recouverte;

3340 Tant ne tardast
Ou sa joie ne retardast,

Se a son proufit ne regardast
Et qu'un grant bien ne lui gardast.'

3344 Lors entretant
Qu'aloie ces faiz racontant,
En la tresbonne confortant,
La quarte s'aloit dementant

3348 Tresasprement
Et dist: 'Je requier jugement
Que leurs diz et leur parlement
Ne me font point d'encombrement.

3352 Toutes trois dïent
Que les fuitifz, que tant maudïent
Et de qui a bon droit mesdïent,
Sont causes qu'en douleurs mendïent

3356 Tousjours nouvelles.
Doncques se leurs douleurs morteles
Par le fait des fuitifz sont teles,
Trop plus pres me touchent qu'a elles.'

3360 Ainsi je vis
Et me fut adoncques advis
Que ne me sceusse estre chevis
D'en jugier, et le feisse envis.

3364 Lors un point ay
Prins, en quoy je les appointay.
De leur debat me despointay;
Autre juge leur acointay

3368 Et diz en hault: 60v
'D'ouÿr mon advis ne vous chault,
Car mon savoir trop petit vault;
Maiz tel juge com il vous fault

3372 Je vous querray,
Et si au vray en enquerray
Que vostre grace y acquerray

3342 Qua son p. *Dc*. 3343 que g. b. *DcOaPh*. 3345 Qu'a.] Que jaloye *Dc*; ses *DbDcOaPh*. 3346 Et *DcOaPcPhQl*. 3347 demandant *Oa*. 3350 ne *Df*. 3351 sont *PcPh*. 3352 *Repeated Db*. 3353 fuictes *DcOaPh*; qui *Db*. 3354 Et de ce qua bon d. m. *OaPh*. 3355 cause *Dc*; douleur *DbDc DdOaPcPh*. 3357 D. sont *Dc*. 3358 fuites *OaPh*; celles *Dc*. 3359 touche *Dc*. 3362 ne me s.] me pense *Oa*, ne (?) pensay *Ph*, ne me peusse *PcQl*. 3363 Dont *Oa*; le fais e. *Dc*. 3365 je les a.] les a. *Oa*. 3370 servir *OaPh*. 3372a Que de par vous en requerray *Df*. 3374 en a. *Db*.

299

Et d'en jugier le requerray.

3376 Chascun tendroit

Que de ce qui appartendroit

Aux dames, dame en son endroit

Trop mieulx jugement en rendroit

3380 Certes que un homme,

Et mieulx entendroit quoy et comme.

Ma dame en juge je vous nomme,

Qui n'a pareille jusqu'a Romme;

3384 Et bien saira

De vous laquele droit aira

Et la verité n'en tayra.

Je demande s'il vous plaira.'

3388 D'accort en furent

Et ma dame en juge receurent,

Quant telz biens dire ouÿ m'en eurent.

Et par mon lengage apperceurent

3392 Que pour le sens

Et la doulceur qu'en elle sens,

A estre tout sien me consens;

Maiz a lui dire ne m'assens,

3396 Et si avra

Tost un an qu'Amours m'en navra.

Par mon cuer durement ouvra,   61r

Qui puis santé ne recouvra,

3400 Maiz aggreiga

Mon mal qui depuis n'alleiga

Et toute douleur m'asseiga.

'Elas, Dieux, oseray ge ja

3404 Lui dire. Oser?

Il me vauldroit mieulx reposer

Que tel folie proposer,

Car je puis assez supposer

3375 *Omitted Df*, A chascune le droit soustendray *OaPh*: len r. *Dc.* 3376 Chascune t. *Ph*, Chascune tendoit *Oa.* 3377 Et *Dd.* 3378 dame] a d. *Ph*, dont *Dc*; son e.] son droit *Oa.* 3380 C. que h. *DcOaPh.* 3382 j. et v. n. *OaPh.* 3383 Que na pareil jusques a r. *Dc*: Quil *OaPh*; nappareille *Oa.* 3386 *Omitted DdOa*: ne t. *Dc.* 3390 Quant tant de b. oiz en e. *Df*: Que *Dc*; tel bien *Ql*; d. ouÿ] d. oyr *DcQl*, oir *OaPh.* 3393 La d. (De la douleur *Ph*) que a elle s. *DfOaPh.* 3397 T.] Tantost *OaPh*; me n. *DbDcOa*, n. *Ph.* 3398 Pour *Pc*, Car *PhQl.* 3399 Que *DcOaPhQl.* 3400 engregea *DcOaPcPhQl*, en gre ja *Df.* 3402 *Omitted Ph.* 3403 D.] et d. *Ph*, dieu *Ql.* 3405 vaulsist *Dc.* 3406 tel f.] telle f. *DcOaPh.*

3408 Qu'el me feroit
Mourir quant me refuseroit;
Son treshault cuer mien ne seroit
Jamaiz, car trop s'abesseroit.

3412 Ne me chaulsist,
Maiz qu'el le sceust: trop me vaulsist,
Ne me donnast ou ne toulsist;
Et ne m'amast se ne voulsist.

3416 Moult ay esté
Pres d'elle et yver et esté,
Maiz un jour fuz admonnesté
Et lui diz de grant volenté

3420 A part, sans fainte,
Qu'amant doit estre un an en crainte
Sans oser descouvrir la plainte
De quoy sa pensee est actainte.

3424 Bien lui souvient
De ces paroles, se devient;
Maiz s'en memoire lui revient,
El scet que le bout de l'an vient.   61v

3428 Or me doint Dieux
Tant plaire une foiz a ses yeulx
Que ses vouloirs me soient tieulx
Qu'a tousjours il m'en soit de mieulx.

3432 Or est arbitre
De ce debat que j'enregistre
Et qu'a jugier lui administre.
Dieu doint qu'a honneur en puist ystre.'

3436 Tant labourerent
Et ma dame tant honnourerent
Qu'en son jugement demourerent.
Au departir de moy plourerent

3440 Et me tendoient
Les mains, et bien me commandoient

3408 Quelle me f. *DbOaPh.*   3411 labesseroit *DcOaPh.*   3413 quelle s. *DbDcDfQl,* quelle le s. *OaPcPh;* moult me v. *Db.*   3414 me t. *DbDcDfOaPcPhQl.*   3415 Ou *OaPcPhQl;* ne m'a.] me amast *Ph;* se ne v.] sel ne v. *DfPcQl,* selle ne v. *DbOaPh,* celle v. *Dc.*   3417 en y. *Dc,* y. *Df.*   3419 grat *Dc.*   3421 sans c. *Ql.*   3425 ses *DbDfPh;* ce *Db.*   3426 M. en m. *Db,* M. sans m. *OaPh;* advient *OaPh,* vient *Ql.*   3427 El s. le b. de lan revient *Ql:* Et *OaPh;* quant *Dc.*   3429 Une f. t. p. a ses y. *Dc.*   3430 telx *Ql.*   3431 me s. *Oa.*   3435 il p. *OaPh.*   3436 T. labourent *Dc.*   3437 h.] honnorent *Dc.*   3438 d.] demourent *Dc.*   3441 bie (*sic*) *Pc.*

301

Dire que se recommandoient
A elle et raison demandoient.

3444 Grant chemin fismes
Tant qu'a un quarrefour venismes
Et la endroit nous departismes,
Car plus un chemin ne tenismes.

3448 A tant tournay
De la, et plus ne sejournay.
Envers Paris m'en retournay,
Car sans y estre, bon jour n'ay.

3452 Pourtant ce livre,
Pour estre de charge delivre,
A ma dame transmet et livre,
Par qui je puis mourir ou vivre.   62r

3456 El le lira
Et pas ne les escondira,
Et puis son avis en dira;
Si sarons comme il en ira.

3460 Maiz pour enqueste
Faire du fait de quoy j'enqueste
Et trouver voie plus honneste,
Lui envoie ceste requeste

3464 Qu'escripte avoie.
'A la plus belle que je voie,
Ou j'ay en espargne ma joie
Et mon cuer, quel part que je soie,

3468 Tousjours lëesce,   62v
Vraie santé, longue jennesce,
Et vers moy monstrer sa largesce
Et vouloir d'oster ma destresce

3472 Tresdure et grande;
De quoy a vous me recommande

3442 quilz *DcPcPh*. 3444 Grans *Dc*; voye *DbDfPcPhQl*, joye *DcOa*. 3445 T. quau (T. qua *OaQl*, T. que *Ph*) chemin fourchu (chemin fourchie *OaPh*) v. *DbDcDfOaPcPhQl*. 3447 tenisme *Dc*. 3448 Adoncq *DcOaPh*. 3449 De la p. je ne s. *Dc*, Et p. ilec ne s. *Ql*. 3449–50 *Inverted Ql*. 3450 me r. *Ql*. 3451 s. la e. *Ql*. 3452 Portant *OaPh*. 3453 *Omitted Oa*, P. e. deschargie et d. *DbPcPhQl*, P. descharge e. et d. *Dc*. 3454 tremect *Oa*. 3455 *Omitted Oa*: et *DbDc*. 3456 Elle le l. *DbPc*, Elle l. *Oa*, Et le l. *Ph*. 3459 savons *Db*, savront *Dc*. 3461 du quel *Pc*; senqueste *DcOa*. 3463 e.] e. je *DbDd*. 3464 *Omitted DfOaPcPhQl*, Dieu la pourvoye *Db*, Comme a la moye *Dc*. 3465 Cest la p. b. *Db*, La tres p. b. *Dc*. 3466 Ou jay espargnee ma j. *Dc*. 3467 quelque p. que s. *DcPh*. 3469 Bonne *DcOa*, Bonte *Ph*. 3470 Envers *Dc*. 3471 v. oster *DcOaPcPhQl*; tristesse *Dc*. 3472 Tresdoure *Dc*.

Quant faire n'ose autre demande.
Il m'est commis que je demande
3476 Vostre avis, Belle,
D'une questïon bien nouvelle
Dont en ce livre la querele
J'ay mise en rime tele quele,
3480 Au long escripte;
Et se si bien ne la recite
Comment elle m'a esté dicte,
Ignorance m'en face quicte.
3484 Or la lisez
S'il vous plaist, afin que disez
De bouche, ou au moins escripsez,
Laquele plus triste eslisez
3488 De quatre amantes,
Dames belles, bonnes, savantes,
Qui sont tristes et desplaisantes
Et de leur debat requerantes
3492 Vostre sentence.
Et vous avez assez scïence;
Pour ce se sont submises en ce
Du tout a vostre conscïence.
3496 Ce hardement
J'ay prins a leur bon mandement,   63r
Car prïé m'en ont grandement,
Que je tien pour commandement
3500 Et suis tenu
D'obeïr; si l'a couvenu.
Ce message m'est advenu
Et g'y suis volentiers venu.
3504 C'est le retrait
Ou je quier joie par long trait,
Et doncques quant le cuer s'y trait,

3475 m'est c.] mest *Db*. 3478 livret *Db*. 3479 mis en r. *DbDcDſOaPcPh*. 3481 Et se (Et si *Dc*) je b. *DcOaPcPhQl*. 3482 Ainsi quelle *Dc*, Comme elle *DbOaPh*. 3484 lisiez *DſOaPcPhQl*. 3485 disiez *DbDſOaPcPhQl*. 3486 ou au m.] au m. ou *Db*; escripsiez *DbDſOaPcPhQl*. 3487 p.] est p. *DcPcPh*, est la p. *Oa*; eslisiez *DſOaPcPhQl*. 3488 Des *DbDcOaPhQl*. 3489 bo. et gentes *Oa*. 3494 su.] soubzmis *DbDcPcQl*. 3495 De *OaPcPhQl*; en *PcQl*. 3497 l. commandement *Db*. 3501 si a c. *DcOaPh*, si la conveu *Db*. 3502 Honneur en ce mest a. *Db*. 3503 Et y s. *OaPhQl*. 3504 regrait *OaPh*. 3505 je qu.] qu. *Db*. 3506 Et adoncq qu. le c. sentraict *Dc*: se t. *Ql*.

303

Les autres membres y actrait.
3508 Bien m'en vendra,
Car lors que vostre main tendra
Ce livre et lire y couvendra,
Du message vous souvendra,
3512 Qui n'a plus rien,
Si non ses douleurs, qui soit sien.
Et pourtant il desire bien
Que ce livre pour son grant bien
3516 Souvent peussiez
Veÿr, et que aussi bien leussiez
En son cuer, par quoy vous sceussiez
Quel pouoir dessuz lui eussiez
3520 Par droit acquis,
Car vostre doulceur m'a conquis
Et je n'y ay remede quis;
Amours l'a bien sceu et enquis.
3524 En gré soit pris
Ce livret pour vous entrepris,
Car se aucun bien y est compris,   63v
Ce a fait l'amour dont suis espris;
3528 Et s'ay emprise
Trop haulte ou trop fole entreprise
De moy mectre en vostre servise,
Faictes du vostre a vostre guise.'

Explicit

3507 si a. *OaPh.* 3508 me v. *Oa.* 3509 Et *DcOaPcPhQl*; quant *Dc.* 3510 il c. *Oa.* 3511 messager *Dc.* 3513 Se *Oa*; sont *Ph.* 3514 il d.] je d. *Dc*, d. il *Oa.* 3515 Quen *DcPh*; livret *Oa.* 3516 pensiez (?) *OaPh*, penses (?) *Ql.* 3517 V.] Voir *DcOa*; quainsi *DcOaPcPhQl*; sceussiez *Db*, le sceusiez *Oa.* 3518 par soy *Ph*, et que *Pc*; leussiez *Oa.* 3519 d.] sur *Oa*, de *Ql.* 3523 Amour *PcPh.* 3525 livre *Dc.* 3526 Et *DcDfOaPcPhQl.* 3527 Ce f. *DbDcOaPcPhQl*; emprins *Oa*, empris *Ph.* 3528 scay *Db.* 3529 Tres *PcQl*; h. et *DcPcQl*, hault et *OaPh.* 3531a Et me prenez *Dc²*, Comme a votre simple novice *Dd².*
...le debat (le livre *Dc²OaPc*) des quatre dames *DbDc²OaPc*, les iiij dames *Ql*, *No explicit DcDdDfPh.*

8

'*Le Debat de Reveille Matin*'

Thirty-seven Manuscripts: *Nc Nf Ng Nj Nl Nn No Nr   Oa   Pa Pb Pc Pd Pe Pf Pg Ph Pj Pk Pl Pn Po Pp   Qa Qb Qd Qe Q f Qg Q j Qk Ql Qn Qo Qp Qq Qr.*

Q j and *Qn* have not been traced and *Qp* has been damaged by fire. All the other manuscripts have been examined.

The poem was included in all the early collected editions and in the Du Chesne edition. Two separate editions apparently exist, of which only one has been traced.[1] The 1489 collected edition, the separate edition in the Rothschild library, and the Du Chesne edition have been examined.

The *Debat de Reveille Matin* is attributed to Alain Chartier in *Pa* and *Qr*, in the collected edition of 1489 from which *Pa* ultimately derives, and in the separate edition in the Rothschild library. In the other manuscripts it is anonymous. The *Debat de Reveille Matin* is edited here from seven manuscripts: *Nf Nj Oa Pc Ph Qd* and *Ql*.

In *Nf Nj Oa* and *Ph* the poem consists of forty-five stanzas, in *Pc Qd* and *Ql* of forty-six; the third stanza is not found in the texts of the first group. The *Debat de Reveille Matin* is a debate between the *Dormeur* and the *Amoureux*, who each speak in turn. The *Dormeur* speaks in stanza II and again in stanza IV, so that, if stanza III is omitted, he speaks in two successive stanzas. Again, stanza IV makes poor sense when it follows directly on stanza II. Stanza III is necessary to the poem for these reasons.

That stanza apart, *Nf* and *Nj* contain complete texts. A large number of readings (lines 33, 38, 42, 54, 74, 102, 118, 133, 144, 157 etc.) is found only in these two texts. *Nj* gives individual readings at lines 37, 227, 248, 271, 295, 305, 348, 349 and 351; it is irregular at lines 90 and 99. Readings peculiar to *Nf* occur at lines 144, 217, 227, 271, 276, 341 and 348. *Nf* is irregular at lines 149, 186, 207 and 264; at line 85 the rhyme is poor.

Oa and *Ph*, which also lack stanza III, are linked with *Nf* and *Nj*. Readings at lines 25, 27, 235 and 309 are found only in these four texts; readings at lines 16, 87, 114, 168, 191, 207, 217, 230, 267, 287 etc. are peculiar to two or more texts of the group. *Oa* and *Ph* contain readings peculiar to themselves at lines 46, 72, 88, 94, 119, 164, 195, 284 and 348. The many individual readings in *Oa* include a number which leave the text irregular: lines 9, 58, 73, 80, 100, 142, 172, 273, 319 and 359; in many cases a word has been omitted. Individual readings are even more numerous in *Ph*, which further lacks line 35 and is irregular at lines 57, 68, 99, 245, 263, 292, 310 and 344. *Ph* rhymes poorly at lines 83, 255 and 367.

Qd contains several readings which link it with *Oa* (lines 6–7, 30, 104, 129 and 310). These readings apart, it is difficult to relate *Qd* consistently to any other text. In *Qd* lines 259 and 317 are omitted and the text is irregular at lines 105, 127, 324 and 357.

[1] Paris, Bibl. Nat., Rothschild 2804. See A. Tchemerzine, *Bibliographie d'éditions originales et rares d'auteurs français des XVe, XVIe, XVIIe et XVIII siècles*, III, Paris, 1929, 333.

The irregular lines and the few individual readings in *Qd* (lines 13, 139, 148, 171, 183, 190, 205, 212, 278, 294 and 318) are very often the result of scribal carelessness.

Pc and *Ql* contain readings peculiar to themselves at lines 19, 23, 26, 34, 36, 38, 71, 111, 120, 164 etc.; both texts further include a large number of individual readings. Lines 183, 186, 203, 271, 318 and 367 are irregular in *Pc*, while at lines 30, 62 and 124, the text contains a poor rhyme. Irregular lines in *Ql* are lines 23, 74, 145, 214, 241, 245, 257, 263 and 264. *Pc* and *Ql* are also linked with *Oa* and *Ph* (lines 30, 193, 275, 329 and 337). Other readings link *Pc* or *Ql* with *Oa* (lines 119, 124, 144, 292, 294 and 300), but above all with *Ph* (lines 39, 92–3, 112, 192, 217, 230, 263, 305, 315, 353 etc.).

Qd has been chosen as base text because it contains stanza III, is generally regular, and has few peculiarities. In these respects it is markedly better than *Pc* or *Nj*. The errors and omissions in *Qd* have been corrected with the help of *Nj* or *Pc*.

LE DEBAT DE REVEILLE MATIN

I   Aprés mynuit, entre deux sommes,   *Qd*, 33r

     Lors qu'Amours les amans resveille,

     En ce païs cy ou nous sommes,

4   Pensoye ou lit ainsi qu'on veille

     Quant on a la puce en l'oreille;

     Si escoutay un amoureux

     Qui a un autre se conseille

8   Du mal dont il est doloreux.

II   Deux gisoient en une couche,

     Dont l'un veilloit qui fort amoit;

     Mais de long temps n'ovrry (*sic*) sa bouche,

12   En pensant que l'autre dormoit.

     Puis oÿ je qu'il le nommoit

     Et huchoit pour mectre a raison,

     Dont l'autre forment le blamoit

16   Et disoit: 'Il n'est pas saison'.

III   Disoit cellui qu'Amours tenoit

     En telle pensee amoureuse

     Que de dormir ne lui tenoit

Le livre de r. m. *Oa*, R. M. *Qd*, *No heading PcQl*. 1 mienuit *NfNjOaPhQdQl*; songes *Ql*. 2 esveille *NfNjOaPcPh*. 4 Pensant *Oa*, Ensoie *Ql*; en lit *Pc*. 6 deux *NfNjPcPhQl*. 7 Dont lun a lautre se c. *NfNjPcPhQl*. 9 D.] Tous d. *Oa*. 11 Et *NfQl*; nouvroit *Pc*. 13 Depuis joy qui *Ql*; je] que *Qd*. 15 Et *Ql*. 16 d. quil *NfNjOa*. *Stanza III omitted NfNjOaPh*. 18 celle *Pc*. 19 challoit *PcQl*.

20 Ne de faire chiere jouyeuse:
'Ce me semble chose honteuse
Que de dormir tant et si fort;
Et pour ce m'est elle ennuyeuse
24 Car il ne sert de riens qui dort'.

IV   L'autre dist, qui dormir vouloit
Et a dormir avoit apris,
Ne de devis ne lui chaloit   33v
28 Car de sommeil estoit espris:
'Frere, se vous avez empris
De veiller a voustre loysir,
Les autres n'y sont pas compris.
32 Face chascun a son plaisir'.

V   'Ha dia', dist l'Amoureux, 'Beau sire,
Tel voulsist veiller qui sommeille;
Tel ploure qui voulsist bien rire;
36 Tel cuide dormir qui s'esveille.
Non pourtant, Bonne Amour conseille –
Et moult souvent le dit on bien –
Q'un bon amy pour l'autre veille
40 Au gré d'autruy, non pas au sien.'

Le Dormeur

VI   Je veillasse moult volentiers,
Beaux amis, pour voustre plaisance,
Si vous peussiez endementiers
44 Dormir pour moy a souffisance.
Mais remectez en oublïance
Jusqu'a demain toute autre chose;
Et dorme qui avra puissance,
48 Car il languist qui ne repose.

20 mener vie *Pc*. 21 Il me s. estre h. *Ql*: Maiz *Pc*. 23 p. ce] de tant *PcQl*; m'e. el. en.] me. en. *Ql*. 24 scet *Ql*. 25 Dist cellui *NſNjOaPh*; que *PcQl*. 26 Et qua d. *PcQl*. 27 Et de parler *NſNj OaPh*. 30 A v. *NſNjPcQl*; pour *NſNjOaPcPhQl*; plaisir *OaPcPhQl*. 32 desir *OaPhQl*. 33 Haa *NſPc*, En (?) *Ql*; dieu *NſNj*. 34 T. v. dormir qui sesveille *PcQl*. 35 *Omitted Ph*: bien vousist *NſNjOaPcQl*. 36 Tel voulsist veillier qui sonmeille *PcQl*. 37 bon *Nj*. 38 Assez s. *NſNj*, Et bien s. *PcQl*. 39 Que lun a. *PhQl*. 41 tres *Pc*. 42 B. a.] Dist lautre et *Pc*, Dist lautre *Ql*; a *NſNj*. 43 pensiez *Oa*. 46 tout *OaPh*. 48 langist *Qd*.

VII
L'Amoureux

Oublïer! Las, il n'entr'oblie
Pas ainsi son mal qui se deult.
Chascun dit bien: 'Oblie, oublie (*sic*)',
52 Mais il ne le fait pas qui veult.
Tel le vouldroit qui ne le puet:
Force lui est, plaise ou non plaise;
Mais ceulx qui la doleur n'aqueult
56 Si en parlent bien a leur aise.

VIII
Le Dormeur

Et quel bien, ne quelle conqueste   34r
Puet il doncques venir a homme
De veiller et rompre sa teste
60 Et ne prendre repos ne somme?
Cela ne sert pas d'une pomme
A ce de quoy on a besoing.
Dormez, et puis aprés en somme
64 Faites ce dont vous avez soing.

IX
L'Amoureux

Le dire ne vous couste guiere,
Mais je le sens bien autrement.
Bien dormir est chose legiere
68 A qui pense legierement.
Pour ce fait on foul jugement
Bien souvent, et a peu d'arrest
Sur ceulx qui ont tel pensement,
72 Quant on n'a essayé que c'est.

X
Le Dormeur

Est ce par jeu ou passetemps
Ou s'il vous en va en ce point?
Je ne pourroye estre contens
76 Quant a moy de ne dormir point.

50 Par *Ph.*   53 vousist *NfNjPcQl*; peust *Pc.*   54 Penser lui (le *NfNj*) fault (fait *Ql*) *NfNjOaPcPhQl*.
55 cilz *Ph.*   56 parlant *Ql.*   57 Que confort ne qu. c. *Ql*: et *NjOaPh*; quel *Ph.*   58 Peust *Pc*; d. v.]
donc v. *Oa.*   62 len *Oa.*   63 le s. *Ql.*   65 gueres *Oa*, gaires *Ph.*   66 M. il men va b. a. *Pc.*   68 Qui
p. l. *Ph.*   69 Pourtant *Ql*; faulx *Oa.*   70 en a peu *Ph.*   71 Sus *PcQl*; fol p. *Ph.*   72 on a e. *OaPh.*
73 Est ce] Est *Oa*; ung p. *NfNjQl.*   74 Ou il *NfNj*; v. en va] v. va *Ql.*   75 Et ne p. *Ph.*

Qu'avez vous? Quel mouche vous point,
Dont tant en vain vous travaillez?
Au fort ja n'yra moins a point
80   Se je dors tant que vous veillez.

XI   *L'Amoureux*

Jouer? Las, nenny. C'est acertes
Si au vif qu'on ne pourroit mieulx,
Puis que tout y va, gaing ou pertes;
84   Il est assez de plus beaux jeux.
Mais quant un bon amy est tieulx
Que vers son amy bien se porte,
A toutë heure, et en tous lieux,
88   Il n'est riens qui tant resconforte.

XII   *Le Dormeur*

Quel resconfort ou quel secours   34v
Vous puet il venir de ma part,
Se voustre mal vous vient d'Amours
92   Ou du trait d'un plaisant regart,
Ou de Reffus, dont Dieu vous gart,
Car mieulx vauldroit tenir prison?
Celle qui a geté le dart
96   Porte avec soy la garison.

XIII   *L'Amoureux*

La garison ne me puet pas,
Amis, venir de vous ne d'ame,
Ne je ne puis passer ce pas
100   Se ce n'est par mercy de dame.
Mais, s'a vous comme amy sans blame
Je di ce qui m'estraint et charge,
En descouvrant ma dure flame,
104   J'en avray le cuer plus au large.

78 en vain tant *Ql*. 80 Se je d.] Se d. *Oa*; t. que v. vueillez *Ph*, et se v. v. *Ql*. 83 gaings *Ql*; perte *Ph*. 85 vray *Pc*; telz *Nf*. 86 Quenvers *Ql*. 87 En toutes heures et t. l. *Pc*: A] Et a *NfNjPh*. 88 t. le (me *Ph*) conforte *OaPh*. 89 Et quel confort *Ph*; ne *NfNjOaPcQl*, et *Ph*. 90 p. il v.] p. v. *Nj*, peust il v. *Pc*. 91 Et *Ph*. 92 dung t. *PcPh*; de p. r. *Pc*. 93 dung r. *PcPh*. 94 plus *OaPh*; vouldroit *Oa*. 97 peust *Pc*. 98 Amy *PcPhQl*; de vous venir *Ph*. 99 je ne p.] ja ne p. *Oa*, je p. *Nj*, ne p. *Ph*. 100 Se ce n'e.] Se nest *Oa*. 102 que *NfNj*. 103 desgorjant la d. f. *OaPcPh*. 104 a l. *NfNjPcPhQl*.

XIV

Le Dormeur

Doncques puis que vous le voulez
Et que le dire vous prouffite,
Et la doleur dont vous doulez
108   Amaindrist d'estre plainte et dite,
Je vous requier que je m'aquite
Envers vous d'en ouÿr le compte;
Et s'a autre je le recite,
112   J'en vueil avoir reprouche et honte.

XV

L'Amoureux

Par Dieu, frere, je vous diray,
Comme a homme en qui je me fie,
De ce dont plus grant desir ay,
116   Soit pour ma mort ou pour ma vie.
J'ay de long temps une servie,
A mon gré sage, bonne et belle,
Et de tous biens tresassuvie
120   Fors que pitié n'est pas en elle.

XVI

Le Dormeur

Certes, puis que Nature a mis   35r
En elle tant de biens en euvre,
Il ne puet estre, beaux amis,
124   Que soubz eulx pitié ne se queuvre.
S'elle si toust ne se descueuvre,
Pourtant ne vous desconfortez,
Car il ne fault pas qui recueuvre;
128   Ne vous, se bien vous y portez.

XVII

L'Amoureux

Portez! Las, qui pourroit jamais
Amer dame plus loyaument
Que j'ay fait elle et que je fais,

105 D. p.] P. d. *Ql*; v. le v.] le v. *Qd*. 108 p. ou d. *Pc*. 109 Je suis dacort que *Oa*. 111 Et se autre chose je r. *Ph*: autres *NfNjOa*; je le r.] le r. *PcQl*. 112 Je v. *PcPhQl*. 114 a qui *NfPh*. 115 Et de riens ne vous mentiray *Ql*. 117 Jen ay l. t. *Ph*; dame s. *Oa*. 118 Sage a mon gre et b. et b. *NfNj*: bonne sage *Ql*. 119 Et en tout tresbien a. *Ql*: en *OaPc*; tout bien *OaPh*. 120 Mais que *NfNjOaPc*; point *PcQl*. 122 bien *Ph*. 123 peust *Pc*. 124 pitie soubz (en *Nj*) eulz *NfNjOa*; se treuve *OaPc*. 127 qui receveuvre (*sic*) *Qd*. 129 Porter *NfNjPcPh*. 131 celle *Ph*.

132 Dont j'ay souffert tant longuement
Dure peine, ennuy et tourment
Qu'il pert que je suis né atout
Et qu'onques ne fu autrement;
136 Et si n'en puis trouver le bout.

XVIII   *Le Dormeur*

Dya, compains, qui se veult soubmectre
Desoubz l'amoureuse maistrise,
Il se fault de son cuer desmectre
140 Et n'estre plus en sa franchise.
Se voustre voulenté s'est mise
En dame ou il ait tel dangier,
Il fault qu'il en soit a sa guise;
144 En vous n'est pas du chalenger.

XIX   *L'Amoureux*

En moy n'en est, n'il ne m'affiert,
Se non de prïer et de plaindre
Comme cellui qui mercy quiert
148 Et qu'Amours fait a ce contraindre.
Mais, s'il est ainsi que par faindre
Plusieurs ont des biens, comme on dit,
Et loyaux n'i puissent actaindre,
152 Je suis maleureux et maudit.

XX   *Le Dormeur*

Qui bien a commencié parface;   35ᵛ
Qui bien a choisy ne se meuve;
Car a la ffin, quoy qu'on pourchace,
156 Qui desert le bien, il le treuve.
Un cuer loyal de fine espreuve
A plus de joye, quoy qu'il tarde,

132 si l. *Pc*.   133 ennuyeux t. *NſNj*.   134 Quil semble que fus nez a. *Pc*: fus *OaPhQl*; o tout *NſNj*.   135 Et quil ne fust onc a. *Pc*.   137 Beau c. *NſNj*.   138 franchise *Ql*.   139 le f. *Qd*.   140 en son servise *Ql*.   141 est *Ph*, cest *QdQl*.   142 il ait] il a *Ph*, il y a *Oa*.   143 en sa g. *Ql*.   144 A vous *NſNj*; de ch. *Nſ*, de la (le *OaPcQl*) changier *NjOaPcQl*.   145 n'en e.] nest il *NſNjPh*, nest point *Pc*; ny ne ma. *Pc*, ne ne ma. *Ph*, ne il naffiert *Ql*.   148 en ce *Qd*.   149 est a. que] est que *Nſ*; pour *NſNj*.   150 du bien *NſNjOaPhQl*.   151 Et les loyaulx ny puet a. *Ql*: pevent *NſNjPcPh*.   154 Qui a bien *Ql*.   155 en la f. *Ql*.   157 Ung loyal c. *NſNj*.   158 A plus de bien combien quil t. *Ql*.

311

Que n'ont ceulx qui font dame neuve
160 De chascune qui les regarde.

XXI   *L'Amoureux*

Un bien de ceulx qui loyaulx sont,
Quant il leur puet d'Amours bien prendre,
Est si grant que les faulx n'en ont
164 Pas la centiesme part du mendre.
Mais le grief mal que c'est d'actendre
En longue douleur la deserte,
Leur fait sembler qu'on leur veult vendre
168 Ce qu'Amours donne ailleurs en perte.

XXII   *Le Dormeur*

Je ne say se trop en enquier,
Mais puis qu'en moy tant vous fïez,
Or me comptez, je vous requier,
172 Quant il avient que vous prïez
La belle et mercy lui crïez
A basse voix et jointes mains,
Pour chose que vous lui dïez,
176 Y trouvez vous ne plus ne moins?

XXIII   *L'Amoureux*

Certes, quant a ceste demande,
Croiez et le saichiez de voir
Que la doulceur d'elle est si grande,
180 Le beau parler et le savoir –
Soit d'esloingnier ou recevoir –
Et sa response si courtoise,
Que plus lui pri sa grace avoir
184 Et mieulx say que ma doleur poise.

159 veuve *Ql.*   161 cueulx *Qd.*   162 leurs *Qd*; peust *Pc.*   164 Mie les cent mil pars du m. *NfNj*, Pas les cent mille pars du m. *OaPh*, Pas la (le *Ql*) cent mille part du m. *PcQl.*   165 le g. m.] le dangier *Ql.*   166 l. paine *Pc*, long demeure *Ql.*   167 Leur semble con leur veulle vendre *Pc*: f. a dire *Ql.*   168 Ou *Oa*; a p. *NfNjOa.*   171 compte *Qd*, dictes *Pc.*   172 Qu. il a.] Qu. a. *Oa.*   178 le s.] s. bien *Ql.*   179 douleur *Ph.*   183 Qui *Qd*, Quant *Ph*; p.] prye *Pc.*   184 scet *Ph.*

XXIV   *Le Dormeur*   36r

> Il n'est point de dame en ce monde,
> S'il avient que l'on la requiere,
> Qu'il ne faille qu'elle responde
> En une ou en autre maniere.   188
> Dame n'est mie si legiere
> Que pour son droit ne se deffende;
> Mais combien que Durté soit fiere,
> A la fin fault il qu'el se rende.   192

XXV   *L'Amoureux*

> Pour plourer, plaindre et souspirer,
> Ne pour riens que je saiche dire,
> Autre chose n'en puis tirer,
> Ne d'octroier ne d'escondire,   196
> Fors sans plus qu'il me doit souffire,
> Sans y reclamer autre droit,
> S'elle veult mon bien et desire –
> Et de chascun en son endroit.   200

XXVI   *Le Dormeur*

> C'est une chose bien sëant
> A dame de tout bien vouloir,
> Et de n'estre a nulli vëant
> Bel Acueil s'il a bon vouloir.   204
> Mais s'un loyal pour mieulx valoir
> De tous poins a elle se donne,
> El se doit de son mal douloir
> S'autrement ne le guerredonne.   208

XXVII   *L'Amoureux*

> Trembler, tressaillir, tressüer,
> Triste de cuer, feible de corps,
> Cuer faillir et couleur müer

185 cest *Pc*.   186 que l'on] que on *NfPc*, que on ne *Ph*, que non *Ql*.   190 de son d. *Ph*; deffendre *Qd*.   191 quen d. *Pc*; si f. *NfNjOa*.   192 A la foiz *PhQl*; f. quelle se r. *NfNj*, f. il quelle se r. *Oa*. 193 Pour plaindre ne pour s. *OaPcPhQl*.   195 ne p. t. *OaPh*, ny p. trouver *Pc*.   196 desconfire *Ql*. 199 Quelle v. *Ql*, Quelle aime *NfNj*.   202 de t. b.] que de b. *Pc*.   203 Et de n'e.] Et ne estre *Pc*; beant *NfNj*.   204 si *PhQd*; sel na *Ql*.   205 son l. *Qd*; avoir *Ph*.   206 A une seulle sabandonne *Pc*: a une *OaPhQl*.   207 Celle si doibt s. m. d. *Pc*: Elle *NjOa*, Il *Ph*; Elle d. *Ql*.

212 M'a veu souvent, et mes yeulx lors
     Plourer ens et rire dehors
     Pour estre aux joyeux ressamblant.
     Et puis n'y treuve je riens fors
216 Courtois parler et beau semblant.

XXVIII   *Le Dormeur*   36v

     Se le beau semblant vient du cuer
     Naïf et non pas contrefait,
     Ne croiez, frere, pour nul feur,
220 Puis qu'elle congnoist voustre fait
     Et, pour l'amer du cuer parfait,
     Vous voit souffrir si dure peine...
     Se le mal d'amours vous meffait,
224 Croiez qu'el n'en est mie saine?

XXIX   *L'Amoureux*

     Nulli ne prent melencolie
     De chose dont il ne lui chault.
     Se j'ay du mal, c'est ma folie;
228 Ce ne lui fait ne froit ne chault.
     Mais au fort, qui plus bee hault,
     Il a plus fort a besoingnier;
     Par Messire Ode et par Machaut
232 Se puet il assez tesmoingner.

XXX   *Le Dormeur*

     Or par la foy que vous devez
     A Dieu et a voustre maistresse,
     Est ce quantque vous y avez
236 D'esperance ne de promesse?
     Avez vous prisé ceste adresse
     De l'amer tousjours sans rappel,

212 Na veu *Qd*; les y. *Ql*. 213 Plorant *Ql*. 214 aux j.] au j. *NfOa*, j. *Ql*. 216 bon *NfQl*, doulz *NjPc*. 217 bon *PcPhQl*; parler *Nf*; de *NjOa*. 219 Ne c. pas que p. n. f. *NfNj*. 221 de *NfNjOaPc*. 222 fait s. *Pc*; s. douleur et p. *Ph*. 223 damer *Pc*. 224 Penses *Ql*; quelle nen est pas s. *NfNjOaPc*, quelle nest mye s. *Ph*. 227 est ma f. *Nf*, par ma f. *Nj*. 228 Il *OaPcPh*. 229 Et *Ph*; monte *Pc*; bee en h. *Ph*. 230 Et (Tant *Ql*) plus a fort a b. *PhQl*: Il] Tant *NfNjOa*, Si *Pc*. 231 eude *Ph*; ou *Ph*. 232 Se peust il *Pc*, Le puet on *Ql*, Le pouez *Ph*. 233 Par le serment que v. d. *Pc*. 235 Se cest *NfNjOaPh*; clamez *NfNj*. 237 prinse *Ql*, prins *Oa*; cest *Ph*.

Et de renoncier a lïesse
240 Pour demourer en ceste pel?

XXXI
L'Amoureux

Se m'aist ores Dieu que je sens
Mon cuer si hors de mon bandon
Que, quoy que soit, folie ou sens,
244 Puis que je le donnay en don –
Et n'eusse jamais guerredon –
Il me convient en ce point vivre.
Se j'en meur, Dieu me doint pardon;
248 Si seray de tous maulx delivre.

XXXII
Le Dormeur

Merci de dame est un tresor   37ʳ
Pour enrichir amans sur terre,
Si ne l'a pas chascun tresor
252 Qui a voulenté de l'aquerre;
Ains le fault a dangier conquerre
Et en souffrir doleur amere,
Car pour prïer ne pour requerre
256 Nul n'a bien s'il ne le compere.

XXXIII
L'Amoureux

Que puis je comparer plus chier
Qu'i mectre cuer, vie et courage?
Je n'ay mieux pour en jeu couchier,
260 Si bon plege ne tel hostaige.
Mais ma dame a trop l'avantaige,
Dont la chose est pis departie,
Car el garde mon cuer pour gage
264 Et fault qu'el soit juge et partie.

240 en telle p. *Oa.* 241 Or ainsy maist dieu *Pc*; ores] or *Ql.* 244 lay donne *NfNj*, luy donne *Ql*; lui donnay un don *Ph.* 245 Et neusse je (Et nen eusse *Ph*) j. guerdon *NfPh*, Et nen eusse j. guerredon *Ql.* 246 Si me fault il *Oa*; cest p. *Pc.* 247 je m. *Ql*; d. le me p. *Pc.* 248 telz m. *Nj*, ces m. *Oa.* 250 amant *NfNj.* 251 nen a pas *Pc.* 252 Qui la v. de la querre *Ql.* 253 Mais *NfNjPcPhQl.* 255 requeste *Ph.* 256 qui ne *Pc*, si ne *Ph.* 257 Qui pourroit c. *Pc*, Que puis c. *Ql.* 258 Que dy m. c. et c. *Pc.* 259 *Omitted Qd*: a jeu *Ql.* 261 a trop davantage *Ql.* 263 Car elle g. *PhQl*, Car elle tient *NfNjOaPc*; en g. *NjPcQl.* 264 quelle *NfQl*, que *Oa.*

XXXIV   *Le Dormeur*

      Aux amans est de bien servir
      A la fin qu'en grace en deviennent,
      Et aux dames de desservir
268   A ceulx qui a droit se maintiennent.
      Puis que les biens des dames viennent
      A elles est deu le service;
      Et est bien raison qu'elles tiennent
272   Sur leurs servans court et justice.

XXXV   *L'Amoureux*

      Je ne dy pas, Dieu m'en deffende,
      Qu'il ne soit raison qu'elle juge
      Sur moy tel peine ou tel amende
276   Qu'il lui plaist, car pour cela fu ge
      Contraint de venir a reffuge
      Vers elle qui ne s'en recorde;
      Mais bien seroit a un tel juge
280   Un peu plus de misericorde.

XXXVI   *Le Dormeur*   37v

      Puis que vous estes si avant,
      Savez vous comme il en yra?
      Il vous fault vivre en la servant.
284   Souffrez tant qu'il lui souffira;
      Et quant elle vous sentira
      Humble, secret et bien amant,
      Par Dieu, son cuer s'adoulcira.
288   Dame n'a pas cuer d'aÿmant.

XXXVII   *L'Amoureux*

      Helas! Je n'ay pouoir n'espace
      D'aler avant ne de retraire.

266 Affin quen grace ilz en d. *Ql.* 267 Aux d. est du d. *Ql*: du d. *NfNjOa.* 268 sy m. *NfNjQl.* 269 dons *Ql.* 270 A celles est *Ph,* A eulx en est *Ql.* 271 Si *Nf*; Et sest b. r. *Nj,* Et b. est r. *Oa,* Et est r. *Pc.* 272 Sus leur servant droit et j. *Pc.* 273 dy pas] di *Oa*; me d. *Ph.* 275 telle p. ou a. *NfNj*; ou] et *OaPcPhQl.* 276 Quil lui plaira car pour ce fuz je *Nf*: car] que *Ql.* 278 len r. *Qd.* 279 bon *Ql*; en *NfNjOaPc.* 282 S. v. c.] S. comment *Ph,* Si (?) v. convient *Ql.* 283 Vives tousdiz en la s. *Pc.* 284 Souffrir *OaPh*; qui *QdQl.* 286 b. cellant (?) *Ql.* 287 P. D.] Espoir *NfNjOa,* Certes *Ql*; s'a.] a. *NfNj.* 288 El na pas c. de dyamant *Pc.*

Je suis le poisson en la nasse,
292 Qui entre ens et ne s'en puet traire.
Vivre en ce point m'est si contraire
Qu'il me fault cuer et corps faillir;
Mais pour mal que je puisse traire
296 N'en puis eschaper ne saillir.

XXXVIII   *Le Dormeur*

En actendant sans soy lasser,
Në autre que vous acuser,
Vous convient il le temps passer;
300 Actendre bien n'est pas muser.
Trop grant actrait fait amuser
Souvent, et deçoit et aluche;
Mais soubz un courtois reffuser
304 Sont les biens d'amours en embuche.

XXXIX   *L'Amoureux*

De long temps a, n'ay sceu ouvrir,
Ne trouver maniere ne tour
De ceste embusche descouvrir,
308 Ou ma joye est en un destour.
J'ay esté emprés et autour,
Mais oncq jusqu'a elle n'avins;
Et quant j'en vien a mon retour
312 Je suis en l'estat que je y vins.

XL   *Le Dormeur*   38r

Bel Acueil n'est mie haÿs
D'Amours qui n'a cure d'orgueil,
Mais le fait franc en son païs,
316 Si que nul si hardi sur l'ueil

291 Je s. comme p. en n. *Oa.*   292 Qui entre et sen p. t. *Ph*: Q. e. e.] Qui y entre *OaQl*; peust *Pc.*
293 cest *Oa.*   294 Qui *Qd*; me fait *OaPcQl.*   295 M. p. chose que p. faire *Pc,* Ne pour mal que gy
saiche t. *Ql*: par *Nj*; jen p. *NfNj.*   297 a soy *Ph.*   298 de v. *Oa.*   299 ce t. *Ql.*   300 De bien actendre
nest m. *Ph*: Bien actendre *OaPcQl.*   301 f. tost muser *Ql.*   302 Les gens et si decort ahuche (?) *Ql.*
303 sur *Ql.*   305 Long t. a que nay s. o. *Oa,* De (Des *PhQl*) l. t. nen ay (je nay *PhQl*) s. o. *PcPhQl*:
Des *NfNj*; nay scey *Nj.*   308 ma j. maint *Oa,* est ma j. *Ph.*   309 au prez *NfNjOaPh*; en tour *NjPc,*
au tour *NfOaPh.*   310 M. a elle oncques na. *Ph,* Et oncques jusques la na. *Ql*: oncques *OaQd*; jusques
a *Oa.*   311 je v. *Ph,* je suis *PcQl.*   312 je v. *Pc.*   315 Ains *Oa*; la f. f. *PhQl.*   316 si] tant *Oa.*

De clamer droit sur Bel Acueil,
Ne chalanger de ses biens fors ce
Qu'il a donné de son bon vueil,
320   Sans faire contrainte ne force.

XLI   *L'Amoureux*

Nully ne puet Amours forcier
A donner les biens qui sont siens,
Ne je ne me vueil efforcier
324   Qu'a requerir grace et plus riens.
Mais tant qu'en loyauté me tiens,
Puet survenir autre servant
Et me reculer de ses biens
328   Que j'ay pourchacez par avant.

XLII   *Le Dormeur*

S'autruy lui plaist, et elle l'ayme,
De tort plaindre ne vous pouez;
Mais s'elle pour servant vous clame,
332   Si l'en mercïez et louez.
Autrement ne vous y jouez,
Car il convient que les dons voysent
Aux sains a qui ilz sont vouez;
336   Ceulx qui n'en ont si s'en apaisent.

XLIII   *L'Amoureux*

Las voire! Mais comme prendra
En gré cuer qui longuement sert,
S'il voit un autre qui tendra
340   La joye du bien qu'il dessert?
S'en bien servant on le dessert,
Son service est mal advenant,
Quant le temps et le loyer pert,
344   Et le reçoit un survenant.

317 *Omitted Qd*: sus *Pc*.   318 Ne ch. de] Ne de ch. *Ph*, Ne ch. *Pc*; des *Qd*.   319 Quil en donra *Ph*, Quil donne *Oa*, Quil a promis *Ql*; a s. b. v. *NſNj*.   321 peust *Pc*.   322 dons *OaPcPh*.   323 men v. *Pc*. 324 Que *Ph*; r.] querir *Qd*.   326 Y peust venir ung seurvenant *Ql*: Peust *Pc*.   328 devant *Ph*. 329 Se autre *OaPcPhQl*, Saucun *NſNj*.   330 De trop p. ne v. debves *Pc*.   331 celle *Ph*; amy *Pc*. 334 biens *Ph*.   335 Aux s. ou ilz furent v. *NſNj*.   336 en a. *Ph*, sen accoisent *NſNjOa*, sen rappaisent *Pc*.   337 comment *OaPcPhQl*.   339 prendra *NſNjPcPh*.   340 des biens *OaPhQl*.   341 il la d. *Nſ*.   343 son t. et son l. *Ql*; et la joye *Ph*.   344 le r.] elle r. *Ph*.

XLIV   *Le Dormeur*

En amours n'a se plaisir non.   38v
Tel y cuide estre receü
Et plaire et avoir bon renon
348   Qui souvent en est deceü;
Et quant une dame a veü
Des gens d'un et d'autre degré,
Puis que le choys lui est deü,
352   Elle doit choisir a son gré.

XLV   *L'Amoureux*

Or je pri a Dieu qu'Il me doint
Selon le bon droit que je y ay,
Et que ja Dieu ne me pardoint
356   S'oncques vers elle varïay;
Mais, puis que premier la prïay
Et qu'elle congnoist mon desir,
Je pri Dieu ou je me fïay
360   Qu'Il ne lui doint pas pis choisir.

XLVI   *L'Acteur*

Ainsi l'aube du jour creva
Et les compaignons s'endormirent,
N'oncques nulx d'eulx ne se leva
364   Tant que huit heures lever les firent.
Si mis en escript ce qu'ilz dirent
Pour mieulx estre de leur butin,
Et l'ont nommé ceulx qui le virent
368   Le debat Reveille Matin.

---

346 e. r.] e. bien r. *NſNjOa.*   347 Et y p. et a. b. nom *Ql*: plaise *Ph.*   348 s. en est] moult s. est *Nſ*, moult s. en est *Nj*, en est s. *OaPh*, y est bien s. *Ql.*   349 Car *Ql*; a v.] a tout v. *Nj.*   351 le ch. est a lui deu *Oa*, le choisir lui est deu *Nj.*   352 Droit est quelle prenge a son gre *Pc*: d. ch.] le d. prandre *Oa*, d. bien prendre *Ph.*   353 je pri] prie je *Pc*, pry je *Ph*; men d. *Oa.*   354 S. ce que deservy ay *Pc.* 355 que jamais *Oa.*   356 Sonq envers elle v. *NſNjQl*, Se onc vers elle v. *Ph.*   357 M. p. qu. p.] M. p. p. *Qd.*   358 congneut *NſOa.*   359 Je prie d. ou tant me f. *Oa*, Je requier d. ou me f. *NſNj.* 360 Qui luy d. ung loyal ch. *Ql.*   363 ne sesveilla *Pc*, ne seclama *Ph.*   365 mist *Oa.*   367 c. qui] c. *Pc*; firent *Ph.*   Explicit *NſNj*, . . . le debat r. m. *Oa*, . . . r. m. *PcQl.*

9

'La Complainte'

Thirty-seven Manuscripts: *Gc Gg Gh   Nb Nf Nj Nl Nm Nq Nr   Oa Oc Ol Pa Pb Pc Pd Pe Pf Ph Pj Pk Pn Po   Qa Qc Qd Qg Qh Qk Ql Qn Qo Qp Qq Qr   Tc.*

The *Complainte* was printed in all the early collected editions and in the Du Chesne edition; there is also an early separate edition of the poem.[1] All the manuscripts have been examined except *Qn*, which has not been traced, and *Qp*, which has been damaged by fire. The printed editions consulted include the collected edition of 1489 and the separate edition. The poem has been edited here from seven manuscripts: *Nf Nj Oa Pc Ph Qd Ql*.

The title, *Complainte*, is that most commonly found. The poem is attributed to Alain Chartier in twenty manuscripts; in the others it is anonymous.

The seven texts used here can be divided into three groups: *Nf Nj Ph*; *Pc Ql*; *Oa Qd*. If *Ph* is disregarded, the twelve stanzas of the poem are presented in a different order by each group.

Nf and *Nj* both contain a complete text of the *Complainte*. Readings at lines 88, 131, 140 (irregular), 170 and 173 make poor sense and are among a number of readings found only in these two texts. *Nj* includes several readings peculiar to itself, of which those at lines 19, 79 and 137 are irregular. A similar number of individual readings is found in *Nf*, those at lines 88 and 157 being irregular.

Readings at lines 9, 27, 40, 74, 89, 91, 93, 119a and 157 are peculiar to *Nf Nj* and *Ph*. The order of the first eight stanzas of the poem in *Ph* corresponds to that in *Nf* and *Nj*. The order of the last four, on the other hand, is the same as in *Pc* and *Ql* and readings peculiar to these three texts occur at lines 128, 157 and 175. Lines 94, 166 and 182 are omitted in *Ph*. The text contains a large number of individual readings, some of which are irregular: lines 18, 24, 55, 75, 106, 111, 122 etc. Some fifteen lines of *Ph* have been corrected in a later hand (*Ph²*), apparently from an early collected edition.[2]

Pc and *Ql* contain very similar texts of the *Complainte*, readings peculiar to the two texts being found at lines 14, 19 (irregular), 31, 33–5, 41, 43, 44, 46 etc. Each text contains in addition a number of readings peculiar to itself. In both texts lines 177–8 are inverted; while *Pc* is complete, *Ql* lacks line 147. *Pc* is irregular at lines 58, 119a, and 180; *Ql* at lines 58, 79, 111 and 180.

The two texts remaining, *Oa* and *Qd*, contain readings peculiar to themselves at lines 22, 25, 29, 75 and 117. Elsewhere, for example at lines 13, 24, 27, 53, 60, 109 and 132, *Oa* agrees with *Pc* and *Ql*; at most of these lines, therefore, *Qd* is to be grouped with *Nf Nj* and *Ph*. In *Oa* lines 31, 70, 83 and 147 are omitted, while the text contains irregular readings peculiar to itself at lines 5, 30, 37, 56, 88, 92 and 178. *Qd* is complete and con-

---

1 GKW 6562.

2 The corrected version is almost always in agreement with the collected edition of 1489.

tains very few individual readings: lines 27 and 91 are irregular and line 75 has a poor rhyme. Almost all the readings peculiar to *Qd* are the result of small scribal errors (lines 16, 55, 72, 159 and 170).

Although the texts of the *Complainte* differ widely, it is impossible in most cases to find any objective reason for preferring one of the versions available to the others. Thus, none of the four orders in which the stanzas are presented is necessarily better than the others. Each stanza of the *Complainte* consists of a variation, or series of variations, on the theme of grief, and there is not always a close or logical connection between them.

Lines 117–20, however, repay examination. At line 119 (119a) in particular, the version of *Oa* and *Qd* is to be contrasted with those of the other five texts. In their versions line 119a is similar in sentiment and expression to line 114 which is found in all seven texts. The version of *Oa* and *Qd* is not repetitive, is better developed and is to be preferred.

Examination of the textual tradition had already suggested that *Qd* was the text most likely to be suitable for use as a base. It contained the smallest number of irregular lines and of individual readings, was complete and generally made good sense. It has therefore been chosen as the base text for this edition of the *Complainte*. The few corrections necessary can be made with the help of *Nj* or *Oa*. Line 132, irregular in all the texts, has been emended.

COMPLAINTE

I   Contre toy, Mort doloreuse et despite,   *Qd*, 83v

       Angoisseuse, maleureuse, maudite,

       Et en tes fais merveilleuse et soudaine,

   4 Ceste complainte ay fourmee et escripte

       De cuer courcié, ou nul plaisir n'abite,

       Noircy de dueil et aggrevé de peine.

       Je t'appelle de traïson vilaine;

   8 De toy me plaing de toute riguer plaine,

       Quant ta durté a tort me desherite

       Du riche don de joye souverainne,

       Et que ton dart a piteuse fin maine

   12 Le chois d'onneur et des dames l'eslite.

II   Tu m'as tolu ma dame et ma maistresse,

       Et as murtry mon cuer et ma lëesse

       Par un seul cop, dont ilz sont tous deux mors.

C. contre la mort *NfNj*, C. que fist lacteur contre la mort *Oa*, C. de la mort a la dame m. alain *Pc*, C. maistre alain *Ph*, C. maistre alain de la mort de sa dame *Ql*.

 Order of stanzas: I–III, V–VII, IV, VIII–XII *NfNj*; I–IV, VII, V–VI, VIII, X, IX, XI–XII *PcQl*; I–III, V–VII, IV, VIII, X, IX, XI–XII *Ph*.

2 A. m. et m. *NfOaPcPhQl*. 4 est f. *Oa*. 5 c.] courrouce *Oa*. 9 Car *NfNjPh* (Quant *Ph²*). 13 oste *OaPcQl*. 14 mas m. *PcQl*. 15 t. d. m.] en destresse *Ph*, t. troys m. *Ph²*.

16   Du cuer n'est riens puis que plaisir le laisse
     Et que je pers la joye de jennesse;
     Ainsi n'ay plus fors la voix et le corps.
     Mes yeulx pleurent ens et rïent dehors,
20   Et tousjours ay le doloreux remors
     Du hault plaisir qui de tous poins me cesse.
     Las! Or n'est plus ce que j'avoye, Amors.
     Je muir sur bout, et en ce point me pors
24   Comme arbre sec qui sur le pié se dresse.

III   Si suis desert, despointé et deffait
          De pensee, de parolle et de fait,
          De los, de joye et de tout ce qui fait
28   Cuer en jennesse a hault honneur venir,
          Quant a celle qui ne t'a riens meffait   84r
          Tu as osté ce qu'el n'a pas forfait
          Et qui jamais ne puet estre reffait.
32   C'est sa vie que tu as fait fenir,
          Dont la mienne se souloit soustenir
          Pour mieulx valoir et plus hault avenir
          Et mectre peine a meilleur devenir.
36   Or as tu tout mon penser contrefait;
          Si ne say plus a quoy me doy tenir,
          Et ne me puet de confort souvenir,
          Quant j'ay perdu sans jamais revenir
40   De tous les biens ce qu'estoit plus parfait.

IV   Qui me pourroit de ce dueil conforter?
          Je n'ay pas cuer a tel doleur porter,
          Car adoulcir ne puis ne supporter
44   Les durs accés de mon dolent mesaise.
          C'est temps perdu que de moy enorter

16 De *Qd.*   18 p. f.] p. *Ph*, p. que *PcPh²Ql*.   19 r. d.] riens d. *Nj*, r. par d. *PcQl*.   21 De deplaisir *Ph²*;
ne c. *Ph²*.   22 or nay *NfNjPcPhQl*.   23 sus *OaPc*; me mors *Ph* (me p. *Ph²*).   24 C. a. s.] C. larbre
PcPh²Ql (C. arbre s. *Ph*) ; sus *Pc*; se seche *OaPcPh²Ql* (se dresse *Ql²*).   25 Or *NfNjPcPhQl*.   26 De parole
de pensee *Oa*.   27 De los donneur *OaPcQl*, De bien de j. *NfNjPh*; et de t.] et t. *Qd*.   28 a haultesse v. *Oa*.
29 Puis qua *NfNjPcPhQl*.   30 ce qui *Nf*, ce que *NjQl*, ce quelle *Oa*.   31 *Omitted Oa*: que *PcQl*;
peust *Pc*.   33–5 Qui plus faisoit la moye soubstenir Pour avoir non et plus hault advenir Et tousjours
tendre a meilleur devenir *PcQl*.   34–5 P. m. v. et meilleur devenir Et m. p. a plus hault avenir *Oa*.
37 me doye t. *Oa*.   38 peust *Pc*.   40 tout le bien *NfNjPh*.   41 Il nest plus rien qui me peust c. *PcQl*:
ce mal *Ph*.   43 a.] endurer *PcQl*.   44 actes *NfNj*, assaux *PcQl*.   45 que de moy] que moy *Ph*.

A m'esjouïr, rire ne deporter:
On ne me puet nouvelles apporter

48 Ne langage si plaisant qui me plaise;
Plaindre et plourer sont mes jeux et mon aise.
Je n'ay soussi jamais comme tout voise;
Il ne me chaut a qui mon fait desplaise.

52 Chascun en puet a son gré rapporter;
Parle qui veult, et qui vouldra se taise,
Et qui avra parlé si se rapaise,
Car ma fortune est telle et si mauvaise

56 Qu'el ne puet pis pour moy desconforter.

V   Jugiez par qui ne pourquoy ce seroit,
Et comme dame ou Amours cuideroit
Qu'aprés sa mort mon cuer autre ameroit,

60 Ou que mon cuer prendroit en riens plaisance,   84v
Car qui tousjours de son bien parleroit
Et d'en parler jamais ne cesseroit,
Le langage ses faiz ne passeroit;

64 On ne la puet louer a souffisance.
Tout s'efforça au jour de sa naissance:
Les elemens y firent alïance;
Nature y mist le hault de sa puissance

68 Et dist qu'alors un chief d'euvre feroit,
Ou tant mectroit sens, honneur et savance
Qu'on vauldroit mieulx de sa seule acointance.
Pardonnez moy de dire oultrecuidance,

72 Mais d'autre amer mon cuer s'abesseroit.

VI   Je ne di pas – ne l'entente n'est telle –
Qu'il n'ait des biens en mainte dame belle,
Et qu'il n'en soit de tresbonnes sans elle,

46 r. ou *PcQl*.   47 On me me p. (*sic*) *Nf*; peust *PcQl*.   48 quil *Oa*.   50 Je nay s. maiz c. (comment *Ql*) t. en v. *PcQl*.   50–1 Il ne me chault j. c. t. v. Je nay soussy a qui m. f. d. *Oa*.   52 p. a s. g.] peust endroit *Pc*, peult en droit soy *Ql*.   53 ou *OaPcQl*.   54 Ou *OaQl*.   55 ma f.] f. *Ph*; est] et *Qd*.   56 Quelle *Oa*; Que ne peust *Pc*.   57 Jugier *Oa*; ne p.] et p. *Nj*, ou p. *Oa*, ne par quoy *Ph*, et pour qui *Nf*, ne comment *PcQl*; se s. *Ph*.   58 Et c. d.] Ou c. d. *Oa*, Que une d. *Pc*; dama (*sic*) *Qd*; ou A.] en a. *Pc*, a. (?) *Ql*.   60 m. c.] jamais *OaPcQl*; a r. p. *Oa*, ailleurs p. *NfNj*.   61 damours me p. *Pc*.   64 peust *PcQl*.   65 Tant *Nf*; le j. *PcQl*.   68 d. alors qun *NfNj*.   69 sc. h. et sa.] h. se. et sa. *OaPcPh²*, de se. et de sa. *NfNj*, dc grace et de sa. *Ph*, h. se. et chevance *Ql*.   70 Omitted *Oa*, Que tout v. m. par (de *Ph²*) son a. *PcPh²Ql*.   71 pour d. *PcQl*, se dy *NfNj*.   73 ne] que *Ph* (ne *Ph²*); mentente *PcPh²Ql*.   74 m. bonne et b. *NfNjPh* (m. d. b. *Ph²*).   75 qui *Ph*; dautres b. que celle (que elle *Ph*) *NfNjPcPhQl*; celle *Oa*.

76 Ou faulte n'a de rien que dame amende.
Ainçois maintien des dames la querrelle,
Pour leur bonté qui croist et renouvelle;
Et se je fail en rien, je m'en rappelle
80 Et cry mercy et engage l'amende.
Mais c'est trop fort que jamais je m'actende
A mieulx trouver, quelque part que je tende
N'en quelque lieu que mon las cuer se rende;
84 Et y faillir seroit douleur mortelle.
En ce point veult Amours que je l'entende
Et qu'a tousjours Loyauté m'en deffende,
Qui tant l'ayma et tant fu de sa bende
88 Que peu s'en fault qu'el n'est morte avec elle.

VII   Helas! Pourquoy me fist Amours emprendre
A tant l'aymer et si hault entreprendre,
Et moy donner tel don pour le reprendre   85r
92 Et de tel joye yssir pour souspirer?
Or me punist Fortune, sans mesprendre,
Pour celle amer, ou n'avoit que reprendre
Et ou Nature et Dieu vouldrent comprendre
96 Ce qu'on savroit a souhait desirer,
Qui tous les biens vouldroit en un tirer;
En elle estoit, sans autres empirer,
Le droit mirouer pour les autres mirer,
100 Ou chascun puet sans riens mectre tout prendre.
Si ne say plus de quel part me virer,
Si non offrir mon cuer a martirer
Et de tous poins d'Amours le retirer,
104 Com chevalier qui ses armes vient rendre.

76 nait *NſOa*, nest *PcQl*; qui *NſNjOaPcPhQl*.   79 Et se je y (se y *Ql*) f. de r. *PcQl*, Et je f. en r. *Nj*; me r. *Ql*.   80 pry *Ql*.   82 avoir *OaPcQl*.   83 *Omitted Oa*: que] ou *Nſ*.   84 Et moins trouver *Oa*, Et lamendrir *PcQl*.   85 lectende *Ph*.   88 quelle *Oa*; que (quil *Ql*) nest mort *NſNjPhQl* (nest morte *Ph²*); avecques(?) *Nſ*.   89 P.] comment *NſNjPh*; my f. *Oa*.   90 si fort *Ph*.   91 me *NſNjPh*; p. le r.] p. r. *Qd*.   92 telle j. *Oa*; yessir *Pc*, yssy *Ph*; par *PcPhQdQl*.   93 Et *NſNjPh* (Or *Ph²*); promist *Oa*.   94 *Omitted Ph*, Par une a. ou il na que r. *NſNj*: Par *Qd*.   95 Ou dieu nature du tout v. c. *PcQl*: vouldroit *Oa*.   97 ses b. *NſNj*.   98 celle *PcQl*; s. nulle aultre e. *PcQl*, s. les autres e. *Oa*.   100 peust *PcQl*.   102 corps *PcQl*.   104 veult *NſOaQl*.

VIII Ainsi mon temps en doleur use et passe,
     Dont le surplus desja m'ennuye et lasse,
     Ne je n'ay jour, heure, lieu në espasse
108 De rien penser qui mon espoir soustieigne.
     Je faiz tresor de regrez que j'amasse,
     Et n'est un bien passé que j'oublïasse;
     J'en rens compte sans q'un seul en trespasse,
112 Par chascun jour, quelque choise qu'avieigne.
     Il est force qu'adés il m'en souvieigne,
     Quel que je soye et quel que je devieigne,
     Tant que l'ame dedans le corps se tieigne;
116 Et n'est chose dont mieulx ne me passasse.
     Fortune veult qu'en ce point me contieigne;
     C'est la leçon qu'il fault que je retieigne.
     J'ay pris ce ploy; force est que le maintieigne,
120 Si seroit fort que jamais le changasse.

IX   Helas! Comment m'est Fortune si dure,   85v
     Ne comme a Dieu souffert ceste aventure
     Que de tous poins met a desconfiture
124 Ma lïesse, mon espoir et ma vie?
     Qui puet mouvoir a ce Dame Nature,
     Qui a souffert qu'on lui feist tel injure
     De deffaire si perfaicte figure
128 Qu'a droit patron avoit faicte assouvie,
     Pour esbahir et desconfire Envie
     Qui mesdisans a mesdire convie?
     Mais s'el en eust cent foiz sa foy plevie,

105 A. ma vie *PcQl*; en d.] folement *Ph*. 106 le s.] le plus *Ph* (le s. *Ph²*). 107 Car je nay pas lieu temps heure ne e. *Ql*: Car *Pc*; j.] temps *OaPc*; ny e. *Pc*. 108 que *Oa*. 109 tresors *Nj*; des r. *OaPcQl*. 110 Nil nest *Oa*; Et nay passe un b. *Ql*. 111 Et r. *Ph*; sans que (sans ce que *Ql*) nul en t. *PcQl*, sans ce qun en t. *Ph*. 113 nen s. *Nj*, me s. *Oa*. 114 Ou que je s. *PcQl*; et (ou *Nf*) quoy que je d. *NfPcQl*. 115 mon c. *Pc*; sy t. *Ph*. 116 Nil nest ch. *Oa*, Et si nest rien *PcQl*. 117 Omitted *NfNjPcPhQl*. 118 Cest la l. qui (quil *Ql*) convient que je tiengne *PcQl*. 119 Jay p. ce plait il fault que le m. *PcQl*. 119a Comme quil soit et comme quil adviengne (en viengne *NjPh*) *NfNjPh*, Comment (Comme *Ql*) quil voise (voit *Ql*) ne comme il en adviengne *PcQl*. 120 Ce *NfNjPcQl*; la ch. *NfPc*. 121 comme *Nj*, pourquoy *Ph*. 122 Et *NfNj*; comment (comme *Ql*) d. seuffre *PcQl*, come doye souffrir *Ph*. 123 Dainsi laissier mectre a d. *Ph*: Qui dung seul coup *PcQl*; mait *Nf*, mecte *Oa*, mectre *Pc*. 125 Et qui a peu m. d. n. *Ph*: peust a ce mouvoir *PcQl*. 126 Quelle a s. mectre a desconfiture *Ql*: Quelle a s. *Pc*, A consentir *Ph*. 127 Et *Ql*; sa p. f. *PcQl*, si parfaire f. *Nj*. 128 Quelle avoit f. a (fait pour *Ph*) p. a. *PcPhQl*: fait *Oa*. 129 A e. *Ph*. 130 mal dire *Ql*. 131 celle *Oa*; en e.] eust *PcQl*; la f. p. *Ph*, a sa p. (*sic*) *NfNj*.

132 Si ne sceut el dire faulte ou laidure.
    Or l'a la mort en jenne aage ravie,
    Et moy, qui l'ay tant loyaument servie,
    Viz en doleur sans l'avoir desservie
136 Et sans savoir pourquoy ma vie dure.

X   Mes semblans sont de joye contrefaiz,
    Tout au rebours du penser et des faiz,
    Et ne me plaist riens de ce que je faiz
140 S'il ne sortist a doulours et a plains.
    Estre tout seul est ma joye et ma paix;
    Je chemine sans savoir ou je vais.
    Qui parle a moy, je l'escoute et me tais
144 Et pense ailleurs s'a force ne me vains.
    J'oy les autres chanter, et je me plains;
    Ilz vont dançant, et je detors mes mains;
    Ilz festoient, et je tout seul remains;
148 J'ay fait leurs tours: maintenant les deffais.
    Plus voy jouer, et tant m'esjouÿs moins;
    Tous mes plaisirs sont de lermes estains.
    Le noir me plaist, car mon cuer en est tains   86r
152 De tainture qui ne fauldra jamais.

XI   Trop dur espart est sur moy esparty,
    Quant esgaré me treuve et departy
    D'un per sans per, qui oncques ne party
156 En faintise n'en legier pensement.
    Oncq ensemble n'avïons riens parti
    Mais un desir, un vouloir, un parti,
    Un cuer entier de deux cuers miparti,
160 Pareil plaisir et commun sentement.
    Mort, or as tu fait le departement
    Dont j'ay pardu mon bien entierement;

132 nen s. *NfNj*, ny s. *OaPcQl*. 133 Or la la m. a tort prise et r. *PcQl*. 134 si l. *Ph*, si longuement *PcQl*. 136 Ne *PcQl*. 137 de j. c.] de joyes c. *Pc*, c. *Nj*. 139 Et ne me p. de r. ce que je f. *PcQl*: Et] Ne il *Oa*. 140 Se il s. *NfNj*, Si me sortis *Oa*; en...en *Oa*, aux...aux *PcQl*; douleur *Ph*. 141 et ma j. *Oa*, est ma vie *PcQl*. 142 Et ch. *Ph*. 145 Joay *Qd*; je ma p. *Nj*. 146 sont *Ql*. 147 *Omitted OaQl*. 149 je me. *NfNj*, plus me. *Ql*. 150 mes desirs *PcQl*; l.] joy *Pc*, joye *Ph*, joyes *Ql*; destains *Pc*. 153 est] et *Nf*. 154 me voy *PcQl*. 155 Du *NjPcQl*; s. par *Qd*. 157 O.] Que *Nf*, Onquez *PcPhQl*; neusmes *NfNjPh*. 159 deux cuer *Qd*. 160 et c. s.] de c. s. *Pc*, dun c. s. *Ql*, c. assentement *Ph*. 162 Et jay *PcQl*.

Si appelle de ton faulx jugement
164 Car tout ce mal m'est avenu par ti,
Dont je renonce a tout esbatement,
Chacié d'Espoir, banny d'Alegement,
Et souhaite la mort tant seulement
168 Disant: 'Mon cuer, pourquoy ne se part y?'

XII   Si prens congié et d'Amours et de Joye
Pour vivre seul a tant que mourir doye,
Sans moy trouver jamays en lieu n'en voye
172 Ou Lïece ne Plaisance demeure.
Les compaignons laise que je hantoie.
Adieu, chançons que voulentiers chantoye
Et joyeux diz ou je me delitoye;
176 Tel rit joyeux qui aprés dolent pleure.
Le cuer m'estraint; angoisse me queurt seure.
Ma vie fait en moy longue demeure;
Je n'ay membre qu'a mourir ne labeure,
180 Et me tarde que ja mort de dueil soye.
Autre bien n'ay, n'autre bien n'assaveure
Fors seulement l'actente que je meure;   86v
Et desire que briefment vieigne l'eure,
184 Qu'aprés ma mort en paradis la voye.

Explicit.

165 ton e. *Ql*.   166 *Omitted Ph* (*Added Ph²*): Charcie *Qd*; Noircy de dueil *Ph²*.   168 ne se p. ty *Ph*, nez
esparty (esparry *Ql*) *PcQl*.   170 P. v. s. t. que m. je d. *PcQl*: m.] nourrir *Qd*, vivre *NfNj*.   171 S.
me t. plus ne en l. ne en v. *Ph*, S. james plus serchier place ne v. *PcQl*.   172 plaisance ne leesse
Oa.   173 Les c. avec qui je h. *NfNj*.   175 Et les beaux diz *PcPhQl*.   176 qui puis de douleur p.
NfNj.   177–8 *Inverted PcQl*.   178 Mon ame en moy fait trop l. d. *PcQl*: l. d.] trop longue d. *Oa*,
trop long d. *Ph*.   179 qua ma mort ne l. *NfNj*, quen langour ne l. *PcQl*.   180 Et] Et si *PcQl*.
181 Rien ne mest bon *PcQl*; ne saveure *Oa*.   182 *Omitted Ph* (*Added Ph²*).   183 Et me tarde que b.
ne vient (b. viengne *OaPh*) leure *NfNjOaPh*, Et ne requier si non que viengne (quaviengne *Ql*)
leure *PcQl*.
...Complainte de la mort *Nf*, ...complainte maistre alain *Ql*.

10

'La Belle Dame sans Mercy', the letters and the 'Excusacion aux Dames'

LA BELLE DAME SANS MERCY

Forty-four Manuscripts: *Gb Ge Gf Gj*   *Nc Nf Ng Nj Nl No Np Nr*   *Oa Oj Om Pa Pb Pc Pd Pe Pf Pg Ph Pj Pk Pl Pn Po Pp*   *Qa Qb Qc Qd Q f Qg Qh Qk Ql Qm Qn Qo Qp Qq Qr.*

The first leaves of *Q j*, which perhaps contained the poem, are missing. *Q j* and *Qn* have not been traced, while *Qp* has been damaged by fire. All the other manuscripts have been examined.

The *Belle Dame sans Mercy* was included in all the early collected editions and in the Du Chesne edition. There are at least six separate early editions.[1] The collected editions of 1489 and 1617 have been examined, as have GKW 6564 and 6565 and the copies in the libraries of Harvard and Yale Universities.

Several modern editions exist of the poem. L. Charpennes republished the text of Du Chesne in 1901. In 1936 the *Belle Dame sans Mercy* was re-edited by A. Pagès, who used *Pe* as base and gave variants from *Qg* and from the Du Chesne edition; Pagès' text was reproduced by A. Berry in 1944. The most recent edition of the poem, that of A. Piaget, is based on *Nj* and, for stanzas LXXXV to XC, *Oa*.[2]

L'EXCUSACION AUX DAMES

Thirty-one Manuscripts:[3] *Nf Nj Nl No Np Nr*   *Oa Oj*   *Pa Pb Pc Pd Pe Pf Ph Pj Pk Pl Pn*   *Qa Qb Qd Q f Qh Q j Qk Ql Qn Qo Qq Qr*

The *Excusacion* was written in reply to criticisms of the *Belle Dame sans Mercy* and all the above manuscripts except *Q j*, which is incomplete, also contain that poem. The criticisms were set out in a letter sent to the ladies of the court. When they forwarded a copy of the letter to Alain Chartier, the ladies added a note of explanation. The two letters are in prose and are never found without the *Excusacion*. They are copied in all the above manuscripts except *Np Ph Qb Q f Q j* and *Qo*. In *Qa* and *Q f* the prose letters are accompanied by metrical versions of them. The metrical version of one letter is

---

[1] GKW 6564–5; Chantilly, Musée Condé, 419; Fairfax Murray, 633; Harvard University, Inc. 8779.5; Yale, U.L., Beinecke, Hfa 19.8f.

[2] See pp. 506–7.

[3] It is possible that *Qp* contains the *Excusacion* and the two letters. See the description of *Qp*.

given in *Qj*. All the manuscripts have been examined except *Qj* and *Qn*, which are untraced.

The *Excusacion* and the prose letters were included in all the collected editions and the Du Chesne edition; the editions of 1489 and 1617 have been examined. Two of the modern editions of the *Belle Dame sans Mercy*, those of L. Charpennes and A. Piaget, further contain editions of the letters and the *Excusacion*, editions made in the same way as those of the *Belle Dame sans Mercy*.

The *Belle Dame sans Mercy* is anonymous in all but two manuscripts, *Np* and *Gj*; in them it is attributed indirectly to Alain Chartier. Many of the rubrics of the letters and of the *Excusacion* mention Chartier's name. A number of manuscripts include, almost as a signature at the end of the *Excusacion*, a quatrain playing on the name Alain.

The title *Belle Dame sans Mercy* is given in the last line of the poem itself. The *Excusacion* has that title most often in the manuscripts, although in several it is called the *Responce*.

The *Belle Dame sans Mercy* has been edited here from nine manuscripts: *Gf Nf Nj Oa Oj Pc Ph Qd* and *Ql*. In the edition of the two prose letters, *Nf Nj Oa Oj Pc Qd* and *Ql* were used and the same manuscripts, together with *Ph*, served for the edition of the *Excusacion*.

Examination of the textual traditions of these four works shows that they are almost as closely connected as the works themselves are historically. It is possible and convenient to discuss them together.[1] The nine texts can be divided into two groups which can, in their turn, be subdivided; such divisions, although useful for discussion, are by no means absolute.

The first group comprises *Nf Nj Oa Ph* and *Qd*. Readings at lines 34, 254, 312, 378 and 786 and at line 149 of the *Excusacion* are given by four of the five texts and are not found elsewhere. There exists in addition a large number of readings peculiar to three or to two of the texts in the group.

Nf and *Nj* both lack stanzas LXXXV to XC and contain readings peculiar to themselves at lines 22, 29–30, 67, 99, 141, 191, 320, 337, 339, 360 etc.; similar readings are found in the other three works, being particularly numerous in the second letter. Individual readings, present in either text, are more frequent in *Nf*. *Nj* is technically irregular at line 295 and at line 77 of the *Excusacion* where it also gives a poor rhyme; readings peculiar to *Nj* are at lines 93, 149, 160, 242, 271, 336, 365, 392, 402, 404 etc. Irregular readings at lines 56, 268, 410, 460, 461, 510, 535, 556 and 660 are found only in *Nf* and the text rhymes poorly at lines 422, 450, 595 and 630. *Nj* and particularly *Nf* have some readings in common with texts of the second group; their relationship with those texts will be discussed later.

Readings peculiar to *Oa* and *Ph* occur at lines 15, 107, 359, 492, 593, 640, 726 and 763 (irregular), and at lines 62 and 103 (irregular) of the *Excusacion*. Both texts contain a large number of individual readings, many irregular. When such readings occur in *Oa* (lines 18, 33, 56, 235, 250, 289, 403, 409, 477, 633 etc.), it is often as a result of an

---

[1] Reference will be made to the *Belle Dame sans Mercy* above all. When lines are cited without the title of the work being mentioned, it is the *Belle Dame sans Mercy* which is intended.

omission. *Ph* is irregular at lines 6, 184, 189, 255, 288, 307, 350, 383, 399, 415 etc. Line 699 is omitted in *Ph*, which also lacks lines 77 and 228 of the *Excusacion*. The connection between *Ph* and texts of the second group will be discussed later.

Qd gives complete texts of the four works; it contains irregular readings peculiar to itself at lines 34, 62, 442, 474, 605, 611, 750 and at lines 31, 236 and 243 of the *Excusacion*. These irregularities result in the main from scribal carelessness; this is also the case with the other individual readings found in *Qd*. *Qd* and *Ph* contain a version peculiar to themselves of stanza XVII of the *Excusacion*.

Gf Oj Pc and *Ql* make up the second group of texts. Readings peculiar to *Gf Pc* and *Ql* are found at lines 16, 70, 160, 229, 293, 338, 360, 369, 380, 412 and 446. *Gf* contains only the first sixty stanzas of the *Belle Dame sans Mercy*, the remaining stanzas having been lost. There exists a large number of readings peculiar to *Pc* and *Ql*, for example at lines 13, 66, 85, 121, 129, 148, 175, 194, 262, 305 etc.

Gf is irregular at line 461 and rhymes poorly at line 159; readings peculiar to *Gf* are at lines 22, 32, 58, 63, 85, 101, 129, 130, 268, 272 etc. Readings peculiar to *Pc* make the text irregular at lines 16, 87, 98, 180, 224 (technically), 408, 483, 675 and 741; poor rhymes are found at lines 253, 557, 695 and 729. *Ql* includes as many individual readings as does *Pc*: those at lines 66, 108, 253, 267, 479, 483, 540 and 626 leave the text irregular; *Ql* rhymes poorly at lines 124, 557, 630 and 729.

Readings at lines 53, 94, 251 and 537 are peculiar to *Oj* and to two at least of the three texts just discussed. Further readings at lines 59, 250, 254, 312, 356, 378, 416, 659 and 708 serve to confirm that relationship, although they are also found in other texts, notably *Nf* and *Ph*. *Gf* and *Oj* are the only texts used in this edition which contain rubrics naming the characters in the poem. Readings peculiar to *Oj* are quite numerous (e.g. lines 5, 19, 83, 84, 88, 106, 112, 144, 145, 214 etc.); the text is irregular at lines 9, 65, 596 and 792 and at line 69 of the *Excusacion*.

It was emphasised earlier that the division of the texts into two groups was not absolute. *Nf* and *Ph*, and to a lesser extent *Nj* and *Oa*, show some kinship with texts of the second group. So far as *Nf* and *Nj* are concerned, readings at lines 267, 280, 580, 585 and 589 indicate that a link exists. If readings linking *Nj* alone are infrequent (e.g. line 786), readings linking *Nf* with the second group are more numerous (lines 23, 44, 59, 250, 284, 356, 381, 410, 411, 461 etc.). Some of the readings just cited also point to a connection between *Ph* and texts of the second group. *Ph* agrees with texts of that group at lines 250, 254, 312, 328, 708 and 740.

It is not easy to choose a base text from which to edit the four works. Although the nine texts just described are at times markedly different, their readings generally make good sense and are acceptable. This is the case in particular with stanza XVII of the *Excusacion*, for which two entirely different versions are available. Where alternative readings differ only in style, it is impossible, in the great majority of cases, to show that one alternative *must* be preferred. Two examples will illustrate the point. At line 585 there is a choice between singular and plural. The singular, *meffait*, seems preferable at first sight for, in using it, the lady recalls line 583 and her remarks serve to link stanzas LXXIII and LXXIV. On the other hand, when the lady goes on with her remarks she refers twice to *les* (line 587), which could be *meffaiz* in the plural. The arguments are of equal weight. At line 729, the version offered by *Oa Oj* and *Ph* gives a rhyme which is less ornate than that offered by *Nf Nj* and *Qd* and their version also involves repetition.[1] It can be argued, however, that the repetition is for emphasis and that the rhyme, though less pleasing than the alternative, is nevertheless regular.

In a few cases, one of the versions available must be rejected on syntactic grounds. A plural may be found where the sense demands a singular or *vice versa*: examples occur at lines 20 (*Oj* and *Pc*), 322 (*Nf Nj* and *Ph*) and 416 (*Gf Nf Oa Oj Pc* and *Ql*). A verb may be used in the wrong person: at line 347 *Nf Nj* and *Ph* give the second person where the sense demands the third.

Such passages are so few in number that, in the choice of a base text, reliance must be placed above all on the characteristics of the texts as they were outlined earlier. It was clear from that discussion that only *Nj* and *Qd* from the first group and *Oj* from the second could be considered as possible base texts. In the passages just examined *Qd* gave a better version than either *Nj* or *Oj*. *Oj* and *Qd* contain complete texts of the four works; in *Nj* six stanzas of the *Belle Dame sans Mercy* are omitted. The number of individual readings and of irregular lines in *Qd* is higher than that in *Oj* or in *Nj*, even when the readings which link *Nj* so closely to *Nf* are also taken into account. When the readings peculiar to each of these three texts are examined in greater detail, however, it is noticeable that those in *Qd* result to a very large extent from scribal errors of a minor character; mis-spellings abound in particular. The number of *substantial* readings peculiar to *Qd* is significantly less than that in *Nj* or *Oj*, which have been copied and revised with greater care. *Qd* has been chosen as base; its defects and errors have been corrected with the help of *Oj* or *Nj*.

Corrections in Oj

The following lines contain corrections in the hand of *Oj*[2];[2] 16 *ne* to *na*; 146 Ne moins; 154 *traveille*; 163 revenoit; 230 *de celle* to *dycelle*; 275 *joyeux*; 288 me*stre*; 332 *moy* to *me*; 347, 350 ser*mens*; 362 *mie* /bien/ *dune*; 365 *meigniee*; 366 venim; 380 on; 395 *le* to *la*; 494 *deux*; 552 *celer* ains /y/ *pert*; 571 *le* gouster; 586 *on* to len; 595, 638 *suis* to *suy*; 623 *quen*; 637 *certif*iez; 640, L II: 5 and 12, EX 198 *refus*; 794 *assemble* to *sassemble*; L I: 7 *a* to de; L II: 4 *leur* to et *leur*; L II: 24 *quon* to *que len*; EX 135 *franc* /cuer/ *na*; 206 *grief* /mal/ *damer*; 212 *mot* /en/ *trespasser*. While most of the corrections are individual, for others (lines 16, 380 and 794) a manuscript akin to *Nf* or *Nj* may have been used.

---

[1] The reading of *Pc* and *Ql* at line 729 is impossible.
[2] On the corrections in *Oj* and the difficulty of distinguishing between the different series, see pp. 94–5 and 157.

LA BELLE DAME SANS MERCY

I

Nagaires, chevauchant, pensoye   *Qd,* 39r
Com home triste et doloreux,
Au dueil ou il fault que je soye
4   Le plus dolent des amoureux,
Puis que, par son dart rigoreux,
La mort me tolly ma maistresse
Et me laissa seul, langoreux
8   En la conduite de Tristesse.

II

Si disoye: 'Il fault que je cesse
De dicter et de rimoyer,
Et que j'abandonne et delaisse
12   Le rire pour le lermoyer.
La me fault le temps employer,
Car plus n'ay sentement në aise,
Soit d'escrire, soit d'envoyer
16   Chose qu'a moy në autre playse.

III

Qui vouldroit mon vouloir contraindre
A joyeuses choses escrire,
Ma plume n'y savroit actaindre,
20   Non feroit ma langue a les dire.
Je n'ay bouche qui puisse rire
Que les yeulx ne la desmantissent,
Car le cuer l'envoyeroit desdire
24   Par les larmes qui des yeulx yssent.

IV

Je laysse aux amoreux malades
Qui ont espoir d'alegement
Faire chançons, diz et balades,
28   Chascun a son entendement,
Car ma dame en son testament   39v
Print a la mort, Dieu en ait l'ame,
Et emporta mon sentement
32   Qui gist o elle soubs la lame.

...ma b. d. s. m. *Nj, No heading Pc.*   5 de son d. *Oj.*   6 me t.] me me t. *Ph,* ma t. *Qd,* ma tollu *Pc.*
9 que je c.] que que je c. *Oj.*   13 mon t. *PcQl.*   14 ny aise *Ql.*   15 soit d'en.] ou den. *OaPh.*   16 Chose
qui a moy nautry (na aultry *Pc*) p. *GfPcQl:* ne a.] na a. *NjOaOj²Ph* (ne a. *Oj*), na autruy *Nf.*
18 A joyeuse chose e. *Oa.*   19 ne s. *Oj.*   20 a le d. *OjPc.*   22 ne le d. *Gf,* ne len d. *NfNj.*   23 lenvoyroit *Nj,* len voudroit *GfNfPcQl.*   24 Pour *Oa.*   29 a son t. *NfNj.*   30 Pris *NfNj.*   32 Qui
gist cele desoubx la lame *Gf.*

332

V   Desormais est temps de moy tayre,
                    Car de dire suis je lassé.
                    Je vueil laissier aux autres faire:
36   Leur temps est; le mien est passé.
                    Fortune a le forcier cassé
                    Ou j'espargnoye ma richesse
                    Et le bien que j'ay amassé
40   Ou meilleur temps de ma jennesse.

VI   Amours a gouverné mon sens:
                    Se faulte y a, Dieu me pardonne;
                    Se j'ay bien fait, plus ne m'en sens,
44   Cela ne me toult ne me donne,
                    Car au trespas de la tresbonne
                    Tout mon bienfait se trespassa.
                    La mort m'assist ilec la bonne
48   Qu'onques puis mon cuer ne passa.'

VII   En ce penser et en ce soing
                    Chevauchay toute matinee,
                    Tant que je ne fu gaire loing
52   Du lieu ou estoit la dinee;
                    Et quant j'euz ma voye finee
                    Et que je cuiday herbergier,
                    J'ouÿ par droicte destinee
56   Les menestriers en un vergier.

VIII   Si me retrahy voulentiers
                    En un lieu tout coy et privé,
                    Mais quant mes bons amis antiers   40r
60   Sçurent que je fu arrivé,
                    Ilz vindrent. Tant ont estrivé,
                    Moitié force, moitié requeste,
                    Que je n'ay oncques eschivé
64   Qu'ilz ne me mainent a la feste.

33 e. t.] e. le t. *Oa*; de me t. *Ph*.   34 de d.] dere (*sic*) *Qd*; je sui *NfNjOaPh*.   36 L. t. et le m. *Ph*.
37 lefforcier *Nf*, le forgier *Ql*.   44 Cela me t. ne ne d. *NfPc*: ne ne d. *GfNjOjPhQl*.   52 ma d.
NjOaPh.   53 ma v. f.] ma v. affinee *GfOjQl*.   54 me c. h. *Ql*.   56 Menestriers (Menestrelx *Oa*,
Menesterelz *Oj*) en ung v. *NfOaOj*, Menestreux dedens ung v. *Pc*, Doulz menestrelz en un v. *Ph*.
58 a p. *Gf*.   59 M. qu.] Mais deux *NfOjQl*, Mes .ij. *Gf*, Maiz deulz *Pc*.   62 force *repeated Qd*.   63 Que
je noy o. acheve *Gf*.

IX

A l'entrer fu bien recueilli
Des dames et des damoiselles,
Et de celles bien acueilly
68   Qui toutes sont bonnes et belles;
Et de la courtoisie d'elles
Me tindrent ilec tout ce jour
En plaisans parolles nouvelles
72   Et en tresgracïeux sejour.

X

Disner fu prest et tables mises.
Les dames a table s'assirent
Et quant elles furent assises,
76   Les plus gracïeux les servirent.
Telz y ot qui a ce jour virent
En la compaignie lïens
Leurs juges, dont semblant ne firent,
80   Qui les tiennent en leurs lïens.

XI

Un entre les autres y vy,
Qui souvent aloit et venoit,
Et pensoit comme homme ravy
84   Et gaires de bruit ne menoit.
Son semblant fort contretenoit;
Mais Desir passoit la raison,
Qui souvent son regart menoit
88   Tel foiz qu'il n'estoit pas saison.

XII

De faire chiere s'efforsoit   40v
Et menoit une joye fainte,
Et a chanter son cuer forsoit
92   Non pas pour plaisir mais pour crainte,
Car tousjours un relais de plainte
S'enlaçoit au son de sa voix;
Et revenoit a son atainte
96   Comme l'oisel au chant du bois.

65 lentree *Oj*, lentrez *Qd*. 66 De d. et de d. (et d. *Ql*) *PcQl*. 67 dicelles *NfNj*; bel a. *OaOj*.
70 le j. *GfPcQl*. 81 Une autre entre les a. vy *Ph*. 83 Et sembloit bien h. r. *Oj*, En pensant c. h.
r. *Ph*. 84 Qui *Oj*. 85 sentretenoit *Gf*, entretenoit *PcQl*. 87 s. son r.] s. r. *Pc*. 88 Telz f. *Oj*.
93 un r. destrainte *Nj*. 94 ou s. *Ph*, au ton *GfOjPc*. 96 ou ch. *Ph*, au son *Ql*.

XIII
    Des autres y ot plaine sale,
    Mais cellui trop bien me sembloit
    Ennuyé, maigre, blesme et pale,
100 Et la parolle lui trembloit.
    Gaires aux autres n'assembloit;
    Le noir portoit et sans devise,
    Et trop bien home ressembloit
104 Qui n'a pas son cuer en franchise.

XIV
    De toutes festoyer faingnoit,
    Bien le fist et bien lui sëoit;
    Mais a la foiz le contraingnoit
108 Amours qui son cuer hardëoit
    Pour sa maistresse qu'il vëoit,
    Que je choysi lors clerement
    A son regart qu'il assëoit
112 Sur elle si piteusement.

XV
    Assez sa face destournoit
    Pour regarder en autres lieux,
    Mais au travers l'ueil retournoit
116 Au lieu qui lui plaisoit le mieulx.
    J'apperceu le trait de ses yeulx,
    Tout empenné d'umbles requestes;
    Si dis a par moy: 'Se m'aist Dieux,
120 Autel fumes comme vous estes'.

XVI
    A la foiz a part se tiroit   4II
    Pour raffermer sa contenance,
    Et trestendrement souspiroit
124 Par doloreuse souvenance.
    Puis reprenoit son ordonnance
    Et venoit pour servir les mes,
    Mais a bien jugier sa semblence,
128 C'estoit un piteux entremés.

98 M. c. t.] M. t. *Pc.*   99 E. m. (m. et *Nj*) blesve et p. *NfNj,* E. b. m. et p. *GfPh.*   101 Guerre aux
a. ne ressembloit *Gf*: ne sembloit *Ph.*   102 p. en sa d. *Ql.*   104 a f. *Oa.*   105 faingnoient *Ph.*
106 moult lui s. *Oj.*   107 a la fin *OaPh.*   108 que *Qd*; h.] ardoit *Ql.*   112 Sus elle moult p. *Oj.*
115 en t. *Ql*; leur r. *Pc.*   118 empennez *Ql*; dumble requestes *Ph.*   120 Autelz f. *Nj,* Autelz sommes
Ph, Autel fusge *Ql.*   121 se trayoit *PcQl.*   124 Pour *Oa*; contenance *Ql.*   128 un petit e. *Oa.*

XVII   Aprés disner on s'avança
              De dancer, chascun et chascune,
              Et le triste amoureux dança
132   Adés o l'autre, adés o l'une.
              A toutes fist chiere commune,
              O chascune a son tour aloit;
              Mais tousjours retournoit a une
136   Dont sur toutes plus lui chaloit.

XVIII   Bien avoit a mon gré visé
              Entre celles que je vi lors,
              S'il eust au gré du cuer visé
140   Autant que a la beauté du corps;
              Qui croit de legier les rappors
              De ses yeulx sans autre esperance,
              Pourroit mourir de mille mors
144   Avant qu'ataindre a sa plaisance.

XIX   En la dame ne failloit riens,
              Ne plus avant ne plus arriere.
              C'estoit garnison de tous biens
148   Pour faire a cuer d'amant frontiere:
              Jeune, gente, fresche et entiere;
              Maintien rassis et sans changier;
              Doulce parolle et grant maniere,   41v
152   Dessoubz l'estendart de Danger.

XX   De celle feste me lassay,
              Car joye triste cuer travaille,
              Et hors de la presse passay;
156   Si m'assis derriere une treille
              Drue de fueilles a merveille,
              Entrelacee de saulx vers,
              Si que nul, pour l'espesse fueille,
160   Ne me peüst veoir au travers.

129 on] lors *Gf*, or *PcQl*.   130 ch. a ch. *Gf*.   132 a... a *Oa*, a... o *Ph*.   135 revenoit *OaPc*. 136 sus *Pc*.   137 Bien a a mon gre advise *Oa*.   140 A. que la b. *Oa*.   141 ses r. *NfNj*.   144 Ainchoiz *Pc*; qua. sa p. *Oj*.   146 Ne moins a. *Oj*².   148 au c. *Ph*; a cueurs damans *PcQl*.   149 f. et legiere *Nj*. 151 et sans m. *Oa*.   153 ceste f. *Gf*; me laissay *Ph*.   154 travaillay *Oa*.   156 Et *NfNj*; dessoubz *Oa*, derreire (*sic*) *Qd*.   157 Dure de f. amerveilles *Ph*.   158 faulx *Ph*.   159 nulz *Ql*; fresle *Gf*.   160 Ne peust veoir au t. *GfPcQl*: peut *NfOa*; a t. *Nj*.

XXI

L'amoureux sa dame menoit
Dancer quant venoit a son tour,
Et puis sëoir s'en revenoit
164 Sur un prëau vert au retour.
Nulz autres n'avoit a l'entour
Assis, fors seulement les deux;
Et n'y avoit autre destour
168 Fors la treille entre moy et eulx.

XXII

J'ouÿ l'amant qui sospiroit,
Car qui plus est pres plus desire,
Et la grant doleur qu'il tiroit
172 Ne savoit taire et n'osoit dire;
Si languissoit auprés du mire
Et nuysoit a sa garison,
Car qui art ne se puet plus nuyre
176 Qu'approucher le feu du tison.

XXIII

Le cuer ens ou corps lui croissoit,
D'engoisse et de pëeur estraint,
Tant qu'a bien peu qu'il ne froissoit
180 Quant l'un et l'autre le contraint.
Desir boute: Crainte restraint;   42r
L'un eslargist: l'autre resserre;
Si n'a pas peu de mal empraint
184 Qui porte en son cuer telle guerre.

XXIV

De parler souvent s'efforça,
Se Crainte ne l'eust destourné;
Mais en la fin son cuer força
188 Quant il ot assez sejourné.
Puis s'est vers la dame tourné
Et dist bas, en plourant adoncques:

163 se r. *Pc*, sen retournoit *Ph*.   164 Sus *Oj*; son vert preau *Ph*.   170 pres est *GfOaOjPcPhQl*.
171 qui *Qd*; sentoit *Pc*, menoit *GfQl*.   173 Et l. *Nf*.   174 muysoit *Qd*; la g. *Ph*.   175 Car aucun
ne se peust (peult *Ql*) p. n. *PcQl*: nuye *Qd*.   176 dun tiron *Ph*.   177 ou c.] en (eu) c. *GfPc*, le c.
Oa.   178 destraint *Ph*.   180 Qu. l'un et] Qu. et *Pc*.   181 refraint *GfNjOaOjPc*, retient *Ph*.   184 tel
g. *Ph*.   185 De vouloir parler se. *Oa*.   189 cest *Ph*; la d. t.] sa d. t. *NfOj*, la d. retourne *Ph*.
190 d. lors *Ph*.

337

L'Amant

Mal jour fu pour moy adjourné,
192   Ma dame, quant je vous vy oncques.

XXV   *Item l'Amant*

Je souffre mal ardent et chault
Dont je muir pour vous bien vouloir,
Et si voy qu'il ne vous en chault
196   Et n'avez d'y penser vouloir;
Mais en trop moins qu'en nonchaloir
Le mectez quant je le vous compte,
Et si n'en pouez pis valoir,
200   N'avoir moins honneur ne plus honte.

XXVI   *Item l'Amant*

Helas! Que vous grieve, ma dame,
S'un franc cuer d'omme vous veult bien?
Et se par honneur et sans blame
204   Je suis voustre et voustre me tien?
De droit je n'y chalenge rien,
Car ma volenté s'est soubzmise
En voustre gré, non pas au mien,
208   Pour plus asservir ma franchise.

XXVII   *Item l'Amant*

Ja soit ce que pas ne desserve
Voustre grace par mon servir,   42v
Souffrez au moins que je vous serve
212   Sans voustre mal gré desservir.
Je serviray sans desservir
En ma loiauté observant,
Car pour ce me fist asservir
216   Amours d'estre voustre servant.

---

191 *Heading in Oj only:* Mal fu j. *NfNj. Stanzas headed in Oj.* 194 Madame p. v. b. v. *Ph:* vo bien *PcQl.* 196 dit p. v. *Ph.* 197 a t. m. *PcPh;* que n. *OaOj,* qua n. *Ph.* 199 ne p. *Ql.* 206 Et ma v. *Oa.* 207 A v. g. *OaOjPhQl.* 210 pour *PhQdQl.* 211 Souffre *Qd.* 214 asservant *Oj.*

338

XXVIII

L'Acteur

Quant la dame oÿ ce langage,
Elle respondy bassement,
Sans müer couleur ne courage
220 Mais tout amesureement:

La Dame

Beau sire, ce foul pensement
Ne vous laissera il jamais?
Ne penserez vous autrement
224 De donner a voustre cuer paix?

XXIX

L'Amant

Nulli n'y pourroit la paix mectre
Fors vous qui la guerre y meïstes
Quant voz yeulx escrirent la lectre
228 Par quoy deffïer me feïstes,
Et que Doulx Regart transmeïstes,
Herault de celle deffïance,
Par lequel vous me promeïstes
232 En deffïant, bonne fïance.

XXX

La Dame

Il a grant fain de vivre en dueil
Et fait de son cuer lasche garde,
Qui contre un tout seul regard d'ueil
236 Sa paix et sa joye ne garde.
Se moy ou aultre vous regarde,
Les yeulx sont faiz pour regarder.
Je n'y prent point aultrement garde;
240 Qui y sent mal s'en doit garder.

XXXI

L'Amant

S'aucun blece autruy d'aventure   43r
Par coulpe de cellui qui blece,

XXVIII *headed* La dame *Gf.* 224 Pour d. *Oj*; a v. *repeated Pc.* *Stanzas* XXIX–LX *headed in Gf.* 225 ne p. *Qd.* 227 rescrirent *Ph.* 229 r. y tramistes *GfPcQl.* 230 de telle d. *Oa,* dycelle d. *Oj²* (de celle d. *Oj*). 232 vostre f. *Ql.* 233 fin *Nf.* 235 un t. s. r.] un s. r. *Oa.* 241 b. aucun *Ph.* 242 quil b. *Nj,* qui besse *Oa.*

339

Quoy qu'il n'en puet mais par droicture,
244 Si en a il dueil et tristece.
Et puis que Fortune ou Rudece
Ne m'ont mie fait ce meshaing,
Mais voustre tresbelle jeunece,
248 Pourquoy l'avez vous en desdaing?

XXXII   *La Dame*

Contre vous ne desdaing n'ataine
N'euz je oncques ne n'y vueil avoir,
Ne trop grant amour ne trop haine,
252 Ne voustre priveté savoir.
Se Cuider vous fait percevoir
Que peu de chose puet trop plaire,
Et vous vous voulez decevoir,
256 Ce ne vueil je pas pourtant faire.

XXXIII   *L'Amant*

Qui que m'ait le mal pourchacé,
Cuider ne m'a point deceü;
Mais Amour m'a si bien chacé
260 Que je suis en voz laz cheü.
Et puis qu'ainsi m'est escheü
D'estre a mercy entre voz mains,
S'il m'est au chëoir mescheü,
264 Qui plus tost meurt en languist moins.

XXXIV   *La Dame*

Si gracïeuse maladie
Ne met gaires de gens a mort,
Mais il siet bien que l'on le die
268 Pour plus tost actraire confort.
Tel se plaint et garmente fort
Qui n'a pas les plus aspres deulx,

243 peust *Pc.* 245 Mais *Ph.* 247 tresplaisant j. *Oj.* 249 C. v. d. (orgueil *Oa*) na. *GfOaOjPcPh* *Ql*: nay d. *Nf.* 250 N'e. je o.] Ne. o. *PcPhQl*; ne ne v. a. *NfOjPcPhQl*, ne v. a. *Oa.* 251 Ne t. g. a. ne h. *GfOjPcQl*, Ne t. g. a. ne grant h. *NfNjPh*, Ne t. a. ne t. h. *Oa.* 253 Ne c. *Ph*; decepvoir *Pc*, devoir (?) *Ql.* 254 Ou puet pou de ch. *Nf*; doit t. p. *GfOjPcPhQl.* 255 vous me voulez d. *Oa*, vous voulez d. *Ph.* 257 ce m. *Ql.* 258 pas *Oj.* 259 fort ch. *Oj.* 262 en m. *PcQl.* 267 chiet *NfNjOjPcQl*; que l'on] quon (?) *Ql*; la d. *Oj*, en d. *Ph.* 268 p. t. a.] p. a. *Nf*, p. t. acquerre *Gf.*

Et s'amours greve tant, au fort
272 Mieulx en vault un dolent que deux.

XXXV
L'Amant

Helas, ma dame! Il vault trop mieulx,   43ᵛ
Pour courtoisie et bonté faire,
D'un dolent faire deux joyeux
276 Que le dolent du tout deffaire.
Je n'ay desir në autre affaire
Fors que mon service vous plaise
Pour eschanger, sans riens meffaire,
280 Deux plaisirs ou lieu d'un mesaise.

XXXVI
La Dame

D'amours ne quier courroux n'aysance,
Ne grant espoir ne grant desir;
Et si n'ay de voz maulx plaisance
284 Ne regart a voustre plaisir.
Choisisse qui vouldra choisir.
Je suis france et france vueil estre,
Sans moy de mon cuer dessaisir
288 Pour en faire un autre le maistre.

XXXVII
L'Amant

Amours, qui joie et dueil depart,
Mist les dames hors de servaige
Et leur ordonna pour leur part
292 Maistrise et franc seigneurïage.
Les servans n'y ont d'aventage
Fors tant seulement leur pourchaz;
Et qui fait une foiz l'ommage,
296 Bien chier en coustent les rachaz.

XXXVIII
La Dame

Dames ne sont mye si lourdes,
Si mal entendans ne si foles

271 grievent *Nj.* 272 un morir que d. *Gf.* 276 lun d. *Oj.* 279 eschiver *Nf.* 280 en l. (lieux *Nj*) *NfNjOjPcPhQl.* 281 c. naissance *NfPh.* 284 Ne regret *GfNfPcQl.* 288 a. le m.] a. m. *Ph.* 289 A. qui j.] A. j. *Oa.* 292 M. et tout f. segneurage *Gf.* 293 ny ont avantage *GfPcQl.* 294 leurs p. *NjOjPhQl.* 295 une fois *repeated Nj;* hommage *Gf,* louvraige *Ph.* 296 Moult *Oⁱ.* 298 Sil *Qd* Tant *Oj.*

Que, pour un peu de plaisans bourdes
300 Confites en belles parolles,
Dont vous autres tenés escoles
Pour leur faire croire merveilles,
Elles changent si tost leurs coles:
304 A beau parler closes oreilles.

XXXIX   *L'Amant*

Il n'est jangleur, tant y meïst   44r
De sens, d'estudie ou de peine,
Qui si triste plainte feïst
308 Comme cellui que le mal maine.
Car qui se plaint de teste saine,
A paine sa faintise cueuvre;
Mais pensee de doleur plaine
312 Preuve ses parolles par euvre.

XL   *La Dame*

Amours est crüel losengier,
Aspre en fait et doulx a mentir,
Et se scet bien de ceulx venger
316 Qui cuident ses secrez sentir:
Il les fait a soy consentir
Par une entree de chierté;
Mais quant vient jusqu'au repentir,
320 Lors se descouvre sa fierté.

XLI   *L'Amant*

De tant plus que Dieu et Nature
Ont fait plaisir d'amours plus hault,
Tant plus aspre en est la pointure
324 Et plus desplaisant le deffault.
Qui n'a froit n'a cure de chault;
L'un contraire est pour l'autre quis,
Et ne scet nul que plaisir vault
328 S'il ne l'a par doleur conquis.

302 leurs *Qd.*   303 leur *Qd.*   304 courtes o. *Oa.*   305 jongleur *PcQl.*   306 et de p. *PcQl.*   307 f.] fist *Ph.*   308 qui *GfNfOaPcQl.*   311 doulceur *Gf.*   312 les p. *Ph*; par leuvre *GfOjPcPhQl.*   314 en m. *NfNjQl*, au m. *Pc.*   315 ce *Oj*; diceulx *Ql.*   319 M. qu. se vient au r. *Ph*: jusqua *Oa.*   320 Alors d. *NfNj*, L. il d. *Oa.*   321 d. a n. *Ph.*   322 plaisirs *NfNjPh.*   326 par *Pc.*   328 acquis *GfPcPhQl.*

342

XLII   *La Dame*

Plaisir n'est mie partout un;
Ce vous est doulx qui m'est amer,
Si ne pouez vous ou aucun
332 A voustre gré moy faire amer.
Nul ne se doit amy clamer
Si non par cuer ains que par livre,
Car force ne puet entamer
336 La volenté france et delivre.

XLIII   *L'Amant*   44v

Haa, ma dame! Ja Dieu ne plaise
Qu'autre droit y vueille querir,
Fors de vous moustrer ma mesaise
340 Et voustre mercy requerir.
Se je tens honneur surquerir,
Dieu et Fortune me confonde
Et ne me doint ja acquerir
344 Une seule joye en ce monde.

XLIV   *La Dame*

Vous et autres qui ainsi jurent
Et se condempnent et maudïent,
Ne cuident que leurs sermens durent,
348 Fors tant comme les moz se dïent
Et que Dieu et les sains s'en rïent,
Car en telz sermens n'a riens ferme,
Et les chestives qui s'y fïent
352 En plourent aprés mainte lerme.

XLV   *L'Amant*

Cellui n'a pas courage d'omme
Qui quiert son plaisir en reprouche,
Et n'est pas digne que on le nomme
356 Ou qu'air ou terre lui atouche.

332 me *Oj*² (moy *Oj*); f. amour *Oa*.   335 peust *Pc*.   336 f. et d.] f. d. *Nj*.   337 a d. ne p. *NfNj*.
338 je v. *GfPcQl*.   339 m. mon m. *NfNj*.   341 Se vostre h. tendz s. *Ph*.   347 cuidez *NfNjPh*;
l. seremens *NfOaPh*, leur serment *Ql*.   348 F. en tant que ses m. se d. *Ph*.   349 en r. *Ph*.   350 Las
Ph; en t. seremens *NfOa*, en tel serement *Ph*.   352 plourant *Qd*.   356 Ne *GfNfOjPcPhQl*; quait
Gf; sur t. *Oj*, en t. *Ph*.

343

Loyal cuer et voir disant bouche
Sont le chastel d'omme parfait,
Et qui si legier sa foy couche,
360 Son honneur pour l'autruy deffait.

XLVI   *La Dame*

Vilain cuer et bouche courtoise
Ne sont mie bien d'une sorte,
Mais Faintise tost les accoyse,
364 Qui par malice les assorte.
La mesnie Faulx Semblant porte
Son honneur en sa langue fainte,
Mais honneur est en leur cuer morte
368 Sans estre plouree ne plainte.

XLVII   *L'Amant*

Qui pense mal, bien ne lui vieigne!   45r
Dieu doint a chascun sa desserte!
Mais, pour Dieu mercy, vous souviengne
372 De la doleur que j'ay soufferte,
Car de ma mort ne de ma perte
N'a pas voustre doulceur envie;
Et se vo grace m'est ouverte,
376 Vous estes garant de ma vie.

XLVIII   *La Dame*

Legier cuer et plaisant folie,
Qui est meilleur quant plus est brieve,
Vous font celle melencolie;
380 Mais c'est un mal dont on relieve.
Faites a vos pensees trieve,
Car de plus beaux jeux on se lasse.
Je ne vous aide ne ne grieve;
384 Qui ne m'en croira, je m'en passe.

357 vray *Ph.*   358 chatel *OjPc.*   359 de l. *OaPh*; touche *Ph.*   360 p. autry *GfPcQl*, p. lautre *NfNj.*
363 racoise *NfNj.*   365 La mesme (mesmes *Oa*) f. s. sa porte (sapporte *Oa*) *NjOa*, La monstre f. s.
sa sorte *Ph*: m.] meigniee *Oj*, mesnies *Qd*, mesure *GfQl*; fault *Qd.*   366 Son venim *Oj²*; et sa l. f. *Ph.*
369 p. m.] ne p. *GfPcQl*, p. a m. *Oj.*   374 Nas pas *Nf.*   377 et p. f.] est p. f. *Gf*, desplaisant f. *Ph.*
378 tant p. *GfOjPcPhQl.*   379 fait *Gf*; ceste *GfNfNjOaOjPcPhQl.*   380 len r. *GfPcQl.*   381 vo
pensee *GfNfPc*, vo pensees *Ql.*   382 yeulx (?) *Ql.*   383 ne ne g.] ne ne vous g. *Ph.*

XLIX

L'Amant

Qui a faulcon, oisel ou chien
Qui le suit, ame, craint et doubte,
Il le tient chier et garde bien
388   Et ne le chace ne deboute:
Et je, qui ay m'entente toute
En vous sans faintise et sans change,
Suis rebouté plus bas qu'en soute
392   Et moins prisé q'un tout estrange.

L

La Dame

Se je fais bonne chiere a tous
Par honneur et de franc courage,
Je ne le vueil pas faire a vous
396   Pour eschever voustre dommaige;
Car Amours est si petit saige
Et de crëance si legiere
Qu'el prent tout a son avantage
400   Chose qui ne lui sert de guiere.

LI

L'Amant

45v

Se pour amour et fëaulté
Je pers l'acueil qu'estranges ont,
Doncq me vauldroit ma loyauté
404   Moins qu'a ceulx qui viennent et vont
Et qui de rien voustres ne sont;
Et sembleroit en vous perie
Courtoisie qui vous semont
408   Qu'amours soit par amours merie.

LII

La Dame

Courtoisie est si alïee
D'Onneur, qui l'aime et la tient chiere,
Qu'el ne veult estre a riens lïee

386 le fuit *Ph.*   387 et ayme b. *PcQl.*   388 Ne ne le ch. *Oa*; ne ne boute *Nf.*   391 deboute *Ph.*
392 prive *Nj.*   395 la v. *Oj²* (le v. *Oj*).   398 tant l. *Oj.*   399 Quelle p. a son a. *Ql*: Quil *GfOaOj*,
Quelle *Ph*; tost *GfNfNjOaOjPc*; en son a. *Oj.*   401 par *NfPh*; est f. *Nf.*   402 Je p. ce questranges sy
ont *Nj*: Je p. le cuer *Nf.*   403 me v.] v. *Oa*, me fauldroit *Qd.*   404 Mieulx *Nj.*   408 Qu'a.] Qui
amours *Pc*; perie *Ph* (merie *Ph²*).   409 si a.] tant a. *Oj*, si liee *Oa.*   410 Do. quelle aime et la t. (et
t. *Nf*) ch. *NfPcQl*: Domme *Ph.*   411 Qua rien ne veult estre liee *Nf*: en rien *Pc.*

345

412   Ne pour devoir ne pour prïere;
       Ains depart de sa bonne chiere
       Ou il lui plaist et bon lui semble.
       Guerredon, contrainte et renchiere
416   Et elle, ne vont point ensemble.

LIII   *L'Amant*

       Je ne quier point de guerredon,
       Car le desservir m'est trop hault:
       Je demande grace en pur don
420   Puis que mort ou mercy me fault.
       Donner le bien ou il deffault,
       C'est courtoisie raisonnable,
       Mais aux siens encores plus vault
424   Qu'estre aux estranges amÿable.

LIV   *La Dame*

       Ne say que vous appellez 'bien' –
       Mal emprunte bien autruy nom –
       Mais il est trop large du sien
428   Qui par donner pert son renom.
       On ne doit faire octroy, se non
       Quant la requeste est avenant,
       Car se l'onneur ne retenon,
432   Trop petit est le remenant.

LV   *L'Amant*

       Oncq homme mortel ne nasqui   46r
       Ou pourroit neistre soubz les cieulx –
       Et n'est autre, fors vous – a qui
436   Voustre honneur touche plus ou mieulx
       Qu'a moy, qui n'atens jeune et vieulx
       Le mien fors par voustre service;

412 Ne p. avoir *GfPcQl*, Ne p. donner *Ph*, Ne par amour *Nf*; par p. *Nf*.   413 Mais *GfNfNjOa OjPcPhQl*.   414 li p. *Qd*.   415 Guerdon *Ph*; c. et r.] c. r. *Oa*, craincte et r. *Ph*.   416 elles *GfNf OaOjPcQl*.   419 et p. d. *NfNj*.   420 P. quamours *Nf*; et mercy *NfNj*.   422 Est c. *PcQl*; raisonnables *Nf*.   426 autre n. *Oa*.   428 pour d. p. *NfPh*, pert par d. *PcQl*.   429 f. o.] f. a autry *Nf*. 432 est (vault *Nj*) le demourant *NfNj*.   433 Oncques homs *Ph*.   434 Ne *Oa*.   435 Et nest pas a. f. a qui *Nj*: Ou *Ph*.   436 t. p. ou m.] t. p. et m. *Nj*, t. ou p. ou m. *Ph*.   437 Par moy *Nf*; j. ou v. *Oa*.   438 Mon bien f. *Ql*; a v. s. *Ph*.

Et n'ay cuer, sens, bouche në yeulx
440 Qui soit donné a autre office.

LVI   *La Dame*

D'assez grant charge se chevit
Qui son honneur garde et maintient;
Mais a dangier travaille et vit
444 Qui en autruy main l'entretient.
Cil a qui l'onneur appartient
Ne s'en doit a autruy actendre,
Car tant moins du sien en retient
448 Qui trop veult a l'autrui entendre.

LVII   *L'Amant*

Voz yeulx ont si empraint leur merche
En mon cuer que, quoy qu'il avieigne,
Se j'ay honneur ou je le serche,
452 Il convient que de vous me vieigne.
Fortune a voulu que je tieigne
Ma vie en voustre mercy close,
Si est bien droit qu'il me souveigne
456 De voustre honneur sur toute chose.

LVIII   *La Dame*

A voustre honneur seul entendez
Pour voustre temps mieulx employer:
Du mien a moy vous atendez
460 Sans prendre peine a foloyer.
Bon fait vaincre et assouployer
Un cuer folement deceü,
Car rompre vault pis que ployer
464 Et esbranlé mieulx que cheü.

439 ny y. *Ph*. 440 Qui soient donnez *Ph*. 441 grans charges *Ql*. 442 gardes *Qd*. 444 en lautry m.
Nf. 446 Ne d. a autre honneur a. *Nf*: Ne se d. *GfPcQl*, Ne sen droit *Ph*. 447 Car trop petit du s.
r. *Gf*: trop m. *Nf*; du s. entretient *Ql*. 448 entedre (*sic*) *Qd*. 449 empris *PcQl*; la m. *Ph*.
450 quil en viengne *Nf*. 452 Et c. *Ph*. 455 men s. *Ph*. 456 amour *Oa*; sus *Pc*. 458 v. honneur
Ql. 460 f.] fouloir (*sic*) *Nf*. 461 B. f. a v. et supploier *Nj*, B. f. craindre a (et *Nf*, et a (?) *Ql*)
souploier *GfNfPcQl*: et a.] et supploier *Ph*.

LIX

L'Amant

Pensés, ma dame, que depuis   46v
Qu'Amours mon cuer vous delivra,
Il ne pourroit – ne je ne puis –
468 Estre autre tant com il vivra.
Tout quicte et franc le vous livra;
Ce don ne se puet abolir.
J'actens ce qui s'en ensuivra;
472 Je n'y puis mectre ne tollir.

LX

La Dame

Je ne tien mie pour donné
Ce qu'on offre a qui ne le prent,
Car le don est abandonné
476 Se le donneur ne le reprent.
Trop a de cuers qui entreprent
D'en donner a qui les reffuse,
Mais il est sage qui aprent
480 A s'en rectraire qu'il n'y muse.

LXI

L'Amant

Il ne doit pas cuider muser
Qui sert dame de si hault pris;
Et se je y doy mon temps user,
484 Au moins n'en puis je estre repris
De cuer failli ne de mespris
Quant envers vous fais ceste queste,
Par qui Amours a entrepris
488 De tant de bons cuers la conqueste.

LXII

La Dame

Se mon conseil voulez oïr,
Querez ailleurs plus belle et gente

466 me d. *Ph.* 468 E. a. (E. autrement *Nj*) tant quil v. *NjPh.* 470 Le don *Ql*; peust *Pc.* 471 ce que *Oj.* 472 ne p. *Oa.* 474 a qui ne le p.] qui ne le p. *Ph,* a qui ne p. *Qd,* son ne le p. *PcQl.* 475 Ains est le don a. *Oj.* 477 T. a dur cuer *Ph,* T. a cuers *Oa.* 479 cil *Nj*; qui enprent *Pc,* et aprent *Ql.* 480 A soy r. *Pc*; quil ne m. *GfNfNjOjPcQl.* 481–800 *Lacking Gf.* 483 Et se je y d.] Et gy d. bien *Oj,* Se (Et *Ql*) je y d. *PcQl,* Se gy devoye *Ph.* 484 ne puis *NfOj,* nen doybz *Pc.* 485 Du c. *Qd.* 486 telle q. *PcQl.* 487 est e. *Ql.* 489 vouler *Qd.*

Qui d'amours se vueille esjouïr
492 Et mieulx sortisse a voustre entente.
Trop loing de confort se tourmente
Qui a par soy pour deux se trouble,
Et cellui pert le jeu d'actente
496 Qui ne scet faire son point double.

LXIII   *L'Amant*

Le conseil que vous me donnez   47r
Se puet mieulx dire qu'exploicter.
Du non croire me pardonnez,
500 Car j'ay cuer tel et si entier
Qu'il ne se pourroit affaictier
A chose ou Loyauté n'acorde;
N'autre conseil ne m'a mestier
504 Fors pitié et misericorde.

LXIV   *La Dame*

Saige est qui folie encommence
Quant deppartir s'en scet et veult;
Mais il a faulte de scïence
508 Qui la veult conduire et ne puet.
Qui par conseil ne se desmeut,
Desespoir se met de sa suite;
Et tout le bien qu'il en requeult,
512 C'est de mourir en la poursuite.

LXV   *L'Amant*

Je poursuivray tant que pourray
Et que vie me durera,
Et lors qu'en loyauté mourray,
516 Celle mort ne me grevera;
Mais quant vo durté me fera
Mourir loyal et doloreux,
Encores moins gref me sera
520 Que de vivre faulx amoureux.

492 sortir *OaPh.* 495 le lieu *Ql.* 498 peust *Pc.* 499 De non c. *Ph.* 500 tel cuer *Ph.* 501 afichier
Ql. 503 Naustre *Qd.* 505 f. commence *Nf.* 508 peust *Pc.* 509 pour c. *Nj*; desmeust *Pc.* 510 De
espoir *Nf.* 511 requeust *Qd.* 512 Est *OaOjPh.* 513 t. que vivray *Nf.* 515 mouray *Qd.*

LXVI

La Dame

De riens a moy ne vous prenez.
Je ne vous suis aspre ne dure
Et n'est droit que vous me tenez
524   Envers vous ne doulce ne sure.
Qui se quiert le mal si l'endure!
Autre confort donner n'y say
Ne de l'aprendre n'ay je cure:
528   Qui en veult en face l'essay.

LXVII

L'Amant

Une foiz le fault essayer   47v
A tous les bons en leur endroit
Et le devoir d'Amours payer,
532   Qui sur frans cuers a prise et droit,
Car Franc Vouloir maintient et croit
Que c'est durté et mesprison
Tenir un hault cuer si estroit
536   Qu'il n'ait q'un seul corps pour prison.

LXVIII

La Dame

J'en say tant de cas merveilleux
Qu'il me doit assez souvenir
Que l'entrer en est perilleux
540   Et encor plus le revenir.
A tart en puet bien avenir:
Pour ce n'ay vouloir de cerchier
Un mal plaisant au mieulx venir,
544   Dont l'essay puet couster si chier.

LXIX

L'Amant

Vous n'avez cause de doubter
Ne suspeçon qui vous esmeuve
A m'esloingnier ne rebouter,
548   Car voustre bonté voit et treuve

527 la prendre *NjOaQl*. 530 a l. e. *Oa*, en son e. *PcQl*. 531 poyer *Ql*. 532 sus *OjPc*; franc cuer *Ph*; doit *Qd*. 533 Qui f. v. *Nf*. 535 un h. c.] ung c. h. *Ql*. 536 cuer *Ql*. 537 Je s. *N Ph*, Jen oy *OjPcQl*. 538 men d. *Ph*. 540 le r.] le revir (*sic*) *Ql*. 541 A t. p. il b. venir *Ph*: peust *Pc Ql*. 542 nay voulente serchier *NfNj*. 544 D. le. cousteroit si ch. *PcQl*. 547 debouter *Ph*. 548 v. bon cuer *Ph*.

Que j'ay fait l'essay et la prouve
Par quoy ma loyauté apert.
La longue actente et forte espreuve
552 Ne se puet celer : il y pert.

LXX   *La Dame*

Il se puet loyal appeller –
Et son nom lui duit et affiert –
Qui scet desservir et celer
556 Et garder le bien s'il l'acquiert.
Qui encor poursuit et requiert
N'a pas loyauté esprouvee,
Car tel pourchace grace et quiert
560 Qui la pert puis qu'il l'a trouvee.

LXXI   *L'Amant*   48r

Se ma loyauté s'esvertue
D'amer ce qui ne m'ayme mie
Et tant cherir ce qui me tue
564 Et m'est amoureuse ennemie,
Quant Pitié qui est endormie
Mectroit en mes maulx fin et terme,
Ce gracïeux confort d'amie
568 Feroit ma loyauté plus ferme.

LXXII   *La Dame*

Un douloreux pense tousdis
Des plus joyeux le droit revers,
Et le penser du maladis
572 Est entre les sains tout divers.
Assez est il de cuers travers
Qu'avoir bien fait toust empirer

549 et lespreuve *NfOjPh*.   551 est f. e. *Nf*, et la demeure *Ph*.   552 Que pieça jay fait en appert *Ph*:
peust *Pc*; ains y p. *Oj²*.   553 peust *Pc*.   554 ce nom *NfNjOaOjPcPhQl*; dit *Oa*.   555 Qui s.] Qui
ne scet *Ph*, Qui soit *Ql*; de servir *Qd*.   556 g. le b.] g. b. *Nf*, garde le b. *Ph*; sil acquiert *Ph*.
557 Qui encore p. et quiert (requiert *Ph*) *PcPhQl*.   559 Tel p. g. et requiert *Ph*.   563–4 *Inverted Ph*.
563 De t. ch. *Oa*, Et t. cheris *Pc*, Et ay chieri *Ql*.   564 Ce mest *Ph*.   565 mest e. *Ph*.   567 Si g. c.
PcQl.   571 le gouster *Oj²*; dung m. *Pc*, des m. *NfNjPh*.   572 le sains *Qd*; tous d. *NfPhQl*.
573 cuer *Oa*; tavers *Nj*, divers *Ph*.   574 Quamours font bien (moult *Pc*) t. e. *PcQl*: fait bien
Nf.

Et loyauté mectre a l'envers,
576 Dont ilz soloient souspirer.

LXXIII   *L'Amant*

De tous soit cellui deguerpis,
D'onneur desgradé et deffait,
Qui descongnoist et tourne en pis
580 Le don de grace et le bienfait
De sa dame qui l'a reffait
Et ramené de mort a vie!
Qui se souille de tel meffait
584 A plus d'une mort desservie.

LXXIV   *La Dame*

Sur tel meffait n'a court ne juge
A qui on puisse recourir.
L'un les maudit, l'autre les juge,
588 Mais je n'en ay veu nul mourir.
On leur laisse leur cours courir
Et commencier pis de rechief,
Et tristes dames encourir
592 D'autrui coulpe, peine et meschief.

LXXV   *L'Amant*

Combien qu'on n'ardë ou ne pende   48v
Cellui qui en tel crime enchiet,
Je suis certain, quoy qu'il actende,
596 Qu'en la fin il lui en meschiet
Et qu'onneur et bien lui dechiet,
Car Faulceté est si maudite
Que jamais hault honneur ne chiet
600 Dessus cellui ou elle habite.

575 en le. *Pc.* 577 De tout *OaPc,* Du tout *Ql.* 578 Damours *NfNjOa.* 580 et de b. *OaQdQl.*
581 le r. *Qd.* 583 ce m. *Pc.* 584 Au p. *Ph.* 585 Sus *OjPc;* telz meffaiz *NfNjOjPcQl.* 586 lon
p. *OaOj*² (on p. *Oj*); on en p. acourir *Ql.* 588 nul veu *Nf.* 589 On les laisse (laisses *Nf*) *NfNjOj,*
Qui leur laisse *PcQl;* leurs c. *Oj.* 590 plus *Oa,* puis *Ph.* 593 C. quon ne pende on quon narde *Nj:*
quon] que len *Oj;* ou ne p.] ne ne p. *OaPh,* ou quon ne p. *Nf.* 594 tel paine *Oa;* e.] chiet *Ph.*
595 Je sui bien c. quoy quil tarde *NfNj.* 596 Qua la f. *Oa;* il lui en m.] quil lui en m. *Nf,* lui
en m. *Oj.* 599 ne ch.] ny eschiet *Ph.* 600 Dessoubz *Oa.*

LXXVI   *La Dame*

De ce n'ont mie grant peür
Ceulx qui dïent et qui maintiennent
Que loyauté n'est pas eür
604   A ceulx qui longuement la tiennent.
Leurs cuers s'en vont et puis reviennent,
Car ilz les ont bien reclamez
Et si bien apris qu'ilz retiennent
608   A changer des qu'ilz sont amez.

LXXVII   *L'Amant*

Quant on a son cuer bien assis
En bonne et loyale partie,
Il doit estre entier et rassis
612   A tousjours mais sans departie.
Si tost qu'amours est mypartie,
Tout le hault plaisir en est hors;
Si ne sera par moy partie,
616   Tant que l'ame me bate ou corps.

LXXVIII   *La Dame*

D'amer bien ce qu'amer devez
Ne pourrïez vous pas mesprendre;
Mais, s'en devoir vous decevez
620   Par legierement entreprendre,
Vous mesmes vous pouez reprendre
Et avoir a raison recours,
Plus tost qu'en foul espoir actendre
624   Un tresdesesperé secours.

LXXIX   *L'Amant*   49r

Raison, Advis, Conseil et Sens
Sont soubz l'arrest d'Amours seellez.
A tel arrest je me consens

605 **Les c.** *PcQl*; revient (*sic*) *Qd.*   607 quil *PcQd.*   608 desquelz *Ql*; clamez *Ph.*   609 on sent *Ql.*
611 Il d. entier et r. *Qd:* On d. *NfNjOaOjPcPhQl.*   613 impartie *Nf*(?)*NjOaPh.*   616 en c. *Pc.*
617 ce que vous d. *Ph.*   618 Vous ne p. en ce m. *Nf.*   619 se ou d. *Oj*, son d. *Qd*, sans d. *Nf Oa*;
detenez *Oa.*   621 debves r. *Pc.*   622 secours *Ph.*   623 qun f. e. *Ph.*   624 Dun *Ph.*   625 conseil
advis *PcQl.*   626 seellees *Ql* ,celez *Nj.*

628 Car nul d'eulx ne s'est rebellés.
Ilz sont parmy Desir meslez
Et si fort enlaciez, helas,
Que ja n'en seray desmeslez
632 Se Pitié ne brise les las.

LXXX   *La Dame*

Qui n'a a soy mesme amitié
De toute amour est deff ïez;
Et se de vous n'avez pitié,
636 D'autruy pitié ne vous f ïez.
Mais soyez tous certiff ïez
Que je suis celle que je fus;
D'avoir mieulx ne vous aff ïez,
640 Et prenez en gré le reffus.

LXXXI   *L'Amant*

J'ay mon esperance fermee
Qu'en tel dame ne doit faillir
Pitié, mais elle est enfermee
644 Et laisse Dangier m'assaillir;
Et s'el voit ma vertu faillir
Pour bien amer, el s'en sauldra.
Lors sa demeure et tart saillir
648 Et mon bien souffrir me vauldra.

LXXXII   *La Dame*

Ostez vous hors de ce propos
Car, tant plus vous vous y tendrez,
Moins avrez joyë et repos
652 Et jamais a bout n'en vendrez.
Quant a Espoir vous actendrez,
Vous en trouverez abestiz,

630 Si tresfort e. es laz *Nf*: e. es las *PhQl*, en laches helas *Pc*.   631 Car ja nen seront d. *Ph*.   632 nen b. *PcQl*; ses las *Oa*, le las *Oj*.   633 Qui a soy m. na a. *Ph*: mesmes *Oa*.   634 tout a. *Oj*.   635 Et se v. nen avez p. *Ph*.   636 Dautre *Oj*.   637 tout c. *NfNjOaPcPhQl*.   638 telle *NfOaPcPhQl*.   640 les r. *OaPh*.   644 Elaisse *Qd*.   645 Dont je mourray certes martir *PcQl*: Celle *Ph*.   646 el s'en s.] et sen s. *Oa*, ou el s. *Pc*, elle sen s. *PhQl*.   647 a t. *PcQl*.   648 servir *Ph*; fauldra *Oa*.   650 Car quant plus (qu. tant p. *Nj*) vous y entendrez (y tendrez *Nj*) *NfNj*.   651 j. et r.] et j. et r. *NfNjOjPcQl*.   652 Et moins j. au b. nen v. *Nf*.   653 actendez *NfNj*.

Et en la fin vous aprendrez
656   Qu'Esperance paist les chestiz.

LXXXIII   *L'Amant*

Vous direz ce que vous vouldrés –   49v
Et du pouoir avez assez –
Mais ja Espoir ne m'en touldrez,
660   Par qui j'ay tant de maulx passez,
Car, quant Nature a enchassez
En vous des biens a tel effors,
El ne les a pas amassez
664   Pour en mectre Pitié dehors.

LXXXIV   *La Dame*

Pitié doit estre raisonnable
Et a nul desavantageuse,
Aux besoingneux tresprouffitable
668   Et aux piteux non domageuse.
Se dame est a autruy piteuse
Pour estre a soy mesmes crüelle,
Sa pitié devient despiteuse
672   Et son amour hayne mortelle.

LXXXV   *L'Amant*

Conforter les desconfortez
N'est pas crüaulté, ains est los;
Mais vous, qui si dur cuer portez
676   En si beau corps, se dire l'os,
Gaingnez le blasme et le deslos
De crüaulté qui mal y siet,
Se Pitié qui depart les los
680   En voustre hault cuer ne s'assiet.

655 trouverez *NfNj*. 657 dictes *Ql*; tant que *Ph*; voulez *Ql*. 658 Car *Ph*. 659 me t. *NfOjPcPh Ql*. 660 Par qui j'ay] Par jay *Nf*. 661 Et qu. *PcQl*; entasses *Pc*. 662 Des biens en vous *PcQl*; telz *Ph*. 663 Elle *PcPh*, Et *NfQl*. 669 a a.] dautruy *Oa*. 671 Se p. *Oa*. 672 Et samour hayneuse et m. *Ph*. 673–720 *Omitted NfNj*. 673 Confortez *Qd*. 674 cruaultez *PhQd*; maiz *PcQl*. 675 M. v. qui] M. qui *Pc*. 676 Et *PcQl*; se b. c. *Qd*. 677 Gaigner *Oa*. 678 chiet *Ql*. 680 En] Qui *Oa*; c. ne s'a.] c. sa. *Ph*.

LXXXVI

La Dame

Qui me dit que je suis amee,
Se bien croire je l'en vouloye,
Me doit il tenir pour blamee
684 S'a son vouloir je ne foloye?
Se de telz confors me mesloye,
Ce seroit pitié sans maniere;
Et depuis se je m'en doloye,
688 C'en est la soulde derreniere.

LXXXVII

L'Amant

Ha, cuer plus dur que le noir marbre   50r
En qui Mercy ne puet entrer,
Plus fort a ployer q'un gros arbre,
692 Que vous vault tel rigueur moustrer?
Vous plaist il mieulx me veoir oultrer
Mort devant vous pour voustre esbat,
Que pour un confort demoustrer
696 Respitier la mort qui m'abat?

LXXXVIII

La Dame

De voz maulx guerir vous pourrez
Car des miens ne vous requerray;
Ne par mon plaisir ne mourrez,
700 Ne pour vous guerir ne gerray.
Mon cuer pour autruy ne herray,
Crïent, pleurent, rïent ou chantent;
Mais, se je puis, je pourverray
704 Que vous në autres ne s'en vantent.

LXXXIX

L'Amant

Je ne suis mie bon chanteur –
Aussi me duit mieulx le plourer –
Mais je ne fu oncques vanteur:

681 On *PcQl*; dist *OaQl*. 682 le v. *Pc*. 684 ne (me *Ql*) souploye *PcQl*. 687 se depuis *Pc*, apres se *Ph*. 688 soulte *Pc*, soubte *Ql*; derniere *Oa*. 689 He *Ph*; Ha a plus dur cuer *Ql*. 690 peust *Pc*. 693 v.] vouloir *Qd*. 695 c. me monstrer *Pc*. 699 *Omitted Ph*. 700 g. men g. *Oa*, g. nen g. *Qd*. 701 Monnour *Pc*, Mon nom *Ql*. 702 et *Ph*. 703 Mais se dieu plaist je p. *Oj*: jy p. *Oa*. 706 A. mavient *Ph*; plus *OaOjPc*. 707 Ne *Ql*.

708 J'ayme plus tost coy demourer.
Nul ne se doit enamourer
S'il n'a cuer de celer l'emprise,
Car vanteur n'est a honnorer
712 Puis que sa langue le desprise.

XC   *La Dame*

Male Bouche tient bien grant court:
Chascun a mesdire estudie;
Faulx amoureux au temps qui court
716 Servent tous de goulïardye.
Le plus secret veult bien qu'on die
Qu'il est d'aucune mescreüz,
Et pour riens qu'omme a dame die
720 Il ne doit plus estre creüz.

XCI   *L'Amant*   50v

D'uns et d'autres est et sera;
La terre n'est pas toute onnye.
Des bons le bien se moustrera
724 Et des mauvais la vilonnye.
Est ce droit, s'aucuns ont honnie
Leur langue en mesdit eshonté,
Que Reffus en excommenie
728 Les bons avecques leur bonté?

XCII   *La Dame*

Quant meschans fol parler eüssent,
Ce mechief seroit pardonnez;
Mais ceulx qui mieulx faire deüssent
732 Et que Noblece a ordonnez
D'estre bien condicïonnez,
Sont les plus avant en la fengue
Et ont leurs cueurs abandonnez
736 A courte foy et longue langue.

708 tout c. *OjPcPhQl.*   712 la l. *Oa.*   714 a (en *Ql*) mal dire *PcQl.*   718 daucunes *OaPcQl*; mescreu
Oa.   719 femme *PcQl.*   720 nen d. *Ph*; creu *Oa.*   721 D'uns] De bons *Oa.*   723 les biens *Ph.*
725 saucun a h. *Pc*, saucuns on h. *Ph.*   726 mesdire *Ql*; m. et honte *OaPh.*   728 a.] avec *PhQl.*
729 m. f. p. e.] m. meschant p. e. *OaOjPh*, m. meschant p. usent *PcQl.*   732 Ce que *Qd.*
733 mieulz *NſNj.*   734 le p. *Oj.*   735 Et tous leurs biens habandonnez *Ph.*

357

XCIII

L'Amant

Or congnois je bien orendroit
Que pour bien faire on est onniz,
Puis que Pitié, Justice et Droit
740 Sont de cuer de dame banniz.
Fault il doncq faire touz onniz
Les humbles servans et les faulx,
Et que les bons soient puniz
744 Pour le pechié des desloyaulx?

XCIV

La Dame

Je n'ay le pouoir de grever
Ne de punir autre ne vous,
Mais pour les mauvais eschever
748 Il se fait bon garder de tous.
Faulx Semblant fait l'umble et le doulx
Pour prendre dames en aguet,
Et pour ce chascune de nous
752 Y doit bien l'escute et le guet.

XCV

L'Amant

Puis que de grace un tout seul mot   51r
De voustre rigoreux cuer n'ist,
J'appelle devant Dieu qui m'ot
756 De la durté qui me honnist;
Et me plaing qu'Il ne parfournist
Pitié, qu'en vous Il oublïa,
Ou que ma vie ne fenist
760 Que si tost mis en oubly a.

XCVI

La Dame

Mon cuer et moy ne vous feïsmes
Oncq rien dont plaindre vous doyez.
Riens ne vous nuist fors vous meïsmes;
764 De vous mesme juge soyez.

<small>738 ont Q*d*, homs Q*l*.   740 cueurs (cuer *Ph*) de dames P*cPhQl*.   741 d. f.] f. P*c*, f. d. Q*l*.   744 Par NfNj; les pechiez O*a*.   749 humble O*a*.   750 baillier P*cQl*; dame Q*d*.   752 d. b.] d. O*a*. 753 que de g.] que g. NfNj.   756 vo d. NfNj.   759 Et Q*l*.   760 Qui Q*l*; oublia O*a*.   761 ne moy P*c*.   762 Ou r. *Ph*.   763 mesmes O*aPh*.   764 mesmes juges NfP*cQl*.</small>

358

Une foiz pour toutes croyez
Que vous demourrés escondit.
De tant redire m'ennoyez,
768 Car je vous en ay assez dit.

XCVII   *L'Acteur*

Adont le dolent se leva
Et part de la feste plourant.
A peu que son cuer ne creva
772 Comme a homme qui va mourant,
Et dist: 'Mort, vien a moy courant
Ains que mon sens se descongnoisse,
Et m'abrege le demourant
776 De ma vie plaine d'engoisse'.

XCVIII   *Item l'Acteur*

Depuis je ne sceu qu'il devint
Ne quel part il se transporta;
Mais a sa dame n'en souvint
780 Qui aux dances se deporta.
Et depuis on me rapporta
Qu'il avoit ses cheveux desroux,
Et que tant se desconforta
784 Qu'il en estoit mort de courroux.

XCIX   *Item l'Acteur*

Si vous pri, amoureux, fuyez   51v
Ces vanteurs et ces mesdisans;
Et comme infames les huyez,
788 Car ilz sont a voz faiz nuysans.
Pour non les faire voir disans,
Reffus a ses chasteaulx bastiz,
Car ilz ont trop mis puis dix ans
792 Le païs d'Amours a pastiz.

765 p. toute *Ph.* 782 Quil a. tire ses ch. *Oa.* 783 sen d. *OjQl.* 786 vanceurs *Qd*; ses m.
NfOaPhQd. 788 en voz f. *Ql*; muysans *Qd.* 789 P. non f. les v. d. *Nj*, P. les f. non v. d. *Oj.*
792 a p.] appatis *Oa*, apatiz *Ph*, a apastiz *Oj.*

C

Item l'Acteur

Et vous, dames et damoiselles
En qui Honneur naist et asemble,
Ne soyés mie si crüelles,
796 Chascune ne toutes ensemble.
Que ja nulle de vous ressemble
Celle que m'oyez nommer cy,
Qu'on appellera, ce me semble,
800 La belle dame sans mercy!

Explicit.

794 croist *Ph*; sassemble *NfNjOaOj²PcPhQl* (assemble *Oj*). 796 de t. *Oa.* 797 nulles *Ql*; de voz r. *Qd*, ne la r. *Oa.* 799 Quon puet (peust *Pc*) appeller *OaOjPcPhQl*; se *NjPcQd.* . . .la belle dame sans mercy *NfNjOaOjPh*, . . .le livre de la b. d. s. m. *Ql.*

COPPIE DES LECTRES ENVOYEES PAR LES DAMES

A ALAIN   *Qd,* 52r

Honnouré frere, nous nous recommandons a vous et vous faisons savoir que nagaires par aucuns a esté baillie aux dames certaine requeste qui grandement touche voustre honneur et le desavancement du tresgracieux los et bonne grace que vous avez tousjours acquis vers
5 elles. Et pour ce que nous vous cuidons tel que bien vous savrez excuser et deffendre de ceste charge quant vous en serez adverti, nous vous envoions le double, esperans que vous mectrez peine a vous geter hors de ce blasme a voustre honneur et a l'esjouissement de ceulx qui plus volentiers verroient voustre los croistre que
10 amendrir. Et comme escript vous a esté par autres lectres de voz amis, journee est assignee au premier jour d'avril a vous et a voz parties adverses, auquel jour vous pensons veoir se vous n'estez mort ou pris, dont Dieu vous gart, laquelle chose vous doubteriez moins que de demourer en ceste charge. Honnouré frere, Noustre
15 Sire vous doint autant de joye comme nous vouldrions et brief

. . .a maistre alain *Ql*, . . .lectres closes que les dames envoierent a lacteur *Oa*; *No heading Pc.* 1 et vous plaise s. *NfNj.* 2 nagaireres *Qd*; n. a este *PcQl*; baille *Oa*, baillee *Oj.* 6 excuser de c. ch. et deffendre *NfNj.* 7 vous en envoyons *NfNjOjPcQl*; esperant *NfOa*; p. de *Oj²* (p. a *Oj*). 8 cest b. *NjOa*; et a l'e.] et le. *Qd.* 9 de celles *NfNj*; vouldroyent (verroient *Nj*) voz loz croistre (acroistre *Nj*) que voz blasmes augmenter *NfNj*; croystre vostre loz *PcQl.* 11 et a voz] et voz *Qd.* 14 que de d.] que demourez *Qd*; N. Seigneur *Nj.* 15 doint comme nous vouldrions pour nous et b. r. *Pc.*

360

retourner, car se vous estiez par de ça, tel parle contre vous qui se tairoit. Escript a Yssouldun, le derrenier jour de janvier.

Et en la marge de dessoubz estoit escript:

19 Les voustres, Katherine, Marie et Jehanne.

16 sen t. *Nj.*   18 *Lacking OjPcQl*: marge dessoubz *NfNj*; est e. *Oa.*   19 et jehenne la toute vostre *PcQl.*

COPPIE DE LA REQUESTE BAILLEE AUX DAMES

CONTRE ALAIN
Qd, 52v

Supplient humblement voz loyaulx serviteurs, les actendans de voustre tresdoulce grace et poursuivans la queste du don d'amoureuse mercy, comme ilz ayent donné leur cuer a penser, leur corps a travaillier, leur vouloir a desirer, leur bouche a requerir, leur temps
5 a pourchacer le riche don de pitié que Dangier, Reffus et Crainte ont embuché et retrait en la gaste forest de Longue Actente, et ne leur soit demouré compaignie ne conduit qui ne les ait laissiez en la poursuite fors seulement Bon Espoir, qui encores demeure souvent derriere lassé et travaillé du long chemin et de la tresennuyeuse
10 queste; et que en un pas qui se nomme Dure Response ont esté plusieurs foiz destroussez de Joye et desers de Leece par les brigans et souldoyers de Reffus, et neantmoins entretiennent tousjours leur queste pour y mectre la vie et le cuer qui leur est demouré, mais que Espoir ne les laisse au besoing; et encores avroient actente de
15 voustre secours et que Bel Acueil et Doulx Actrait les remeissent sus, se ne fust qu'il est venu a leur congnoissance que aucuns ont escript en vers rimés certaines nouvelletez ou ilz n'ont gueres pensé. Et puet estre que Envye, rebutement d'amours ou faulte de cuer qui les a fait demourer recreuz en chemin et laissier la queste qu'ilz
20 avoient encommenciee avecques nous les fait ainsi parler et escrire. Et ont tant fait, comme l'on dit, pour destourner aux autres la joye a quoy ilz ont failli que leurs escriptz sont venuz en voz mains et,

...r. faicte et b. aux d. c. maistre a. *Ql*, C. des lectres envoyees aux d. c. a. *Nf*, C. des lectres de la r. envoyee par les amans aux d. c. a. *Nj*, ...supplicacion qui fut b. aux d. c. lacteur *Oa*; *No heading Pc*. 2 v. doulce g. *PcQl*; la requeste *Ql*.   3 m. que comme *NfNjOa*; leurs cueurs *PcQl*; l. corps] leurs corps *NfNjQl*, leurs cuers *Qd*.   4 l. b. a r. l. v. a d. *Pc*; r. et l. t. *Oj²*.   6 et si ne *NfNj*.   7 demouree *Ql*.   8 seulement espoir *OjPcQl*; demeure derriere *Ql*.   9 tout desriere *Pc*; derreriere *Qd*; ch. de la t. qu. *NfNj*, ch. et la t. qu. *Pc*; tresmerveilleuse qu. *Oa*.   10 ung trespas qui sappelle *NfNj*; dure requeste *OjPcQl*.   11 es desers de l. *NfOa*.   12 leurs questes *NfNj*.   14 avoient (aroient *Nj*) ilz a. *NfNj*.   15 le r. s. *Pc*.   16 se ne f.] ne f. ce *Nj*, ne f. *NfOa*; qui leur est v. *Oa*, quil v. *Pc*.   18 peust e. *Pc*; et f. *Nf*; du c. *Oa*.   19 affait demourez *Qd*; et ont laissie *Nf*.   20 encommence *NfNj*, commancee *Oa*; les a fait *NjOaPcQl*; rescripre et tant ont f. *PcQl*.   21 ont dit *Nf*, on dit *Oa*; destourber *Oj*; destourner la j. *PcQl*.   22 a qu. ilz ont f.] quilz ont f. *Ql*; en vous m. *Qd*.

pour l'actrait d'aucunes parolles doulces qui sont dedans, vous ont
amusees a lire leur livre que on appelle *la* (53r) *Belle Dame sans*
25 *Mercy,* ouquel, soubz un langaige afaictié, sont enclos les commence-
mens et ouvertures de mectre rumeur en la court amoureuse et
rompre la queste des humbles servans et a vous tolir l'eureux nom
de pitié qui est le parement et la richesse de voz autres vertuz. Et en
aviendra dommage et esloingnement aux humbles servans et
30 amandrissement de voustre pouoir se par vous n'y est pourveu.
Qu'il vous plaise de voustre grace destourner vos yeulx de lire si
desraisonnables escriptures et n'y donner foy ne audience, mais les
faire rompre et casser partout ou trouver se pourront et des faiseurs
ordonner telle punicion que ce soit exemple aux autres, et que
35 voz humbles servans puissent leur quéste parfaire a voustre honneur
et a leur joye, et moustrer par euvres qu'en vous a mercy et pitié.
Et ilz prieront Amours qu'il vous doint tousjours tant de leece que
aux autres en puissez repartir.

24 amusez *Oa,* amuse *PcQl;* que len *Oj²* (quon *Oj);* quilz appellent *Oa.* 25 ausquelx *Oa;* soubz
l. *Nf;* s. e. les o. de remectre r. *Oa.* 26 couvertures *Qd;* rimeur *NfNjPcQl.* 27 et v. t. *NfNj;* don
de p. *Oj.* 28 la riche *Qd.* 29 aviedra *Qd.* 31 de v. benigne g. *NfNj;* destourner de lire *Pc.*
33 f. derompre *Nf,* faites rompre *Oa;* des (de *Nf*) faisans *NfNjOj.* 34 ordonnes *PcQl;* si que
voz *NfNj,* et vos *Pc.* 36 moustres par oeuvre *Pc;* m. par oeuvre quen eulx (m. que en eulz *Nj*) a
pitie et mercy *NfNj;* que a v. *Ql.* 37 p. a. pour vous quil *Oj.* 38 departir *NfNj.*

L'EXCUSACION AUX DAMES

L'Acteur

I Mes dames et mes damoiselles,   *Qd,* 53v
Se Dieu vous doint joye prouchaine,
Escoutés les durez nouvelles
4 Que j'ouÿ le jour de l'estraine.
Et entendez ce qui me maine,
Car je n'ay fors a vous recours;
Et me donnez par grace plaine
8 Conseil, confort, aide et secours.

Item l'Acteur

II Ce jour m'avint en sommeillant,
Actendant le soleil levant,

E. faicte envers les d. (E. envers les d. faicte *Nj*) par alain *NfNj,* Aux d. *Qd,* ... e. maistre alain aux
d. *Ql,* La Responce a la Belle dame sans mercy *Ph; No heading OaPc.* 5 ce quil *Qd.* 7 Et mes
dames par g. p. *Oa.* 9 Ung j. *Ql;* me vint *Pc.*

Moitié dormant, moitié veillant,
12 Environ l'aube ou peu avant,
Qu'Amours s'apparut au devant
De mon lit a l'arc tout tendu,

Le Dieu d'Amours

Et me dist: 'Desloyal servant,
16 Ton loyer te sera rendu.

Le Dieu d'Amours

III   Je t'ay long temps tenu des miens
A l'eure que bien me servoyes,
Et te gardoye de grans biens
20 Trop plus que tu ne desservoyes;
Et quant ta loyauté devoyes
Vers moy garder en tous endroiz,
Tu fais et escriz et envoyes
24 Nouveaulx livres contre mes droiz.

IV   Es tu foul, hors du sens ou yvre,
Ou veulx contre moy guerre prendre,
Qui as fait le maleureux livre,
28 Dont chascun te devroit reprendre,
Pour enseigner et pour aprendre   54r
Les dames a geter au loing
Pitié la debonnaire et tendre,
32 De qui tout le monde a besoing?

V   Se tu as ta merencolie
Prise de non amer jamais,
Doivent achater ta folie
36 Les autres qui n'en pevent mais?
Laisse faire autruy et te tais!
Que de dueil ait le cuer nercy
Qui ja croira, comme tu fais,
40 Qu'oncques dame fust sans mercy!

12 ung p. a. *Nf.* 13 *Omitted Oa.* 16 Ton loyal *Nf.* 19 des g. b. *OaPc.* 20 tu nen d. *OjPc.*
21 Et qu. ta desloyaute desvoyes *Nf.* 25 foult *Qd.* 26 De vouloir a moy g. p. *Oj*: Qui v. *PcPhQl.*
31 P. d. et t. *Qd*: le d. *Oa.* 32 De quoy *NfNj.* 36 puent *Nf.* 37 f. a autruy *Oa.* 40 dames *Nf.*

363

VI

Tu mourras de ce peché quicte;
Et se briefment ne t'en desdiz,
Prescher te feray comme herite
44 Et bruler ton livre et tes diz.
En la loy d'Amours sont maudiz,
Et chascun m'en fait les clamours.
Les lire est a tous interdiz
48 De par l'inquisiteur d'Amours.

VII

Tu veulx mon pouoir abolir
Et qu'onneur et bonté s'efface,
Quant tu quiers des dames tolir
52 Pitié, mercy, doulceur et grace.
Cuides tu doncques que Dieu face
Entre les hommes sur la terre
Si beau corps et si doulce face
56 Pour leur porter rigueur et guerre?

VIII

Nenny non, Il n'y pensa oncques,   54v
Car ja faites ne les eüst
Plus plaisans que chose quelconques
60 Que sur terre faire deüst,
S'Il ne veïst bien et sceüst
Qu'elles doivent l'eür porter,
Qui par droit les hommes deüst
64 Resjouïr et resconforter.

IX

Ne seroit ce pas grant dommaige
Que Dieu, qui soustient homme en vie,
Eust faite si perfaite ymage
68 Par droite excellence assouvie,
Que la pensee en fust ravie
Des hommes par force de plaire...
Se Dieu leur portoit telle envie
72 Qu'Il leur donnast pour adversaire?

45 la foy *Ql.* 47 Le lire *NfPcPhQl.* 49 Te v. *Qd,* Veulx tu *Ph.* 52 douleur *Ph.* 57 N. n.]
Nenny *Nf.* 59 choses quelzconques *NjPcPhQl.* 60 sus *Oj;* f. peust *Ql.* 62 devoient *OaPh,*
devroient *Oj.* 63 Que *Ph.* 67 fait *NjPh;* si plaisant y. *OjQl.* 68 excellente *Ph.* 69 p. en f.] p.
ne f. *Oj,* p. f. *PcQl.* 70 p. f. desplaire *OaPh.* 72 *Omitted Oa:* par *Qd.*

X

    Cuides tu faire basiliques,
    Qui occïent les gens des yeulx,
    Ces doulx visages angeliques
76 Qui semblent estre faiz es cieulx?
    Ilz ne furent pas formez tieulx
    Pour desdaingner et nonchaloir,
    Mais pour croistre de bien en mieulx
80 Ceulx qui ont desir de valoir.

XI

    Doulceur, courtoisie, amitié
    Sont les vertuz de noble femme,
    Et le droit logeis de Pitié
84 Est ou cuer d'une belle dame.
    S'il failloit par ton livre infame
    Pitié d'entre dames bannir,
    Autant vauldroit qu'il ne fust ame
88 Et que le monde deust finir.

XII

    Puis que Nature s'entremist   55r
    D'entailler si digne figure,
    Il est a croire qu'elle y mist
92 De ses biens a comble mesure.
    Dangier y est soubz couverture;
    Mais Nature la tresbenigne,
    Pour adoulcir celle pointure,
96 Y mist Pitié pour medicine.

XIII

    Pour garder honneur et chierté,
    Raison y mist Honte et Dangier,
    Et volut Desdaing et Fierté
100 Du tout des dames estrangier;
    Mais Pitié y puet chalengier
    Tout son droit car, quant el fauldroit,
    El feroit la bonté changier,
104 Puis que nulli mieulx n'en vaudroit.

75 Des d. v. *Ph.* 76 semblant *Qd.* 77 *Omitted Ph,* Il ne les eust pas f. t. *Nf,* Ilz ne furent formez pas formez telz (*sic*) *Nj.* 82 dame *PcQl.* 84 eu c. *PcQl;* noble *NfOjPcQl;* femme *PcQl.* 85 S'il f.] Cuides tu *NfNj.* 90 Detailler *Ph;* sa d. f. *Ql,* si noble f. *NfOjPh.* 91 Il nest acroire quil y m. *Qd.* 92 ces *Oa.* 93 courverture *Qd.* 95 painture *Oa.* 96 Y m. raison *NfNj;* m.] me desdire *Oa.* 99 Et en voult *Ph.* 100 les d. *Oa.* 101 peust *Pc.* 102 car qu. el f.] qu. elle f. *NfNj,* qu. el f. *Oa;* fauldra *Ph.* 103 Elle *OaPh.*

XIV

Tu veulx, par ton oultrecuidance
Et les faulx vers que tu as faiz,
Tolir aux dames leur puissance,
108 Toutes vertuz et tous bienffaiz,
Quant ainsi leur pitié deffaiz,
Par qui maint loyal cuer s'amende;
Si vueil chastier tes meffaiz
112 Ou que tu m'engages l'amende.'

XV

L'Acteur

Quant j'euz ces parolles ouÿ
Et je vi la fleche en la corde,
Tout le sanc au cuer me fouÿ.
116 Oncq n'eu tel paeur dont me recorde,
Et dis: 'Pour Dieu misericorde,
Escoutez moy excuser, sire'.

Le Dieu d'Amours

Il respondi: 'Je le t'acorde.
120 Or dy ce que tu vouldras dire'.

XVI

L'Acteur

' Ha, sire, ne me mescroiez
Ne les dames semblablement,
Se vous ne lisez et voyez
124 Tout le livret premierement.
Je suis aux dames ligement,
Car ce peu qu'oncques j'euz de bien,
D'onneur ou de bon sentement,
128 Vient d'elles et d'elles le tien.

XVII

Avant que faire ceste faulte
Mon cuer choisiroit qu'il mourroit.
La folie seroit si haulte
132 Que ja nul ne le pardonroit.

55v

106 le f. v. *Qd.*   113 Qu. je ces p. ouy *Oj.*   114 Et je] Je *Ph.*   115 ou c. *Nj.*   116 O. n'eu] Oncques
neuz *Ph.*   117 Si dy *NſNjOaOjPcPhQl.*   119 Il respond je le ta. *Ph.*   121 Ha a s. ne me croyez
Oa: Ha s.] He s. *Nſ*, Ha a s. *PcQl.*   123 lisies *PcPhQl.*   124 Le (Ce *Ph*) livret tout p. *NſPh*: livre *Oa.*
126 Car tel poy que onc jeuz de b. *Pc*, Car tel peu que jeus euz oncques de b. *Ql.*   127 ou] et
NſNjPcPhQl.   129 c. chose *Ph.*   131 trop h. *Ph.*   132 ne la p. *Ph.*

> Bien est vil cellui qui vourroit
> A l'onneur des dames meffaire,
> Sans lesquelles nul ne pourroit
> 136 Jamais bien dire ne bien faire.

XVIII
> Par elles et pour elles sommes:
> C'est la sourse de noustre joye;
> C'est l'espargne des nobles hommes;
> 140 C'est d'onneur la droite monjoye;
> C'est le penser qui plus resjoye;
> C'est le chief des mondains plaisirs;
> C'est ce qui d'espoir nous pourvoye;
> 144 C'est le comble de noz desirs.

XIX
> Leur serviteur vueil demourer
> Et en leur service mourray,
> Et ne les puis trop honnourer
> 148 N'autrement ja ne le vourray;
> Ains, tant qu'en vie demourray,
> A garder l'onneur qui leur touche
> Employeray ou je pourray
> 152 Corps, cuer, sens, langue, plume et bouche.

XX
> Pitié en cuer de dame siet   56r
> Ainsi qu'en l'or le dÿamant,
> Mais sa vertu pas ne s'assiet
> 156 Tousjours au plaisir de l'amant;

133 cellui vil *Ph*; quil *Qd*. 135 on ne p. *Ph*. 137 Pour *Qd*; pour elle s. *Nj*. 138 la seurte *Oa*, le confort *Oj*. 139 ladresse *Ph*; des (de *Nf*) vaillans h. *NfNjOaOjPcQl*. 141 Cest ce qui les bons cuers r. *Ph*. 142 Et *Nf*. 143 ce que *Oa*; d'e.] desespoir *Ph*. 144 Et *NfNjOaOjPcQl*. 148 ne le feray *Oa*. 149 Et t. *NfNjOaPh*. 150 A g.] G. *Ph*; les t. *PcQl*. 151 Complayeray *Oa*; mourray *Nf*. 152 Cuer corps *NjOj*. 155 Et sa v. *NfNj*.

Alternative version of stanza XVII in NfNjOaOjPcQl:

> De leur bonté vient et habonde   *Oj*, 102r
> Eur en joye et confort en dueil.
> C'est l'exemple des biens du monde,
> 132 Aysc de cuer et deduit d'oeil.
> C'est le rabais de tout orgueil
> Et le patron pour les bons faire,
> Sans qui nul franc cuer n'a le vueil
> 136 De rien bien dire ne bien faire.

130 Cueur *Oa*. 134 Et se p. *Nf*, Cest le p. *Oa*; les b. plaire *PcQl*. 135 Sans le quel f. c. na nul v. *Pc*, Sans lequel nul f. c. na v. *Ql*: Sans que *Nf*; n'a le v.] ait le v. *NfNj*, ne le v. *Oa*.

Ains fault deffermer un ferment
Dont Crainte tient Pitié enclose
Et, en ce fermouer deffermant,
160   Souffrir sa douleur une pose.

XXI   Pitié se tient close et couverte
Et ne veult force ne contraintes,
Ne ja sa porte n'est ouverte
164   Fors par souspirs et longues plaintes.
Actendre y fault des heures maintes,
Mais l'actente bien se recueuvre,
Car toutes dolours sont estaintes
168   Aussi tost que sa porte s'euvre.

XXII   S'el ne gardoit sa seigneurie,
Chascun lui feroit l'ennuyeux;
Et sa bonté seroit perie,
172   Car el avroit trop d'envïeux.
Pour ce son tresor gracïeux
N'euvre pas a toutes requestes,
Neant plus q'un joyau precïeux
176   Qu'on ne doit moustrer qu'aux grans festes.

XXIII   Se j'osoye dire ou songier
Qu'onques dame fust despiteuse,
Je seroye faulx mensongier
180   Et ma parole injurïeuse.
Jamais de dame gracïeuse
N'ait il ne mercy ne respit,
Qui dit de voix presumpcïeuse
184   Qu'en dame ait orgueil ne despit.

XXIV   Comme la rose tourne en lermes   56v
Au forneau sa force et valeur,
Ainsi rent Pitié aux enfermes,
188   Par feu d'amoureuse chaleur,

159 Et en] En *Oa*; ce fermant *Ql*.   162 forces *PcQl*; contrainte *OaPh*.   163 Et *NfNj*.   166 lentente *Qd*.   168 la p. *OaPcQl*.   169 Selle *Ph*.   174 Neuvrent *Oa*.   177 Se] Et se *Oa*.   178 Que d. fust onc d. *Ph*: Qu'o.] Que oncq *Ql*.   184 Que d. ait dorgueil ne d. *Oa*.   187 Aussi receut p. aux e. *Ph*.

Pleurs qui gairissent la doleur,
Tant est leur haulte vertu digne;
Mais au cuer gist la pitié leur
192 Plus parfont que l'or en la mine.

XXV   Mon livre, qui peu vault et monte,
A nesune autre fin ne tent
Si non a recorder le compte
196 D'un triste amoureux mal content
Qui prie et plaint que trop atent,
Et comme Reffus le reboute;
Et qui autre chose y entent,
200 Il y voit trop ou n'y voit goute.

XXVI   Quant un amant est si estraint,
Comme en resverie mortelle,
Que force de mal le contraint
204 D'appeller sa dame crüelle,
Doit on penser qu'elle soit telle?
Nenny, car le grief mal d'amer
Y met fievre continüelle
208 Qui fait sembler le doux amer.

XXVII   Puis que son mal lui a fait dire,
Et aprés lui pour temps passer
J'ay voulu ses plaintes escrire
212 Sans un seul mot en trespasser,
S'en doit tout le monde amasser
Contre moy a tort et en vain,
Pour le chestif livre casser
216 Dont je ne suis que l'escripvain?

XXVIII   S'aucuns me veulent acuser
D'avoir ou failli ou mespris,

                                                              57r

189 Par plours qui gardent la d. *Ph.*   190 T. est leur v. haulte et d. *NfNj*, Par leur v. puissant et d. *PcPh.*   191 ou c. *NfNjOaOj.*   191–2 Mais quant le dangier nest pas leur Plus en prisent la medicine *Ph.*   193 livret *NfPc*; vault poy *Nj*, plus vault *Oa.*   197 Qui pleure *Ph*; que] et *Qd.* 198 rebute *Qd*, deboute *Ph.*   200 Il y noit *Qd.*   201 contraint *Nf*, astraint *PcQl.*   206 Nenny non car le mal damer *Nf.*   210 empres *Qd.*   211 ces p. *Ph.*   212 atrespasser *Oa.*   214 Comme *Oa.*   215 le povre livret *NfNj.*   216 je nen s. *Oa.*

Devant vous m'en vueil excuser,
220 Que j'ay pieça pour juge pris;
Et, combien que j'ay peu apris,
S'ilz en ont rien dit ou escript
Par quoy je puisse estre repris,
224 Je leur respondray par escript.'

XXIX   Quant Amours ot ouÿ mon cas
Et vit qu'a bonne fin tendi,
Il remist la flece ou carcas
228 Et l'arc amoureux destendy,
Et tel response me rendy:

Amours

Puis qu'a ma court tu te reclames,
J'en suis content et tant t'en dy
232 Que j'en remet la cause aux dames.

XXX   *L'Acteur*

Lors m'esveillay subit et court
Et plus entour moy riens ne vy.
Pour ce me rens a voustre court,
236 Mes dames, et la foy plevy
D'obeïr a droit sans envy,
Ainsi qu'Amours l'a commandé;
Et se je n'ay mal desservy,
240 Ayez moy pour recommandé.

Voustre humble serviteur Alain
Que Beauté print pieça a l'aim
Du trait d'uns tresdoux rïans yeulx,
244 Dont il languist, actendant mieulx.

221 Et c. quaye poy a. *Ql.*   223 Pour quoy *Pc*; peusse *Qd.*   226 que b. f. *Qd.*   227 sa f. *Nj*; eu c. *Pc.*
228 *Omitted Ph.*   231 Je s. *Ph*; t. en di *OaOjPh.*   232 je r. *NfNjPc*, jen renvoie *OjQl.*   234 Et plus
riens en tour moy ne vy *Ph.*   236 et la f.] la f. *Qd.*   237 s. e.] s. (et s. *PcQl*) ennuy *NfOaPcQl.*
239 Mais *NfNjOaOjPcQl*; jen ay *Oa.*   ...la response de lacteur *Oa*, ...la responce maistre alain
Ph, Explicit *OjQl.*   241–4 *Lacking OaOjPhQl.*   242 Qui *Pc.*   243 Dun t. dun t. d. y. *Qd.*   244 je
languis *Nf.*

11

'Rondeaulx et Balades'

The twenty-three rondeaux and five ballades have been numbered consecutively in Roman figures.

RONDEAUX

Eighteen Manuscripts:[1] *Nf*(IX, XI, XXIII) *Nh*(I, IV) *Nj*(I–XXII) *Nm*(V–VIII, XVII) *Om*(IV) *Ph*(XVII) *Qd*(I–XXII) *Qg*(XIII–XIV) *Qr*(I–II, XXIII) *Ta*(VI) *Tb*(V, XIX) *Tc*(III, V–VIII, XII–XIII, XV–XVII, XXI–XXII) *Td*(I–X, XII–XIV, XVI–XXIII) *Te*(V, VIII) *Tf*(XXI) *Tg*(V) *Th*(VIII) *Tq*(XXI).

All the manuscripts have been examined. The *Jardin de Plaisance*, which includes fourteen of the rondeaux printed together as a collection, has also been consulted,[2] as has the *Complainte du Prisonnier d'Amours*, a later separate edition of the same collection.[3] None of the rondeaux was included in the early collected editions of Chartier's works. André du Chesne included in his collected edition two rondeaux from *Pe*, which are not by Chartier.

BALLADES

Twenty-six Manuscripts:[1] *Ba*(XXVIII) *Nf*(XXIV–XXVII) *Nj*(XXIV–XXVII) *Nl*(XXV–XXVII) *Nm*(XXIV) *Oa*(XXIV–XXV) *Oc*(XXVIII) *Ol*(XXVIII) *Om*(XXVIII) *On*(XXVIII) *Oq*(XXVI) *Ph*(XXIV) *Pp*(XXVIII) *Qa*(XXVIII) *Qd*(XXIV–XXVI) *Qr*(XXVI) *Tc*(XXVIII) *Td*(XXIV–XXVI, XXVIII) *Tg*(XXVIII) *Tj*(XXVIII) *Tk*(XXVIII) *Tl*(XXVIII) *Tm*(XXVIII) *Tn*(XXVIII) *To*(XXVIII) *Tp*(XXVIII).

All the manuscripts have been examined except *Tp*. None of the ballades was included in any of the early collected editions of Chartier's works. The *Jardin de Plaisance* contains ballade XXVIII.

The other early anthologies which contain copies of lyrics by Chartier, principally rondeau VI and ballades XXV and XXVIII, have been listed by C. J. H. Walravens.[4]

The collections of lyrics in *Nf Tc Td* and *Nj* have all been published.[5] The only previous

---

[1] It is possible that *Qn*, which has not been traced, contains some of Chartier's rondeaux and ballades; see the description of the manuscript.

[2] The facsimile edition has been used above all: E. Droz et A. Piaget (eds.), *Le Jardin de plaisance et fleur de rhétorique*, I–II, Paris, 1910–25 (*SATF*). The second volume (pp. 271–5) contains a bibliography of manuscripts containing the lyrics.

[3] Paris, Bibl. Nat., Rothschild 3174. See also A. Piaget, 'La Complainte du prisonnier d'amours', *Mélanges Emile Picot*, II, Paris, Morgand, 1913, 155–62.

[4] Dr Walravens has also published a bibliography of the modern editions (*Alain Chartier, études biographiques*, 254–7; 257–61).

[5] [Marquis Ph. de Chennevières (ed.)], *Rondeaux et ballades inédits d'Alain Chartier*, Caen, Poisson et fils, 1846; L. Clédat, 'Ballades, chansonnettes et rondeaux', *Lyon-Revue*, décembre 1886, 307–20 (unexamined); M. Löpelmann (ed.), *Die Liederhandschrift des Cardinals de Rohan*, Göttingen, 1923 (*Gesellschaft für Romanische Literatur*, XLIV); Piaget, *La Belle Dame sans mercy*.

critical edition of the lyrics is that by E. J. Hoffman, who relied on the *Jardin de Plaisance*, on the Du Chesne edition, and on the editions of *Nf Tc* and *Td*.[1]

The attribution of the lyrics

The lyrics are very often copied at the end of the collected manuscripts in which they appear; this is the case in *Nf Oa* and *Qd*. Elsewhere they may be used to fill up space remaining at the end of a quire, as in *Ol Qg* and perhaps *Qr*. Material considerations of this kind help to explain the variation in the size of the collections which survive.

Nj and *Qd* contain the largest collections; smaller ones are found in *Tc* and in the *Iardin de Plaisance*. The many lyrics copied in *Td* are not grouped together, being scattered throughout that *chansonnier*. In the manuscripts and the edition mentioned so far, the lyrics are anonymous. The smaller collection in *Nf* and some of the lyrics in *Nm* and *Ph* are attributed to Alain Chartier. *Tk* and *To*, which each contain one ballade, ascribe it to Chartier. If these attributions are taken together, then six of the twenty-three rondeaux edited here and all five ballades are attributed to Chartier in at least one manuscript or contemporary work.[2] In only one instance is a lyric, rondeau XXI, said to be by another poet; its case will be examined separately.

The almost identical collections in *Nj* and *Qd* include all the lyrics attributed to Chartier except rondeau XXIII and ballade XXVIII. These collections have been accepted as authentic because they are copied in two good and early manuscripts of Chartier's works, manuscripts which, the lyrics apart, contain exclusively (*Nj*) or almost exclusively (*Qd*) works by Alain Chartier.[3] Collections in other manuscripts, for example the two rondeaux in *Pe* published by Du Chesne or the other lyrics copied in *Nl*[4] or *Qr*, do not meet these conditions and have therefore not been included in this edition.

In *Tf* and *Tq* rondeau XXI is copied as part of a collection of lyrics in French composed by Lord Suffolk 'whylest he was prysonnier in Fraunce'; the two manuscripts contain an almost identical rubric. The rondeau is the only poem common to *Tf* and *Tq*, and to the collections in *Nj* and *Qd* which have just been accepted as authentic. Both *Tf* and *Tq* contain collections of Middle English works and were copied in England. The attribution in them of one rondeau to Lord Suffolk does not invalidate the arguments used earlier about the authenticity of the collections in *Nj* and *Qd*, taken as a whole.

The authenticity of ballade XXVIII must also be considered separately, since the ballade is not included in *Nf Nj* or *Qd*. On the other hand it does appear in *Oc Ol Pp Tc* and *Td*, which contain other works by Chartier; it is also included in the *Jardin de Plaisance*, though at some distance from the collection of rondeaux. The ballade is attributed to Chartier in *Tk* and *To*. Again the fact that an English translation of it was printed by Caxton in 1484 at the end of the translation of the *Curial* suggests that Caxton considered

---

[1] Hoffman, *Alain Chartier, his Works and Reputation*, 325–53.

[2] In the following list the attributions are in brackets: V(*Nm*) VII(*Nm*) IX(*Nf*) XI (*Nf*) XVII(*Ph*) XXIII(*Nf*) XXIV(*NfNmPh*) XXV (*Nf*) XXVI (*Nf*) XXVII(*Nf*) XXVIII(*TkTo*). Rondeau V is also attributed to Chartier by Jean Regnier: see E. Droz (ed.), *Les Fortunes et adversitez de Jean Regnier*, Paris, 1932, 154 (*SATF*).

[3] The fact that these two manuscripts belong to different traditions gives their testimony a certain independence.

[4] See p. 84, n. 1.

the ballade to be by Chartier. Most critics have until now been sceptical about the ballade's authenticity, being aware only of the Caxton translation and of the attribution in *To*, an early sixteenth century manuscript. The attribution in *Tk* strengthens the case, even though it is of the same period as that in *To*. In the absence of evidence to the contrary, the ballade must be considered authentic. Too much significance should not be attached to the absence of the ballade from *Nf Nj* and *Qd*, for it is clear that no complete collection of Chartier's works exists. The subject of the ballade is such that it would not readily fit into a collection of love poems.

The textual tradition

The rondeaux and ballades have been edited from the five manuscripts which contain the largest collections, *Nf Nj Qd Tc* and *Td*,[1] and from *Oa Ph* and *To*; these last each contain only one or two lyrics.

Nf and *Nj* contain readings peculiar to themselves in IX (lines 3, 4 and 11), XXIV (line 25), XXV (refrains and lines 11, 27 and 33) and XXVI (lines 2, 6 and 32). *Nf* contains poor rhymes in XXIV (lines 6 and 7); that at line 6 is found also in *Nj*. *Nf* is irregular in XXIV (line 16), XXVI (lines 32 and 40) and XXVII (lines 5 and 14) and further contains a number of individual readings. *Nj*, which contains the larger collection, gives irregular lines in III (line 4), XI (line 9), XVI (line 12), XVIII (line 4), XXIV (line 34) and XXVI (line 26). There are in addition a number of readings peculiar to *Nj*.

Nj and *Tc* contain readings peculiar to themselves in III (lines 9 and 10), VII (lines 10 and 11), VIII (lines 3 and 11), XIII (line 12) and XVII (lines 13 and 15). The two texts rhyme poorly in VII (line 5) and XXII (line 16). Irregular lines occur in *Tc* in XXI (lines 2 and 12) and XXII (line 14). The first five lines of VI are damaged in *Tc* and difficult to read; in XVII, line 8 is omitted. In *Tc*, individual readings occur quite frequently.

Qd and *Td* are generally in agreement and opposed to *Nf Nj* and *Tc*. Both texts contain individual readings, *Td* to a much larger extent than *Qd*; in some cases, for example in II (lines 5–6), V (line 9) and VIII (line 9), *Td* differs markedly from the other texts. *Td* is irregular in I (line 5), IV (line 7) and V (line 4). Irregular lines are more frequent in *Qd* and occur in II (line 11), IX (line 1), XVII (lines 2 and 3), XXI (lines 1 and 5) and XXVI (lines 35 and 39); in many cases, a word or letter has been omitted.

Since *Oa Ph* and *To* each contain only one or two lyrics, their place in the textual tradition cannot be determined accurately. The choice of a base text lies between *Nj* and *Qd*. On grounds of accuracy there is little to choose between them; *Nj* contains one ballade more than *Qd*. *Qd* has been chosen as base for poems I–XXII and XXIV–XXVI, because it generally makes good sense and because it contains slightly fewer individual readings than *Nj*. XXVII has been edited from *Nj*; XXIII and XXVIII from *Td*.

---

[1] Repeated efforts to obtain a microfilm of *Td* produced a film of the recto of each leaf, but not of the verso. Some use has therefore had to be made of the diplomatic edition by M. Löpelmann (*Die Liederhandschrift des Cardinals de Rohan*).

The refrain in the rondeau

The length of the refrain is not indicated in *Nf Nj* or *Qd*. Elsewhere, for example in *Nm Ph* or *Td*, the first few words of the refrain followed by *etc.* are copied at the appropriate points in the rondeau, showing that there is a refrain but not indicating its length. Here the full refrain, as used when the rondeau was set to music, is given in italics; rondeaux v, ix and xiii show how skilfully it could be used.[1]

RONDEAULX   *Qd*, 100r

I
   Pres de ma dame et loing de mon vouloir,
   Plain de desir et crainte tout ensemble,
   Le cuer me fault et le parler me tremble
4 *Quant dire doy ce qu'il me fault vouloir.*

   Seul dis, 'Belle, vous me faictes douloir';
   Mais au besoing Crainte mon propos m'emble,
   Pres de ma dame et loing de mon vouloir,
8 *Plain de desir et crainte tout ensemble.*

   Or ay je mis toutes a nonchaloir
   Pour une seule en qui tout bien s'assemble.
   Oseray je ja desbucher du tremble
12 Pour requerir ce qui me puet valoir?
   Pres de ma dame et loing de mon vouloir,
   Plain de desir et crainte tout ensemble,
   Le cuer me fault et le parler me tremble
16 *Quant dire doy ce qu'il me fault vouloir.*

II
   Comme oseroit la bouche dire
   Ce que le cuer pas penser n'ose?
   Comment requerray je la chose
4 *Que je n'ay hardement d'escrire?*

   Se prïere actrait escondire,
   Ma joye me sera forclose.
   Comme oseroit la bouche dire
8 *Ce que le cuer pas penser n'ose?*

I 2 emsemble *Qd.* 5 Sent dis *Nj*, Seul je dy *Td.* 6 emble *Td.* 9 en n. *Td.* 11 moy d. *Nj.* 12 ce quil *Qd*; peust *Td.* II Rondin *Nj.* 5–6 Se p. a. lesconduyre Dont ma j. en fut las f. *Td.*

[1] On the length of refrains see N. Wilkins, 'The Structure of Ballades, Rondeaux and Virelais in Froissart and Christine de Pisan', *French Studies*, XXIII, 1969, 337–48, esp. 343.

Mais, en doye plourer ou rire,
Ma pensee sera desclose,
Car se je la tenoye close,
12 Desir me pourroit bien occire.
Comme oseroit la bouche dire
Ce que le cuer pas penser n'ose?
Comment requerray je la chose
16 *Que je n'ay hardement d'escrire?*

III   *Au pouvre prisonner, ma dame,*
           Donnez l'aumosne de lïece.
           J'ay du tout, en ceste destraisse
        4 *Despendu mon plaisir, par m'ame.*

           Crainte m'assault, Desir m'enflamme.
           Dangier eslargier ne me laisse.
           Au pouvre prisonner, ma dame,
        8 *Donnez l'aumosne de lïece.*

           C'est pour trop craindre et doubter blame
           Que si dure prison me blesse.
           Faites ycy voustre largesse,
       12 Car oncques mais n'en requis ame;
           Au pouvre prisonner, ma dame,
           Donnez l'aumosne de lïece.
           J'ay du tout, en ceste destraisse
       16 *Despendu mon plaisir, par m'ame.*

IV   *Ou mon desir s'assouvira*
           Ou ma tristece m'occira
           Par vous, belle, prouchainnement,
        4 *Se mon cuer quiert l'alegement*
           Du mal que pour vous servir a.

           Un de ces deux me souffira,
           N'Espoir plus ne me mentira
        8 Se j'ay de parler hardement.

9 en d.] ou d. ou *Td.*   11 Car sainsi la t. plus c. *Td*: tenoy c. *Qd.*   III Rondel *Nj.*   4 par m'a.] par
madame *Nj.*   6 eslargir *NjTcTd*; ne me l.] riens ne l. *Td.*   9 par *NjTc*; ou d. *Tc.*   10 my b. *NjTc.*
11 Mostrez ycy *Nj.*   12 amt *Qd.*   IV Rondeau *Nj.*   1 massouvira *Nj.*   5 nous *Nj.*

Ou mon desir s'assouvira
Ou ma tristece m'occira
Par vous, belle, prouchainnement.

12 Tout bien ou tout mal m'en yra
Car, quant voustre bouche dira
Ouÿ ou nenny seulement,
El asserra le jugement
16 Dont mon dueil ou moy finera.
Ou mon desir s'assouvira
Ou ma tristece m'occira
Par vous, belle, prouchainnement,
20 *Se mon cuer quiert l'alegement*
Du mal que pour vous servir a.

V   *Triste plaisir et doloreuse joye,*
Aspre doulceur, resconfort ennuyeux,
Ris en plourant, souvenir oublïeux,   101r
4 *M'acompaignent combien que seule soye.*

Embuschez sont, affin qu'on ne les voye,
Dedans mon cuer en l'ombre de mes yeulx
Triste plaisir et doloreuse joye,
8 *Aspre doulceur, resconfort ennuyeux.*

C'est mon tresor, ma part et ma monjoye,
De quoy Dangier est sur moy envïeux.
Bien le sera s'il me voit avoir mieulx,
12 Quant il a dueil de ce qu'Amours m'envoye.
Triste plaisir et doloreuse joye,
Aspre doulceur, resconfort ennuyeux,
Ris en plourant, souvenir oublïeux,
16 *M'acompaignent combien que seule soye.*

VI   *Mort sur les piez, faingnant d'avoir plaisir*
Et estrenné de doloreuse estraine,

---

12 Tout mal ou tout bien *Nj*.   15 Il a. *Td*.   V Chancon *Nj*.   4 Si ma. c. que seul je s. *Td*.
5 Embuchie *Tc*.   9 Ce sont les biens dont je fais ma m. *Td*: et ma monoye *Tc*.   10 est encore
e. *Td*.   VI Rondel *NjTc*.   1–5 *Damaged Tc*.   1 Mourant sur p. *Td*; le pie *Tc*.

Ce jour de l'an renouvelle ma paine
4 *Ou par trop craindre ou par trop hault choisir.*

J'ay peu d'espoir et beaucop de desir,
Le corps failly et la parole saine,
Mort sur les piez, faingnant d'avoir plaisir
8 *Et estrenné de doloreuse estraine.*

Acouché gist en lit de Desplaisir
Mon dolent cuer; et le corps se pourmaine
Pour vëoir ce qui si griefment me maine
12 Qu'il m'en convient en cheminant gesir.
Mort sur les piez, faingnant d'avoir plaisir
Et estrenné de doloreuse estraine,
Ce jour de l'an renouvelle ma paine
16 *Ou par trop craindre ou par trop hault choisir.*

VII   *Riche d'espoir et pouvre d'autre bien,*
Comble de dueil et vuide de lïesse,
Je vous suppli, ma loyale maistresse,
4 *Ne me tollez ce que je tiens pour mien.*

Se je le pers, je n'avray jamais rien –
C'est l'espargne de toute ma richesse –
Riche d'espoir et pouvre d'autre bien,
8 *Comble de dueil et vuide de lïesse.*

Souffrir pour vous? Helas, je le vueil bien!
Je n'aim riens tant que le mal qui me blesse.   101v
J'ayme trop mieulx l'endurer qu'il me lesse,
12 Mais que Pitié me retieigne pour sien.
Riche d'espoir et pouvre d'autre bien,
Comble de dueil et vuide de lïesse,
Je vous suppli, ma loyale maistresse,
16 *Ne me tollez ce que je tiens pour mien.*

3 j. de laon *Qd.*   4 part t. h. ch. *Qd.*   9 Au couchier g. *Tc.*   11 P. v. ce que si griefvement me m.
Td.   12 Donc me c. *Nj,* Quil me c. *TcTd.*   VII Rondelet *Nj,* Chanconnete *Tc.*   5 la pers *Nj;* bien
NjTc.   10 Je nay riens mieulx que *NjTc,* Riens n'ayme tant que *Td.*   11 t. m.] encor m. *NjTc;* qui
me l. *Tc.*

VIII

Je n'ay pouoir de vivre en joye
Et si ne puis meurir de dueil;
Ne ne puis haïr ne ne vueil
4 *Celle qui tel doleur m'envoye.*

Helas, et comment gariroye
De la doleur dont je me dueil?
Je n'ay pouoir de vivre en joye
8 *Et si ne puis meurir de dueil.*

S'un jour Amours abandonnoye,
Bien say q'un gracïeux acueil
Me retrairoit par un doulx oeil;
12 Et puis je recommenceroye.
Je n'ay pouoir de vivre en joye
Et si ne puis meurir de dueil;
Ne ne puis haïr ne ne vueil
16 *Celle qui tel doleur m'envoye.*

IX

Helas! Ma courtoise ennemie
Et mon gracïeux adversaire,
Dont vous puet mon desplaisir plaire
4 *Qui m'occit, et si n'en meurs mie?*

Mon cuer qui de doleur lermie
Ne cesse de crïer et braire:
'Helas! Ma courtoise ennemie
8 *Et mon gracïeux adversaire!'*

Est Pitié en vous endormie
Ou s'elle a autre part affaire?
Fu je donc fait pour tel mal traire
12 Sans avoir joye ne demie?
Helas! Ma courtoise ennemie
Et mon gracïeux adversaire,
Dont vous puet mon desplaisir plaire
16 *Qui m'occit, et si n'en meurs mie?*

VIII Rondeau *Nj*, Rondinot *Tc*. 3 Et ne scey h. *NjTc*. 6 d. tant me d. *Td*. 9 Se ung tout seul jour labandonnoie *Td*: damours a. *Qd*. 11 My r. *NjTc*; son d. o. *Td*. 12 recommaceroie *Td*. IX Rondelet *Nf*, Rondel *Nj*. 1 H. ni courtoisie e. *Qd*. 3 peust *Td*; ce d. *NfNj*. 4 ne m. *NfNj*. 9 en vous *repeated Nf*. 10 Ou elle *Nf*. 11 tout mal *NfNj*, tant mal *Td*.

X

    De quoy me sert le regart de mes yeulx
    Loing de tout ce qu'il leur plaist que je voye,
    Quant je ne puis d'eulx avoir autre joye,
4 *Ne je ne suis d'autre bien envïeux?*

    S'un tout seul jour ilz me font plus joyeux,   102r
    Tout le surplus, quanque je voy, m'emoye.
    De quoy me sert le regart de mes yeulx
8 *Loing de tout ce qu'il leur plaist que je voye?*

    Ce me seroit le plus seur et le mieulx
    S'au deppartir de tous poins les clöoye
    Jusqu'au retour, car point n'en jouïroye,
12 Et en eusse cent millïons de tieulx.
    De quoy me sert le regart de mes yeulx
    Loing de tout ce qu'il leur plaist que je voye,
    Quant je ne puis d'eulx avoir autre joye,
16 *Ne je ne suis d'autre bien envïeux?*

XI

    Je vi le temps que je souloye
    Vivre en espoir d'estre joyeux,
    Et pensoye qu'il m'en fust mieulx;
4 *Mais je pers ce que j'actendoye.*

    J'ay par espoir eu de la joye;
    Je ne soule plus, se m'aist Dieux.
    Je vi le temps que je souloye
8 *Vivre en espoir d'estre joyeux.*

    Un autre a ce que demandoye,
    Qui maintenant m'est ennuyeux;
    Il fu de mon bien envïeux
12 Des lors que premier me douloye.
    Je vi le temps que je souloye
    Vivre en espoir d'estre joyeux,
    Et pensoye qu'il m'en fust mieulx;
16 *Mais je pers ce que j'actendoye.*

X Rondeau *Nj*. 6 Et le s. *Td*; mennoie *NjTd*. 12 de ytieulx *Nj*. XI Rondel *Nf*, Chanconnecte
Nj. 2 espoix *Qd*. 6 s. mais *Nf*. 9 Ung a. ce que je d. *Nj*. 10 emuieux *NjQd*.

XII

Deshors! Deshors! Il vous fault deslogier,
Desir sans joye et Pensee d'Amours.
Tant avez fait en mon cuer de voz tours
4 Qu'il n'y a plus pour vous que fourrager.

Nonchaloir vueil desormais harberger
Avec Oubli, pour moy donner secours.
Deshors! Deshors! Il vous fault deslogier,
8 *Desir sans joye et Pensee d'Amours.*

Je vous receu un peu trop de legier.
Departez vous! Alez logier ailleurs!
N'aprouchez plus de mon cuer les forsbours!
12 Trop ay vescu soubz voustre dur dangier.
Deshors! Deshors! Il vous fault deslogier,
Desir sans joye et Pensee d'Amours.
Tant avez fait en mon cuer de voz tours
16 *Qu'il n'y a plus pour vous que fourrager.*

XIII

'Cuidez vous qu'il ait assez joye
Qui est loing de ce qu'il desire,
Et pense ce qu'il n'ose dire,

102v

4 Et voit et ne lui chault qu'il voye?'

'Voulentiers le conforteroye.
Et que vous en semble, beau sire?
Cuidez vous qu'il ait assez joye
8 *Qui est loing de ce qu'il desire?'*

'Que diriez vous se j'estoye
Cellui qui porte tel martire?
Un cuer qui loing d'espoir souspire,
12 N'est il pas en piteuse voye?
Cuidez vous qu'il ait assez joye
Qui est loing de ce qu'il desire,
Et pense ce qu'il n'ose dire,
16 *Et voit et ne lui chault qu'il voye?'*

XII Chanczon *Nj*, Rondelinet *Tc.* 1 desloyer *Qd.* 3 de vous t. *Qd.* 5 deshors mais h. *Tc.*
6 donneur *Qd.* 10 Deportez *Nj.* 12 vesu *Qd.* XIII Chanczon *Nj*, Rondel *Tc.* 1 quil est *Tc.*
10 ce m. *NjTd.* 12 en mauvaise v. *NjTc.*

XIV

La bonne volenté que j'ay
De bien amer voustre beauté,
Avec espoir de loyauté,
4 *Me font tenir vers vous plus vray.*

A mon pouoir vous moustreray,
Non pareille en toute bonté,
La bonne volenté que j'ay
8 *De bien amer voustre beauté;*

Ne jamais autre ne seray
Car en ce point suis arresté
Sans y penser desloyauté,
12 Pour ce que point ne changeray.
La bonne volenté que j'ay
De bien amer voustre beauté,
Avec espoir de loyauté,
16 *Me font tenir vers vous plus vray.*

XV

Belle, qui si bon cuer avez
Que jamais haïr ne savez
Et si ne voulez rien amer,
4 *Dont vient ce que j'ay tant d'amer*
Pour vous et ne le parcevez?

Maugré pitié, fort me grevez,
Dont bien petit preu recevez;
8 Et si ne vous en puis blamer,
Belle, qui si bon cuer avez
Que jamais haïr ne savez
Et si ne voulez rien amer.

12 De mourir me parachevez,
Ou du dur mal me relevez,
Ou Amours me fait enflammer.
Ne me souffrez tant affamer
16 Se ja bien faire me devez.

XIV Rondelet (62v), Chanczon (63r) *Nj*. 2 Damer vostre belle b. *Nj*. 4 fait *Nj*; vers vous tenir *Td*. 12 P. ce jamais ne ch. *Td*. XV Rondel *Nj*, Rondinet *Tc*. 4 jay tart (?) *Tc*. 5 ne la p. *Tc*, ne lappercevez *Nj*.

Belle, qui si bon cuer avez
Que jamais haïr ne savez
Et si ne voulez rien amer,
20 *Dont vient ce que j'ay tant d'amer*
Pour vous et ne le parcevez?

XVI

Puis qu'autre rien ne me puet plaire   103r
Ne le gré de mon cuer actraire
Fors voustre beauté seulement,
4 *Helas et pourquoy ne comment*
La me veult Fortune fortraire?

Je ne say qu'elle pense a faire
Mais, s'elle m'est tousjours contraire,
8 Je ne puis vivre longuement,
Puis qu'autre rien ne me puet plaire
Ne le gré de mon cuer actraire
Fors voustre beauté seulement.

12 Vous servir est tout mon affaire;
Vous me pouez faire ou deffaire.
Je suis en voustre jugement,
Et ne sera point autrement
16 Se la mort ne m'en fait retraire,
Puis qu'autre rien ne me puet plaire
Ne le gré de mon cuer actraire
Fors voustre beauté seulement.
20 *Helas et pourquoy ne comment*
La me veult Fortune fortraire?

XVII

Joye me fuit et Desespoir me chace.
Je n'ay plaisir ne je ne le pourchace.
J'ay mes bons jours passez et ma lëesse,
4 *Puis que la mort m'a tolu ma maistresse*
De qui seule j'esperoye la grace.

Quant plus me trouve en mainte bonne place
Ou chascun rit et s'esbat et soulace,

XVI Chancon *Nj*, Rondel *Tc.* 1 Pour quaultre bien ne me peust p. *Td.* 4 H. mais p. et c. *Tc.*
6 p. a f.] p. f. *Td*, p. affaire *Qd.* 12 V. s. est mon a. *Nj.* 15 Et ne seray ja a. *Td.* XVII Chanczon
Nj, Rondel... *Ph*, Chanconnete *Tc.* 2 ne le p.] ne p. *Qd.* 3 mes b. j.] b. j. *Qd.*

8   Et plus me croist mon mal et ma destresse.
Joye me fuit et Desespoir me chace.
Je n'ay plaisir ne je ne le pourchace.
J'ay mes bons jours passez et ma lëesse.

12   Si pri a Dieu que vray pardon lui face
Car, sans qu'en rien le bien d'autruy efface,
Aprés sa mort sa pareille ne lesse.
Mon cuer la plaint et mon regret ne cesse
16   Quant Souvenir me presente sa face.
Joye me fuit et Desespoir me chace.
Je n'ay plaisir ne je ne le pourchace.
J'ay mes bons jours passez et ma lëesse,
20   Puis que la mort m'a tolu ma maistresse
De qui seule j'esperoye la grace.

XVIII   *Quant un jour suis sans que je voye*
Un seul plaisir que mes yeulx ont,
Toutes les lëesses qui sont
4   *Ne me mectroient pas en joye.*

Plus me dueil que se je perdoye   103v
Tous les biens qui ja m'aviendront,
Quant un jour suis sans que je voye
8   *Un seul plaisir que mes yeulx ont.*

Mais s'il lui plaist que la revoye,
Mes doleurs tout a coup s'en vont,
Qui au departir reviendront
12   *Plus dures que je ne vouldroye.*
Quant un jour suis sans que je voye
Un seul plaisir que mes yeulx ont,
Toutes les lëesses qui sont
16   *Ne me mectroient pas en joye.*

XIX   *Au feu! Au feu! Au feu, qui mon cuer art*
Par un brandon tiré d'un doulx regart,

8 *Omitted Tc.*   13 que r. *NjTc.*   14 la p. *Td.*   15 se p. *NjTc.*   XVIII Rondelet *Nj.*   4 Ne mectroient pas mon cuer en j. *Nj.*   6 T. les b. que jamaiz viendront *Td.*   9 M. si *Qd*, M. quant *Td.*   XIX Chancon nouvele *Nj.*

Tout enflambé d'ardant desir d'amours.
4 *Grace, Mercy, Confort et Bon Secours,*
Ne me laissiez bruler, se Dieu vous gart.

Flamme, chaleur, ardeur partout s'espart.
Estincelles et fumee s'en part;
8 Embrasé suis du feu qui croist tousjours.
Au feu! Au feu! Au feu, qui mon cuer art
Par un brandon tiré d'un doulx regart,
Tout enflambé d'ardant desir d'amours.

12 Tirez, boutez, chacez tout a l'escart!
Ce dur dangier getez de toute part!
Eaue, pitié, de lermes et de pleurs!
A l'ayde! Helas, je n'ay confort d'ailleurs.
16 Avancez vous ou vous vendrez trop tart!
Au feu! Au feu! Au feu, qui mon cuer art
Par un brandon tiré d'un doulx regart,
Tout enflambé d'ardant desir d'amours.
20 *Grace, Mercy, Confort et Bon Secours,*
Ne me laissiez bruler, se Dieu vous gart.

XX   *S'oncques beaux yeulx orent celle puissance*
          De donner dueil et de promectre joye,
          J'ay de l'un plus que porter n'en pourroye
4   *Et de l'autre je vif en esperance,*

Car les plus beaux et les plus doulx de France
Ont de mon cuer fait amoureuse proye,
S'oncques beaux yeulx orent celle puissance
8 *De donner dueil et de promectre joye.*

Et s'une foiz l'ueil de mon cuer s'avance
Et ceulx du corps devers la belle envoye,
Son doulx regart qui le mien reconvoye
12 Me navre a mort et si m'offre alegence.
S'oncques beaux yeulx orent celle puissance

6 Flambe *Nj.*   14 E. p.] Eaue de p. *NjTd.*   15 A laide las *Td.*   XX Chancon *Nj.*   1 telle p. *NjTd.*
3 ne p. *Td.*   11 le m. ransonnoie *Nj.*

De donner dueil et de promectre joye,
J'ay de l'un plus que porter n'en pourroye
16   *Et de l'autre je vif en esperance.*

XXI   Loyaument et a tousjours mais,   104r
             De pieça et plus qu'oncques mais
             Je suis voustre et voustre me tien,
4   M'amour, ma joye, mon seul bien,
             Mon espoir, mon desir, ma paix.

             Ma volenté, mes diz, mes fais
             Sont telz et seront a jamais;
8   C'est la leçon que je retien.
             Loyaument et a tousjours mais,
             De pieça et plus qu'oncques mais
             Je suis voustre et voustre me tien.

12   Ou que je suis, ou que je vais,
             Quoy que je dy ou que je tais,
             Vous avez le cuer qui fu mien.
             Or nous entr'amons doncques bien,
16   Si seront noz plaisirs parfais.
             Loyaument et a tousjours mais,
             De pieça et plus qu'oncques mais
             Je suis voustre et voustre me tien,
20   *M'amour, ma joye, mon seul bien,*
             Mon espoir, mon desir, ma paix.

XXII   *Ainsi que bon vous semblera*
             Et que voustre plaisir sera,
             Me vueil a voustre grace actendre,
4   *Car, soit mon mal greigneur ou mendre,*
             Quant vous vouldrés, il cessera.

             Ce que de moy ordonnera
             Voustre doulceur, il se fera
8   Se mon pouoir s'i puet estendre,

XXI Rondel *Nj*, Rondelinet *Tc.*   1 L. et a t. (*sic*) *Qd.*   2 Despiece *Tc.*   4 Ma joie mon soulas mon b.
Nj: ma j. et mon s. b. *TcTd.*   5 ma p.] p. *Qd.*   12 je s.] s. *Tc.*   13 je die *Td.*   15 entramours *Tc.*
XXII Rondeau *Nj*, Rondelet *Tc.*   1 Aussi *Tc.*   4 grefveur *Tc.*   8 se p. *Tc,* sy peust *Td.*

Ainsi que bon vous semblera
Et que voustre plaisir sera;
Me vueil a voustre grace actendre.

12 En ce point mon temps passera
Ne mon cuer ne s'en lassera,
Et devoit il de doleur fendre.
Il s'est venu a mercy rendre.
16 Que, s'il vous plaist, en pensera?
Ainsi que bon vous semblera
Et que voustre plaisir sera,
Me vueil a voustre grace actendre,
20 *Car, soit mon mal greigneur ou mendre,*
Quant vous vouldrés, il cessera.

XXIII   *Du tout ainsi qu'il vous plaira*   Td, 91v
A moy commander ou deffendre,
Mon cueur jusqu'au partir et fendre
4 *Pour nulle autre ne vous lairra;*

Ains tousjours vous obeÿra
Et vous servira sans offendre,
Du tout ainsi qu'il vous plaira
8 *A moy commander ou deffendre.*

Maiz du doulx bien et cetera –
Vous me poués assés entendre –
Y doibs je renoncer ou tendre,
12 Ou se ma bouche se tayra?
Du tout ainsi qu'il vous plaira
A moy commander ou deffendre,
Mon cueur jusqu'au partir et fendre
16 *Pour nulle autre ne vous lairra.*

14 Et d. il] Et doit il *Tc*, Et deubt il bien *Td*.   15 A vous se vient a m. r. *Td*: Il est v. *Qd*.   16 Ainsi que bon vous semblera (*sic*) *NjTc*.   XXIII Rondinet *Nf*.   2 Sur moy *Nf*.   4–6 Tousjours mais vous obeira Et pour nulle autre ne laira De bien vous servir fresche et tendre *Nf*.   9 et ce taira *Nf*.

XXIV

Aucunes gens m'ont huy araisonné,
En tournoiant, ainsi que je songoye,
Pour quel cause j'ay si habandonné
4 Joyeuseté, plaisir, lëece et joye,
Et dont ce vient que je ne me resjoye
Et plus ne fais dit ne chançon nouvelle,
Et que j'ay mis soubz le banc ma vïelle
8 Et renoncé au service amoureux.
Je n'en dy plus, mais mon cuer pense et sele
Que les loyaulx sont les plus doloreux.

Je suis dolent, triste et dessaisonné;
12 Je n'ay plaisir de chose que je voye.
J'ay plus pardu que Dieu ne m'a donné
Et suis desert de plus que je n'avoye.
J'ay oublïé ce peu que je savoye.
16 Nulle chose fors penser ne m'est belle.
Je n'ay chançon fors que la kyrïelle
Ne je n'atens jamais estrë eureux.
Fortune veult, dont nul homme n'appelle,
20 *Que les loyaulx sont les plus doloreux.*

C'est mon ordre qu'estre desordonné;
Je voys avant comme home qui forvoye.
Ce que je fais doit estre pardonné:
24 Je ne suis plus cellui que je souloye,
N'il ne me chaut qu'on cuide que je soye,
Puis que la mort m'a departy de celle
Que tant valoit que tous furent en elle
28 Les biens qu'autres choisiroient pour eulx.
Or m'a moustré la mort dure et crüelle
Que les loyaulx sont les plus doloreux.

XXIV Autre balade *Nf*, Balade *Nj*, Balade dalain *Ph*, No heading *Td*.   3 quelle c. *OaTd*.   5 ne me desjoye *Oa*.   6 ny f. *Oa*; dis *Td*; diz ne chancons nouvelles *NfNj*.   7 la v. *Td*, mes vielles *Nf*. 11 desraisonne *Nf*.   13 D.] plus *Qd*.   14 navouye *Qd*.   16 N. ch.] Et n. ch. *Nf*.   18 Ne ne matens j. destre e. *Td*.   20 soient *Td*.   25 Il *NfNj*; men ch. *OaTd*.   27 Qui *NfNjOaPhTd*.   29 d. et c.] d. tuelle *Oa*.

Prince, ay je tort, puis que j'ay choisi telle   105r
32   Qui n'avoit si fors qu'elle estoit mortelle,
Se je fais dueil treslong et rigoreux
Et se je tien envers tous la querelle
Que les loyaulx sont les plus doloreux?

XXV   AUTRE

J'ay un arbre de la plante d'amours
Enraciné en mon cuer proprement,
Qui ne porte fruit si non de doleurs,
4   Fueilles d'ennuy et fleur d'encombrement;
Mais, puis qu'il fu planté premierement,
Il est tant creu de racine et de branche
Que son umbre qui me porte nuysance
8   Fait au dessoubz toute joye sechier.
Et si ne puis pour toute ma puissance
Autre planter ne cellui arracher (sic.).

De si long temps l'ay arrousé de plours
12   Et de lermes tant doloreusement,
Et si n'en sont les fruiz de riens meilleurs
Ne je n'y truis gaires d'amendement.
Je les recueil neantmoins songneusement;
16   C'est pour mon cuer amere soustenance,
Qui trop mieulx feust en freche ou en souffrance
Que porter fruit qui le deüst blecier,
Mais pas ne veult l'amoureuse ordonnance
20   *Autre planter ne cellui arrachier.*

S'en ce primtemps que les fueilles et fleurs
Es arbreceaulx percent nouvellement,
Amours vouloit moy faire ce secours,
24   Que les branches qui font empeschement
Il retrenchast du tout entierement   105v

Only first four words of envoy included Oa. 33 Et *Ph*; treslont *Qd.* 34 Et se je t.] Et je t. *Nj*, Et je maintiens *Nf*; e. vous *Ph*. XXV A. balade *NfOa*, Balade *Nj*, *No heading Td.* 2 En racine *NjQd.* 3 si non fruit *Oa.* 4 flours *NfNjTd*, fruit *Oa.* 6 Il est creu de r. et de b. *Nj.* 9 par *Oa.* *Refrains* Autre y p. *NfNj.* 11 Des l. t. a lay a. de p. *NfNj*, De l. t. lay bien a. de p. *Oa*: est a. *Td.* 14 ne t. *Qd.* 15 pourtant s. *Td.* 16 Cest de mon c. la mere s. *Td.* 17 fut *Td.* 18 f. qui d. b. *Oa*, fruis qui le deussent b. *Td.* 19 l'a. o.] la. plaisance *Oa.* 20 cestuy *Nj.* 21 qui *Qd.* 22 Et a. *Td.* 25 rentrenchast *Qd.*

Pour y anter un raimseau de plaisance,
Il geteroit bourjons de souffisance;
28 Joye en ystroit, dont il n'est riens plus chier,
Et ne fauldroit ja par desesperance
Autre planter ne cellui arrachier.

Ma princesse, ma premiere esperance,
32 Mon cuer vous sert en dure penitance.
Faites le mal qui l'aqueult retrenchier,
Et ne souffrez en voustre souvenance
Autre planter ne cellui arrachier.

XXVI   AUTRE

J'ay voulentiers oÿ parler d'amours
Tousdis en bien, et enviz en mesdire,
Et le parler m'en a semblé tousjours
4 Un passetemps bien gracïeux pour rire;
N'oncques n'en sceu riens fors par oÿr dire
Et rencontrer ceulx qui en revenoient,
Dont l'un content, l'autre non, s'en tenoient,
8 Jusqu'environ quinze jours davant mars
Qu'Amours transmist Desir et Doulx Regars
Disant: 'Desir, il me plaist que tu t'armes
Contre cellui qui desprise mes dars'.
12 *Je n'en doy pas parler comme clerc d'armes.*

Alors Desir vint logier es forsbours
De mon vouloir en approchant de tire,
Et j'esbahy de ses estranges tours
16 Levay un pont qui Crainte se fait dire.
La me tira Doulx Regart mainte vire
Dont les unes feiblement m'assonnoyent,   106r
Les autres mieulx, car tost et dru venoyent.
20 La fu Beauté qui print un de ses ars,
Trait a mon cuer et le perce en deux pars
Par un plaisir plus fort qu'erbes ne charmes,

26 ruisseau *NfOa.*   27 a s. *NfNj.*   29 pour d. *Oa.*   33 quil (qui *Nj*) la seult *NfNj*, qui lassault *Oa.*
34 souffrer *Qd.*   XXVI A. balade *Nf*, Balade *Nj*, *No heading Td.*   2 T. en b.] Entre dames *NfNj*;
ennuys *Td.*   5 Noncq nen s. r. f. que par o. d. *Td.*   6 Et rencontray *NfNj*, Et recontrer *Qd.*
13 fosbours *Qd.*   20 dars *Nf.*   21 Trait en *Nf*; le part *Td.*

Si apperceu qu'Amours n'estoit pas gars;
24 *Je n'en doy pas parler comme clerc d'armes.*

Riens n'y valu garnison ne secours;
Assailli fu et prest de desconfire.
A l'assaillir fit Desirs mains estours,
28 Honte rougir et Päeur soy deffrire;
Ne plus Raison n'y savoit contredire.
Los et Renom l'assault en hault sonnoyent,
Et Souvenir et Pensee minoyent,
32 Qui en mine prindrent tous les souldars;
Et puis Franc Cuer qui de riens n'est eschars
Lascha le pont dont je languis en larmes.
Desir entra a flambans estandars;
36 *Je n'en doy pas parler comme clerc d'armes.*

Ma maistresse, je suis au lit ou j'ars,
Prins de Desir dont je ne me depars;
Mais se j'avoye et cent corps et cent armes,
40 La prise est voustre, et valoit mille mars.
Je n'en doy pas parler comme clerc d'armes.

XXVII   BALADE   *Nj,* 55v

Je ne fu nez fors pour tout mal avoir
Et soustenir les assaulz de Fortune.
Qu'est ce de bien? Je ne le puis savoir
4 N'onques n'en eus – ne n'ay – joie nesune.
Je fusse mieulz tout mort cent fois contre une
Que de vivre si douloureusement.
Ce que je vueil me vient tout autrement,
8 Car Fortune a pieça ma mort juree.
Il me desplaist de ma longue duree
Ne je n'ay plus de vivre grant envie,
Mais me murtrit douleur desmesuree
12 *Quant je ne voy ma doulce dame en vie.*

26 et pres de *Nf,* et deprez de *Nj.*   32 Qui par m. *NfNj*; t. les s.] t. s. *Nf.*   35 entra *repeated Qd;*
en f. e. *Nf.*   37 ou l. *NfNjTd.*   39 et c. corps] et corps *Qd.*   40 La p. est vallist m. m. *Nf.*
Explicit *Qd.*   XXVII 5 c. f. c.] c. c. *Nf.*

390

J'ay perdu cuer, sentement et savoir.
Plourer a part, c'est mon euvre commune.
Plains et regrez sont mon plus riche avoir
16 Ne je ne compte en ce monde une prune.
Tout m'ennuye: ciel et soleil et lune
Et quanqui est dessoubz le firmament.
Je desire le jour du jugement,   56r
20 Quant ma joie est soubz la tombe emmuree
Et que la mort m'est rude et aduree,
Qui m'a toulu celle que j'ay servie;
Donc j'ay depuis longue peine enduree,
24 *Quant je ne voy ma doulce dame en vie.*

Je n'attens riens que la mort recevoir;
Mon cuer a pris a ma vie rancune.
La mort en fait lachement son devoir
28 Quant el n'occit et chascun et chascune
Sans espargnier ne beauté ne peccune;
Mais, malgré lour, tout efforceement.
Je la requier craignant duel et torment;
32 Et elle soit par rigueur conjuree!
Elas! Pourquoy m'a elle procuree
Mort a demy sans l'avoir assouvie?
Vie en langueur, telle est ma destinee,
36 *Quant je ne voy ma doulce dame en vie.*

XXVIII   BALADE   Td, 41r

Il n'est danger que de villain,
N'orgueil que de povre enrichi,
Ne si seur chemin que le plain,
4 Ne secours que de vray amy,
Ne desespoir que jalousie,
Ne hault vouloir que d'amoureux,
Ne paistre qu'en grant seignorie,
8 *Ne chere que d'omme joieux;*

Ne servir qu'au roy souverain,
Ne lait nom que d'omme ahonty,

---

14 mon envie c. *Nf.* XXVIII B. faicte et composee par le doulx poete maistre Alain charretier *To, No heading Td.* 3 Ne suivir ch. *Tc.* 6 Ne h. v. questre amoureux *Tc.* 9 qu'au r.] que de r. *Tc.*

Ne menger fors quant on a fain,
12 N'emprise que d'omme hardi,
Ne povreté que maladie,
Ne hanter que les bons et preux,
Ne maison que la bien garnie,
16 *Ne chere que d'omme joieux.*

Ne n'est richesse qu'estre sain,
N'en amours tel bien que mercy,
Ne que la mort riens plus certain   41v
20 Ne meilleur chastoy que de luy,
Ne tel tresor que prodommie,
N'engoisse qu'en cueur convoiteux,
Ne puissance ou n'y ait envie,
24 *Ne chere que d'omme joieux.*

Prince, que voulés vous que die?
Il n'est parler que gracïeux,
Ne louer gens qu'aprés leur vie,
28 *Ne chere que d'omme joieux.*

13 que m.] que de m. *Tc.*   17 Et *To.*   23 Ne p. ou il nait e. *Tc,* Ne p. ou nait e. *To.*   Lenvoy *To.*
25 Que voulez vous que je vous die *TcTo.*   26 Il n'est que parler g. *To.*

12

'Le Breviaire des Nobles'

Fifty-three Manuscripts: *Ba Bb Bc Bd Be Bf Bg Bh Bj Bk   Na Ne Nf Nh Nj Nk Nl Nq
Oa Oc Od Oe Og Oj Om On Oo Op Oq   Pa Pb Pc Pd Pe Pf Ph Pk Pl Pm Pn Po Pp
Qa Qd Qe Qk Ql Qm Qn Qo Qp Qq Qr.*

Qn has not been traced and *Qp* has been damaged by fire. All the other manuscripts, except *Oo*, have been examined. *Ba* contains extracts from the poem, *Bk* only a fragment.

The *Breviaire des Nobles* was included in all the early collected editions and in the Du Chesne edition. There are at least four separate early editions of the poem.[1] The collected editions of 1489 and 1617 have been examined, as have three of the separate editions extant.

In 1951 W. H. Rice published a list of thirty-six manuscripts containing the poem; three years later, he published editions of the *Breviaire des Nobles* and of Michault Taillevent's riposte to it, the *Psaultier des Vilains*.[2] The edition of the *Breviaire des Nobles* is based on *Pn*, with variants from *Pd* and *Po*; in special circumstances, further variants are given from *Om* and *Qa*, from the Du Chesne edition and from the collected edition of 1529 published by Du Pré.

The *Breviaire des Nobles* is attributed to Alain Chartier in twelve manuscripts;[3] in the others the poem is anonymous. The title, *Breviaire des Nobles*, is that found in almost all the manuscripts.

The poem has been edited here from eight manuscripts. Essentially three groups of texts can be distinguished: *Nf Nj*; *Pc Ql*, *Qd*; *Oa Ph*, *Oj*. At the same time it is clear that the three groups are all interlinked and that the textual tradition of the *Breviaire des Nobles* is extremely complicated.

Nf and *Nj* contain readings peculiar to themselves at lines 7, 15, 91, 122, 154, 162, 193, 208, 226, 249 etc.; that at line 7 makes the rhyme unsatisfactory. The text in *Nj* is complete and includes few individual readings (lines 71, 96, 144, 149, 281, 286, 330, 389 and 437); *Nj* is irregular at lines 246 (technically), 280 and 284 and rhymes badly at line 58. *Nf* lacks the final rondeau and contains many more readings peculiar to itself than does *Nj*. At lines 140, 315, 322, 330, 355, 359, 389, 394 and 395 *Nf* is irregular and at lines 94, 206 and 395 it rhymes unsatisfactorily.

Nf and *Nj* contain at lines 95 and 409 readings peculiar to themselves and to *Pc* and *Ql*; further readings at lines 195 and 439 are found only in these four texts and in *Qd*. *Nf* is more closely linked to *Pc* and *Ql* than is *Nj*; readings at lines 88, 319, 391 and 431 are found only in these three texts. Like *Nf*, *Ql* lacks the final rondeau.

Pc and *Ql* are themselves closely linked; there are many readings peculiar to the two texts (lines 11, 13, 32, 82, 91, 97, 130, 154, 165, 167 etc.). Individual readings are more

---

[1] GKW 6560–1; Pellechet 3525; Chantilly, Musée Condé, 420 (unexamined).
[2] W. H. Rice, 'Pour la bibliographie d'Alain Chartier', *Romania*, LXXII, 1951, 380–6; 'Deux poèmes sur la chevalerie...', *Romania*, LXXV, 1954, 54–97.   [3] *Ba Bb Bc Bd Bf Bk Nq Pa Pd Pn Qo* and *Qr*.

frequent in *Pc* (lines 6, 14, 19, 58, 65, 87, 88, 104, 144, 179 etc.) than in *Ql* (lines 168, 172, 179, 207, 209, 233, 244, 246, 261 etc.).

Qd bears some relationship to *Pc* and *Ql* as is shown by readings at lines 98, 173, 268, 282 and 432; the degree of relationship is not clear. *Qd* contains a considerable number of readings peculiar to itself, many of which are of small importance and result from scribal errors. Lines 155, 222, 252, 254, 315, 319, 375, 432 and 433 are irregular in *Qd*.

Oa and *Ph* both lack lines 315–17 and contain readings peculiar to themselves at lines 282 and 302. *Oa* further lacks lines 131, 140, 200–1, 346 and 354–7. Of the many individual readings in *Oa*, those at lines 5, 41, 87, 176, 182, 194, 224, 240, 275 and 348 make the text irregular; in several cases a word has been added. *Ph* lacks line 120 and contains irregular readings peculiar to itself at lines 164, 176, 180, 203, 205, 246, 268 and 357. A number of corrections have been made in a second hand (*Ph²*), for example at lines 5, 25 and 38, apparently from an early printed edition.

Oa and/or *Ph* have some readings in common with *Oj*, for example at lines 75, 88, 95, 98, 173, 195, 268, 383, 409, 434, 435 and 439. At these points and elsewhere *Oa Ph* and *Oj* generally stand apart from the tradition represented by *Pc* and *Ql*.

Oj is complete and contains very few individual readings (lines 11, 40, 109, 152, 210, 213, 292, 305, 324, 406 etc.); its text is entirely regular.

The different readings offered at the lines where the texts of the *Breviaire des Nobles* diverge most, are almost all acceptable. At lines 154 and 415, however, the readings given by *Pc* and *Ql* strain the syntax and make poor sense; at line 339 the sense demands a feminine pronoun and the version of *Oa Pc* and *Ql* must therefore be rejected. On several occasions texts give rhyme words which are unsatisfactory according to fifteenth-century practice. *Nf Oa* and *Ph* give poor rhymes at line 96; *Pc* and *Ql* at line 167; *Ql* at line 240; *Oa* and *Ph* at line 302.

It was already clear from the description of the texts that *Oj* was likely to be the most suitable base text for an edition of the *Breviaire des Nobles*. That view is confirmed by an examination of these lines. The few corrections to *Oj* which have proved necessary have been made from *Qd* or *Nj*.

Corrections in Oj

The corrections follow the same pattern as those in the *Debat des Deux Fortunés d'Amours* and have been treated in the same way in this edition.[1] The scribe has made good omissions in lines 19 (*duit*), 185 (*nous*) and 202 (*le cuer*). Certain other changes may have been made by him: 2 *preuz* to *preux*; 205 *autre* to *autry*; 423 *puniz* to *punis*. The alterations made by the second hand (*Oj²*) are as follows: 140 ser*ment*; 156 et; 265 de*sert*; 282 en; 309 *vile*; 344 *donner*; 419 *failli*; 420 *Quantquilz*; 421 *ront* to *ronpt*; 428 *commence* /et/ *ne*; 435 *Et le bon* to *Et* /son/ *bon*. While the corrections are altogether less substantial than those in the *Debat des Deux Fortunés d'Amours* or the *Belle Dame sans Mercy*, that at line 282 also suggests that use may have been made of a manuscript akin to *Nf* or *Nj*.

Form of ballades IV, V and X

In certain texts, ballades IV, V and X have a longer envoy than that usually found, and ballade V is differently arranged. Details are given in the notes.

[1] See p. 157.

LE BREVIAIRE DES NOBLES *Oj*, 65r

I   *Noblesce*

Je, Noblesce, dame de bon vouloir,
Royne des preux, princesse des haulx faiz,
A tous qui ont volenté de valoir
4   Paix et salut par moy savoir vous faiz.
Que, pour oster les maulx et les torfaiz
Que Vilennie a entreprins de faire,
Chascun de vous s'il veult estre refaiz
8   *Ses heures die en cestui breviaire!*

Je me doy bien de plusieurs gens douloir
Qui ont du tout mes estaz contrefaiz,
Et en mettant vertu en nonchaloir,
12   Prennent mon nom et laissent mes bienffaiz,
Et ont leurs cuers avilez et deffaiz
Et enclinez a mesdire et meffaire;
Mais qui vouldra pardon de ses meffaiz,
16   *Ses heures die en cestui breviaire.*

Qui est des bons le successeur ou l'oir
Ne doit avoir la terre sans le faiz,
Et s'il n'est duit a bien faire et vouloir,
20   Les biens d'autruy sont en lui imparfaiz;
Ains a du tout los et honneur forfaiz
Quant il n'ensuit des nobles l'exemplaire,
Et s'aucun s'est en cest endroit meffaiz,
24   *Ses heures die en cestui breviaire.*

Pour entendre comme nobles sont faiz
Douze vertuz monstrent cy leur affaire;
Doncques qui veult estre noble parfaiz
28   *Ses heures die en cestui breviaire.*

No *heading Oa.* 2 de h. f. *Qd.* 5 Car *Ph* (Que *Ph²*); et les t.] et t. *Oa.* 6 a f. *Pc,* defaire *NjQd.*
7 parfaiz *NſNj.* 11 mectent *PcQl*; vertuz *Oj*; a non ch. *OaPcPhQdQl.* 13 nons *PcQl.* 14 mal
faire *Pc.* 15 pardon vouldra *NſNj.* 17 et *Ph.* 18 tenir *Oa.* 19 ou v. *Oa,* et valoir *Pc.*
23 scet *Qd.* 25 Prince entendez *Ph².* 27 nobles p. *NjOaPcQl.*

Foy

Dieu tout puissant, de qui Noblesce vient
Et dont descent toute perfeccïon,
A tout crëé, tout nourrit, tout soustient
32   Par sa haulte digne provisïon;
Mais, pour tenir la terre en unïon,
A ordonné chascun en son office:
Ly un seigneur, l'autre en subjectïon
36   *Pour Foy garder et pour vivre en justice.*

Et qui de Dieu le plus hault honneur tient
Par seigneurie ou dominacïon,
Plus est tenu et plus lui appartient
40   D'avoir en lui entiere affectïon,
Crainte et honneur, bonne devocïon
Et vergoigne de meffait et de vice,
Et faire tout en bonne entencïon
44   *Pour Foy garder et pour vivre en justice.*

Cil est nobles et pour tel se maintient,
Sans vanterie et sans decepcïon,
Qui envers Dieu obeïssant se tient
48   Et fait le droit de sa professïon.
Qui quiert Noblesce en autre oppinïon
Fait a Dieu tort et au sang prejudice,
Car Dieu forma noble condicïon
52   *Pour Foy garder et pour vivre en justice.*

Povre et riche meurt en corrupcïon,
Noble et commun doivent a Dieu service;
Mais les nobles ont exaltacïon
56   *Pour Foy garder et pour vivre en justice.*

Loyaulté

Pourquoy furent les nobles ordonnez
Et establiz seigneurs sur les menuz,
Et leur furent les haulx honneurs donnez

31 et s. *Qd.*   32 promission *PcQl.*   34 a son o. *Ph.*   35 Li uns *OaQd.*   38 ordonnacion *Ph* (d. *Ph²*).
39 Est plus *Ph.*   40 a lui *Oj*; parfaicte *Nf.*   41 b. d.] et b. d. *Oa.*   43 a b. e. *NjOaQd.*   45 Se il *Nf*;
noble *PhQd.*   48 possession *Oa.*   50 au sien *Ph* (au s. *Ph²*).   53 richu *Qd.*   58 sus *Pc*; meneurs *Nj.*
59 leurs f. *Qd*; leurs h. h. *Ph.*

60 Et hommages qui d'eulx sont attenuz?
    Ilz ne sont pas si treshault advenuz
    Pour rappiner et par leur force prendre;
    Mais sont de droit et par raison tenuz
64 *Servir leur roy et leurs subgez deffendre.*

    Et quant plus sont de honneur guerredonnez
    Et a plus grant dignité parvenuz,
    Doivent estre mieulx conditïonnez
68 Et tous leurs faiz en raison maintenuz,
    Leurs cuers fermes, leurs diz entretenuz,
    Ne faire tort a plus grant në a mendre,
    Car ilz doivent, sans varïer pour nulz,
72 *Servir leur roy et leurs subgez deffendre.*

    S'ilz varïent, s'ilz sont desordonnez
    Et leurs subgiez ne sont d'eulx soustenuz,
    Ou se leur roy est d'eulx abandonnez
76 Par lascheté qui les a detenuz,
    Je di qu'ilz sont plus villains devenuz
    Que un bon bouvier qui sa rente vient rendre
    Et qui paie pour ceulx qui sont venuz
80 *Servir leur roy et leurs subgez deffendre.*

    En Noblesce sont les droiz contenuz
    De Loyaulté, ou ceulx doivent entendre,
    Qui ces deux poins ont par cuer retenuz:
84 *Servir leur roy et leurs subgez deffendre.*

IV   *Honneur*   66v

    Hault Honneur est le tresor de Noblesce,
    Son espergne, sa privee richesce,
    Et ce que un cuer noble doit desirer:
88 Son seurconduit, sa guide et son adresce,
    Son reconfort, son plaisir, sa lÿesce,
    Et le mirouer ou il se doit mirer.

61 treshaulx *Ph.* 62 et pour *NfOaPhQd.* 65 Et tant *Oa*; sont (sent *Pc*) plus *PcPhQl.* 66 grans digni-
tez *Ph.* 69 L. faiz f. *Nf.* 71 Car ne d. point v. *Nf*; pour v. *Nj.* 73 cilz s. *Nf.* 75 Et *NfQd.* 77 vaillans
Ph. 78 un b. b.] ung bouvier *Oa.* 82 ou tous *PcQl*; actendre *Nf.* 83 ses d. *Nf.* 87 Et ce] Et en ce *Oa*;
noble cueur *Pc.* 88 Sour s. *Pc*, Son sens conduit *Nf*; sa garde *NfPcQl.* 90 ou on *Nf*, dont ilz (*sic*) *Qd.*

Rien ne pourroit un bon cuer empirer
92   S'il ayme Honneur, ne jamais n'ara honte,
Car c'est le bien qui les autres seurmonte.

Qui n'a Honneur, tost dechiet sa haultesce,
Bon los perit, renommee le lesse,
96   Et mespris fait son pouoir descirer.
Ou Honneur fault, pert son nom Gentilesce,
Car vergoigne, vilennie ou rudesce
Font cuer gentil fremir et souspirer.
100   On ne peut plus un bon cuer aÿrer
Qu'enfraindre Honneur qui l'omme a vertu dompte,
Car c'est le bien qui les autres seurmonte.

Ou Honneur est, tort et injure cesse;
104   C'est le chemin pour venir a proesce
Qui fait les bons a hault estat tirer
Et met en eulx atrempee lÿesce,
Courtois parler et loyale promesse,
108   Sans varïer, chanceller ne virer.
Trop mieulx vauldroit se souffrir martirer
Que avarice sus l'onneur d'omme monte,
Car c'est le bien qui les autres seurmonte.

112   Nobles hommes, tenez en plus grant compte,
Car c'est le bien qui les autres seurmonte.

V   *Droitture*   67ᵣ

Raison, equité, mesure,
Loy, Droitture
116   Font les puissances durer;
Et honneste nourreture,
Par nature,
Fait bon cuer amesurer
120   Et tout meffait forjurer,
Et jurer

91 son b. c. *NfNj*, ung franc c. *PcQl*. 94 d. de h. *Ph*, d. sa noblesce *Nf*. 95 Son los p. *NfNjPcQl*, Son bon los pert *Qd*. 96 povoit *Nj*; desirer *NfOaPh* (dessirer *Ph²*). 97 son non pert *PcQl*. 98 et *PcQdQl*. 99 Fait *Nf*. 100 peust *Pc*; ayer *Qd*. 101 homme *Qd*. 104 a v. *Pc*. 107 et loyaute p. *Qd*. 109 soy s. *NfNjOaPcPhQdQl*. 110 sur *NfNjOaPhQdQl*; honneur *OaPcQl*. 119 Font *Oa*. 120 *Omitted Ph (Added Ph²)*: forvoier *Oa*.

De garder en son endroit
A chascun son loyal droit.

124   Pour ce ne doit faire injure
Ne laidure,
N'en torfait s'aventurer,
Toute noble crëature
128   Dont la cure
Doit estre a droit mesurer.
Mieulx vault son cuer adurer
D'endurer
132   Que tollir, car Dieu rendroit
A chascun son loyal droit.

Noble homme se desnature
Et procure
136   A son sang deffigurer,
Qui s'arme en querelle obscure,
Faulse et sure,
Pour pratique procurer:
140   C'est le serment parjurer.
Forjurer
Justice, qui rent tout droit
A chascun son loyal droit!

144   Ne faisons pas murmurer,   67v
Conjurer;
Et n'ostons plus orendroit
A chascun son loyal droit.

VI   *Proesce*

148   Proesce fait aux nobles assavoir,
Qui ont le cuer de suyvre sa banniere,
Que nul ne peut par elle pris avoir
N'estre receu a sa grant court plenniere
152   S'il n'a en soy trop plus fait que maniere,

122 Et *NſNj*. 130 vaulx *Qd*; corps *PcQl*; adjurer *Oa*. 131 *Omitted Oa*. 140 *Omitted Oa*: serement *NſPh*. 144 par *Nj*; mururer *Pc*. 146 pas *NſOa*. 149 leur c. *Nj*; densuivir *Nſ*, de suivir *Nj*, de suir *OaPcQl*, de suivier *Qd*; la b. *Oa*. 150 peust *PcQl*. 152 lui *NſNjOaPcPhQdQl*.

399

Sens pour choisir bon parti justement
Et, a l'exploit, conduite et hardement,
Ferme propos et arresté courage,

156 Diligence, secret et peu langage;
Et qu'en l'estour rien fors Dieu ne ressoigne,
Mais choisisse, comme pour avantage,
Honneste mort plus que vivre en vergoigne.

160 Bon renon est son tresor, son avoir
Et la chose que Proesce a plus chiere,
Ne ja homme n'y fera bien devoir,
Qui en armes quiert praie la premiere,

164 Car Couvoitise est tousjours coustumiere
D'amer honneur assez escharcement
Et tout a coup par son aveuglement
Entrerompre l'ordre de bon ouvrage.

168 L'onneur lesse, qui entent au pillage
Et pour prouffit pert soy et sa besoigne,
Dont par aprés regrete a grief dommage
Honneste mort plus que vivre en vergoigne.

172 Elle ne veult nul servant recevoir,
Qui par long trait a travail ne l'acquiere;
Et se tu veulx les siens appercevoir,
Ilz n'ont souvent teste ne main entiere.

176 Doulce aux foulez est elle et aux fiers fiere,
Et aux simples ne fait empeschement.
Si di que cil la poursuit laschement
Et porte armes en meschant vasselage,

180 Qui s'espreuve sur povre labourage
Et des assaulx des ennemis s'esloigne;
Ains desirer devroit, s'il estoit sage,
Honneste mort plus que vivre en vergoigne.

68r

154 conduit et h. *NfNj*, conduire h. *PcQl*.   155 et a. c.] a. c. *Qd*, a. jugement *Oa*.   157 Et qui en le.
f. d. ne r. *Oa*: Si quen *Ph*.   158 par a. *Qd*.   160 t. et a. *Qd*.   162 ne f. *Ph*; bon *NfNj*.   164 C. est
t.] t. est c. *Ph*.   165 Davoir *PcQl*, Dame *Nf*.   166 Et tant *Oa*; pert *Ph* (par *Ph²*).   167 Entrerompt
tout (lordre *Ql*) dun chacun bon courage *PcQl*: Dentre rompre *Qd*; courage *Oa*.   168 Honneur *Ql*.
169 *Omitted Qd*.   170 au g. d. *Ph*.   172 sergent *Ql*.   173 Que *Qd*; par ung t. *Oa*, par l. temps *PcQdQl*;
la quiere *Pc*.   176 D. aux f. et aux f. f. *Oa*, D. aux f. elle est aux f. f. *Ph*, D. aux souefs elle est et
aux f. f. *PcQl*.   178 sil *Ph*.   179 Et povre en armes et cest hault v. *Ql*: Qui p. *Ph*; petit v. *Pc*.
180 Qui s'e.] Et qui se. *Ph*, Qui se prendra *PcQl*; sus *Pc*.   182 A. d. devroient silz estoient s. *Oa*:
desiroir *PcQl*.

184 D'oultrage meurt cil qui vit par oultrage;
Raison le veult et Dieu le nous tesmoigne.
Donq doit amer homme de hault lignage
Honneste mort plus que vivre en vergoigne.

VII   *Amour*

188 Digne chose est Bonne Amour sans amer,
Plaisant confort et vie delettable,
Car Bonne Amour ne se peut entamer
En noble sang d'omme ferme et estable.

192 C'est largesce de hault cuer honnourable,
Qui de soy fait a ce qu'il ayme part;
C'est la bonté qui soy mesmes espart
Et qui acquiert autry cuer pour le sien.

196 Hayne porte le feu dont elle s'art;
Qui n'a Amour et amis, il n'a rien.

Si la doit bien tout noble reclamer
Et querre amis par service amïable,
200 Son roy, sa terre et ses amis amer   68v
Et au besoing leur estre secourable;
Mais quant le cuer n'est au semblant semblable,
C'est fiction plaine de mauvais art,
204 Qui descueuvre sa fraude tost ou tart
Et dont ne vient a soy n'a autry bien.
Gentilz hommes, aiez y bien regart;
Qui n'a Amour et amis, il n'a rien.

208 Or se puet donq cellui chetif clamer,
Et son estat est dolent et dampnable,
Qui grieve et nuit et se fait diffamer
Et n'aime rien fors d'amour prouffitable.
212 Telz gens suyvent au gaing et a la table,

---

186 d. avoir *Nf*; grant l. *Nf*, hault parage *PcQl*.   188 bon a. *NjOa*.   190 bon a. *Nj*; peust e. *Pc*.
192 Car *Qd*.   193 ce quelle a. *NfNj*.   194 soy m.] de soy m. *Oa*.   195 lautry *NfNjPcQdQl*.
198 Sil *Nf*, Cil *Oa*.   199 pour *Nf*.   200-1 *Omitted Oa*.   201 aux besoing *Nf*.   203 f. plain *Ph*.
204 sa faulte *PcQl*.   205 na (ne *Ph*) autre *NfNjOaPcPhQdQl*.   206 a. y mieulx r. *Pc*, a. ly (?)
bien esgart *Nf*.   207 a. ne a. *Ql*.   208 peust bien *PcQl*; cil pour ch. *NfNj*.   209 Et son honneur
est douleur et d. *Ql*.   210 nuit et grieve *NfNjOaPcPhQdQl*; ce f. *Ph*.   211 samour *Ph*.
212 sieuvent *Pc*.

Mais en fortune ilz tournent a l'esquart.
Par tromperie est trompé le renart:
Amour retourne a cil qui ayme bien.
216 Homme haÿ doit vivre en grant esgart;
Qui n'a Amour et amis, il n'a rien.

C'est amittié qui trop tost se depart,
Quant elle fault des qu'on ne dit plus: 'Tien'.
220 Prïez donq Dieu que de ce mal vous gart;
Qui n'a Amour et amis, il n'a rien.

VIII   *Courtoisie*
Qui veult Noblesce esprouver,
Ou nul vil homme n'attaint,
224 Il la doit querre et trouver
La ou Courtoisie maint,
Qui tous ses envïeux vaint
Par sa doulceur gracïeuse,
228 Et n'est ennuyeuse,   69r
Fiere n'orgueilleuse,
Mais humble et joyeuse,
Et plaisant toudis
232 *En faiz et en dis.*

Par les faiz seult on prouver
Ce qui est ou cuer empraint;
L'euvre fait tel reprouver
236 Vilain qui gentil se faint,
Car la noblesce s'estaint
Des que la vie est honteuse,
Et lengue oultrageuse,
240 Pensee envïeuse
Et main perilleuse
Font gens estourdis
En faiz et en dis.

213 Et *NfNjOaPcPhQdQl.* 215 Amy *PcQl*; a cilz qui *Oa*, a ce quil *PcPhQl.* 216 d. estre *Pc.*
220 Prions...nous g. *PcQl*: qui *Oa.* 222 Qui v. noble e. *Qd.* 224 d. qu.] d. acquerre *Oa.* 226 ces
e. *Oa*, ses ennemis *NfNj.* 228 El *Qd*; enuieuse *NfNjOaPc.* 233 ses *Ql*; puet *OaPh*[2], peust *PcQl.*
234 en c. *PcQl*, au c. *Qd*, es cuers *Oa.* 237 sa *Qd.* 240 Et p. e. *Oa*: ennuyeuse *PcQl.*

244 Les courtois font approuver
Leur bien par mainte et par maint;
Et en eulx ne peut couver
Mauvaistié qui n'y remaint.

248 Ilz n'ont jamais semblant faint
Ne maniere desdaigneuse,
Mais chiere amoureuse,
De tout bien soigneuse,

252 A nul dangereuse,
Et sans escondis
En faiz et en dis.

Teste trop fumeuse,
256 Rigour despiteuse,
Bouche rïoteuse
Font les contredis
En faiz et en dis.

69v

IX   *Diligence*

260 Puis que vertu se parfait d'avoir paine,
L'ame en vault mieulx et la vie est plus saine;
L'omme en devient saige, seur et expert.
Et Paresce est laide, nice et vilaine,

264 Despourveue, non sachant, incertaine,
Qui los, ne pris, ne grace ne desert.
On puet jugier que Noblesce se pert
En lasche cuer qui en riens ne traveille,

268 Car pour neant vit qui n'ensuit en appert
Diligence qui les vertuz esveille.

Diligence est a Noblesce prochaine,
Car c'est celle qui conduit et demaine
272 Tous haultains faiz dont Gentilesce appert.
C'est fol cuider et vanterie vaine
Pour digne sang ou lignee haultaine

244 aprouvoir *Ql.*   246 Et en] Et en en *Nj*, En *Ph*; peust *Pc*; couvier *Ql.*   247 y r. *PcQl.*   249 parolle
NfNj.   251 tous biens *NfNjOaPcPhQl.*   252 De nul d. *Oa*, A nul bien d. *Qd.*   253 Et faiz e. *Oa.*
254 ne en *Qd.*   256-7 *Inverted PcQl.*   258 Sont *PcQl.*   261 Lame en v. m. la vie en est p. s.
Oa: sa v. *Ql.*   263 est l. n.] est n. l. *NfNjOaQd*, est rude l. *Ph.*   264 Desprouveue *Qd.*   266 peust *Pc.*
267 qui en r.] qui r. *Oa.*   268 ne suit *PcQdQl*; en a.] a. *Ph.*   274 en *Nf.*

403

De soy tenir pour noble, s'il n'y pert.
276 Cil qui du tout a Oyseuse s'assert,
Son nom dechiet et sa vertu sommeille;
Et meurt tout vif, s'a amer ne s'ahert
Diligence qui les vertuz esveille.

280 Que vault homme qui muse et se pourmaine,
Et veult avoir mol lit et pance plaine
Et demourer en repos a couvert;
Et passe temps sepmaine aprés sepmaine
284 Et ne lui chault en quel point tout se maine –   70r
Qui soit perdu ne qui soit recouvert –
Et veult que on soit devant lui descouvert
Et que on die qu'il est noble a merveille?
288 Mais qui noble est, il aprent de quoy sert
Diligence qui les vertuz esveille.

Le raisin meur se queult parmy le vert,
Et le meschief l'omme avise et conseille;
292 Et au travail, fait du rude un appert
Diligence qui les vertuz esveille.

x   *Necteté*

Cuer qui a haultesce tire
Et ou Noblesce est assise,
296 Doit toute ordure despire,
Laidure et goulïardise,
Car sa noblesce desprise,
Quant nettement ne la garde,
300 *Cellui ou tous prennent garde.*

Il ne doit faire ne dire
Chose dont on le mesprise,
Ne qui l'autry bien empire
304 Ne dont son los amenuyse.

275 s'il n'y p.] sil ny appert *Oa.*   277 deschief (*sic*) *Qd.*   278 tous vifs *Oa*; ne sa ert *Oa.*   280 et se p.] et p. *Nj.*   281 Qui *Oa*; mot lit *Nj.*   282 a r. *OaPh*, au r. *PcQdQl.*   283 passer *NfNjPh.*   284 t. se m.] se m. *Nj*, se demaine *Nf.*   285 ou *PcQl.*   286 devers *Nj*, davant *Qd.*   288 est noble *NfNj OaPcPhQdQl.*   291 a. et c.] a. c. *Nf.*   292 dun r. *NfNjOaPcPhQdQl.*   298 Et *Oa.*   299 autrement *Nf*; se g. *NfNj.*   *Refrains* C. ou t. se p. g. *Oa.*   302 desprise *OaPh.*   304 Ne qui *NfNj.*

Pense donq bien et avise,
Et sur soy mesmes regarde,
Cellui ou tous prennent garde.

308   Lait parler et trop mesdire
Sont une vile devise
Sur homme ou chascun se mire
Et ou tout le monde vise.

                                                      70v

312   Honnesteté est requise
Pour tenir en sauvegarde
Cellui ou tous prennent garde.

    Par nette et plaisant cointise,
316   D'ordure se contregarde
Cellui ou tous prennent garde.

XI   *Largesce*

    Tant est Largesce en tous cas advenant,
Qui a soy plaist et a autry prouffite,
320   Que c'est rente d'onneur bien revenant
Dont l'un acquiert gaing et l'autre merite:
Au preneur vault et au donneur delitte;
Chascun des deux endroit soy en amende.
324   Bien n'est perdu que Largesce despende,
Car tous ses biens se despendent par sens.
Le prodigue gaste sans nul pourpens:
Et au large le bien sourt et habonde,
328   Dont il rent soy et les autres contens;
C'est l'enseigne des vertuz en ce monde.

    Don receü oblige le prenant,
Et le donneur sa grant bonté acquite;
332   Le donné vault plus que le remenant
Car bien mucé porte joye petite.
Et pourtant est Avarice mauditte,

305 Si (Sil *NfNjPh*) pense b. *NfNjOaPcPhQdQl.*   306 Se *Oa*; sus *PcQl.*   308 Par nectete et plaisant cointise (*sic*) *Oa*: ou *PcQl.*   310 Sus *OaPc. Envoy omitted OaPh.*   315 Par nectete et p. c. *NfQd*, Par (Pour *Ql*) nectete et c. *PcQl.*   319 Que a *NfPcQl*; et a a.] et a. *Qd.*   320 Car *Ph.* 321 g. et l'a. m.] g. la. m. *Ql*, gaaing la. m. *Pc.*   322 Au p. et au d. d. *Nf*: prenner (premier) *Qd*; donnant *OaQl.*   323 deulz deux *NfNj.*   324 Nest rien *Nf*, Rien nest *NjOaPcPhQdQl.*   326 prodigoys *PcQl.*   327 sien *Ph.*   329 en cest m. *Oa*, de cest (ce *Ql*) m. *PcQl.*   330 D. r.] D. qui est r. *Nf*, D. quest r. *Nj.*   331 Et fait le droit de sa profection *Pc*: a g. b. *Oa.*   332 v. mieulx *Qd.*

Qui le poing clot que nul ne s'i attende,
336   Et lui avient que un autre gaste ou vende
Ce qu'elle acquiert et garde a griefz tourmens.
Et s'il lui sourt peril, guerre ou contens,   711
A nul ne chault qui la greve ou confonde,
340   Mais Largesce treuve amis en tous temps;
C'est l'enseigne des vertuz en ce monde.

Pour ce ne doit estre eschars ne tenant
Un franc cuer d'omme en qui Noblesce habite,
344   Mais a donner plus joyeulx qu'en prenant,
Car Largesce secourt l'omme et respite.
Escharceté est a noble interditte;
Tout gentil cuer tient au large sa bende.
348   Bienfait est tel que droit veult qu'il se rende
Dont il parti, et retourne dedens;
Jamais bienfait ne se pert en nul sens
Mais quelque foiz sur son maistre redonde.
352   Largesce tient l'estendart sus les rens;
C'est l'enseigne des vertuz en ce monde.

Riche qui laisse honneur pour les despens,
Tout bien lui faille et son avoir lui fonde.
356   A Largesce voit on le cuer des gens;
C'est l'enseigne des vertuz en ce monde.

XII   *Sobresse*

Quant bon desir, qui veult hault avenir,
Meut la pensee a monter en valeur,
360   L'omme se doit lors sobrement tenir
Et eschiver le vin et sa chaleur,
Qui fait changer bon advis en foleur,
Force grever et a nature tort,
364   Troubler la paix et mouvoir le descort

337 g. a grief t. *Pc.*   338 guerre peril *Oa.*   339 nen (ne *Oa*) ch. qui le g. *OaPcQl.*   341 de cest (ce *Ql*) m. *PcQl.*   343 ouquel n. *Oa*, qui en n. *Ql*, qui a n. *Pc.*   344 au d. *PcQl.*   346 *Omitted Oa.*   347 a l. *PcQl.*   348 dieu v. *NfNj*, il v. *Oa*; que se r. *Qd.*   349 et] puis *Nf.*   350 J. nul bien *Oa.* 352 sur *NfNjOaPhQdQl.*   353 en cest m. *Oa*, de ce m. *PcQl.*   *Envoy omitted Oa.*   342 *Repeated at head of envoy Ph.*   355 Tous biens lui faillent et son a. lui f. *Nf.*   357 de ce m. *PcQl*, en m. *Ph.* Sobriete *NfNjPh²* (S. *Ph*).   359 Mait *Pc*, Met *Ql*; a (en *Ql*) m. et v. *PcQl*, a monte en v. *Nf.* 360 s. t.] s. maintenir *Oa.*   361 la ch. *Qd.*   362 font *Ph.*

Et delaisser toute chose imparfaitte;   71v
Mais qui bien a a soy Sobresse actraitte,
Elle est propice et de peu assouvie,
368 *Ayde de sens et de santé la gaitte,*
Garde de corps et concierge de vie.

De faire excés ne puet il bien venir,
Ne corps ne los n'en puet estre meilleur;
372 Ains en pert on maniere et contenir,
Voix, alaine, legiereté, couleur.
Et tousjours a glouton quelque douleur
Et est pesant, replet et gras et ort;
376 Sa vie abrege et approuche sa mort.
Nul n'en a dueil; homme ne le regraitte
Se vers Sobresse il ne fait sa retraitte,
Car c'est celle par qui nul ne devie:
380 *Ayde de sens et de santé la gaitte,*
Garde de corps et concierge de vie.

Et qui ne scet mesure retenir
Sur sa bouche qui est l'uissier du cuer,
384 Comme peut il bien savoir parvenir
A conduire chose de pesanteur?
Gloutonnie laisse toute haulteur
Et seulement a soy paistre s'amort,
388 Et ventre saoul n'est ayse s'il ne dort,
Car d'autre bien ne songe, pense ou traitte;
Mais Sobresse, en souffisance reffaitte,
Est preste a tout quant vertu lui convie,
392 *Ayde de sens et de santé la gaitte,*
Garde de corps et concierge de vie.

Sobresse duit les faucons et affaitte   72r
A hault voler; si est ditte et plevie:

365 de laissir *Qd.* 366 actraire *Qd.* 370 nen p. nul b. *Oa*; peust *Pc.* 371 peust *Pc.* 373 l. c.] legierte et c. *Nj*, et la greslecte c. *Oa.* 375 Et est p.] Et sest p. *Nf*, Et p. *Qd*; poussif r. *PcQl.* 376 apresse *PhQd.* 377 Nul en a *Qd*; ame *PcQl.* 378 nul ne f. *Oa*; sa rectaite *Qd.* 382 ne soit *PcQl.* 383 Sus *PcQl*; la b. *NfNjQd*; de c. *Qd.* 384 peust *Pc*; b. s. p.] b. p. *Oa.* 389 Car da. chose ne soigne p. ou t. *Nf*: ne soigne *Nj.* 390 en souffisant retraite *PcQl.* 391 quanque v. c. *NfPcQl*; la c. *Oa.* 394 d.] dompte *Nf*; f. et a.] f. a. *Ql.* 395 voloir *PcQl*; est si *Oa*; droicte et pleine *Nf*, a ce p. *Ph*, duite et plaine *Oa.*

396   *Ayde de sens et de santé la gaitte,*
     Garde de corps et concierge de vie.

XIII   *Perseverance*

     O excellent, haulte vertu divine,
     Qui tout parfait, acomplit et termine,
400   Royne puissant, Dame Perseverance,
     Cil qui retient ta loyalle dottrine,
     Sans forvoyer le droit sentier chemine
     De los, de pris, de paix, de souffisance,
404   Car tu vains tout par ta ferme constance
     Qui de souffrir n'est foulee ne lasse,
     Mal eur confont et sus Fortune passe
     Et en tous lieux la vittoire te donne,
408   Dont tu acquiers par raison la couronne
     Quant les vertuz toutes la main te tendent.
     Par ton conduit a hault louyer s'estendent,
     Si te doivent pour patron advouer
412   *Puis que la fin fait les euvres louer.*

     Tu es celle qui les cuers examine
     Et, comme l'or ou croisel, les affine
     En loyaulté par ton humble souffrance;
416   Et qui a toy s'asseure et determine,
     Tu le ressours quant il fault et decline
     Et lui donnes confort et soustenance.
     Mais cuer failli, lascheté, varïance,
420   Quantqu'ilz ont fait gastent en peu d'espace:
     Ennuy les ronpt; faulte de foy les lasse;
     Vertu leur fault; honneur les abandonne.   72v
     Ilz sont punis: et Dieu te guerredonne,
424   Car les bons ont du bien, quoy qu'ilz attendent.
     Et tous nobles qui a haultesce entendent,
     Se ilz sont sages, se vont a toy vouer
     Puis que la fin fait les euvres louer.

398 O e.] E. *Oa.*   399 parfais acomplis *Nf.*   405 f.] saoulee *Oa*, recreant *PcQl.*   406 confort *Oa*, confons *Ph*; sur *NfNjOaPcPhQdQl.*   407 en tout lieu sa v. *Ql.*   408 Car *NfNj.*   409 les mains *NfNjPcQl.*   410 descendent *PcQl.*   411 donnent *Qd*; par raison a. *Nf.*   414 en c. *Pc.*   415 Et *PcQl.*   417 ou d. *NfNjOaPcPhQdQl.*   420 Quant ilz *Qd*; gaste *Oa*; un *Ph* (en *Ph²*).   421 Euvre *Oa.*   423 ainsi d. les g. *Ph²* (et d. te g. *Ph*); leur g. *PcQl.*   426 acoy *Qd*; louer *Oa.*   427 laffin *Qd.*

408

428   Il ne fait rien, qui commence et ne fine;
       Et des que aucun a varïer s'encline,
       Son bien passé demeure en oublïance.
       Et quant l'euvre est haulte, louable et digne,
432   S'on l'entreprent sans ce qu'on l'enterine,
       C'est reprouche de lasche oultrecuidance.
       La pert l'omme son nom et sa fïance,
       Et le bon los tantost se brise et casse;
436   Mais qui a droit ses affaires compasse,
       Oultre poursuit cë a quoy il s'ordonne
       Et jusque au bout en loyaulté foisonne,
       Dont ses bienffaiz au parfournir s'amendent.
440   Ceulx qui tantost a Fortune se rendent
       Veult Noblesce du tout desadvouer,
       Puis que la fin fait les euvres louer.

       Ceulx sont nobles qui corps et biens despendent
444   En loyaulté, et leur seigneur deffendent
       Sans le droit neu de leur foy desnouer,
       Puis que la fin fait les euvres louer.

       Vostre mestier recordez,
448   *Nobles hommes, en ce livre.*

       Quant vous serez descordez,
       Vostre mestier recordez.

       Voz faiz aux moz accordez.
452   Se noblement voulez vivre,
       Vostre mestier recordez,
       Nobles hommes, en ce livre.

428 ne c. et f. *Ph* (c. et ne f. *Ph²*).   431 loyalle et d. *NſPcQl.*   432 S'on l'e.] Et on le. *Qd*, Et on lenprent *PcQl.*   433 reprouch (*sic*) *Qd.*   434 La p. homme *PcPhQl*, La perit loms *NſNj.*   435 Et son *Oj²Ph* (Et le *Oj*).   436 ses affaire *Qd.*   437 cë] cen *Nj.*   438 jusques au b. *Oa.*   439 les *NſNjPcQl*; au p.] au poursuir *Oa.*   441 fortune *Oj*; du tout noblesse *Oa*; d.] adesnouer *Pc.*   442 laffin *Qd.* 444 Et *Ph*; leurs seigneurs *Oa.*   445 veu...desvouer *Ph.*   446 laffin *Qd.   Rondeau lacking NſQl.* Rondel *NjPh.*   448 cest l. *Oa.*   451 au (ou *Ph*) nom a. *NjOaPcPhQd.*   ...breviaire des nobles *NſNj.*

13

'Le Lay de Paix'

Forty-eight Manuscripts: *Fa Fb Fc Fd Fe Ff Fg   Na Nb Ne Nf Nh Nj Nk Nl Np Nq Oa Ob Oc Od Oe Of Oj Ol Om Oq   Pa Pb Pc Pd Pe Pf Ph Pj Pk Pl Pn Po Pp   Qd Qh Qk Qn Qo Qp Qq Qr.*

All the manuscripts have been examined except *Qn*, which has not been traced, and *Qp*, which has been damaged by fire.

The poem was included in all early collected editions, in one separate edition,[1] and in the Du Chesne edition. The 1489 collected edition, the separate edition, and the Du Chesne edition have been examined.

The title, *Lay de Paix*, is that found in most of the manuscripts. The poem is attributed to Alain Chartier in ten manuscripts and also in the edition of 1489; in the other manuscripts it is anonymous. *Fe Nq Pe* and *Qo* state that the *Lay de Paix* was given or sent to the Duke of Burgundy.[2]

The poem has been edited from seven manuscripts: *Nf Nj Oa Oj Pc Ph* and *Qd*. The texts which they contain can be divided into two groups: *Nf Nj, Oa Ph; Pc, Oj Qd*. The division is by no means absolute, however, and there is evidence of contamination.

A complete text of the poem is contained in *Nj*, which includes many readings peculiar to itself and to *Nf* (lines 2, 16, 71, 110, 112, 154–7, 176 etc.); at lines 16, 112 and 200, both texts give poor rhymes. In *Nj* the rhyme is also poor at lines 227, 281 and 283, while at lines 5, 173, 200 and 258 the text is irregular. Individual readings are found in *Nj* at lines 22, 33, 54, 62, 183 and 199; several of them result from scribal carelessness. *Nf* lacks line 15 and is irregular at lines 11, 163, 173, 188 and 284. Readings peculiar to *Nf* occur at lines 16, 38, 62, 194, 198–9, 202, 233 and 263.

Nf and *Nj* often agree with *Oa* and *Ph*, for example at lines 16, 100, 147, 173 and 279. Lines 73, 84, 94, 106, 126, 137 etc. are also important in this connection, although there the agreement is only partial. In *Oa* lines 126 and 135 are omitted and lines 128–32 are in an order different from that of the other texts. *Oa* is irregular at lines 6, 151, 173, 193, 194, 213 and 284, and rhymes poorly at lines 16, 31, 193 and 280; it contains readings peculiar to itself at lines 10, 22, 69, 132, 150, 154 etc. Individual readings are more frequent in *Ph* (lines 25, 31, 55, 84, 122, 127 etc.). *Ph* lacks lines 11, 87, 101, 116 and 168, and contains several irregular lines (lines 32, 151, 173, 188, 254, 258, 273 and 279) and poor rhymes (lines 16, 109, 193 and 227).

In *Pc* lines 82 and 110 are omitted and lines 273–5 are in an order not found in the other texts; lines 10, 127, 151, 173, 254, 258 and 284 are irregular and the text contains poor rhymes at lines 16 and 193.

---

[1] GKW 6566. The volume was reprinted in 1826 by J. Didot aîné, in an edition limited to sixteen copies.

[2] See p. 11.

Oj and *Qd* contain readings peculiar to themselves at lines 100, 173, 254 and 275; they further agree at lines 94, 193 and 280. At other lines (lines 40, 106, 126, 137, 147, 151, 167 etc.) one or both texts is in agreement with *Pc*, but the degree of relationship is not clear. Both *Oj* and *Qd* are complete and contain few individual readings. *Oj* is irregular at lines 151 and 211, and contains readings peculiar to itself at lines 13, 40, 109, 148, 153, 283 and 284. Most of the readings found only in *Qd* (lines 7, 19, 36, 44, 73, 142, 168, 188 and 212) seem to be the result of scribal carelessness; *Qd* is irregular at lines 46, 84 and 151, and rhymes poorly at lines 16 and 52–3.

The texts of the *Lay de Paix* differ most noticeably at lines 123–7 and 153–9; nevertheless, the different versions available for these passages all make good sense. The choice of a base text is made easier by reason of the poem's complicated metres and rhyme-schemes. It is clear that, of the seven texts, *Oj* and *Qd* are most accurate and least individual in these respects and that *Oj* is a little better than *Qd*. *Oj* has been used as base text in this edition. Any corrections necessary have been made with the help of *Qd* or *Nj*.

Corrections in *Oj*

The corrections are similar to those in the *Debat des Deux Fortunés d'Amours* and the *Breviaire des Nobles*, and have been treated in the same way as in those editions. In line 199 *liz* has been changed to *lis*; in line 225 where the scribe wrote *fiers cuers*, *cuers* has been scored out. Three corrections are in the hand of *Oj*[2]: 188 *serment*; 273 *a.* /et/ *f.*; 275 *vicieux*.

LE LAY DE PAIX

I   Paix eureuse, fille du Dieu des dieux,   *Oj, 60r*

Engendreë ou trosne glorïeux,

Et transmise par le conseil des cieulx

4   Pour maintenir la terre en unité,

Exilliee de France et d'autres lieux

Par oultrages et descors furïeux;

A vous, Princes nez du lis precïeux,

8   Tresexcellens en toute dignité,

Jadis loez, haulx et vittorïeux,

Et a present de vostre eur enuieux,

Et contre vous mesmes injurïeux,

12   En guerroiant vostre felicité

Par faulx debaz et faiz malicïeux

Qui tant durent que trop sont ennuieux;

L. de p. aux seigneurs de france *Pc, No heading OaOj.* 2 E.] Et e. *NfNj*; en t. *Pc.* 5 Essillie *Nj*; de... d'a.] de... et a. *Pc.* 6 oultrage *Oa.* 7 A nous (Avons) *Qd.* 10 de v. eur] de v. cuer *Oa*, de v. *Pc.* 11 *Omitted Ph*: Et c.] Et encontre *Nf.* 13 Par f. discors *NfNjOaPcPhQd.* 14 trop...tant *Pc*; qui *Pc.*

Pour radrecer voz courages en mieulx
16 Transmet ce lay d'amour et d'amité.

II Pensez de qui vous venistes
Et yssistes,
Et dont voz armes prenistes,
20 Et tenistes
Honneur, terre, nom et gloire.

Et de ceulx par qui nasquistes
Et vesquistes,
24 Dont les biens vous vindrent quittes
Que n'acquistes,
Aiez aucune memoire.

Et par voz guerres despites,
28 Leurs merites
Ne deffaittes ou desdittes,   60v
Qui escriptes
Sont et durent jusqu'a ore.

32 S'autrement faittes ou dittes,
Voz conduittes
Seront en honneur petites,
Et maudittes
36 En cronique et en hystoire.

III S'entre vous a des torfaiz,
Des debaz et des meffaiz,
Contrefaiz
40 Par volenté et par fait
Qui deffait
Ce qu'amour y deüst faire,

En doivent estre deffaiz
44 Ceulx qui ne se sont meffaiz

15 *Omitted Nf.* 16 Transmetz *Nf*; lay de paix *NfNj*; et dunite *NfNjOaPcPhQd.* 19 vous *Qd.*
22 diceulx *Oa*; nacquistes *Nj.* 25 Et *Ph.* 30–1 *One line Ph.* 31 jusques ore *Ph*; ores *Oa.* 32 f.] ne
f. *Ph.* 33 condites *Nj.* 36 En croniques et h. *Pc*: in h. *Qd.* 38 De…de *Nf.* 40 ou *PcQd*;
de f. *Oj.* 44 sen s. *Qd.*

412

Par voz faiz,
Et qui de tout ce meffait
N'ont forfait,
48 Et si en ont tel affaire.

Visez que par voz forfaiz
Voz ennemis sont refaiz
Et si faiz
52 Que maint exploit et torfait
En ont fait
Pour la fleur de lis deffaire.

Si vous seroit trop grief faiz
56 Que vous, qui en fustes faiz
Si parfaiz   61r
Et en avez le bienfait
Au parfait,
60 Lui souffrissez tant meffaire.

IV   Discorde hayneuse
Fait vie attayneuse
Et souspeçonneuse,
64 Tousjours angoisseuse,
Melencolieuse,
Plaine de douleur et d'ire;

A l'ame greveuse,
68 Au corps perilleuse,
Au cuer chagrineuse,
A l'onneur doubteuse,
Aux biens dangereuse,
72 Et au courage martire;

De bien ennuyeuse,
De mal desireuse,
De soing planteureuse,
76 D'ayse souffreteuse,
D'autry besoigneuse,
A qui rien ne peut suffire;

46 Et de qui ce m. *Qd.*   52 mains esplois et tort fait *NjOj*, mains exploiz et torfaiz *Qd.*   53 faitz
Qd.   54 lir *Nj.*   55 Ce *Ph.*   62 Et v. *Nf,* Est v. *Nj.*   67–8 *Inverted Ph.*   69 corps (*sic*) *Oa.*
71 dommageuse *NfNj.*   73 enuieuse (envieuse) *NjOaPh*; ennueuse *Qd.*   78 peust *Pc.*

413

Pensee soigneuse,
80 Paine merveilleuse,
Despense oultrageuse,
Charge coustageuse
Et si poy eureuse
84 Que soy et autry empire.

V   Dieux, quelz maulx et quelz dommages,   61v
Quelz meschiefs et quelz oultrages,
Quelz ouvrages,
88 Quelz pillages
Et forsaiges,
Et quans petis avantages
Sont venuz par voz debas!

92 Quantes dames en veufvages,
Orphenins sans heritages
Ne mesnages;
Labourages
96 Et villages,
Bourgs, villes, chasteaulx, passages,
Ars, destruis, et mis au bas!

Les vaillans hommes et sages,
100 Mors, prisonniers ou hostages
En servages;
Pastissages
Et truages,
104 Tailles pour paier les gages
Ou se font les grans cabas;

Faultes de foys et d'ommages,
Meschans mis en haulx estages,
108 Cuers volages,
Foulx messages,
Faulx langages:
Si pensez en voz courages
112 Que trop durent telz esbas.

82 *Omitted Pc.* 84 Et qui soy et autre e. *Ph*: autre e. *Qd*, autre en e. *NʃNjOa.* 85 Dieu *Nʃ.* 87 *Omitted Ph.* 90 quant *PhQd.* 94 Et *NʃNjOaPc.* 100 en *NʃNjOaPcPh.* 101 *Omitted Ph.* 106 Faulte *Nʃ NjOaQd*; foy *NʃNjPh.* 109 Faulz *NʃNjOaPcPhQd*; mesnaiges *Ph.* 110 *Omitted Pc:* Folz *NʃNj.* 112 debas *NʃNj.*

VI   Quant en France estoie,
Je l'entretenoie
Seure par la voye,
116   Par les villes coye,
Si que nulz n'y meffaisoient.
Toutes gens aloient
Quel part qu'ilz vouloient,
120   Et ne se mesloient
Ne ja ne parloient
Fors de lÿesse et de joye.

De gens la peuploie,
124   La foy augmentoie,
Justice y gardoye,
Labourer faisoie;
Et tous en seurté vivoient.
128   Les marchans gaignoient,
Nobles voiageoient,
Clercs estudïoient,
Les prestres chantoient;
132   Et chascun planté mouvoie.

Riche la tenoie,
Les bons soustenoie,
Honneur maintenoie,
136   Gens y admenoie.
Tous estrangiers y venoient,
Les princes donnoient,
Les grans despendoient,
140   Povres y partoient,
Tous en amendoient;   62v
C'estoit d'onneur la montjoye.

Las! Trop fort m'ennoie
144   Que bannie en soie,
Et qu'el se desvoie
Du tout et forvoie;

116 *Omitted Ph.*   122 ou de j. *Ph.*   126 *Omitted Oa,* Science y mectoye *NfNjPh.*   127 tout *Ph;* v.]
y v. *Pc.*   128 *between* 131 *and* 132 *Oa.*   132 ch. avoit *Oa;* monnoye *OaOj.*   135 *Omitted Oa.*
137 estranges *NfOaPhQd.*   139 Les gens *Ph.*   142 le m. *Qd.*

Si que les estrangiers voient
148 Ceulx qui en avoient
L'onneur, qu'ilz devoient
Garder s'ilz savoient,
Qui la desavoient,
152 Se Dieu des cieulx n'y pourvoie.

VII   Don vient cest aveuglement
Qui si maleureusement
Et tant douloureusement,
156 Par fautte d'entendement,
D'advis et de sentement,
Maintient cest esloignement
Si longuement?

160 Entendez l'enseignement
Du Crëateur qui ne ment,
Qui pardonna largement
Et vous fait commandement,
164 Par loy et par testament,
De vivre paisiblement.
Helaz! Comment

Chiet en voz jours si griefment,
168 Et par voz faiz seulement,
Vostre maison mesmement,   63r
Qui estoit le parement
D'onneur soubz le firmament
172 Et de foy le fondement?
Son detriment

Est a vostre dampnement
Et un honteux vengement;
176 Et se bon advisement
Et piteux consentement
N'y mettent amendement,

147 estranges *NfNjOaPhQd*. 148 Que ceux qui a. *Pc*: envoient *Oj*. 150 G. la souloient *Oa*: s'ilz] ilz *Ph*. 151 Qui du tout la (le *Qd*) d. (desvoyent *Qd*) *OaOjPcPhQd*. 154 Qui si doulereusement *NfNj*: Que *Qa*. 155 *Omitted NfNj*: si *OaPh*. 156a De sage gouvernement *NfNj*. 163 c.] le c. *Nf*. 167 cueurs *PcQd*. 168 *Omitted Ph*: par voiz fait *Qd*. 172 Et de la foy fondement *Pc*. 173 destruisement *Pc*, destruiement *NfNjOaPh*. 176 Se tost bon a. *NfNj*, Et si bien a. *Ph*.

416

Vous en soufferrez tourment
180   Au jugement.

VIII   Quel plaisir et quel lÿesse,
Quel honnourable richesce
Ou quel renom de proesse
184   Vous puet il d'ailleurs venir,
En souffrant mal avenir
A ce dont vostre haultesse
Et tout vostre bien vous vient?

188   Est il serment ne promesse,
Fait par ire ou par tristesse,
Qui puisse rompre la tresse
Ou droit de sang retenir
192   Vous fist et entretenir
Par la naturele lesse
Dont le lÿen vous retient?

Pitié et Raison confesse
196   Qu'il n'est dangier në aspresse,
Peril de mort ne destresse   63v
Que ne doiez soustenir
Pour le beau lis maintenir,
200   Dont l'onneur et la noblesse
A garder vous appartient.

Et se par vostre paresce,
Fautte d'advis ou simplesce,
204   Chascun verser la delesse,
Que cuidez vous devenir
Ne quele seurté tenir?
Car qui soy mesmes se blesse
208   D'autry deffïé se tient.

IX   Voz debaz ennuyent.
Les bons cuers les fuyent

181 ou *NfNjOaPcPhQd*.   183 prouuesce (*sic*) *Nj*.   184 peust *Pc*.   188 Et il *Qd*; serement *Nf* (?) *Ph*.
191 Qui *Pc*.   193 Par la n. leesse *Oa*, Par n. liesse *PcPh*.   194 le l. v.] le bien v. *Oa*, tout le bien v.
Nf.   196 ny a. *Pc*.   197 ou d. *Pc*.   198 Que nen doye s. *Ph*.   198–9 s./m.] m./s. *Nf*.   199 soustenir
Nj.   200 et la n.] et la haultesce (et h. *Nj*) *NfNj*.   202 rudesse *Nf*.   204 vous d. *NfNjNj*, le d. *PhQd*.
208 deffier *Ph*.

Et pour la paix prïent,
212 Et vous en supplïent:
Faictes y devoir.

Les vertuz s'oublïent;
Erreurs multiplïent.
216 Ennemis espïent
Tousjours, quoy qu'ilz dïent,
A vous decevoir.

Droiz excommenïent
220 Et les lois maudïent
Ceulx qui Paix desdïent.
Nature et Droit crïent
Et font assavoir

224 Que tous se rallïent –
Les fiers s'umilïent;
Les durs s'amolïent;
Les rigoureux plïent –
228 Pour la paix avoir.

64r

X Aiez des maulx repentance
Et des biens recongnoissance;
Toute ire et fureur cassez.
232 Oublïez les temps passez
Et reprenez ordonnance.

Donnez au peuple allejance
Et a Dieu obeïssance.
236 Vous en avez fait assez
Pour devoir estre lassez;
Relessiez Lui la venjance.

Ne croiez oultrecuidance;
240 Peu dure fiere puissance.
Dieu pardoint aux trespassez:
Par la fault que vous passez;
C'est nostre commune dance.

211 Qui pour vous la p. p. *Oj*.   212 suppliant *Qd*.   213 Faicte *Oa*.   222 droiz *Ph*.   225 Les bons *Ph*.
225–6 *Inverted NfNj*.   227 prient *NjPh*.   231 Tout *NfPc*.   233 lordonnance *Nf*.   235 obedience *Ph*.
240 vostre p. *Ph*.   241 les t. *NfNjPcQd*.   243 vostre *NfPc*.

244 Guerre la mort vous avance:
Paix tient vo vie en souffrance,
Par qui temps est relaxez.
Ensemble vous amassez;
248 Monstrez qu'estes nez de France.

XI   Qui veult que sa vie dure
En murmure,
Et trop se lesse abuser
252 A user
Son temps dessoubz la fortune,   64v

El se tourne vers lui dure
Et obscure,
256 Et le lesse cabuser
Sans muser,
Car el n'est pas tousjours une.

Homme, qui de Paix n'a cure,
260 Se procure
Que Paix le doit reffuser
Et ruser;
C'est la venjance commune.

264 Raison lui nuist et Nature
Par droitture,
Ne on ne puet desacuser
N'excuser
268 Qui la lesse pour rancune.

XII   Si vous requier par desir curïeux:
Fuyez rappors faulx et suspicïeux;
Querez moyens doulz et concordïeux;
272 Vainquez rigour par vostre humilité;

Laissez aigreur et faiz contencïeux,
Orgueil, fierté, vouloir ambicïeux,

245 voz vie *Oa*, la vie *Pc*. 246 Par quoy *Ph*. 250 Sans m. *Ph*. 252 Et u. *Pc*. 253 sa f. *Pc*.
254 Elle *NſNjPcPh*, Et *Oa*; a lui *NſNj*. 256 se l. *NſPh*. 258 elle *NjPcPh*. 260 Si *NſNj*, Et
Ph. 263 Et *Nſ*. 266 Ne on ne sen peust excuser *Pc*: desencuser *OaPh*. 267 Ne accuser *Pc*. 268 la
l.] le l. *Ph*, l. paix *Pc*; par *NſOa*. 271 moyen *Oa*. 273 et f. c.] et c. *Ph*. 273–5 *In order* 274, 275,
273 *Pc*. 274 f. et faiz a. *Ph*.

Affettïons, appetit vicïeux,
276 Pensez que tout n'est que une vanité,

Et que les durs et les presumpcïeux
Vivent dolens et melencolïeux;
Mais les benings, courtois et gracïeux
280 Se gouvernent selon humanité.

Leurs faiz durent et leurs estaz sont tieulx
Que honneur leur croist et meurent seurs et vieulx,
Si qu'a l'issir des fraeles corps mortieulx
284 Leur ame est sauve avec la Deïté.
Amen.

Explicit.

275 apetis *NfNjOaPcPh*.   279 Et *NfNjOaPcPhQd*; benignes *Ph*.   280 Soy gouvernans *NfNj*; se non *Pc*; lumanite *NfNjPc*, humilite *Oa*.   281 telz *Nj*.   282 sains *NfNjPh*.   283 Si que a loysir leur fault leur c. m. *Pc*: Et *NfOaPh*; des f.] leurs f. *Oj*; mortelz *Nj*.   284 L. a. est s.] L. a. et s. *Oj*, L. a. est sauvee *Oa*, Lame est sauve *Nf*, Leurs ames sauves *Pc*.   Amen *only in OaOj*.   *No explicit NjPhQd*, . . .le lay de paix *Nf*, . . .le livre de paix eureuse *Oa*.

14

'Le Debat du Herault, du Vassault et du Villain'

One Manuscript: *Of*.

The debate was discovered and edited by S. Lemm in 1914.[1] It was re-edited in 1961 by J. E. White, who relied on Lemm's edition rather than the manuscript. For this edition, photographs of *Of* have been used.

In *Of* the poem is anonymous and has no title. It is copied immediately after works by Chartier and just before two poems by Pierre de Nesson. The last two stanzas of the debate show that the author was called 'Alain' and that he was on friendly terms with 'Neczon', 'le vaillant bailly d'Aigueperse'. These details, together with the content of the poem, indicate that it is by Alain Chartier.

The poem was entitled the *Debat Patriotique* by A. Thomas[2] and that title has been used by critics since then. 'Patriotique' is anachronistic: the first examples of the word in French date from the middle of the eighteenth century.[3] The title has been changed to that above which, though longer, is more in keeping with fifteenth-century practice.

The text given by *Of* is generally satisfactory. The corrections which have been made are few and generally suggested themselves. Lines 95 and 424, however, gave some difficulty. Words which have been added to the text (lines 27, 57, 83, 95, 277, 335 and 424) are printed within square brackets. Rejected readings are given in the usual way, save that in this case their source need not be stated.

[1] See pp. 92–3.
[2] A. Thomas, 'Une œuvre patriotique inconnue d'Alain Chartier', *Journal des savants*, 1914, 442–9.
[3] Robert, v, 191; FEW, VIII, 24.

LE DEBAT DU HERAULT, DU VASSAULT ET DU VILLAIN

I   Naguieres q'ung prudent herault,   *Of*, 87a
            Grant voyageur, homme ancïen,
            Parloit a ung jeune vassault
4   Qui ne savoit q'ung peu de bien;
            Si estoit il de bon hostel
            Et filz d'ung vaillant chivallier,
            Mais l'enfent n'estoit mie tel
8   Quoy qu'il feüst son heretier.

II   A l'enfent estoit grant chevance
                    Par la mort de son pere escheue,
                    Maiz de son honneur et vaillance

12   Avoit il petite part eue.   87b
                    Le herault le trouva tançant
                    A ung bon homme de villaige,
                    En l'appellant 'Villain püant',

16   Cuidant faire beau vassellaige.

III   Le herault estoit froit et cault
                    Et vit que ce jeune seigneur
                    Estoit oultrecuidé et chault

20   Et avoit en lui pou d'onneur,
                    Dont il estoit bien esbaÿ
                    Car il avoit cogneu le pere.
                    Doulcement vers lui se traÿ

24   Pour s'acquiter et devoir faire,

IV   *Le Herault*

                    Disant: 'Mon seigneur, je vous prie!
                    Car il ne vous vueille desplaire,
                    Pour Dieu, chouse que [je] vous die,

28   Car je ne m'en puis ne doy taire!
                    Les vostres m'ont fait largement
                    Des biens; si doiz de mon pouvoir
                    Amer l'ostel, principalment

32   Vous, chief des armes et seul hoir.

V   Et deussiez vous maintenant estre
                    Villenant villains en villaige?
                    Ne deussiez vous servir ung maistre

36   Vaillant, avant estre son paige?
                    Le bon mareschal de Sancerre,
                    Que je vis puis bon connestable,
                    Faisoit bien gesir sur le feurre

40   Vostre pere, et mangier sans table.'

VI   *Le Vassault*

                    'Voy, mon seigneur fut renommé,
                    Ung des meilleurs que l'on veist oncques.

Vous avez tresbien sermonné,

44   Mais le temps n'est pas tel qu'adoncques;
Vëez vous comme il nous en baille.
Dieu ait l'ame des trespassés!
Ilz n'eussent pas geu sur la paille

48   S'ilz eussent des moulz liz assés!'

VII   *Le Herault*

Lors lui respondy le herault:
'S'ilz se fussent tousjours tenu,
Ainsi que vous, blanc, moyte et chault,

52   L'onneur ne leur fust pas venu,
Car on n'a jamaiz bien sans peyne;
Pour ce lasches n'ont pris ne loz'.
'Voy', dist l'aultre, 'Que vault avoyne

56   Au jour d'uy pour les bons? Trois soulz?'

VIII   *[Le Herault]*

'Mieulx valent trois soulz en bon nom
Que cent mille frans en reprouche.
Que les bons n'ayent guerredon

60   Ne vous saille jamaiz de bouche,
Car ung vaillant pouvre sans doubte
A plus de bien de ce qu'il sent
Qu'on l'aime, louë et redoubte,

64   Que n'ont lasches riches ung cent.'

IX   *Le Vassault*

'A ce loz et honneur conquerre
A souvent des perilz assez,
Et bien souvent en l'alant querre

68   Sont, sans l'avoir, mains trespassez.
Dieu par sa grace les assoille!
Or maintenant par sa vaillence
Nul bon ne treuve qui l'acueille

72   Comme l'on souloit faire en France.'

45 comment.

423

X   *Le Herault*

    'Or s'on fait es vaillans devoir   87d
    Ne s'ilz ont offices ne dons,
    Vous ne le devez pas savoir,
76 Car il ne le scet que les bons;
    Et croy, mais qu'il ne vous desplaise,
    Que l'onneur n'est ne ne tient compte
    De nul home qui quiere l'aise,
80 Et fust cent fois roy, duc ou conte.'

XI   *Le Vassault*

    Au vassal despleut du herault
    Dont il parle si haultement,
    Mais au vieillart petit [en] chault.
84 Lors lui dit rigoureusement
    Le jeune vassal: 'Or ça, sire!
    Je prens que j'aye le vouloir
    De faire quantqu'on pourroit dire,
88 M'armer, servir en tout devoir.

XII
    Il ne me fauldra pas actendre
    Que le roy m'aide a mectre suz;
    Ains me fauldra mes baguez vendre,
92 Espoir engagier le surplus.
    Et s'aucun essoyne me sourt,
    Ou une perte toute seule
    Ces humeurs [de] broez de court
96 S'en mocqueront a pleine gueule.'

XIII   *Le Herault*

    'De teulz souillars la mocquerie
    Ne vous doit de riens retarder,
    Car mal que nulz d'eulx de vous die
100 Ne fait se non vous avancer.
    Gormandent, flatent, estudïent
    A rendre villains fellons motz;
    Quand de vous ou aultre mesdïent,
104 Leur blasme vous est ung grant loz.'

95 Ces souillars h. b. de c.

XIV

Le Vassault

'Je ne sçay, maiz le plus souvent
Les flateurs sont bien des seigneurs,
Et ont tout a leur gré le vent
108   Et raboutent tous les meilleurs;
Et cela pluseurs bons retarde
D'avoir bon vouloir a leur maistre,
Car a chief qui riens ne regarde
112   Autant vault maulvaiz que bon estre.'

XV

Le Herault

'M'aist Dieu, sire, sauf vostre grace,
Fault il, se je sers ung seigneur
Lasche, failli, qui ne pourchasse
116   D'estre vaillant ne son honneur,
Ou se j'ay ung prince si beste
Que les bons il ne recognoisse,
Qu'a sa folie je m'areste
120   Tant que mon honneur je n'acroisse?'

XVI

Le Vassault

'Je croy bien que son honneur croistre
Doit vouloir chascun gentilhomme
Pour soy faire amer et cognoistre,
124   Quoy que la sayson n'est pas comme
Elle estoit du temps noz ancestres,
Car ceulx qui les vaillans faysoient
Estoient les bons vaillans maistres
128   Qui les vaillans recognoissoient.'

XVII

Le Herault

'Qu'il ne soit pour vaillans sayson?
Si est trop meilleur que jamaiz
Et je vous diray la rayson:
132   Il en est trop moins qu'oncques maiz.
Et s'il en estoit ung venu,
Tel que furent les trespassez,

125 Ellestoit (*sic*).

425

Il seroit trop plus chier tenu
136 Que s'il estoit des preux assez.'   88b

XVIII   *Le Vassault*

'Or ça! Je prens q'ung de ces preux
Revenist maintenant en vie.
De quoy s'aideroit il? De ceulx
140 Qui tiennent ceste pillerie?
Car quant il s'en vouldroit aidier,
Tous trayroient le cul arriere,
Qu'il n'y a ung tout seul rotier
144 Qui ne fuÿsse la frontiere.'

XIX   *Le Herault*

'Quant ces hommes vaillans vivoyent,
Dieu leur donnoit a tous ung don;
C'est car es charges qu'ilz avoient,
148 Ilz faisoient d'un maulvaiz bon.
Maintenant on fait le rebours,
Car des bons on fait les maulvaiz:
Les chiefs se soillardent es cours;
152 Leurs gens pillent païs de paix.'

XX   *Le Vassault*

'Pour ce, des nobles du païs
Les seigneurs qui ces pillars tiennent
Sont petitement obeïz,
156 N'a leurs mandemens plus ne viennent.
Aussi ne verrés vous seigneur
Qui teulz gens advoue ne tiegne,
Qui face riens de son honneur
160 N'emprise dont mal ne lui viegne.'

XXI   *Le Herault*

'Dea', dit le herault, 'Les emprises
Sont aucunes foiz vaillemment
Et par grant prouesse avant mises,
164 Dont il advient estrangement

141 ilz sen vouldroient.   144 fuyssent.   156 viegnent.   160 emprinse.   161 emprinses.

426

Et bien souvant que l'an a veu   88c
Que la plus feible et plus petite
Partie, qu'on n'eust jamaiz creu,
168 A la plus grande mise en fuyte.'

XXII   *Le Vassault*

'Je croy bien qu'il ait es batailles
Aucunes foiz des meseürs,
Car, lou sont telles larronnailles,
172 Dieu n'envoye pas les eürs;
N'oncq je ne veiz – ne leur desplaise,
Sy en ay je cogneu beaucop –
Nul dont la fin n'en feust maulvaise,
176 Se ne fust le bastard Bigot.'

XXIII   *Le Herault*

'Beau sire, vous ne devez mie
Vous eslïessier d'oïr dire
Q'ung homme de meschante vie
180 Face meschant fin, ou mal muyre.
Espoir est il en paradis –
La voie en est a tous ouverte –
Et s'il n'est vray ce que je diz,
184 Je croy qu'il n'y a pas grant perte.'

XXIV   *Le Vassaulx* (sic)

'Se les maulvaiz des vices plains,
Qui oncques fors tout mal ne firent,
Estoient autant des gens plains
188 Que ceulx qui vaillemment vesquirent,
L'en feroit es vaillans grant tort,
Car leur guerredon et debvoir
Est de les plaindre aprés leur mort
192 Et leurs beaulx faiz rementevoir.'

XXV   *Le Herault*

'Mectez dont peyne d'estre bon
Et voz vaillans parens ensuyvre,   88d

176 Ce.   186 Quoncques.   190 guerdon.

Pour acquerir ce guerredon
196 Qui aprés leur mort fait gens vivre.
Suyvés tousjours les plus vaillans
De quelque baz estat qu'ilz soient,
Car aucunes foiz les plus grans
200 Ne font pas tout ce qu'ilz devroient.'

XXVI   *Le Vassault*

'Dëa, se mon prince me mande,
Il fault que je l'aille servir
Et aille soubz qui il commende;
204 En moy n'en est pas le choysir,
Car se soubz aultre chief de guerr
Plus avant me mectz ou alie,
L'en me confisquera ma terre
208 Et reprandra de foy mentie.'

XXVII   *Le Herault*

'Soubz princes laschez et failliz
Et en armes meseüreux,
Sont bien aucunes foiz sailliz
212 Mains vaillans et chivallereux,
Et tel fois que d'une journee
Cil qui est chief le non avra,
Qui sera de toute l'armee
216 Cellui qui moins d'armes fera.'

XXVIII   *Le Vassault*

'Et doncques, par ce que vous dictes,
Ce loz et pris que les chiefz ont
Ne vient mie par leurs merites,
220 Quant ce sont ceulx qui moins en font.
Et je cuideroye q'ung chief
Ne deust d'estre preux nom avoir,
Tant venist la chouse a bon chief,
224 Fors selon qu'il feroit devoir.'

206 a. je me m. 208 reprandon (?). 220 se. 224 celon.

XXIX

Le Herault

'Chief qui entreprent hardiment,
En tenant gens en ordonnence,
Actent le peril vaillemment
228 Contre une plus grande puissance.
Prennons qu'il ne face aultre chouse:
Si est ce a lui grant hardïesse,
Dont l'avanture actendre il ose;
232 Et se bien en vient par lui est ce.'

XXX

Le Vassal (sic)

'Bien? Doncques doit ung chief de guerre,
Qui se moustre vaillant tout oultre,
Grant loz et grant honneur acquerre,
236 Quant cellui qui riens ne se moustre
Et qui sera de la journee
Cellui qui le moins fera d'armes,
Avra toute la renommee
240 Du bien que feront ses gens d'armes!'

XXXI

Le Herault

'Or, pensés doncques, quel dueil est ce
A ung prince chevallereux
Qui, soy moustrant plain de prouesse,
244 Se voit desemparé de ceulx
Qui lui doyvent service et foy,
Dont il est et chief et seigneur?
Et, par mon serement, je croy
248 Qu'il n'est nul si grant crevecuer.

XXXII

Que peult ung cuer panser en lui,
Qui se moustre vaillemment preux,
Et voit que la faulte d'aultrui
252 Lui met le nom de malheureux?
Et, quant a moy, je ne croy mie
Qu'au seigneur, pour jeune qu'il soit,
N'en souviegne, quoy qu'on en die,
256 Toutes les fois qu'il les revoit.'

241 doncq.

XXXIII *Le Vassault*

'Ung chief, doncques, quant il prent charge
Doit bien eslire gens de fait,
Et soy garder qu'il ne se charge
260 De gens par qui il soit deffait;
Non pas de jeunez pinperneaux
Car, comme ont dit ly ancïen,
Qui fait sa chace de chëaux,
264 C'est avanture s'il prent rien.'

XXXIV *Le Herault*

'Dëa, ce n'est mie merveille,
S'un seigneur quelque chouse emprent
Et par jeunez foulz se conseille,
268 Se honteusement lui en prent;
Et quant le cas est advenu,
Tant soit bon et chevallereux,
Chascun le fuit et est tenu
272 En ses emprinses malheureux.

XXXV Et au rebours, s'il advient bien
Et que pour lui soit la journee,
Tout le pris et loz en est sien
276 Du bien que se fait en s'armee,
Et quant Dieu [lui] donne ung tel bruyt,
Il a plus qu'il ne veult de gent;
Chascun tel pouvre pour neant suyt
280 Plus tost q'ung riche pour l'argent.'

XXXVI *Le Vassault*

'Je cuide bien, se sa parsonne
A une grande seignourie,
Cela ne lui tost ne lui donne
284 Le renom de chevallerie;
Et ce, les ancïens ne doubtent,
Ainçois tiennent, et est certain:
Scïence et vaillance se boutent
288 Souvent en gens de basse main.'

265 merveilles. 268 emprent. 285 a. pas ne d. 287 Que s.

430

XXXVII   *Le Herault*   89c

'On le voit souvent advenir
Que cil qui n'a q'ung peu vaillant,
Met plus grant paine a acquerir
292   Scïencë, ou d'estre vaillant,
Que le filz d'ung roy ou d'ung comte;
Si ne diz je pas q'ung seigneur
Qui de vaillence ne tient compte
296   Ne viengne bien tart a honneur.'

XXXVIII   *Le Vassault*

'Il leur souffit d'estre grans maistres
Sans avoir honneur et vaillance;
Et s'ilz font de leurs enfens prestres,
300   C'est sans lecture ne scïence.
Pouez pancer q'une pollice
Qui est conduyte par teulx chiefs,
Par lasche prince et prelat nyce,
304   Est cause de mains grans meschiefs.'

XXXIX   *Le Herault*

'Prince sans vaillence est peu craint;
Aussi chascun destruit sa terre,
Chascun ses trevez lui enfraint,
308   Trop mendre de lui lui fait guerre.
Ses subgetz lui desobeïssent;
Et ceulx qui par sa lascheté
Il laisse destruire, maudissent
312   L'eure de sa nativité.'

XL   *Le Vassault*

'Et le prince vaillant et saige
Enrichist en paix ses subgeiz.
En sa terre pillart ne paige
316   N'arrançonne ne prant logeiz.
Il n'a ne parent ne voysin
Qui ne le voye voulentiers

314 subgetz.

431

Ne ja ne perdra ung poucin,
320 Tant le craingnent les estrangiers.'

XLI *L'Acteur*

Le villain qu'on avoit tancé,
Lequel ilz ne vëoient pas,
Si s'est maintenant avancé
324 Et se veint mectre en leur soulaz
Disant: 'Ores, ne vous desplaise...'
Puis hosche le chief et s'escoute:
'Il me couvient mectre a mon aise'.
328 Lors se veint seoir sur une moute.

XLII *Le Villain*

Et quant il se fut acouté,
Sans fairë aultre reverence:
'J'ay bien ouÿ et escouté
332 Vostre soulaz, mais quant je y pense,
Tout ne vault ung bouton de haye.
Vous ne parlés point de la taille.
Pour quoy est [ce] que l'on la paye,
336 Se n'est pour faire la bataille?

XLIII En quoy a l'en tant despendu
D'argent comme l'en a levé,
Que par le col soit il pendu
340 Qui loyaulment l'a gouverné?
Ilz dïent que c'est pour le roy,
Maiz il va bien en aultres mains,
Car par mon serement, je croy
344 Que c'est cil qui en a le moins.

XLIV Et queulx gens d'armes avons nous
En la frontiere, se Dieu plaist?
Il me semble qu'ilz fuyent tous
348 La guerrë; elle leur desplaist!
Tous ceulx que le roy a suz mis,
L'en les puisse par les coulz pendre;

432

Nous sont pis que les ennemis,　　　　　　　　90a
352　Et si ne nous ousons deffandre.

XLV　　　Ou est celle belle conqueste
Que l'en a fait sur les Angloiz?
He Dieu, et que le peuple est beste
356　Quant il accorde teulx octrois!
De l'or qu'on a eu de la taille
On eust achecté Angleterre!
Et par Dieu, tant qu'on la leur baille,
360　Ilz ne feront exploit de guerre.

XLVI　　Mais quant on les refusera,
A quoy l'on a trop actendu,
Alors tout besoing leur sera
364　D'aler conquester du perdu;
Et par mon serement, je croy
Que, tant qu'on leur vueille octroyer,
Les gens qui se dïent au roy
368　N'aprendront de riens guerroyer.

XLVII　　Et le peuple a trop bel respondre
Au roy quant il requier ses aydez:
"Sire, tez gens se vont escondre
372　Quant il est temps que tu t'en aydez".
Maiz ou quierent ilz leurs mussoires?
A desrouber pouvres marchans;
En guectant les marchiez et foires
376　Et destroussant gens par les champs!'

XLVIII　　　　　L'Acteur
Puis s'entrerompi le soulaz
Des trois, car le saige vieillart
Se print lors a parler moult bas
380　Et tirer le vassault a part;
Et sembloit qu'il eust grant desir
De blasonner ne sçay lesqueulx.
Qu'il dit, je n'en peuz riens oïr,　　　　　　90b
384　Fors qu'il dit: 'Croyés, ilz sont teulx'.

354 Quon a. f.　376 destroussans.
433

XLIX   *Le Vassault*

         Dont le vassault lui respondy:
         'Il fault doncq que tout soit desert'.
         Et le herault lui dist aussi:
   388   'Vous voiez bien que tout se pert'.
         Le vassal lui dist: 'Quel remede,
         Que pensés vous, que ce sera?'
         'Par ma foy, a ce que je cuide',
   392   Dist le herault, 'Tout se perdra.'

L   *Le Villain*

         'Perdra? Mais est il ja perdu!
         Que le deable en soit adouré!'
         Leur a le villain respondu,
   396   Qui loing d'eulx estoit demouré.
         'A la bataille, a la bataille,
         Entre vous aultres gentillastres;
         Non pas au roy tollir sa taille
   400   Et vous groppir gardant voz astres!

LI   Car se les gentilhommes feissent
         Aussi bien que nous leur debvoir,
         Que le roy des corps ilz servissent
   404   Ainsi que nous de nostre avoir,
         Les estrangiers pas ne pillassent;
         Mais les nobles mesmes, subgeiz
         Du roy, vont vers eulx quant ilz passent
   408   Faire rançonner les logeiz.

LII   Que le grant deablë y ait part!
         Chascun dit qu'ilz sont a butin.
         Il se peut tresbien lever tart
   412   Qui a nom de lever matin;
         Et par le sang Dieu, les François
         Avront fait cincq cens mille biens   90c
         Et destruit trestous les Angloiz,
   416   Qu'on dira qu'il n'en sera riens.'

         401 genltilhommes (*sic*). 407 panssent (?). 410 s. habutin.

LIII

L'Acteur

Le vieulx herault adoncq s'en rit,
Dont le villain ainsi s'avence.
Lors le jeune vassal despit
420　Lui dist: 'Beau sire, quant je y pense
Il me semble que ces villains
Ont trop beau compter sans rabatre,
Car ilz ne sont jamaiz contraings
424　[De soy] faire tüer ne batre'.

LIV

Me sembloit d'eulx ouÿr parler
Qu'antr'eux jouassent une farce,
Et lors il me va remambrer
428　Du vaillant bailly d'Aigueperse
Qui me dist une foys: 'Alain,
J'ayme trop mieulx paier la taille
Et vivre longuement villain,
432　Que noble mourir en bataille'.

LV

On pourroit avoir souspeczon
Que je voulsisse cecy dire
Pour mon bon compaignon Neczon.
436　Pour ce, quant je l'ay fait escripre,
J'ay a l'escripvain deffendu
Du moustrer. Au fort, s'on lui baille,
Bien assailly, bien deffendu;
440　Face, s'il scet, de pire taille!

Explicit.

421 ses.　424 Deulx aler f.　425 Il me s.

Notes and Glossary

Il n'est si bon chartier
qui ne verse
Morawski 934

The notes and the glossary are intended to complement each other and should be used in conjunction.

The notes are in two sections. In the second section are discussed points of interest or difficulty which affect individual lines or groups of lines. The first section is made up of general notes on Chartier's language. These general notes should be seen as a convenient way of treating in more detail points which would otherwise have had to be made in separate and scattered notes. Even if space had permitted, a more detailed study of Chartier's language would be premature and inappropriate here. To be complete, any such study must also take account of his prose works. A critical edition of the *Livre de l'Esperance* is now available, but similar editions are still lacking of the *Quadrilogue Invectif* and of the *Curial*, if the French version of that work proves to be by Chartier.

The general notes draw attention to what may appear to be inconsistencies and even irregularities in the language of Chartier's poems. Taken together they form a large enough corpus for it to be possible to distinguish between the normal and less usual features of his language. It is with the latter that these notes are chiefly concerned. Rhyme-words are cited if possible and bear an asterisk as a distinguishing mark: thus, DF 1*. They are emphasised because they are less likely than other words to have been altered by scribes. Nonetheless, spellings, even of rhyme-words, vary, the more so since use is made in this edition of no less than five base manuscripts.

There are dangers in laying too much emphasis on alternative and unusual forms, and on inconsistencies. Chartier and his contemporaries attached great importance to form and rhyme, and like them he cast his net wide to find forms which would help make his lines rhyme and scan. But that is not the only reason why he chose unusual forms or spellings. They are also used for stress and emphasis: some of the examples cited below show this clearly; others may have been intended to have that effect.

The general notes are followed by notes on each of the poems. Where necessary, the notes on particular lines are preceded by an account of the way in which the poem is decorated in the different manuscripts used in

436

the edition. If a detailed note deals with a whole line or several lines together, the line(s) are not quoted. When a word or phrase is discussed, it is cited in italics at the beginning of the note.

In the detailed notes and the glossary use is made of a small number of abbreviations. Those which refer to standard editions and works of reference are explained in the bibliography. The abbreviations used to refer to Chartier's poems are listed below. It should be noted that when reference is made in a note to another line of the same poem, only the number of the line is given; references to lines of other poems consist of the abbreviation for the poem and the number of the line.

Le Lay de Plaisance	PL
Le Debat des Deux Fortunés d'Amours	DF
Le Livre des Quatre Dames	QD
Le Debat de Reveille Matin	RM
La Complainte	CO
La Belle Dame sans Mercy	BD
Les Lectres des Dames a Alain	L I
La Requeste Baillee aux Dames contre Alain	L II
L'Excusacion aux Dames	EX
Rondeaulx et Balades	RB
Le Breviaire des Nobles	BN
Le Lay de Paix	PA
Le Debat du Herault, du Vassault et du Villain	HV

GENERAL NOTES

MORPHOLOGY

Nouns, articles, pronouns, adjectives and adverbs

Declension. The two-case declension system has almost entirely disappeared. Masculine subject forms occur above all as rhyme-words, plural forms being found less frequently than singular ones: *amis* (PL 23), *Homs jolis* (PL 97), *tresententis* (DF 313*: cf. 314*–15*), *tous seulx* (QD 201*), *advenuz* (QD 372*); *faisant* (QD 101*), *entreprenant* (QD 2903*), *negligent* (QD 3196*), *ancïen* (HV 262*). Singular forms, but not apparently plural ones, are sometimes used incorrectly in order to scan or rhyme: *homs* (PL 55 and 179), *un vert prez* (QD 382*), *despeschans* (QD 1004*). Singular forms with final *s* are especially common with *amour* and *rien*, and are used as subject or object.

Examples of the older imparisyllabic declension are also found: *ancestre* (DF 74*), *ancesseurs* (QD 2870); *compains* (DF 397*), *compaignon* (DF 390); *homs* (PL 55 and 179: DF 561*), *hom* (QD 1194*), *homme* (DF 720 and 936); *sire* (DF 227*), *seignieur* (DF 73);

437

they are not always used correctly. The Third Lady makes some play with imparisyllabic forms in QD 2391*–3*.

Gender. Certain nouns are of variable gender. *Amour* can be masculine or feminine and singular or plural (DF 62, DF 450, QD 2419, QD 2679, QD 2953–4, BD 397); when it is personified it is generally masculine and is often written *amours. Honneur* is masculine or feminine: see PL 195, DF 1084, QD 3007. *Mesaise*, feminine in DF 121, QD 2951 and BD 339, is masculine in CO 44 and BD 280; *aise* is masculine on the only occasion when its gender is clear (QD 2313). Adjectives which precede *gens* are feminine (DF 944, RB xxiv:1, PA 118); those which follow are masculine (QD 3174, BN 242).

Article. The older definite article *li* is found four times. In each case its presence avoids a hiatus, for the following noun or pronoun begins with a vowel or *h*: DF 561, DF 1063, BN 35, HV 262; only the last example is plural. Four examples of *un(g)s* occur, twice with *homs* (PL 55, QD 2889), twice with plural nouns: *uns yeulx* (EX 243) and *uns carneaulx* (DF 1040); in the first case it describes a pair, in the second a group thought of as a unit. There are no comparable examples of *unes.*

Personal pronouns. Elle and *el* are alternative subject forms (PL 37 and 55). Of the disjunctive pronouns, *my* (QD 554*) and *ty* (QD 566* and CO 164*) are variants of *moy* and *toy* which are found only at the rhyme; *ly* (QD 502*) and *lui* (PL 27, PL 106 and QD 507*) are rare feminine forms, while *ly* occurs once as a masculine (QD 1124*).

Possessive pronouns and adjectives. (Toute) moie (QD 1371*) and *(les) voz* (QD 2053) are the only examples of these older accented forms. *Vo* is found four times (QD 2851, BD 375, BD 517, PA 245) as an alternative to *vostre.*

Indefinite pronouns and adjectives. The pronouns *autr(u)y, cellui* and *null(u)y* are alternative forms, longer and more emphatic, of *autre, cil* and *nul*; like them they can be used in all positions. *Nulluy* occurs once as an adjective (QD 506*). There are only two examples of *cestui*, once as an adjective in the refrain of the first ballade of the *Breviaire des Nobles*, once as a pronoun in QD 1961; it is emphatic in both instances. The pronouns *icelle* (QD 525) and *iceulx* (QD 491 and 950) are almost as rare.

Relative pronouns. Que and *qu'* are found quite commonly as subject forms: DF 500, 788 and 816; QD 173, 319 and 787. The only example of the dative *cui* is in PL 43. *Qui* can be accusative plural (RM 55).

Adjectives. Adjectives derived from the Latin third declension may have the same form for both genders in the singular and plural, as may present participles when they are used adjectivally: *grant joye* (DF 138), *griefz penances* (QD 3087), *quel lÿesse* (PA 181), *tel peine* (RM 275), *hystoires ne sont faillans* (QD 2925). Feminine forms in -*e* and -*es* are found less frequently: *nouvelle...grande* (DF 162*), *pensee greve* (QD 1722*), *quele seurté* (PA 206), *teles gens* (DF 944). Such forms are rare with present participles: *sont...requerantes* (QD 3491*); the rhyme in -*antes* is likewise unusual and emphatic. The plural of adjectives in -*el* varies: *telz* (PA 112), *tieulx* (EX 77*); *mortelx* (DF 203), *mortieulx* (PA 283*); *tieulx* also occurs as a nominative singular (RM 85*).

Adjectives may take alternative forms: *nuisable* (PL 166*), *nuysible* (DF 1072*); *songeux* (DF 210*), *songeur* (QD 2086*); *felle* (DF 890), *felonnes* (DF 559*).

Adverbs. Two forms exist for adverbs formed from adjectives derived from the third

General notes

Latin declension: *briefment* (CO 183), *brievement* (QD 1937★); *granment* (DF 1★), *grandement* (QD 3498★).

Some adverbs are of variable length: *encor* (DF 512★), *encore* (DF 826★); *onc* (PL 10), *oncques* (DF 46); *donc* (PL 65), *doncques* (DF 218★).

Tres is with few exceptions written by the scribes as an adverbial prefix, and has been treated as such in the poems. In the variants the prefix is not always given.

Verbs

Conjugation. Some verbs exist side by side in different conjugations: *despendu* (RB III: 4), *despensee* (QD 2334★); *despire* (BN 296★), *despite* (QD 1038★); *eslargier* (RB III: 6), *eslargi* (QD 1957); *finera* (RB IV: 16★), *finir* (EX 88★); *fremie* (DF 791★), *fremir* (BN 99); *yssir* (QD 162), *istre* (QD 1989★); *ouvrir* (DF 11), *ouvrera* (QD 1381★); *poursuyent* (QD 495★), *poursuivent* (QD 2439★).

Infinitive. Alternative forms of an infinitive are found: *fuÿr* (QD 2609), *fuire* (QD 1844★); *querre* (DF 804★), *querir* (BD 338★) and compounds; *remanoir* (QD 2370★), *remaindre* (QD 2194★).

Present indicative. Two forms exist for the first person singular of verbs in *-er*, the form with final *-e* being the more common: *aym* (QD 979), *ayme* (QD 188★); *os* (QD 694★), *ose* (QD 193★); *pors* (CO 23★), *porte* (QD 108); *suppli* (RB VII: 3), *supplie* (DF 1239★); *truys* (QD 1524), *treuve* (QD 126). From *mourir*, both (*je*) *meur* (RM 247) and (*je*) *muir* (CO 23) are found.

The effects of stress and analogy can be seen in the co-existence of forms such as: (*il*) *convie* (CO 130★), (*il*) *convoie* (PL 102★); (*il*) *devie* (BN 379★), (*el*) *desvoie* (PA 145★); (*il*) *greve* (QD 1041★), (*il*) *grieve* (PL 165★); (*il*) *lermie* (DF 792★), (*je*) *lermoie* (QD 1372★); (*je*) *parle* (QD 1628), (*il*) *parole* (QD 1959★); *parlent* (RM 56), *parolent* (QD 2702★).

Present subjunctive. Third person singular forms without *-e* are found, often in stylised phrases: *doint* (QD 340★) and *pardoint* (RM 355★), *gart* (RB XIX: 5★), *octroit* (QD 388), *puist* (QD 775), *ramaint* (QD 1256★; see note), *represent* (QD 2667★). For the second person plural, forms in *-ez* occur: *louez* (QD 2027★), *disez* (QD 3485★), *escripsez* (QD 3486★). Other noteworthy subjunctive forms include: (*il*) *acquierge* (QD 816★), (*el*) *chiece* (QD 2143★), (*il*) *meschiece* (QD 2144★), *comprengiez* (QD 3103★), (il) *muyre* (HV 180★). *Aille* (DF 530★), *voise* (QD 1674★) and *voit* (QD 3216★) are all third person singular forms from *aller*. *Aist* (QD 1368) and *aÿe* (QD 1573★), both from *aider*, form part of a set phrase.

Future and conditional tenses. From verbs in *-er* short and long forms exist: *demourra* (DF 1054★), *dourra* (QD 1920★), *dourroient* (QD 786★), *envoyroit* (BD 23), *ordonnera* (RB XXII: 6★), *pardonroit* (EX 132★), *retournera* (DF 826), *retourra* (DF 1051★). The spelling does not always reflect the pronunciation: *emploieroie* (QD 456★) counts as three syllables (feminine), *celeroie* (QD 451) as three; *conforteroye* (RB XIII: 5★) and *recommenceroye* (RB VIII: 12★) are of four and of five syllables (feminine) respectively.

The older future of *estre* is found on four occasions: (*elle*) *ert* (PL 190), (*il*) *yert* (QD 1080★), (*elle*) *yere* (QD 1285), *yerent* (QD 2421★).

Past tenses. The following forms co-exist but may reflect the practice of scribes rather than of the author: *dirent* (QD 2491★), *distrent* (QD 358); *mirent* (QD 2493★), *mistrent*

(DF 1189*: cf. lines 1187–8 and 1190). The older past tense of *estre* is rare: (*je*) *yere* (DF 1231*), (*elle*) *yert* (QD 718), (*elle*) *yere* (QD 2384*).

Past participles. Rompue (QD 2880*) is to be compared with *rouptes* (QD 2128*), *derompue* (QD 2882*) with *desroux* (BD 782*), *loié* (QD 3036*) with *l̈iez* (DF 702*). *Entaillie* and *travaillie* (QD 1587*–8*) are rare feminine forms: *eslacie* (QD 2680*) is probably a third example.

PHONOLOGY

A word may appear in different guises, especially when used at the rhyme. Sometimes a change of spelling serves to make the rhyme more satisfying to the eye: thus, the past tenses *fist* (DF 434*) but *fit* (QD 2151*), or the past participles *desconfist* (DF 436*) but *desconfit* (QD 2153*). Other cases point to differences of pronunciation: *crerre* (QD 3180*), *croirre* (QD 1655*); *maindre* (QD 1312*), *mendre* (QD 151*); *moitié* (DF 115), *moitie* (QD 2682*); *moult* (QD 212), *mont* (QD 1809*); *nonny* (QD 2776*), *nenny* (RM 81); *sara* (QD 268* and 2966), *saira* (QD 3384*).

Many examples result from an alternation between *c* and *ch*: *avancer* (QD 2004), *avanchié* (QD 2787*); *entrelacee* (QD 1420*), *entrelachiez* (QD 1168*); *lasse* (QD 2005*), *lasche* (QD 2512*); *parface* (RM 153*), *parfache* (QD 2971*).[1] Such examples are particularly common in the *Debat des Deux Fortunés d'Amours* and the *Livre des Quatre Dames*.

Certain words have a variable number of syllables, it being possible to treat *ea* and above all *eu* as a monophthong or a diphthong. The longer forms are often emphatic and found at the rhyme, which they necessarily enrich. Thus *s'asseure* (BN 416), *m'asseür* (QD 1107*); *espeüre* (QD 1899*), *espeuré* (QD 2962*); *eur* (DF 649), *eür* (DF 434); *eureuse* (PA 83*), *eüreuse* (QD 302*); *dea* (DF 227), *dëa* (HV 201); *neantmoins* (DF 463), *nëantmoins* (DF 1139*); *neant* (EX 175), *noiant* (QD 993*). *Saoul* and *saouler* vary in length: *saoul* (BN 388), *säoul* (QD 1666); *saouleroient* (QD 1642), *säoulees* (QD 2692*). *Eaue* now has two syllables (QD 64 and 89), now one (DF 404). Certain spellings may mislead: *aage* (CO 133), *autouers* (QD 69), *mirouer* (CO 99), *logeis* (DF 66) and *seellez* (BD 626*) are each of two syllables.

SYNTAX

Verbs

Number. A singular verb may have more than one subject: see DF 78, DF 98, BD 439–40, and BN 53–4, where singular and plural verbs are used successively.

Progressive tenses occur frequently, for example in DF 396*, QD 1002* and QD 1332*. Where they are formed with part of *estre*, the present participle usually agrees (QD 1332*, QD 2925* but QD 104*); where part of *aller* is used, it generally does not (DF 85, QD 910*; DF 789 is a doubtful case).

Past participles. When preceded by a direct object, past participles do not always agree: QD 349*, QD 679* and QD 827*. They can agree in anticipation of a direct object (QD 245*, QD 1341* and QD 1845) and can sometimes be inflected for no very clear reason (QD 723*).

---

[1] C. T. Gossen has also noted the co-existence of these two pronunciations and the use made of them by poets (*Petite Grammaire de l'ancien picard*, Paris, Klincksieck, 1951, 75–7, esp. 77).

Mood. Some conjunctions, for example *combien que* 'although' or *tant que* 'as long as', are followed by either the indicative or the subjunctive mood. Details are given in the glossary, where it has been possible to determine the mood. Unusual examples of the subjunctive in subordinate clauses are discussed in the notes.

Nouns and pronouns

Direct object pronouns must frequently be understood, especially where an indirect object pronoun is expressed (DF 406, DF 797 and QD 3404).

Genitive. Examples of the genitive by juxtaposition are frequent (DF 1018, DF 1229 and QD 2636–7) and particularly with *autry* (DF 234, DF 924 and DF 926).

LE LAY DE PLAISANCE

14–15	'No lady at all will be troubled this day... nor shall I (be troubled) on account of any lady.'
17	The heading above the second stanza in *Nj* is not found in any other manuscript of the *Lay de Plaisance*. It is to be compared with headings found in two manuscripts of the *Lay de Paix*, again before the second stanza: 'Premier lay' in *Nk*, and 'Le lay' in the early printed edition of the poem, GKW 6566. It is not clear why a heading should be inserted at that point and only in these three texts.
27	'He who rejoices in it (*Plaisance*).' *Lui* is here used as a stressed feminine disjunctive pronoun; cf. line 106 and QD 507.
31–2	'Him who conducts himself and behaves graciously.'
35–6	'Gay rejoicing suits and becomes her.'
43	*Cui*, here dative, is the only example of this form found in Chartier's poetry; it is very rare indeed at this period (GG, 79).
45–9	In line 49 *Nj* probably reads *En fumant* (as do *Nf* and *Ph*), but *En suivant* is also possible; *Oa* has *Ensuivant*. While *En fumant* makes no obvious sense and has been rejected, neither of the alternative readings is entirely satisfactory.
	En suivant could be taken in the sense of 'imitating' and would echo *contrefaire* in line 48. (Chartier uses similar doublets in lines 35–6 and 41–2). The passage then means: 'Pleasure causes many a trick to be done, then undone, then re-done; causes one man to imitate another, in imitation (*literally* imitating) to bear devices'.
	Ensuivant is attested by Godefroy (III, 243a–b) with the meaning 'next', but examples are rare.
71	*Eschace* 'Mean', is written thus to fit the rhyme. (Cf. *bonne*, 'boundary-stone', DF 560 and BD 47.) Elsewhere, e.g in RB XXVI: 33 and BN 342, *eschars* is found.
85–95	These lines all depend on *fait* in line 81.
91	Similar phrases occur in line 194, in QD 571 and in RM 99. The sense is either 'to travel many a journey' or 'to experience many a predicament'. For the possible meanings of *passage* (and *passee* and *pas*) see the glossary.

92–5   In *Nj* the lines were written twice by the scribe; the second copy has been erased.

100–2   'Feels the point of Love, which is anointed with a sweet hope which accompanies (*or* guides) it.'

104   *La* It is not clear whether *Amours* (line 100) or *Plaisance* (line 98) is intended. For the gender of *Amours*, see page 438.

115   The subject is still *Plaisance* (line 109), *le* being a reprise of *qui* in line 113.

115–16 'It brings him to, and reconciles him to, a true purpose.' Parts of *amener* and *amai(s)nier* are juxtaposed.

126   *Pouoir* See page 145.

137   *Feroit* is used as a *verbum vicarium*. Cf. BD 20.

157   *Avra* See page 145.

163, 167 *Prouffitable* is used as rhyme-word in both lines. In the first it means 'health-giving, beneficial', in the second 'profitable, advantageous'.

176   *Musable* The sense is probably 'which makes one preoccupied'; cf. G, V, 456b–c. La Curne (VII, 454) and Godefroy (V, 452b) each cite one and the same example of the word, suggesting for it 'bewildered, lost' and 'in search of amusement' respectively.

182   Chartier used hiatus sparingly but consistently, for emphasis. Other examples include DF 219 and 322, which also occur at the caesura.

194   *Passer mainte passee* See the note to line 91.

The *explicits* will be found complete in the descriptions of the manuscripts concerned.

LE DEBAT DES DEUX FORTUNÉS D'AMOURS

DECORATION

Line 189, in which is introduced the lady who suggests the topic for debate, is in capitals in *Ph* and *Qd*. The beginning of the first speech of the Fat Knight (line 218) is marked by an initial in *Nf* and *Nj*. The end of his second speech was to be indicated at line 671 in *Ph*, where room for an initial has been left. *Nf* and *Nj* contain an initial at line 688, the third line of the Thin Knight's reply. The scribe of *Qd* has indicated the end of that speech and the beginning of the Fat Knight's rejoinder by writing line 1111 and part of line 1114 in capitals; there is an initial in *Nj* at line 1116. Initials in *Nf* and *Nj* mark the final speech of the Thin Knight, at line 1147 in *Nj*, in *Nf* at the following line. Line 1156, where the conclusion begins, has an initial in *Pc*.

In *Oj*, the base text, changes of speaker are indicated by a mark in the margin at lines 226, 241, 671, 686, 1111, 1117 and 1147. The other indications in the margin of *Oj*, at lines 669 and 1108, have been reproduced in the edition of the poem.

1   *Fu* 'I was'.

2–4   *Assis*, *duisant* and *que* are all dependent on *chastel*.

28   'What is love.' For similar examples of *de* see RB XXVII: 3 and lines 472–3; see also H, II, 710–11 and Shears, 211–12.

29	*Que* 'Why'. Cf. QD 414.
32	*Don*, which also occurs in QD 508, 949, and 3314, and in PA 153, has been taken not as *d'ou*, but as a variant of *dont*; that spelling is given by most texts for each of these lines. In line 32 in *Oj*, *dont* has been changed to *don*.
37	Cf. CO 176 and Morawski 2368.
50	'And the dreamer to imitate him who is joyful.' For *contrefaire de* see H, II, 497–8; cf. Shears, 149–50.
60	Both nouns depend on *fait* (line 57). 'Now hurts them, now does them good.'
67	*Il y veult faire* The scribe of *Oj* first wrote *Il veult faire*, the reading given also by *Nf Oa Ph* and *Qd*. He then inserted *y*, presumably as part of the first series of corrections to the text. The reading of the base is unsupported but, since it makes good sense, it has been accepted. The alternative, *Il veult fairë*, has a good deal of support but involves a rather awkward hiatus.
93–7	The stanzas of five lines are discussed in the introduction to the poem.
96	*Ces* is intended to make the description more vivid. Cf. line 359 and Christine de Pisan, *Cent Ballades*, XXXIV. The reading *espesses mailles*, found only in *Oj*, has been rejected. It is likely that *espesses*, the penultimate word in line 94, has been copied a second time in error. Cf. lines 809 and 810 (variant), 1209 and 1210 (variant), PA 282 and 283 (variant). One cannot be sure that these apparent errors were not in the exemplar of *Oj*.
101	*Fait* The subject is *Amours* (line 90).
160–1	'And if they bear whatever pleasant words he asks them to.'
164	*Cent* is to be taken as an indeterminate large number. Cf. QD 1240.
172	*Et s'ainsi est que* 'And if it is the case that'. Cf. lines 426, 518–19 and RM 149.
175	*Qu'es tiers cieulx* 'Than in the third heaven', i.e. paradise.
187	*Profont* The scribe's abbreviation of the first syllable is not clear; in line 97 he had written *profont* in full. In line 920, however, *parfont* is found, again in full.
227	*Dea* 'Now then, well now'. It is not necessarily an exclamation of surprise, as Godefroy suggests (II, 431a–b).
229	*A par vous* 'In your opinion, personally'. Cf. QD 1056, BD 119 and BD 494 where the meaning is 'by, to oneself'.
255	'Neither faithful service nor suffering would be of value.'
274–6	The Fat Knight quotes successively three proverbs. The first resembles Morawski 113.
275	*Pos* 'Mugs, tankards'. The line means 'And great thirst makes one drink deep'.
282	*Rosiers*, given only by *Oj*, has been retained in view of QD 1894–7.
283	'And in this the insect (bee) resembles them closely.'
290	*Au...a* depend on *viens* (line 286).
342	*Maniere et contenance* 'Manners and good behaviour'; cf. BN 372.
352	*Deviser* probably means 'to devise, design' (G, II, 703c–704c); 'to adorn with a device' is another possibility.

358   *Les grans saulx* 'With great leaps', see G, x, 618c–619c.

379   *Tasse* 'Purse'. Line 383 contains another dry aside.

380   *Sur la nuyt* 'At night' (Shears, 111–12).

382, 384 *Vient* The two rhyme-words scarcely differ in meaning.

383   *Tient* recalls *s'entretient* (line 381).

401   *Blasonner* occurs in line 453, in QD 3172 and in HV 382. Both Godefroy (VIII, 330b–c) and Huguet (I, 599–601) suggest 'to praise' or 'to blame', but those meanings are perhaps too specific. The sense 'to proclaim, speak at length about' fits all the examples listed above, the context indicating whether praise or blame is involved. The English verb *to blazon* has a similar sense, but only from the sixteenth century (OED, I, 909).

424   *S'esjouÿr* is the rhyme-word here and in line 421. In the first case it is the lover who rejoices, in the second *les autres*. Cf. note to QD 3064, 3066.

440   *L'acointance* is the reading in *Nf Oa Pc* and *Ph*; in *Nj Oj* and *Qd* the scribes have written *la cointance*. Both words are attested, the first more commonly than the second. *Acointance* occurs elsewhere in Chartier (PL 151 and CO 70), but the only example of *cointance* is as a variant to PL 151. After some hesitation *acointance* has been preferred. The meaning is not affected.

453   See the note to line 401.

466–81 These lines make up one conditional sentence. The protasis, which occupies lines 466–78, is to be taken in two parts; lines 472–8 depend on *tant que*. Cf. lines 521–34.

      Two versions are available for line 476. That of the base, found also in *Nf Nj* and *Pc*, introduces a new statement and leaves the previous one in the air. Since it reads less well than the alternative and involves an anacoluthon, it has been rejected.

472–3 'Until she sees that what he says is no pretence.' Cf. line 28.

499   *Pendant* can precede or follow the noun which it qualifies. See H, v, 711.

502   *Elle* is clearly the lady, although her reappearance is not very well prepared.

508   'And takes greater care not to lose it.'

521–34 These lines form another long conditional sentence; the protasis occupies lines 521–33. Cf. lines 466–81.

532   *Et que* The clause depends on *Si bon* (line 529).

535   'And if he has no heart, Love makes him an entirely new one.'

561–2 'Presently the man's disposition improves as a result.'

564–8 These lines qualify *homs* (line 561).

566–7 'Desiring to do better than all others and (desiring) that what he does should be more fitting for him.'

572–89 *Comme* (line 572) and *doncques* (line 577) mark off the two parts of a simile.

574   'By means of reboilings and many a different method of preparation.'

576   The subject of *fait* is *sucre* (line 572).

578   *Jennesse* On all other occasions the scribe of *Oj* has written *jeunesse* or *jeune*;

see lines 370, 584–5 etc. *Jennesce* is the form used by the scribe of *Dd* (QD 1235 and 3469); see also the note to CO 17.

583–5   *Est* is to be understood. 'And the presumption of which Youth can never tire, is destroyed in young people.'

595   *Reclamer* here has the technical sense 'to reduce (a hawk) to obedience' i.e. 'to teach, tame' (OED, VIII, 248–9). Cf. BD 606. Godefroy (VI, 667b–668a) and Huguet (VI, 391–2) both suggest 'to call a falcon back to the lure', a meaning which fits the two contexts less well.

601–4   (*Celui*) *qui* (line 604) is to be taken as the subject of the singular verbs in lines 601–3.

634   *Quant est de moy* 'So far as I am concerned'.

638   *Bel* presumably agrees with *deduit* (line 637).

639   *Va au change* 'Loses those who hunt it, by starting a fresh beast'.

676   *Assez sus l'escolier* 'Looking very like a scholar'. For similar examples of *sus*, see Shears, 39 and 59–60.

680   'And did not laugh, and was not festive or merry.' For similar examples of *mener*, see line 268.

684   See the note to line 896.

687   'Are to be praised, are praiseworthy.'

690–1   'Nor can I give you my approval concerning the purpose at which you are aiming.'

713   'Of this topic which arises between us.'

729–30   'And if a person goes to seek his pleasure there, the benefit which he has is sold to him at too high a price.'

748   *Seellees* counts as two syllables (feminine). Cf. QD 2260 and BD 626.

750   *Ilz* is here used instead of *elles*; Huguet (IV, 543–4) lists many similar examples.

762   *Bon jour* is well attested; the plural might have been expected, to go with *bonnes nuis*.

808   *Verte* 'Green', here contrasted with black, indicates joy. Cf. QD, line 2369 and H, VII, 450.

823–6   Only *Oa* and *Pc* rhyme consistently, the first in *-oire*, the second in *-ore*. All the other texts have *ore* (*oire* in *Qd*) in line 823 and *encore* in line 826. Cf. QD 2768, where only *Dd* and *Ql* have *encoire*, and PA 31, where only *Qd* has *oire*.

830   *Vez* 'See', an imperative form.

839   'However long the night may be.'

843   'He eats when he is not hungry.' *Meng(e)ut* is well attested as a present indicative form (H, V, 124).

849–50   There is a want of sequence here as the Thin Knight tries to convey vividly the instructions given by the Lover to his messenger. Cf. QD 451.

858   'And that he is mad in not giving up at once.'

886   *L'enaigre* 'Irritates him.' The verb appears in various guises: *lenesgre NfNj, le naigre OaPh, len aigre Oj, lennaigre Qd*. (In *Pc* the line is omitted.) This is the

only example of *enaigrer* given by Godefroy (III, 81a), although *enaigrir* is well attested.

896   *Aspis* may be plural; it is more likely, however, that the nominative singular form has been used for the sake of the rhyme. Cf. line 684.

908   *Ne que si* 'Any more than if'. Cf. QD 1228 and 1340.

916–17 'If a man lets himself be attacked by Jealousy, she causes the loss of all honour in him.'

926   'And wishes to turn another's benefit into income for himself as a reserve.'

984   *Veir* 'To see'. Cf. QD 3015.

996   *Tout* 'Entirely, completely'.

1005   *Reseront* 'Will again be'.

1035   *Mucera* None of the texts has *muchera*, the spelling which might have been expected here at the rhyme: see QD 1906 and 3177.

1051   *Retourra* 'He will return'; see page 439.

1065   *Dechié*, given by *Nj Oj* and *Pc*, is to be interpreted as a form of *dechiet* 'decline, collapse'; see Rouy, *Alain Chartier: Le Livre de l'esperance*, 207.

        Chatel 'Asset, property'; *Nf* and *Qd* have the homonym *chastel* 'castle'. The play on words also involves *rabas* 'reduction' or 'destruction'; cf. BD 358.

1068–78 The infinitives depend on *fait* (line 1068).

1073   *Impossible* 'Powerless'; cf. FEW, IX, 239.

1076   In *Nj* the first three letters of *souvent* (see the variants) have been added by a second hand in a space left by the scribe; the letters are spaced out in order to fill the gap.

1077   '(Make him) pay heed to what is harmful to him, deaf to his advantage.'

1110   *Qu'* is modified both by *soustien* (line 1109) and by *maintien* (line 1107).

1113   *Peut* is here past historic. Cf. QD 1852 and 3254.

1125   *D'Amours* It is not clear whether or not the initial letter has been erased in *Qd*.

1138   Other versions of this proverb, No. 1966 in Morawski, are found in QD 1352 and QD 3079.

1176   *Truffois* 'Jest'. No other example of the word is given by Godefroy (VIII, 99b). *Truffer* 'to jest, mock' is well attested.

1187–90 The rhyme in *-istrent* is unusual. Elsewhere, for example at QD 2491–4, *-irent* is found; see pages 439–40.

1199   *Son port* 'What he wears'. *Port* means literally 'the act of wearing'.

1207   This important line is discussed on page 31.

1223   'As I think'; cf. G, X, 662c–663b.

LE LIVRE DES QUATRE DAMES

DECORATION

In *Dd*, the base text, lines which have a decorated initial are written in capitals, at least in part. Details of the initials are given below. The scribe of *Dd* has indicated a change of speaker by setting marks in the margin at lines 385, 467, 497, 527, 540, 1046, 1066, 1849 and 2483.

Introduction (lines 1–164). At the beginning of the poem there are miniatures in *Dc Dd* and *Df*, and space has been left for one in all the other texts except *Ql*. All the texts contain initials, except *Ph*, in which space has been left.

The divisions between the stanzas of the introduction are marked in all the texts, sometimes incorrectly as in *Pc*, sometimes with initials as in *Db* and *Dc*.[1]

Narrative (lines 165–384). Where the narrative begins there is a space of one line in *Dd*; there are initials in *Db Dc Oa* and *Pc*. Space is left for an initial at line 169 in *Ph*. *Oa* has an initial at line 201. In *Dc* a space of one line has been left before line 291.

The Poet and the First Lady (lines 385–1045). The different stages in the conversation between the poet and the First Lady are indicated by notes in the margin of *Ql*.[2] In *Pc* lines 391, 497 and 537 have initials; in *Ql* only the last two. Line 389 has an initial in *Dc* and *Oa*; the speaker is named in a rubric in *Dc* and room is left to do so in *Oa*. A gap of one line has been left in *Db* at the end of the First Lady's speech.

The Poet (lines 1046–96). In *Dc* a rubric and an initial at line 1046 mark the change of speaker. There are indications in the margin of *Ql* at lines 1046 and 1066 to show that the poet is speaking. Initials are found in *Pc* and *Ql* at line 1066.

The Second Lady (lines 1098–848). The beginning of her speech is marked with a miniature and an initial in *Dd* and *Df*; in *Dd* the first word of line 1098 is on fol. 20r with the miniature below, and the rest of the line (and the initial) is on fol. 20v. The speaker is named in a rubric in *Dc* and room is left to do so in *Oa*.[3] Both these texts have initials at line 1098 and in *Ph* there is space for one. There are initials in *Pc* and *Ql*, but in the previous line.

The Poet (lines 1849–2014). The change of speaker is indicated by a rubric in *Dc* and by a note in the margin of *Ql*. Both texts have an initial, as does *Db*.

The Third Lady (lines 2015–482). Miniatures in *Dd* and *Df* mark where the speech begins; there is room for a miniature in *Db* and *Ph*. All the texts have initials except *Ph*, in which space has been left. The speaker's name is given in a rubric in *Dc* and in the margin of *Ql*; space for a rubric is left in *Oa*. In *Dd* line 2015 is divided between ff. 36r and 36v; the second part of the line contains the initial and is copied under the miniature.

Line 2099 has an initial in *Db* and space has been left, apparently for a miniature.

The Poet (lines 2483–543). The change of speaker is indicated by a rubric and an initial in *Dc*, by an initial in *Db*. Space for a miniature is left in *Ph* before line 2527.

The Fourth Lady (lines 2544–3099). *Dd* and *Df* have miniatures at the beginning of her speech. All the texts except *Ph* and *Ql* contain initials at line 2544: in *Ph* space is left; *Ql* has space for an initial in the previous line. The speaker's name is given in a rubric in *Dc* and in the margin of *Ql*.

The Third Lady (lines 3100–24). All the texts except *Ph* mark the lady's first words with an initial: at line 3100 in *Dd Df Pc* and *Ql*; in the next line in *Db Dc* and *Oa*. The

[1] The first eleven stanzas have initials in *Db*, in *Dc* all twelve. In *Pc* and *Ql* the twelfth stanza has an initial. [2] At lines 385, 437, 497 and 540.

[3] In *Pc* a later hand has indicated the change of speaker at lines 1098, 2015 and 2544.

change of speaker is indicated by a rubric in *Dc*. At line 3101 there is room for a miniature in *Db*, and for an initial and a miniature in *Ph*.

The Poet and the First Lady (*lines 3125–99*). All the texts have an initial at line 3125 except *Dc* and *Ph*; there is room for an initial and a miniature in *Ph*.

The Second Lady (*lines 3200–75*). *Dd* and *Df* contain an initial at line 3200. *Db Oa Pc* and *Ql* have initials at line 3201, where space has been left for a miniature in *Db* and *Ph*.

The Poet (*lines 3276–343*). Line 3276 is marked by an initial in *Dd Df Oa Pc* and *Ql*, and in *Ph* space has been left; in *Db* the initial is in the following line. There are initials at line 3317 in all the texts except *Dc* and *Ph*; room has been left for an initial in *Ph* and for a miniature in *Db*.

The Poet and the Fourth Lady (*lines 3344–59*). *Dd Df* and *Pc* mark line 3344 with an initial; the initial is in the following line in *Db*.

The Poet (*lines 3360–464*). Line 3360 has an initial in *Dd Df* and *Pc*, and room for one is left in *Ph* and *Ql*; in *Db* line 3361 has the initial. There are initials in *Dd Df* and *Pc* at line 3452, and at line 3460 in *Dd* and *Df*.

The Poet's request (*lines 3465–531*). The opening line is marked by a miniature in *Dd* and *Df* and by initials in all the texts except *Db Dc* and *Ph*; in the last, space has been left.

4	The reference is to the First of May. Cf. Christine de Pisan, *Autres Ballades*, xxv.
11–12	'With the strange colours of which the earth had been bare for so long during winter.'
111	'But if I enjoyed this benefit.'
135	'In the hope for which I have failed', i.e. 'which I hoped to have and have failed to receive'.
163	*Atour* 'Head-dress'; the hats of the ladies are prominent in the miniatures in *Dd* and *Df*.
167–8	*Dont...Qui* Both clauses depend on *doeil* (line 166).
175	*Combien que* 'Because, (the more so) since'. See LaC, iv, 111.
177	'Who on that account has so much grief.'
181–2	The subject of *s'y tieigne* and *devieigne* is *cuer* (line 176).
186–200	These lines make up one sentence. *Ce m'est assez bien* introduces three clauses, each beginning with *que* (lines 186, 188 and 190). At the end of the third clause, the poet gives his reasons (lines 192–8) and reaches a conclusion (lines 199–200).
188–9	'And that I love her only in thought, within myself.'
192–4	'Since I can do nothing else and since I dare not so much as think that...'
221	*Il ne demourroit guiere...Que* 'It would not be long before'.
238	*Eüsse* is subjunctive by attraction. Cf. lines 3310 and 3519.
250	'Even if I were to die as a result.'
255	*Amer* 'Bitterness' is frequently rhymed with *amer* 'to love' in courtly poetry. Cf. RB xv: 4; see TL, i, 346.
259	*Quant* 'If'. Cf. lines 485 and 624.

264–6   *A quoy* (line 266) probably refers to *grace* (line 263), in which case lines 264–5 must be taken together and *entreprendre* means 'to overcome, attack'. Alternatively, the clause in line 266 could depend on *entreprendre* and mean '(to undertake) even that which I dare not aspire to', *Et* being emphatic.

268   'My lady will know nothing of this.'

290   *Et deüst il jouÿr* 'Even if he had reason to rejoice'.

295   'And the thought would never occur to me.' Cf. LaC, III, 369 (*cheut au coeur*).

297   *Se* 'Thus; indeed'; La Curne (IX, 360) cites examples from Froissart. Cf. line 1067 (*si*).

326   'Which I have received for two years past.'

327   'Which is plain to see.' Cf. Mod. Fr. *Cela se voit au doigt et à l'œil.*

330–1   *Fers et fustz* '(Iron) tips and (wooden) handles'. The rhyme demands a plural form, even if the dart is singular.

338   'And she was concerned with what was best for her.' For *le meillieur* in the sense of 'best course', see G, V, 216c–218a and H, V, 194–5.

346   *Lay* 'I leave', from *laier*.

359–60   'And they were not interested in picking violets.'

370   *Le* i.e. *encontre* (line 369).

371   *Encontre* 'Chance, adventure'.

414   'That I do not know why it does not break them.' Cf. DF 29 (*que*).

415–16   'Every one of them is close to melting and close to breaking.' Cf. line 686.

426   *Ennuit* is probably part of *ennuire* 'to harm, hurt', of which only one example is given by Godefroy (III, 209b). The phrase 'Il m'ennuy de voz sacrifices' occurs in the *Livre de l'Esperance* (*ed.* Rouy, 175, lines 111–12); *ennuy* is there thought to be part of *ennuyer*, though *ennuire* is also a possibility.

434   *A mon gré revenoit* probably 'pleased me' (cf. H, IV, 366), though the idea of 'revenue' or 'return' may also be implied.

451   There is a want of sequence here as Chartier begins to use indirect speech. Cf. DF 849–50, and the note to line 1894.

485   *Quant* 'If'. Cf. line 259.

489   *Targe* 'Shield, protection'.

507   'That she should be good enough to tell me' (cf. H, I, 571).

509   *Il la couvient* The use of the accusative in such constructions is well attested; see TL, II, 981.

520   'If one confides it.' Cf. Mod. Fr. *s'ouvrir de qch. à qn.*

523   *Et que* 'And if'.

535   'We can endure it better together.' For similar examples of *pouoir* see TL, VII, 1410–11.

565–7   The texts vary greatly; different versions are available for certain lines and different orders are possible. *Dc Pc* and *Ql* agree, but every other text contains a version peculiar to itself.

     The lady, considering the two hearts now separately, now as an entity, uses first the plural, then the singular: 'And (have) separated one far from the other when it was not through you that they came together, that which was a single party.'

571   See the note to PL 91.

576–7   'You have willed this rather than done it.' See LaC, x, 189, 'Volonté est reputée pour le fait'. Cf. PA 40.

582–4   'Why have you not killed me, who am not the stronger, as soon as my sweet mate?'

586   *Que* 'Why?'

589, 590   *Son…sa* i.e. of the dart.

610   'And you utterly consume me with care.' Cf. line 593.

624   *Quant* 'If'. Cf. line 259.

632   *Pourquoy* 'Wherefore, for which reason'.

636   'However it may be.'

643   *Quelconques* The form with final *s* is found as late as the sixteenth century; see H, vi, 276. Cf. EX 59.

659   *Et que…defface* 'And that He may loose'.

673   'That in everything he behaved well towards me.'

686   See the note to lines 415–16.

697   *L'assëoit* 'Disposed it, ordered it'.

698   'For he hated every sort of dishonour.'

701   'He did not long refrain from coming.'

705–9   The stanzas of five lines are discussed in the introduction to the poem.

732–40   The construction is complicated. 'And she (Fortune) allows many a man to have, in abundance and entirely at his pleasure, whatever he likes; and Fortune is not at all displeased and he does not know what unhappiness is, he who has not deserved to be served with the blessings which Love distributes, for his heart is not in subjection but free from it.'

754   'That on some occasion, which falls very appropriately.'

760   'In love which does not pass to a third party.'

773–6   'For Love, to reward good lovers, wishes to ordain that one lady can give as great a benefit as a hundred ladies can, and can give (have) benefits in abundance.' *Foisonner* can be transitive or intransitive (G, iv, 46c–47a; TL, iii, 1993–4).

789–92   For similar rhymes see lines 1929–32; cf. H, iii, 183.

793–5   'And if they had not enjoyed it, as though joyful they would boast that, yes, they had.'

812   *Nuz piez et en lange* A classic description of the dress of a pilgrim or penitent (see G, iv, 714a–c). Cf. lines 367–8 and 1259.

828   *Reposé* can be taken literally, the coward being 'rested' as opposed to the man of valour who is exhausted by his labours. Alternatively, it may mean 'hidden, in hiding' and be contrasted with *exposé* in the preceding line (see G, x, 549c, who cites the same example as LaC, ix, 169; the example dates from 1416).

831   *Baillant* In *Df* the first letter could be either *b* or *v*.

833   *Assez affaire* 'A great deal of trouble'.

835   *Soy deffaire* 'To destroy oneself in a moral sense', i.e. 'to bring shame upon oneself' (see TL, II, 1580).

836   *N'eüssent peu.* An alternative is *n'eussent peü.*

868   *Amonnestoit* 'Urged; told'. The verb conveys both meanings and governs two clauses, the verbs of which are respectively subjunctive and indicative.

870   *Racointe* A noun from *racointier*, 'to get to know again *or* well'. La Curne (IX, 10) and Godefroy (VI, 538b) give only this example and suggest the meanings 'rapprochement charnel' and 'commerce amoureux' respectively; they are more explicit than is the lady.

872   *Estoit* (line 871) is to be understood.

879–80   The scribe of *Dd* has shown how these lines are to be punctuated. The lady is blinded with tears and grief. Cf. lines 2535–7.

        En amouree 'As one in love' (G, I, 278c–279a); *s'amourer* also occurs in line 1346. Only *Oa* has *enamouree.*

891   *Que* probably means 'In such a way that, so that'; it would also be possible to take it as a nominative form of the relative pronoun.

897–900   'For in droves, the cries and summonses of the good knights notwithstanding, you covered the tops of your helmets.' They did so, presumably, to conceal their crests or some other sort of insignia.

        Cruppeaulx has been taken as a diminutive of *cruppe* or *croppe*, 'rounded top' (LaC, IV, 406); *coppeaulx*, the alternative reading, has a similar sense (G, IX, 192c).

908   *Cens* is ambiguous. The basic sense is 'feudal dues'; its homonym 'hundreds' provokes the wry addition *et milles.*

933   *Quel rousee* probably 'What a soft lot they are!' Cf. Mod. Fr. *tendre comme* (la) *rosée.*

985–6   'I am greatly grieved, harsh Death, by the fact that you do not sooner sting...' *Mors* has been taken to be part of *mordre*, but there may also be some play on *mourir*; see TL, VI, 254, for similar examples.

993–6   'In fact it cannot be; that is why my life is wearisome to me without his life, for the more favoured it was, the more fitting it would be.' For other examples of (*Il*) *est noiant*, see G, V, 512b and *Roman de la Rose*, lines 2761 and 6187.

1011   In *Ql* there is a small suprascript addition, difficult to read, between *qui* and *son amourer.*

1015   'Love has so rewarded me that...'

1019   'For they must not see them any more.'

1043   *L'aggreve* In *Oa* and *Ql* the reading is *la griefve.*

1047   *Puis* 'Well', here used figuratively.

1075–7   'For grief's nature is such that it is reduced if a person reveals it where it is fitting to do so.'

1080–1   'The more it is shared, the shorter a sad thought will be.'

1092–5   'And I was suggesting to the three others likewise that they should comfort her in such a way that...'

1128–30   'And he came to that age after ten years had gone by when...'

1151–2   *Mal baillir* Although Godefroy (I, 557c) cites this example separately, suggesting 'être tourmenté, agité', the usual sense, 'maltraiter, malmener', fits just as well. We can translate: 'Grief and Anger who have made him tremble often and have caused him to be ill-treated.'

1178   *Erse* 'A harrow' hence 'a type of portcullis'. The latter, taken figuratively, is the more likely meaning. La Curne (VII, 38–9) lists both meanings and adds a third, 'peine, fatigue', quoting this line as his sole example; FEW (IV, 431) suggests 'action fâcheuse' for a single example, presumably this one, from Alain Chartier.

1196–200   The verbs in line 1200 govern the sequence of nouns in the preceding lines. The past participles agree with the majority of the nouns.

1208   *N'a y* i.e. *N'a il*; cf. lines 2566 and 2727.

1211   *Cuer* 'Desire'. Cf. BD 710 and BN 149.

1217–19   There is a want of sequence here. Line 1219 must be taken as an alternative to lines 1217–18. A possible rendering is 'Without being seen to blame, hurt or deceive others but to receive them kindly'.

1220   *Nully* 'Anyone'. Cf. line 2561.

1223   *Sur* 'Towards, against', here used to emphasise Fortune's hostile intentions. Cf. RB V: 10.

1228   'Without hurting anyone, any more than he would his own head.' Cf. line 1340.

1240   *Cent paires* lit. 'One hundred pairs'; on *cent* see the note to DF 164. At lines 2042–3, *cent paire* is found with a singular verb. Both forms were found at this period (see TL, VII, 49–53), as they still are in spoken English.

1243   *Abrevé* probably 'Vexed, tormented'. See TL, I, 65 (*abriver*) and the note to BD 63.

1256   'And I pray God that He may bring him back to me.' The old subjunctive form is used here in a time-honoured phrase. For other examples, see TL, VIII, 246–8.

1272   *En amours coulez* 'Fallen in love'. Cf. *coler en une heresie* (G, IX, 216b).

1302   'Consumed as regards each joy.'

1304   *A lee* are written thus in *Dd*, but are run together in the other texts.

1340   'Any more than are mills which mill in all winds.' Cf. line 1228.

1352   See the note to DF 1138.

1356   *Ne mal* Part of the verb *estre* must be understood.

1363–4   'But my love never had recourse to him (the God of Love) to make a complaint; neither did I.' Cf. G, VI, 728c–729b.

1369   *Que* A verb, e.g. 'I declare', must be understood. Huguet (VI, 273–4) cites similar examples which also follow an affirmation or oath. Cf. line 1678 and RM 241.

1377–9   'Unless God takes action and puts an end to the evil which I find difficult to conceal, provided that I have him back.' *Cesser* is transitive; see TL, II, 142.

1385   *Par abbregié* 'Quickly' is the most likely meaning; see LaC, I, 26–7 (*abregier*) and G, V, 733a–c (*par*). Cf. line 1805.

1386   *Ainsi que* 'In such a way that'.

1399   *Mal fait* is written as two words in all the texts consulted. *Fait* can be taken either as noun or verb: in the first case it is governed by *semble* (line 1397); in the second, the subject of *fait* (as of *m'emble*) is *Fortune* and *il me semble* is in parenthesis.

1416   'He did not cease thinking them (amorous thoughts) on account of them (his pains).'

1419   *L'autre* 'The other (fever).'

1462, 1464 *Wide* is spelt so in *Dd Ph* and *Ql*; the other texts all have *vuyde* (*vuide*).

1464   In *Oa* the third word is indecipherable; the leaf has been damaged.

1480   *Joieux semblant* is governed by *J'ay fait* (line 1478).

1489   *Eschequier* It is not known what type of musical instrument is meant. Godefroy (III, 385b) and La Curne (V, 478) cite examples from Machaut and Deschamps respectively. In his edition of Deschamps, G. Raynaud suggests 'instrument de musique, tambourin qu'on râclait avec l'ongle' (VIII, 34 and 36), but the context is far from clear.

1499–500 'I should not have been wearied by dancing, nor tired, dejected or exhausted.'

1505   The sense is not clear. Possible renderings are 'Everything was involved in it, everything contributed to it'.

1526   *Du long et des lez* gives a leonine rhyme and is the correct reading. Chartier has re-cast *du long et du lé*, the more usual form of the expression.

1527   *Reslez* 'Watered'. Godefroy (VII, 99a) suggests 'flooded' for this line and cites only one other example of the verb, with the meaning 'to drizzle'.

1534–5 *Acomte* 'Account' or 'reason, motive' (TL, I, 102); while *acointe* and *acomte* are easily confused, only *Pc* clearly has *acointe* (*Dc* has *acointer*); no text has *aconte*. *Enchiere* 'Increase in price' or, less likely, 'delay' (H, III, 398–9).

       There is a play on two meanings of *chiere*. The primary sense is 'dear, beloved'; the secondary sense 'dear, expensive' suggests, or is suggested by, the financial terms in line 1535.

1554   *Ce que* 'The fact that'. Cf. RB xv: 4.

1567   *Empirement* 'Deterioration' is personified.

1575   *D'une envaÿe* lit. 'With one attack', that is 'at one fell swoop'.

1582   *Rente* 'Rent, regular payment'.

1589   *Et que* 'And in such a way that, And so that'.

1606   · *Se tient* 'Remains *or* Holds together'.

1610   *Delés* has a legal sense. It is not clear whether it means 'acts of renunciation' (G, II, 480a) or 'bequests' (H, II, 766–7: *delaisser*); given the context, the latter is the more likely.

1626–7 'That one's actions have much greater consequences than one thinks beforehand.'

1635   *Et servie m'assers* 'And, though I am one who is served, I subject myself'.

1637   *Mez* All the texts, except *Dc Dd* and *Ph*, have *mais*.

1656   *Accroirre* 'To lend' is contrasted with *donner*.

1657   *Jeuns* 'Hungry'.

1674   *Car* 'Because'.

1675   *En un, que* 'In one of such a kind that'.

1678   See note to line 1369.

1697   *D'aguet* probably 'on watch', though *en aguet* is the usual expression. Huguet
        (I, 122–3) and La Curne (I, 225–7) both suggest 'prudently, cautiously' for
        d'aguet, a sense which scarcely fits here.
          En tant 'Thus, in that way'. Cf. line 3170.

1709–16 These lines are complicated and can be read in several ways. *Penser* (line 1710)
        has been taken to be the subject of *fait* (line 1710) and of *puet* (line 1712); line
        1716 supports this interpretation. The punctuation of lines 1711–12 is that
        given in *Dd*.

1720   *Penser* (line 1716) is the subject of the two verbs.

1735   *Sans l'aviser* 'Without my noticing him'.

1742   *Rendue* 'Devoted servant' rather than 'nun', the usual sense (TL, VIII, 803).

1746   'That my fortunes are in decline.' Cf. *Roman de la Rose*, line 8324.

1755–70 These lines make up one conditional sentence. The division is marked at line
        1762 by the repetition of *Au moins*, previously used in line 1756.

1764   *De demain en demain* 'For one tomorrow after another'. Cf. *de jour en jour*,
        on which the phrase has been modelled. Only one other example of the phrase
        has been found, in TL, II, 1350, with the sense 'transiently'.

1767   *M'envoysasse*, given only by *Df*, has been adopted because it makes better sense
        and provides a better rhyme than the alternative.

1776   'What I can least procure.' See H, IV, 111–12.

1781   'And thereby, and for that reason.'

1782   'Since the time when his misfortunes were renewed'. Cf. CO 78.

1792   *Remanant* At line 2901, where it is also used as rhyme-word, and elsewhere,
        the form is *remenant*.

1804   *Tel* Foulet (§ 495) gives similar examples of the omission of the relative pronoun.
        The example in line 2727 is probably part of a standard phrase.

1805   *Par vray* 'Truly'. Cf. line 1385.

1815   *En rabatant* recalls *En combatant* (line 1813). The lady has suffered as a result of
        the fighting; the English ladies may also suffer if their loved ones are struck
        down and the French begin to gain the upper hand.

1820   *Tant pour tant* 'Proportionately, to an equivalent extent'.

1822–3 'I can only have recourse to them, and may that be of greater help to me.'

1840   *Quë Espoir faut.* This reading, which is given by *Oa* and *Pc* and may underlie
        those of *Db* and *Dd*, has been accepted after some hesitation. In other lines where
        que does double duty (see lines 2206 and 3078), the sense is 'than that'; here it
        must mean 'than when' or 'than if'.

1849–52 The same four rhymes are found in DF 1111–14. *Peut* (line 1852) is past historic.
        In *Oa Pc* and *Ql* the stanza rhymes in *-eust*.

1876–7 'And by her nose I laid all of it, very close indeed.' For *joignant* see G, IV, 648b.

1884–93 The first part of the sentence is complicated by asides and afterthoughts. 'Then
        I told them all, and I recollected, just as the words came to me on account of the
        instance which then occurred of the wild-rose by which she recovered her
        senses, that it is right that in love there should be joy and burning pain.'

1894	The poet moves from indirect to direct speech. Cf. note to line 451.
1896–7	'By which they prevent us from picking them without hurt.'
1907	'Tightly hived with the sweet honey.' Although *estroit* could be taken as an adjective governing *miel*, the rhythm of the line is improved if it is understood as an adverb. See TL, III, 1483–6.
1937–8	'And in short: Pleasure is sweet, but timorously so.'
1964	*Lesse* 'Leash'. Cf. PA 193.
1968	*Dommaine* Only *Dd* has this spelling; the others have *demaine*.
1984	'And it is not in his power to speak properly.' See TL, III, 1457; cf. RM 144–5.
2007	*Në arrest* 'Nor do I stop'.
2029	'But don't be rash and disparage someone else's.' For *se jouer a* see L, III, 197; cf. RM 333. *Autry* has been taken as *autry* (*mal*).
2043	See the note to line 1240.
2049	*Tenant* 'Wearying'; cf. line 1791. *Ten(n)er* makes better sense than *tenir*.
2053	*Aucun* is contrasted with *tous*.
2064–5	*Deserte*, used as rhyme-word in either line, means 'forsaken' and 'ravaged' respectively.
2067	'Not to mention Despair who cannot be trusted.'
2073	*Aprés* Lines 2077 and 2101 *et seq.* show that *aprés* is intended and not *apres* (*âpres*).
2084–5	'For she never had any experience of changing her affections nor did the idea appeal to her.' *Change* implies 'change of love, transfer of affections' (H, II, 185).
2099	*Hors d'estat* 'Out of sorts'. It is tempting to replace *estat* with *esbat*, which is given by five texts and would provide a richer rhyme. In describing the Second Lady as *hors d'esbat*, the Third Lady would be echoing *triste* and playing on the more usual expression. *Estat* has been retained, however, since it is found in *Db Dc* and *Dd*; as the preceding stanza shows, Chartier does not always use rich rhyme.
2114	Some of the stages in the Third Lady's speech are marked by signs in the margin of *Dd*, here and at lines 2138, 2154 and 2166. The signs are of the type used elsewhere to indicate a change of speaker; see pages 446–7.
2137	*La presse* is given by *Dd* and *Oa*; *Db Dc* and *Df* have *laspresse*, *Ph* and *Ql lapresse*, while *lapresse* in *Pc* can be read as one or two words. *Presse* is well attested with the sense of 'sorrow, distress' (TL, VII, 1810).
2191	*Griesche* 'Harsh, terrible'; the meaning is clear from the context. It is less clear whether the word is associated with *gries* 'Greek' or a dialect form of *gris* (LaC, VI, 427). Cf. Middle English *grise* (OED, IV, 432).
2195	'Beset by enough ills to cause my death.'
2205–7	'If nothing more was explained to him than that Grief is breaking the heart...' For a similar use of *que*, see line 3078.
2233	*Elles* i.e. *mort* and *prison* (line 2224).
2237	*Craintiveté* 'Fear'. No other example of the word has been found.
2245	*S'entrematent* 'Check-mate, defeat one another'. Only this example is listed in LaC, V, 428, and G, III, 290a.

2255 *En petit nombre* 'In small quantity'.

2260 See the note to DF 748.

2279 *Cours* 'Courses, passages at arms' recalling *tournoiz* (line 2276).

2284–6 'I hold from him only one heart; and it also, by God, is set, and I shall set it, in only one place.'

2293 Although *emploiee* rhymes satisfactorily, Chartier may well have intended a leonine rhyme, as is suggested by *empliee*, the spelling in *Pc* and *Ql*. Cf. G, IX, 444a, and H, III, 375–6.

2326 *Hardie* is part of *hardier* 'to embolden' or 'to attack, ambush' (G, IV, 420a–c); it is used here in both senses.

2328 *Recoeuvre* means both 'covers again' and 'makes good'.

2331–2 'And if anyone has pictured Love's qualities in which reflection plays small part.'

2349 'He forges him in such a fashion or of such a size.'

2352 Cf. Isaiah, II: 4.

2355–8 The rhyme, in *-oule* in *Dd* and *Df*, is in *-o(s)le* in the other texts.

2369 See the note to DF 808.

2380 *Droit charier* 'To be circumspect, proceed with care' (TL, II, 287).

2383 *Et de maniere* 'And in a fitting manner'.

2385 *Qui* here does double duty, being equivalent to *que qui*. Cf. the note to lines 2205–7.

2400 *La dance basse* 'A slow and rather stately dance' (H, I, 494). The Third Lady's description (lines 2401–2) is not very specific.

2406 *En dragiee* 'Combined, blended; as a dragee (?)'. *Dragiee* can mean a mixture, often of grains (LaC, V, 252; G, IX, 413c–414a), or a dragee or sweetmeat (*ibid.*). The meaning 'sugar-coated pill' seems to be a modern one.

   Db Oa Ph and *Ql* have *endragee* which is listed by La Curne (V, 360) and Godefroy (III, 134b) with the meanings 'mingled' and 'excessive' respectively; this line is the only example quoted.

2409–14 Cf. Morawski 745 and 1364.

2411 'Not without smoke' (G, II, 460b). No other example has been found of *deffumé* in this sense.

2423 'Travelling the same road.' *Pareil* is probably an adjective agreeing with a cognate accusative understood. Only one (modern) example has been found of *pareil* used as an adverb (R, V, 118).

2426 *Loiens* In BD 78, where it is again the rhyme-word, the spelling is *liens*. Here *Ph* has *liens* and *Db Oa Pc* and *Ql* give *leans*.

2429 *Trestours* 'Detours, delays' (G, VIII, 63a–b).

2431–4 'A trembling heart, in which sorrows are gathering, shares some of them out among behaviour, actions and appearance or else these sorrows go and appropriate them all.'

2438 A verb must be understood, as is also the case in the version of the proverb in Morawski (No. 2249). A third version was used by Christine de Pisan as the refrain of *Autres Ballades*, XXXVIII: 'Selon seigneur voit on maignée duite'.

2440	*Desuivent* 'Pursue'. Only two other examples of the verb have been found (LaC, v, 151; TL, II, 1620).
2469	*Espoire* 'I hope'. This form of the present tense is well attested (H, III, 671).
2480	*Fouÿe* 'Dug, hollowed', here used figuratively. Cf. Mod. Fr. *creuser* (R, I, 1030).
2484	*Fait* here 'Words, speech'.
2487–9	Although the style is abrupt, almost telegraphic, the meaning is clear.
2498	'That the mouth talks on at such length about it.'
2507	There is a mark in the margin of *Dd* to indicate that a new development is beginning. See the note to line 2114.
2512	*Se lasche* is a variant of *se lasse*. *Se lascher* is attested, though rarely (G, x, 65c–66a), with the meaning 'to relax, weaken'.
2523–4	*N'entendoye* is found only in *Db*. *Ne pensoye*, the reading in the other texts, gives a poorer rhyme and brings two parts of *penser* into proximity.
2535–8	In *Dd* the rhyme is in *-ëoit* throughout, in *Ph* in *-oyoit*. The other texts have now one rhyme, now the other.
2541–3	'And her grief is double because she doubles it in the telling of her shame, by saying to them...'
2558–60	'That through me her grief is greater or through him whom I thought better than he was.'
2561	*Nulluy* 'Anyone'. Cf. line 1220.
2566	'And people say: "Why was he there?"' Cf. line 1208.
2587	*Courouchié* is used again as rhyme-word in line 2589. The respective meanings are 'angered' and 'grieved'.
2644	*Couvoie*, used as rhyme-word here and in line 2647, means first 'accompanies', secondly 'leads, directs'.
2645–8	'I did not realise your treachery or that you would set out except when the heart leads you to do so at long intervals.' *Lengage* (line 2640) is still personified; the image of the journey is developed in lines 2649–52. When she talks of long intervals, the lady may be recalling that the lover was traditionally tongue-tied or alluding to the fact that lovers often met infrequently for fear of the *mesdisans*.
2665	'Many make a present in words.'
2680	*Eslacie* 'Spread (?)' is well attested, being given by *Db Dd* and *Df* (the reading is not *eslatie*, which would give a better rhyme). It may be part of *eslasier* 'to spread, widen' (G, III, 476a; TL, III, 1082).
2682	*Par la moitie* 'In two'. Examples of this pronunciation are given in TL, VI, 168.
2685	'Keeping company with them and seeing them.'
2719–20	'Whereby anyone and everyone hears (*or* knows) all about the affair.' For (*il*) *y a qui* see H, I, 438.
2726	*Vent* probably 'Reputation'. Cf. Cl. Lat. *ventus*.
2727	*Telz y a y* i.e. *Telz* (*qu'*)*il y a* probably 'Such as these', though for *telz y a* Godefroy (VII, 662a) suggests 'quelques-uns'. For similar examples of *y* see lines 1208 and 2566; see also line 1804 (*tel*).
2768	See the note to DF 823–6.
2776	All the texts, except *Dd*, have *nenny*.

457

2777   *Tout onny* 'Equally'. *Onny* is the spelling in *Dd Df* and *Pc*; the other texts have *uny*.

2778–9   *Pour ce* and *que* are to be taken together.

2783   Bertran du Guesclin (*c.* 1320–80), Constable of France (1370–80).

2792   *Tiré* The sense is not clear; 'attracted' or 'drawn' are possibilities. 'Acted as a tyrant' should also be considered, although no such example is attested; *regné* occurs in the preceding line; *tirant* 'tyrant' is the normal spelling at this time (see Christine de Pisan, *Autres Ballades*, XLIX, 24).

2801   *Tantare* La Curne (X, 28) and Godefroy (VII, 681c) list only this example. The former suggests 'fanfare'; the latter is at a loss. Only one example, a different one, is listed by Huguet (VII, 183) who considers it an onomatopoetic formation. *Aler a la tantare* probably means 'to make merry, go on a spree'. Cf. Engl. *tantara* 'the sound of a flourish on a trumpet' (OED, XI, 80); the first three examples, all from the sixteenth century, link it with joy or jollification.

2809   *Sautereles* 'A type of dance' (G, VII, 331b). It may also have had at this time the sense of 'bird-trap' which it has in Modern French.

2818   *Ont* is to be understood.

2823   'And little can be expected from actions like those.'

2826   *Lis* 'I read'.

2847   *Hers* 'Heirs'.

2848–9   'And they had such ill fortune that they ended their lives there.' For similar examples of *rencontrer*, see H, VI, 490–1.

2862   *Cachier* 'To pursue'.

2876–7   Cf. St John, XX: 25.

2876–9   In *Df Oa Pc Ph* and *Ql* the rhyme is in *-oyon*.

2882–3   'That if one's clothes are ragged, even if one is good, nonetheless one appears to stink.'

2902   'They are lovers of the current variety.'

2913   *Guignoient* The imperfect indicative is used for vividness. See also the note to RB XXII: 14.

2920   'For anyone who had been censured.'

2923   *Que tant* 'How greatly (?)'.

2933–4   *En . . . la* i.e. *amour* (lines 2926 and 2943).

2945   *Present* 'At present'.

2954–5   'The pleasing troubles brought by love strengthen hearts and improve them.'

2969   *Cache* 'Pursuit'.

2980–1   'Would my heart not have declared that it would love him always?'

2989   *Nouvelle* 'News'.

2990   *En bien* 'To his credit'.

2997   *Le mal* i.e. *d'amours*.

3005   *Fuÿt* 'He fled'.

3015   *Veÿr* is a spelling peculiar to *Dd*, the other texts having *veoir*. Cf. DF 984.

3016–17   'So I say fie upon my heart and trust it no more.'

3019   *Fy* 'I did'.

3020–1 'That I loved him first, two years ago in May', i.e. 'that he was the first person that I ever loved'.

3026–30 The Fourth Lady is saying that if ever she can withdraw her heart from Love, she will never again allow her heart to relapse.

3033 *Qu'il...amie* Since the lady is talking in general terms, *amie*, given only by *Dd*, makes better sense than *amy*, which is found in all the other texts; no text has *Qu'el*.

3038 'For it to go so far astray.'

3040 'I make great efforts to.'

3047 *Maistrise* 'An action which requires skill' (G, v, 102c).

3049 *Meurt* is apparently indicative, although a subjunctive would be more usual.

3064, 3066 *Ouvrant* is in either case part of *ouvrer* 'to act, work'. The difference in function makes it possible to use them both as rhyme-words in the same stanza. Cf. note to DF 424.

3068–70 'The shameful recovery of him is deliverance from him; recovering him is separation from him.'

3078 See the note to lines 2205–7.

3079 See the note to DF 1138.

3090 *Loz* 'Share'.

3109 *Anvel* Probably a series of requiem masses said daily for a year (DuC, I, 260; R, I, 163).

3139 'That death does not cause much greater grief (than it).'

3145 *A droiz* 'Rightly'. The usual form of the expression, *a droit*, has been modified to fit the rhyme. Cf. note to line 1526.

3158 The punctuation is that given in *Dd*.

3170 *En tant que* 'In such a way that'. Cf. line 1697.

3172 See the note to DF 401.

3175 The reference is to a standard form of punishment, in the course of which the miscreant was exposed to view and sermonised; see G, III, 378a.

3180 *Crerre* is found in *Dd* and *Df*; the other texts have *croire* or *croyrre* (*PcQl*).

3198 *Refuz de gent* 'Outcasts' (FEW, x, 199).

3216 *Voit* must be taken as part of the present subjunctive of *aller*. Elsewhere (lines 1674 and 2948) *voise* is found, but examples of *voist* occur in contemporary authors; see Raynaud, *Les Cent Ballades*, XI, 16.

3242 *Plas*, given only by *Dd*, has been preferred to *plus*, which is found in the other texts but does not make very good sense. *Plat* is often derisive in Old and Modern French. The phrase *plat pays* in the sense of 'countryside' or perhaps better 'backwoods' is well attested (G, X, 353a–c; H, v, 692; FEW, IX, 46), and line 3242 would probably have suggested that phrase to a contemporary reader. We can translate 'Or bumpkinly justiciars'.

3252–5 In *Oa* and *Ph* the rhyme is in -*eust*.

3263 *N'a eu* The reading of *Db Dd Pc* and *Ql* has been retained, although the alternative provides a richer rhyme.

3264–9   Entirely different versions are available for line 3269, and both make good sense. That of *Db* and *Dd*, apparently less attractive because it involves a verbless sentence, has been accepted. The Second Lady's speech has become increasingly abrupt and it is appropriate for her now to begin a list in the way she does. The version of *Db* and *Dd* also provides a richer rhyme.

3282   *Amenrir son cuer* Cf. *grossir le coeur* 'to give heart, courage' (H, IV, 393).

3298   *Puis dix ans* 'For the last ten years', a reference to the strife which had first begun in the summer of 1405. See above, pages 35-6.

3306–7   The subjunctive mood following *monstrer* is unusual.

3310   *Eüssent* is subjunctive by attraction. Cf. lines 238 and 3519.

3320   *Fist* The subject of the verb is the clause which follows.

3320–3   In the other texts the rhyme is in *-fist* throughout.

3341–3   *Sa...son...lui* refer to the lady's lover.

3403–35   These lines have been taken as a soliloquy. The end of the monologue is more clearly defined than the beginning.

3412–15   'It would not matter to me, provided that she knew it: that would avail me much, even if her reaction was neither favourable to me nor unfavourable; and she would not love me unless she wished to.' For another phrase combining *donner* and *tollir*, see BD 44.

3452   *Pourtant* 'For that reason' (G, VI, 313b).

3470–1   In the margin of *Dd* there is the following inscription in a near contemporary hand 'Nota pour madame de vandome'.

3470–3   *Sa...vous* The address once over, the lady is referred to in the second person. Cf. lines 3519–21.

3515   *Son* i.e. of the poet, as in line 3518. It is much less likely that *son* refers to the book: see lines 3479–80.

3519   See the note to line 3310.

3519–21   *Lui...m'a* The poet, having talked of himself as a messenger and thus in the third person, changes to the first. Cf. lines 3470–3.

LE DEBAT DE REVEILLE MATIN

The *Debat de Reveille Matin* and the *Belle Dame sans Mercy* were translated into Italian by Carlo del Nero at Montpellier in 1471. See W. Söderhjelm, 'La dama senza mercede', *Revue des langues romanes*, 4ᵉ série, V (XXXV), 1891, 95–127.

14   'And called to him to make him speak.' For *mectre a raison* see DuC, VII, 24.

37   *Non pourtant* 'However, nevertheless'.

39   Morawski includes a similar proverb: 'Amy pour aultre veille' (No. 81).

41   Headings are found in only five texts: *Nc Pp Qe Qr* and the separate early edition. The lover is called *l'Amoureux* in line 33, and four of the texts use that heading; in *Pp* he is called *l'Amant*. The name of the sleeper is not given in the poem. In *Pp*, he is *le Compaignon*; in *Nc*, *le Dormant*; in *Qe Qr* and the edition, *le Dormeur*. The last has been adopted.

74   'Or does it really affect you like this?'

77	*Quel mouche vous point?* 'What is the matter with you?'
79	'After all, things will not become worse.'
83	*Tout y va* 'Everything is at stake, everything is involved'.
99	*Passer ce pas* 'Pass through this pass', i.e. 'overcome this difficulty'. See the note to PL 91.
104	'My heart will be easier as a result.'
109–10	'. . . that I may do my duty by you in hearing . . .'
127–8	'He who extricates himself does not fail, nor will you, if you conduct yourself well.' Line 127 contains another of the wise saws of which the *Dormeur* is so fond; cf. lines 48, 153–6 and 334–5.
144–5	'It is not in your power to make claims.' 'It is not in my power nor is it fitting for me.' Cf. QD 1984.
154	Cf. Morawski 1841.
155	*Ffin* The spelling at lines 192 and 266 is *fin*.
185–8	The syntax is obscure, particularly the relation of the clause *Qu'il ne faille* to the previous two lines; the meaning is clear, however. Here and elsewhere, the *Dormeur* uses a markedly conversational style; cf. lines 219–24.
196	'Neither acceptance nor refusal.'
209–11	The infinitives and adjectives all depend on (*Elle*) *m'a veu* (line 212).
219, 224	*Croiez* (line 224) recalls *Ne croiez* (line 219); the *Dormeur* has at the same time modified the construction. Chartier uses anacoluthon in this way to convey the style and pace of conversation. See also the notes to lines 185–8 and to EX 71.
228	'It is of no concern at all to her.' Cf. *Roman de la Rose*, line 3182.
231	*Messire Ode*, Oton de Granson (*c.* 1345–97); *Machaut*, Guillaume de Machaut (*c.* 1300–77). Both poets aspired to the love of high-born ladies: Granson sang of his love for Isabelle 'la non pareille de France'; in the case of Machaut, the Lover may be thinking of any one of a number of poems, for example the *Voir Dit* or the *Remede de Fortune*, which recount an affair such as he describes.
237	'Have you assessed this course of action?'
240	Literally 'to remain in this skin', that is 'to remain in this present condition or frame of mind'. Godefroy (x, 307c–308a) cites similar examples.
241	See the note to QD 1369.
256	Cf. *Roman de la Rose*, line 2584.
260	Both nouns expand on *mieux* (line 259).
264	'And she must be judge of the suit and a party to it'; the phrase is still current in Modern French.
279	*Seroit* (a) could be from *estre* or *seoir*, and would thus mean 'belong' or 'be fitting'; the latter fits the context better.
281–2	'Since you have gone so far, do you know what will be the result?'
301–4	The *Dormeur* is contrasting the lady who accepts a suitor readily and may deceive him (lines 301–2), with the lady who refuses at first but may relent later (lines 303–4).
305	*De long temps a* 'For a long time now'. Cf. the variant to RB xxv: 11.

316   *Hardi* is almost certainly an adjective and part of the verb *estre* must be understood; cf. DF 583–5 and QD 1356. It is less likely that *hardi* is part of *hardir* 'to be, make bold'; in either case the meaning would be the same.

        Sur l'ueil 'At the risk of losing his eye'; for similar examples of *sur*, see Shears, 155. *Ueil* is probably singular in order to rhyme; cf. BD 439, where the opposite occurs.

333   'Otherwise don't be foolish enough to do so' (L, III, 197); cf. QD 2029.

334–5   'Gifts must go to the saints to whom they are dedicated.' This is another of the *Dormeur*'s wise sayings, meaning that things must be as they must be. Cf. lines 48, 127–8, 153–6.

353   *Doint* In Qd the vowels are largely obscured by a blot.

LA COMPLAINTE

Of the lyrical poems, numbers XVII, XXIV and XXVII are contemporary with the *Complainte*, as is shown by their use of a common stock of themes and expressions.

17   *Jennesse* In Qd both *jennesse* (CO 17 and 28, BD 40) and *jeunece* (BD 247) are found, as are *jenne* (CO 133) and *jeune* (BD 149 and 437). See the note to DF 578.

61   *Son bien* 'Her worth', i.e. the worth of Chartier's lady.

63   Chartier, using the topos of inexpressibility, is saying that the lady's actions cannot be described adequately in words. 'His words would not surpass her actions.'

72   *Amer* In Qd the scribe has corrected the final letter, having first written *amez*.

87   *De sa bende* 'In her company, following'. Cf. BN 347.

96   *Savroit* See page 145.

111   'I keep account of them without omitting a single one.' *Trespasse* is first person.

132   No text contains a regular line; *elle*, given by all seven texts used in this edition, has been replaced by *el.*

137   'I put on a joyous appearance.'

153   Chartier is playing on two meanings of *espartir*: 'to separate' and 'to flash (of lightning)'. *Espart* can be taken likewise in the sense of 'thunderbolt' or 'separation'; the former is its usual sense.

157   'Together we never had anything divided.'

159   *Miparti* The reading in Qd is clearly *imparti*; in Pc and Ql it could be taken as either *imparti* or *miparti*. The scribes of Nf Nj Oa and Ph have used the spelling *myparty(i)*. Cf. BD 613.

168   'Saying, "Why does my heart not break?"' See the note to QD 1208.

176   See the note to DF 37.

181   'I have no other blessing, nor do I find any other blessing to my taste.'

LA BELLE DAME SANS MERCY

The *Belle Dame sans Mercy* dates from the same period as the *Complainte* and lyrics XVII, XXIV and XXVII.

The edition of the *Belle Dame sans Mercy* by A. Pagès also includes an edition of the translation into Catalan made by Francesch Oliver. A translation of the poem into Middle English, perhaps by Sir Richard Ros, has been edited several times: see C. Brown and R. H. Robbins, *The Index of Middle English Verse*, New York, Index Socy., 1943, 1086. Details of an Italian translation made in 1471 are given in the notes to the *Debat de Reveille Matin*.

The rubrics in the editions of the *Belle Dame sans Mercy* and the *Excusacion aux Dames* have been taken from *Oj*. Further headings, not in *Oj*, have been added at lines 119 and 121 of the *Excusacion*.

23   *L'envoyeroit* See page 439.

29   *En son testament* 'By the terms of her will'. Chartier's suggestion is that her legacy to him was not so much a bequest as an expropriation.

43, 46   There is a play on two senses of *bien fait*. In line 43 it is best taken as 'done right', contrasting with *Se faulte y a* in the previous line. However, 'profit, benefit', the sense in line 46, is also implicit in line 43.

44   'It has no effect upon me.' Cf. QD 3414.

56   *Les menestriers* The line has been corrected in *Qd*; the scribe first wrote *Menestrerelz*, a reading similar to that in *Oj*.

63   *Eschivé* Cf. BN 361. *Eschever* occurs in line 396 and as rhyme-word in line 747.

70   See the note to line 355.

137, 139 *Viser* first has the sense 'to aim', secondly 'to reflect on, consider'.

147   *Garnison* is to be taken both in its basic sense of 'store, supply' and in the sense of 'garrison'.

148   *Faire frontiere* 'To attack, wage war on' (G, IV, 163b–c).

181   *Restraint* has been corrected from *refraint* by the scribe of *Qd*.

249, 251 When the scribe of *Qd* first copied these lines, *ne* (line 249) and *grant* (line 251) were not included; both words were added later by the scribe, but in a finer pen.
       The crucial difference between the versions available for these lines is the rhyme, on the one hand *ataine/haine*, on the other *ataïne/haïne*. *Nf Nj* and *Qd* give the former rhyme but contain different versions, especially for line 251; *Gf Oa Oj Pc* and *Ql*, which give the second rhyme, show some disagreement likewise at line 251; *Ph* offers a combination of the two rhymes. The readings in *Qd* have been accepted following the earlier decision that the base text should be changed as little as possible. Other examples in Chartier of *haine*, *ataine* and derived forms argue against the second form of the rhyme. Nevertheless, the way in which the lines are written in *Qd* casts some doubt on the validity of the version accepted.

262   *Mercy* In *Qd* the *e* is badly misshapen.

301   'Which you (men) teach', i.e. 'At which you men are past masters'. Cf. La Fontaine, *Fables*, X: 16.

318   'By being at first endearing' is the most likely sense. *Entree* could also mean 'look, appearance' (H, III, 511–12).

326–36   A small tear on folio 44r of *Qd* goes through these lines; they can be reconstructed with a little difficulty.

333–4   The lady's view is that, in love, heart-felt emotion is much more important than the rules laid down in some manual.

355   *Que on* The scribe of *Qd* first wrote *que lon* and then deleted the *l* by putting a dot underneath. He followed the same procedure at line 70 (*teindrent*) and line 365 (*mesgnies*).

358   *Chastel* 'Stronghold, castle'; *Oj* and *Pc* have *chatel*. See the note to DF 1065.

365   See the note to line 355.

384   *Je m'en passe* probably 'I shall make the best of it' rather than 'I can dispense with him'; see H, V, 670, and G, X, 290a–291b.

390   See the note to QD 2084–5.

391   'I am held in the lowest esteem', almost certainly a standard phrase, although the other examples attested are later (G, VII, 562c; FEW, XII, 372).

418   'For deserving (*or* to deserve one) is beyond my reach.'

439–40   It is not uncommon to find a singular verb with more than one subject; see page 440. It is less usual to find a plural subject immediately before a singular verb. The rhyme calls for the plural form.

472   The lover can neither add to the gift nor take it away.

496   *Point* Here 'point' or 'score' following *jeu* in the previous line.

529–30   'All good men must at some time try it so far as they are concerned.'

541   '(Any) benefit from it may be late in coming.'

543   *Au mieulx venir* 'At best'.

574–5   Lit. 'Whom the having of some benefit causes to...', i.e. 'Who, through having some benefit, quickly grow worse and turn loyalty upside-down'.

606   *Reclamez* See the note to DF 595.

607–8   *Retiennent a changer* 'Are again anxious to change'. *Retenir a* is to be taken as a compound of *tenir a*.

613   *Mypartie* The reading in *Nf* could be either *mipartie* or *impartie*; cf. CO 159. *Mypartie* and *partie* (line 615) mean 'divided, shared'. The lover is telling what happens when a lover divides his attentions.

626   See the note to DF 748.

642, 645   *Faillir* used twice as rhyme-word, means first 'to be lacking' then 'to fail, weaken'.

648   *Mon bien souffrir* 'My suffering well borne'.

654   *Vous en trouverez abestiz* 'You will become stupid as a result'.

686   'I should be bestowing (*lit.* it would be) pity without moderation.'

702   *Pleurent* In *Qd* the first *e* is misshapen. Cf. line 262.

710   *Cuer* 'Desire, intention'. Cf. QD 1211.

716   *Goulïardye* is listed by Godefroy (IV, 306a) with the meaning 'gluttony'; his one example is from Chartier's *Livre de l'Esperance*: 'Ils sont a l'escole de

gouliardies et viles paroles'. The meaning 'loose, coarse talk' suits both contexts better. Cf. BN 297.

717, 719   *Die* occurs as rhyme-word in both lines with little, if any, difference in meaning.

729   In *Qd*, *meschent* (*parler*) has been corrected rather untidily to *fol* (*parler*); the alteration may be in a second hand. The corrected reading, which is also given by *Nf* and *Nj*, gives a better rhyme than the alternative.

LECTRES DES DAMES A ALAIN

8, 11   Although *Qd* makes good sense at these lines, the readings of the other texts have been preferred, since they are clearer and more in keeping with the style of the letter.

14–15   *Noustre Sire* In *Oa* and *Pc Sire* is written out in full; elsewhere the scribes have used a contracted form of the word. The abbreviation in *Nj* is to be expanded to *Seigneur* rather than *Sire*.

19   As Champion has pointed out (*Histoire poétique*, 1, 71), the names correspond to those of three of the Queen's ladies, Catherine de l'Isle-Bouchard, Marie and Jeanne Louvet. The coincidence is striking, but in the absence of other evidence the identification must remain tentative.

LA REQUESTE BAILLEE AUX DAMES CONTRE ALAIN

10   *Que...ont esté* It is best to take *que* as a conjunction recalling *comme* (line 3); the mood is indicative, however, and not subjunctive.

26   *Rumeur* The alternative form *rimeur*, given by four texts, has the advantage of being ambiguous, meaning both 'tumult' and 'rhymer'.

L'EXCUSACION AUX DAMES

In *Nj* the poem has what amounts to a subsidiary title. The rubric of the second letter concludes: '...et puis la response par alain'.

4   i.e. New Year's Day. The line helps to date the *Excusacion*; see pages 7–8.

9–16   The three rhymes are respectively -*eillant*, -*vant* and -*endu*. It is unusual for Chartier to employ two so similar rhymes in the same stanza.

60, 63   *Deüst* is used twice as a rhyme-word with little, if any, difference in meaning.

71   *Se Dieu* The God of Love recalls *Que Dieu* (line 66) and takes the opportunity to alter the construction. Cf. the note to RM 219 and 224.

72   'That He should have given it (the image) to them to be their enemy.'

108, 111 *Bienffaiz* and *meffaiz*. It is not clear whether the scribe wrote *sf* or *ff*. Other examples in *Qd* suggest that *ff* was intended.

113   Of the texts used in this edition, only *Oj* contains a rubric; in *Ph* a gap has been left between stanzas xiv and xv. Some other texts of the *Excusacion* contain a rubric at this point: 'Comment le Dieu d'amours tient l'arc entexé et la fleche en la corde oyant l'excusacion de maistre Alain' *Pa Pk* and the 1489 collected

edition (an almost identical heading has been added by a later hand in *Pc*); 'Response faicte par maistre Alain chartier au dieu d'amours en soy excusant de ce qu'il l'accusoit avoir escript et fait livres nouveaux contre ses droiz' *Pd*; 'La responce que maistre Alain fist au dieu d'amours' *Qa*; 'Response de l'acteur' *Qb*.

191   *La pitié leur* 'That pity of theirs', i.e. 'the pity they have'. The unusual word-order makes the phrase more emphatic.

RONDEAULX ET BALADES

I: 11   Chartier is playing on words. *Desbucher* means 'to come down, come out (from a hiding-place in a wood or tree)'; cf. QD 1908. *Tremble* means either 'trembling' or 'aspen, trembling poplar'.

II: 9   'But, whether I must weep or laugh as a result...'

III: 6   *Eslargier*, although it is attested, is a much rarer form than *eslargir*, given by *Nj Tc* and *Td*. The sense here is apparently 'to go free, take flight'.

IV: 12   'I will fare well or ill – there will be no half measures.'

IV: 16   While *finera* rhymes satisfactorily, it is likely that Chartier wrote *finira* which is given by *Td*.

V: 4   *Seule* This rondeau, exceptionally, is written from the lady's standpoint.

VI: 3   *Renouvelle* 'I increase (my pain)'.

VII: 2   *Comble*, which is also found in EX 92, has been adopted rather than *comblé*; *vuide* could similarly have been read as *vuidé*.

VII: 11   *Qu'* 'Than that'. See the note to QD 2205–7.

IX: 12   'Without having the least little joy.'

X: 12   'Even if I had a hundred million like them.'

XIII   The rondeau is in dialogue. The lover speaks first; in lines 5–8 the lady replies and then asks the lover to answer his own question.

XV: 4   *Ce que* See the note to QD 1554.
        Amer is ambiguous, meaning both 'love' and 'bitterness'.

XVII: 13–14   *Efface* is first person singular. Cf. CO 73–84, where similar thoughts are expressed.

XIX: 14   *Pitié* 'For pity's sake' (R, v, 359).

XXI: 1–2   The rhymes are satisfactory, if the adverbial phrases at the end of either line are taken to be equivalent to a single word.

XXI: 4   In *Nj* the line is in two hands. The words 'Ma joie m   mon seul bien' are in the scribe's hand. A second hand has inserted *on soulas* in the space, and *seul* has been scored out.

XXII: 14   'Even if it must split with grief.' The imperfect indicative is used for vividness. Cf. the notes to XXVI: 40 and to QD 2913.

XXIV: 5   *Me resjoye* 'I rejoice' is present indicative. For Huguet (VI, 535) *resjoye* is part of *resjoyr*. The much rarer *resjoier* (FEW, IV, 77) is more likely, although it is not listed by any of the other standard dictionaries. Cf. *esjoie* (PL 75) from *esjoier*, which is well attested.

XXIV: 9 *Sele* 'Conceals'.

XXIV: 17 *Kyrïelle* The word is closely associated with the liturgy and often means 'litany'. It was also used to denote a lyric poem similar to the *ballade*. Here the meaning seems to be 'penitential song' or 'lament'.

XXIV: 32 *Si* 'Fault, defect'.

XXVI: 7 *Non* It is impossible to be certain that the scribe of *Qd* has written *non* and not *nen*.

XXVI: 8 i.e. St Valentine's Day.

XXVI: *Refrain* 'I must not talk of it as one without experience', i.e. 'I have experience enough to draw on'. See H, II, 310–12.

XXVI: 23 *Gars* 'Boy, youth' conveys the same idea of inexperience as does *clerc d'armes* in the refrain.

XXVI: 39 *Armes* 'Souls'.

XXVI: 40 'The prize is yours, even if it were worth a thousand marks.' Cf. XXII: 14.

XXVII The ballade has no envoy. The envoy, though usual by this time, was by no means obligatory. Christine de Pisan and Charles d'Orléans both wrote ballades without them.

XXVII: 3 'What is good?' See the note to DF 28.

XXVII: 14 *Euvre* and *envie* (line 10) are written almost identically in *Nj*. A closer examination reveals a slight difference in the *ductus* of the last two letters; in line 10 the *i* is dotted.

XXVII: 27–32 These lines, especially lines 30–2, give difficulty. *Malgré lour* (*M. leur* in *Nf*) means 'in spite of them' (G, V, 121a–b) and must refer to *beauté ne peccune* (line 29). *Efforceement* has the sense 'eagerly; with all one's strength' (TL, III, 1047). If *tout* is taken as an adverb, the lines do not make very good sense; *tout* is better understood as part of *tollir* (*toulu* is in line 22; *toult* occurs in BD 44).

The lines may mean: 'In this matter Death does her duty irresponsibly since she does not kill each and every one without sparing either beauty or wealth; but eagerly carries people away, beauty and wealth notwithstanding. I call upon her, fearing grief and torment; and may she be summoned forcibly.' The poet appears to be saying that if Death is going to be so irresponsible as to bear off a person of beauty and substance (the poet's lady), then Death ought to carry off each and every one. It is unfortunate that only *Nf* and *Nj*, of the manuscripts used here, contain the ballade. *Nl*, the only other text available, is of no help.

LE BREVIAIRE DES NOBLES

An anonymous abridged version of the *Breviaire des Nobles*, entitled *Les Douze Vertus de Noblesse*, exists in *Oh Oq* and *Ql*; in Paris, Bibl. Nat., f. fr. 17527; and in London, Brit. Mus., Cotton, Julius C IX. Another adaptation of the poem, by Jean le Masle, was published at Paris in 1578 by Nicolas Bonfons; there is a copy in the Rothschild Library (No. 445: see Tchemerzine, *Bibliographie d'éditions originales et rares*, III, 274).

A translation of the poem into Scots prose, made by Andrew Cadiou, was published in Edinburgh in 1508 by Chepman and Myllar under the title of the *Porteous of Noblenes*;

the only copy extant is imperfect (see Wm. Beattie, *The Chepman and Myllar Prints*, Edinburgh, Bibliogr. Socy., 1950). The later Asloan MS also contains a copy of the translation probably taken from the 1508 edition (see W. A. Craigie, *The Asloan Manuscript*, I, 1923, 171–84 [*STS*]).

The first ballade has a title in only two of the texts used in this edition, *Oj* and *Qd*. The virtues described in the poem are numbered in *Pc*, in which the ballades have headings of the following type: 'Foy la premiere des xii vertus aux noblez'; 'Loyaulté la ij⁰ vertu'; 'Honneur la iij⁰ vertu' etc. None of the ballades is headed in either *Oa* or *Ql*.

In some texts, for example *Oj*, the refrain is given in full only at the end of the first stanza of a ballade.

1–4   The *Breviaire* begins with an address. The beginning of the *Lay de Paix* is not dissimilar in form.

1–28   See the note to PA 37–60.

5–8   *Que...die* The sentence is to be understood as an exhortation.

53–4   The contrast between a singular and a plural verb is deliberate and further emphasises the antithesis.

68–70   *Doivent* (*estre*) must be understood; *doivent* is repeated in line 71.

89, 106   *Lÿesce* is used twice as a rhyme-word with no clear distinction in meaning.

110   *Que* 'Than that'. See the note to QD 2205–7.

112   'Noble men, take greater account of it (Honour).'

112–13   In *Qe* the envoy is of four lines:

> Nobles hommes tenés en plus grant compte
> Pour vostre honneur noblement maintenir
> Car c'est le bien qui les aultres seurmonte
> Affin que paix puissés entretenir.

The envoy is of four lines in *Pa*:

> Qui garde honneur on le doit honnorer.
> Nobles hommes tenez en plus grant compte
> Que de tresor que puissez procurer,
> Car c'est le bien qui les autres surmonte.

Envoys of four lines are also found in *Ba*, in *Bj*, in GKW 6561 and in Pellechet 3525.

114–47   In some texts, for example *Bc* and *Bd*, ballade v is rearranged so that the stanzas are of seven lines and the envoy of three.

120, 141   *Forjurer* The infinitive occurs twice as a rhyme-word. It is clear that at line 120 the sense is 'to forswear'. The same sense is possible at line 141 and lines 140–2 could be construed as meaning 'The result is to perjure one's oath and to forswear justice'; Chartier uses chiasmus elsewhere. A much rarer meaning of *forjurer* is 'to defend' (H, IV, 164). If it is accepted, then the infinitive has imperative force. The rhyme is then regular and the word-order straightforward.

128–9   'Whose concern must be to weigh things up correctly.'

134–6   'A noble man acts unnaturally and seeks to disfigure his blood (i.e. race, family).'

144–7   In *Pa* the envoy is of five lines:

> Ne faisons par murmurer
> Conjurer
> Contre nous en quelque endroit,
> Mais faisons pour plus durer
> A chascun son loial droit.

149   *Cuer* See the note to BD 710.

152   *Fait...maniere* The contrast is between action and the semblance of action.

156   'Diligence, discretion and few words.'

157   *Et que...ne* 'And unless'.

163   *Praie* The spelling *proye* is given by *Nf Nj Pc Ph* and *Ql*.

205   'And from which no benefit is derived whether for oneself or for anyone else.

212–13   'Such people pursue profit and gaming; faced with misfortune, they turn away'; cf. RB XIX: 12. There is also some play on words, for *esquart* can mean 'the action of discarding in a game of cards'.

219   Cf. *Roman de la Rose*, line 1130.

276   *Oyseuse* 'Idleness', an allusion to the character in the *Roman de la Rose* (line 523 et seq.). Cf. QD 2767.

282   *En* The reading in *Oj* is not clear, having been altered by the second hand (*Oj²*).

290   Cf. Morawski 693–4.

315–17   In *Qe* the ballade has an envoy of four lines:

> Par necte plaisant coinctise
> D'ordure se contregarde
> Et maintient tousjours franchise
> Cellui ou tous prennent garde.

347   *Tient au large sa bende* 'Keeps company with the man of generosity'. Cf. CO 87.

348–9   'A good action is such that justice demands that it be returned (*or* that it should go) to the place from which it came and that it go in there again.' Cf. Morawski 298 and 1146.

352   *Rens* 'Ranks'.

355   'May all profit fail him and may his property be destroyed.'

372   *Maniere et contenir* Cf. DF 342.

376   'He shortens his life and brings his death nearer.'

391   'Is ready for all that virtue directs to it.'

405–7   The verbs are all dependent on (*constance*) *Qui*...

LE LAY DE PAIX

1–16 The first stanza, addressed by Peace to the Princes of France, is made up of a single sentence. The subject is *Paix*, described in lines 1–6. The verb and object are in line 16; the indirect object in lines 7–14. In line 15 *Paix* outlines her aim in sending the *lay*.

10 *Enuieux de* 'Tired of, irritated with'; cf. line 73, where the spelling is *ennuyeuse*, however. The readings given here (ennuyeux *NfOaQd*, enuyeux *NjPc*, enuieux *OjPh*) suggest that *enuieux* is intended rather than *envieux*, which makes less good sense. The spelling *enuyeux* is attested (H, III, 465–6).

17 See the note to PL 17.

25 *Que n'acquistes* 'Which you did not acquire'. The idea expressed in the previous line is repeated.

31 See the note to DF 823–6.

37–60 The rhymes in *-faiz* and *-aire* are also used in the first ballade of the *Breviaire des Nobles* and many rhyme-words are common to both poems.

   The meaning of this complicated stanza is as follows: 'If among you there are misdeeds, disputes and crimes which are imitated in will and in action, destroying what influence love ought to have, even those people must be destroyed by your actions, who have done no wrong and who in all this wrongdoing have done none, and yet have so much trouble as a result. Consider that by your crimes your enemies are restored and put into such a position that they have carried out many an exploit and misdeed to destroy France. And it would be too grievous a burden to you, that you, who were made so perfect and perfectly benefit from her, should suffer so much ill to be done to her.'

40 See the note to QD 576–7.

61–84 The stanza consists of a single sentence. The subject is *Discorde* (line 61). The feminine adjectives in lines 62–71 and in 73–7 agree with *vie* (line 62). The nouns in lines 72 and 79–82 are in apposition with *vie*. Cf. PL 81–95.

106 *Faultes de foys* 'Breaches of faith; broken pledges'.

113–52 Each quarter of stanza VI is further divided in *Oj*, making eight sections of five lines. These subdivisions are not found in any of the other texts used here.

113–15 'When I (Peace) was in France, I kept her safe...'

132 'I caused everyone to have plenty.' In many texts the last word in the line could be read as *mouvoie* or *monnoie*: in *Oj* it is clearly *monnoie*.

145 *El* i.e. France.

190, 193 *Tresse* 'A plait or braid of hair'; *lesse* 'a lead or leash'. Both words are to be taken figuratively in the sense of 'link' or 'tie'. Cf. QD 1964.

204 *Verser la delesse* 'Leaves her to collapse (come to grief)'. *La* refers to *maison* (line 169) or to *France* (lines 113 and 151), or to both of them.

275 *Appetit* The singular form is surprising after *affettions*; it is given by both *Oj* and *Qd*.

282 See the note to DF 96.

LE DEBAT DU HERAULT, DU VASSAULT ET DU VILLAIN

Space has been left for a title between the decorated border and the miniature at the beginning of the poem.

1	*Naguieres que* 'It is not long ago that.' In BD 1 and L 1: 2 *nagaires* is used adverbially.
3	*Parloit* The last three letters are largely obscured.
26	*Car* is used to introduce the Herald's request.
32	*Chief des armes* 'Head of the family', i.e. the person who could bear its arms undifferenced. La Curne (II, 153) cites *chief d'armes* with this sense, but gives no examples.
37	Sancerre was appointed Constable on 26 July 1397 and died on 6 February 1402 (Champion, *Histoire poétique*, I, 42).
45	'See how time deceives us.'
78–9	*N'est...de* 'Does not belong to'.
85	*Or ça* 'Come now! Now then!' (TL, II, 2); cf. line 137.
90	'Until the King helps me out.' For a similar example of *mectre suz* see J. Misrahi et C. A. Knudson (eds.), *Antoine de la Sale: Jehan de Saintré*, Genève, Droz; Paris, Minard, 1965 (*TLF*), page 16, line 8.
95	The corrected line is modelled on a sentence from *Le Jouvencel* quoted by both Godefroy (IV, 528b) and La Curne (VII, 74): 'Vela le mengeur de soupe et le humeur de brouets de court'. The disadvantage of the correction is that *souillars* is not repeated.
106	'Flatterers are in good favour with lords.'
108	*Raboutent* Godefroy (VI 532c) cites one example of the verb and suggests *rebuter* 'to rebuff, discourage', a sense which fits here. Elsewhere (TL, VIII, 126 and 384–5), it is linked with *rebouter* 'to repulse, reject', but no examples are given.
115–16	*Pourchasse* modifies both *d'estre* and *honneur*.
119	*Que* is modified by *Fault il* (line 114).
129–30	The *Herault* resumes the point made by the *Vassault* in order to contradict it the more forcibly.
132	'There are many fewer of them than ever before.'
147	*C'est car* 'That is to say that' (TL, II, 40–2).
152	*De paix* 'At peace' or 'in peace-time'.
160–1	*Emprise* is the spelling demanded by the rhyme. *Emprinses* has been left in line 272.
167	*Que* 'Which thing'.
171	*Lou* is a shortened form of *la ou*; for other examples see TL, V, 14–16.
176	*Le bastard Bigot* The identity of Bigot is uncertain. He is perhaps Jean le Bigot who quit the siege of Saint-Sauveur in 1374, but who was pardoned after Du Guesclin, the Constable, had interceded. See Baron Kervyn de Lettenhove, *Œuvres de Froissart*, VIII, Bruxelles, Devaux, 1869, 453.
187	*Plains* 'Mourned'.
201	*Dëa*, here and in line 265, counts as two syllables. In line 161 and elsewhere (see the note to DF 227), it is a monosyllable.

258   *Gens de fait* 'Men of action'.

263–4   'A man who hunts with puppies is lucky if he catches anything.'

265   *Dëa* See the note to line 201.

283   Cf. BD 44.

314, 316 The rhyme has been corrected with the help of lines 406 and 408. *Subgetz* has been left in line 309.

324   *Soulaz* 'Conversation'; cf. lines 332 and 377. It is surprising to find this sense, so strongly reminiscent of Old Provençal; no similar example has been found in Middle French.

337–40 The *Villain* is probably using an asymmetrical construction, in which *tant* governs first *comme*, then *que*. Is he suggesting that dishonest officials, not content with spending all that they have raised, have put honest officials to death in order to lay hands on their funds?

349   *Suz mis* 'Raised, levied'.

373   *Mussoires* 'Reserves, savings'; other derivatives of *mucer* have this sense (FEW, VI: 3, 195). The only other example of the word which has been found is *muçoire a l'aissele* 'a type of dance'.

382   See the note to DF 401.

389   *Remede* Huguet (VI, 473–4) gives examples of *remede* rhyming with words ending in *-ide*; *remide* is also found.

394   *Deable* counts as two syllables; cf. line 409.

398   'You sorry lot of gentlefolk.' *Entre* is expletive; cf. H, III, 500–1. *Gentillastre* is derogatory.

399–400 The infinitives have imperative force. Cf. note to BN 120 and 141.

400   *Vous groppir* probably 'to remain, stay put'; see FEW, XVI, 419.

411–12 This proverbial expression is very similar to Morawski 1802.

413–16 'And, by God's blood, the French will be supposed to have had five hundred thousand successes and killed every single Englishman, and then we'll be told that they've done nothing of the kind.'

424   The correction has been made with the help of line 123.

438–40 These lines are discussed on pages 37–8.

GLOSSARY

The glossary is not exhaustive. Where a word has the same meaning in Modern French as it had for Chartier, that meaning (and thus often the word itself) is not listed. Each sense of a word is followed by a reference to the first line or lines where it clearly has that sense. If possible two, and sometimes three, references are given; the abbreviations used to refer to the poems are listed on page 437. Where it may be that a word has more than one meaning, the different meanings are separated by a semicolon. Entries are frequently grouped, adverbs with the appropriate

Glossary

adjective, for example, participles with the infinitive; sub-entries are separated by a colon. The entries are in normal alphabetical order, except that *y* has been treated as *i* throughout.

The following abbreviations are used: *adj.* adjective; *adv.* adverb; *conj.* conjunction; *excl.* exclamation; *f.* feminine; *i.* impersonal; *indic.* indicative; *m.* masculine; *n.* noun; *p.p.* past participle; *pl.* plural; *prep.* preposition; *pres.p.* present participle; *pron.* pronoun; *subj.* subjunctive; *v.* verb; *v.n.* verbal noun.

abestir v. to become dull, stupid BD 654

abrever v. see note to QD 1243

accés see *acez*

accoyser v. to calm, soothe BD 363

accouter (*s'*) v. to rest on one's elbows DF 140, HV 329

accroirre v. to lend QD 1656: *acroire sur* to put trust in PL 93

accueillir v. to receive, welcome QD 1631, BD 67; attack, assail QD 1915, RM 55

acez n.m. (periodic) pain, attack QD 153, QD 1415

achaison n.f. opportunity DF 467; reason QD 1426

achever v. to make complete, fulfil PL 175, QD 1276

acointable adj. approachable, friendly PL 172

acointance n.f. acquaintance PL 151, DF 440

acointe adj. acquainted, intimate DF 179, QD 871

acointer v. to get to know DF 339; make known QD 3367: *s'acointer de* to become acquainted with PL 98, DF 178

acomte n.m. see note to QD 1535

acoucher v. to lie down RB VI: 9

acoupé p.p. besotted DF 799

acoustrer v. to arrange, prepare QD 1739

acouter see *accouter*

acquerre v. to acquire QD 667, QD 1799; see page 439

acquester v. to acquire QD 2299

acquierge from *acquerir*; see page 439

acquiter v. to fulfil, discharge DF 1217,

QD 823; free, discharge QD 2691: *s'acquiter* to do one's duty QD 1037, RM 109

acroire see *accroirre*

actendre a v. to wait for HV 362: *s'attendre a* to aspire to DF 757, QD 266; count on, rely on BD 446, BD 459

actraitte n.f. attraction, charm QD 1730

adens adv. on one's face DF 144

adez adv. always QD 1261, QD 3329: *adés...adés* now...now DF 59, DF 112

adjourner v. to dawn DF 152, BD 191

adjouxter v. to add QD 1396, QD 2520

administrer v. to present, provide QD 1988, QD 3434

admonnester see *amonnester*

adonner v. to direct DF 390, DF 455

adonq, adoncques adv. then DF 226, DF 217

adont see *adonq*

adouler v. to sadden DF 832, QD 1271

adrechié see *adresser*

adresce n.f. (right) road, direction PL 123, BN 88; course of action RM 237

adresser v. to direct DF 180, DF 330: *s'adrecer vers* to go towards QD 1299: *adrechié* p.p. & adj. (well) brought up, educated QD 1136

adurer v. to harden BN 130: *aduré* p.p. & adj. harsh RB XXVII: 21

advisement n.m. sense, reflection PA 176

advouer v. to consider, esteem QD 1138, QD 2028: *advouer qn. de qch.* to give s.o. approval concerning sth. DF 690

473

affaictier v. to tame, train DF 595, BN 394: *s'affaictier a* to reconcile o.s. with BD 501: *affaitié* p.p. & adj. false, affected QD 1231, L II: 25

affaire n.m. business, concern PL 51, BD 277; trouble, difficulty QD 833, QD 1239

afferir v. to be fitting, appropriate DF 191, QD 966

affermer v. to strengthen QD 2955, QD 2957; affirm QD 2980: *affermé* p.p. fixed, set QD 717

affetardir (s') v. to become soft, lazy QD 2761

afficher v. to fix, set DF 813

affïer (s') de v. to trust in, rely on BD 639

affilouere n.f. oilstone, hone QD 2104

affonder v. to swallow up DF 920

affuÿr v. to come running DF 360, DF 942

aggregier v. to grow worse QD 1388, QD 3013

aggrever v. to overwhelm, burden QD 1043, CO 6

aguet n.m. watch DF 909; trick, deceit QD 857, BD 750: *d'aguet* see note to QD 1697

aherdre (s') a v. to apply o.s., devote o.s. to BN 278

ahonty p.p. & adj. shamed, dishonoured RB XXVIII: 10

ahurter (s') v. to attack, clash QD 982

ayde n.f. aid, tax HV 370

aider v.: *(se) m'aist Dieu, se Dieu m'aÿe* so God help me QD 1368, QD 1573, RM 241, HV 113

aÿe see *aider*

aim n.m. hook EX 242

aÿmant n.m. hard steel; diamond (i.e. a proverbially hard substance) RM 288

ainchois que conj. (subj.) before QD 2611

ainçois adv. but, rather DF 216, QD 820

ains adv. but, rather PL 64, PL 72

ains que conj. (subj.) before QD 1126, QD 1912

ainsi que conj. (subj.) so that QD 1386

aÿr n.m. irritation, anger DF 899, QD 2943

aira from *avoir*

aÿrer v. to anger, irritate BN 100

aysance n.f. solace, comfort BD 281

ayse n.m. pleasure, ease DF 287, QD 385; see also *baigner*

aise adj. content, at ease DF 123, QD 623

ayser v. to make happy, please DF 649: *s'aiser* to find pleasure QD 1766

aist see *aider*

alangouré p.p. languishing QD 1471

alechier v. to attract DF 810, QD 2754

alegance n.f. relief, comfort PL 155, RB XX: 12

allegement n.m. relief, comfort QD 1095, QD 2201

allegier v. to relieve QD 1386; decrease, ease QD 3401

allier v. to bind QD 2291

aloigne n.f. delay, respite QD 3142

aloignier v. to prolong QD 972

alucher v. to confuse, deceive RM 302

amandrissement n.m. reduction, diminution L II: 30

amati p.p. & adj. downcast, defeated QD 1344, QD 1836

ambedeux adj. both QD 1603

amende n.f. satisfaction, amends QD 1359, RM 275

amendement n.m. improvement DF 290, DF 619

amender v. to improve, benefit DF 497, DF 562

amendrir v. to reduce, lessen DF 1130, QD 1374

amenuyser v. to diminish, reduce QD 514, BN 304

amer n.m. bitterness DF 224, QD 255

amesurement adv. moderately, with moderation BD 220

amesurer v. to moderate, restrain BN 119

amïable adj. amiable PL 173, QD 1214

amoistir v. to water QD 63

amolïer v. to soften PL 80, DF 1125

amonnester v. to urge, exhort QD 868, QD 3418

amordre v. to accustom QD 987: *s'amordre a* to apply o.s. to BN 387

amortissement n.m. deadening, weakening QD 2124

amourer (s') de v. to fall in love with QD 1346: *amouré* p.p. see note to QD 880

amuser v. to deceive QD 3224, RM 301; amuse L II: 24

ancesseurs n.m.pl. ancestors QD 2870; see page 437

anter v. to graft RB xxv: 26

antier see *entier*

anvel n.m. see note to QD 3109

äourner v. to adorn, furnish with QD 2600, QD 2847

apaisier (s') de v. to content o.s. with RM 336

apert see *apparoir*

appaier v. to appease, satisfy DF 697

appaillardir v. to become loose, slack QD 2763

appaire(nt) see *apparoir*

appareiller v. to prepare, cause QD 1058

apparer v. to appear PL 196, QD 1306

apparïer (s') a v. to make o.s. equal to QD 2382

apparoir v. to appear, be evident DF 1074, QD 327: *s'apparoir* to appear EX 13

appartenir v. to suit, be appropriate PL 35, QD 183

appeller de v. to appeal against DF 1210, CO 163: *appeller qn. de* to accuse s.o. of CO 7

appendre v. to belong to, be appropriate to QD 2889

appensé p.p. & adj. thoughtful, prudent QD 2332

apperroit see *apparoir*

appert adj. open, clear DF 706, QD 1198; skilful, valiant QD 1144, BN 292:

en appert openly, clearly DF 452, QD 1143

appert see *apparoir*

appertement adv. quickly QD 1926

appliquier v. to direct DF 1149; use QD 1490

appointer v. to prepare, put in good order DF 180; reconcile QD 3365: *s'appointer* to prepare o.s. PL 103, QD 2457

apprentif n.m. apprentice DF 316, QD 860

apprest n.m. (method of) preparation DF 574

aqueult see *accueillir*

aquiter see *acquiter*

aquouärdir (s') v. to become cowardly QD 2762: *aquouärdi* p.p. & adj. cowardly QD 2373

ardre v. to burn QD 1652, BD 175: *ardant* pres.p. & adj. burning, ardent DF 16, DF 112

ardure n.f. ardour, burning desire DF 577, QD 1890

argu n.m. quarrel DF 904

argüer v. to press, beset QD 1709

arme n.f. soul RB xxvi: 39

arraisonner v. to address, speak to DF 389, RB xxiv: 1

arrançonner v. to put to ransom HV 316

arrester (s') a v. to fix on, decide on QD 805, QD 866; heed, take notice of HV 119: *arresté* p.p. & adj. determined, resolute QD 2324, BN 155: *pou arresté* immoderate, immoral QD 2749

arroi n.m. manner, conduct QD 2750

arrouter (s') v. to gather together DF 946; *s'arrouter a* to direct o.s. to, go in the direction of QD 743

aspic n.m. asp DF 896

aspresce n.f. torment QD 398; difficulty QD 927, PA 196

assaveurer v. to find to one's taste, to enjoy CO 181

assavoir v.: *faire assavoir* to make (it) known BN 148, PA 223

assegier v. to besiege, beset QD 398, QD 1387

assener a v. to succeed in, manage to QD 2966: *mal assené* badly provided for DF 870

assent n.m. assent, agreement DF 1226

assentir (s') a v. to consent to QD 1943, QD 2280

asseoir v. dispose, order QD 697; to set, place QD 1407, BD 47: *asseoir un jugement* to pass judgement RB iv: 15

asseurer (s') v. to find assurance QD 1107: *s'asseurer a* to trust in, count on BN 416

assez adv. much, plenty, very DF 29, DF 192

assoille see *assoudre*

assonner v. to strike RB xxvi: 18

assorter v. to join together BD 364: *s'assorter a* to join together with QD 1120

assoudre v. to absolve HV 69

assouployer v. to soften, overcome BD 461

assourdi p.p. dazed QD 1882

assouvir v. to complete, accomplish RB xxvii: 34; satisfy BN 367: *s'assouvir* to be satisfied QD 2295, RB iv: 1: *assouvi* p.p. & adj. replete, full QD 215, RM 119; perfect CO 128, EX 68

assuvie see *assouvir*

astre n.m. hearth; home HV 400

ataine n.f. animosity BD 249

atie n.f. animosity QD 1342

atoucher a v. to touch BD 356

atour n.m. hat, headgear (of noblewoman) QD 163

atout adv. therewith RM 134.

atremper v. to temper, moderate DF 1141, BN 106

attayner v. to annoy, irritate DF 968

attayneux adj. disagreeable, irritating PA 62

attainte n.f. purpose, aim DF 471, BD 95

attenir v. to hold, possess BN 60

attraire v. to attract DF 809, QD 197

audience n.f.: *donner audience a* to listen to, give credit to L ii: 32

autouer n.m. goshawk QD 69

autr(u)y see pages 438 and 441

avaller v. to go down QD 347

avancer (s') v. to hurry RB xix: 16

avant adv. first of all HV 36: *plus avant* further, more DF 130, DF 958; cf. BD 734: *mectre avant* to further HV 163

avantager v. to give an advantage to PL 84

avencer (s') v. to make bold HV 418

avenir v. to suit, be becoming PL 37; happen PL 38, DF 362

aventurer (s') v. to put oneself at risk, venture QD 876, BN 126: *aventuré* p.p. & adj. unfortunate, wretched QD 721

aviler v. to dishonour BN 13

aviner v. to fill with wine QD 914

aviser v. to advise, tell QD 1092, BN 291; perceive, notice QD 1735, QD 2477; reflect BN 305: *aviser a* to consider QD 257: *s'aviser* to consider, reflect QD 512, QD 1085

avoir n.m. possession(s), wealth QD 3034, QD 3302

avoir v.: *ot* ago QD 3021

bacinet n.m. basinet QD 2597

baguez n.f.pl. possessions, baggage HV 91

baigner v.: *se baigner d'aise* to be overjoyed QD 2712–13

bailler v. to give QD 831, QD 1946: *en bailler a* to deceive HV 45

baillir v. to give QD 1586, L i: 2: *mal baillir* to ill-treat, ill-use QD 278, QD 1152

bandon n.m. power, authority RM 242

barater v. to trick, cheat DF 871

basilique n.f. basilisk EX 73

bassement adv. in a low voice BD 218

baster a v. to be equal to, manage to QD 1661

batant adv. at top speed QD 2003

baut adj. proud, bold QD 2962

bëer v. to desire, aspire DF 566, RM 229

bejaunie n.f. foolishness DF 591

bel adj.: *avoir bel faire qch.* to be easily able to do sth. HV 369, HV 422

bende n.f. company, following CO 87, BN 347

benoist adj. blessed, holy DF 404

besoigne n.f. need, necessity DF 278, QD 1555; concern, affair QD 2967, QD 3049: *mettre en besoigne* to set to work DF 494

besoignier v. to work, strive DF 1009, RM 230

besoingneux adj. needy, needful BD 667, PA 77

bestourner v. to turn over, upset DF 1068

bienfait n.m. profit, benefit DF 1020, BD 46; good action QD 1355, BD 580

blandices n.f.pl. blandishments, caresses QD 799

bobant n.m. presumption QD 909

bonne n.f. boundary (-stone), limit DF 560, BD 47

bouhourt n.m. combat, tourney DF 654

bouleurs see *boulierres*

boulierres n.m. cheat, trickster QD 2393

bourde n.f. lie, nonsense QD 2687, QD 3222

bout n.m.: *sur bout* upright DF 761, CO 23

bouter v. to push DF 386, DF 945: *se bouter en* to enter, fall into DF 13, DF 1076

bouton n.m.: *bouton de haye* rose-hip HV 333

braire v. to shout DF 631, RB IX: 6

brief adv. soon, quickly DF 858, QD 587; in short DF 955: *a brief compter, parler* to be brief QD 1465, QD 3121

briefment adv. soon, quickly CO 183, EX 42

brievement adv. in short QD 1937

broet n.m. thin soup, gruel HV 95

broudeure n.f. embroidery DF 677

buhoreau n.m. heron QD 2802

butin n.m. booty, spoils RM 366: *a butin* in common QD 1176; in league, in partnership HV 410

ça adv.: *depuis en ça* thereupon, thereafter QD 2532

cabas n.m. trick, deceit PA 105

cabuser v. to deceive, trick PA 256

cache n.f. pursuit QD 2969

cachier v. to pursue QD 2862

carcas n.m. quiver EX 227

carneaulx see *quarneaulx*

casser v. to put an end to PL 183, DF 583; suppress EX 215

causer (se) de v. to rely on, base o.s. on QD 2517

caut adj. prudent, sagacious DF 498, HV 17

cautele n.f. wile DF 726

cauteleux adj. cunning, sly DF 548

celeement adv. in concealment QD 108

cellui see page 438

cemondre v. to exhort QD 1811, QD 2552

cens n.m. feudal due QD 908

cep n.m. fetter QD 2394

cerchier v. to seek, search for DF 85, DF 261

cerne n.m. circle DF 54

certes adv.: *a certes, a droittes certes* really, truly DF 721, DF 703

certiffïer v. to assure BD 637

cesser (se) de to refrain from DF 1168

cestuy pron. this (one) QD 1961: adj. this BN 8; see page 438

chalenger v. to demand, claim RM 144, RM 318

chaloir v.n. to be of concern, of interest DF 90, DF 532

change n.m. change, exchange QD 810, QD 2085; see notes to DF 639 and QD 2084–5

changierres n.m. changer QD 2392

chappellet n.m. chaplet, garland QD 1611

charïer v.: *droit charïer* to be circumspect, proceed with care QD 2380

chastel n.m. castle DF 2, DF 828

chastoy n.m. warning; punishment RB XXVIII: 20

chatel n.m. asset, property QD 1035, QD 2898; see note to DF 1065

chau(l)droit, chaulsist, chau(l)t see *chaloir*

chëaux see *chëel*

chëel n.m. puppy HV 263

chëoir v. to fall DF 994, DF 1040; happen QD 754: v.i. to befall QD 1817

cherra, cherroit, cherront see *chëoir*

chevance n.f. wealth, possessions HV 9

chevir de v. to win through, manage QD 1552: *se chevir de* to win through, succeed in, cope with QD 1444, QD 3362, BD 441

chiece see *chëoir* and page 439

chief n.m. head QD 466, QD 1862; height, top EX 142; leader HV 111, HV 205: *de chief en chief* from beginning to end DF 957: *venir a bon chief* to come to a successful conclusion HV 223

chiere n.f. face, countenance DF 369, DF 832: *faire chiere* to be pleasant, cheerful, welcoming QD 1226, BD 89, BD 133: *de sa bonne chiere* out of kindness BD 413

chierté n.f. affection BD 318, EX 97

chiet see *chëoir*

chivallereux adj. valiant, valorous HV 212, HV 270

choisir v. to see, perceive QD 165, BD 110

cil pron. he (who), the one (who) PL 27, PL 31; this one QD 2895; see page 438

clamer v. to call QD 190, QD 948; claim QD 1289, RM 317: *clamer pour* to accept, recognise as QD 606, RM 331: *se clamer* to call o.s., be called DF 870, QD 1847

clamour n. m. or f. (loud) complaint DF 31, EX 46

clerc n.m.: *clerc d'armes* see note to RB XXVI: refrain

cochet n.m. weather-cock QD 1719

coing n.m. stamp, die DF 973

cointe adj. attractive, smart PL 97, DF 177

cointise n.f. elegance, smartness QD 2790, BN 315

cointoier (se) v. to bedeck, adorn o.s. DF 446

cole n.f. humour, disposition QD 1960, BD 303

combien que conj. (indic. or subj.) although QD 48, QD 183; (indic.) because, the more so since QD 175

comble n.m. height, culmination EX 144

comble adj. full to the brim EX 92, RB VII: 2

commant n.m. representative QD 2974

comme conj. (subj.) in that, since L II: 3

comme que conj.: *comme qu'il soit* however it may be QD 636: *comme qu'il voise* however it may turn out QD 2948

compains n.m. companion DF 397; see page 437

comparagier v. to compare PL 96

comparer v. to compare PL 9, QD 2032; appear PL 193; buy, acquire QD 559, RM 256-7

compasser v. to arrange, fashion PL 191, QD 1155

complaint n.m. complaint, lament QD 1051

comprengiez from *comprendre*; see page 439

comqueste n.f. conquest, gain, DF 265, QD 2300

condicïonner v.: *bien condicïonné* p.p. & adj. of good behaviour, well-mannered QD 2361, BD 733

condicïons n.f.pl. disposition DF 562

conduit n.m. escort L II: 7; guidance BN 410

conduite n.f. guidance BD 8; leadership BN 154

confermer v. to strengthen QD 719, QD 2958

confire v. to compose, make up QD 2150, BD 300

confuz p.p. overwhelmed, overthrown QD 331

connin n.m. rabbit QD 54

conquerre v. to gain, acquire DF 65, DF 272

conqueste see *comqueste*

conquester v. to win, conquer HV 364

conseiller (se) a, par v. to seek counsel from RM 7, HV 267

consentir a v. to agree with, fall in with BD 317: *se consentir a* to consent to QD 2279, QD 3394

contenance n.f. countenance, bearing, composure PL 158, DF 342

contencïeux adj. contentious PA 273

contenir (se) v. to behave PL 31: *se contenir en* to keep to CO 117: *contenir* v.n. composure BN 372

content n.m. quarrel, dispute QD 1646, BN 338

contraint p.p. & adj. constrained, ill at ease QD 517, QD 1068

contrecuer n.m. aversion, distaste QD 3010

contredit n.m. contradiction, denial QD 527, BN 258

contrefaire de v. to imitate DF 50

contregarder (se) v. to save, preserve o.s. QD 1264, BN 316

contretenir v. to support PL 42; contain, moderate DF 1113, BD 85

contreuve n.f. invention QD 2672, QD 3289

controuver v. to invent DF 992

converser v. to live, dwell QD 2765

convi n.m. banquet, feast DF 937

convie see *convoier*

convoy n.m. escort QD 1779

convoier v. to accompany PL 102, DF 364; lead, direct QD 2647, CO 130, BN 391

corrompre (se) v. to be destroyed, break QD 2418

coste n.f. slope QD 382: *de coste* aside DF 821; at hand, close by QD 3134

costoier v. to escort, accompany DF 448, QD 1277

couchier v. to stake RM 259

couler v. see note to QD 1272

coulpe n.f. fault, responsibility QD 3072, BD 242

coup n.m.: *a coup* suddenly DF 120, DF 138

courage n.m. heart (as seat of emotions, will) PL 83, DF 86; courage DF 552, RM 258

courcier v. to distress, grieve DF 950, DF 1088; become distressed QD 2538

courir v. to be current, in fashion QD 1348, QD 2781: *courir seure (a)* to rush at DF 39, QD 683: *au temps qui court* at the present time BD 715

courouchier see *courroucer*

couroux n.f. distress, vexation DF 231, DF 435

courroucer v. to anger DF 901, QD 2587; distress, grieve QD 2547, QD 2589

cours n.m. course, passage at arms QD 2279, QD 3189 (?)

courtine n.f. curtain DF 656, QD 97

coustageux adj. costly PA 82

couvent n.m. promise QD 1717

couvoier see *convoier*

couvrir v. to hide, conceal DF 807, QD 1073: *couvert* p.p. & adj. covert, secret DF 997, QD 1199: *couvertement, a couvert* covertly, secretly QD 1927, BN 282

craintiveté n.f. fear QD 2237

cremeteux adj. fearful, afraid QD 863

cremir v. to fear QD 1983

cremour n.f. fear QD 2217

crerre i.e. *croirre* QD 3180

crevecuer n.m. heartbreak HV 248

croisel n.m. crucible BN 414

crouler v. to shake, agitate QD 2357

cruppel see the note to QD 897–900

cuer n.m. desire, intention, will DF 304, DF 1027

cuidance n.f. opinion, presumption DF 583

Glossary

cuider v. to think, believe DF 48, DF 51: v.n. thought, opinion DF 370, DF 1097

cure n.f. care, concern RM 314, BD 325

curïeux adj. anxious, concerned PA 269

dance n.f.: *dance basse* see note to QD 2400

dangier n.m. power, dominion DF 33, RB XII: 12

dart n.m. dart, javelin QD 331, QD 586

davant prep. before RB XXVI: 8

dea excl. see note to DF 227

debat n.m. debate, dispute DF 712, DF 1064

debatre v. to debate DF 196, QD 2162; contest QD 1830; assert QD 2098

debouter v. to expel, chase away, drive away QD 741, QD 1394

decepcïon n.f. deception QD 3229, BN 46

decevance n.f. deception QD 128, QD 747

dechëoir v. to decline, diminish DF 1042, QD 1408: *se dechëoir* to hurt, injure o.s. QD 2614

decherra see *dechëoir*

dechié n.m. decline DF 1065

dechiet, dechois see *dechëoir*

dedentre adv. within DF 894

deduire v. to recount DF 673: *se deduire* to amuse o.s., take pleasure DF 186

deduit n.m. delight, pleasure DF 637, DF 645

defaillir v. to fail, be wanting, lacking DF 917, QD 241

deffaire v. to undo, destroy PL 46, DF 183: *deffaire de* to separate from, deprive of QD 659, CO 25: *se deffaire* to bring shame upon o.s. QD 835

deffermer v. to open, unfasten EX 157, EX 159

deffïance n.f. distrust DF 953; challenge, defiance QD 2637, BD 230

deffïer v. to reject, repudiate DF 954; challenge, provoke QD 1531, QD 3018

deffrire (se) v. to become alarmed RB XXVI: 28

deffumé adj. smokeless QD 2411

definer v. to die QD 422; end QD 2346

defondre v. to melt DF 98

defouler v. to insult QD 2693

defuire v. to flee, shun DF 1186, QD 492

degoiser (se) v. to sport QD 88

degré n.m. rank, station RM 350

deguerpir v. to abandon QD 1577, BD 577

delé n.m. see note to QD 1610

delectable adj. agreeable, pleasant QD 991, BN 189

delit n.m. delight QD 2825, QD 3227

delitter v. to delight BN 322: *se delicter* to take delight QD 2688: *se delitter en* to enjoy, delight in DF 1216, CO 175

delivre adj. free QD 481, QD 3071

demain n.m.: *de demain en demain* see note to QD 1764

demaine n.m. power, control PL 119, QD 1968

demaine see *demener*

demener v. to conduct, lead DF 976, QD 2965; beset DF 771, QD 1571: *se demener* to become upset DF 869, QD 1866

dementer (se) v. to lament QD 2500, QD 3347: *se dementer de* to desire to QD 3287

demeure n.f. tarrying, delay CO 178, BD 647

demie n.f. see note to RB IX: 12

demour n.m. delay QD 2216

demourant n.m. part remaining DF 1242, QD 1828

departement n.m. separation CO 161

departie n.f. departure QD 1596, BD 612

departir v. to separate QD 564, QD 579; share, distribute QD 739, QD 2434: *se departir* to depart QD 1562, RB XII: 10; part QD 3446: *se departir de* to give up, abandon DF 858, QD 684: *departir* v.n. departure QD 2459, RB XVIII: 11

deport n.m. joy, pleasure DF 1201

deporter (*se*) v. to rejoice, take delight CO 46, BD 780: *se deporter en* to rejoice, delight in PL 27, DF 166: *se deporter de* to cease to PL 20, QD 840

derompre v. to tear QD 2882, BD 782

deronger v. to bite DF 836

derrier adv. & prep. behind QD 2447, QD 2866

derroi n.m. misdeed, misconduct QD 2748

des prep. *des adonques* at once QD 642: *des lors que* (indic.) from the time when QD 2278, RB XI: 12

desacuser v. to exonerate, exculpate PA 266

desavancement n.m. ruin, harm L I: 3

desavantageux adj. disadvantageous BD 666

desavoier v. to turn aside, lead astray PA 151

desbuchier v. to take from a hiding-place (in a wood or tree) QD 1908; see note to RB I: 11

descarchier (*se*) *de* v. to free o.s. (from a burden) QD 2212

desceler v. to reveal DF 1094

descherpir v. to separate QD 1580

descirer v. to rend, divide QD 2793; split, break apart BN 96

descliquer v. to utter DF 1150

desclore v. to reveal DF 996, QD 194: *se desclore de* to reveal QD 520

desconfire v. to discourage, dishearten DF 436; defeat, overwhelm QD 487, QD 1403: *desconfire* v.n. defeat RB XXVI: 26

desconfiture n.f. defeat, discomfiture QD 645, CO 123

desconforter v. to dishearten, distress QD 581, CO 56: *se desconforter* to be disheartened, distressed QD 838, QD 1863

descongnoistre v. not to recognise QD 2275: *se descongnoistre* to lose control over o.s. QD 884, BD 774

descorder v. to disunite, put into discord BN 449

descort see *discort*

descoulourer v. to grow pale, lose colour QD 1062, QD 1472

descoulper v. to disculpate, clear from blame QD 3073

descouvrir v. to discover, uncover, reveal DF 993, DF 1105: *descouvert* p.p. bare-headed BN 286: *a descouvert* openly QD 1566

desdire v. to contradict DF 476, BD 23; deny PA 221: *se desdire de* retract, disavow EX 42

desemparer v. to abandon HV 244

desert p.p. & adj. ravaged QD 470, QD 2065; forsaken QD 2064, CO 25

deserte n.f. reward, desert RM 166, BD 370: *sans deserte(s)* undeservedly DF 705, QD 471

deservir see *desservir*

desgorger v. to disgorge QD 2506

desgrader v. to degrade, lower BD 578

deshaitier v. to sadden, distress QD 1795

deslier v. to free, release from PL 76

deslogier v. to change one's lodging RB XII: 1

deslos n.m. blame, disapproval BD 677

deslouer v. to blame, criticise DF 689

desmantir v. to contradict BD 22

desmectre (*se*) *de* v. to renounce one's rights over QD 321, QD 2987

desmouvoir v. to turn aside, dissuade DF 171, DF 484

desnaturer (*se*) v. to change, act contrary to, one's nature BN 134: *desnaturé* p.p. & adj. unnatural DF 622

despecier (*se*) v. to be destroyed QD 2145

despendre v. to spend BN 324, PA 139: *despendre en* to spend on QD 2888, HV 337; use, employ in RB III: 4, BN 443

desperance n.f. despair QD 2067

despire v. to despise BN 296

despit adj. noxious, evil DF 897, CO 1; irritated HV 419

despit n.m. vexation DF 1002; scorn EX 184

despiter v. to despise QD 1038

despiteux adj. pitiless BD 671, EX 178

desplachier v.n. moving off QD 2860

desplaisance n.f. sadness, grief QD 273, QD 1702

desplaisant adj. wretched, unhappy QD 3490

desplaisir n.m. grief, sorrow DF 111, DF 243

desploier v. to reveal, uncover QD 3037

despointer de v. to remove from, deprive of PL 107, CO 25: *se despointer de* to detach, dissociate o.s. from QD 3366

despourveu p.p. & adj. destitute, deprived BN 264

desprisier v. to scorn, despise QD 800, QD 2546

desrivé p.p. & adj. disorderly, wanton QD 1543

desrouber v. to rob, despoil HV 374

desroux see *derompre*

dessaisonné p.p. & adj. upset RB xxiv: 11

desservir v. to deserve, be worthy of DF 450, DF 930; free from servitude QD 740; serve ill QD 2937, RM 341, BD 213: *desservir a* to reward RM 267

desseure n.m.: *estre au desseure* to be successful DF 38

dessevrance n.f. separation QD 3070

dessevrer v. to quit, leave PL 189

dessus adv.: *par dessus* into the bargain QD 3270

dessus prep. above DF 361, QD 2103; upon DF 486, QD 382; over QD 3519

destendre v. to unbend (bow) EX 228

destour n.m. isolated spot QD 157; difficult situation RM 308; obstacle BD 167

destourber de v. to turn away from QD 2759: *se destourber* to hinder o.s. DF 1121

destraindre v. to torment, beset QD 516

destroit n.m. place difficult of access QD 1909

destruire v. to kill QD 3236, HV 415

desuivre v. to pursue QD 2440

desvoier (se) v. to become bewildered, lost QD 1777; go astray, become lost PA 145: *desvoié* p.p. bewildered QD 3002

detenir v. to keep, keep control of PL 30, BN 76

determiner (se) a v. to decide on, settle on BN 416

detordre v.: *detordre ses mains* to wring one's hands DF 836, CO 146

detraire v. to remove, take away PL 62

deu n.m. due QD 1391

deule(nt), deult see *douloir*

deulx see *dueil* and *douloir*

devenir a, en v. to come to QD 510, RM 266: *se devient* perhaps DF 524, QD 3425

devier v. to go astray; die BN 379; *cf. desvoier*

devis n.m. liking, intention DF 938; talk, conversation RM 27

devise n.f. (heraldic) device, love-token PL 49, DF 482

deviser v. to describe QD 1736, QD 2475; see note to DF 352: *deviser a, avec* to talk to, with DF 188, QD 1086, QD 1091: *deviser de* to talk of QD 515

devoier v. to prevent QD 1896

dextre adj.: *a dextre* to the right QD 2447

dia excl. see note to DF 227

dicter v. to write, compose PL 128, DF 1243

dictié n.m. poem QD 824

diffame n.m. dishonour, ignominy DF 593, QD 963

diffameur n.m. defamer, slanderer QD 2775

dinee n.f. dinner BD 52

discort n.m. discord, disagreement DF 1064, BN 364

dit n.m. (short) poem DF 306, DF 319

divers adj. varying, different DF 547, DF 574; cruel, evil QD 1177, QD 1522

doy n.m. finger DF 513, DF 865: *apparoir au doy et a l'oeil* to be plain to see QD 327

doie(nt), *doiez* from *devoir*

doint from *donner*; see page 439

domageux adj. harmful, hurtful BD 668

dommage n.m. harm, hurt, damage PL 86, DF 85

dommageable adj. harmful QD 2568

dommaine see *demaine*

dompter *a* v. to school in, to DF 1128, BN 101

donner (se) *a* v. to give o.s. to, be taken up with QD 2359, RM 206

dont conj. at, from the fact that; because QD 986, HV 82, HV 231

doubler v. to sing the second part; copy QD 26

doubte n.f. fear DF 1012, DF 1076

doubter v. to fear DF 965, DF 1075: *se doubter de* to be afraid of DF 15, DF 137

doulçaine n.f. dulcian, type of flute QD 1488

douloir v. to suffer pain, grieve DF 104, QD 509: *se douloir (de)* to grieve (over), complain (at) DF 432, QD 175

doulx n.m. sweetness DF 224, DF 280

dourra, *dourroient* from *donner*; see page 439

dragiee n.f. see note to QD 2406

droit n.m.: *a droit*, *a droiz* rightly, properly DF 356, DF 543, QD 3145: *faire le droit de* to comply with BN 48

droitture n.f. right, justice DF 1104, QD 1889: *par droitture* in justice, rightly DF 620, PA 265

dueil n.m. grief, sorrow PL 70, DF 10

dueil(le) see *douloir*

duire v. to suit, be appropriate DF 3, BD 554; lead DF 570, QD 2438; instruct, teach QD 24, BN 19: *duit* p.p. & adj. skilled, experienced DF 571

duppliquer v. to reply to the reply of the defendant DF 1147

durer v. to endure QD 1421

efforceement adv. with all one's might RB XXVII: 30

effors n.m. company, troop BD 662

el see page 438

ele n.f. wing QD 2808

embatre (s') v. to be at issue, in dispute DF 713; struggle QD 2244: *s'embatre en* to enter into, break into DF 194; rush into QD 2101

embesoigner v. to employ DF 493

embler v. to steal QD 534, QD 749: *s'embler de* to depart, fly away from QD 29, QD 669: *en emblant* covertly, secretly DF 394, QD 1478

embucher (s') v. to hide, conceal o.s. DF 1036, QD 1905

embusche n.f. ambush QD 2326, RM 307: *en embuche* hidden RM 304

emoyer see *esmoier*

empenner v. to feather, fit with feathers QD 1497, BD 118

empeschement n.m. obstacle RB xxv: 24, BN 177

empeschier v. to preoccupy DF 1032, QD 1456; hamper, hinder QD 1002, QD 2190: *s'empeschier en* to be involved in, taken up by DF 262

emplaige n.m.: *au fuer l'emplaige* in proportion, as appropriate QD 2677

empraindre v. to stamp, imprint DF 748, DF 973

emprendre de, *a* v. to undertake to, resolve to RM 29, CO 89

emprés adv. nearby RM 309

emprinse see *emprise*

emprise n.f. enterprise, undertaking QD 246, QD 3528

enaigrer v. to irritate, upset DF 886

enamourer (s') v. to fall in love PL 5, QD 1011: *enamouré* p.p. & adj. in love DF 1086 *encerchier* v. to seek QD 2211

enchacer v. to dispel PL 70

encheoir en v. to fall into BD 594

enchiere n.f. see note to QD 1534–5

enchiet see *encheoir*

encombrement n.m. harm, ill QD 3351, RB xxv: 4

encommencier v. to begin BD 505, L II: 20

encontre n.m. chance, adventure QD 371: *aler a l'encontre* to go to meet QD 369

encontre prep. & adv. against QD 830, QD 1343

encontrer v. to meet QD 975

encoulper v. to accuse QD 3075

encuser (s') v. to denounce, betray o.s. DF 1121

endementier adv. meanwhile QD 1873, RM 43

endroit n.m. respect DF 332, QD 3144: *en son (leur) endroit, endroit soy* for his (their) part, so far as he is (they are) concerned QD 3378, RM 200, BN 323: *cy endroit* here QD 497: *la endroit* there QD 3446

enferme adj. weak, sick QD 539, EX 187

enferrer v. to pierce (with an iron point) QD 2227, QD 2836

enflamber v. to inflame RB xix: 3

enforcer (s') v. to become stronger QD 1186

engaignier v. to irritate, hurt DF 1010

engregier v. to become worse DF 782

engreige n.f. aggravation, irritation QD 3015

enhaÿr v. to conceive a hatred for DF 1028, QD 424

enhenner v. to weary QD 1500

enhorter v. to encourage, exhort PL 23, DF 420

enjouer (s') v. to enjoy o.s. DF 502

enmy prep. amid QD 1995; see note to DF 275

ennuit see note to QD 426

enorter see *enhorter*

enquerir v. to enquire, ask DF 949, DF 957

enquerre v. to enquire, ask QD 1800, QD 2211

enquester de v. to enquire, ask about QD 3461

enroncher v. to scratch (with brambles) DF 1037

enruchier v. to put in a hive QD 1907

ens adv. inside, within RM 213, RM 292: *ens en* prep. inside, within BD 177

enserrer v. to enclose; wring (of heart) QD 2226

ensuÿr v. to follow QD 3303

ensuivre v. to follow, imitate PL 113, QD 482

entailler v. to sculpt, carve QD 1587, EX 90

entalentif adj. desirous of, anxious to DF 314

entamer v. to impair, harm DF 222, QD 946

entechié p.p. & adj. having a certain quality QD 2753: *bien entechié* endowed with good qualities QD 1135

entencïon n.f. intention DF 294, DF 563

entendre v. to understand DF 301, DF 308: *entendre a* to attend to, concern o.s. with DF 407, QD 1555: *entendre en* to direct one's thoughts towards DF 756: *entendant* pres.p. & adj. intelligent, knowledgeable DF 498

entente n.f. intent, desire DF 478, QD 430

ententif adj. attentive, intent DF 313, DF 1238

enteriner v. to finish off BN 432

entier adj. sincere, true DF 1179, QD 759

entre prep. see note to HV 398

entree n.f. see note to BD 318

entremater (s') v. see note to QD 2245

entremettre (s') de v. to attend to, concern o.s. with DF 784, QD 782

entremez n.m. dish, entertainment between the courses of a banquet QD 1640, BD 128

entreprendre v. see note to QD 264–6: *entreprendre contre* to take measures against QD 592: *entrepris* p.p. smitten QD 38 *entrepreneur* adj. enterprising, venturesome DF 538, QD 2927

entrerigoler (s') v. to make merry (together) QD 2703

entrerompre v. to interrupt, break into QD 1860, BN 167

entretailleur n.m. carver, engraver DF 491

entretant adv. in the meantime QD 1768: *entretant que* conj. (indic.) while QD 3344

entretenir (s') a v. to hold on to DF 381

entrevescher (s') a v. to become tangled, confused with QD 1455

entroigne n.f. (piece of) nonsense QD 3140

entr'oublier v. to half forget, forget for a space QD 166, RM 49

enuieux de adj. tired of, irritated with PA 10, PA 73

envaÿe n.f. see note to QD 1575

envaÿr v. to attack DF 901, QD 426

envers adv. on one's back DF 144: *mectre a l'envers* to turn topsy-turvy BD 575

envy n.m.: *a l'envy* vying with one another QD 2691

environner v. to walk around DF 403

enviz adv. reluctantly QD 1380, QD 3363

envoysier (s') v. to become joyous QD 1767

equal adj. equal QD 1281

erbe n.f. herb (with magic properties) RB XXVI: 22

erragier v. to become mad, enraged QD 1997, QD 2405

erre n. m. or f.: *grant erre* in haste QD 3182

erse n.f. see note to QD 1178

ert see page 439

esbat n.m. amusement DF 410, DF 700

esbatement n.m. amusement DF 3, DF 652

esbatre (s') v. to enjoy o.s. DF 22, DF 502: *pour esbatre* for fun, for amusement DF 193, DF 688, DF 1109

escart n.m.: *a l'escart* aside, away RB XIX: 12, BN 213

eschace see *eschars*

escharcement see *eschars*

escharceté n.f. meanness QD 1336, BN 346; scarcity QD 958

eschars adj. mean PL 71, RB XXVI: 33: *escharcement* adv. sparingly BN 165

escheoir v.i. to happen DF 1039, QD 753: *escheoir a* to fall to, come to HV 10

eschequier n.m. see note to QD 1489

eschever v. to avoid, escape DF 200, BD 396

eschiver v. to avoid, escape BD 63, BN 361

escïent n.m.: *a droit escïent* truly QD 2012

escole n.f.: *tenir escole* to teach DF 316, BD 301

escondire v. to refuse QD 3457, RM 196: *escondire* v.n. refusal QD 197, RB II: 5

escondit n.m. refusal DF 474, BN 253

escondre (s') v. to hide, conceal o.s. HV 371

escoute n.f. watchman DF 909, QD 2129; watchfulness BD 752

escouter (s') v. to husband one's strength, take care of o.s. HV 326

escouvenir v.i. to be necessary, needful QD 313

escueillir (s') v. to rush, hasten QD 1913

escute see *escoute*

esgart n.m. care, attention BN 216

eshonté p.p. & adj. shameless BD 726

esjoier v. to fill with joy, rejoice PL 75

esjoÿssement n.m. rejoicing QD 118, L I: 8

esjouÿr v. to rejoice QD 289; gladden QD 1712: *s'esjouÿr* to rejoice DF 166, DF 366: *esjouÿ* p.p. & adj. joyous, merry QD 794, QD 2481

eslacie p.p. see note to QD 2680

eslargier v. see note to RB III: 6

eslargir v. to set free QD 1957; expand, extend BD 182: *s'eslargir en* to bestow freely QD 1326

esliessier (s') de v. to rejoice to HV 178

eslite n.f. choice QD 2612, CO 12

eslongié p.p. & adj. distant, faraway QD 2265

esmaier see *esmoier*

esmerillon n.m. merlin QD 69

esmoier v. to be moved, feel upset QD 1055; trouble, alarm QD 1389, QD 3001: *s'esmaier* to become troubled, alarmed QD 3325

espace n.m. space of time DF 208, QD 478; space, room QD 1679, CO 107

espargne n.f. store, reserve, treasure, QD 3466, EX 139

espart n.m. see note to CO 153

espartir v. to divide, separate QD 565; see note to CO 153: *s'espartir* to be divided, shared QD 1080; spread QD 2506, RB XIX: 6

espasse see *espace*

espergne see *espargne*

espeürer v. to frighten QD 1899, QD 2962

espie n.f. spy DF 909, QD 1579

espïer a v. to seek to PA 216

espieu n.m. hunting-spear DF 631

esplourer v. to bathe with tears QD 1063: *esplouré* p.p. & adj. tearful DF 1083, QD 879

espoindre v. to pain DF 10

espoir adv. perhaps HV 92, HV 181

esprendre v. to seize, overwhelm QD 154, QD 593: *estre espris de* to be seized with, overcome by QD 3527, RM 28

espreuve n.f. worth, value RM 157

esprouver v. to prove, try QD 803, QD 2218: *s'esprouver* to prove o.s. BN 180

esquart see *escart*

essemplaire n.m. example, model PL 58, BN 22

essoyne n.m. difficulty, accident HV 93

essorer (s') v. to take wing, soar DF 639, QD 1667

estable adj. firm, stable DF 1081, BN 191

estage n.m. position, station PA 107

estaindre v. to extinguish, put an end to DF 120, CO 150; die QD 676, QD 2195

estant n.m. standing position QD 1816

estat n.m. condition, estate PL 121, QD 1802; rank, dignity QD 887, BN 10: *hors d'estat* in a poor state QD 2099

estonner v. to stun DF 391

estouper v. to stop, close DF 800, QD 1858

estour n.m. attack, fight QD 158, QD 2430

estourdi adj. and p.p. thoughtless, foolish BN 242: *a l'estourdi* in a confused, dazed manner QD 1883

estraindre v. to beset, pain QD 1110, CO 177

estraine n.f. present (given on New Year's Day) RB VI:2: *le jour de l'estraine* New Year's Day EX 4

estrangier v. to estrange, alienate DF 901, EX 100: *s'estrangier de* to abandon, quit DF 780; become a stranger to QD 1250

estre n.m. place, abode DF 72, QD 1668; condition, state QD 2448

estrener v. to give a New Year's gift PL 3, PL 15

estrief n.m. stirrup QD 1147

estrif n.m. quarrel, dispute QD 2530

estrivee n.f. contest, dispute QD 1544: *a l'estrivee* vying with one another QD 18

estriver a, contre v. to strive, struggle against DF 1237, QD 85

estudie n.m. study, care BD 306

eur n.m. (good) fortune, happiness DF 434, DF 649: *mal eür* ill fortune QD 50, QD 306

euré p.p.: *bien euré* fortunate QD 2963

euvre see *ouvrir*

exaulcement n.m. exaltation QD 3335

exaulcer v. to exalt, glorify QD 2921

excercer (s') a v. to occupy o.s. in QD 2764

excommenier v. to exclude BD 727; excommunicate PA 219

exemplaire see *essemplaire*

exiller (s') v. to ruin o.s. QD 2895

exoigne n.f. delay; dispensation QD 3143

experir v. to experience, suffer QD 1200

explet n.m. revenue, return QD 2495

exploitter v. to carry out, achieve DF 501, BD 498

expondre v. to expound QD 2553

extaindre see *estaindre*

façon n.f. face QD 1870

fade adj. pale DF 318, QD 1410

faillir v. to fail PL 126, DF 58; err, make a mistake QD 2925, EX 218: *faillir a* to fail to DF 15, QD 279: *faillir a, en qch.* to fail in sth. QD 135, QD 430, CO 79: *faillant* pres.p. & adj. failing, weakening DF 540: *failli* p.p. & adj. weak, cowardly QD 1007, QD 2858: *sans faillir* without any doubt DF 915

faintise n.f. pretence, deceit PL 64, QD 133

faire pour v. to be favourable to, support QD 2492

fait n.m. case, condition, situation DF 764, DF 993: *de fait* in fact, in deed DF 534, QD 577

faiz n.m. burden, responsibility QD 2023, QD 2626

farser (se) de v. to mock, poke fun at DF 941

faulsaire adj. or n.m. false, disloyal (person) QD 2249

fëable adj. reliable, faithful QD 3292

fëauté n.f. good faith, fealty DF 1082, BD 401: *fëauté de* faithfulness, fealty towards QD 854

fel adj. treacherous, disloyal DF 890

felon adj. treacherous, disloyal DF 559, DF 884

fengue n.f. mud, filth BD 734

fer n.m. iron tip (of weapon) QD 330

ferir v. to strike QD 1078, QD 2328: *se ferir en* to rush into DF 744, QD 2420

ferment n.m. clasp EX 157

fermer v. to fix, set, establish QD 718, QD 2956

fermouer n.m. clasp EX 159

festëoit see *festoier*

festoier v. to make merry DF 416; fête, greet warmly DF 445, QD 699

feur n.m.: *pour nul feur* on no account DF 1028, RM 219

feurre n.m. straw HV 39

fevre n.m. blacksmith QD 2350

fez see *faiz*

fy see note to QD 3016

fiance n.f. trust DF 954, QD 2167

fichier v. to fix DF 728

fiction n.f. invention, lie BN 203

fier (se) de v. to trust in BD 636

fieu n.m.: *tenir en fieu* to hold in fee QD 2282

fin adj. pure DF 1002, QD 89; true RM 157

finer v. to end, finish QD 92, QD 423; die RB IV: 16: *finer de qch.* to find, procure QD 1776

flair n.m. smell QD 59

flajol n.m. flageolet, small flute QD 2388

foy n.f. promise, pledge DF 877, QD 823

fois n.f. turn DF 1177: *sa foys* in his turn DF 34: *a la foiz* sometimes BD 107, BD 121

foison adv. in great quantity DF 1010

foison n.f. a great deal QD 784

foiz see *foys*

foleur n.f. folly, foolishness DF 582, DF 669

folez see *fouler*

foloyer v. to act foolishly BD 460, BD 684

forcier n.m. coffer, strong-box BD 37

forclore v. to prevent, exclude, banish DF 998, QD 2454

forfaire v. to forfeit, lose CO 30, BN 21; do wrong PA 47

forfait n.m. crime PA 49

forjurer v. see note to BN 120 and 141

fors conj. & prep. except DF 856, DF 933: *fors de* except DF 543, QD 46, BN 211

fors que conj. (indic.) except that QD 142, QD 418

forsaige n.m. act of violence PA 89

forsbour n.m. outlying part of town, suburb RB XII: 11, RB XXVI: 13

fort n.m.: *au fort* after all, in fact DF 700, QD 169: *venir au fort* to come to the point QD 248

fortraire v. to remove, take away QD 1731, RB XVI: 5

fortuner v. to bring (good or ill) fortune upon DF *title*, QD 542, QD 2061

forvoier v. to stray from the road, lose one's way QD 2444, QD 3038

fouÿr v. see note to QD 2480

foul adj. mad, foolish RM 69, BD 221

fouler v. to tread down, crush, harm DF 1132, QD 1269: *foulé* p.p. & adj. downcast, down-trodden, wearied DF 834, DF 1222, BN 176

fourrager v. to pillage RB XII: 4

franc adj. free, free-born DF 932, RM 315

franchise n.f. liberty, freedom DF 61, DF 87; generosity, goodness QD 2304: *grans franchises* outstanding qualities PL 59

frapper (se) v. to rush QD 2841

freche n.f.: *estre en freche* to lie fallow RB XXV: 17

fremier v. to tremble DF 791

frire v. to tremble, shudder DF 98

frisson n.f. fear, fright QD 1439

frivole n.f. frivolity, nonsense QD 800

froisser v. to vex, hurt QD 882, QD 2273; break BD 179

frontiere n.f. line of battle, front DF 806; see note to BD 148

fuer n.m.: *au fuer l'emplaige* see *emplaige*

fuire v. to flee QD 1844, QD 2595

fuitif n.m. & adj. fugitive QD 886, QD 2585

fumeux adj. irascible, choleric BN 255

fust n.m. wooden handle of weapon QD 330

gabe n.f. jest, joke DF 1176

gaillart adj. bold, gallant DF 857

gale n.f. merriment, amusement DF 657, DF 680

galer v. to make merry PL 94

garde n.f.: *ne se donner garde de qch.* not to expect sth. QD 1920

garmenter (se) v. to lament, complain BD 269; cf. *guermenter*

garnison n.m. store, provision BD 147; garrison RB XXVI: 25

gars n.m. see note to RB XXVI: 23

gart from *garder*; see page 439

gast adj. waste, deserted L II: 6

gehiner v. to torment QD 1974

genglerie n.f. gossip, prattle QD 3288

gengleur n.m. gossip, prattler QD 2903, BD 305

gent adj. fair, pleasing PL 40, DF 588

gentillastre n.m. see note to HV 398

gerray see *gesir*

gesir v. to lie (sick) DF 110, BD 700

geu from *gesir*

giet n.m. jess, fastening, bond QD 1658, QD 2291

gieu n.m. game, jest QD 390, QD 703

gormander v. to guzzle; squander HV 101

goulee n.f. (evil) word, remark QD 2694

gouliardye n.f. see note to BD 716

gouliärdise n.f. loose, coarse talk BN 297

goute n.f. gout DF 139, DF 908

gouverner (se) v. to conduct o.s. PA 280

gré n.m. will, pleasure DF 82, DF 86: *bien en gré, en (bon) gré* favourably, with pleasure DF 430, DF 527, QD 980: *prendre en gré* to take in good part QD 129, RM 337–8, BD 640

gref see *grief*

greignieur adj. larger, greater QD 1312, RB XXII: 4

gresillon n.m. cricket QD 66

gresse n.f. fat DF 643, DF 833

grevable adj. harmful DF 1079

grief adj. grievous DF 1048, QD 464: *griefment* adv. grievously RB VI: 11, PA 167

griesche adj. fem. see note to QD 2191

groppir (se) v. see note to HV 400

guenchier a v. to avoid, dodge QD 2784

guermenter (se) de v. to lament, bemoan QD 137, QD 1758

guerredonner v.: *guerredonner qch. a qn.* to reward s.o. for sth. QD 1324

haÿ excl. alas QD 2724

haÿr v.: *haÿr de mort* to have a deadly hatred for QD 2871

haitié adj. content, happy QD 1229

hantise n.f. keeping company with, company QD 2685

haquart adj. haggard DF 635

harberger see *herbergier*

hardement n.m. boldness DF 106, DF 343

hardïer v. to attack, ambush BD 108: see note to QD 2326

hardïesce n.f. boldness DF 1100, HV 230

harnois n.m. armour DF 96, QD 2598

harper v. to harp, make music QD 36

hastif adj. pressing, urgent DF 1099, QD 633

haultesce n.f. glory QD 745, BN 94

haussaire n.m. brigand QD 2246

havir v. to burn DF 936

hemy excl. alas QD 552

her n.m. heir QD 2847, BN 17

herbergier v. to halt BD 54; give lodging to RB XII: 5

hericement n.m. bristling (of hair) QD 2123

herite n.m. heretic EX 43

herray, herroit from *haïr*

hober (se) v. to move, bestir o.s. QD 912

hom(s) see page 437

honnir v. to shame, dishonour QD 2778, BD 725

hontage n.m. shame, dishonour QD 972

hontoier (se) v. to become ashamed QD 2538

hors adv.: *estre hors* to be spent, be past QD 1786, BD 614.

hostel n.m. house, family HV 5, HV 31

hostellage n.m. hospitality DF 1056

huchier v. to call to QD 3179, RM 14

huyer v. to abuse DF 941, BD 787

humeur n.m. one who sips, sipper HV 95

hurt n.m. shock, blow DF 540, QD 2149

hurter v. to clash; spur QD 984

y = il see note to QD 1208

icelle, iceulx pron. that (one), those QD 525, QD 491, QD 950; see page 438

yere(nt), yert see pages 439 and 440

ilec see *yleq*

yleq adv. in that place DF 20, BD 47

impossible adj. see note to DF 1073

inconvenient n.m. difficult situation, misfortune QD 2011, QD 2799

yssir v. to leave, come out, issue DF 519, QD 162

istre v. to leave, come out, issue QD 1989, RB XXV: 28

yvire n.m. ivory QD 1296

ja adv. already QD 39, QD 378; ever QD 1539, QD 3403: *ne...ja* not, never DF 242, DF 244, DF 436: *ja soit ce que* conj. (indic. or subj.) although QD 443, BD 209

jangler v. to gossip DF 49

jangleur see *gengleur*

joyeuseté n.f. joyfulness RB XXIV: 4

joignant adv. close QD 1877

joincture n.f. union QD 644

jouëllier n.m. jeweller DF 492

jouer (se) a v. see notes to QD 2029 and RM 333

jouste n.f. joust DF 654, QD 3189

justicier n.m. justiciar QD 3242

kyrïelle n.f. see note to RB XXIV: 17

labourage n.m. arable, cultivated land BN 180, PA 95

lacher v. to lace, tie QD 1658

laidure n.f. unseemly, offensive remark CO 132, BN 297; evil action BN 125 *laier* v. to let, allow QD 270, QD 3251; leave QD 346, RB XXIII: 4

lair(r)a see *laier*

lait adj. evil, harmful DF 183, DF 897

lame n.f. tombstone, tomb QD 2132, BD 32

lange n.m. woollen garment, cloth DF 641, QD 812

larris n.m. rough ground DF 735

larronnaille n.f. band of robbers HV 171

las see *laz*

lascher (se) v. to grow weary, faint QD 2512

lasnier n.m. lanner (falcon) QD 69

laz n.m. bond, snare DF 81–2

lé adj. wide DF 747, QD 1304

ledengier v. to insult, abuse QD 3232

lëesce n.f. joy, gaiety DF 286, QD 399

lente n.f. nit QD 2576

lermëoit see *lermoier*

lermie see *lermoier*

lermoier v. to weep DF 792, QD 1054: *lermoyer* v.n. tears BD 12

lerroit see *laier*

les n.m. legacy QD 1609

lesse n.f. leash, bond QD 1964, PA 193

lez n.m. side DF 150, QD 1526

lez prep. beside DF 8

li article see page 438

ly pron. see page 438

lie adj. happy PL 73, DF 369

lïen n.m. bond, fetter BD 80, PA 194

lïens see *loiens*

lierres n.m. robber, thief QD 2391

lÿesce see *lëesce*

lieu n.m.: *avoir lieu* to have place, effect DF 69

lige adj. liege QD 1316: *ligement* adv. like a liege man EX 125

lignee n.f. line, lineage BN 274

lis n.m. fleur-de-lys PA 7, PA 199

lober v. to deceive, trick QD 911

loberie n.f. trick, deception QD 798

loiens adv. there QD 2426, BD 78

loier v. to bind QD 3036

loyer see *louyer*

loirre n.m. lure, bait DF 595, QD 1654

loirrer v. to lure; train QD 1653

loisir n.m.: *a son (voustre) loisir* at his (your) pleasure DF 109, RM 30

loisir v. to be allowed QD 454

loit see *loisir*

los n.m. praise, honour DF 222, DF 276

los see *lot*

losengier n.m. flatterer, deceiver BD 313

lot n.m. lot, share QD 3090, BD 679

louyer n.m. reward, recompense QD 1360, QD 1637

lour i.e. *leur*

loz see *los* or *lot*

luicte n.f. fight QD 2436

lus n.m. lute PL 136, QD 1489

main n.m. morning PL 113, QD 1763

maindre see *mendre*

maine(nt) see *mener*

maint see *manoir*

maintenir (se) v. to behave, act QD 849, QD 1267: *maintenir* v.n. behaviour QD 691

maintien n.m. conduct, behaviour DF 63, DF 343; composure DF 126

mais adj. evil QD 2694

mais adv.: *a tousjours mais* for ever (more) DF 132, BD 612: *oncques mais* ever DF 434, RB XXI: 2: *ne...oncques mais* never RB III: 12: *n'en pouoir mais* see *pouoir*

maistrise n.f. authority, power DF 64, DF 969; action requiring skill QD 3047

maiz que conj. (subj.) provided that, if only QD 148, QD 3413

maladif adj. & n.m. sick (person) DF 684, BD 571

malefaçon n.f. misdeed DF 905

malmener v. to ill-treat DF 869

malmetre v. to ill-treat DF 1011

malparler see *mauparler*

mandement n.m. instruction, command QD 3497

mander v. to inform, instruct DF 164; command QD 3169

maniere n.f. manner, appearance QD 366, BD 151; manners, behaviour DF 342; measure, moderation BD 686: *de maniere* properly, in a fitting manner QD 2383: *perdre maniere* to lose one's composure BN 372

manoir v. to remain QD 1253; reside QD 1790, QD 2367

manoir n.m. dwelling, abode QD 2368

mare n.f. mere, pool QD 2802

maronnier adj. of the sea QD 1286

marrir v. to sadden DF 736, QD 1373

marrisson n.f. grief, sadness QD 1438

martire n.m. martyrdom, (intense) suffering PL 156, RB XIII: 10

martirer v. to make a martyr QD 2464, QD 2618

mat adj. checkmated, beaten DF 1158, QD 1829; dejected, downcast QD 366, QD 1500

maugré i.e. *malgré*

maugreer v. to blaspheme against QD 924

maulouyer n.m. ill reward DF 1137

mauparler n.m. slander, calumny DF 568, DF 752

mauvaistié n.f. wicked, evil deed DF 914, QD 1199; wickedness DF 922, QD 1230

mechief see *meschief*

medecine n.f. remedy QD 421, QD 1930

meffaire v. to do wrong BD 279, BN 14: *meffaire (a)* to harm, hurt DF 435, QD 2313, QD 3323: *se meffaire* to do wrong BN 23, PA 44

meffait n.m. misdeed DF 182, DF 533

mehaigner v. to wound, hurt QD 1936

mehaing n.m. wound, hurt QD 2020, BD 246

meillieur n.m. best course QD 338

mendier (de) v. to be bereft, deprived (of) QD 560, QD 3355

mendre adj. lesser, smaller QD 151, QD 1312: *le mendre* least DF 19, QD 264

mener v. make (a noise) QD 86, BD 84; to be in (a mood, state) DF 268, QD 361, QD 1865; see note to DF 680

menestrier n.m. minstrel BD 56

menterie n.f. lie, lying QD 3290

merche n.f. mark DF 66, BD 449

merchier v. to mark QD 2160

merele n.f. pay, winnings QD 2810

merir v. to repay, reward BD 408

merveilleux adj. terrible, violent QD 2430, CO 3; strange, extraordinary BD 537

mes n.m. dish, course QD 1639, BD 126

mesaise n. m. and f. sorrow, unhappiness DF 121, QD 736, CO 44

meschance n.f. ill luck, misfortune DF 952

mescheoir a v.i. to go badly, turn out badly DF 1041, QD 756

mescherra see *mescheoir*

meschiece see *mescheoir* and page 439

meschief n.m. misfortune DF 913, DF 956

meschiet see *mescheoir*

mescroire v. not to believe, refuse to believe BD 718, EX 121: *mescroire de* to suspect of QD 893: *mescreü* adj. faithless, untrustworthy QD 2067

meseür n.m. misfortune HV 170

meseüreux adj. unlucky HV 210

meshaing see *mehaing*

mesler (se) v. to quarrel, argue DF 770, PA 120: *se mesler de* to concern o.s. with BD 685

mesmement adv. especially, above all QD 3332, PA 169

mesnie n.f. household, followers QD 2438, BD 365

mesprendre v. to make a mistake, do wrong DF 967, QD 267: *sans mesprendre* without any doubt CO 93

mesprison n.f. mistake, error QD 1195, BD 534

message n.m. messenger DF 158, QD 3511; message DF 330, QD 1996

messeoir v. to suit ill DF 886

mesure n.f.: *par mesure* in a regular fashion QD 72

meür adj. ripe QD 1900, BN 290

meürer v. to mature QD 2961

mez see *mes*

my see page 438

mignot adj. soft, self-indulgent QD 2774

mignotise n.f. softness, self-indulgence QD 2788

mine n.f. (facial) expression QD 1931

mipartir v. to share, divide CO 159, BD 613

mire n.m. physician BD 173

mirer v. to mirror; instruct CO 99: *se mirer a, en* to learn from, take as an example QD 2795, QD 3031

mirouer n.m. mirror; model CO 99, BN 90

moie see page 438

moyte adj. flabby, limp HV 51

moitoier adj. having a half share in QD 1280

monjoie n.f. culmination PL 105, EX 140; highest aspiration RB V: 9

monnoie n.f. coin DF 973

monstre n.f. show, ostentation QD 368

mont n.m.: *en un mont* all together QD 1810

mont adv. much QD 1809

monter v. to avail, be worth DF 258, QD 1468

montjoye see *monjoie*

mort n.m. bite, sting QD 1930

moute n.f. clod, mound HV 328

mouver v. to set in motion DF 991

mu adj. dumb DF 630

mucer v. to hide, conceal QD 517, QD 1906: *se mucer* to conceal o.s. DF 1035, QD 3183

muchier v. see *mucer*

müer v. to change DF 395, DF 594; moult DF 643

muir, muyre from *mourir*

murmure n.f. quarrel; complaint PA 250

murmurer v. to murmur, complain QD 1424, BN 144

murtrir v. to kill CO 14, RB XXVII: 11: *se murtrir* to kill o.s., be in agony DF 128, DF 924

musable adj. see note to PL 176

musart adj. foolish, thoughtless DF 1102

muser v. to muse, reflect DF 205; waste time DF 1115, QD 1613, QD 2947

muserie n.f. foolishness, nonsense DF 1102

mussoire n.f. see note to HV 373

nagaires adv. not long ago, recently BD 1, L I: 2; see note to HV 1

naÿf adj. genuine, true QD 3241, RM 218: *roche naÿve* bare rock QD 82

namie adv. not long ago, recently DF 1

nasse n.f. net RM 291

neant see *nient*

nenny see *nonny*

nëoit from *noyer*

nercy adj. *black*, gloomy DF 808, EX 38

nesun adj. any QD 2058; (with *ne*) no QD 48, EX 194

neu n.m. knot BN 445

nice adj. simple, raw, inexperienced DF 19, DF 591

nient n.m. see note to QD 993–6: *pour nient* to no purpose QD 682, BN 268: *neant plus que* no more than EX 175

noiant see *nient*

noise n.f. noise DF 648, DF 904

nonchaloir n.m. negligence, lack of interest RB XII: 5: *mectre en, a nonchaloir* to take little account of, think little of DF 103, DF 295

nonchaloir v. to disdain, neglect QD 3007, EX 78

nonny adv. no QD 2776, RM 81: *nenny non* certainly not EX 57

nourreture n.f. upbringing DF 618, BN 117

nuyeux adj. cloudy QD 19

nuisable adj. harmful PL 166

nuysance n.f. harm RB XXV: 7

Glossary

nuitie n.f. night QD 2681

null(u)y adj. any QD 506: pron. anyone QD 1220, QD 2561: (with *ne* etc.) no one PL 63, PL 165–6; see page 438

o prep. with DF 726, QD 1287

obster v. to be an obstacle: see note to QD 898

occire v. to kill QD 486, QD 489

octroi see *ottroy*

octroier v. to grant QD 388, QD 819

oeuvre from *ouvrir*

oeuvre see *ouvrer*

offendre v. to offend RB XXIII: 6

oir see *her*

oïr see *ouÿr*

oiseuse n.f. idleness, laziness QD 2767, BN 276

oncques adv. ever DF 220, QD 2601: *ne...oncques* never DF 46, DF 74

onny adj. even, level BD 722; equal BD 741: *tout onny* equally QD 2777

onniz see *honnir*

onq adv. ever QD 1848: *ne...onc* never PL 10, DF 636

or adv.: *tresor* straight away DF 511, RM 251

ordonnance n.f. discipline, self-control DF 343, BD 125, PA 233; order, ranks QD 2865

ordonner (s') a v. to prepare, dispose o.s. for QD 2814, BN 437

ordure n.f. wrong, dishonest action BN 296, BN 316

ore adv. now DF 823, PA 31

orendroit adv. now BD 737, BN 146

ores adv. now RM 241, HV 325

orfenté n.f. destitution, affliction QD 1707

orphenin n.m. orphan PA 93

orra see *ouÿr*

ort adj. filthy BN 375

ot see *avoir*

ot see *ouÿr*

ottroy n.m. permission DF 878; gift, grant QD 1912, BD 429

oublïance n.f. oblivion BN 430: *(re)mectre en oublïance* to forget (again) QD 2638, RM 45

oublïeux adj. forgetful RB V: 3

ouÿe adv. yes QD 2482

ouÿr v. to hear DF 7, DF 134

oultre adv. further, onwards QD 2841, BN 437: *plus oultre* more QD 2161: *tout oultre* entirely, through and through HV 234

oultrecuidance n.f. presumptuousness QD 1483, EX 105; presumptuous remark CO 71, PA 239

oultrecuidé p.p. & adj. presumptuous QD 2978, HV 19

oultrer v. to destroy, put an end to QD 973, QD 2849: *oultré* p.p. & adj. excessive, large QD 1740

ourne n. m. or f.: *a ourne* together QD 1992

ouvrer v. to work, act PL 182, QD 1377

ouvrer (s') v. to open QD 1381

paix n.f. pax, osculatory DF 405

par prep.: *a par soy* by oneself QD 1056, BD 494; to oneself BD 119; see note to DF 229

parcevez see *percevoir*

parçonnier adj. sharing in QD 1288

pardoint from *pardonner*; see page 439

pardu from *perdre*

parfaire (se) v. to perfect o.s., grow perfect DF 184, QD 2971

parfait n.m. fulfilment DF 612

parfournir v. to provide in full BD 757, BN 439

parlement n.m. talk QD 3350

parlementer v. to talk QD 2501

paroir v. to appear QD 2883, RM 134

part n.f. side, party DF 1116, QD 2048: *les trois pars* three (parts) out of four DF 724: *a part* apart, aside DF 855, QD 3420 *parti* n.m. position, situation DF 760, QD 132; side (in dispute) DF 977, DF 1241; party QD 567; resolve CO 158: *par tel party que* (indic.) so that DF 99

partie n.f. beloved QD 2095, BD 610; party (to dispute) RM 264, L I: 12: *quant de ma partie* for my part QD 1594

partir v. to divide QD 136, CO 157: *partir a, en* to share in, have a part in QD 2461, CO 155, PA 140: *se partir* to split, break QD 687, CO 168: *partir (se) de* v. to leave, issue from RB XIX: 7

pas n.m. pass, passage DF 734, QD 1993; pass, difficulty QD 571, RM 99; see note to PL 91

passage n.m. pass, difficulty PL 91; pass, ford PA 97; see note to PL 91

passee n.f. passage, journey; difficulty PL 194: see note to PL 91

passer v. to undergo, suffer DF 579, QD 1153

pastissage n.m. tax, tribute PA 102

pastiz n.m. tax, tribute QD 1835, BD 792

peautraille n.f. rabble, riff-raff QD 3305

peccune n.f. money, coin RB XXVII: 29

pel n.m. skin: see note to RM 240

pener v. to be in pain QD 1867: *se pener de, a* to strive to QD 1518, QD 2964

pennetiere n.f. shepherd's scrip QD 2386

pensement n.m. thought, reflection RM 71, CO 156

percer v. to show through RB XXV: 22: *tresperchié* pierced through QD 2161

percevoir v. to perceive, see DF 525, BD 253

perchier see *percer*

pers adj. (dark) blue QD 76

pert see *paroir*

perte n.f.: *donner en perte* to give away, squander RM 168

peser v. to weigh, have value DF 1146, RM 184: v.i. to be disagreeable, painful DF 1145, QD 91, QD 1279

peu adv.: *a peu que* see note to QD 415–16

peu p.p. of *paistre* DF 368

pieça adv. for some time past QD 1298; some time ago QD 2116, QD 2136: *de pieça* for a long time now DF 756, RB XXI: 2

piece n.f.: *longue piece* a long time QD 2142

pillerie n.f. pillaging HV 140

pinpernel n.m. fool, nincompoop HV 261

piquant n.m. thorn QD 1895

piteux adj. charitable, piteous DF 1222, QD 861

plaint n.m. complaint, lament QD 1049, CO 140

planter v. to leave, abandon DF 340, QD 1245

planteureux adj. abundant, plenteous QD 303, PA 75

plat adj. worthless QD 3242

pleger v. to be surety for QD 1957

plennier adj. full, entire QD 223; plenary BN 151

plet n.m. words, talk QD 2498

plevir v. to pledge, promise CO 131, EX 236; certify, warrant BN 395

ploy n.m. decision CO 119

plus adv.: *sans plus* only, no more than DF 363, DF 1151, QD 194: *trop plus* see *trop*

poindre v. to prick, pierce DF 280, QD 342: *poignant* pres.p. & adj. poignant, pungent QD 1880

point n.m. state, condition PL 17, QD 530; favourable moment QD 3364; score BD 496: *bien a point* well, appropriately DF 488, QD 754: *en bon point* plump DF 212, DF 709: *de tous poins* entirely, completely DF 813, DF 1149: *venir, aler a point* to go well DF 522, QD 343, RM 79: *(re)mettre a point* to put right, in good order DF 379, QD 3331

pointe n.f. (sharp) point PL 100, QD 1922

pointure n.f. sting, wound QD 1892, BD 323

poise see *peser*

polir v. to remove, steal QD 1591

pollice n.f. government HV 301

pollu p.p. soiled DF 1132

porchier n.m. swineherd QD 904

port n.m. see note to DF 1199

porter v. to bear, endure QD 108, QD 313: *se porter* to conduct, behave o.s. QD 673, QD 2835

pose n.f.: *une pose* for a time EX 160

poulx n.m. pulse QD 2339

poulz n.m.pl. lice QD 2576

pouoir v. see note to QD 535: *n'en pouoir mais* to be unable to do anything about sth. DF 765, BD 243; see page 145

pouoirs n.m.pl. troops, forces QD 3169

pourcacher see *pourchacer*

pourchacer v. to strive after, seek for, pursue PL 66, QD 1659; procure, cause DF 624, BD 257: *pourchacer de* to strive to QD 2968, HV 115

pourchaz n.m. pursuit, quest BD 294

pourmaine see *pourmener*

pourmener v. to pursue, torment DF 772, QD 1570: *se pourmener* to walk about, take a walk RB VI: 10, BN 280

pourparler v. to discuss QD 2530

pourpens n.m. thought, reflection BN 326

pourpris n.m. (enclosed) area QD 33

pourprise n.f. (enclosed) area QD 2306

poursuir v. pursue QD 495

pourtant adv. for that reason QD 3452, BN 334: *non pourtant* nonetheless RM 37

pourtraire v. to portray, represent QD 2317

pourvoir v. to provide QD 1894: *pourvoir a* to take thought for QD 2445; look, see to L II: 30: *pourvoir de* to provide with QD 3122, EX 143: *pourvoir que* to take care, see to it that BD 703: *pourveu* p.p. & adj. prepared, ready QD 2799

praie see *proie*

pratique n.f. skill; practice BN 139

prëau n.m. meadow DF 655, BD 164

prendre v. to assume, suppose DF 823, DF 978: v.i. to befall, happen DF 765, QD 1934: *prendre a* v. to begin to QD 369, QD 1715: *se prendre a* to be attached to DF 18; begin to DF 226, HV 379: *se prendre a qn. de qch.* to reproach, criticise s.o. for sth. QD 1672, QD 2622, BD 521: *se prendre garde* to take care DF 508

present adv. at present QD 2945

present n.m. present, gift QD 991, QD 2665

presse n.f. press, thick (of a fight) DF 531, QD 928; sorrow QD 2137: *faire presse* to press DF 644

prestement adv. promptly DF 674

presumpcïeux adj. presumptuous EX 183, PA 277

preu n.m. advantage, profit DF 607, DF 948

preux adj. worthy, valiant DF 1219, RB XXVIII: 14

prindrent, prins, print see *prendre*

pris n.m. worth, reputation DF 246, QD 34

priser v. to esteem DF 252, DF 269; count the cost of RM 237

priver v. to tame PL 85

priveté n.f. friendship DF 443, BD 252

procurer (se) a v. to seek to, strive to BN 135

prodommie n.f. honour, worth RB XXVIII: 21

proie n.f. prey QD 1660, QD 1663; prize, booty QD 2300, RB XX: 6, BN 163

prouffitable adj. see note to PL 163 and 167

provision n.f. foresight BN 32

puce n.f.: *avoir la puce en l'oreille* to be disturbed, troubled RM 5

puis adv.: *puis...puis* now...now PL 46-8, DF 60

puis prep.: *puis deux mois* these last two months QD 321: *puis dix ans* for the last ten years QD 3298, BD 791 *puis que* conj. (indic.) after, since (the time when) QD 1129, QD 1299–300, QD 1715

puis n.m. well QD 1047

quanqui, quanque pron. all that DF 514, QD 1786, RB XXVII: 18

quant adj. how many PA 90, PA 92

quant adv.: *quant de* as for DF 1125, QD 707: *quant plus* the more... BD 378, RB XVII: 6

quant conj. if QD 259, QD 485

quant pron.: *tout quant* all that BN 391

quantque see *quanque*

quarneaulx n.m.pl. battlements DF 360, DF 1040

quarrel n.m. square stone (for paving) DF 359

quartain adj.: *fievre quartaine* quartan fever QD 936

que adv. why QD 586, QD 642

que conj. why DF 29, QD 414; (= *ce que*) what DF 396, DF 666; (with expressions of time) when DF 467, QD 4; in that, because, for DF 858, QD 1019, QD 1162; (subj.) in order that DF 1017, QD 884, QD 2736; in such a way that QD 476, QD 891; (= *que que*) QD 1840, QD 2206: *ce que* the fact that QD 1554, RB XV: 4, HV 62; (= *ce que*) which HV 167

que pron.: *ne que* any more than DF 908, QD 1228, QD 1340

querele n.f. case, side QD 2811, CO 77; dispute QD 3478

querir v. to seek DF 336, QD 2220

querre v. to seek DF 804, QD 3372

queste n.f. request BD 486

queult see *cueillir*

queur(en)t from *courir*

queuvre from *couvrir*

qui pron. the person who, anyone who PL 39, PL 68, QD 844; if anyone PL 113, DF 649; (= *ce qui*) DF 1204, QD 1823; (= *que qui*) DF 1242, QD 2385

quicte adj. quit, absolved QD 2586, QD 3483; free, unburdened BD 469, PA 24

quicter v.: *quicter qch. a qn.* to yield, abandon sth. to s.o. QD 323

quoy que conj. (indic. or subj.) although QD 228, QD 1116, QD 1960

quoquart n.m. fool DF 627, QD 917

quouärdie n.f. (act of) cowardice QD 2324, QD 2577

rabais n.m. reduction EX 133 (var.)

rabas n.m. reduction; destruction DF 1065

rabatre v. to reduce (price, total) DF 714, HV 422; strike down QD 1815

rabouter see note to HV 108

rachat n.m. redemption BD 296

racointe n.f. see note to QD 870

radrecer v. to put back on the right path PA 15

raembre v. to ransom, redeem QD 999

raffermer v.: *raffermer sa contenance* to regain one's composure BD 122

raim n.m. branch QD 1315, QD 1875

raimseau n.m. small branch RB XXV: 26

raint see *raembre*

ralïer v. to unite QD 4: *se ralïer* to become reconciled PA 224

ramaint see note to QD 1256 and page 439

ramentevoir v. to recall DF 1114, QD 1851

rapaiser (se) v. to calm down CO 54

rapasser v. to pass again DF 377, QD 2401

rappeaulx see *rappel*

rappel n.m. call, summons QD 898: *sans rappel* irrevocably RM 238

rappeller (se) de qch. v. to retract sth. CO 79

rappiner v. to steal BN 62

rassis p.p. & adj. composed, calm, collected DF 588, QD 2961; wise QD 777

ratirer v. to pull, hold back QD 1564

ravir v. to carry off DF 776, QD 1441; transport, delight DF 42, DF 175: *ravy* p.p. bemused, beside oneself BD 83 *rebours* n.m. opposite QD 310, QD 2613: *au rebours* in a contrary way QD 1267; conversely HV 273

rebouter v. to reject, spurn DF 1078, BD 391

rebutement n.m. rejection L ɪɪ: 18

reclamer v. see note to DF 595: *se reclamer a* to appeal to EX 230

reconvoier v. to escort back, bring back RB xx: 11

recorder v. to recall BN 447; record QD 2489, EX 195: *recorder une leçon* to go over a lesson DF 312: *se recorder de* to remember RM 278, EX 116

recort adj. mindful QD 2490

recort n.m. recollection, memory DF 542

recouvrance n.f. recovery QD 3068

recouvrer v. to recover, gain, find PL 184, QD 48; repair, make good QD 469, QD 3339; see notes to QD 2328 and RM 127–8

recrëant adj. recreant, cowardly QD 958

recroire v. to weary, exhaust QD 2066, L ɪɪ: 19: *recreü* p.p. & adj. faithless, cowardly QD 894.

recueillir (se) v. to retire, retreat QD 1916

recuitte n.f. reboiling DF 574

redonder v. to abound QD 1511: *redonder en mal a* to cause harm to QD 731: *redonder sur* to redound on BN 351

referir (se) v. to rush QD 1079; flow QD 2422

refraindre v. to check, restrain DF 119, QD 410

refuge n.m.: *estre a refuge a qn.* to have recourse to s.o. QD 1363

refui n.m. refuge QD 3193

regaler v. to repair, make good QD 2111

regarder a v. to take care of, attend to QD 1262, QD 3342

regenter v. to rule QD 2820

regorger v. to be disgorged, overflow QD 2505

relais n.m. remains, residue BD 93

relessier v. to leave PA 238

remaindre v. to remain, stay DF 1140, QD 1164, QD 2194

remanant see *remenant* and *remanoir*

remanoir v. to remain, stay QD 1789, QD 2370

remenant n.m. remains, residue DF 878, QD 1792

remerir v. to reward QD 1356

remis p.p. & adj. subdued, quiet DF 1014

remonstrer v. to reveal DF 1170: *se remoustrer* to reveal o.s. QD 1737

remüer v. to change QD 2353, QD 2357

rencheoir v. to relapse QD 3027

renchiere n.f. (increasing) difficulty BD 415

rencontrer v. see the note to QD 2848–9

rendre (se) pour v. to declare o.s. QD 2016

rendue n.f. see note to QD 1742

renforchier (se) v. to regain one's strength QD 903

renommer v. to celebrate, glorify DF 960, DF 1172

renouvel n.m. return of spring QD 3108

renouveler v. to be renewed QD 1782, CO 78

rente n.f. rent, revenue, return DF 926, QD 431: *de rente* regularly QD 1582

repaire n.m. resort, dwelling QD 143

repairer v. to return, repair QD 2042

repartir v. to grant, distribute (in return) L ɪɪ: 38

repas n.m. return (journey) DF 733, QD 569

replet adj. filled QD 2496

reposé p.p. see note to QD 828

reprouver v. to reprove QD 2219; prove BN 235

requerre v. to request QD 1797, QD 3375

requeult from *recueillir*

resbaudir v. to encourage, cheer DF 685

reschapper v. to escape QD 2121

resconfort n.m. comfort, consolation RM 89, RB v: 2

rescourre v. to rescue QD 920, QD 2250

reseront see note to DF 1005

resler v. see note to QD 1527

resourdre v. to restore, renew, help DF 660, QD 1513

respasser v. to cure, heal DF 582, DF 709

respit n.m. respite, delay DF 895, EX 182

respiter v. to delay, defer DF 1215, BD 696; spare, save BN 345

ressoigner v. to fear, be apprehensive about QD 1104, QD 1553

ressourdre see *resourdre*

restraindre v. to shut off from, remove from QD 1112

resverie n.f. distraction, madness EX 202

retenir v. to retain, accept service of QD 298, QD 319: *retenir a* see note to BD 607-8

retraire v. to draw back PL 61, DF 592; retreat QD 2608, RM 290; take away L II: 6: *se retraire* to retire, retreat, draw back DF 321, QD 1916

retrait n.m. retreat DF 322, QD 2316

retrenchier v. to cut down, destroy RB XXV: 25, 33

revel n.m. pleasure, delight QD 3110

revenant adj. and pres.p. producing income, revenue BN 320

revenir v. to regain consciousness QD 1888

reverchier v. to scrutinise QD 2159

revers n.m. contrary, opposite BD 570

reverse n.f.: *a la reverse* upside-down QD 1180

rien n.m. anything QD 1211, QD 2854

rien adv. (with negative) in no way DF 967, CO 29

rigoler (se) de v. to be amused at QD 1617, QD 2999

rimoier v. to sing; set to rhyme QD 1053, BD 10

rïote n.f. quarrel DF 1064

rïoteux adj. quarrelsome DF 884, BN 257

ris n.m. laugh, laughter DF 30, DF 658

rober v. to steal QD 792; rob QD 910

rompre v. to tear DF 641, DF 865; (of heart) break, be broken DF 989, QD

414, QD 1961; break, destroy QD 2128, QD 3107, L II: 33; interrupt QD 2529, L II: 27: *rompre sa teste* to rack, cudgel one's brains DF 146, RM 59

rotier n.m. mercenary, soldier of fortune HV 143

roule n.m.: *mectre en son roule* to enroll QD 2358

rouptes see *rompre*

rouver v. to seek DF 911, QD 801

rüer v. to throw, cast DF 631, QD 2906

ruser v. to reject, deny PA 262: *se ruser de* to leave, abandon DF 625, DF 1117

sachier v. to draw QD 2861

sacouter v. to whisper (a secret) DF 943

sade adj. agreeable, pleasing QD 1412

saillir v. to escape, depart DF 56, RM 296; leap, jump DF 359, QD 2119; issue DF 918: *se saillir de* to escape from, depart from DF 782, BD 646: *saillant* pres.p. & adj. energetic, active DF 538

saing n.m. sign QD 2021

saira from *savoir*

saison n.f. favourable, opportune moment DF 70, DF 466

sans prep.: *sans plus* see *plus*

sans que conj. (subj. or indic.) without DF 484, DF 930, QD 1724-5

sauldra see *saillir*

sauls n.m. willow-tree BD 158

sault see *saillir*

sauterele n.f. see note to QD 2809

sauvable adj. saving, salutary PL 164

savance n.f. knowledge, wisdom CO 69

scïent adj. wise, knowledgeable QD 2010, QD 2797

seeller v. to seal DF 748, QD 2260

seigneurïage n.m. dominion, authority BD 292

seignieurie n.f. lordship, dominion, authority DF 969, EX 169

Glossary

seignorie see *seignieurie*

semblant n.m. mien, appearance, expression DF 117, DF 214

semblence n.f. appearance BD 127

semille n.f. deception, trick QD 2892

semondre see *cemondre*

sené adj. wise, sensible DF 868

sensible adj. intelligent, sensible QD 2091

sentir (se) de v. to feel the effects of BD 43

sëoir v. to suit, be fitting DF 26, DF 488, DF 689: se sëoir to sit DF 678, BD 163: sëant, soiant pres.p. & adj. fitting DF 567, QD 996, RM 201

serchier see *cerchier*

sery adj. soft QD 60, QD 141

serre n.f. prison QD 1531: en serre enclosed DF 803, QD 666

servir a v. to serve DF 558

seul(en)t see *souloir*

seurconduit n.m. safe-conduct BN 88

seure see *courir (seure)*

seurprendre v. to seize, capture by surprise QD 37, QD 513

seurquerir v. to press excessively, impose upon QD 445, QD 1688

seurté n.f. surety, promise DF 878

si n.m. fault, defect RB xxiv: 32

si adv.: par si que on condition that QD 1379

si conj. & adv. and, so PL 137, PL 148; indeed QD 1067: et si and so, and thus DF 51, DF 105; and yet BD 195, BD 199

si non que conj. (subj.) unless DF 695

si que conj. (indic.) so that DF 517, DF 571; just as QD 1337

simplesce n.f. foolishness PA 203

sirent see *sëoir*

sis see *sëoir*

soeil see *souloir*

soiant see *sëoir*

soillarder (se) v. to sully one's reputation HV 151

soing n.m. care, anxiety, concern DF 213, DF 961

somme n.f. load, burden QD 2035

somme n.f.: mectre en somme to add together QD 1682

sommer v. to sum, add up DF 1174

songeart n.m. dreamer DF 50

songeur adj. pensive QD 2086

songeux adj. pensive DF 210, DF 851

songier v. to think of, dream of, imagine DF 781, QD 2186, QD 2263

sorte n.f. company PL 24, QD 580: par dures sortes harshly QD 1545

sortir a v. to result in CO 140; match, suit BD 492

soubtif adj. subtle, skilful DF 1102: soubtivement adv. subtly, skilfully DF 776, QD 1940

souëf adj. sweet DF 514

souffrance n.f.: en souffrance quiet, at peace QD 2731, RB xxv: 17, PA 245

souffreteux de adj. deprived of, lacking PA 76

souillart n.m. sloven HV 97

soulacer v. to cheer PL 75: se soulacer to rejoice RB xvii: 7

soulas n.m. pleasure QD 231; conversation HV 324, HV 332

souldart n.m. soldier, mercenary QD 2120, RB xxvi: 32

soulde n.f. pay, reward BD 688

souldoyer n.m. soldier, mercenary L ii: 12

souloir v. to be wont, be accustomed QD 167, QD 174

sourdre v. to rise, arise, spring DF 659, DF 1064: se sourdre to arise QD 1881

soustenance n.f. sustenance RB xxv: 16; support BN 418

soute n.f. lowest part BD 391

souvenance n.f. memory, recollection QD 3084, BD 124

suÿr v. to follow DF 627

suyvre a v. to follow BN 212

supplir v. to supply, make good DF 1242

sur prep. (of time) at, in DF 380; towards, against QD 1223, RM 275, RB v: 10 (see note to RM 316): *conquerre sur* to capture from QD 1530

surquerir see *seurquerir*

survenant n.m. see *survenir*

survenir v. to come along, come after RM 326, RM 344

sus adv.: *mectre qch. sus a qn.* to accuse s.o. of sth. QD 3269: *mectre suz* see notes to HV 90 and HV 349: *remectre sus* to restore (to health) L II: 15–16

sus prep. upon DF 357, QD 932; tending towards DF 676; against DF 907; over, above QD 1179, BN 110

table n.f. (gaming-) table BN 212

taille n.f. tax, toll PA 104, HV 334

taindre v. to change colour, grow pale QD 677

tancer see *tenser*

tandiz que conj. as long as QD 2309

tant adv.: (*de*) *tant plus* the more QD 535, QD 1730, QD 2146: *tant moins* the less QD 1652, BD 447: *a tant* at this point QD 1046, QD 1814: *en tant* in that way, thus QD 1697: *tant pour tant* in like measure QD 1820

tant com(me) conj. (indic. or subj.) as long as DF 45, DF 1236: *de tant comme* in that, to the extent that QD 2299

tant que conj. (indic. or subj.) as long as DF 132, QD 58; (indic. or subj.) until DF 427, DF 472: *a tant que* (indic. or subj.) until QD 1383, QD 1924, CO 170: *en tant que* (subj.) in such a way that QD 3170: *de tant plus que...tant plus* the more...the more BD 321–3

tantare n.f. see note to QD 2801

targe n.f. shield, protection QD 489, QD 2315

targer v. to be slow to QD 488

tasche n.f.: *en tasche* in the mass, all together QD 2514

tasse n.f. purse DF 379

tauxer v. to accuse, censure QD 2920

tel pron. see note to QD 2727

tempester (*se*) v. to storm, rage DF 145

tenant adj. mean, avaricious BN 342

tencer see *tenser*

tençon n.f. quarrel, argument DF 904

tendre a v. to aspire to, aim at DF 302, DF 691, QD 587

tenir v. to consider DF 345, DF 613: (*il*) *ne lui tenoit de* he was not anxious to, interested in QD 360, RM 19: *se tenir* to behave, conduct o.s. PL 32, RB XIV: 4; see note to QD 1606: *se tenir de* to refrain from DF 984, DF 989: *se tenir a* to hold to CO 37: *tenu* p.p. beholden, indebted QD 1026; obliged BN 39, BN 63

ten(n)er v. to exhaust, weary QD 1499, QD 1791, QD 2049

tenser v. to argue QD 924; rebuke HV 321: *tenser a* to argue with QD 109, QD 2534

termine n.m. (space of) time QD 420

teulx from *tel*; see page 438

ty see page 438

tieulx from *tel*; see page 438

tire n.f.: *de tire* at once, immediately RB XXVI: 14

tirer a v. to strive after DF 297, QD 2709: *se tirer a part* to retire, withdraw BD 121

tissir v. to weave QD 10, QD 3268

tixu see *tissir*

tollir v. to take away, remove DF 1133, QD 655

tonnelle n.f. arbour, bower DF 656; trap (for partridges) DF 788

torchier v. to beat QD 902

torfait n.m. misdeed BN 5, BN 126

tortant from *tordre*

toudis adv. always DF 683, BD 569

touldrez, touldroie, toulsist, toult, toulu see *tollir*

tour n.m. resource QD 159

tourner (*se*) v. to return DF 738, QD 3302

tournoiement n.m. tournament DF 654

tournoier v. to walk up and down DF 682, RB XXIV: 2

tousdis see *toudis*

touser v. to shear QD 935

tout adj. & n.m.: *trestout* (absolutely) every, all QD 698, QD 2426; see note to QD 1876–7: *du tout* entirely, completely PL 29, PL 67

traictier v. to draw, drag QD 1794

traire v. to draw, pull, take DF 513, DF 855; bear, endure QD 1732, RM 295; fire (arrow) QD 1940, QD 1947; *se traire a, vers* to go towards QD 3506, HV 23: *se traire de* to withdraw from RM 292

trait n.m. time QD 3505, BN 173; shaft RM 92, BD 117: *a trait* slowly, at leisure DF 323

transporter (*se*) v. to go, betake o.s. QD 839, BD 778

travaillier v. to pain, weary, exhaust QD 1588, BD 154: *se travailler* to exhaust o.s. RM 78

travers n.m.: *au travers* across QD 209, BD 115; through BD 160

travers adj. troublesome, perverse BD 573

treille n.f. trellis DF 655, BD 156

tremble n.m. aspen, quivering poplar; trembling RB 1: 11

tres adv. prefix: very, greatly; words beginning with *tres* are listed under their second syllable; see page 439

tresaler v. to consume, destroy QD 1302, QD 2112

tresor n.m. treasure (-house) EX 173

trespas n.m. (narrow or difficult) passage DF 732; death QD 570, BD 45

trespasser v. to pass (beyond) DF 560; die DF 710, QD 476; omit CO 111, EX 212: *se trespasser* to die, pass away BD 46

tresse n.f. see note to PA 190 and 193

tressüer v. to sweat; become agitated troubled QD 1710, RM 209

trestour n.m. detour; delay QD 2429

tribouler v. to torment, vex QD 1270

trieve n.f. truce, respite BD 381

tristour n.f. sadness, grief QD 107, QD 1075

trop adv. greatly, very QD 517, QD 2026, QD 2191: *trop plus* much more DF 91, DF 175

truage n.m. seigneurial dues PA 103

truffois n.m. jest DF 1176

truÿs from *trouver*

turtre n.f. turtle-dove QD 671

uller v. to howl DF 644

us n.m. usage DF 1153

vaillant adv. of value, worth HV 290

vaillemment adv. valiantly HV 162, HV 188

valoir a v. to avail QD 199, QD 455

value n.f. worth, value DF 1131

vantance n.f. boasting QD 2055

vanteur n.m. braggart, boaster BD 707, BD 711

varïance n.f. vacillation BN 419

varïer v. to vacillate, waver QD 2379, RM 356, BN 71

vassal see *vassault*

vassault n.m. young man of noble birth HV 3, HV 81

vassellaige n.m. valiant, worthy deed HV 16

vëer v. to refuse, forbid RM 203

vendoise n.f. dace QD 87

vener v. to hunt DF 774

vengement n.m. vengeance PA 175

venue n.f.: *d'une venue* at one go, at one fell swoop QD 1027

verbler v. to give voice to QD 27

verser v. to collapse, come to grief QD 2767, PA 204

vïaire n.m. face DF 516

vïelle n.f. viol PL 139, RB XXIV: 7

villener v. to treat with scorn, vilify QD 3053, HV 34

villenie n.f. boorish action DF 568; boorishness BD 724, BN 6

vilonnye see *villenie*

vinee n.f. wine QD 915

vire n.f. arrow QD 1294, RB XXVI: 17

virer v. to turn QD 1293, BN 108: *se virer* to turn CO 101

vis n.m. face QD 1063, QD 1472

viser v. to observe, reflect, consider QD 1733, PA 49: *viser de* to aim to, seek to DF 350: *viser a* to aim at, seek QD 1087, QD 1353; reflect on, consider QD 2156, BD 139: see note to BD 137, 139

vo adj. your QD 2851, BD 375; see page 438

voy excl. indeed, to be sure HV 41, HV 55

voiement n.m. seeing, sight QD 2685

voier v. to go, make one's way QD 2423

voir n.m. truth DF 837, DF 1197: *voir disant* truthful DF 1004, QD 2157: *pour, de voir* in truth QD 260, QD 977, RM 178

voise, voit from *aller*; see page 439

volentif adj. desirous, eager DF 1101

voste n.f.: *tourner la voste* to turn around DF 822

vouer v. to vow, swear DF 131, QD 1140

vourra(y), vourroit from *vouloir*

voz see page 438

vray adj. *de, par vray* truly QD 1021, QD 1805

vueil n.m. will, desire DF 113, DF 1098

vuide see *wide*

wide adj. empty QD 1464, RB VII: 2

wider v. to empty, clear QD 1462, QD 2979

y has been treated throughout as *i*

Select Bibliography

MANUSCRIPTS

A list of the manuscripts of Alain Chartier is given on pp. 45–8. Details of other manuscripts consulted will be found in the index.

PRINTED WORKS

The abbreviations shown in brackets at the end of some entries are those used in the notes and the glossary.

1. *Palaeography, textual criticism etc.*

Bédier, J., 'La tradition manuscrite du *Lai de l'ombre*. Réflexions sur l'art d'éditer les anciens textes', *Romania*, LIV, 1928, 161–96, 321–56.

Bischoff, B., G. I. Lieftinck, G. Battelli, *Nomenclature des écritures livresques du IXe au XVIe siècle*, Paris, CNRS, 1954.

Briquet, C. M., *Les Filigranes. Dictionnaire historique des marques du papier*, I–IV, Leipzig, Hiersemann, 1923². (Briquet)

Bühler, C. F., 'Sir John Paston's *Grete Booke*, a Fifteenth-Century "Best-Seller"', *Modern Language Notes*, LVI, 1941, 345–51.

   The Fifteenth-Century Book, the Scribes, the Printers, the Decorators, Philadelphia, U.P., 1960.

Bulletin de la Société des Anciens Textes Français, 1875–1936.

Bulletin d'information de l'Institut de Recherche et d'Histoire des Textes, I–XV, 1952–68.

Chaytor, H. J., 'The Medieval Reader and Textual Criticism', *Bulletin of the John Rylands Library*, XXVI, 1941–2, 49–56.

Delisle, L., *Le Cabinet des manuscrits*, I–III, Paris, Imprim. Nat., 1868–81.

Ham, B., 'Textual Criticism and Common Sense', *Romance Philology*, XII, 1959, 198–215.

Hector, L. C., *The Handwriting of English Historical Documents*, London, Arnold, 1958.

Knudson, C. A., 'The Publication of Old French Texts: Some Comments and Suggestions', *Speculum*, XXIV, 1949, 510–15.

Langlois, E., *Les Manuscrits du 'Roman de la Rose'*, Lille, Paris, 1910 (*Travaux et mémoires de l'Université de Lille*, n.s., I: VII).

Maas, P., *Textual Criticism*, Oxford, Clarendon P., 1958.

Mayer, C. A., *Bibliographie des œuvres de Clément Marot*, I (*Manuscrits*), II (*Editions*), Genève, 1954 (*Travaux d'humanisme et renaissance*, X, XIII).

Notices et extraits..., I–XLII, 1787–1933.

Samaran, Ch. et R. Marichal, *Catalogue des manuscrits en écriture latine portant des indications de date, de lieu ou de copiste*, Paris, CNRS, I, 1959; II, 1962; V, 1965; VI, 1968.

Scriptorium, I, 1947–

Stevenson, A. (ed.), *C. M. Briquet: Les Filigranes…Jubilee Edition*, I–IV, Amsterdam, Paper Publs. Socy., 1968.

Wormald, F., and C. E. Wright (eds.), *The English Library before 1700*, London, Athlone P., 1958.

Wright, C. E., *English Vernacular Hands from the Twelfth to the Fifteenth Centuries*, Oxford, Clarendon P., 1960.

2. Early printed books

Beattie, W., *The Chepman and Myllar Prints. A Facsimile…* Edinburgh, Bibliogr. Socy., 1950.

Brunet, J. C., *Manuel du libraire…*, I, Paris, Didot, 1860.

Burger, K., *Beiträge zur Inkunabelbibliographie (Supplement zu Hain und Panzer)*, Leipzig, Hiersemann, 1908.

Claudin, A., *Histoire de l'imprimerie en France au XVe et au XVIe siècle*, II, Paris, Imprim. Nat., 1901.

Copinger, W. A., *Supplement to Hain's 'Repertorium bibliographicum'*, I–II, London, Sotheran, 1895–1902.

Davies, H. W., *Catalogue of a Collection of Early French Books in the Library of C. Fairfax Murray*, I–II, London, Privately printed, 1910. (Fairfax Murray)

Delalain, P., 'Notice sur Galliot du Pré…', 15 pp.; 'Notice complémentaire sur Galliot du Pré…', 24 pp.; offprints from *Journal général de l'imprimerie et de la librairie*, 6 décembre 1890 and 3 octobre 1891.

Delisle, L., *Chantilly, Le Cabinet des livres: Imprimés antérieurs au milieu du XVIe siècle*, Paris, Plon-Nourrit, 1905. (Chantilly)

Deschamps, P. et G. Brunet, *Manuel du libraire: Supplément*, I, Paris, Didot, 1878.

Gesamtkatalog der Wiegendrücke, VI, Leipzig, Hiersemann, 1934. (GKW)

Graesse, J. G. T., *Trésor de livres rares et précieux*, Dresden etc., II, 1861; VII, 1869.

Hain, L., *Repertorium bibliographicum*, I: ii, Stuttgart, Paris, 1827.

Macfarlane, J., *Antoine Vérard*, London, Bibliogr. Socy., 1900 for 1899.

Panzer, G. W., *Annales typographici*, II, Norimbergae, Zeh, 1794.

Pellechet, M., *Catalogue général des incunables des bibliothèques publiques de France*, II, Paris, Picard, 1905. (Pellechet)

Polain, M.-L., *Catalogue des livres imprimés au quinzième siècle des bibliothèques de Belgique*, I, Bruxelles, Soc. des Bibliophiles, 1932. (Polain)

Renouard, P., *Imprimeurs parisiens…*, Paris, Claudin, 1898.

Tchemerzine, A., *Bibliographie d'éditions originales et rares d'auteurs français des XVe, XVIe, XVIIe et XVIIIe siècles*, III, Paris, Plée, 1929. (Tchemerzine)

3. Works used in the notes to the poems

Brunot, F., *Histoire de la langue française*, I, Paris, Colin, 1905.

Burger, A., *Lexique de la langue de Villon*, Genève, Droz; Paris, Minard, 1957.

Du Cange, *Glossarium mediae et infimae latinitatis*, I–X, Niort, Favre; Londres, Nutt, 1884–7. (DuC)

Bibliography

Ewert, A., *The French Language*, London, Faber & Faber, 1949².

Foulet, L., *Petite Syntaxe de l'ancien français*, Paris, 1930³ (*CFMA*). (Foulet)

Gardner, R. and M. A. Greene, *A Brief Description of Middle French Syntax*, Chapel Hill, 1958 (*University of North Carolina Studies in the Romance Languages and Literatures*, XXIX). (GG)

Godefroy, F., *Dictionnaire de l'ancienne langue française*, I–X, Paris, Vieweg, Bouillon, 1881–1902. (G)

Gossen, C. T., *Petite Grammaire de l'ancien picard*, Paris, Klincksieck, 1951.

Huguet, E., *Dictionnaire de la langue française du XVIe siècle*, I–VII, Paris, Champion, Didier, 1925–67. (H)

La Curne de Sainte-Palaye, *Dictionnaire historique de l'ancien langage françois*, I–X, Niort, Favre; Paris, Champion, 1875–82. (LaC)

Littré, E., *Dictionnaire de la langue française*, I–IV, Paris, Hachette, 1878. (L)

Morawski, J. (ed.), *Proverbes français antérieurs au XVe siècle*, Paris, 1925 (*CFMA*). (Morawski)

The Oxford English Dictionary, I–XII, Oxford, Clarendon P., 1933. (OED)

Poirion, D., *Le Lexique de Charles d'Orléans dans les ballades*, Genève, Droz, 1967 (*Publs. romanes et françaises*, XCI).

Robert, P., *Dictionnaire alphabétique et analogique de la langue française*, I–VI, Paris, Soc. du Nouveau Littré, 1966. (R)

Shears, F., *Recherches sur les prépositions dans la prose du moyen français (XIVe et XVe siècles)*, Paris, Champion, 1922. (Shears)

Tobler–Lommatzsch, *Altfranzösisches Wörterbuch*, I–VIII, (IX), Berlin *later* Wiesbaden, Steiner, 1925–72 [in progress]. (TL)

Wartburg, W. von, *Französisches etymologisches Wörterbuch*, I– , Bonn, Klopp *later* Leipzig *and* Basel, 1928– [in progress]. (FEW)

4. *Editions of other writers*

Champion, P. (ed.), *Charles d'Orléans: Poésies*, Paris, I, 1956²; II, 1927 (*CFMA*).

Crow, J. (ed.), *Les Quinze Joyes de mariage*, Oxford, 1969 (*Blackwell's French Texts*).

Droz, E. (ed.), *Les Fortunes et adversitez de Jean Regnier*, Paris, 1923 (*SATF*).

Droz, E. et A. Piaget (eds.), *Le Jardin de plaisance et fleur de rhetorique*, I–II, Paris, 1910–25 (*SATF*).

Dupire, N. (ed.)., *Les Faictz et dictz de Jean Molinet*, I–III, Paris, 1936–9 (*SATF*).

Fourrier, A. (ed.), *Jean Froissart: L'Espinette amoureuse*, Paris, 1963 (*Bibl. française et romane*, B: 2).

Kervyn de Lettenhove, Baron (ed.), *Œuvres de Georges Chastellain*, I–VIII, Bruxelles, Devaux, 1863–6.

Lecoy, F. (ed.), *Le Roman de la Rose*, I–III, Paris, 1965–70 (*CFMA*).

Longnon, A. (et L. Foulet) (eds.), *François Villon: Œuvres*, Paris, 1932⁴ (*CFMA*).

Neal, Y. A. (ed.), *Le Chevalier poète Jehan de Garencières (1372–1415)*, I–II, Paris, Nizet, 1953.

Paris, G. (ed.), *Chansons du XVe siècle*, Paris, 1875 (*SATF*).

Piaget, A., *Oton de Grandson, sa vie et ses poésies*, Lausanne etc., 1941 (*Mémoires et documents publiés par la Soc. d'Hist. de la Suisse romande*, IIIe série, I).

Piaget, A. et A. Picot (eds.), *Œuvres poétiques de Guillaume Alexis*, I–III, Paris, 1896–1908 (*SATF*).

Queux de Saint-Hilaire, Marquis de and G. Raynaud (eds.), *Œuvres complètes de Eustache Deschamps*, I–XI, Paris, 1878–1903 (*SATF*).

Raynaud, G. (ed.), *Rondeaux et autres poésies du XVe siècle*, Paris, 1889 (*SATF*).

(ed.), *Les Cent Ballades...par Jean le Seneschal*, Paris, 1905 (*SATF*).

Roy, M. (ed.), *Œuvres poétiques de Christine de Pisan*, I–III, Paris, 1886–96 (*SATF*).

Rychner, J. (ed.), *Les Arrêts d'amour de Martial d'Auvergne*, Paris, 1951 (*SATF*).

Varty, K. (ed.), *Christine de Pisan's Ballades, Rondeaux, and Virelais: An Anthology*, Leicester, U.P., 1965.

Wilkins, N. (ed.), *One Hundred Ballades, Rondeaux and Virelais from the Late Middle Ages*, Cambridge, U.P., 1969.

Winkler, E. (ed.), 'Französische Dichter des Mittelalters: I, Vaillant', *Sitzungsberichte der Kais. Akademie der Wissenschaften in Wien: Phil.-hist. Klasse*, CLXXXVI: i, 1918.

5. Editions of Alain Chartier later than 1550

Berry, A. (ed.), *La Belle Dame sans merci*, Paris, 1944.

Bouvier, R. (ed.), *Alain Chartier: le Quadrilogue invectif*, Paris, Editions Universelles, 1945.

Charpennes, L. (ed.), *Alain Chartier: la Belle Dame sans merci, avec une notice*, Paris, Laval, Barnénoud, 1901 (*Les Livres et poèmes d'autrefois*).

Chartier, D. (ed.), *Le Curial de M. Alain Chartier*, Paris, Chevillot, 1582.

[Chennevières, Marquis Ph. de (ed.)], *Rondeaux et ballades inédits d'Alain Chartier*, Caen, Poisson et fils, 1846.

Clédat, L., 'Ballades, chansonnettes et rondeaux', *Lyon-Revue*, décembre 1886, 307–20 (unexamined).

Denifle, H. et Æ. Chatelain, *Chartularium universitatis parisiensis*, IV, Paris, Delalain, 1897, 381–2.

[Didot, J. (ed.)], *Le Lay de paix* [Paris], Didot aîné [1826].

Droz, E. (ed.), *Alain Chartier: le Quadrilogue invectif*, Paris, Champion, 1950² (*CFMA*).

Du Chesne, A. (ed.), *Les Œuvres de Maistre Alain Chartier*, Paris, le-Mur *or* Thiboust, 1617.

Furnivall, F. J. (and P. Meyer) (eds.), *The Curial made by Maystere Alain Charretier*, London, 1888 (*EETS, Extra Series*).

Hemeryck, P., *Alain Chartier, poète et penseur, d'après 'Le Debat des deux fortunes* (sic) *d'amour' et les œuvres latines*, Paris, 1970 (Thèse de l'Ecole Nationale des Chartes).

Heuckenkamp, F. (ed.), *Le Curial par Alain Chartier...*, Halle s. S., Niemeyer, 1899.

Hoffman, E. J., *Alain Chartier...*, 1942, 325–53. (See section 6, below.)

Laidlaw, J. C., *The French and Latin Manuscripts of Alain Chartier: A Bibliographical Study, together with Editions of Four Poems*, 1963 (Cambridge University Ph.D. Thesis).

Lamius, Io., *Deliciae eruditorum...*, IV, Florentiae, Vivianii, 1737, 38–42, 164–9.

Lemm, S., 'Aus einer Chartier-Handschrift des Kgl. Kupferstichkabinetts zu Berlin', *Archiv für das Studium der neueren Sprachen und Literaturen*, CXXXII, 1914, 131–8.

Löpelmann, M. (ed.), *Die Liederhandschrift des Cardinals de Rohan*, Göttingen, 1923 (*Gesellschaft für Romanische Literatur*, XLIV).

Martène, E. et U. Durand, *Veterum scriptorum et monumentorum...amplissima collectio*, II, Parisiis, Montalant, 1724, 1459–65.

Pagès, A., '*La Belle Dame sans merci* d'Alain Chartier: texte français et traduction catalane', *Romania*, LXII, 1936, 481–531.

Piaget, A. (ed.), *Alain Chartier: La Belle Dame sans mercy et les poésies lyriques*, Lille, Genève, 1949² (*TLF*).

Quicherat, J., *Procès de condamnation et de réhabilitation de Jeanne d'Arc*, V, Paris, 1849, 131–6 (*Société de l'Histoire de France*).

Rice, W. H., 'Deux poèmes sur la chevalerie: *le Bréviaire des nobles* d' Alain Chartier et *le Psautier des vilains* de Michault Taillevent', *Romania*, LXXV, 1954, 54–97.

Rosenthal, G. (ed.), *Dialogus familiaris amici et sodalis super deploratione gallice calamitatis, ab Alano Auriga* (sic) (*Alain Chartier*) *editus*, Halle-a.-S., John, 1901.

Rouy, F. (ed.), *Alain Chartier: Le Livre de l'esperance*, 1967 (Paris Thesis).

Viriville, Vallet de (ed.), *Le Livre des quatre dames*, Paris, 1858 (unexamined).

Walravens, C. J. H., *Alain Chartier: études biographiques...*, 1971, 263–73. (See section 6, below.)

White, J. E., Jr. (ed.), *The Major Poems of Alain Chartier: A Critical Edition*, 1962 (University of North Carolina Ph.D. Thesis).

6. *Critical works on Alain Chartier*

Aubrun, C. V., 'Alain Chartier et le marquis de Santillane', *Bulletin hispanique*, XL, 1938, 129–49.

Blayney, M. S., 'Sir John Fortescue and Alain Chartier's *Traité de l'Espérance*', *Modern Language Review*, XLVIII, 1953, 385–90.

'Alain Chartier and Joachism?', *Modern Language Notes*, LXX, 1955, 506–9.

Blayney, M. S. and G. H. Blayney, 'Alain Chartier and *The Complaynt of Scotlande*', *Review of English Studies*, n.s. IX, 1958, 8–17.

'*The Faerie Queene* and an English Version of Chartier's *Traité de l'Espérance*', *Studies in Philology*, LV, 1958, 154–63.

Busquet, R., 'Une épitaphe d'Alain Chartier', *Mémoires de l'Institut Historique de Provence*, VI, 1929, 179–87.

Champion, P., *Histoire poétique du XVe siècle*, I, Paris, 1923, 1–165 (*Bibliothèque du XVe siècle*, XXVII).

Chesney, K., 'Some Notes on the Lyrics of Alain Chartier', *Mélanges de linguistique et de littérature romanes offerts à Mario Roques*, I, Bade, Paris, Didier, 1950, 27–35.

Delaunay, D., *Etude sur Alain Chartier*, Rennes, Oberthur, 1876.

Denifle, H. et Æ. Chatelain, 'De legatione Alani Chartier in Germaniam', *Chartularium universitatis parisiensis*, IV, Paris, Delalain, 1897, XIII–XIV.

Du Fresne de Beaucourt, G., 'Les Chartier: recherches sur Guillaume, Alain et Jean Chartier', *Mémoires de la Société des Antiquaires de Normandie*, 3e série, VIII (XXVIII), 1870, 1–59.

Bibliography

Garapon, R., 'Introduction à la lecture d'Alain Chartier', *Annales de Normandie*, IX, 1959, 91–103.

Hannappel, M., 'Poetik Alain Chartiers', in G. Körtig und E. Koschwitz (eds.), *Französische Studien*, Heilbronn, Henninger, 1881, 261–314.

Hemeryck, P., *Alain Chartier, poète et penseur...*, 1970. (See section 5, above.)

Hirschel, G., '*Le Livre des Quatre Dames*' *von Alain Chartier: Studien zur französischen Minnekasuistik des Mittelalters*, Heidelberg, 1929.

Hoffman, E. J., *Alain Chartier, his Works and Reputation*, New York, Wittes Press, 1942.

Joret-Desclosières, G., *Un Ecrivain national au XVe siècle: Alain Chartier*, Paris, Fontemoing, 1899[4].

Kastner, L. E., 'Concerning an Unknown Manuscript of Alain Chartier's Selected Works', *Modern Language Review*, XII, 1917, 45–58.

Kussmann, L., *Beiträge zur Überlieferung des* '*Livre des Quatre Dames*' *von Alain Chartier*, Greifswald, Abel, 1904.

Laidlaw, J. C., 'English Translations of Alain Chartier', *Modern Language Review*, LVI, 1961, 222–4.

  'The Manuscripts of Alain Chartier', *Modern Language Review*, LXI, 1966, 188–98.

  'André du Chesne's Edition of Alain Chartier', *Modern Language Review*, LXIII, 1968, 569–74.

  'Master Alain Chartier and Master Alain Lequeu', *French Studies*, XXII, 1968, 191–200.

Mancel, G., *Alain Chartier: Etude bibliographique et littéraire*, Bayeux, St Ange Duvant fils, 1846[1], 1849[2].

Moldenhauer, K., *Zur Überlieferung des* '*Livre de l'Espérance*' *von Alain Chartier*, Greifswald, Abel, 1904.

Perot, F., *Recherches sur la filiation de Guillaume, Alain et Jean Chartier: leur généalogie de 1290 à 1900*, Vannes, Lafolye, 1900.

Perret, P.-M., 'L'ambassade de l'abbé de Saint-Antoine de Vienne et d'Alain Chartier à Venise d'après des documents vénitiens', *Revue historique*, XLV, 1891, 298–307.

Pezet, M., 'Recherches historiques sur la naissance et la parenté d'Alain, Jean et Guillaume Chartier', *Mémoires de la Société d'Agriculture, Sciences, Arts et Belles-lettres de Bayeux*, I, 1842, 243–64.

Piaget, A., 'La *Quistione d'amore* de Carlo del Nero', *Romania*, XXI, 1892, 431–3.

  'L'épitaphe d'Alain Chartier', *Romania*, XXIII, 1894, 152–6.

  'Notice sur le manuscrit 1727 du fonds français de la Bibliothèque Nationale', *Romania*, XXIII, 1894, 192–208.

  'Un prétendu manuscrit autographe d'Alain Chartier', *Romania*, XXV, 1896, 312–15.

  '*La Belle Dame sans merci* et ses imitations', *Romania*, XXX, 1901, 22–48, 317–51; XXXI, 1902, 315–49; XXXIII, 1904, 179–208; XXXIV, 1905, 375–428, 559–97.

  (ed.), *Le Miroir aux dames*, Neuchâtel etc., 1908 (*Académie de Neuchâtel, Faculté des Lettres, Travaux*, II).

  'La Complainte du prisonnier d'amours', *Mélanges offerts à M. Emile Picot*, II, Paris, Morgand, 1913, 155–62.

Requin, Abbé, 'Jean de Fontay et le tombeau d'Alain Chartier', *Bulletin archéologique du Comité des Travaux Historiques et Scientifiques*, 1892, 434–43.

Rice, W. H., 'Pour la bibliographie d'Alain Chartier', *Romania*, LXXII, 1951, 380–6.

Seznec, J., 'L'Alain Chartier de Sainte-Beuve', *Romanic Review*, XXXV, 1944, 203–19.

Söderhjelm, W., 'La dama senza mercede', *Revue des langues romanes*, 4e série, V (XXXV), 1891, 95–127.

Thomas, A., 'Alain Chartier chanoine de Paris, d'après des documents inédits', *Romania*, XXXIII, 1904, 387–402.

'Un document peu connu sur Alain Chartier (5 juillet 1425)', *Romania*, XXXV, 1906, 603–4.

'Encore Alain Chartier', *Romania*, XXXVI, 1907, 306–7.

'Alain Chartier en Hongrie', *Romania*, XXXVIII, 1909, 596–8.

'Une œuvre patriotique inconnue d'Alain Chartier', *Journal des savants*, 1914, 442–9.

Thuasne, L., '*Le Curial* d'Alain Chartier et la traduction de Robert Gaguin', 7 pp., offprint from *Revue des bibliothèques*, janvier–mars 1901.

Toustain, Vicomte de, 'Notice historique et généalogique sur la famille d'Alain Chartier', *Revue nobiliaire historique et biographique*, n.s. II, 1866, 5–13.

Wahlund, C., 'La Belle Dame sans mercy', *Skrifter Kongl. Humanistiska Vetenskaps-samfundet i Upsala*, V: viii, Upsala, 1897.

Walravens, C. J. H., *Alain Chartier: études biographiques, suivies de pièces justificatives, d'une description des éditions et d'une édition des ouvrages inédits*, Amsterdam, Meulenhoff-Didier, 1971.

7. General works

Anselme (Le père), *Histoire généalogique...*, I–IX, Paris, Compagnie des Libraires, 1726–33. (Anselme)

Aschbach, J., *Geschichte Kaiser Sigmunds*, III, Hamburg, Perthes, 1841.

Bennett, H. S., 'The Author and his Public in the Fourteenth and Fifteenth Centuries', *Essays and Studies by Members of the English Association*, XXIII, 1938, 7–24.

'Caxton and his Public', *Review of English Studies*, XIX, 1943, 113–19.

Briquet, A. (ed.), *Lettres de Jean Besly (1612–1647)*, Poitiers, 1880 (*Archives historiques du Poitou*, IX).

Champion, P., *La Librairie de Charles d'Orléans*, Paris, 1910 (*Bibliothèque du XVe siècle*, XI).

Histoire poétique du XVe siècle, I–II, Paris, 1923 (*Bibliothèque du XVe siècle*, XXVII).

Coville, A., *Gontier et Pierre Col et l'humanisme en France au temps de Charles VI*, Paris, Droz, 1934.

La Vie intellectuelle dans les domaines d'Anjou-Provence de 1380 à 1435, Paris, Droz, 1941.

Dickinson, J. G., *The Congress of Arras 1435: A Study in Medieval Diplomacy*, Oxford, Clarendon P., 1955.

Doutrepont, G., *La Littérature française à la cour des ducs de Bourgogne*, Paris, 1909 (*Bibliothèque du XVe siècle*, VIII).

[Droz, E., Y. Rokseth, G. Thibault], *Trois Chansonniers français du XVe siècle*, Paris, 1927 (*Documents artistiques du XVe siècle*, IV).

Droz, E. et G. Thibault, *Poètes et musiciens du XVe siècle*, Paris, 1924 (*Documents artistiques du XVe siècle*, I).

Bibliography

Du Fresne de Beaucourt, G., *Histoire de Charles VII*, Paris, Libraire de la Soc. Bibliogr., I, 1881; II, 1882.

Jeanroy, A. et E. Droz, *Deux manuscrits de François Villon*, Paris, 1932 (*Documents artistiques du XVe siècle*, VI).

Langlois, E., *Recueil d'arts de seconde rhétorique*, Paris, Imprim. Nat., 1902.

Lote, G., *Histoire du vers français*, II, Paris, Boivin, 1951.

MacCracken, H. N., 'An English Friend of Charles of Orleans', *Publications of the Modern Language Association of America*, XXVI, n.s. XIX, 1911, 142–80.

Mattingley, G., *Renaissance Diplomacy*, London, Cape, 1955.

Morel, O., *La Grande Chancellerie royale... (1328–1400)*, Paris, 1900 (*Mémoires et documents publiés par la Société de l'Ecole des Chartes*, III).

Pagès, A., 'Le thème de la tristesse amoureuse en France et en Espagne du XIVe au XVe siècle', *Romania*, LVIII, 1932, 29–43.

Paris, G., 'Un poème inédit de Martin le Franc', *Romania*, XVI, 1887, 383–437.

Patterson, W. F., *Three Centuries of Poetic Theory. A Critical History of the Chief Arts of Poetry in France (1328–1630)*, I–II, Ann Arbor, Michigan U.P., 1935 (*Univ. of Michigan Publications, Language and Literature*, XIV–XV).

Piaget, A., 'Pierre Michault et Michault Taillevent', *Romania*, XVIII, 1889, 439–52.

'Oton de Granson et ses poésies', *Romania*, XIX, 1890, 237–59, 403–48.

'Remarques sur Villon à propos de l'édition de M. A. Longnon', *Romania*, XXI, 1892, 427–31.

'Michaut pour Machaut', *Romania*, XXI, 1892, 616–17.

'Simon Greban et Jacques Milet', *Romania*, XXII, 1893, 230–43.

'Jean de Garencières', *Romania*, XXII, 1893, 422–81.

'Pierre Chastelain dit Vaillant', *Romania*, XXIII, 1894, 257–9.

'*Le Songe de la barge* de Jean de Werchin, sénéchal de Hainaut (1404)', *Romania*, XXXVIII, 1909, 71–110.

'Balades de Guillebert de Lannoy et de Jean de Werchin', *Romania*, XXXIX, 1910, 324–68.

'Oton de Granson, amoureux de la reine', *Romania*, LXI, 1935, 72–82.

Piaget, A., et E. Droz, *Pierre de Nesson et ses œuvres*, Paris 1925 (*Documents artistiques du XVe siècle*, II).

'Recherches sur la tradition manuscrite de Villon. I: Le manuscrit de Stockholm', *Romania*, LVIII, 1932, 238–54.

Poirion, D., *Le Poète et le prince: l'évolution du lyrisme courtois de Guillaume de Machaut à Charles d'Orléans*, Paris, 1965 (*Univ. de Grenoble: Publs. de la Faculté des Lettres et Sciences Humaines*, XXXV).

Rice, W. H., 'Two Poems of Michault Taillevent: *Le Congié d'Amours* and *La Bien Allée*', *Modern Philology*, XLII, 1944, 1–8.

Schutz, A. H., *Vernacular Books in Parisian Private Libraries of the Sixteenth Century according to the Notarial Inventories*, Chapel Hill, 1955 (*University of North Carolina Studies in the Romance Languages and Literatures*, XXV).

Shapley, C. S., *Studies in French Poetry of the Fifteenth Century*, The Hague, Nijhoff, 1970.

Thomas, A., 'La date de la mort de Thomas de St Pierre', *Romania*, XXXIII, 1904, 606–9.

Bibliography

Valois, N., *Histoire de la pragmatique sanction de Bourges sous Charles VII*, Paris, Picard, 1906 (*Archives de l'histoire religieuse de la France*).

Watkins, J. H., 'Michault Taillevent – a *mise au point*', *Modern Language Review*, XLVI, 1951, 361–7.

Wilkins, N. E., 'The Structure of Ballades, Rondeaux and Virelais in Froissart and in Christine de Pisan', *French Studies*, XXIII, 1969, 337–48.

Indexes

INDEX TO THE POEMS

The index is divided into the following sections:

1. *Proper names*
2. *Personified figures*

As in the glossary, *y* has been treated as *i* throughout.

1. *Proper names*

Aigueperse (Bailly d') HV 428
Aise DF 124
Alain DF 1245; EX 241; HV 429
Angleterre QD 1798; HV 358
Anglois (les) QD 836, 896; HV 354, 415
Auffrique DF 124
Bertran (du Guesclin) QD 2783
Bigot (Le bastard) HV 176
France QD 274, 619, 831, 2573, 2922, 3197,
   3210, 3215, 3263, 3301; RB xx: 5; PA 5, 113,
   248; HV 72
François (les) HV 413

Yssouldun L i: 17
Jehan (de Grailli, comte de Foix) DF
   1180
Jehanne L i: 19
Katherine L i: 19
Marie L i: 19
Neczon (Pierre de) HV 435
Paris QD 3450
Phebus (Gaston III, comte de Foix) DF 1180,
   1218, 1229
Romme QD 3383
Sancerre, Mareschal de HV 37

2. *Personified figures*

The many references to the Deity (more than 130) and to *Amours* (more than 130) are not listed.

Accueil DF 810; *see also* Bel Accueil
Adversité QD 2061
Advis BD 625
Aigreur PL 177
Alegement CO 166
Amoureux Soing DF 972
Ardant Desir DF 570; QD 2256; *see also*
   Desir
Avarice BN 334

Beau Parler DF 933
Beauté EX 242; RB xxvi: 20
Bel Accueil DF 467; RM 204, 313, 317; L ii:
   15; *see also* Accueil
Bon Espoir L ii: 8; *see also* Espoir, Vain
   Espoir
Bonne Amour RM 37; BN 188, 190
Bon Secours RB xix: 4
Bon Vouloir QD 1952; *see also* Franc Vouloir,
   Hault Vouloir

Chagrin PL 178
Confort RB xix: 4
Conseil BD 625

Couroux QD 1151
Courtoisie DF 862, 960; BD 407, 409; BN 225
Couvoitise QD 2791; BN 164
Crainte DF 257; QD 1969, 1976; BD 181,
   186; L ii: 5; EX 158; RB i: 6, iii: 5, xxvi:
   16
Cuider BD 253, 258; *see also* Fol Cuider

Dangier DF 809, 1016; QD 2445; BD 152, 644;
   L ii: 5; EX 93, 98; RB iii: 6, v: 10
Decevance QD 128
Desconfort QD 1014
Desdaing EX 99
Desespoir QD 3133; BD 510; RB xvii: 1
Deshonneur QD 2829
Desir DF 83, 300, 418; QD 154, 158, 254, 680,
   683, 702, 1685, 1795, 1835, 1843, 1940, 1947,
   1959, 2000, 2065, 2101, 2105, 2107, 2109,
   2436, 2441, 2446, 2456; BD 86, 181, 629;
   RB ii: 12, iii: 5; xii: 2, xxvi: 9, 10, 13, 27,
   35, 38; *see also* Ardant Desir
Desperance QD 2067
Desplaisir RB vi: 9
Destinee QD 540

513

INDEX OF MANUSCRIPTS, DOCUMENTS
AND EARLY PRINTED BOOKS

The index is divided into the following sections:

1. Manuscripts of Alain Chartier
2. Scribes
3. Names in Chartier manuscripts: owners, inscriptions etc.
4. Devices in Chartier manuscripts
5. Manuscripts and documents – general
6. Books printed before 1617

1. Manuscripts of Alain Chartier

The sigla are explained and listed on pages 44–8; the index does not include any references to pages 50–1 and 57.

Index

Index

2. Scribes

Bodin 128
Bonnefoy 110
Bosco, Ja. de 119
Bosco, Jo. de 119n
Bosco, L. de 119n
Deffez, Fraer 86

Herlin, Jehan 95n
Herlin, Lois 95
Herlin, Pierre 95n
Jeunesse 93
Nicholaus plenus amoris 72
Panier, Jehan 87

3. Names in Chartier manuscripts: owners, inscriptions etc.

Alebret, Yzabeau d' 71, 108
Alençon, Marguerite d'Orleans, Duchesse d' 137
Andon, Seigneur d' 120
Angoulême, Jean, Comte d' 56, 71, 108
Angoulême, Marguerite de Rohan, Comtesse d' 56, 108
Ashburnham, (fourth) Earl of 76–7, 85, 127
Aubais, Marquis d' 77
Austria, Margaret of 125
Auvergne, Jehan d' 115n

B...(?), Maistre Bertran, secretaire du roy 134
Barbantane family 69
Barrois 76–7, 127
Beaujeu, Anne de 131–2
Béhague, Comtesse de 118
Berry, Jean, Duc de 140
Besançon, Capucin House 119
Béthune, Philippe de 90
Blossete 108
Bourbon, Connétable de 80
Bourbon, de 108
Bourbon, Francoys de 80
Bourbon, Pierre de, Dauphin d'Auvergne 132
Bourdon, F. 112
Brieux, de 118
Brodeau, 92
Bruges, Louis de, Sr. de la Gruthuyse 65
Burrus, M. 132

Castellane, Rene de 120
Castellane family 120
Castres, Abbé de 72
Charles VIII, King of France 65
Chastelain, George 64
Cherysy, Charlot de 124
Clèves, see Orleans
Coquille, Gilbert 117
Coulonges, Jehanne de 108
Crassier, Baron de 73
Croy family, 123

Daillon, Loyse de 114
Daillon, Renee de 114

Dany (Dauy), Jehan 76
Deciternes 62
Despeaux (?), Loyse 114
Devillers, Jehan 86
Diesbach family 128
Dinteville, House of 70
Drieu, Metre Robert 71
Droz, Mlle E. 97
Du Bonaiffiard (?), Jacques 109
Dubrovsky, Peter 130
Duclaux (?), Maistre Francoys 92
Du Lude, Madamoyselle 114
Du Puy, Brothers 106

Espinay, Anthoine d' 75
Espinay, Charles d' 75
Espinay, Rene d' 75

Fauchet, Claude 75
Francoys, Jehan 71
Francoys, Martin 71
Frederick III the Wise, Elector of Saxony 72

Gaignat, L.-J. 132
Gaignières, R. de 72n
Gerard, G. J. 128
Grassay, Marie de 114
Graville, Anne de 74, 138n
Graville, Louis Malet de 138n
Graville, Malet de, family 138
Guillemot, Jan, Sr. de l'Argentaye 68
Guilliaume 92
Guyard, Jehan 71

Hamilton, (tenth) Duke of 99
Hauweel, Florencius 124

Jacquemart-André, Mme 118
Joly, Claude 70

Kirbet, F. 97

L...(?), Maistre Bertran, secretaire du roy 134
Laborde family 141

Index

4. Devices in Chartier manuscripts

See also the description of *Pj*.

The index is divided into the following sections:

1. Historical and literary figures

References to Alain Chartier are not included.

2. *Scholars and critics*

The index does not generally include the references in pages 61–144 to the critics listed on page 60.

3. Names of places, institutions, events etc.

References to France are not included.

Index

4. Works of Alain Chartier

The index does not include any references to pages 61–144.

5. Works other than those by Chartier

Index